The Colonel

Richard Norton Smith

The Colonel

The Life and Legend of

ROBERT R. McCORMICK

1880–1955

Northwestern University Press

EVANSTON, ILLINOIS

Northwestern University Press
Evanston, Illinois 60208-4210

Northwestern University Press edition published 2003
by arrangement with Houghton Mifflin Company. Copyright
© 1997 by Richard Norton Smith. All rights reserved.

Printed in the United States of America

10 9 8 7 6 5 4 3 2 1

ISBN 0-8101-2039-9

Book design by Robert Overholtzer

Library of Congress Cataloging-in-Publication data are available
from the Library of Congress.

The paper used in this publication meets the minimum require-
ments of the American National Standard for Information
Sciences—Permanence of Paper for Printed Library Materials,
ANSI Z39.48-1992.

For Bob and Elizabeth Dole

Contents

Illustrations

"In this and like communities, public sentiment
is everything. With public sentiment, nothing can fail;
without it, nothing can succeed. Consequently,
he who molds public sentiment goes deeper than he
who enacts statutes or pronounces decisions."

ABRAHAM LINCOLN

"Europe extends to the Alleghenies;
America lies beyond."

RALPH WALDO EMERSON

"I give you Chicago. It is not London —
and Harvard. It is not Paris — and buttermilk.
It is American in every chitling and sparerib
and it is alive from snout to tail."

H. L. MENCKEN

"I like to stir up the animals."

COLONEL ROBERT R. MCCORMICK

Medills, Pattersons, McCormicks

A PARTIAL FAMILY TREE

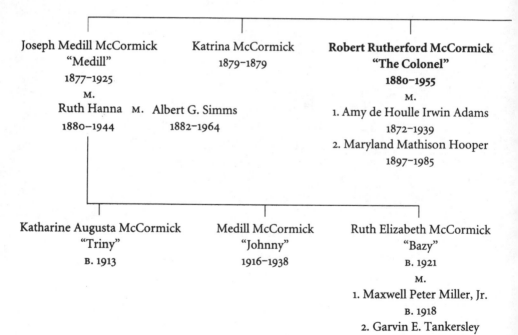

Cyrus Hall McCormick —— William Sanderson McCormick   M. Mary Ann Grigsby
1809–1884   1815–1865   1828–1878

Joseph Medill McCormick   Katrina McCormick   **Robert Rutherford McCormick**
"Medill"   1879–1879   **"The Colonel"**
1877–1925   **1880–1955**
M.   M.
Ruth Hanna   M.   Albert G. Simms   1. Amy de Houlle Irwin Adams
1880–1944   1882–1964   1872–1939
                                                                    2. Maryland Mathison Hooper
                                                                       1897–1985

Katharine Augusta McCormick   Medill McCormick   Ruth Elizabeth McCormick
"Triny"   "Johnny"   "Bazy"
B. 1913   1916–1938   B. 1921
                                                                       M.
                                                                       1. Maxwell Peter Miller, Jr.
                                                                          B. 1918
                                                                       2. Garvin E. Tankersley
                                                                          1911–1997

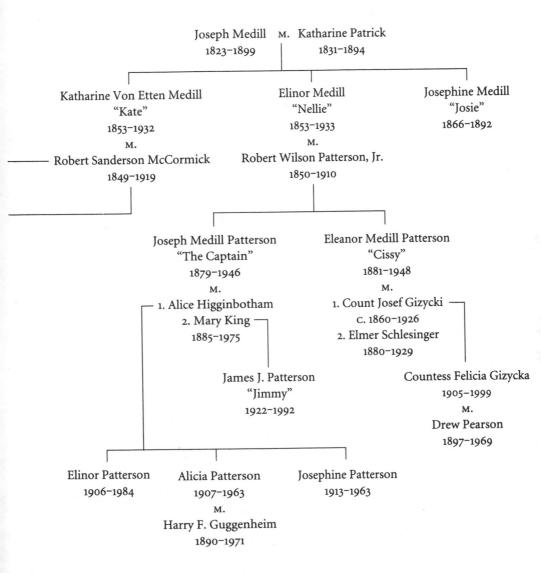

Joseph Medill M. Katharine Patrick
1823–1899 · 1831–1894

Katharine Von Etten Medill
"Kate"
1853–1932
M.
Robert Sanderson McCormick
1849–1919

Elinor Medill
"Nellie"
1853–1933
M.
Robert Wilson Patterson, Jr.
1850–1910

Josephine Medill
"Josie"
1866–1892

Joseph Medill Patterson
"The Captain"
1879–1946
M.
1. Alice Higginbotham
2. Mary King
1885–1975

Eleanor Medill Patterson
"Cissy"
1881–1948
M.
1. Count Josef Gizycki
c. 1860–1926
2. Elmer Schlesinger
1880–1929

James J. Patterson
"Jimmy"
1922–1992

Countess Felicia Gizycka
1905–1999
M.
Drew Pearson
1897–1969

Elinor Patterson
1906–1984

Alicia Patterson
1907–1963
M.
Harry F. Guggenheim
1890–1971

Josephine Patterson
1913–1963

Prologue:
The Voice of America

It was clear that Colonel Diver . . . cared very little what Martin or anybody else thought about him. His highspiced wares were made to sell, and they sold . . . Nothing would have delighted the colonel more than to be told that no such man as he could walk in high success the streets of any other country in the world: for that would only have been a logical assurance . . . of his being strictly and peculiarly a national feature of America.

— Charles Dickens, *Martin Chuzzlewit*

WHEN DICKENS sent his impressionable young Englishman across the Atlantic to take the pulse of Jacksonian America, the traveler could barely conceal his astonishment at the eye-gouging ferocity of Yankee journalism, as personified by Colonel Diver and his jingoistic *New York Rowdy Journal.*

"I am rather at a loss," Martin finally tells a sympathetic interpreter of the local scene, "to know how this colonel escapes being beaten."

"Well, he has been beaten once or twice," replies the New Yorker, clearly believing such chastisement an inadequate deterrent for someone of the colonel's recidivist tendencies.

Had Martin's shade returned to the United States a century later, he would have found Franklin Roosevelt in Andrew Jackson's place and Colonel Diver's lineal descendant still bearding the British lion — not in New York, but a thousand miles to the west, in a vast inland empire called Chicagoland by Colonel Robert R. McCormick and his fire-breathing *Chicago Tribune.* Stretching from Des Moines, Iowa, on the west to Battle Creek, Michigan, on the east, and along a north-south line running from Eau Claire, Wisconsin, to Terre Haute, Indiana, Chicagoland was in 1940 home to 10 percent of the American people. In McCormick's rendering it was "the vital center of America," a glorified Frank Capra village of county fairs and corner drugstores, where everyone worked hard and went to church on Sundays and voted the straight Republican ticket.

Proudly insular, the Colonel's neighbors shared his distrust of life outside the American heartland. "The trouble with you people out there is that you can't see beyond Ohio," McCormick told a *New York Times* reporter in 1947. "And when you think of taking a trip farther west than Ohio you think you're Buffalo Bill. Out there the people think they have got to be for Russia or they have got to be for England. Here, we are for America first, last and all the time."[1]

Believing the East to be gripped by a paradoxical alliance "of international capital and international communism," McCormick looked to the Midwest to preserve the republican form of government. This explained the 144-point-type thunderbolts the publisher of the *Tribune* hurled against New York City, with its "gigolo magazines" and "steam-heated Socialists." To McCormick, New York was "a Sodom and Gomorrah of sin; it is the octopus which battens on the rest of the United States and strangles the free enterprise of competitors ... its young people are immoral and its mature people burned out. It is the reservoir of evil from which disintegrating revolutionary doctrine spreads over the country."[2]

McCormick justified the *Tribune*'s self-proclaimed status as the World's Greatest Newspaper through its circulation, advertising, and political muscle; above all, through its furious Americanism. "What the Chicago *Tribune* reminds me of most is the state of Texas," wrote John Gunther, a Chicagoan born and bred. "Like Texas, it is aggressive, sensitive in the extreme, loaded with guts and braggadocio, expansionist, and medieval. Also, like Texas, it has its own foreign policy — though one very different."

If Colonel McCormick's boasts excited ridicule outside Chicagoland, if a poll of Washington correspondents concluded that the *Tribune* was no more reliable than the despised Hearst organization and hardly as credible as the Communist *Daily Worker*, it only confirmed the Colonel's opinion of the nation's capital as a nest of tax-eaters and "mental dope fiends," built upon the swamp of compromise.

Today, sixty years on, those anesthetized by the compressed blandness of *USA Today* or a thousand interchangeable editions of *Eyewitness News* may find it hard to imagine the emotional violence roused by McCormick's implacable chauvinism. To be sure, there were other American newspapers whose circulation topped one million (although in the 1940s no full-size paper in America could match the *Trib*'s readership or ad revenues). There were — and are — other media outlets accused of blatant bias. But there was only one *Chicago Tribune*, pugnacious, hugely readable, a thorn in the flesh of liberals, One Worlders, and do-gooders of every stripe.

The Colonel's life was a one-man Age of Anxiety. His phobias included, in no particular order, the New Deal; the Fair Deal; Prohibition; Wall Street; the United Nations ("anyone who speaks up for the United Nations is obviously either a Communist or misinformed"); Huey Long (the sole difference between FDR and the demagogic Kingfish, said McCormick, was that "between a Harvard accent and nigger talk"); Wisconsin ("the nuttiest state in the Union, next to California") and its capital, Madison, a liberal hotbed McCormick called New Leningrad;[3] Henry Luce; Herbert Hoover ("the greatest state socialist in history" — before FDR); grand opera; the Nuremberg trials; Walter Winchell; "Buster" Tom Dewey, New York's liberal Republican governor; NATO; State Department functionaries "dead from the neck up"; and cringing "he-debutantes" in his country's foreign service who were more eager to curry favor with an exhausted British empire than to uphold the muscular nationalism of the Mississippi Valley.

Consensus was a dirty word to Robert Rutherford McCormick, regarded by millions of admirers as an ardent patriot and a fearless, if lonely, dissenter from the collectivist anthill. Slack-jawed detractors viewed him with equal fervor as a prototypical reactionary whose defamatory skills endangered the very freedom of expression to which he devoted his life. Both camps were right, yet neither grasped the complexities of this life-long maverick cum pillar of the establishment, whose *Tribune* reflected America as in a funhouse mirror. "I contain multitudes," Walt Whitman had written. So did Colonel McCormick.

• His military title was earned in the trenches of World War I and later called into question by critics who accused McCormick of faking his battlefield exploits. For the rest of his life, McCormick cherished his wartime associations, particularly those with the famed Big Red One, or First Division of the U.S. Army, which held a place in his affections second only to the *Tribune.* In countless articles, books, speeches, and radio broadcasts, he presented himself unblushingly as the greatest strategic thinker since Hannibal. Yet the old soldier who revered martial virtues despised martial force — at least when applied in any cause other than the defense of American territory. The most bellicose of military champions, McCormick was simultaneously the most strident of isolationists.

• "The un-American insect press is continually buzzing around us," declared the *Tribune* in 1950, singling out for criticism the *Chicago Sun-Times, St. Louis Post-Dispatch,* and *Saturday Review of Literature* as publications "conducted by the strange inferiority complex of auburn millionaires." Yet it could also be said that McCormick, the liberals' scourge, was the First Amendment's best friend. Sensibly defining the constitutional position of the press as "freedom from coercion by the government, and not freedom from human frailty," the Colonel spent lavishly to persuade the United States Supreme Court in 1931 to overturn the notorious Gag Law, under which a scruffy small-town weekly in Minnesota had been suppressed as a public nuisance by resentful politicians.[4]

• As befitting "An American Paper for Americans," the *Tribune*'s masthead gave prominent position to Old Glory. The Flag of the Day contest ranked just behind the canine-loving publisher's Dog of the Week feature. But when New Dealers in 1935 seized control of the Rhode Island Supreme Court, threatening the rule of law as defined by the Colonel, he abruptly ordered that state's star cut out of the enormous banner hanging in the lobby of Tribune Tower. Only a warning from his lawyer that he could be prosecuted for flag desecration moved McCormick to restore Little Rhody to her rightful place.

• The Colonel assumed God to be a Presbyterian, but almost never tested his theory by going to church. Only once did he discuss his sins with a friendly pastor. He grumbled that the experience left him feeling like "a fool."[5]

• As a boy, McCormick experienced firsthand the wave of fear and repression that swept Chicago following the Haymarket bombings of 1886. Half a century later, he directed that strikers outside the city's Republic Steel plant be referred to in print as "rioters." Yet his *Tribune* paid some of the highest wages in the profession. Its paternalistic boss shared his profits through annual bonuses and generous benefits. Sick or injured members of the *Tribune* family could expect to be cared for free of charge. Those who went off to fight in the wars McCormick deplored knew that jobs would be waiting for them on their return.

• Learning that a much-married woman was about to take her seventh husband, the Colonel lashed out at pleasure-seekers, "promiscuous as alley cats," whose behavior brought the institution of marriage into contempt. This did not keep him from persuading the wives of two close friends to divorce their husbands and marry him, in scandalous transactions greased by large cash payments.[6]

• McCormick was both visionary and anachronism. Decades before farm-belt politicians jumped on the ethanol bandwagon, he maintained that alcohol could be profitably manufactured from cornstalks. In the 1920s he suggested that elevated highways would alleviate traffic congestion. He named all three Chicago airports, adapted airplane seatbelts for use in automobiles thirty years before Detroit stumbled onto the idea, and, during World War II, came up with a desperately needed synthetic rubber called — what else? — Tribuna. The publisher of the *Chicago Tribune* was a pioneer in wireless news transmission, the use of color, and a primitive version of fax technology. He had seven patents to his name. He could take apart and reassemble a printing press. Yet more than once McCormick summoned *Tribune* engineers to his Astor Street townhouse to change the channel of his television set. With equal sang-froid he rang for a servant to retrieve a pencil inches out of reach. He could as easily turn his back on puffed-up dignitaries to shake hands with Canadian millhands. On Christmas Eve he was likely to be found in the *Tribune* printing plant greeting blue-collar workers. And the Colonel went to his grave mourned chiefly by house servants and a Japanese valet.

For much of the first half of this century, Robert McCormick was one of the most powerful, controversial men in America. He got to be so by emulating one of the most powerful, controversial men in the second half of the nineteenth century — his grandfather Joseph Medill, an early *Tribune* editor who helped elect Abraham Lincoln president in 1860. Like the *Tribune*'s circulation, the influence of the Medills and McCormicks extended far beyond the shores of Lake Michigan. Among the Senate Irreconcileables who doomed American participation in the League of Nations was McCormick's older brother, Medill. Medill's wife, Ruth Hanna, the daughter of one president-maker, blazed political trails in Congress and as Thomas E. Dewey's 1940 presidential campaign manager. McCormick's cousin, Joseph Patterson, founded the *New York Daily News* in 1919 with *Tribune* capital and quickly built the *News* into the most successful tabloid in America. Another Patterson cousin, Cissy, entertained capital readers for a generation with her Auntie Mame antics as publisher of the *Washington Times-Herald*.

Together, the McCormicks and the Pattersons were the Barrymores of American journalism, every bit as gaudy, accomplished, and quarrelsome as that lustrous stage clan. It was no accident that the young Joe Patterson wrote polemical plays denouncing capitalism or that the flamboyant Cissy, a self-described "mean old Irish shanty bitch," considered taking to the stage after her failed marriage to a penniless Polish count. Even Colonel McCormick, an introvert who generally held life at handshake's length, invited himself into millions of homes every Saturday night. For fifteen years, beginning in 1940, radio listeners who tuned in to *The Chicago Theater of the Air* were treated, between snatches of "Naughty Marietta" and "Rosemarie," to the old artilleryman's pronouncements on military tactics and obscure heroes of the American Revolution, delivered in an artless baritone and with characteristic disregard for the stopwatch.

By then McCormick was synonymous with Chicago, as famous as Al Capone or Mrs. O'Leary's cow. In 1940, America's second city was the world's fourth largest metropolis, home to 3.4 million people and second to none in its brash disregard for knockers and pessimists. And why not? This was the city whose motto was "I will"; the city that had raised itself out of the mud in the 1850s, invented the skyscraper, and wrested the World's Columbian Exposition away from New York; the city that produced more food, printed more books, nominated more presidents, welcomed more rail passengers, and created more myths about itself than any other on earth.

As with Chicago, so everything about Colonel McCormick was larger than life, from the outsize American flag that fluttered atop Tribune Tower to the publisher's exaggerated claims to have introduced machine guns to the U.S. Army and ROTC to the nation's classrooms. "I was determined to lead a great life, an exotic life," McCormick once wrote. In fact, he lived many different lives, as city official, engineer, inventor, soldier, military historian, woodsman, civic booster, athlete, radio performer, world traveler, Arctic explorer, experimental farmer. He founded one of Chicago's most successful law firms. He wrote a provocative biography of Ulysses Grant. His study of the battle of Gettysburg was taught at West Point.

But it is as a controversialist that McCormick is best remembered, especially in the grim thirties and martial forties, when the United States underwent dizzying transformation and the Colonel cast himself as defender of an idealized and dying social order. He had little time and less use for clones; the Century of the Common Man was a stench in his nostrils. To dramatize his opposition to Social Security in the 1930s, he printed a dog tag on the *Tribune's* front page. Soon, he insisted, every recipient of New Deal largesse would be required to wear one.

Over time, the *Tribune's* meanness became a national scandal, as when McCormick accused postmaster general James Farley of working "behind the smiling mask of Franklin Roosevelt to bring the end of self-government in the world." Taking their cue from the Colonel, *Tribune* reporters baited Roosevelt mercilessly. Typical was the front-page headline spread across five columns after the first lady found herself in a minor traffic accident: REVOKE MRS. FDR'S DRIVER'S LICENSE. And *Tribune* operators are still remembered for their apocalyptic greeting during the closing weeks of Alf Landon's hopeless 1936 campaign against Roosevelt: "Did you know that there are only *x* more days to save the country?"

Spitefully, FDR spread stories that the Colonel's hatred could be traced to the fact that he had stolen a girlfriend away from his onetime Groton schoolmate, a claim McCormick dismissed as "another one of Frank's shallow lies." On the eve of Pearl Harbor, after Roosevelt had goaded Marshall Field III into challenging the *Tribune's* dominant position with a morning rival, the *Chicago Sun*, McCormick struck back with what he modestly labeled "the greatest scoop in history." The *Sun* rose on December 4, 1941, but most Chicagoans were fixated on that morning's *Tribune*, which revealed the War Department's top-secret plans for a global campaign against Hitler enlisting ten million American soldiers, sailors, and airmen.

Following the Battle of Midway in June 1942 and a *Tribune* sidebar detailing the composition of the shattered Japanese fleet, a livid Roosevelt briefly considered sending Marines to occupy Tribune Tower. On reflection, he ordered that a grand jury be convened, in the hope of indicting the paper's managing editor for revealing wartime secrets to the enemy. Harry Truman carried on in FDR's footsteps, excoriating the Colonel as a traitor who deserved to be hauled before a firing squad.[7]

Yet McCormick went on spitting into the wind of polite convention, assailing political correctness forty years before it had a name. His denunciations of the servile "wood pussy press" sharpened with age. His personal assignments to reporters, signed "RRMC," veered from the quixotic to the bizarre. "Fix Europe," he directed one of his overseas correspondents days before FDR left for Yalta. Another man was dispatched to the traffic island in front of Tribune Tower to learn where policemen bought their whistles and to obtain expert instructions in the art of whistle-blowing. A mixup in communications, exacerbated by McCormick's indecipherable handwriting, resulted in half a dozen *Tribune* reporters and photographers being ordered to Cantigny, the Colonel's estate in suburban Wheaton, to observe a lilac hedge.[8]

At Cantigny, McCormick swam in the nude, sang nonsense songs in his vegetable garden, and kept a pet goldfish named Tojo (after Japan's doomed wartime prime minister) "because he is a poor fish." When Russia supplanted Japan in the pantheon of American adversaries, the Colonel converted Tribune Tower into the world's largest fallout shelter, complete with rooftop steamboat whistle to summon the people of Chicago the moment Soviet planes were sighted in the vicinity. In the basement he stockpiled thousands of cans of pineapple juice, said to be highly effective in treating radioactive burns.[9]

McCormick was drawn to conspiracy theories like a small boy to a burning building. With the cold war raging, he launched a campaign to eliminate the wearing of babushkas. These were described by A. J. Liebling as "a colored kerchief that girls, especially schoolgirls, put over their heads and tie under their chins, producing an effect that does not strike me as specifically Russian." The *Tribune* disagreed. "We propose a city-wide burning of babushkas!" it raged. "Those regimenting rags, which convert pretty, young Chicago faces into moon-faced parodies of peasants, have made the teen scene resemble potato digging time on a

Soviet collective . . . To the torch then, and the burning of the babushkas!"[10]

McCormick's bluster had a way of obscuring his commitment to principle. Once a *Tribune* advertising manager asked editors to downplay the
divorce of a wealthy department store owner. The phone rang late that
night in the Colonel's bedroom at Cantigny.

"Keep the story and throw out the advertising," McCormick replied
without hesitation.

But this would mean the next day's paper had to be torn up.

"Tear it up," said the Colonel.

But the store had a major advertising contract with the *Tribune*.

"Tear up the contract."[11]

Over the fireplace in his baronial Tribune Tower office, McCormick
carved his declaration of principles, reminding visitors that newspapers
like his were created "to furnish that check upon government which no
constitution has ever been able to provide." But to whom, if anyone, was a
newspaper accountable? Four decades after his death, it is tempting to sen-
timentalize McCormick as an editor of the old school, answerable to the
millions who read his columns or took umbrage at his rantings. Certainly
as a practitioner of personal journalism, tomahawking his enemies while
feathering his arrows with wit, he was the last of his kind.

And yet . . . in 1946, 133 newspapers were sold for every 100 American
homes. Today that figure has been cut in half. Fewer Americans subscribe
to newspapers than in 1965. In an age of declining cultural literacy and
instantaneous communication, journals everywhere struggle to survive.
Often they seek relevance through the very features, from beauty tips and
movie reviews to household and financial planning, that McCormick and
Joe Patterson used early in this century to reinvent the *Tribune*.

Together McCormick and Patterson transformed Chicago's third-
ranking newspaper into the most widely read full-size journal in the
land — the heart of a communications empire that included nearly 7,000
square miles of Canadian timberland, three company towns, state-of-
the-art paper mills and power dams, a fleet of ships to transport foreign newsprint to McCormick's Lake Michigan docks, a large chunk of
the Mutual Broadcasting System, successful radio and television stations
bearing the inevitable call letters WGN (for World's Greatest Newspaper),
and invaluable parcels of downtown Chicago real estate. In the process
McCormick himself became as widely feared or followed as anyone in a
generation of media titans that included William Randolph Hearst, Harry
Chandler, Joseph Pulitzer, and Henry Luce.

Those moved to burn the *Tribune* in the streets of Chicago found
its publisher, brooding in his tower perch, forever holding the modern
world at bay, a subject of endless fascination. McCormick managed his

celebrity like a business, deliberately lending himself to caricatures like the long-running series of Colonel McCosmic cartoons that enlivened the rival *Chicago Daily News.* Even puppeteer Burr Tillstrom got into the act by presenting a fanciful Colonel Crackie to complement Kukla, Fran, and Ollie.

During McCormick's lifetime, profiles of him generally fell into two categories: rancorous and condescending. Since his death, in 1955, passions have cooled. Yet would-be biographers have been frustrated by a lack of access to his personal and business papers. In the summer of 1990, I was approached by officials of the Robert R. McCormick–Tribune Foundation, to which he left the bulk of his estate. They asked if I might be interested in undertaking a full-scale biography of the Colonel. If so, they promised, for the first time, to make available all of McCormick's papers — totaling several hundred thousand pages — as well as *Tribune* corporate records vital to any accounting of the Colonel's business career.

Quickly and unanimously, we agreed that the credibility of the project would depend on its absolute independence of the newspaper and foundation. Since then no one at either organization has seen anything I have written, nor has anyone asked to.* For this, as much as for the original grant of unlimited access to the McCormick archives, I am grateful.

With the opening of the Colonel's papers came a fresh set of challenges, for a biographer has dual obligations. Without empathy for his subject (not to be confused with admiration, let alone affection), he cannot possibly break through to understanding, the key to intelligent speculation about individual character, motives, and inner life. At the same time, he owes his reader an unsparing candor, keeping in mind Lytton Strachey's maxim: "Discretion is not the better part of biography." McCormick poses a particularly high hurdle for any biographer interested in fairness and balance, qualities rarely associated with his *Tribune.* Associates found him hard to know, harder still to take completely seriously. I have tried to do both, depicting him against the backdrop of protean Chicago and a turbulent century of American journalism. Moreover, McCormick's story is also that of a great American dynasty, one whose impressive achievements were equaled by its capacity for self-indulgence.

To understand Robert McCormick, then, one must first inhabit the world of his grandfather, Joseph Medill, the world of Dickens's *New York Rowdy Journal,* and an era when newspapers were read not for their

---

*The sole exception is Kristie Miller, a grandniece of the Colonel's and the biographer of his sister-in-law, Ruth Hanna McCormick Simms. A current member of the board of Tribune Company, Kristie has been generous with her time, her insights, and her encouragement. It goes without saying that she bears no responsibility for the conclusions I have reached.

objectivity but for their personality. That this rococo brand of journalism should survive in the pages of McCormick's *Tribune* long after changes in public taste and professional canons rendered it extinct nearly everywhere else makes the Colonel historically significant. So does his legacy as a champion of Middle America in the political and cultural wars which continue to divide a nation far less homogenous than it pretends.

When McCormick died on April Fool's Day, 1955, eulogists unable to think of anything positive to say called him "an American Original." Few bothered to look over their shoulders at an equally distinctive figure in the history of American news-gathering, upon whom the dead man had patterned his life and whose ancient stand-up writing desk occupied a place of honor in McCormick's office in Tribune Tower, alongside a marble bust of Lincoln and the gun used to murder a corrupt *Tribune* reporter at the height of Chicago's mob era.

For almost a century, Joseph Medill and Robert McCormick personified a distinguished, if raucous, newspaper tradition of alienating the powerful. Medill lectured American presidents from Franklin Pierce to William McKinley; his grandson picked up where he left off, abusing with fine impartiality chief executives of both parties and all ideological persuasions. Closer to home, Victorian-era Chicagoans cheered Mayor Carter Harrison when he hurled Medill's *Tribune* to the ground and stomped on the paper as if it were a venomous snake. Forty years later the clownishly venal Republican mayor William "Big Bill" Thompson denounced all McCormicks as moral degenerates.

Both publishers thrived on controversy, never doubting their place on the side of the angels. What the *Tribune* correspondent James O'Donnell Bennett wrote of Medill in 1926 was at least as applicable to McCormick: "He believed that the United States was the finest country on earth, that Chicago — despite Democrats — was the finest city in the country, and that the *Tribune* had more character and sense of service than any other newspaper in the world."

It is the final irony of McCormick's paradoxical career that this reactionary in love with the First Amendment, this urbane provincial, this uniformed martinet who conceived a dread of militarism, this passionate, if quirky, student of history, was described as *sui generis* by contemporaries quick to apologize for the strutting journalistic traditions from which he and his vanished kind had sprung. There would have been a *Chicago Tribune* without Joe Medill, but there would have been no *Tribune* legend to inspire Robert McCormick or provoke millions of *Tribune* readers to spasms of outrage punctuated by laughter.

PART I

Splendid Monsters

1823–1903

"Never take the defensive. It is an indication
of a bad conscience. Always attack."

JOSEPH MEDILL

1

The House of Medill

"Go in boldly, strike straight from the shoulders, hit below the belt as well as above, and kick like thunder."

— Joseph Medill to Abraham Lincoln, September 10, 1859

JOSEPH MEDILL traced his family origins to the sixteenth century, to a band of French Huguenots who crossed the English Channel to avoid persecution by a Catholic king. Medill's grandfather found work in the famous Belfast shipyards that launched Britannia as a great seagoing power. His father, William Medill, was born in 1792 on a farm near Dram and Coothill, County Monaghan. Reared a devout Calvinist, William passed on to his son not only the Medill obstinacy and moral courage but also his creed's stern insistence on making civic life conform to God's will.

Something else flowed in the Medill blood as well — a disdain for lordly Britain that drove William and his bride, Margaret, to forsake Ulster for the New World soon after their 1819 wedding. Joseph, their eldest son, was born on April 6, 1823, near the town of St. John in a disputed region of northern Maine later awarded to British Canada under the Webster–Ashburton Treaty. Beginning life on foreign soil deprived Joseph Medill of any chance to become president of the United States. This caused a lifelong grudge, worn like a birthmark, against America's hereditary enemy. But it also inflamed the outsider's identification with his adopted homeland, making Medill *plus royaliste que le roi.*

In 1832, William and Margaret Medill resumed their westward travels, part of a broad migratory river that surged up and over the Appalachians until Ohio became the third most populous state in the young republic.

Memories of the War of 1812 were still fresh along the frontier, even around established communities like Massillon, where the Medills bought a farm after a cholera epidemic diverted them from their original destination of St. Louis. In a later autobiographical sketch, only recently uncovered, Joseph Medill remembered Massillon as "a very lively place populated by energetic and pleasant people." The Medills resided there six years, until William bought a farm in nearby Pike township. During this period young Joseph heard bloodcurdling tales of Indian atrocities caused by British provocateurs.[1]

A schoolboy rhyme of the period captures both the pride and the justifiable sense of military inferiority with which upstart Yankees confronted their haughty former masters:

> We love our rude and rocky shore
> And here we stand
> Let foreign navies hasten o'er
> And on our heads their furies pour
> And peal their cannons' loudest roar
> And storm our land
> They still shall find our lives are given
> To die for home, and leant on Heaven
> Our hand.

If the adult Joseph Medill often behaved as if he had a personal pipeline to heaven, he came by his self-assurance the hard way, having assumed responsibility for two sisters and three younger brothers as their father's health declined and his attempts to farm the scrubby hill country of northeastern Ohio proved unprofitable. An intellectually precocious boy, Joseph befriended an elderly Quaker whose extensive library served as his first classroom. Impressed by the tall, spare youth with rust-colored hair and an insatiable appetite for books, the older man let Joseph feast on thick volumes of history and biography, supplementing his literary diet with the likes of Milton, Shakespeare, Pope, Shelley, Dickens, and Irving. Each Saturday the youngster walked nine miles "hunting up some teacher at Canton to recite to or help me out of hard places in Mathematics, Latin, Chemistry, Natural Philosophy, Law, etc." On the side he took subscriptions for Horace Greeley's influential *New York Weekly Tribune.*[2]

"It was hard work and what education I obtained came by self-denial and application," Medill reminisced half a century later. He developed a hero worship for Benjamin Franklin, another self-taught, self-made poor boy who never hesitated to challenge the conventional wisdom of his time. With something of Franklin's mental versatility, if little of his bubbling wit or generosity of spirit, the future editor considered the Bible "the most wonderful astrological book we have" and the electricity that powered humming telegraph wires as a direct gift from God. Making a fetish out of common sense, Medill decided that there was nothing sensible about English orthography, so he devised his own rules of spelling, arbitrarily dropping all silent letters.[3]

His fascination with ancient Rome and the crumbling republic immortalized by Edward Gibbon prompted an extravagant admiration for Roman order and a corresponding suspicion of anyone who did not share his belief in a strong central government as the engine of American greatness. In Medill's *Tribune*, the word *Nation* was always capitalized and the United States referred to in the singular, as an integrated federal republic and not the loose confederation of sovereign states enshrined in Jeffersonian dogma. Like many Scots-Irish newcomers, young Medill brought with him a disdain for slavery and the southern aristocracy so reminiscent of caste-conscious Britain.

Wherever Medill came by his ideas, he didn't get them from classroom instructors, his formal education being limited to a few months in a district school and a brief sojourn at Massillon Academy. In February 1844, a fire wiped out his family's homestead and his own hopes of pursuing a college education. His longing to escape the drudgery of Ohio farm life survived the flames, however, as did the stubborn will and lonely sense of duty imparted by his Presbyterian ancestors.

To assist his struggling family, he landed a teaching position in a rural schoolhouse at $25 a month. Something of his frustration, as well as his rich polemical talents, is conveyed by an angry editorial of somewhat later vintage. "Teacher's wages are jewed down to that delicate point at which a lazy ignoramus is puzzled whether to teach or maul rails," Medill sputtered, the memory still rankling. "In the name of common sense, how can one person be expected to hear a dozen branches recite twice, three, or four times in a single day, out of as many different kinds of schoolbooks? And all this in a single room, densely jammed, wretchedly heated, unventilated, some roasting, others shivering, all breathing an atmosphere foul as a glue factory."[4]

In the classroom Medill earned his spurs by thrashing three reluctant scholars on the first day of school. His pugilistic exploits caught the attention of his future bride, Miss Katharine Patrick, the daughter of a county judge who doubled as editor of the *Tuscarawas Chronicle*. Pining for the refinements of life in his native Belfast, James Patrick had books and oysters in the shell brought over the mountains in saddlebags. Miss Patrick's mother, also named Katharine, was descended from Hudson Valley grandees who had fought in the Revolution and moved west as their fortunes steadily declined. One thing that did not diminish was the family's sense of entitlement. According to tradition, Katharine Van Etten Westfall always carried a bag of gold dollars for distribution to anyone who could provide her with a chicken dinner.[5]

In time, Medill began hanging around newspaper offices, where he learned to set type, work a hand press, and write an occasional article or editorial. At the age of twenty-one the industrious young man apprenticed himself to a Canton lawyer. Two years later he entered into a partnership with George McIlvaine, a future chief justice of the Ohio Supreme Court. His new calling brought him face to face with his fellow attorneys Salmon P. Chase and Edwin M. Stanton, both destined, as mainstays of Lincoln's cabinet, to become invaluable sources for the *Chicago Tribune*. Chase and Stanton were gifted public performers, able to draw upon forensic talents denied to Medill. Given the choice, Medill would rather argue his convictions from the cloistered confines of an editor's office. There, alone with his pen and a bottomless capacity for moral indignation, he could hurl *obiter dicta* with impunity.

Never hesitant to assert his historical claims, Medill in later years took credit for the ensuing political revolution. As he put it, "The honor of giving birth to the Republican party ought to be divided between Steve Douglas and myself. I began by preaching the death of the Whig party in my little Whig paper; Douglas hastened it by pulling down the bars and letting the South into the free territory."[6]

This was not as far-fetched as it might sound. Quickly abandoning his tepid pursuit of the law, Medill in 1849 purchased the *Coshocton Whig*. His first act as publisher was to rename his acquisition the *Republican*. As such, it lent powerful support to a nascent fusion movement of antislavery elements in the region. Seeking a broader stage for his talents, Medill looked to Cleveland, a handsome city of rapidly expanding influence on the shores of Lake Erie. In the fall of 1851 he established a morning paper there called the *Forest City*, later merged with a local abolitionist sheet to form the *Cleveland Leader*. Hoping to repeat his earlier political success, the editor campaigned for General Winfield Scott, the vainglorious Mexican War hero nominated by the Whigs in 1852 to oppose the aggressively mediocre Democratic presidential candidate, Franklin Pierce. In November, Scott suffered a crushing defeat, losing even Whiggish Ohio by more than 30,000 votes.

Scott's rejection strengthened Medill in his belief that the time had come to bury the Whig party, whose English antecedents made it anathema to Irish voters, and raise up in its place a new political organization pledged to resist the spread of slavery. Encouragement in these party-building efforts came from Horace Greeley and his *New York Tribune*. Greeley was a professional eccentric, in the vanguard of every mid-century reform campaign from vegetarianism to the utopian ideas of the

French socialist Fourier. Greeley's idealism had its limits: once asked to contribute to a fund that would save sinners from going to hell, the editor snapped, "I won't give you a cent. There don't half enough go there now." With his pink skin, piping voice, and trademark chin whiskers, Greeley did not look formidable, but his crusading zeal rivaled Medill's own, and no one laughed at the *Tribune's* nationwide circulation of 50,000.

Greeley employed Medill as his Cleveland correspondent, visiting him on trips to the Western Reserve and beaming with approval as the *Leader* rallied Ohioans dismayed by the bumbling incompetence of the Pierce administration. Medill's grassroots organizing accelerated during the winter of 1852–53. After sampling antislavery opinion, he formally proposed the establishment of a new party, to be known as the National Republicans (a title previously applied to the short-lived anti-Jackson coalition of the early 1830s, uniting eastern commercial interests and western advocates of Henry Clay's ambitious program of internal improvements). One night in March 1854, he called a meeting of Ohio politicians. Although fewer than a dozen responded, it was more than enough to fuel a tedious debate about what the new party might be called. Hoping to attract dissatisfied former Democrats like himself, Salmon P. Chase argued for the name Free Democrats, but a majority agreed with Medill that any party committed to the natural-rights philosophy of the founding fathers should bear the name Republican. A similar gathering held the month before at Ripon, Wisconsin, had anticipated what an outdoor convention at Jackson, Michigan, that summer only ratified, replacing the enfeebled Whigs with a movement whose youthful fervor was undiminished by its sectional appeal.[7]

At the age of thirty-two, Joseph Medill was a force to be reckoned with, a seasoned journalist with a taste for politics and a talent for organizing other men to do his bidding — exactly the sort of upwardly mobile American whom Horace Greeley advised to "go West, young man, and grow up with the country." Some early *Tribune* histories claim that Greeley's famous counsel was originally directed at Medill himself. This seems unlikely; still, it was only natural that the New York editor should urge his western protégé to go where he might lend the greatest assistance to their common cause.

In the winter of 1854–55 that meant Chicago, a crude but promising town boasting 85,000 people, more than 500 saloons, and 110 brothels. Less than forty years had passed since the Indian massacre of inhabitants of Fort Dearborn, near the mouth of the Chicago River. In the 1830s the fort had been rebuilt to serve as Winfield Scott's headquarters in a burlesque war against the Fox and Sauk Indian tribes. Scott had assembled his strategists at Rat Tavern, a frowzy house of public entertainment presided over by Long John Wentworth. At six feet, seven inches tall, and weighing over three hundred pounds, the Democrat-turned-Republican Wentworth was another of the race of giants who created Chicago, then and for years afterward called Mudtown by unfortunate pedestrians in clawhammer coats and freshly pressed linen trousers.

As it happened, Greeley knew of another enterprising journalist who might be willing to enter into a Chicago partnership with Medill. Charles H. Ray was a former medical doctor who was less interested in conventional surgery than in ridding his country of the cancer of slavery. For the past three years he had edited the Galena, Illinois, *Jeffersonian*, a maverick Democratic newspaper opposed to the repeal of the Missouri Compromise implicit in Douglas's Kansas-Nebraska Act. As clerk of the Illinois state senate in February 1855, Ray had announced the narrow victory of Lyman Trumbull over the downstate lawyer Abraham Lincoln in their contest for a U.S. Senate seat. Now he dreamed of starting a penny newspaper in Chicago, both to further the sacred cause of freedom and to shatter Senator Douglas's presidential ambitions.

Greeley, anxious to have a Chicago acolyte, wrote mutual letters of introduction for Medill and Ray. By the time these were exchanged in a corridor of the Sherman House in March 1855, Medill had already received an independent feeler from Captain J. D. Webster, one of the owners of the faltering *Chicago Daily Tribune*, an outgrowth of the weekly *Gem of the Prairie*. The *Tribune* had been born in a third-floor room at the corner of LaSalle and Lake streets eight years earlier with a promise to be "neutral in nothing; it will be independent in everything." Investigation revealed that the paper could be had for much less than the cost of launching a new sheet.

The reasons why said volumes about Chicago's combustible mix of ethnic and religious rivalries. The *Tribune*'s noisy hostility to foreigners, especially Irish Catholics, and its ham-handed opposition to saloons patronized by the foreign-born, had done nothing to endear it to immigrants. Indeed, only a few weeks earlier the city editor had been challenged to a duel after he criticized a ship's captain for transporting the papal nuncio, the future Cardinal Bendini, on his expedition into the American wilderness.

Medill needed little persuading to buy a one-third interest in the venture. Ray and Medill's Cleveland bookkeeper, Alfred Cowles, came in for most of the rest. As befitting one of his statewide visibility and extensive political contacts, Ray became editor-in-chief of the revamped *Tribune*. Medill was named managing editor, at $40 a week. In June 1855, the new team, an uneasy alliance in a city poised on the brink of greatness, commenced business.

✧ 2

When assessing his paternal ancestors and their contentious progeny, Colonel McCormick was more than usually blunt. "All the McCormicks are crazy except me," he insisted, mindful that not everyone would rush to accept his qualification. One could with equal candor and greater charity say that the McCormicks were a family in which emotional balance and intellectual (or any other) modesty were notable chiefly for their absence. This turbulent clan had its roots on the bleak, windswept island of Mull, carved by the sea off the northwest coast of Scotland. Long before Robert Louis Stevenson made Mull famous in *Kidnapped*, the visiting Samuel Johnson had concluded that "in this country every man's name is MacLean" (usually spelled MacLaine). The McCormicks were a sept of this dominant clan. Their motto, "Meat and Drink to McCormick," was, in the Colonel's puckish telling, "a privilege they received from the MacLaines for a very, very fine job of cattlestealing."[8]

Whether or not they were outlaws in the technical sense, a love of combat undoubtedly flowed in the McCormicks' blood, and the seventeenth century afforded no shortage of opportunities for born fighters like Captain James McCormick. Leaving Mull for battle-scarred Ulster, he plunged headlong into the sectarian strife that seems a permanent part of Irish history. In 1690 he took up arms against James II, the feckless Catholic monarch who had been chased out of England the year before. McCormick distinguished himself in the defense of the Protestant stronghold of Londonderry. He played a hero's part at the Battle of the Boyne, the decisive encounter that secured the English throne for the Protestant contender, William of Orange (after which James, the last in a line of Stuart kings dating to 1603, scurried back to France with the immortal concession speech, "I do now resolve to shift for myself"). For his exploits, James McCormick was memorialized in a Londonderry church window and given a coat of arms featuring a mailed fist clutching a spear.

Adoption of the Toleration Act of 1689 calls into question the subsequent family tradition that Captain McCormick's son, Thomas, shook the dust of unhappy Ireland from his boots and sailed for America in 1735 in search of religious freedom. Perhaps, as a good Calvinist fearing God and nothing else, Thomas McCormick did forsake idolatrous Britain for religious liberty in the New World. But it is just as likely that he was lured across the ocean by the promise of cheap, abundant farmland. Settling on two hundred acres near what is now Harrisburg, Pennsylvania, he raised crops and children in equal profusion. His fifth son, Robert, the first of his line to bear that name, was also the great-great-grandfather of our subject.

"McCormicks always marry their betters," the Colonel maintained; if so, the pattern may have been set by his eighteenth-century eponym, whose bride, Martha Sanderson, brought to the altar a handsome dowry and the managerial skills to run a large farm and family while her husband was away fighting British redcoats in the Carolinas. In 1779 the McCormicks moved south, to the fertile Shenandoah Valley of Virginia. A change of scenery did nothing to lessen Robert McCormick's unwavering adherence to the Scottish piety of his forebears; appalled by local Presbyterian hymn-singing, he founded a rival congregation faithful to the old ways. In years to come, liturgical infighting ranked alongside disputed patents, contested fortunes, and savage political feuds as a source of McCormick family acrimony.[9]

Robert and Martha McCormick contributed handsomely to the new nation's exploding population. In July 1780 they welcomed a sixth son, also named Robert, who would more than validate the flippant tribute his great-grandson made to the upward mobility of McCormick men. At the age of twenty-eight, Robert II wed Mary Ann Hall, an uncommon woman commonly known as Polly. A soldier's daughter with expensive tastes that were rarely gratified in the barracks hall or officers' quarters, Polly appeared to her loving family as distinctive as the peacocks preening themselves on the lawns of Walnut Grove, the 532-acre McCormick estate.

Hoping for still greater riches, Polly's husband devised a horse-powered thresher, a blacksmith's bellows, and other machines intended to ease the backbreaking labors of the American farmer. Yet the proprietor of Walnut Grove was repeatedly frustrated in his search for a reliable, affordable horse-drawn reaper, which, by replacing the ancient sickle and heavy cradle, could vastly multiply each year's wheat harvest during the few short days before a crop ripened and shattered. Such a device would revolutionize the agricultural economy, so it is hardly surprising that tinkerers besides Robert McCormick should pursue the grail for themselves. What is strange, or would be among all but the combative offspring of Captain James McCormick, is that long after Robert's death in 1846, his work was at the center of a controversy involving him and his eldest son, Cyrus.

Born at Walnut Grove in February 1809, Cyrus McCormick inherited his father's mechanical gifts and aptitude for business. ("If inventive genius is hereditary," Colonel McCormick commented late in life, "I got it from the McCormick side. None of the Medills knew a fence from a lawn mower.") While his father struggled for twenty years to master the technology of vibrating knives and grain platforms, Cyrus looked on. Evidently he learned something, for in 1831 he was able to supply the critical missing element, a wheel to operate the reaper's complex gears. Beyond this innovation, it was Cyrus's ability to absorb and integrate the discoveries of others that formed the basis of his claims to be inventor of the reaper.[10]*

Still, the world did not exactly beat a path to his door, even after Cyrus patented his new machine in 1834. Father and son opened an iron furnace, succeeding only in draining the family's resources. Soon Walnut Grove was heavily mortgaged. In 1844, Cyrus left home to pursue new customers for his reaper. His efforts were rewarded in the fast-growing northwest, the monotonously flat terrain of which proved much better suited to the device than the gullied hills of Virginia. In 1847, seeing where his future markets lay, Cyrus descended on Chicago, a human whirlwind in size 55 trousers, armed with a letter of introduction from his political twin, Stephen A. Douglas.

That June, Douglas's journalistic nemesis, the *Chicago Tribune*, published its initial run of four hundred copies. Delegates to the city's first political convention howled in protest over President Polk's veto of a harbor and river improvements bill. The executive in distant Washington was not the only thing in bad odor with Chicagoans that summer. Owing to the proliferation of meat-packing plants along its banks, the Chicago River had become an open cesspool, as deadly to local inhabitants as the inky lake waters delivered through wooden pipes, which invited periodic epidemics of cholera. Life in early Chicago required intestinal fortitude, of which Cyrus McCormick had more than his share. Erecting a showplace factory on three hundred feet of lakeshore property just south of the modern-day Tribune Tower, McCormick sold 1,500 reapers and cleared $50,000 in his first year. The mill suffered extensive damage in an 1851 fire. Rebuilt within six months along more elaborate lines than ever, its thirty-horsepower engine became one of the local wonders routinely displayed to out-of-town visitors.

McCormick himself was something of a Chicago attraction. Admirers credited him with channeling nature "to the benign end of civilization and bringing bread to the mouths of the poor." In reality, his chief interest was bringing money to himself. This he did in spectacular fashion, anticipating the Fields and Armours, Wrigleys and Pullmans, who would make Chicago what H. G. Wells called "the most perfect presentation of 19th century individual industrialism I have ever seen." By 1856 the McCormick firm could report annual profits of $300,000, a figure that might have been higher still if not for the proprietor's hobby of suing his enemies. Having persuaded his younger brothers William and Leander to leave Walnut

---

*Over the years a vast amount of ink has been spilled, much of it by argumentative McCormicks, contesting Cyrus's title as "father of the reaper." Thirty years after his death, his vinegary niece by marriage, Kate McCormick, aided by her newspaperman son, Robert, waged an unsuccessful campaign to keep Cyrus out of the Hall of Fame.

Grove and take a hand in running the Chicago operations, Cyrus was free to indulge himself in an endless round of lawsuits.

By no means all of these dealt with patent infringement. For example, the reaper king pursued the Pennsylvania Railroad for twenty-one years over some luggage he said had been damaged by a lightning bolt. The officers of the New York Central were more adroit; they wrote out a check the moment they heard a McCormick writ was in the offing. In 1854 the litigious inventor went up against Abraham Lincoln, the prairie lawyer who had been engaged by a competitor from nearby Rockford, Illinois. Before the case could go to trial, Lincoln was silenced by Joseph Medill's attorney friend, Edwin Stanton, who took one look at the gawky westerner in his sweat-stained linen duster and asked, "Where did that long-armed baboon come from?" No matter; Lincoln's side won the case and the Springfield attorney pocketed $2,000. It was, as events would show, a down payment on future battles with the Chicago industrialist, whose southern sympathies made him and his family personae non grata among sworn foes of slavery like Medill.

✧ 3

It was inevitable that Medill, like McCormick convinced that he was doing the Lord's work and sharing the vision of a great city lurking within the untidy straggle of wooden buildings ranged along the stinking river, should cross swords with the transplanted Virginian who railed against "Abolitionist Chicago." It was just as predictable that Medill and his *Tribune* partners would forge an alliance with Lincoln, whose visit to their offices in the spring of 1855 became part of the corporate mythology inherited by Colonel McCormick and his blood relations.

"Can you tell me when I can see Dr. Ray?" the tall stranger inquired. Ray, it turned out, was away from the building.

Might the visitor be speaking, then, to "the new editor from Cleveland — McDill, Medill or something?"[11]

He was indeed. On learning of this, Lincoln handed over four dollars for a *Tribune* subscription, along with compliments to the new management for having abandoned the nativism of their predecessors. The talk soon turned to current politics, in particular to Medill's campaign to attract disaffected Whigs such as Lincoln into Republican ranks. "From that day until his death I enjoyed a peculiar and close intimacy with Mr. Lincoln," Medill asserted long afterward.[12] He was not the first political follower to mistake access for influence, or to fill Lincoln's pregnant silences with his own thoughts, interpretations, or objectives. *The Collected Works of Abraham Lincoln*, ten volumes regarded as definitive, contain but four letters from Lincoln to Medill, while Medill's papers, with their generous helpings of unsolicited counsel, illustrate the one-sided relationship existing between the two men during the convulsive decade leading up to and including Lincoln's wartime presidency.

In the turbulent mid-fifties, Medill helped to raise money and rifles for antislavery forces in Kansas, where a border war between Missouri Bushwhackers and Kansas Jayhawks served as a dress rehearsal for a vastly bloodier conflict looming on the horizon. Closer to home, he and Ray utilized the "horse blanket" format of four immense pages, each nine columns wide, with a scattering of advertising on each page, to make their *Tribune* into a combination town crier, purveyor of gossip, Chamber of Commerce promoter, and scold. When a Mrs. Wheeler, married just a month, twice attempted suicide, the editors demanded that her abusive husband spend a year in jail, breaking rocks. Under the heading SERVED HIM RIGHT, the paper poured scorn on a Chicagoan judged guilty of cruelty toward a horse, than which there was hardly any crime more "despicable or cowardly."

To one of Medill's outlook, the greatest crime of all was slavery, and the worst offender sat in the White House. James Buchanan was only the latest doughface — a northern man with southern principles — to defile the place of Washington. The president's brazen attempts to recognize the pro-slavery government imposed on Kansas by border ruffians made him a latter-day Judas. Adding to Buchanan's sins was the worst depression yet experienced by the American people. As panic swept the marketplace and money went into hiding, even Chicago felt a momentary check in its hitherto unstoppable expansion. Cyrus McCormick continued to pay his workforce every Saturday night, but the city's journalistic establishment trembled.

In July 1858, the *Tribune* was driven to a merger with the *Democratic Press*, operated by "Deacon" William Bross, a future lieutenant governor of Illinois, whose extravagant brows and flowing beard gave him the appearance of an Old Testament prophet, and young John Locke Scripps. The new concern borrowed heavily to meet its obligations, including payment for one of Richard Hoe's new high-speed rotary presses and the first copper-faced type to be used in Illinois. Thus girded for battle, the *Tribune* looked forward to besting its rival, the *Chicago Times*, on the streets and at the polls.

✧ 4

Eighteen fifty-eight was an election year. All eyes were on Illinois, where Stephen Douglas, having broken with Buchanan over the turmoil brought on in Kansas by the senator's theories of squatter sovereignty, was made an unlikely Republican hero. Overheated blood boils easily; in the feverish climate touched off by Bleeding Kansas, Horace Greeley and other easterners hoped to detach the Little Giant from Buchanan's fast-sinking administration. Medill was incredulous that such "political wetnurses" had so little faith in "the barbarians of Illinois" as to choose their advocates for them.

Lincoln shared his dismay. That June, after disposing of Long John Wentworth's senatorial claims, the Springfield lawyer entered the fray with the *Tribune* at his side. The marriage had its stormy moments. "How, in God's name, do you let such paragraphs in to the *Tribune?*" wrote an exasperated candidate after Medill and Ray urged upon Indiana Republicans a course almost identical to what Greeley had tried to fob off on Illinois. "I confess it astonishes me."[13]

More useful to Lincoln's cause were *Tribune* attacks on Douglas as one who "would rather go about the country like a strolling mounteback, with his cannon, toadies and puffers . . . than to stand up to the work with a full-grown man to confront." On July 22 the paper challenged the incumbent senator to a series of debates "in the old western style." Beginning at Ottawa in mid-August, Lincoln and Douglas argued their differences before tens of thousands of spectators assembled in courthouse squares and at county fairgrounds. Attentive voters appeared mindful, in the words of the *Richmond Enquirer*, that they were witnessing on the Illinois prairies "the great battle of the next Presidential election."[14]

As usual, Medill was full of advice. "Put a few ugly questions at Douglas," he urged Lincoln at the start of the series, "in as sharp, pointed and offensive a form as possible." The candidate must pitch into his opponent "dogmatically and unqualifiedly. Be saucy with the 'Catiline' and permit no browbeating — in other words give him h — l." Lincoln should discard all thoughts of personal modesty, for he was dealing with "a bold brazen lying rascal" peddling theories of self-government no better than "humbug, slang and trash."[15]

While Lincoln and Douglas exchanged body blows on platforms across the state, their journalistic seconds indulged in verbal fisticuffs. "If mutilating public discourses were a criminal offense, the scamp whom Douglas hires to report Lincoln's speeches would be a ripe subject for the Penitentiary," said the *Tribune* of the *Chicago Times*. The most recent scholar of the debates, Harold Holzer, has argued persuasively that each side polished the words of its respective favorite and left the opposition to the tender mercies of rushed stenographers and partisan headline writers. DRED SCOTT CHAMPION PULVERIZED, the *Tribune* declared of the first debate. LINCOLN BREAKS DOWN. DOUGLAS SKINS "THE LIVING DOG," countered the *Times*.[16]

In the weeks leading up to the voting, the *Tribune* contrasted the plain ways of Mr. Lincoln, who eschewed paid libelers and traveled quietly from one meeting to the next, with the hired puffers and lavishly outfitted railroad cars favored by his opponent. Hoping to compensate for a superior Democratic organization, Medill joined a committee that dispatched so-called floating voters from Chicago to doubtful districts downstate. It wasn't enough. In November, Republican legislative candidates outpolled their rivals by 4,000 votes, but the ancient, if less than honorable, device of the gerrymander assured Douglas of sufficient strength to retain his place in the Senate.

Yet Lincoln had won far more than he lost. Overnight the obscure lawyer was transformed into a national figure. "No man could have done more," the *Tribune* asserted in the gray dawn of defeat. "His speeches will become landmarks in our political history; and we are sure that when the public mind is more fully aroused to the importance of the themes which he has so admirably discussed, the popular verdict will place him a long way in advance of the more fortunate champion by whom he has been overthrown."

For the next year the *Tribune* rowed with muffled oars toward its objective — a western, Republican president. It didn't necessarily have to be Illinois's favorite son. Indeed, throughout most of 1859 Medill touted his Ohio acquaintance Salmon P. Chase, at one point assuring Chase that he would "work underground for you, and openly for a western man." But the painfully upright governor of Ohio inspired little enthusiasm, even in his own state. The other leading contender, Senator William Seward of New York, not hitherto regarded as a slave to principle, surprised his supporters and delighted his enemies by imprudently warning of an "irrepressible conflict" between southern slaveowners sheltering behind the Constitution and antislavery forces motivated by a "higher law." John Brown's quixotic raid on Harper's Ferry, staged in the hope of igniting a slave rebellion, succeeded only in rousing southern fire-eaters and discrediting the higher-law theories espoused by Seward and his fellow Black Republicans. Thus Seward became a victim of timing and his own verbal incontinence.

To a growing number of pragmatists, Abraham Lincoln appeared less intractable than either Chase or Seward, a blank slate on which men of all persuasions were free to write their ideological desires. Lincoln doubted his White House prospects. "Aren't you an optimist, Joe?" he once asked Medill. The editor boldly — and self-servingly — replied, "A man ought to be an optimist and you must be." This has the sound of retrospective myth-making. Lincoln's fatalism did nothing to smother his ambition for office, which now took him on a well-publicized tour of Ohio, Wisconsin, Iowa, Indiana, and Kansas. As for the presidency, he privately acknowledged in the fall of 1859, "the taste *is* in my mouth a little."[17]

Yet it was also in Lincoln's interest to appear no more than a regional candidate, lest Medill and the Illinois Republican chairman, Norman Judd, be frustrated in their scheme to obtain the party's 1860 convention for Chicago. Three days before Christmas 1859, the conspirators got their wish from Republican National Committee members persuaded that Lincoln was a mere favorite son. This cleared the way for the *Tribune*'s February 16, 1860, editorial endorsing the man from Springfield. After paying tribute to Lincoln's character, intellect, and, less predictably, "executive capacity," the paper got down to brass tacks. Principles were fine, but parties existed to win elections, and Lincoln was far more electable than any of his competitors; his very obscurity would be an asset in such pivotal states as Indiana, New Jersey, and Pennsylvania.

The candidate helped his cause with a celebrated address at New York City's Cooper Union. Before heading east, Lincoln invited Medill and Ray to examine his text. They urged numerous improvements to the manuscript, none of which passed muster with Lincoln. Lincoln took New York by storm. "With a sickly sort of smile," Ray looked at Medill and remarked that "old Abe must have lost out of the car window all our previous notes." "This must have been one of his waggish jokes," said Medill.[18]

No one was laughing that spring as Chicago voters prepared to elect a mayor. "Great things are expected of Chicago," wrote Medill from Washington. "She is the pet Republican city of the Union — the point from which radiate opinions which more or less influence six states. The city must be saved." Chicago Democrats performed this noble mission themselves, by splitting down the middle between a pro-Buchanan faction led by Cyrus McCormick and a majority loyal to Senator Douglas. In the wake of Harper's Ferry, the reaper king had bought a controlling interest in the *Chicago Herald*. A few months later he purchased the *Chicago Times*. McCormick merged the two papers as part of his plans to forestall a Republican victory in 1860 and crush "that dirty sheet," the *Tribune*. Violently opposed by the *Tribune*, he failed to win his party's nomination for mayor. In April, Long John Wentworth, a Republican convert, scored a decisive triumph at the polls.

A month later thousands of Republicans assembled in Wentworth's city to choose a president. For $5,000, Chicagoans had erected the Wigwam, a barnlike structure holding 10,000 delegates and partisan onlookers. Thanks to Norman Judd, a disproportionate number of those were Lincoln supporters, their presence facilitated by free rail tickets and illegally obtained convention passes. Medill, too, helped stack the deck against the officious New Yorkers lined up behind Seward. Assigned responsibility for seating arrangements, he isolated the big New York delegation in a remote corner of the Wigwam and surrounded doubtful Pennsylvania with a *cordon sanitaire* of Lincoln men from Illinois, Indiana, and New Jersey. It was, he said afterward with evident satisfaction, "the meanest trick I ever pulled."[19]

Medill played little role in buttonholing delegates, until his talent for being in the right place at the right time reasserted itself with historic consequences. "I took my seat among my old friends of the Ohio delegation," he recalled, "but Joshua Giddings without ceremony ordered me out. My friends came to my rescue; we had a nice little argument and I stayed." At the end of the third ballot, with Lincoln a handful of votes shy of the nomination, Medill leaned over and whispered in the ear of a wavering Ohioan named Carter, "Now is your time. If you throw the vote to Lincoln, Chase can have anything he wants." What assurance could Medill offer him, Carter demanded. "I know," Medill replied melodramatically, "and you know I wouldn't promise it if I didn't know."[20]

Thus convinced, the erstwhile Chase supporter jumped to his feet and announced a switch of four votes to Lincoln. A cannon on the roof of the Wigwam boomed the news to crowds outside the convention hall. In the streets of Chicago, jubilant Republicans carrying hand-split rails — an inspired campaign emblem loathed by the candidate — did a snake dance of victory. Inside the brightly lit *Tribune* offices, editors put the finishing touches on an editorial awarding exclusive credit for Lincoln's nomination to the people. "Neither personal effort, neither private pledges, neither promise of office or of patronage, were used to secure the end," they intoned, in blatant disregard for the truth. In the same issue the *Tribune* declared, "The age of purity returns."[21]

To insure that it would last beyond November, Medill and his colleagues swung their heaviest guns into line. Senior editor John L. Scripps wrote a 4,000-word campaign biography which formed the basis for a nationally syndicated profile of the little-known Illinoisan by William Dean Howells. On its own the *Tribune* printed fourteen pro-Lincoln pamphlets. Medill carried sums of money to doubtful Illinois counties. He also traveled east, hoping to neutralize "his satanic majesty," James Gordon Bennett of the *New York Herald*. He warned Lincoln that some "subtle Jesuitical articles" by the unreliable Wentworth might yet show up in Bennett's newspaper.[22]

Other Chicago publishers pursued different agendas that fall. Following his party's Baltimore convention, at which he tried unsuccessfully to broker a compromise between Douglas and Buchanan, Cyrus McCormick was reduced to hoping that the election of a president might be thrown into the House of Representatives. "The Southern position is now, without doubt, *sound and just*," he wrote at the start of the fall canvas, "and I think they are determined to maintain it." The *Tribune* accused McCormick, as chairman of the Cook County Democrats, of conspiring to take Douglas's place in the Senate. Both Democratic factions were disappointed in November, when Lincoln swept Chicago by 4,500 votes and Illinois by 12,000. "We are no prophets if the result of Tuesday does not settle disunion work," declared a self-satisfied *Tribune*.[23]

✧ 5

Throughout the tense winter of 1860–61, men looked with suspicion on friends of a lifetime. Among Medill's targets was Representative William B. Kellogg, an Illinois lawmaker close to Lincoln. Kellogg hoped to avert fraternal bloodshed by amending the Constitution to ease restrictions on slavery in the territories. For his troubles he was pilloried in the *Tribune* as a treacherous swindler. The congressman from Peoria took the earliest opportunity to express his displeasure, by knocking Medill to the floor of Washington's National Hotel. At age thirty-eight, too old to enlist, handicapped by spinal rheumatism and encroaching deafness, Medill fought back with the sharpest weapon at his command, his tongue. He denounced James Buchanan as a whiskey-soaked coward drinking "to drown remorse and stupefy his brain as he staggers along with the treasonable gang who have possession of him."[24]

Six weeks after the election, Medill combined deference with a whiff of sarcasm in a brisk letter to the new president, "the first one I ever have ventured to send to so *august* a functionary." Formalities over, the *Tribune*'s Washington correspondent plunged ahead with his real reason for writing, which was to urge Lincoln to put Salmon P. Chase in his cabinet and keep William Seward out. His appeal went for naught, as Lincoln took both men into his official family. Medill proposed Norman Judd for postmaster general or secretary of the interior. The president-elect excluded Judd from the cabinet table. Before his inauguration, said Medill, Lincoln must stay at the National Hotel, "the Fremont House of Washington" and a favorite haunt of Henry Clay. Lincoln registered at the rival Willard. Under no circumstances must he admit Pennsylvania's itchy-fingered political boss Simon Cameron to his inner circle, Medill told Lincoln; "Sinner Cameron and Honest Abe don't sound well together."[25]

Events would prove this a shrewd assessment, but Lincoln, not Medill, was president, and he was in no mood to be dictated to by Illinois cronies. Cameron was made secretary of war, until gross ineptitude and a depressing lack of battlefield success made it necessary to pack him off to the czar's court at St. Petersburg.

So much for the age of purity.

With precious little to show for his president-making, an angry Medill accused Lincoln of forgetting his place. The new chief executive, he groused, "never could have been heard of except as a retired, played-out country politician but for the favors of the *Tribune* and its friends." Lincoln did not become notably more generous. For a while even the Chicago postmastership seemed beyond reach. "If we get the office for four years we shall vastly increase our newspaper business," Medill reminded his colleague Alfred Cowles. "I could run up our weekly circulation to 50,000 or 60,000." This was far more than one might expect of Medill's intraoffice rival, John L. Scripps. Besides having a poor business head, Scripps was entirely "too conscientious" to carry out the necessary purge of political opponents.[26]

In true Chicago fashion, Medill tried to bribe the new president, telling Cowles to contact Lincoln secretly and "show him that while I would make a good postmaster I would put money in his purse. If I had charge of the Chicago Post Office you can bet high that I would make about 5000 Western Postmasters do some begging for the *Tribune*, or off went their d—d heads." In the end, Scripps got the job and with it the whip hand over rural postmasters throughout the region.[27]

On the day after Christmas 1860, Medill warned the president-elect of rebel plans to seize Washington before Inauguration Day. Describing himself modestly as "a volunteer sentinel on the walls," he pleaded with Lincoln to slip into the capital two months early, thereby showing disunionists that "they had a second Jackson to deal with." Lincoln remained in Springfield until the third week of February, when rumors of an assassination plot prompted the famous all-night train ride that took him through hostile Baltimore. He arrived in Washington on the morning of February 23, having lost nothing more serious than his dignity. The next day Medill informed his Chicago associates that he had yet to lay eyes on the president-elect: "The rush of vultures on him is tremendous."[28]

With America coming apart at the seams, the new occupant of the White House had cause to regret his ambition to live there. Medill's emotions were more complex. If bad news is proverbially good for journalists, then the Civil War proved a godsend to the *Tribune*, as it did to Chicago, whose stockyards supplied beef and pork to feed northern armies, and whose status as a railroad hub and manufacturing center made it a pivotal part of the Union war-making machine. On February 18, as Lincoln's train rattled across upstate New York and jubilant secessionists met in Montgomery, Alabama, to inaugurate Jefferson Davis, five men joined Medill in formally incorporating the Tribune Company. Two hundred shares of stock were issued, valued at $1,000 apiece.

The action could not have been more suspiciously timed. Over the next few months circulation soared, as readers throughout the northwest fixed their attention on the first fumbling attempts by green soldiers to kill each other in Virginia cornfields and the *Tribune*, with more eyes than Argus, transported them to the front lines. To the president, Medill offered personal assurances that "the Northwest will back you with their last man, dollar and bushel of corn." In the same letter he admonished Lincoln, "Do your duty, the *people* are with you."[29]

Editorial support was more equivocal. In contrast to its historically accepted image as Lincoln's shield and defender, the *Tribune* in fact showed robust disenchantment with many administration policies. When John Charles Frémont, that quintessential political general, sought to free Missouri slaves unilaterally early in the conflict, the radicals at the *Tribune* were ecstatic. Their joy was quickly replaced by shrill anger directed at the conservative chief executive, who countermanded Frémont's order. Lincoln's action had inflicted on the Union a worse defeat than Bull Run, they argued.

Medill blamed such caution on Secretary of State Seward, the de facto president, who "has kept a sponge saturated with chloroform to Uncle Abe's nose." Dissatisfied with the "rotten cabinet and a blind, cowardly Congress," Medill was made equally gloomy by the battlefield exploits of "copperhead Grant and crazy Sherman." Early in 1862, he crisply informed Lincoln that the United States was on the brink of ruin. "Any steamer may bring the news of European intervention — the people know that when that happens the Union is gone and the curse of posterity will rest on the memory of those who fooled away the day of grace. The verdict will be, 'the harvest is past, the summer is ended, but the nation is not saved.' To placate a few hundred Kentucky slavemasters this great Republic was allowed to be shivered by rebellion and foreign intervention."[30]

Edwin Stanton was called out of retirement to shake up the War Department. Medill warned his friend that he would encounter "rottenness and rascality from top to bottom. You will discover scores of lukewarm, half-secession officers in command who cannot bear to strike a vigorous blow lest it hurts their rebel friends or jeopardizes the precious practice of slavery." Medill's fury overflowed in blunt sentences about "a contractor's war — a war on Chinese principles . . . a war of horrible grimaces, of shocking expenditures, of sickening blunders, of quasi-loyalty, of lumbering inaction, of discouraging torpidity."[31]

At other times even this tower of patriotic resolve wavered. Eighty years after the fact, a New Hampshire congressman weary of being abused in the pages of Colonel McCormick's *Chicago Tribune* placed in the *Congressional Record* a remarkable plan that the Colonel's grandfather had advocated for ending the Civil War while preserving slavery. "I can understand the awful reluctance with which you can be brought to contemplate a divided Union but there is no help for it," Medill had written to Representative Elihu B. Washburne, chairman of the powerful House Ways and Means Committee, in January 1863. Barely two weeks after Lincoln signed the Emancipation Proclamation, transforming a war about states' rights into a war for human rights, Medill dismissed the president as a milk-and-water type inclined to "do the right thing always too late and just when it does no good."[32]

No such indecision palsied *his* hand. "An armistice is bound to come during the year '63," said Medill; it would be the unavoidable product of a depleted treasury, a hostile Congress, and a war-weary populace. With this in mind, he proposed that the capital's defenses be weakened in order to establish a heavily patrolled line from Cairo, Illinois, to Vicksburg, Mississippi. The Confederacy would thus be reduced to seven slave states and the Lincoln government left sovereign over Delaware, Maryland, Western Virginia, Tennessee, Missouri, Arkansas, Texas, and Louisiana — "as much slave territory as we can digest for a few years." The United States should indemnify its losses by seizing Canada. "England deserves this punishment and someday must catch it," Medill contended. Then, having gratified their sense of manifest destiny at the expense of an ancient enemy, northerners could sit back and await southern application "in a few years" for readmittance to the splintered national family.[33]

Medill's scheme, unlike the Union armies, went nowhere. From abject pessimism the editor veered toward premature jubilation as the much-maligned Grant closed in on Vicksburg. Writing to his brother William in May 1863, Medill envisioned a golden future for the American republic. A thousand European immigrants daily made their way to New York. Crush the rebellion, abolish slavery forever, and Medill expected a comparable migration from industrial North to agrarian South. His hatred of slavery did not translate into a love of slaves. Come the final Union triumph, he predicted, "the niggers in the South will all float off into the Gulf States, like blackbirds when the frost comes." In future wars, he continued, "black and yellow men will be freely used to fight. We will not be so careful about spilling the blood of niggers . . . Old Abe says 'bring on your niggers. I want two hundred thousand of them to save my white boys, as soon as I can get them.' "[34] For Medill, human freedom, like racial justice, was an abstraction, a subject generating mostly verbal passion.

Not so with relations between nations. On the eve of Gettysburg, Medill anticipated not one but two future North American conflicts, "one to clear the British out of Canada and the other to clear the French out of Mexico. This continent belongs to the Free American race and they are bound to have it — every inch of it, including the West Indian Islands." British insults would thus be avenged. As for the France of Louis Napoleon, "she has taken a mean and cowardly advantage of this nation to crush poor Mexico, which will not be allowed. We shall permit no nation to abuse Mexico but ourselves. We claim the right to turn her up on Uncle Sam's knee and spank her bottom."[35]

Clamoring for faster progress in recruiting black troops — not least because the new regiments would relieve pressure for an unpopular draft of white men — Medill put his views in writing to the president. He did so, he informed Lincoln, "not having either time or inclination to hang around waiting rooms among a wolfish crowd seeking admission to your presence for office or contracts or personal favors." Medill mourned his brother William, who had been killed in the Gettysburg campaign. Returning to Chicago, he found the *Tribune* embroiled in a war of its own with the rival *Chicago Times*, under new management since Cyrus McCormick had sold it to a forty-two-year-old Vermont-born printer's devil named Wilbur F. Storey. Formerly the editor of the *Detroit Free Press*, Storey had achieved journalistic immortality by declaring that "it is a newspaper's duty to print the news and raise hell."[36]

Storey wasted no time in testing his theory on Chicago readers. Besides praising Jefferson Davis, the *Times* offered demands for the impeachment of the despotic King Abraham the First. General Ambrose Burnside ordered the paper suppressed, a gross violation of First Amendment rights that the *Tribune* endorsed warmly. That night 20,000 Chicagoans assembled in Court House Square to protest the repressive action and threaten violence against Storey's competitor if it were not reversed. Burnside executed a hasty *volte face* on orders from the White House, provoking fresh *Tribune* grumbling about Lincoln's "timid, vacillating policy."

As if he didn't have enough quarrels going, Medill launched a bitter feud with the Associated Press, based in New York. (In time he would help found a western rival to the AP.) His resentment of the dandified East surfaced anew when the *New York Herald* floated a presidential trial balloon for General Grant. "We claim the right to tell this organ of the Five Points and the Thugs of New York, that it must keep its copperhead slime off our Illinois General," barked the *Tribune*. Not to be outdone, the *Herald* called its Chicago antagonist "the sewer into which goes everything too dirty for its New York namesake to print."

In November 1863, Medill bought out his partner, Charles Ray. For all his disappointment with the Lincoln administration, the new editor-in-chief displayed a pragmatic allegiance to the president to whose fortunes he and his paper were so closely tied. However flawed, Lincoln was indispensable to continued Republican rule. This shrewd reading of the political compass guided Medill's course throughout the 1864 election campaign. Anytime enthusiasm flagged, all he had to do was consider the Democratic alternative: the cocky yet sluggish George B. McClellan, a poor man's Napoleon supported by an unholy alliance of Wall Street money-brokers and "the great unwashed of the Celtic persuasion."[37]

In November, Lincoln thrashed McClellan, sweeping all but three states. Medill resumed his admonitory ways. The disgraced Frémont should be sent to Paris, he wrote to the president early in 1865, the disgraceful Benjamin Butler made secretary of the navy. Congress must guarantee black Americans their full rights of citizenship, by constitutional amendment if necessary. Lincoln should reconsider his inflationary fiscal policies and show more patience in making peace. "Don't coax the rebel chiefs but pound them a little more," Medill counseled Lincoln, in flat contradiction of his earlier advice. "The starch is not sufficiently taken out of the devils yet."[38]

Between them, Grant and Sherman managed that feat decisively. Five days after Lee's surrender, Medill again put pen to paper, this time to urge the hangman's noose for Jefferson Davis and to take a swipe at "the cruel vindictive millions who starved to death with devilish malice 25,000 of our brave, patriotic sons and brothers. There can be no forgiveness for them on this side of the grave." In the same letter he invited Lincoln to visit Chicago. "You have stayed in Washington long enough without a furlough," he told the exhausted president. As for his Illinois neighbors, "we will agree not to shake you to death," Medill wrote teasingly, "but will not pledge to refrain from pretty loud cheering."[39]

The cheers turned to sobs that night, when John Wilkes Booth fired a bullet into Lincoln's brain. Once the immediate shock subsided, the grieving *Tribune* found something providential in the election of Vice President Andrew Johnson, a militant Unionist from Tennessee. "Johnson's little finger will prove thicker than were Abraham Lincoln's loins," Medill predicted. "While he whipped them gently with cords, his successor will scourge them with a whip of scorpions."

Within two months the *Tribune* would repudiate this judgment and the accidental president who inspired it. Incensed over Johnson's conciliatory overtures to former slavers, Medill demanded an end to rations for General Lee. As far as the *Tribune* was concerned, the defeated general could earn his bread hammering rocks in some northern penitentiary. Should Lee nevertheless persist in his desire for liberty, "we will hire him to tote paper in the *Tribune* press rooms provided no Union soldier applies for the job."[40]

❖ 6

April 1865 saw another tragedy, as poignant as if less portentous than the death of a president. William Sanderson McCormick, the younger brother of Cyrus, had long been a soul in torment. For fifteen years the sensitive William had labored incessantly to build the family firm and fortune while deriving scant pleasure from either. Lured to Chicago with visions of instant wealth, he never emotionally left the Old Dominion of his youth. Along with his wife, Mary, the daughter of a Virginia planter, he remained a stranger in a city with little to recommend it save the money to be made from selling reapers and buying house lots.

"Chicago is destined to be the great city of the West," he wrote shortly after the birth of his son, Robert Sanderson McCormick, in 1849, "though I do not think I should like to make my living by farming here. The west wind is too cold for me, or would be if I had to be in the field in the winter." The brutal climate contributed to the death of his eighteen-month-old daughter, Mary, from whooping cough. It may also have exacerbated William's depression — what his wife called, in the euphemistic language of the time, "nervous headaches, low spirits, and general debility."[41]

It didn't help that William, like his more forceful brother Leander, was frequently at odds with the domineering Cyrus. "Bro. C. H. is having a say-so in almost everything nowadays," he acknowledged. Besides launching the *Chicago Times* as a Democratic rival to the hated *Tribune*, Cyrus founded the *Presbyterian Expositor* as a conservative voice within the church of his youth. Outraged by the abolitionist sentiments emanating from Chicago pulpits, Cyrus also took the first steps toward establishing the landmark theological seminary that would bear his name.[42]

When the war came, it found Cyrus pursuing claims at the Patent Office in Washington. Actual hostilities he regarded as a tiresome distraction from money-making. Upon his discontented brothers fell the burden of defending the reaper king against *Tribune* allegations that Cyrus was a slaver in league with southern traitors. As the fighting escalated, William McCormick became a virtual prisoner of his blood, afraid of the economic as well as political future. With Lincoln in the White House and emancipation on the lawbooks, he regarded public bankruptcy and social revolution as unavoidable. He contemplated transferring company assets to England, where Cyrus, in between triumphant demonstrations of his reaper, was hobnobbing with young J. P. Morgan and the Rothschilds.

On his return from Europe in the summer of 1864, Cyrus was forced to negotiate a new arrangement guaranteeing each of his brothers an annual salary of $6,000. The revival of his dormant political aspirations guaranteed him yet another scorching round of abuse from the *Tribune*. The announcement of his candidacy for Congress found Joseph Medill lying in wait. "Mr. McCormick has not an instinct that is not in sympathy with the rebellion," claimed the *Tribune*. "Like all poor white trash of Virginia, he left the State a better friend of slavery than the slaveholders themselves, and the prejudices of his youth have built upon a defective education, a perfect monomania in behalf of man-stealing." Following a brutish campaign in which "the Copperhead candidate" was accused of pirating the reaper from a poor New York mechanic named Obed Hussey, Cyrus was crushed at the polls.[43]

His outlook remained defiant. As late as March 4, 1865, four weeks before the fall of Richmond, Cyrus told William of his intention to visit the Confederate capital and negotiate peace between North and South. He simultaneously urged his brother to buy gold and ride the market up, "if Sherman be whipped, which I think probable." By then, however, the younger McCormick was taking orders only from doctors treating him for "nervous dyspepsia." A diet of stale bread, milk, and vegetables improved neither the patient's mood nor his constitution. Electrical treatments proved futile. So did a two-month regimen at a New York hydropathic institute and a second water cure in Cleveland.

At the end of April 1865, William's despair spilled over in a confused letter to Cyrus. "I am extremely nervous," he wrote. In August he went to Jacksonville, Illinois, and the State Hospital for the Insane. Before his death the following month, his mind cleared enough for him to compose a final appeal to Cyrus and Leander, imploring his brothers to bury their differences and live for something beyond worldly wealth. In death, William Sanderson McCormick proved no more adept at providing for his family than he had during his abbreviated life. His widow returned to Virginia, placing her four children at the mercy of their uncles. Whatever else divided them, Cyrus and Leander were as one in their reluctance to share the family business. In return for $400,000, the surviving McCormicks obtained undisputed control of the reaper and the substantial real estate holdings assembled largely through the dead man's labors.

On no one did this exclusion from responsibility fall more heavily than on William's oldest son, Robert. The last of his line to be born at Walnut Grove, Robert Sanderson McCormick retained to the end of his days a slightly faded aura of aristocratic pretense, a trait passed on in exaggerated form to his son and namesake. Young Rob McCormick displayed the equestrian habits of a country squire. He rode each day to a school on South Wabash Avenue. After classes let out, he and his brother, also named William, hunted pigeons and rabbits in a swampy district later occupied by Marshall Field's department store. When the boys crossed the Chicago River by boat, they were as close as they would ever get to the McCormick factory perched at the mouth of the river.

Refused a place in the family enterprises, Rob turned to literary pursuits befitting the proper southern gentleman he fancied himself to be. He began a career as a bibliophile and collector of historical prints, Napoleon being a special obsession. He became something of an authority on French literature. Had his father's estate been larger, he might have followed his natural bent as an amateur scholar and dedicated man of fashion. Instead, upon graduation from the University of Virginia in 1872, he staked his siblings' $400,000 inheritance on the grain futures market — no place, as it turned out, for a gentleman.

In due course he fell in love, with the unlikeliest girl in Chicago.

✧ 7

Joseph Medill emerged from the war years retaining the fierce egotism of youth, yet otherwise aged beyond his years. Although still in his mid-forties, the editor was bent with rheumatism. A black ebony ear trumpet, used as a prop to enrage or humiliate tedious visitors, reinforced an appearance of dour integrity. After 1866, Medill was deprived of purposeful activity, his dominant position at the *Tribune* having been awarded to Horace White, a younger journalist of equal vigor and far less reluctance to criticize Republicans for squandering the moral high ground gained through wartime sacrifice.

For the next eight years, Medill stalked the fringes of power. He clashed with Andrew Johnson in Washington and with his erstwhile partners at the *Tribune*. Blocked from editorial crusading, he conquered his natural diffidence long enough to seek political office. As a member of the Illinois state constitutional committee, he championed river and canal transport in opposition to powerful rail interests. After an unsuccessful campaign for Congress, he won a seat on the U. S. Civil Service Commission, a somewhat ironic gift from President Grant, whose commitment to reform of any sort was open to question.

Then came Sunday evening, October 8, 1871.

On the third floor of Chicago's pink marble courthouse, a night telegraph operator named William Brown looked out a window and saw a faint orange glow on the southwest horizon — the death throes of the previous night's fire, he thought, the latest of three dozen to plague the drought-stricken city since the end of September. For the moment he was unconcerned. So, apparently, was the watchman in his tower, high above the telegraph office.[44]

But as Brown fixed his gaze on the orange light, it seemed to swell in size and intensity. At 9:32 the tower watchman sprang to life, sounding an alarm but also misdirecting fire crews to a spot more than a mile from the corner of Jefferson and De Koven streets, where the ramshackle two-story barn of Patrick O'Leary had been burning for nearly an hour. Later reports would blame the fire on Mrs. O'Leary's cow, said to have kicked over a lamp while being milked for the second time that day. In fact, not a cow but a negligent civil servant caused Chicago's destruction — a fitting commentary on a city whose slapdash growth was inseparable from its rampant political corruption.

Superlatives came naturally to Chicagoans like Medill, inhabitants of the fastest-growing city in the land. Visitors found the place lacking in modesty of scale or demeanor — the *Tribune* correspondent Elias Colbert compared it to Pompeii — but it was undeniably exciting and, for all the babble of exotic tongues, thoroughly American. For one thing, Pompeii never published seven newspapers all at once. Chicago in 1871 did. No fewer than thirteen rail lines brought 120 passenger trains a day to Union Station, the busiest terminal on earth. Fourteen miles of river docks made Chicago the nation's greatest inland port and the northwest's chief marketplace. Sprawling stockyards on the city's West Side established "Porkopolis" as a worthy rival of Cincinnati, while local factories led by Cyrus McCormick's sprawling reaper works turned out one farm wagon every seven minutes.

Chicago was unique, according to a contemporary observer, in that all its inhabitants "have come for the one common, avowed object of making money. There you have its growth, its end and its object." Prosperity so quickly and thoughtlessly gained did not come without a price. Chicago had been built on the cheap. Two thirds of its 60,000 buildings were made of wood, many of them little more than green-pine shanties. Such elegance as the commercial sector boasted was mostly of the ersatz variety, the result of stucco fronts, flimsy veneer, and wooden cornices painted to resemble stone. For years the Police Board had pleaded with officials to enact a uniform building code, to require metal roofs in place of the ubiquitous tar and felt, and to increase the size of the woefully under-manned fire department. All such advice had been ignored, leaving the *Tribune* to fulminate about the dangers posed by walls a hundred feet high but only a single brick wide.

The summer of 1871 broke all records for dryness. On the morning of October 8, *Tribune* readers encountered a front-page advertisement for a local insurance company: "Fire — fire — prepare for fall and winter fires!"

Even so, few people paid attention to the alarm bell belatedly rung that night. The business district was largely deserted, save for churchgoers sauntering home after evening services. Medill was in his bed at ten o'clock, when a howling southwest wind carried sparks from O'Leary's barn four blocks to the roof of St. Paul's Catholic Church. Many fire-fighters, worn down after spending seventeen hours battling Saturday night's blaze, were hung over from the traditional postfire drunk with which they purged the horrors of their job. By the time the misdirected companies finally reached the O'Leary neighborhood, hundreds of miles of wooden sidewalks were feeding the flames. Additional fuel was provided by vast stockpiles of pine lumber and shingles heaped alongside the banks of the Chicago River.

With the wind acting as arsonist, the fire played a deadly game of hop-scotch, flinging red-hot embers and burning boards in front of its advance. At one in the morning, Medill reached the fireproof citadel of the *Tribune* at the corner of Dearborn and Madison streets. His appearance coincided with the return of night police reporter G. P. English from the O'Leary neighborhood.

"Where's the fire?" English was asked.

"Everywhere."

"Write it up."[45]

English did as he was told until ordered to the roof, where Medill was putting out small fires and Elias Colbert was dictating notes on the progress of flames that had all but encircled the building. From the vantage point they could see a vision of hell — a red snow, some called it afterward. Hoping to escape the rain of fire, thousands of terrified Chicagoans poured into the Washington Street tunnel; overhead, the river itself seemed to boil. Those who could ran toward the vast prairies lapping the city from the west. Others made their way north to huddle in a Catholic cemetery. An estimated 30,000 refugees spent a miserable night in Lincoln Park.

Five million rats, flushed from their subterranean nests, perished in the flames. So did Ramrod Hall, the city's largest bordello, leaving Madam Kate Hawkins and her trademark horsewhip powerless over her flock of fifty girls. The Chicago Historical Society burned to the ground. With it went the original draft of Lincoln's Emancipation Proclamation. As Monday dawned, prosperous members of the Chicago Club, organized two years earlier in a parlor of the Sherman House, sat down to a champagne breakfast. Suddenly the fire changed course, forcing them to evacuate to the lakefront, where the celebration continued, fueled by as much liquor and as many cigars as the diners had been able to stuff into their pockets.

At the *Tribune*, grimy pressmen labored by candlelight, oblivious to the shattering of first-floor plate-glass windows. The blowtorch heat melted press rollers. Around seven o'clock that Monday, Medill and his coworkers discovered a small blaze smoldering beneath a neighboring barbershop. By then Horace White, believing the worst to be over, had gone home for breakfast. So had Deacon William Bross, who left hoping to salvage his North Side residence.

This left Joseph Medill as the captain of a sinking ship, a role for which he was perfectly cast. For the better part of a decade, Medill, accustomed to advising and abusing American presidents, had seen his editorial authority eroded by his junior White, a liberal Republican at odds with the Grant administration. Now, at last, he was in undisputed control. Like White and Bross, he had a family to worry about, but having long since channeled his passions into politics and journalism, he wasn't about to forsake the *Tribune* in its hour of need.

From the corner of Madison and Dearborn, employees watched in awe as the towering brick Palmer House was reduced to ruins. Moments later the fire devoured McVickers' Theatre, within spitting distance of the *Tribune*. Medill ordered everyone off the roof of the building (after rescuing a telescope he used for observing sunspots, which he viewed as the cause of human behavior). A little before nine o'clock — almost exactly twelve hours after William Brown had first observed the orange light from his courthouse window — an exhausted Medill headed home to the corner of Morgan and Washington streets. Waking from a fitful two hours' sleep, he found the *Tribune* building gutted.

Deacon Bross described what happened next. "On reaching Canal Street ... I was informed that while Mr. White and I were saving our families on Monday afternoon Mr. Medill, seeing that the *Tribune* office must inevitably be burned, had sought for and purchased Edwards' job printing-office, No. 15 Canal Street, where he was then busy organizing things. When I arrived I found Mr. Medill in the upper stories among the types and printers, doing all he could to get ready to issue a paper in the morning."[46]

Learning of a four-cylinder press in Baltimore, Medill purchased it by telegraph. While the fire raged to the north, a clerk announced the arrival of some anxious advertisers seeking lost friends. By 4 P.M. the stoves were up, Horace White was back in his usual place of command, borrowed paper was going into the basement, and printing arrangements were being made with the undamaged *Chicago Journal.* That evening Bross was dispatched east to secure scarce printing materials and reassure doubters of Chicago's future.

It is often said that the verdict of history depends on who writes the history. In the aftermath of the disaster, Medill's nemesis, Wilbur Storey of the *Chicago Times,* perpetuated the story of the incendiary cow. Storey called Mrs. O'Leary, an industrious woman in her thirties, "an old hag about seventy" who had set the fire to avenge her removal from the city pension rolls. In much the same way, for as long as Robert McCormick lived, his grandfather was exclusively credited with the most famous editorial in *Tribune* history. Published early on Wednesday morning, October 11, 1871, its appearance testified to the abundant optimism with which Chicagoans greeted their humbling:

CHEER UP

In the midst of a calamity without parallel in the world's history, looking upon the ashes of thirty years' accumulations, the people of this once beautiful city have resolved that CHICAGO SHALL RISE AGAIN.

Less important than the identity of the author was the devastation that belied such journalistic cheerleading. More than 17,000 structures and nearly four square miles of urban landscape had been incinerated. South of the river, only two buildings were left standing in a 460-acre wasteland. At least 250 people were dead. One hundred thousand Chicagoans were without homes.

No greater disaster had ever befallen an American city. To the Reverend

Granville Moody of Cincinnati, the hellfire was divine punishment for Chicago's refusal to close 2,000 saloons on the Lord's Day, "a retributive judgment on a city that has shown such devotion in its worship of the Golden Calf." Adding to local misfortune, no sooner had the ruins stopped smoking than it was time to elect a mayor and common council. Perhaps on the theory that desperate times called for measures and men to match, a nonpartisan group meeting in an undamaged schoolhouse proposed Joseph Medill, a force of nature almost equal to the fire, for the city's top administrative position.[47]

Medill responded in character. First he sent word to the convention that he would not accept the nomination. Then, prodded by future mayor Carter Harrison, he relented, on one condition: that he be given sufficient powers to dominate both the council and the various boards that operated as so many independent fiefdoms. Delegates grateful for a strong leader to tell them what to do accepted his terms. A month later the electorate followed suit, choosing Medill and his Union-Fireproof slate of city council candidates by an overwhelming majority. In his inaugural address, the new mayor promised that a new Chicago would rise like a phoenix from the ashes. He insisted, moreover, that it be constructed of brick, not wood. That same month the *Tribune* demanded and got an investigation of municipal corruption. On Christmas Eve, Medill shut down all unlicensed saloons. Six days later, during a visit by Russia's Grand Duke Alexis, five current and former aldermen were indicted for embezzlement.

The die was cast. During the course of a single stormy term in office, Medill displayed the blunt honesty and tenacious vision for which he was known among his fellow editors, and which rallied public support so long as the crisis mentality engendered by the fire remained in effect. He founded an impressive public library system. He practiced municipal economy in place of aldermanic boodling. Most predictably, Mayor Medill expanded the power of his office, relying on a liberal use of his veto pen and a special grant of legislative authority to reorganize the fire and police departments.

Less successful was his campaign against public drunkenness and the criminal activities associated with 3,000 saloons. Medill's police superintendent recommended closing these well-patronized establishments at 11 P.M. instead of midnight and keeping them closed on Sundays. A tenfold increase in saloon license fees caused German voters, among the most dependable in their Republican loyalties, to protest this heavy dose of Yankee Protestant moralizing. Uproar ensued. The police chief was suspended from his duties. Mass meetings led to the creation of an anti-Medill People's party. Adding mockery to impotence, the mayor was denounced in German-language newspapers as Dictator Joseph I.

Exhausted by the endless controversies swirling about him, Medill left

Chicago in the summer of 1873, four months before the scheduled conclusion of his term. In his absence the *Tribune* asked voters, "Do you want your city converted into a German principality?" On election day they replied overwhelmingly in the affirmative. For Medill, the wound of rejection never healed. Asked many years later to run for the U. S. Senate, he refused, explaining, "Politics and office seeking are pretty good things to let alone for a man who has intellect and individuality." In more honest moments the failed politician lashed out at "the rabble" that had repudiated his moral tutorship.[48]

✧ 8

Abandoning Chicago temporarily, the Medills sailed for Europe. There Joseph nursed his grievances and dreamed of regaining control of the *Tribune*. He also became better acquainted with his family. With his wife, Katharine, he enjoyed a relationship of uncomplicated Victorian dominance. His daughters were another story. Alternatively spoiled and neglected, each grew up to resemble her father at his most commanding. The eldest, Kate, was especially willful. Along with her sister, Nellie, Kate Medill was as ambitious as a robber baron and as subtle as Niagara Falls. Together they inspired Medill's plaintive retort, "Is it my fault that I'm the father of the worst two she-devils in all Chicago?"[49]

Only slightly less beautiful than her dazzling sister, Kate more than compensated with a biting wit and a precocious aptitude for the masculine world of business and politics. Writing to her absent husband in January 1860, her mother mingled talk of Washington's smoke-filled rooms with the latest "droll speeches" out of the mouth of their six-year-old daughter. Sitting before the fire one evening, young Kate was struck with an idea. What if her parents should move to Ireland and while there have another child?

"It would be a little *Irish* boy, wouldn't it?" she asked.

"Yes, Katie," her mother replied.

"Oh, wouldn't that be dreadful!"

"Why so, Katie?"

"Why, because when it grew up then it would *vote* for Douglas." Added the observant mother, "What a *rank little Republican she is.*"[50]

In this as in so much else, she was her father's daughter. A girlhood friend recalled "a splendid, vibrant creature . . . the most democratic, brilliant girl in her class," who was nevertheless "very executive." At the age of fifteen, Kate was sent by her parents to St. Mary's Catholic Academy in South Bend, Indiana. "I am so anxious you should grow up to be not only an accomplished, but what is of much more consequence, a *truly good* woman," her mother wrote. "I want you to be *happy*, and to be *happy* you must be *good — truthful above all things*." It would cause Mrs. Medill much grief to hear that her daughter had neglected either her studies or her religious devotions. "I will know just how much you love me by your obedience in these little things." Unconsciously stoking the budding rivalry between Kate and Nellie, she asked her namesake, "I wonder if you will be as popular here as your sister is — everybody loves Nellie — she is so *prudent* and obliging."[51]

In a letter of her own, perhaps more revealing than intended, Kate sought assurances that her mother would have no more children — the competition would unnerve her. She graduated from St. Mary's in June 1869. Her father was too busy to attend the commencement ceremonies. Being mayor of Chicago left Medill little time for his family, a situation that changed only with their European travels of 1873–74. In Paris, the Medills visited art galleries and indulged a vicarious sense of superiority to the underdressed girls back home. Across the Channel they stayed in British country houses and befriended Andrew Carnegie at his Scottish castle.[52]

Amid such splendors, Kate's thoughts were not exclusively focused on Titians or Highland grouse. Even before their departure, Medill had detected in his older daughter a chronic restlessness. "Housekeeping is not a thing she dotes upon," he noted drily. Nor was he above deflating the young woman's social pretensions by puffing up his own. "I think she begins to realize that all the beaux who used to come did not solely call on her account," he told his wife. In the meantime, "she continues to dodge her most devoted admirer and grows more fervent at each approach."[53]

Exactly how Kate Medill first encountered her future husband is uncertain. One story had them meeting on the dance floor of the Grand Pacific Hotel. In a more dramatic version, Rob McCormick, washed out of a rowboat on storm-tossed Lake Michigan, looked up from the shore to find Miss Medill gazing sympathetically into his eyes. Whatever its origins, their improbable courtship progressed rapidly, notwithstanding Medill's evident disapproval of a Virginia Copperhead for a son-in-law. Sometime early in 1876 the relationship was sealed, in Munich, where the musically gifted Kate had gone to study voice and piano.

On June 9 of that year, in the presence of seventy-five family members and friends, the nephew of Cyrus McCormick was wed to the daughter of Joseph Medill. A heavy downpour marred the elaborate reception, attended by three hundred guests in sodden laces, silks, and white tulle. Their carriages took fully two hours to deposit them outside the Medill residence. Dozens of elegant gifts, among them a magnificent gilt clock from Cyrus and Nettie McCormick, testified to the dynastic implications of the match. While Kate's bridal wardrobe received minute attention in the local press, the groom was rather hastily described by the *Chicago Times* as being "actively engaged in the insurance business . . . and also interested in grain elevators in St. Louis."[54]

One week after the nuptials, Rob McCormick wrote a jaunty note to his new sister-in-law. Kate had been ready to abandon her honeymoon at Detroit or Toledo, he told Nellie, and rejoin her mother for a Medill family Sunday. Only after considerable effort had he been able to prevail upon her to continue as far as Montreal. He would not always be so persuasive.

❖ 9

It was a matter of national significance when, in October 1874, using $300,000 loaned at 10 percent interest by Marshall Field, Joseph Medill bought a controlling interest in the *Tribune* from his former partners, Horace White and Alfred Cowles. Declared the *Cincinnati Daily Times*, "we are glad to see the most influential of the *Tribunes* . . . at length giving up its guerrilla warfare and resuming its once powerful position as a pronounced Republican journal." Less friendly was the *Louisville Courier-Journal*. The paper unfavorably contrasted Medill's staunch support of Grant with the independent ways of White. "The era of rancorous partisan journalism is gone," it concluded.[55]

Medill disproved such notions with his first issue, in which he sang a familiar hymn of praise to the Grand Old Party of Union and Manifest Destiny. Acknowledging that "it is not essential to the prosperity or influence of a party paper that it should willfully misrepresent its opponents, and behold nothing but evil and depravity in all their actions, or discover only treasonable designs in all they propose to do," he nevertheless insisted that for any truly principled editor, neutrality equaled cowardice.

Others took note and took aim. In December 1875, the *Chicago Daily News* made its first appearance with a banner headline:

FOR PRESIDENT
OF THE UNITED STATES, ALASKA, THE WESTERN ISLAND,
AND PERHAPS CUBA.
HON. JOSEPH MEDILL OF ILLINOIS.

To Joseph Medill (as to his descendents), there was no such thing as bad publicity. (Similarly, when *Time* made him the object of a snide cover story in June 1947, Colonel McCormick seemed genuinely delighted, holding up a copy of the magazine's unflattering cover and chortling, "How is that for free national publicity?") In an age of intensely personal journalism, when savage feuds among editors were profitably prolonged, Medill literally thrived on the attention. Among his Chicago contemporaries, for example, none was more offensive than eccentric old Wilbur Storey of the *Times*. "What can possibly ail that venerable lunatic," Medill wondered out loud in June 1881, "if not a consciousness of the inferiority of his own newspaper in any respect to the *Tribune*?" Storey's death from syphilis not long after removed an ancient enemy.

No matter; Medill was resourceful in finding replacements. The times were with him, as the rapid growth of Chicago bred inequities to match its parvenu fortunes. Sixty years before Franklin Roosevelt accused Colonel McCormick of seeing Communists under his bed, McCormick's grand-father imagined them in the streets of Chicago. "If the chief end of man is to become a lazy lout, a shiftless vagabond, a brawling, long-haired idiot, a public nuisance and an enemy of the human race, let him turn Commu-nist," he said.

Yet in his private correspondence, Medill, the apologist for big business, could lash out angrily at exploitative "railroad plutocrats" subsidized by taxpayers. Declaring his concern for the millions rather than the million-aires, the *Tribune* publisher cast himself as a spokesman for plain-living midwesterners victimized by his own party's high tariff policies. For years he jousted with eastern manufacturers and protectionist politicians such as Benjamin Harrison and William McKinley. Medill was honestly shocked by conditions prevailing in Dickensian neighborhoods like the nineteenth ward, a grim collection of filthy shanties unfortunately spared by the Great Fire. "Make those monsters who collect rents of these slum tenants put in sewers and plumbing," he demanded.[56]

Fearlessness was a deserved part of Medill's journalistic legend. A young correspondent covering a juicy scandal roiling North Shore society was once summoned to the old man's office.

"Your name Fullerton?" Medill asked the cub.

"Yes, sir."

"Any relation to the Rev. Thomas Fullerton?"

"Yes, sir, he was my uncle."

"Is that so? I went to school with Tom Fullerton. How is he?"

Small talk over, Medill bore in on the youth.

"Did you write that story?"

"Yes, sir."

"We are sued for $50,000 in damages for libel."

"Is that so?" asked the reporter, his distress painfully apparent.

Medill nodded his head, then asked, "Is the story true?"

"Yes, sir, it is true."

"Well then, libel him for about $100,000 more tomorrow."[57]

Such aggressiveness served the *Tribune* well. In 1876 it scooped other newspapers on the failed attempt by some counterfeit artists to steal Abraham Lincoln's remains from their Springfield tomb. Seven years later the paper installed its first telephones. Line drawings printed from chalk plates became a regular feature. And all the while Medill flailed away at familiar targets: the "Bourbon city" of New York, the British empire in all its wickedness, and "Viper Altgeld," the courageous if politically foolhardy governor of Illinois, John Peter Altgeld.

Altgeld earned the *Tribune*'s undying enmity by pardoning three anarchists accused of complicity in the Haymarket bombings of 1886. To Medill, it was simple. The bombs were thrown because Chicago had become the world capital of "socialistic, atheistic, alcoholic European classes." As for Altgeld, "he does not reason like an American, not feel like one, and consequently does not behave like one." Medill was just as dismissive of "snarling fault-finding mugwumps" inside the GOP. He worried that the saloon was supplanting the church in its influence over the proletariat. He decried prizefighting as a contest between "two whiskey-soaked professional plug-uglies in soft gloves."[58]

"Sam," he admonished his brother, "you are giving too damned much space to baseball." Two columns a day was excessive for "a rowdy game that interests very few."

Sam Medill would have none of it. "I am going to give more," he told Joe. "We ought to give a page."[59]

A generation after Appomattox, Medill advised hotheaded southerners to "take the ice out of their juleps and put it on their heads." His own head remained feverish with panaceas. Investigation of the aging process convinced Medill that lime was the chief agent of human decay. As he explained it, "the whole process of growing old and wearing out is due to a superabundance of this white mineral substance — a liming up 'till finally a man lies down — a brittle mummy a hundred years before his time."[60]

With the benefit of this insight, Medill retreated for several weeks a year to the bone-dry air around Pasadena, California. High in the San Bernardino Mountains, he hoped to purge all traces of lime from his system. Not even a distance of two thousand miles, however, could diminish the old man's influence on the newspaper that had long since become his personal organ. When in Chicago, it was Medill's custom to arrive at work each morning with pockets bulging with clippings and half-written editorials. A visiting journalist captured the scene one day as *Tribune* employees dutifully lined up to receive their instructions. "The argument is not merely suggested, but is marked out step by step and often articles appear in almost the identical language of the chief. Many subjects Mr. Medill writes upon himself, treating them in terse and vigorous, though not always graceful style. Beginning an article sitting at a table, he is apt to finish it at a window, one foot on a chair bringing the knee into position to be used as a desk."[61]

The observant visitor caught the odd mix of tradition and novelty that characterized Medill and his paper. The editor clung tenaciously to personal habits — refusing for twenty years to be photographed — even while enthusing over technological advances. According to this flattering profile, Medill possessed "all the insistence, stubbornness and shrewdness of men educated in the old school of journalism and all the push and enterprise of those educated in the new. He is proud of the *Tribune*, but almost as proud of the fact that early in his career he walked from Toledo to Chicago."[62]

2

A Second Son

"Solitary trees, if they grow at all, grow strong."

— Winston Churchill

I N CHICAGO as elsewhere, the decades after the Civil War were transforming years in the dissemination of news. The literacy rate among
Americans doubled between 1870 and 1900. Simultaneously, a sharp
decline in the average workweek spurred the growth of newspapers and
other forms of mass entertainment. Typesetting machines came into general use. Presses were operated electrically. Newsprint made from wood
pulp, a revolutionary advance first employed in Germany, left whole
forests vulnerable to urban readers. A literate populace and the national
mania for party politics combined to give big-city editors a visibility and
influence never since equaled. Indeed, long after Horace Greeley's death it
was said that upstate New York farmers went on reading his newspaper in
the belief that "Uncle Horace" was still providing its editorial voice.

Medill's imprint on the *Chicago Tribune* was no less profound. Daily circulation tripled under his leadership. By the time of his death in 1899, the
Sunday edition was being read in 179,000 homes. All this made the *Tribune*
a valuable property and its publisher a modestly wealthy man. Yet while
the merchant princes of Chicago raised astonishingly ugly mansions beside
Lake Michigan, their vulgar displays contributing to the local reputation
for "cash, cussing and cuspidors," after 1885 Medill lived simply in a solid
thirty-six-room brownstone at 101 Cass Street. Instead of pursuing riches
for their own sake, he worked overtime to free himself from Marshall
Field's extortionate loan and the crippling lien it placed on his editorial
authority.

His heirs were less disinterested. We have already made the acquaintance of the firstborn, Kate Medill, and her polished, ineffectual husband, Robert S. McCormick. Medill's youngest child, Josephine, inherited the reddish hair and independent spirit of her father. She displayed his sharp tongue as well, until death from tuberculosis prematurely silenced it in 1892. This left Elinor, known from infancy as Nellie. In an era when few women could hope to assert themselves in the executive suite, Nellie and Kate waged a shadowy competition over the *Tribune* through the men in their lives.

Here Nellie had a distinct advantage, for her husband, Robert W. Patterson, was already a promising journalist when Rob McCormick was courting disaster in the grain business. Like McCormick, Patterson had his roots in the South. His Tennessee-born father, the founder of Chicago's elite Second Presbyterian Church, had more recently led emigrating Protestants to Lake Forest, a North Shore refuge from the Irish Catholic tide lapping at Chicago City Hall. Young Patterson began his journalistic career on Wilbur Storey's *Chicago Times*. He worked briefly at the *Interior*, a religious weekly, before going to the *Tribune* in 1873. Over the next few years he served as night telegraph editor, drama and book critic, and Washington correspondent.

He also began courting the boss's daughter. In January 1878, Patterson became the second Confederate sympathizer to infiltrate the Medill household. Behind his genial exterior, the bookish newcomer had a stubborn streak, unforgettably revealed during the Pullman strike of 1894. Giving free rein to the hysteria of the times, Medill insisted that the Socialist leader Eugene Debs be labeled Dictator Debs in all *Tribune* news columns. Patterson countermanded the order, in the process piercing his father-in-law's aura of cranky omnipotence.

Patterson's professional stock rose as his marriage crumbled. Little seemed to please Nellie Patterson, least of all the mirthless entertainments and empty travel that substituted for meaningful involvement in the family business. Like many women stymied by the social conventions of the era, she became a monument of convention. Her correspondence depicts an arid environment of unreliable servants, common houseguests, and stultifying routine. New York left her predictably dissatisfied. In opulent Newport, Rhode Island, she found herself "rather outside the inner circle . . . I must associate with swells or nobody!"[1]

But if the eastern beau monde relegated her to a place below the salt, Nellie could always impress her Chicago neighbors. Her Gold Coast mansion, with its marble bathrooms and foot-thick walls, evoked nearly as much comment as Mrs. Potter Palmer's granite-turreted castle on the lakefront. At Mrs. Palmer's Thursday evening receptions, Nellie indulged her queenly prerogatives, frowning upon "a large number of queer-looking lady managers" in attendance. Her sister was not immune to her fanatical quest for respectability. "We went to Kate's for tea," Mrs. Patterson informed her mother, hastening to note the drab presence there of "three Frenchmen — all rather ordinary. She has Mrs. Fish to dinner tonight but Kate is always so careless. Her dinners are not nearly so nice as mine. For instance last night she was short two people." Adding to her offense, Kate had been seen smoking cigarettes with male guests after dinner. Such flouting of convention scandalized the Reverend Patterson's daughter-in-law.[2]

Nellie wasn't a bad woman, merely a silly one. She summed up her approach to life by telling her husband — already seeking solace from his marriage in the well-lubricated fellowship of the Chicago Club — "not to worry about anything but illness or *disgrace* — nothing would break me down but these."[3]

Even by these standards, Nellie's sister had considerable cause for alarm. If not disgraced, Rob McCormick was most certainly discouraged as he tried to make his way in the grain business during the hard years following the panic of 1873. Hoping to establish a life beyond Medill's long shadow, he and a cousin operated a grain elevator in St. Louis, the city to which Rob took his bride in the autumn of 1876. The venture was not a success. McCormick blamed its failure on a combination of "my own mistaken judgment" and a trusted associate's fraud. Whatever the cause, the firm of McCormick and Adams was dissolved with heavy losses. The sale of his residual interest in Walnut Grove to his Uncle Cyrus was not enough to restore Rob's spirits or liquidate $130,000 in debts owed to his sisters Ruby and Lucy. A job as the *Tribune*'s literary critic only emphasized his dependence on his father-in-law.[4]

So did the birth in May 1877 of a son, inevitably christened Joseph Medill McCormick and confusingly known as Medill to family and friends. With his arrival, Kate McCormick regained the ground lost to her sister through Rob's financial embarrassments. She moved quickly to consolidate her gains. By the time Nellie gave birth to *her* first child, Joseph Medill Patterson, in January 1879, Kate was on the verge of delivering again. "My nurse predicts a boy for me," she told her mother, "which plunges me into despair. I long for a girl." A week later she got her wish, only to have it cruelly snuffed out; the infant Katrina McCormick lived less than six months. The grieving mother never got over her loss — or forgave her next child for being born male.[5]

Within months of Katrina's death, Kate discovered that she was again pregnant. This time she returned to Chicago for her confinement, which took place in a three-story, thirty-foot-wide house on Ontario Street, just east of today's Michigan Avenue. Built a few years earlier on the site of a former baseball field, 363 Ontario belonged not to Kate but to Nellie, who had received it as a gift from Joe Medill. There, in an upstairs chamber known as the Green Room, Kate's second son was born, on July 30, 1880.

According to family tradition, the baby was christened Robert Sanderson McCormick, Junior, but no such name appears on his birth certificate, undated until the end of August. In an unpublished autobiographical fragment, Colonel McCormick, whose middle name had long since been changed to Rutherford to conform with his mother's supposed blood ties to Sir Walter Scott, asserted that Kate had been forced to take refuge under Nellie Patterson's roof because "my father had met financial disaster." But why forgo the comforts of the much grander Medill establishment, just a few block away? The most likely explanation is one bruited about at the time and dusted off nearly a century after the event by a *Tribune* researcher, namely, that Kate had moved out of her father's place after a quarrel with Rob.[6]

The Colonel did little to clarify the mysterious circumstances surrounding his birth. Just the opposite. So uncomfortable was that steamy Friday morning in July 1880, he later claimed, that his father had hitched up the family carriage and driven downtown to purchase every electric fan he could locate. And so it was, explained McCormick, that he had begun life as the world's first air-conditioned baby. Few of his listeners knew, and fewer still would have told him if they did, that the electric fan made its first appearance in 1882.

✧ 2

C. S. Lewis once observed that happy childhoods are usually forgotten. When Colonel McCormick unspooled his memoirs over the *Tribune* radio station WGN early in the 1950s, he was noticeably silent about childhood happenings. Whether such neglect was in obedience to Lewis's rule is questionable. To begin with, there were his parents, of whom he saw little. The McCormicks subscribed to aristocratic notions of child-rearing: let the servants do it. Except that Rob and Kate could barely afford servants. By the time their second son, whom they called Bertie, was born, they had few emotional resources for him to draw on either.

The boy's earliest education came at the hands of a Scotch Presbyterian nurse "who frightened me almost to death." McCormick's Scottish thrift long outlasted any youthful interest in Presbyterian ritual. As a publishing tycoon worth many millions, he collected string, of which he had never had enough to play with as a boy. What toys the child did own were paid for, along with the offending nurse and the roof sheltering them both, by

Joseph Medill. In his will, Medill forgave loans to Rob McCormick totaling $90,000. It was this money, together with the still more valuable political influence wielded by the *Tribune*, that launched the failed brokerage dealer and frustrated literary critic on a diplomatic career ideally suited to one of his well-tailored amiability.[7]

Before setting foot in Europe's chancelleries, however, the future ambassador experienced more than his share of humbling setbacks. In the spring of 1881, Rob abandoned plans to settle permanently in St. Louis, thus acknowledging his continuing dependence on Joseph Medill's largesse. Signs of strain in the McCormick household appear in a message from Kate to her mother, dispatched that summer from the fashionable resort of Newport. Combining faint praise for the Narragansett climate with scorn for the local cuisine, Kate ridiculed the "horrid people at our table" from Baltimore and likened a new acquaintance to "a walking cotton ball." "I am deadly *deadly* sick of this place" she wailed, "and don't expect to ever return. If I don't go abroad I will go to New London — if I live."[8]

The mother of two young children, Kate did not see fit to mention either. "I didn't go to Bertie's musical, but of course Nellie did," she notified her mother on another occasion. "It was a terrible night too but Nellie went all the way over from Astor Street in a storm to find it dull and scantily attended." Over the years many such messages flowed from her pen, an unappealing blend of acidic social reporting and blank self-pity. To Kate's younger son, already sensitive about the special status his brother enjoyed as heir apparent, these spoke eloquently of parental neglect.[9]

A photograph from the era shows Kate and her children in an unintentionally revealing pose. The young mother dominates the studio portrait, her rich clothing and elegantly styled hair not obscuring a tendency to plumpness. Her boys, dressed in sailor suits, stare soulfully into the camera. Bertie wears a particularly wistful expression. Kate looks off to one side. The effect is to make her and not her children the focus of attention.

Being married to poor but proud Rob McCormick only intensified Kate's need to see herself as a member of the Chicago meritocracy. Bertie never forgot the sight of his mother boarding a horse-drawn streetcar for the short ride from the dreary Ontario Flats, in which the McCormicks resided, to the South Water Street Market. For a three-year-old whose legs were too short to reach the floor, the straw-lined cars were a tantalizing source of warmth. Other women might walk the half-mile distance, but Kate refused to trail her skirt through the mud of an unpaved thoroughfare.[10]

Grimmer recollections flooded over the adult McCormick as he toyed with his autobiography. After sixty years, he could still hear hacking sounds coming from the apartment across the hall, where his great-uncle Sam Medill lay dying of tuberculosis. When Bertie joined a gang of home-owners' sons in waging war against neighborhood squatters, snowballs quickly gave way to more lethal weapons. "Once I opened a boy's head with a stone, and, terrified, hid in the attic until I became hungry," he remembered. "I do not know whether I was the more relieved or disap-pointed that my feat of arms had not been reported."[11]

Bicycles were ungainly novelties in the 1880s, their riders shooed away from wooden sidewalks by killjoy police. So Bertie repaired to the circle at Chicago and Michigan avenues, close by the waterworks, which had sur-vived the Great Fire to become an urban landmark. Like his grandfather, who counted Thomas Edison among his close friends, the boy was fasci-nated by electricity. He installed an electric doorbell at Medill's Cass Street residence and strung telegraph wires between his own house and that of a neighbor. His career as a telegrapher ended abruptly one morning when a tapping messenger inadvertently woke Kate McCormick from her pre-dawn sleep.

Bertie made his first European journey at the age of five. "Everybody falls in love with him," said his father. His earliest known letter, composed in London on stationery topped by a horseman in full pursuit of a fox, conveys both loneliness and a boyish capacity for mischief-making. "Dear Grandma," it reads, "I wish I was home. I would then be happy. The police said he would arrest us if we got into the tree again. We were in St. James Park. Yesterday we went — " Here the letter abruptly breaks off so that Bertie can visit the zoo, accompanied by his "cranky" nanny.[12]

In the fall of 1885 the McCormicks returned to Chicago, a city of explo-sive energy, infinite possibilities, and colliding interests. During Bertie's first ten years the local population would more than double, moving Chicago past Philadelphia as the second largest metropolis in the United States. In the summer of his birth, Republicans meeting in Chicago had rejected a third term for Ulysses Grant, stampeding instead to a dark-horse congressman from Ohio named James Garfield. The platform they adopted demanded, in language Joseph Medill himself might have com-posed, "legislation for the United States and not for the whole world."

Bertie's first formal schooling unfolded at the University School for Boys, whose imitation frieze from the Parthenon testified to the city's cul-tural immaturity. "Having seen it I urgently desire never to see it again," Rudyard Kipling wrote of Chicago when young Bertie McCormick and his family were shivering at the Ontario Flats. "It is inhabited by savages. Its air is dirt." Local attempts at sophistication ran afoul of nouveau riche dis-play and corruption. In the 1880s Chicago dog owners paid more for their licenses than the politically well-connected streetcar companies did.

Already the Garden City of memory had given way to an industrial giant draped with a pall of soot. Through the grimy alchemy of modern capitalism, Chicago's smokestacks sustained three universities, two dozen theaters, and a symphony orchestra. Captain A. H. Bogardus, "wing shot champion of the world," was admitted to the pantheon of local heroes after shooting five hundred pigeons in less than nine hours. On a visit to his grandparents in California, Bertie McCormick was presented with a twenty-gauge single-barrel shotgun. When he protested that he wanted a more adult double barrel, his father replied, "No, learn to hit them with a single shot." In time McCormick would fire almost every kind of weapon, and most of his hits were made on the first shot.[13]

❖ 3

That his parents favored Bertie's handsome, high-strung older brother was as obvious as their continuing grief over the loss of Katrina. Writing from Europe in September 1888, Kate contrasted Medill's latest achievements with the intellectual shortcomings of eight-year-old Bertie. When the younger boy finally learned to read, a few months later, it helped to dissipate his growing sense of isolation. Among other things, books offered companionship to a child uprooted from familiar surroundings and placed in an alien culture.

After November 1888 Bertie had need of such friends as his literary imagination could supply. That fall American voters put Indiana's Benjamin Harrison in the White House. Like every other midwestern Republican, the new president could not ignore the *Chicago Tribune* and the insistent claims for preference made by its editor. Egged on by Kate, Joseph Medill pressured Harrison and his secretary of state, James G. Blaine, to initiate Rob McCormick into the foreign service. In April 1889, these efforts were rewarded with McCormick's appointment as second secretary to the American legation in London. The selection was cleared through the resident minister, Medill's neighbor and friend of thirty years, Robert Todd Lincoln.

For Bertie, the ocean crossing aboard the White Star liner *Adriatic* was enlivened by the presence of an Arctic explorer named William Emory. The boy was less impressed by Robert Lincoln, a remote, unimaginative figure best remembered today as the president of the Pullman Car Company. McCormick never forgot the sight of Abraham Lincoln's son dressed for court in satin knee breeches, ruffled shirt, and black buckled shoes. Much later he claimed that his fellow citizens ably represented the Great Republic so long as they shunned such outlandish costumes, "but after the rank of Ambassador was established the State Department became snobbish and un-American and has been so for half a century."[14] (His father's natural dignity was much offended by velvet pants and silk stockings, McCormick maintained. His fashion-conscious mother, however, seemed "delighted" with the elaborate garb prescribed at Victoria's court.)

The McCormicks arrived in an imperial capital at the peak of its glory. One quarter of the human race bowed low before the squat, frog-eyed Widow of Windsor. As the world's greatest naval power, Britain launched a thousand merchant vessels annually. Clocks around the globe were set according to Greenwich time. Ten mail deliveries a day served London, the undisputed hub of international finance, trade, and banking. Beneath the unceasing drone of commercial activity that Londoners called "the Hum" lay another, more sinister metropolis. Eighty thousand prostitutes infested squalid neighborhoods such as Cheapside and Blue Gate Fields. Outside the elegant townhouse of the Prince of Wales, the empire's most notorious philanderer, street sounds were deadened by rubber pavement. Elsewhere the urban racket competed with the disorienting effects of blinding fogs, dubbed "London particulars" by Charles Dickens.

British hegemony in the palmy days of empire admitted no such confusion. According to the historian Carl Beckson, Victorian imperialism was the political equivalent of Darwinian natural selection, a civic religion that could take the place of waning Christianity. Fanning the flames of dominion was the blustering new penny press, which reached absurd heights at the time of Victoria's Jubilee. "How many millions of years has the sun stood in heaven?" asked the *Daily Mail.* "But the sun never looked down until yesterday upon the embodiment of so much energy and power."

It was against this backdrop that Rob McCormick and his family took up residence in London. British arrogance held little appeal for a homesick boy of eight reared in a household where twisting the tail of the British lion was an honored tradition. The adaptable Rob McCormick quickly learned when to exchange a top hat for a more comfortable "pot" and how to converse with social butterflies in drafty country houses and stuffy gentlemen's clubs. "I can venture to take a seat on top of a bus east of Charing Cross," he wrote half seriously, "but must never be seen in so undignified a position up Pall Mall or Piccadilly Way." It is hard to imagine that this kind of ironic disapproval did not communicate itself to his children.[15]

In fact, transport was the least of his frustrations. Blocking his path to diplomatic promotion was the legation's first secretary, Henry White, a suave New Yorker and close friend of the wife of Vice President Levi Morton. With little else to occupy her time, Kate enlisted Robert and Nellie Patterson in a fumbling attempt to remove White. Secretary Blaine professed sympathy for the McCormicks but was unwilling to offend Robert Lincoln, who, far closer to White than he let on, feigned ignorance as his subordinate refused to introduce McCormick to other members of the diplomatic community.

After six months, the newcomer remained mired in trivialities. "I would like the place better if there was real work to do," he wrote wistfully, "but I may find my hands full later." In November 1889, with his fortieth birthday behind him and little hope of advancement to brighten the future, Rob moved his family into a "bijou residence" near Hyde Park. Increasingly, his hopes were being transferred to his elder son. Medill McCormick, he wrote, "by avoiding my mistakes and profiting by advantages his grandfather places within his reach," must one day attain power and influence through the *Tribune*.[16]

The father's pride was pardonable. Handsome and precocious, Medill possessed a scattershot intellect and omnivorous curiosity. His charm inspired a crush in his tomboy cousin Eleanor Patterson, to whom he gave the nickname Cissy. By contrast, Miss Patterson haughtily dismissed Medill's younger brother as "Bertie the Swipe." Besides a bedroom overlooking Grosvenor Square, the two boys shared little but a distaste for their new surroundings. Kate's sons were "miserably unhappy" in London, she reported shortly after their arrival. "Dear Grandma," Bertie wrote in confirmation of this one Sunday afternoon in July 1889, "I don't like it here. I am going to Madstone [sic] tomorrow. Affectionately yours, Bertie."[17]

Whether because of or despite their disenchantment, Kate arranged to place her children "where they can be near me yet in the country." Evidently Bertie resisted, for six months passed between Medill's enrollment at Elstree, a highly regarded boys' school perched on a hillside fourteen miles from London, and his own entry into Langley, in the appropriately named community of Slough. Langley was a latter-day Dotheboys Hall, complete with a sadistic proprietor and a master named Collins, remembered by one classmate as a "priceless brute." Within a month Bertie was reciting for his cousin Joe Patterson a depressing litany of hardship. For breakfast he was subjected to "bad sossiag and a bad cup of coffee and some dry bred and butter." Lunch consisted of mutton or beefsteak. In the evening there was more of the ubiquitous bread and butter, prompting the hungry child's forlorn inquiry, "Do you have dinner at the school you go to?"[18]

✧ 4

The stress of life abroad, coupled with their unrealized expectations, began to tell on the McCormicks. In March 1891, Rob refused a State Department offer to represent his country in Portugal, saying that he preferred being secretary in London to being minister in Lisbon. With rather greater candor he explained to friends that Kate would feel compelled to travel most of the time in Portugal, "taking the children with her, as she would have to do, for the sake of respectability." Appearances mattered greatly in the McCormick household; judging from the family's surviving correspondence, maternal affection ran a distant second.[19]

Bertie in particular seems to have passed a largely unsupervised childhood. At the age of eleven, while vacationing at Nice, he taught himself the rudiments of sailing. With a friend he hazarded a Mediterranean crossing in a small sloop. Several hours out of port the boys were overtaken by a ship's captain, well short of the African coast. Equally resourceful on land, Bertie traveled alone from Nice to Paris, where he befriended a black American clown named Chocolat at a circus in the rue St.-Honoré. After being talked out of his only five-franc piece by the circus performer, the boy somehow made his way to Calais, crossed the Channel, and boarded a train for London before a final stage deposited him at his school in the Middlesex countryside.

The only surprising thing about his odyssey, McCormick reminisced afterward, was that it didn't seem surprising at all. In his memoirs he devoted more space to royal mistresses and British fortune-hunters than to the splendid monsters who inhabited the McCormick household. Yet he also took more than the usual pains to put a good face on a family already beginning to disintegrate.

Unable to evict Henry White from the London legation, Rob McCormick tendered his resignation in June 1891. Thereafter he practiced a different brand of diplomacy, as resident commissioner in the British capital for the approaching Columbian Exposition. Here at last, McCormick boasted, was a chance to show millions of visitors "that there is something in Chicago beside pork packaging establishments!" He heatedly denied reports that he was drinking too much. "I understand and appreciate the spirit of your advice about the 'Seduction Cocktail,'" he assured his mother-in-law, "but the discomfort which the 'vile habit' produces, and my own mature views on the subject, are sufficient restraint."[20]

Prodded by Rob, Bertie simultaneously announced a fresh enthusiasm of his own. "I am going to try and learn the Constitution," he excitedly wrote to his cousin Joe. "Papa is willing to give us ten francs for the job." Both messages were premonitory, the first of Rob McCormick's slow dissolution from drink, the second of his son's near-religious feeling for America's organic charter.[21]

The death of her sister Josie in January 1892 sent Kate into an emotional tailspin. Ten months later Rob reported that his wife's mental health was more fragile than ever. "I am put to my wits ends sometimes to convince her that she must not let her imagination run riot in picturing as her own every conceivable disease that flesh is heir to," he confessed dejectedly. In a panic that young Medill might overexert himself in school, Kate now withdrew the boy from Elstree and dispatched him to California to stay with his Medill grandparents.[22]

Bertie was less fortunate. In May 1892 he entered Ludgrove, "an aristocratic institution which I got into because my father was a diplomat." High-toned the school may have been; exclusive it was not, being populated mostly by the sons of Norfolk squires. Ludgrove was the brainchild of Arthur Dunn, a product of Eton and Cambridge who had enjoyed passing celebrity as England's greatest amateur football player. According to Shane Leslie, Winston Churchill's cousin and Bertie McCormick's Ludgrove classmate, Dunn was "Sir Galahad in flannels," with an athlete's physique of chiseled ivory and a singing voice too robust for the rural chapel.[23]*

To modern eyes, Dunn appears the proverbial good fellow, more decent than profound. In his quarters he displayed a favorite verse from Ecclesiastes: "Whatsoever thy hand findeth to do, do it with all thy might." He read his Bible with an absorption that almost made up for the fact he read nothing else. He taught his charges to love God and hate Harrow. His creed was frankly evangelical, wrote Leslie. "Bible History he accepted as a prelude to Victorian England . . . the heroes or scoundrels of Israel or Judah he fitted into categories of gentlemen or cad." Assisting this minor-league Arnold was a sweet-faced wife who inspired in Bertie a lifelong devotion. Helen Dunn showed the introverted boy a solicitude and disregard for pretense wholly missing in his mother. (Once asked if her modest wardrobe could stand the test of a royal occasion, the headmaster's wife replied, "Give me a pocket handkerchief and I dare face the world!")[24]

Dunn was thirty-two years old in 1892, the luster of his playing-field achievements beginning to dim, when he decided to found a school for boys at Ludgrove, an East Barnet estate once owned by Henry VIII. The present manor house was of more recent vintage, built shortly after Dickens immortalized the surrounding landscape in the pages of *Oliver Twist*. Under Dunn's supervision, a hillside opposite Hadley Wood was leveled to make way for a football field; stables were turned into changing rooms; a carriage house became a racquet court.

On Sunday mornings Bertie McCormick joined other boys in scratchy Eton jackets and stiff white collars to attend services at nearby Cockfosters. His Sabbath reading was limited to such self-improving volumes as *Ben-Hur* and *The Pilgrim's Progress*. During the week he and his classmates were taught by the sarcastic, asthmatic T. C. Weatherhead, whose jokes occasionally found their way into *Punch*, and Henry Hansell, an uninspired instructor of French so bored with his subject that he occasionally

---

*Leslie advanced a theory of his own to explain the adult McCormick's emotional violence toward the British empire. It could be traced, he claimed, to the fact that Lord Salisbury snubbed McCormick's father by refusing to receive him at Hatfield, the country home of the Cecil family since Elizabethan times. But for one cup of tea in a stately English house, concluded Leslie, the whole tone of Chicago journalism in the next century might have been radically altered. The reasoning is charming but far-fetched.

slept through class. (Hansell earned dubious fame as a tutor to the Prince of Wales. "He never taught us anything at all," recalled the Duke of Windsor in 1953. "I am completely self-educated.")

Ludgrove boys who excelled in class received tickets marked VG, a sufficient number of which admitted holders to the master's quarters for a tea party and parlor games. Bertie made his share of appearances. "He seems to me to be a boy of no ordinary merit," Dunn wrote to Rob McCormick in May 1892, "of a most affectionate disposition and particularly anxious to please and obey me in every little detail." Because of his aptitude for mathematics, the young American was drilled in algebra and Euclid. Within two months of his arrival, he won a prize for "continued steady work throughout the term."[25]

In the Dunn regime, athletics were on a par with scholarship. Bertie practiced cricket six days a week, without ever gaining much proficiency in the game. A revenge of sorts came when an American baseball team played an exhibition game at Ludgrove and it fell to him to explain the pitcher's curve ball.

Over time, Ludgrove developed into a typically British establishment of high collars, indifferent food, and peer-sanctioned brutality. (The school gardener habitually bowed before the sons of gentlemen who crossed his path.) To those seeking Freudian explanations for McCormick's later anglophobia, the Colonel stoutly denied that he had been beaten during his school days. In truth, he remembered Dunn with affection and his school with respect. Less convincingly, he insisted that classmates extolling the glories of English, Irish, or Scottish civilization had left unmolested the Stars and Stripes that covered his bed. (Of course, the fact that he slept under an American flag says something about boyish alienation.)

Certainly he knew enough of his country's history to despise the red-coated soldiers standing guard outside Buckingham Palace. While still in Chicago he had devoured fiercely nationalistic works such as *The Boys of '76*, in whose pages heroic colonists rose up and whipped their British oppressors. Nor was he swayed by the sight of ancient Queen Victoria riding in an open carriage through the gates of Hyde Park. The crowd of cheering subjects reminded him of a comic opera.

Inevitably exposed to Dickens, Thackeray, and Scott, Bertie thought the first two wrote by the yard, an unfortunate habit perpetuated by certain editorial writers. More happily, he developed an addiction to the *London Illustrated News*, whose pictures he extolled decades later to *Chicago Tribune* staffers as models of their art. "In an effort to remain American," he revealed, "I read and reread *Tom Sawyer* and *Huckleberry Finn* and all of the Mark Twain writings." He came to regard *Pudd'nhead Wilson* as the great American novel.[26]

Influenced by the example of his classmates, Bertie dreamed of joining the navy. Among his acquaintances, several would fall in the Great War. One was devoured by a lion in a Norfolk game park. Another became viceroy of India. A third was shot in bed by an actress. After leaving school, McCormick, by his own admission, never again set eyes on his closest friend at Ludgrove, a clergyman's son named Theo Pelly. The impression of youthful shyness curdling into adult isolation is unmistakable.

Indeed, perhaps the most important thing that McCormick learned at Ludgrove was how to conceal feelings of emotional deprivation. "Joe is grand but for occasional bursts of homesickness," Bertie told his mother in a letter about his Patterson cousin, recently enrolled at Groton School, in Massachusetts. "I never let such sad thoughts come to the surface." This was a brave but false front. In June 1893, claiming that he was unhappy there, Kate McCormick withdrew Bertie from Ludgrove. "I don't like the place," she wrote. "They are reduced gentility keeping up. Servants in livery and not enough to eat."[27]

✧ 5

In the last years of his life, determined to edit history as he had the daily reporting of news, Colonel McCormick destroyed many of his father's papers and a trunkful of correspondence from his mother — the former, one suspects, to protect a dead man, the latter to protect himself. By then Rob McCormick's alcoholism jostled for place alongside other skeletons in the family closet.

According to Janet Woititz's *Adult Children of Alcoholics*, such concern for appearances is common among the children of alcoholic homes. "You begin to live in a fairy-tale world, with fantasies and dreams," she writes. A sense of normality is as rare as emotional intimacy. "Because [these people] lack reliable and consistent love from one or both parents, building a relationship with another person is very painful and complicated. Because they have been disappointed and manipulated, however subtly, many of them wind up with 'the colossal terror of being close.' " In burning his mother's letters, Colonel McCormick turned his back on a relationship that had been anything but nurturing.

In the fall of 1892, Joseph Medill saw to the Groton admission of his namesake and grandson. Originally Bertie was to have enrolled at the opening of the winter term, but Kate's "dreadfully nervous temperament" had made it impossible for Rob McCormick to accompany his twelve-year-old son across the Atlantic, so Medill substituted for his brother at the New England academy. It was decided that the autumn 1893 term would be soon enough for Bertie to follow in Medill's footsteps. Once more separated from her beloved Medill, Kate began to haunt European spas, seeking a cure for her multiplying complaints. Easily bored, she left Switzerland for Italy, then turned around before reaching Florence, declaring herself tired of Italian hotels. Back in Geneva, Rob wrote that "brave Bertie" had his heart set on a naval career. Rather than Groton, Bertie hoped to attend "some school like the Poly-technic," followed by Annapolis.[28]

Pronouncing the English climate unsuitable, Kate packed the boy off to Paris. Bertie spent the summer of 1893 studying French under the tutelage of a war widow named Madame Passa, who startled her pupil by taking regular doses of arsenic as a stimulant. Equally memorable were the brightly lit fountains of Versailles and the pronounced lack of deference shown to a young marquis by his predominantly American schoolmates.

It was about this time that Bertie, already tall for his age, was singled out in a German park by the visiting Prince of Wales and his cousin, Germany's Kaiser Wilhelm. The future King Edward VII spotted the youth in his sailor suit and a hatband bearing the letters HMS. "Ah, a nice little English boy," he remarked. "I am not," shot back Bertie. "I am an American." The kaiser laughed heartily. Afterward Bertie applied to his mother — "who was not much interested in what kind of cap I wore" — for a hatband commemorating his own country's navy. He dined out for years on this early example of patriotic insolence.[29]

That summer the McCormicks joined 28 million other visitors to the World's Columbian Exposition in Chicago. Intense competition over the fair had prompted New Yorker Charles A. Dana to deride Chicago as "that windy city," an epithet that long outlived the fair's plaster-and-lath palaces along the lakefront. Equally grating was the superior tone adopted by Ward McAllister, the self-proclaimed arbiter of New York's cultural elite. McAllister raised aesthetic complaints over midwestern feed-store millionaires who put ballrooms in their attics and bowling alleys in the basement. "I would suggest that Chicago society import a number of fine French chefs," he sniffed. "I should also advise that they do not frappé their wine too much." A Chicago journalist reassured McAllister that his city's mayor "will not frappé his wine too much. He will frappé it just enough so the guests can blow the foam off the top of the glass without a vulgar exhibition of lung and lip power."

"Chicago was like no other city in the world," claimed Theodore Dreiser, "a city which had no traditions but which was making them." In retrospect, its fair can be seen as a crowning achievement of Joseph Medill's Roman republic. To the end of his life, Medill's grandson cherished memories of the summer when, as a thirteen-year-old expatriate, he boarded an electric railway and rode naphtha-powered boats through shimmering waterways. The boy's astonishment was shared by his countrymen. Henry Adams, for one, thought the Chicago fair more remarkable than Niagara Falls, the geysers of Yellowstone, and the nation's railway system combined. Concluded Adams, "Chicago asked in 1893 for the first time the question whether the American people knew where they were driving."

To Bertie McCormick, as to millions of gaping fair-goers, the question answered itself in the 127,000 electric lights scattered throughout Jackson Park and the hundred-ton locomotives displayed cheek by jowl with the printing presses, cash registers, typewriters, adding machines, and safety bicycles spawned by a relentlessly inventive people. Chicago's fair celebrated scientific genius and prosperity without limit. Mayor Carter Harrison said as much in a speech delivered on October 28, hours before he was assassinated by a disappointed office-seeker. "Genius is but audacity," he argued, "and the audacity of the 'wild and wooly west' and of Chicago has chosen a star and has looked upward to it, and knows nothing that it cannot accomplish."

Yet even before the fair closed its gates, the American economy was plunged into a severe depression. In time the forces of beleaguered wealth would look askance at the pushing inhabitants of the recently closed frontier. They would rally to the safe, if unexciting, governor of Ohio, William McKinley, until then known chiefly for his sponsorship of high tariffs designed to benefit eastern manufacturers at the expense of western and southern interests. These protectionist policies had greatly complicated Rob McCormick's task of persuading the British to display their wares in Chicago.

During the winter of 1893–94, Rob and his family came to know McKinley better. Joseph Medill, forever in search of the next Lincoln, spent the cold-weather months in Thomasville, Georgia, at the invitation of Mark Hanna, McKinley's campaign manager. The visit had consequences over and above the *Tribune*'s support for McKinley in 1896, for it was in Thomasville that young Medill McCormick fell in love with Hanna's daughter Ruth. Nine years passed before the two were married, in a ceremony postponed by the disapproval of Medill's mother. As for Bertie, his Thomasville recollections included the chilling sight of the epileptic Mrs. McKinley sitting frozen at the dinner table while her husband draped her face with a napkin and the conversation went on all around her as if nothing untoward had happened.

"Bertie wants an electric motor — whatever that is," his mother reported just before Christmas of 1893. "I haven't the faintest idea in the world what my darling Medill will want." In the end she settled on a pair of skates for each. Medill soon after returned to Groton, where he and his irrepressible cousin Joe Patterson earned notoriety as the Gold Dust Twins. "My husband says I did Bertie a great injustice in saying that he was less clever than Medill," Kate wrote to Groton's headmaster, Endicott

Peabody. "He says that he is less quick but has more concentration and 'arrives' just as well!" To which Rob McCormick added his hope that Bertie might one day join "a triumvirate of Grotonians" entrusted with the destiny of the family newspaper.[30]

In March 1894, a telegram arrived announcing a place for Bertie — now called Rutherford by his mother — in Groton's second form. The hopes thus raised were abruptly dashed when Bertie failed the school's entrance examination. Throughout the summer he worked diligently with a Harvard-trained tutor, only to fail a second time in September. His grandfather was "keenly disappointed." So was Kate, although for a different reason: she had hoped that Bertie would be a college freshman when Medill, as a senior, could exert his admirable influence over his sibling. In the next three months, aided by a pair of glasses prescribed by a Boston oculist, Bertie redoubled his efforts. Finally, a few days before Christmas 1894, the McCormicks were told to send the boy east.

For Bertie, now Rutherford, membership in Groton's third form meant yet another upheaval. A stranger abroad, he would soon be regarded as an alien in his own land. He reacted much as Joseph Medill had in overcompensating for his Canadian birth, displaying a patriotism so extreme as to raise doubts about his sense of identity. The larger significance of his English years lay in the fact that he never outgrew them. In maturity he provided a stunning example of cognitive dissonance — wearing English clothes, following cricket scores religiously, speaking with an accent more reminiscent of Mayfair than of Kankakee. In private he recreated the very society that had so wounded him as a child, becoming in the process Lord McCormick of Wheaton, master of hounds, pursuer of foxes, a squire tweedy enough to meet even Ward McAllister's exacting standards. McCormick the editor based his defense of press freedoms on liberties first codified in the Magna Carta. He imported to his rural seat the sexual double standard of titled nobility.

Yet McCormick's antipathy toward the British, and especially the British upper crust, whose rural customs he reenacted in the Chicago suburbs, became one of the governing passions of his life. He justified his purchase of $50,000 in Irish bonds as a contribution toward the dissolution of a despised empire. Armchair psychologists attributed his hostility to unhappy experiences at an English public school. It would be more accurate to say that McCormick loved the *idea* of England, the manly virtues of G. A. Henty and the imperial nationalism of Kipling, while loathing the insufferable pride of a people drunk with their own sense of superiority. Moreover, the heart of McCormick's unapologetic Americanism was to be found in an enterprising culture as old as Jefferson's aristocracy of talent and virtue. Whatever dammed economic dynamism and the fluid society it both sustained and reflected, this was his mortal enemy.

It was in England, McCormick joked, "where I first learned how to browbeat the lower classes." This was only the start of his education. On a personal level, he discovered while abroad just how insignificant a figure he cut in the lives of his parents, and how scant their interest in his future possibilities was. He learned other things, in their way just as shattering: a fear of personal intimacy and an abiding suspicion of those whose love ought to be unconditional. Thereafter his affections were directed along institutional lines; he loved a corporation or a country, necessarily idealized, where rejection could only come at the polls and might even then be subject to later reversal.

England brought McCormick face to face with family hypocrisy and social pretense. He would spend the rest of his life denying truths too painful to acknowledge. Small wonder that as an old man, alone except for his memories and aristocratic self-justifications, he should burn the documentation of his boyhood misery.

✧ 6

Groton would not, at first glance, appear to be the ideal place to send a shy, emotionally delicate boy of fourteen whose sense of self was as fragile as an eggshell. Reflecting the muscular piety of its formidable headmaster, Endicott Peabody, the school employed genteel regimentation to produce a type — the moderately useful gentleman who would serve his country and his kind in keeping with "the Rector's" code of noblesse oblige. The place was as expensive as it was exclusive. Annual tuition and board cost $600. Boys customarily enrolled for six years and were assigned to either the Harvard or the Yale Division.

To the casual observer, Groton might seem an extension of Bertie's experience at Ludgrove, another raw school straining for venerability. But there was a critical difference. At Ludgrove the diplomat's son had been welcomed as an honored guest from abroad. To the proud, provincial youths of New England, he was a freakish intruder, neither Yankee fish nor English fowl. The class of 1899 included a DuPont, a Roosevelt, an Alsop, a Bowditch, and a Griswold. Bertie McCormick was the only member born west of the Hudson River. Condescension shot from his classmates like ink from a squid. It left the interloper permanently embittered against New Englanders as latter-day colonials infatuated with their mother country.

Bertie's independence, coupled with his defiant assertions of midwestern superiority, made him a rank outsider. Inevitably he stuck his nose all the higher in the air. But if Groton increased his isolation, it also gave him the courage to go it alone. When the clannish sons of the codfish aristocracy taunted him as an "Illinois Indian," he fell back on some advice from his father. "Tell them they are descendants of Boston tradesmen and you are descended from Virginia gentlemen," Rob McCormick had instructed his son. It was a lesson Bertie took to heart, with fateful implications.[31]

Ancestral pedigrees aside, New England winters proved devastating to the newcomer's health. McCormick blamed his lifelong vulnerability to respiratory ailments on the arctic dormitories of Groton. Colder still was the school's social climate. Both could be traced to the headmaster, "an Episcopalian puritan" of lofty conviction and uncertain humanity. No one better embodied the Emersonian dictum that an institution is but the lengthened shadow of an individual. Peabody was twenty-seven years old in October 1884, when he took the reins of the brand-new school for boys located just outside the quiet Massachusetts village of Groton, thirty-five miles northwest of Boston. The youthful headmaster had conceived his American counterpart to Thomas Arnold's Rugby while enrolled as a senior at the Episcopal Theological School in nearby Cambridge. Peabody's contagious enthusiasm extracted $40,000 from a board of trustees that included J. P. Morgan. The Lawrence family of Groton donated one hundred acres of land on a wooded ridge overlooking the sluggish Nashua River.

Within a few years of its founding, the school boasted a cluster of red brick buildings in vaguely neoclassical style, flanked by handball courts and a mock Tudor chapel, all designed to reproduce faithfully the ambiance of Peabody's English schooldays. The Rector was a muscular blond, exactly six feet tall and straight as a gun barrel, with broad shoulders, icy blue eyes, and a majestic stride. Dressed in his habitual blue shirt and low, soft collars, he radiated confidence. His virtue, like his self-assurance, was impregnable. Between Cambridge and Groton he had gained practical ministerial experience at a church in unrefined Tombstone, Arizona. "Well," the *Tombstone Epitaph* had concluded, "we've got a parson who doesn't flirt with the girls, who doesn't drink beer behind the door, and when it comes to baseball, he's a daisy."

In common with his friend Theodore Roosevelt, to whom he had unsuccessfully offered a teaching position, Peabody showed strenuous disregard for human frailty. Dreading adolescent impurity, he forbade his youthful charges to read Voltaire. Along with Harvard's Charles William Eliot, he held that a successful headmaster must be something of a bully. Admirers of the Rector liked to tell of the night he was driving along a dark country road and a would-be thief leaped out of some bushes. Instinctively Peabody stepped on the gas and nearly ran the man over. His approach to intellectuals was similarly direct. "I am not sure I like boys who think too much," he acknowledged.[32]

Having built his implacable reputation, Peabody made it work for him (a lesson not lost on the adult McCormick). Behind his unbending perfectionism was a man willing, under the right circumstances, to look the other way, as Bertie discovered one day when he and a friend, examining a package of cigarettes left on the school golf course, unexpectedly encountered the headmaster. "You *found* them?" Peabody inquired, none too hopefully. The boys hastily replied in the affirmative. "Give them to Mr. Cushing," said Peabody. "He smokes cigarettes."[33]

Peabody's Groton was a conformist's paradise. Individualism was only slightly less sinful than impurity. "A certain amount of sadism appears to be inseparable from boys' boarding schools," McCormick later observed. The singular contributions of Groton included the boot-box, a locker large enough to accommodate a pair of boots — or a doubled-up newcomer whose deviance from social norms led to his disciplining by upperclassmen. Then there was "pumping," the exclusive right of sixth formers to terrorize an insufficiently deferential younger boy by holding him over a black soapstone sink and pouring vast amounts of water down his throat until this produced in the panicky offender the sensations of drowning.

Two notable exceptions to the prevailing order were the Rector's cousin, William Amory Gardner — "Billy Wag" to hundreds of Grotties — and the Reverend Sherrard Billings, popularly known as "Beebs." Both men joined enthusiastically in the rituals of school life, Mr. Billings entertaining generations of students with his spirited conducting of the nonsense song "Blue Bottles." Gardner, an accomplished yachtsman, was sometimes seen on the river dressed in spats, orange shoes, and green waistcoat. His charges had to make do with Sunday uniforms of blue suits and stiff collars, varied each Memorial Day when they put on blue coats, white duck trousers, and straw hats and marched through the village in tribute to Civil War veterans.

Another kind of heroics was supplied by campus visitors such as Booker T. Washington and Theodore Roosevelt, who regaled students with his adventures as New York City's police commissioner. "If some Groton boys do not enter political life and do something for our land, it won't be because they have not been urged," said Peabody. The message resonated with TR's distant cousin from Hyde Park. Enrolling at Groton one year after Bertie McCormick, Franklin Roosevelt labored against multiple disadvantages. Like his future rival, he entered Groton two years after most of his classmates, thereby lagging far behind in the race for friends and reputation. Both boys joined a student body predisposed to hostility thanks to the unorthodox behavior of older relations (McCormick's cousin Joe Patterson struck one Groton instructor as "a chronic revolutionary"; far worse was FDR's half-nephew, James Roosevelt "Taddy" Roosevelt, an object of universal derision among the school population).[34]

But while McCormick instinctively rebelled against collective life, receiving seventeen black marks in his first term alone, Roosevelt worked all the harder to fit in. He captured the school's punctuality prize three years running. He readily complied when a pack of boys cornered him in a hallway and ordered him to dance for their amusement. Eight months passed before he earned his first black mark. "I am very glad of it, as I was thought to have no school spirit before," he told his parents, conforming even in his lawlessness. Throughout his Groton years, young Roosevelt emulated the Rector's unquestioning faith in God and in himself. This was hardly surprising: as an only child, groomed for success like a colt bred to win the Derby, he had enjoyed the undivided love and attention of doting parents.

Bertie McCormick, by contrast, arrived at Groton as something of an afterthought within his own family. His unusual height made him the subject of unwelcome attention. His vaguely English accent inspired ridicule. So did his awkwardness on the playing field and his extreme sensitivity to criticism. In the spirt of E. M. Forster, who once wrote, "I don't feel *of* anywhere. I wish I did," Bertie made few friends at Groton. No surviving account testifies to any triumph he may have enjoyed in compulsory debating. He did not play baseball or football. He did not go rowing on the Nashua, or join the Missionary Society, or sign up for the campus newspaper, *The Grotonian* — this last an abstention he later attributed to an unduly harsh writing instructor, who frightened him off any journalistic efforts for twenty years. Instead, Bertie pursued the solitary recreation of canoeing, at its best when riverbank elms flamed in brilliant autumnal shades of orange and scarlet. In the winter he strapped on ice skates and flew against a stiff northeast wind. Then the Nashua became a scenic highway of escape — or the cause of yet another illness and confinement to Groton's bleak student infirmary.[35]

When not in rude health, Bertie could be plain rude. The outbreak of the Spanish American War coincided with a scarlet fever epidemic at Groton. In the runup to war, he found himself under quarantine. He just missed being kept company in misery by Franklin Roosevelt, whose solicitous mother, denied personal contact with her son, challenged school regulations by perching on top of a stepladder outside the infirmary window and reading aloud to him each day. But Bertie McCormick had no visitors. He found diversion in naming bedpans after school functionaries. His undisguised impatience with hospital food provoked a stern reprimand from the Rector, leading to a bitter confrontation and a rare Peabody apology. "If I was not just I am sorry for it," wrote the headmaster. "It is my wish that the school should supply you and all who are ill with food. I believe that the food is generally well cooked and abundant. If it should happen as you say . . . that an egg should not be fresh then you may tell the nurse of it and she will get you another." Peabody's real complaint was that the boy had been "lacking in consideration and courtesy" toward the nurses. He was more than willing to listen to any civil complaint, said the

Rector, "but I must insist that you act in a manner which the nurses expect from a Groton boy and that you carry out conscientiously the regulations in regard to the hours of putting out lights and talking."[36]

Groton answered to Peabody, but it was governed by bells. Their insistent clanging roused students at seven o'clock each morning, sending them to a frigid shower of river water pumped up from the Nashua by windmill. They announced breakfast at seven-thirty and chapel forty-five minutes later. They ushered scholars from the pew to the first classes of the day, where the Rector was on hand to read notices before the balance of the morning was given over to study and recitations. Peabody returned before lunch to hand out detentions and lead the boys in calisthenics. He presided over the midday meal, carving the roast in the presence of his wife, Fanny, and the senior prefect, all seated upon a raised platform in the dining room of Hundred House, Groton's recently completed dormitory cum library building.

The iconoclastic Joe Patterson, two forms ahead of his Chicago cousin, described his afternoon routine with terse irreverence:

11:45–1:15	Do what we please, wash, etc.
1:15–1:30	(Though about two seconds are spent in washing, etc.) the rest in reading, fighting, etc.
1:30–2:15	Lunch
2:45–5:00	Study
5:00–5:45	Fool exercise, etc.
5:45–6:00	Same as before lunch

Here Patterson broke off long enough to mention that "some big fellows are blackmailing a first former of an orange saying if they [sic] did not give it to them they would throw it at their face."[37]

After six o'clock supper and a half-hour recess came evening prayers, enunciated by the Rector in his mellow Anglican voice. Yet another period of study preceded the nightly ritual in which each Grotonian shook hands with the businesslike Peabody and his sympathetic wife. The student day ended a little before nine o'clock, in a spartan, doorless cubicle just large enough to hold a bed, bureau, chair, and rug. (Only fifth- and sixth-formers had private studies.) No pictures personalized the drab brown walls. Wall hooks served in place of clothes closets.

Groton's curriculum was less functional than its architecture. In his first year Bertie studied Latin, Greek, algebra, English literature, French history, and some elementary science. His worst subject was sacred studies, traditionally opened by the Rector's peremptory command, "Nails and notebook, boy!" Bertie missed several weeks that winter and spring on account of pneumonia. Before departing for the healthier climate of Georgia, he scored a creditable 7.47, receiving a perfect 10 in neatness. It was a measure of his growing dissatisfaction with Groton that over the next three years his grades declined steadily, until he dwelled regularly in the bottom quarter of the class.

The problem lay as much in the school's classical priorities as in Bertie's highly practical brain. Exposed to the Greek historian Xenophon, *Oman's Greek History*, and *Allen's History of the Roman Republic*, young McCormick learned nothing of Jamestown, Gettysburg, or the industrial revolution even then transforming American society. He read Shakespeare, Scott, Pope, and Molière but no American author except for the favorite son of New England, Nathaniel Hawthorne. He studied Edmund Burke's "Speech on Conciliation with America" but left Groton otherwise ignorant of Revolutionary history. His writings fell short of profundity even by schoolboy standards, yet they are richly revealing of the timidity and belligerence that coexisted behind a bullying facade.

In one autobiographical essay, Bertie described his encounter with a poacher trespassing on his grandfather's farm west of Chicago. Hearing a shot fired close by, he was overcome by a fit of rage. "I started toward the spot from which the gunshot had come," he wrote. Anger quickly gave way to fear. "Supposing I should be shot! I stopped, turned to retreat, then, ashamed of my cowardice, shut my teeth hard, cocked my gun, and advanced toward the poacher."

"What are you doing here?" Bertie demanded of his quarry, a young rabbit hunter abruptly reduced to a "picture of terror."

"Just walking home, sir," the boy told him.

"You liar," said Bertie — "bold now that I saw my opponent's cowardice."

The accusation of unlawfully shooting rabbits on Medill's property led to boyish protestations of innocence. To no avail. Bertie grabbed the offender's rifle and a brace of bloodied rabbits, "even though I believed his story." Intending to return the weapon the next day, assuming that the young miscreant would come around to ask forgiveness, on second thought Bertie concluded, "I hope he will never come, for I need a good rifle."[38]

For all the adolescent bravado the scene contains, it is not difficult to imagine the youthful antagonists reversing roles.

Bertie's weekly themes foreshadowed his adult preoccupations. He expressed sympathy for the Elizabethan poet Dryden, compelled for economic reasons to write "flattering odes to the ruler moguls." Reflecting his love of all things martial, the boy criticized John Milton for beginning the narrative of *Paradise Lost* in the middle, thereby skipping the battle of Lucifer and his fallen angels. "Why Harvard Always Loses" diagnosed excessive Ivy League pride as the source of gridiron humiliation. The influence of Joseph Medill could be seen in his grandson's diatribe against Confederate treatment of northern prisoners as "an outrage of civilization," and in Bertie's demand for a strong navy to contest Queen Victoria's supremacy on the waters of the world.[39]

The schoolboy essayist showed flashes of old Medill's temper as well as his fervent nationalism. Anticipating war with Spain, he imagined himself making the eagle scream on the floor of the Senate in Washington. "How long are we going to suffer our national honor to be trampled on?" demanded Senator McCormick. Toward President McKinley, a peace-loving executive "laboring between the demands of the people and the orders of Hanna," he felt the contempt of an adolescent moralist. "It is time for Congress to act. It is time to give independence to struggling Cubans. It is time to send the murdering Spaniards back to Spain. It is time to call in grim visaged war, if necessary, and retrieve our national honor."[40]

Bertie was in Washington, D.C., during the third week of February 1898. It was the height of the capital's social season. At dawn on the seventeenth, a naval officer roused President McKinley with terrible news: a few hours earlier the battleship *Maine* had been torn apart by an explosion in Havana harbor. More than 250 of her crew lay entombed in the shattered hulk. War fever swept the nation, with Joseph Medill in full-throated cry against the "diabolical insult" inflicted on the United States by Spain. To contemplate a financial settlement with the nation responsible for such villainy, he snapped, "is enough to make a dog vomit." Medill got his war; his equally militant grandson was denied admission to Annapolis by a navy oculist.[41]

An alternative presented itself in Yale College, where Medill McCormick was already enrolled as a member of the class of 1900. Citing Bert's continuing susceptibility to winter colds, Rob and Kate decided to withdraw him from Groton before his last year. Given his aptitude for mathematics, he seemed to his father a logical candidate to run the *Tribune's* business operations, perhaps to oversee the paper's mechanical department. By May 1898 it was all fixed: Bert would spend the coming fall and winter in San Antonio, preparing for Yale while keeping a close eye on his ailing grandfather.

The boy's last set of grades at Groton was undistinguished. With a cumulative average of 6.27, he stood sixteenth out of nineteen boys, barely ahead of the laughable Taddy Roosevelt. Looking back, McCormick claimed that the most important thing he had gained from the school was the ironic result of punishing New England winters. Annual bouts with pneumonia had caused him to spend most cold weather months in the South and West. There he took advantage of every possible opportunity to improve his shooting. This youthful exposure to large-bore, black powder rifles made McCormick, in his immodest words, "one of the modern military writers able to comprehend battles in the days before smokeless powder."[42]

Estimates of McCormick's nonacademic performance differed widely. To one classmate he seemed "a likeable lad who wasn't especially noteworthy in any way." Another recalled him as "an ebullient, warm-hearted boy, full of mischief, with greater interest in the outside world than the rest of us." Endicott Peabody's appraisal was, characteristically, a model of precision: Rutherford McCormick was "distinctly able intellectually, not more than fairly industrious . . . keen about games, physically powerful," and possessed in abundance that "wide-awake quality which one connects with his native city."[43]

And what did the object of such measured praise think about Groton? In fact, the lessons Bert McCormick learned there were almost entirely negative. He hated the caste system of the school, the rigid hierarchy that terrorized new boys and lionized sixth-formers; the regulations, as pervasive as the broad *a* of the Yankee dialect; the loss of privacy and the assault on individualism that buttressed Peabody-style social engineering. McCormick's lifelong antipathy for the East as an insular and backward-looking region can be traced to his Groton years. He never forgave the instructor, as ignorant of trans-Mississippi America as McCormick was contemptuous of New England, who equated western support for the Spanish war with greed for military pensions. "While I only had a small allowance," McCormick subsequently wrote in defense of his schoolboy patriotism, "I remember the pleasure it gave me to pay for the stamps on checks."[44]

As an adult he would embark on a career of revenge against Groton, profaning nearly everything the school held sacred, especially after Franklin Roosevelt's New Deal came to be identified with Peabody's religion of public service. During the 1932 campaign, McCormick recalled for the Rector the first McKinley-Bryan contest, when the forces of capitalism had pointed in terror at the farmer-labor coalition that threatened social upheaval. "We are going through similar times, it appears," he grimly told Peabody. In later years he insisted that Roosevelt had been merely a bit player at Groton, overshadowed within his class by a boy who went on to design airplane motors for Charles Lindbergh and another who graduated to a Philadelphia medical practice.[45]

Before he became America's preeminent Roosevelt hater, McCormick was sufficiently attached to his old school to donate a canoe for use on the Nashua and to provide scholarships for the sons of army officers. The Depression made him rethink his generosity; the New Deal transformed his relationship with Groton into an adversarial one. A classmate soliciting contributions in the fall of 1936 got a blunt rejection. "This year all of my funds must be spent in an endeavor to get our schoolmate out of the White House," McCormick explained. He would rather invest his overtaxed resources in changing the political outlook than in supporting a school doomed, along with the rest of private education, by "the famous graduate of the Class of 1900."[46]

For all his resentments, McCormicks' never fully escaped the Rector's spell. "At the last Groton dinner in New York, I looked around the room and thought how far the graduates had strayed from the ideals you had formed for us," he wrote to Peabody in 1930. "And then I thought how much further we would have strayed if it had not been for your teaching." When the headmaster stepped down after nearly six decades at the helm, McCormick contributed $250 to a retirement fund. Following Peabody's death (and his own escalating battle with the Roosevelt administration), he allowed his bias to crowd out his charity. "The Rector certainly was a foreigner, " he told his cousin and fellow Grotonian Chauncey McCormick. Moreover, the record of Groton in public life was hardly commendable "when you consider Frank Roosevelt and his sons and Dean Acheson. I try to blame the Roosevelts on Harvard, but I cannot do that for Acheson."[47]

3

Fitting In

"Assumed responsibility for himself in Chicago, Illinois, July 30th, 1880. He fitted himself at Groton School and came to Yale to 'fulfill his destiny' and incidentally to be president of the University Club and write for the *Chicago Tribune* . . . His greatest college grievance is 'Mediaevalism' and he believes 1903's weak point to be over-conservatism."

— from McCormick's 1903 Yale classbook

NOT LONG before his death, Colonel McCormick appeared at a *Tribune* awards banquet, one of those unabashedly sentimental occasions that helped foster his belief in the company as an extended family, the only real family he had ever known. When his turn came to speak, he indulged an old man's privilege to rewrite the past more to his liking. As he had so often before, he conjured up the final days of his grandfather, finally breaking down as he described the poignant scene at the deathbed of "the old hero" in March 1899.[1]

The truth of their relationship was more complicated. Like the rest of his clan, Bertie McCormick looked up to Joseph Medill with mingled awe and terror. Boys did not speak to the white-haired patriarch unless spoken to; one might just as easily address the bronze statue of Benjamin Franklin that Medill donated to the people of Chicago for placement in Lincoln Park. It didn't matter; in a life nearly devoid of emotional ties, Bertie was instinctively drawn to the stooped figure who entertained him with anecdotes of Lincoln and Grant. It was as if, having been frozen out of his parents' life, Robert McCormick retreated a generation and uncritically celebrated his kinship with the great publisher-editor.

A flag flown over the *Tribune* during the Civil War graced McCormick's inner sanctum on the twenty-fourth floor of Tribune Tower, and in the vaulting lobby he had chiseled the words of his ancestor beside quotations from James Madison, Patrick Henry, and John Milton. Joe Medill gave him a window on history and an exalted view of his family's place in it. Medill provided the son of self-absorbed globetrotters with a stable home, or rather homes, the big brownstone on the North Side of Chicago alternating each summer with Red Oaks, the simple Wheaton farmhouse that, enlarged to the same dimensions as the White House, was rechristened Cantigny in memory of the sole World War I battle in which McCormick took part. Outside today's rose-brick mansion stands a monument wrongly identifying Joseph Medill as the founder of the *Tribune*. If nothing else, it conveys the highly personal approach to the past shared by Cantigny's builders.*

Curiously, neither Medill nor McCormick set out to become an editor or publisher. Trained in the law, each became a law unto himself, at least within the tightly knit *Tribune* organization, where memos signed MUST, JM carried the same force as story "suggestions" bearing the initials RRMC. When an out-of-town paper reprinted a story Medill had somehow overlooked, he ordered it run a second time, on the theory that anything not appearing in the *Tribune* for three weeks was news all over again. The same comedy was played out during the McCormick reign, with even less pretense of editorial democracy. "When the Colonel wants a drink of water," explained a successful managing editor, "we turn the fire-hose on him."[2]

Neither opinion-maker was inclined to play second fiddle when he could conduct or, better yet, own the orchestra hall. As mayor, Medill promoted a canal connecting the Great Lakes with the Mississippi River, an engineering marvel his grandson pushed toward completion as president of the Chicago Sanitary District. Yet neither man came close to realizing his early political promise, or to forgiving the tendency of the average voter to sell his birthright for a leaf-raking job or Social Security card. "Anyone who calls the United States a democracy shamefully traduces our Republic," Colonel McCormick thundered. For him as for his grandfather, the advantage of republican institutions was not that they expressed the popular will so much as that they restrained it.

✧ 2

In a taped interview with a *Tribune* employee chosen to write his biography in the 1940s, McCormick acknowledged that he and his grand-

---

*Invited late in life to choose the greatest events in recorded history, the Colonel selected four: the birth of Christ, the invention of printing, the discovery of America, and the founding of the American republic.

father had been something less than intimates. "In my younger days he didn't talk to me," he said of the aging martinet. At the age of thirteen Bertie watched as gloomy-faced visitors came to the house on Cass Street to see the old man, then plagued by heart disease and imprisoned by deafness. In happier times he observed a parade of supplicants, Marshall Field and George Pullman among them, dropping by to seek Medill's advice or solicit *Tribune* editorial support. In later life the Colonel credited Medill with inspiring his lifelong interest in Ulysses Grant by insisting that he read Grant's memoirs instead of an adventure tale from the pen of Arthur Conan Doyle.[3]

Following the death of his wife in 1894, Medill entertained an offer to buy the *Tribune* for $6 million. He decided against selling on the counsel of his daughters, each of whom had reasons to retain the newspaper and the wealth and status it conferred. Well aware of the tensions under his roof, Medill wrote a will intended to perpetuate his hold on the *Tribune* as "a party organ, never to be a supporter of that party which sought to destroy the American union or that exalts the state above the nation."[4]

Several revisions ensued before the final document was ready for signing in the spring of 1898. Under its terms a trust was established, with 1,050 shares (out of a total of 2,000 distributed among all *Tribune* owners) nominally overseen by Medill's two sons-in-law, aided in their administrative duties by William G. Beale, Robert Todd Lincoln's law partner and a pillar of the Chicago establishment. As arranged by Beale, restraints on the sale of stock would prevent Kate or Nellie from singlehandedly disposing of the paper or dictating its editorial policies. The trust would continue until such time as both women died or the trustees decided to sell their shares. In this way, McCormicks and Pattersons might live comfortably off the dividends of stock that, technically speaking, belonged to none of them.

But no legal codicil could still the intense rivalry afflicting the House of Medill. In 1896, partly to compensate Kate for her sister's downtown mansion, Medill began construction of a summer residence near Wheaton, "a nice country place twenty miles from Chicago ... beyond the reach and influence of the smokey atmosphere of the city." He employed the Boston architect Charles A. Coolidge to create a spacious New England–style house flanked by porches. Carpenters were paid a dollar and a half a day to lay down floors of quartered oak and sheathe the exterior in white pine clapboards. It was here, at the rustic five-hundred-acre estate dubbed Red Oaks, that young Bert McCormick spent his happiest days. Walking with his grandfather over miles of dusty roads, the boy listened as Medill, in a voice thickened with age, stirred the fires of ancient controversies.[5]

For McCormick, Red Oaks became a place of indoctrination as well as recreation. His grandfather's mind was a magpie's nest of misinformation and prejudices, whose truth he asserted with bulldog tenacity. To Medill, the Midwest was a bastion of self-respecting independence. The East, by contrast, was a fertile breeding ground for snobs, toadying diplomats, and traitors. Republican reformers were a pink tea set of jabbering moralists. James G. Blaine was the greatest statesman since Lincoln.

In the summer of 1896, Bert accompanied his grandfather to Bar Harbor, Maine, where he heard the old man describe his friendship with the Plumed Knight, by then three years in his grave. William Jennings Bryan, his free-silver nostrums, and his Populist allies occupied a menacing position in Medill's thoughts that summer. In a moment of inspiration he dubbed the crazy-quilt coalition supporting Bryan's insurgency the Popocrats. Bert McCormick, equally upset with the workmen at Red Oaks for their Democratic loyalties, reassured himself about Republican campaign prospects by polling suburban train passengers.

On breathless summer days, Bert drove stock to the DuPage River and hauled back water for barnyard and household use. With his brother he rode horses and bagged game in the neighboring woods. Discovering that Billy the Kid had been killed by a sheriff who heard him moving in the dark, Bert taught himself to shoot at sound. He improved his marksmanship by blasting off the heads of chickens destined for the family dinner table.[6]

Eighteen ninety-seven marked the *Tribune*'s golden jubilee. Feeling his mortality, Medill relaxed his long-standing rule against being photographed and sat for a picture with his four grandchildren, standard-bearers of a dynasty in the making. In the fall of 1898 the editor went to San Antonio; Bert kept him company at the fashionable Menger Hotel. The youth sat transfixed as Medill reminisced with his doctors and questioned returning officers about the splendid little war recently concluded on Cuban soil. "My day for useful work is nearly over," Medill wrote to Robert Patterson in February 1899. But he could still strike fire from his flint. "The prosperity of Chicago is bound up with the essential improvement of the Chicago River," he admonished his son-in-law. Under no circumstances should the *Tribune* neglect the city's waterborne commerce.[7]

To the White House, Medill fired off equally imperious telegrams, warning McKinley not to relax his grip on America's fledgling empire. Bert McCormick carried one such message to a nearby telegraph office on the night of March 16. The next morning, Medill, his faltering heart further weakened by acute prostate trouble, was not at his customary place on the hotel veranda. Yet even propped up in bed, the dying editor was capable of a star turn. "Bring me the papers," he commanded those around him. The exertion of reading left him comatose. Shortly after nine o'clock he muttered, "My last words shall be, what is the news?"[8]

McCormick duly reported this final request, without mentioning its theatrical preface. He also exaggerated his part in the deathbed scene, claiming that he had been alone with Medill when the end came. (He was actually out of the room and had to be summoned by a nurse.) Other McCormick stories improved even more with the telling. According to the adult McCormick, he had mourned his grandfather by killing a man in a San Antonio bar, then hiding the murder weapon in Medill's casket.[9]

Only now, almost a century later, is it possible to point to a likely explanation for this bizarre story, contained in an unpublished manuscript in the McCormick archives. It is a self-consciously literary short story, complete with references to Homer, about an innocent Anglo boy who stumbles into San Antonio's notorious "MexTown." Offended by the sight of prostitutes in adobe huts, the young man and his friends take refuge in a neighborhood bar. He is drawn into a brawl between a drunken soldier and a bartender trying to eject him from the establishment. Fearing the contempt of female onlookers, the unarmed boy throws his hands behind him as if to seize an imaginary pair of guns. "Don't shoot, for God's sake!" the soldier slurs before hightailing it into the night.[10]

"I wrote this with the idea of publishing it," McCormick later informed his father, then serving as U.S. ambassador to Austria-Hungary, "but I rather hesitate to offer it to the publisher. However, as you are representing these people, I send it to you that you may understand them."[11]

In fact, it was not until 1901, a full two years after Joseph Medill breathed his last, that the elder McCormick went to Europe in one of the diplomatic posts purchased with Kate's money and the *Tribune*'s influence. Either Bert McCormick waited a long time to produce a sanitized version of his crime for paternal review, or else he inflated the story in later years to enhance his reputation for bravado. Short of exhuming Medill, there is no way to verify his narrative. In a way it doesn't really matter, for whatever its provenance, the tale reveals much about the half real, half invented persona of Robert McCormick and his curious balance of aggressive self-regard and almost morbid self-doubt. Not yet twenty years old, he was already sustained by illusions. The taste for manufactured reality never left him.

❖ 3

Two days after Medill's death, the managing editor of the *Tribune* received a bulky envelope addressed in a familiar scrawl; inside were half a dozen clippings and proposed editorials. The entire packet was printed as written. The Illinois legislature adjourned out of respect for the dead man. The Chicago Press Club, over which Medill had once presided, honored him as "the last remaining representative of the old order of things, the journalism of the city in its infant and adolescent stages, which gives place to that of the metropolitan city of the West."[12]

Against these fulsome tributes the reporter Ben Hecht registered a stiff protest. Hecht could scarcely credit the last words attributed to Medill. "The old buzzard didn't give a good goddamn about real news," he angrily told a friend. "He was always trying to project some crackbrained spurious scheme and attacking first and second generation Americans who didn't belong to his clubs or had the wrong shaped nose. To most Chicago newspapermen he was a cantankerous sonofabitch."[13]

Medill would have worn such criticism as a badge of honor. Throughout life he had rationalized his friendlessness as the price of editorial integrity. He passed this misanthropic pride on to his grandson, who used it, in turn, to mask the alienation and loneliness at the heart of his own personality. "I had so few friends before I went to college," McCormick once confided, "that I took up companionship at the expense of my studies." In this he reflected the prevailing mood among Yale undergraduates at the turn of the century. It was with more than the usual parental misgivings that Rob and Kate McCormick sent their sons to the New England school. On a preliminary visit, Rob had been shocked by the lack of supervision accorded boys from schools such as Groton, "where they had been entirely free from the temptations which literally walk the streets of New Haven."[14]

Sexual license was not the only vice stalking local streets. To the ordinary trials and hazards of student life — intemperance, gambling, sloth, blasphemy, class envy — was added the confusion of a venerable institution struggling to escape the chrysalis of religious orthodoxy in which it had been born. A generation had passed since President Noah Porter had granted William Graham Sumner permission to teach the agnostic and Darwinian ideas of Herbert Spencer. At Yale, as elsewhere, religion was losing its war with science. Empiricism crowded out revelation as a source of light in the university's credo, *"Lux et Veritas."* To tradition-loving alumni, Yale was little better than notoriously free-thinking Harvard.

McCormick attributed his decision to enroll in the class of 1903 to the influence of *Frank Merriwell at Yale.* In an age when college men were popularly derided as "cigarette dudes," the athletic hero of nearly a thousand stories was a model of disciplined virility. But if the Merriwell brothers, Frank and Dick, made student recruitment easy, they hardly prepared callow freshmen for the dangers and delights of New Haven. Still less did their competitive fantasies relate to a university in the throes of an identity crisis.

According to one of McCormick's Yale contemporaries, "The college of my day was a combination of sporting resort, beer garden, political convention, laboratory, factory of research, and nurse of liberal arts." In the 1911 novel *Stover at Yale*, the protagonist is warned, "Now you've got to do a certain amount of study here. Better do it in the first year and get in with the faculty." Illustrating the bleak logic of Sumner's survival of the fittest, just over half the class of 1903 completed the first year's course. Few who remained had their world substantially broadened.

In the last week of September 1899, Bert took up residence in Pierson Hall, on Chapel Street. His arrival coincided with the elevation of Yale's thirteenth president, a forty-three-year-old economist whose flailing arms and strident voice reminded onlookers of Theodore Roosevelt, another well-bred reformer with a pugilistic style and conservative instincts. Around New Haven it was said that Arthur Twining Hadley combined the mind of Saint Paul with the manner of Saint Vitus. His absentmindedness caused him to trip over wastebaskets while dictating in his office or lecturing students on whom he had turned his back. The president assured visiting clergymen that while no time limits were imposed on chapel eloquence, "we have a feeling here at Yale" — and Hadley sliced the air with his trademark pump-handle gesture — "that no souls" — slash — "are saved" — slash — "after the first twenty minutes."[15]

As the first lay president in two centuries, Hadley in his academic robes faced the same thorny issues of personal liberty and social obligation that confronted Roosevelt and other opinion-makers at the dawn of the Progressive era. Simply put, how could materialistic Americans reconcile their competitive ethic with their professed egalitarianism? As a student of economics, Hadley anticipated Roosevelt's verbal pummeling of "malefactors of great wealth." The freedom to achieve must not degenerate into destructive selfishness, Hadley reminded the class of 1903. Character and service must take precedence over the mindless accumulation of profits.

College presidents have issued such ringing challenges since time immemorial, perhaps because conformity, not conscience, is the companionable guide used by most students as they confront the riddle of life. Class spirit, after all, is a euphemism for the herd instinct. It would be both gratifying and inaccurate to claim that these sermons had an appreciable impact on nineteen-year-old Bert McCormick. They were no match for the individualism bordering on eccentricity Joseph Medill had bequeathed to his grandson. Moreover, one could hardly expect a repressed second son to forgo entirely the tribal rituals that, at Yale as at virtually every American college of the period, threatened to make the lonely pursuit of knowledge a campus sideshow.

For the first and last time, McCormick made a conscious effort to be like everybody else. He reveled in his euphonious nickname, Rubberfoot. He pretended to enjoy the beer and smoke of Tontine's restaurant. There was nothing feigned about his enthusiasm for football. These were the glory days of college athletics. Walter Camp, employed during the week in a New Haven watch factory, revolutionized the game through the forward pass and other innovations he pressed upon Yale's coaches. To the class of 1903, gridiron stars were demigods. Players who lost a game by fumbling the ball avoided their class reunions for years.*

For undergraduates, Yale operated as a strict hierarchy ruled by upperclassmen. Commencement honors meant less than success on Tap Day — the defining moment when Yale men learned whether they had been invited to join one of the senior societies, such as Skull and Bones or Scroll and Key, which dominated campus life and, many thought, distorted student priorities. Freshmen languished at the bottom of the greasy pole. Banished from campus proms and segregated in the galleries at glee club concerts, first-year students compensated with their own rituals. On Washington's Birthday in 1900, Bert McCormick exposed his towering frame, topped by a comical plug hat, to a volley of snowballs fired by upperclassmen. On May 1, Dewey Day, he and other freshmen fought sophomores for possession of a fence in front of Durfee Hall. At the height of the battle he and his classmates successfully flanked their older tormentors, seizing their objective at the cost of one assailant knocked unconscious. Rowdy students then demolished a building on College Street before toasting their courage around a bonfire.

Unamused professors clamored for abolition of Dewey Day and the Pass of Thermopylae, another springtime rite of humiliation forced on freshmen, who were made to run a gauntlet of hostile upperclassmen. In the face of faculty opposition, Thermopylae fell more quickly, if less nobly, than its classical namesake. On his own initiative, in December 1900, Hadley disbanded the once sacred sophomore societies. Yet neither the president nor his exasperated faculty could eliminate Bottle Night, when hundreds of bottles of drinking water that were cooled on undergraduate windowsills suddenly and inexplicably rained down on pedestrians. All this was part of being a Yale man.

So were campus eating clubs such as Mory's, descended from a pre–Civil War establishment known as Mrs. Moriarty's Quiet House. The quiet had long since evaporated, replaced by youthful high spirits and the boisterous singing of Civil War tunes and instant Spanish-American War standards like "Goodbye, Dolly Gray." Alcoholic excess fueled much of Yale's musical patriotism (ale and champagne forming an essential part of

---

*"What has happened to Yale since . . . I do not know," McCormick lamented in 1947. "Perhaps it was the Harkness Memorial that feminized and Anglicized it." Even so, his alma mater was preferable to Harvard, which, as long ago as his undergraduate days, had been "heading in the direction of Oscar Wilde."

athletic conditioning). When not devouring fried egg sandwiches for break-fast, Bert happily lent his baritone to the likes of "Glorious, Glorious, One Keg of Beer for the Four of Us" and "A Highball at Nightfall." Cole Porter was still a decade in the future, and the Whiffenpoofs had yet to go astray. This left Bert to exercise his creative powers by producing a three-act parody entitled "The Three Musketeers, or Booze and the Queen's Garter." It was set in a beer garden outside the mythical establishment of Snorey's, and the script was studded with the terrible puns and preposterous situa-tions that earn sophomoric humor its bad name. But McCormick's play-writing ambitions, unlike those of his cousin Joe Patterson, began and ended at Yale.[16]

McCormick's thirst was less easily quenched. By his own estimate, his crowning achievement at Yale was election to Mory's Velvet Cup Com-mittee. To this elite group was entrusted a six-handled pewter receptacle filled with a potent mix of champagne, ale, and liqueurs. Whoever touched the cup to the table was required to replenish its contents. Given the scarcity of automobiles, rented horses pulled McCormick and his friends to late-night dinners at the Cheshire Inn. On the way back the animals drove without human interference. This was not without danger, to man and beast. Once an inebriated roommate narrowly escaped injury when he fell off the box; fortunately, he landed on a horse.

In the spring of his freshman year, McCormick passed up a lecture by the New York publisher Whitelaw Reid on the state of American news-papers. He chose instead to hear Justice David J. Brewer of the Supreme Court praise William Howard Taft and other Yale-educated lawyers for their contributions to the life of the nation. McCormick credited Brewer with sparking his subsequent interest in the law. At other times he traced his legal career to an eagle-eyed geology instructor who flunked his row-mates after he caught them cheating. Admittedly indifferent to fossils, Bert insisted that he alone was not guilty. He had failed the exam honestly. "If you do not pass me," he pleaded with the instructor, "you will ruin my reputation for honesty." His ingenious argument had its effect. The young man from Chicago might not be much of a geologist, but he showed defi-nite promise as a lawyer.[17]

McCormick's academic performance improved once he shed the intel-lectual straitjacket of freshman year. Having pronounced the classics "stupid," he welcomed the opportunity to pursue subjects more in line with his mathematical and engineering interests. He did well enough in higher math so he could later conduct a World War I course in French artillery techniques. His navigational studies served him in good stead when exploring the Gulf of St. Lawrence and adjacent timberlands, seeking reliable paper supplies for the *Tribune*. McCormick undertook his first experiment in hydraulics as a freshman, when meerschaum pipes were an undergraduate fad. No smoker, he put his pipe to better use. He punctured a hole in the bottom of a gallon jug filled with water, then watched as it smoked the pipe for him.

He performed creditably enough in an academic environment where scholarship was viewed as unfashionable. Abandoning poker in response to a dean's prodding, he concentrated on French, history, and English literature. He took William Graham Sumner's famous "Science of Society" course, although it would be a mistake to attribute the wintry conservatism of his later years to this "preacher of force in a world of fate." No grandson of Joseph Medill had to join the Sumner cult to gain an appreciation of social Darwinism. It bears noting that McCormick, whose adult devotion to the Constitution assumed cultish intensity, confessed to having little formal training in constitutional history, a deficiency he blamed on "a very old professor, too feeble for his work" and a Yale administration too impoverished to pension the man off.[18]

Perhaps the most telling evidence of McCormick's newfound sense of purpose lay in the steady improvement of his grades. It was the exact reverse of his unhappy experience at Groton.

✧ 4

On New Year's Day 1900, more than three hundred *Tribune* employees gathered at Auditorium Hotel in Chicago for a ritualistic changing of the guard. Holding center stage were Robert Patterson, draped at last in the mantle of editorial superintendent, so jealously guarded by Joseph Medill, and James Keeley, a thirty-two-year-old prodigy recently elevated to the post of managing editor. Reduced to walk-on parts in the celebration were Rob McCormick and his gangling second son, misidentified for *Tribune* readers as Rutherford S. McCormick.

On the same day the *Tribune* family ushered in the post-Medill era, other Chicagoans released a brace of terrified Kansas jackrabbits at the corner of 47th and West to be hunted down by greyhounds as public sport. Such contrasting scenes were typical of Chicago. The city had grown a hundredfold since 1847; during one rainy twenty-four-hour period, a *Tribune* correspondent counted 210,692 people passing by the corner of State and Madison streets. Yet for all its polyglot diversity, the place remained close to its frontier origins — in the words of Theodore Dreiser, "a maundering yokel with an epic in its mouth." As the old century expired, the *Tribune* cast itself as respectable chaperon to Dreiser's bawdy, extroverted, red-faced city, "singing of high deeds and high hopes, its heavy brogans buried deep in the mire of circumstance."

Chicagoans rivaled Texans in their fondness for hyperbole. Local residents boasted of "the greatest boulevard system in the world," notwith-standing $25 million in pending damage suits caused by wooden sidewalks. Sixty local residents owned automobiles in 1900, enough to inspire *Tribune* demands for a speed limit of twelve miles per hour. Faithful to Medill's pseudoscience, the paper argued for "the perfect combustion of coal" and compressed air as energy sources preferable to electricity. Municipal cor-ruption was an editorial perennial; Editor Patterson denounced shoddy work by politically favored contractors and railed against gambling houses and opium dens in such unlovely districts as Whiskey Row, Bloody Max-well, and Dead Man's Corner. Although the *Tribune* opposed women's suffrage, it conceded that the president of Stanford University, David Starr Jordan, was probably correct in asserting that a college education did not, by itself, disqualify a woman for matrimony.*

In keeping with its image as the paper of record among Chicagoans of high caste, the *Tribune* devoted column one on page one to "News and Views of the *London Times*." It printed the highly colored dispatches of Winston Churchill, an upstart war correspondent anxious to parlay his South African heroics into a seat in Parliament. Sharing the editorial page was a gossipy "Letter of Marquise de Fontenoy" detailing the latest activi-ties of European royals and nobility. Not surprisingly, the *Tribune* liked to think itself above grubby commercial realities. From Medill's heyday the paper had taken a dim view of rivals employing "bummers who call sub-scribers and seek ads for their sheets." As for its own advertisements, lumped unappealingly together apart from the news, "they come as the wind comes, on it own accord and unsolicited."

By 1900 the wind had changed course, forcing even Rob Patterson to accept circulation-building giveaways. He would play the game, he reluc-tantly decided, but according to his own rules. When choosing a set of dishes to be offered as an incentive to subscribers, he unerringly selected the most expensive. "By God," he said, "if we're going to be a whore, we're going to be a good one."[19]

In an age when cub reporters earned $12 a week, the editorial superin-tendent of the *Tribune* paid himself an annual salary of $15,000. Patterson made his brother Raymond the paper's Washington correspondent, in which role Raymond exercised considerable authority whenever Repub-lican administrations occupied the White House. To be sure, occasional threads of political liberalism lent color to the *Tribune* tapestry. The paper was outspokenly critical of Charles T. Yerkes, the traction company mo-

---

*In this the *Tribune* reflected the tidy complacencies of the genteel class for which it was edited. That spring the Chicago Horse Show decreed that all female contestants must ride sidesaddle — no more divided skirts to divert attention from the horses. Simultaneously, men at the University of Chicago were permitted for the first time to attend a women's basketball game, a privilege limited to department heads accompanied by their wives.

nopolist who, in his drive to obtain absolute mastery over lucrative street-car franchises, had widely corrupted state and city officials. It sided with striking Pennsylvania coal workers in the summer of 1902, all the while decrying government ownership of the mines as "flapdoodle and non-sense." Patterson the moralist lavished praise on employers such as Swift and Company for their refusal to hire cigarette smokers.

Despite, or perhaps because of, such high-minded conservatism, the *Tribune*'s influence was disproportionate to its readership. A new seventeen-story headquarters at Madison and Dearborn, opened in May 1902, testified to this fact. But no building, however impressive, could hide the paper's runner-up status behind Victor Lawson's *Daily News* and *Morning Record* and the Scripps-owned *Evening Journal.* Nor was there any secret to the Lawson formula for success: his were mass journals, aimed squarely at the swelling immigrant population and priced accordingly. Publishers of the era, taking daily losses for granted, hoped to recoup by selling Sunday editions fattened with lucrative advertising.

The new century brought an unwelcome intruder to upset the competitive balance. Thirty-seven-year-old William Randolph Hearst, staked to the game with a $17 million inheritance from his father, entered national politics by launching the *Chicago American* on July 2, 1900. On the face of it a Democratic party organ loyal to William Jennings Bryan, the new paper, like all Hearst sheets, was first, last, and always for William Randolph Hearst. To meet his deadline, its publisher raided rival news organizations in Chicago and imported a flying squadron of editors, reporters, and pressmen from New York. In the process he raised journalistic wages as he lowered journalistic standards.

Specializing in lurid exposés of dubious veracity, the Hearst press boxed the compass of human weakness and depravity. The publisher, according to his biographer W. A. Swanberg, liked to carpet the floor with his newspapers, turning their pages with his feet. Finding an issue lacking in blood, sensation, or erotic appeal, Hearst moped like an unhappy child. "This is like reading the telephone book," he grumbled. In the view of one critic, Hearst's ideal newspaper would be one "in which the Prince of Wales had gone into vaudeville, Queen Victoria had married her cook, the Pope had issued an encyclical favoring free love . . . France had declared war on Germany, the President of the United States had secured a divorce in order to marry the Dowager Empress of China . . . and the Sultan of Turkey had been converted to Christianity — all of these being 'scoops' in the form of 'signed statements.' "[20]

Confronted with so flamboyant a disturber of the peace, tightwad publishers had no choice but to loosen their purse strings. As the competition for readers escalated, the *Tribune* operated at a special disadvantage; competent, colorless Robert Patterson was increasingly absorbed in the business of the bottle — a preoccupation, it must be acknowledged, that seemed as much a staple of big-city newspapering as tenement fires and love nests.

Stepping forward to fill the vacuum was James Keeley, a cigar-chomping, ambulance-chasing newshound straight out of *The Front Page*. Like many in his profession, Keeley could never resist making a good story better. So he fabricated his biography, portraying himself as a penniless English orphan instead of the son of a London schoolteacher who had been deserted by her husband. Sent to live with American relatives, young Keeley worked for newspapers in Kansas City, Memphis, and Louisville before joining the *Tribune* in 1889. Six years later he became city editor.

A short, bullet-headed man with limitless energy and a robust curiosity to compensate for his spotty formal schooling, Keeley claimed that a good newspaperman never rested. As city editor he proved his point by remaining at work until midnight or later to get the first edition out. Early on the morning of May 7, 1898, he turned his penchant for long hours to spectacular advantage. Shortly before 4 A.M., ahead of the American command and just minutes too late to appear in New York publications, a Manila correspondent flashed word of Admiral Dewey's naval triumph over the superannuated Spanish fleet. A jubilant Keeley phoned President McKinley at the White House with his scoop.

When it came to getting their man, Canada's Mounties had nothing on Jim Keeley. In the most audacious of his stunts, he pursued one crooked banker all the way to Tangier, Morocco, where he persuaded the distraught man to give himself up. Back in Chicago, he arranged a rapid trial through the state's attorney, predicated on a guilty plea and immediate incarceration. Following the banker's parole — also secured by Keeley — the reformed embezzler was hired by the *Tribune* and sent on an inspection tour of southern forests to find a pulp tree adaptable to papermaking.

Such scoops alone were not enough to win a war with Hearst. Other bait was needed to catch and retain fickle readers. Throughout urban America, Progressive-era politicians were wrestling with democratic institutions that had grown remote from those they were designed to represent. With his incomparable flair for self-dramatization, Theodore Roosevelt was a newspaperman's dream. In the White House he made the federal government an instrument of popular assertiveness and the presidential office a kind of national ombudsman. By the same token, Keeley and likeminded journalists transformed newspapers with a newfound emphasis on public service *and* private utility. "The big development of the modern newspaper," Keeley declared before an audience at Notre Dame University, "will be along lines of personal service. The newspaper that not only informs and instructs its readers but is of service is the one that commands attention, gets circulation, and also holds its readers after it gets them."[21]

Here, then, was a formula for combatting peephole journalism: to avert the reader's gaze from scandal to the demands of big-city living in an era of rapid growth, when much of the population felt alienated from familiar sights, customs, and accents. Joseph Medill's ink-stained contemporaries had, with apostolic zeal, instructed readers in what they should think and how they should vote. To these vital functions was now united practical advice for urban residents treated, above all else, as news *consumers*. Keeley's *Tribune* would offer its hand as friend, protector, assimilator, and guide to the strange new world of twentieth-century America. As such, it hoped to become indispensable, even in those households deaf to its political harangues.

Under Patterson, the paper unbent long enough to run a weekly "good roads bulletin" for bicyclists who were heading through "summer resorts" — never suburbs — such as Highland Park and Lake Forest. It also sponsored a correspondence school providing home instruction in "educational, technical, and commercial subjects — conducted by a corps of experienced and able teachers." These less than trailblazing features were mere condiments in a steady news diet of tarriff reform, bimetalism, and Balkan war clouds. Keeley aggressively diversified the *Tribune*'s contents, salting hard news with soft features, many aimed at female readers. His first great coup was to land the actress Lillian Russell, no stranger to the headlines, as the *Tribune*'s beauty editor. The Divine Lillian told readers how she had found the secret of health in exercise, generously supplemented by facial creme, lipstick, and hairdressing. In addition to writing her popular column, the stage star lectured on beauty and charm before capacity audiences in Orchestra Hall.

Keeley next snagged Laura Jean Libby, the author of several saccharine novels, to write a column on problems of the heart. In two years Miss Libby received 50,000 letters from romantically deprived *Tribune* readers. Having addressed Chicago's beauty and love needs, Keeley hired Marion Harland, a national authority on domestic economy, to supervise a new cookery department. Other columns dealt with child care, gardening, and the latest fashions. "A Day with a Wage Earner," a you-are-there account of life in the workplace, began in 1901. The *Tribune* devoted two columns on page one to "Poems You Ought to Know."

Only a modestly gifted writer himself, Keeley gave employment to James O'Donnell Bennett, Ring Lardner, and other wordsmiths. Bert Leston Taylor, a popular columnist specializing in topical verse, was lured away from Victor Lawson's *Journal*. His "Line-O-Type" feature, signed with the initials BLT, became must reading in thousands of Chicago homes. An even bigger acquisition was scored in 1903. "We've got McCutcheon!" Keeley exalted, as well he might, since the much-loved cartoonist John T. McCutcheon had been among Lawson's most prized (if least appreciated) assets.

That same year the *Tribune* established a free ice fund with assistance from Jane Addams and other urban reformers ministering to the poor. It founded summer hospitals for convalescent women and impoverished children. A worker's magazine aimed at manual and office employees was started in 1904. The "Voice of the People" department fostered a dialogue between readers and their friends and counselors at the *Tribune*. Vacation guides, astrology charts, and a sports section printed on pink paper each played a role in cementing readers' loyalty.

Keeley's interests ranged far beyond how-to journalism. The assassination of President McKinley in September 1901 inspired a *Tribune* campaign to ferret out local anarchists. Keeley praised McKinley's successor for his efforts to bolster American military strength and cut a canal through the Isthmus of Panama. With TR in the White House, the *Tribune* lent its voice to a swelling chorus raised against "odious monopolies" in sugar, tobacco, barbed wire, and anthracite coal. "The enemies of a newspaper are its best advertisers — if it's an honest newspaper," Keeley maintained. The paper turned a pitiless spotlight on medical quacks, mediums, and loan sharks. It conducted bacteriological tests of water at public schools, with alarming findings subsequently confirmed by board of education chemists.

Whether staging a playwriting contest, demanding a new city charter, or raising funds for victims of an Italian earthquake, the *Tribune* under Keeley made as much news as it reported. Sitting by his daughter's sickbed one July 4, the editor became incensed over the sounds of firecrackers popping outside his window. He picked up a phone, called the *Tribune* newsroom, and ordered a survey of thirty American cities (later raised to one hundred) to learn how many holiday revelers had been injured by unregulated explosives. As it happened, more Americans had lost their lives celebrating the country's birthday than wearing its uniform in the war with Spain. Out of this impulsive act by a distraught father came the Safe and Sane Fourth movement, which, although no more successful than Colonel McCormick's later crusade for simplified spelling, helped define the *Tribune* for a nationwide readership.

As the weight of editorial responsibilities increased, Keeley drew back from the casual intimacy of his early years at the *Tribune*. Around the city room it was whispered that he had begun to think himself irreplaceable, a potentially fatal miscalculation in the House that Medill Built. However contentious they appeared to outsiders, Medill's daughters were only too willing to adjourn their quarrel and unite against anyone who might threaten their dynastic aspirations.

❖ 5

In October 1900, Bert McCormick joined other members of the Yale Republican Club in a torchlight parade through the streets of New Haven on behalf of the McKinley-Roosevelt ticket. If the president's majority at the polls a month later fell short of his nine-to-one landslide among conservative Elis, it was more than adequate to rekindle Kate McCormick's old dream of abandoning Chicago, where her sister Nellie reigned socially and Robert Patterson ran the *Tribune*, to establish her own court on foreign soil.

The past few years had severely tested her wiles. At the age of fifty-one, Rob McCormick was without visible means of support. In fact, he subsisted on an annual allowance of $6,000 from his wife, supplemented by the meager crumbs of recognition that came his way as a member of the Chicago library board. Completion in 1897 of a palatial new library, complete with Tiffany mosaics and soaring glass dome, left him at a loose end. Kate sought help from her brother-in-law in obtaining a fresh sine-cure with the Lincoln Park Commission, a course that Governor Altgeld — "Viper Altgeld" to *Tribune* readers — was understandably reluctant to abet.

In the afterglow of McKinley's triumphant win over that other *Tribune* nemesis, William Jennings Bryan, the resourceful Kate had another idea. She and Rob fancied a diplomatic appointment, "a small mission like Belgium," she assured Robert Patterson, hastening to add, "We only want it one year — just for the experience." Securing so modest a plum should be easy for one of Patterson's standing. All he had to do was drop by the president's house in Canton, Ohio, and remind the chief executive of how much the *Tribune* had done over the years for the GOP.[22]*

Patterson, reluctant to purchase party spoils at the cost of editorial independence, didn't see it that way. Yet the relentless pressure exerted by his sister-in-law soon caused him to yield. McKinley proved a tougher nut to crack. At length the president offered Patterson the Rome embassy for himself, an invitation as unwelcome as it was unsought. It took the *Tribune* editor two trips to Canton before the wary McKinley finally granted Kate's wish. And so it was that on March 7, 1901, Robert S. McCormick reentered the diplomatic lists as U.S. minister to the Austro-Hungarian empire, a jerrybuilt kingdom of fifty million people stretching "from the Venetian lagoons to the Bohemian forests and from the Swiss cantons to the minarets of Montenegro."

*True to form, Kate didn't rely exclusively on Patterson to press her claims. Working through Illinois senator Shelby Cullom and others, she left the impression that she was the *Tribune*'s majority stockholder — a marked departure from the facts.

Taking up residence in Vienna, the romantic, frivolous, rigidly stratified capital of this empire in twilight, the new minister found his duties less than onerous. He had plenty of time to polish his German — one of six major tongues that made Vienna a Babel of clashing ethnic identities — and haunt local antique shops. "Frightfully lonely and homesick," Kate derided Viennese society as a clutch of highborn wastrels. "No dinners, no musicales, no teas! Only balls," she complained to her stateside niece, Cissy Patterson.[23]

Rob and Kate stare out from century-old photographs, he overdressed in a braided jacket, with a full beard and a high forehead, clutching a plumed hat under his right arm; she as elegant as a beaded gown, tiara, and neck collar can make her, given her continuing fleshiness and close-set eyes. Much later Colonel McCormick would claim that his parents had been splendid diplomats "because they had no inferiority complex." At the time, however, Rob and Kate seemed as dazzled by Hapsburg glitter as any member of *Die Adeligen* — the Noble Ones, two hundred elite families who gave Vienna's carnival atmosphere its tone of frothy artifice. Characteristically, Rob inflated his intimacy with Emperor Franz Joseph, a septuagenarian autocrat from a ruling family stained by scandal, personal tragedy, and madness.[24] (His son followed suit, fabricating a story that his father had arrived at the Hofburg Palace a mere minister in a carriage and departed an ambassador in an ornate coach driven by mild-white horses. The actual elevation was far more prosaic, the result of bureaucratic rather than royal intervention.)

As Kate's craving for power and status went unsatisfied, her fears multiplied. At one point she believed her son Medill to be on the transport ship *Hancock* in Japanese waters. "Suppose he is *drowned!!!* Oh what anxiety our children give us, and how *little* consideration," she cried to Nellie. In the event, Medill returned safely to Chicago, where he and Joe Patterson read copy for church notices and performed humble tasks on the *Tribune* local staff. Christmas 1901 was "awfully blue," Kate lamented, since it was the first time she had been separated from her sons on that quintessential child's day. On second thought, what with holiday callers and musings about a possible promotion from Vienna to St. Petersburg and the court of Czar Nicholas II, "it wasn't quite as bad as I had anticipated." She then proceeded to fill eight pages without returning to the subject of her absent children.[25]

Blind to the obvious, Kate denied the seriousness of Medill's long courtship of Ruth Hanna. Her relations with her second son were strained for reasons that did neither party credit. "Bertie cannot get over the feeling that he and [Joseph Medill's] other grandchildren have been done out of their inheritance," confessed Rob McCormick. Bert's distrust compounded his isolation within the family, but Kate held her ground, refusing to increase his allowance — or independence — until the new *Tribune* building was paid for and dividends resumed. On the eve of his twenty-first birthday, Bert was fast assuming the distant, self-absorbed air of one at home in his own mind and nowhere else.[26]

More lay behind his social inadequacies than a periodic compulsion to withdraw from the world around him. Like Melville's Ishmael, McCormick often experienced November in his soul, and his periodic bouts of depression were reinforced by frequent maternal warnings about the "weak spot on the McCormick brain." Hadn't Grandfather William died in a state asylum? she never tired of pointing out. McCormick's response was a chronic restlessness that made him, in time, the most widely traveled man in Chicago. The habit was implanted early; while still an undergraduate, he gladly forsook Chicago to join an Arizona cattle drive, being careful to observe the gentlemanly code burned into him by Endicott Peabody.

The city dude looked on in disgust as a cowhand roped and tied a bull, then started to ride away from the helpless creature. "You're not going to leave that bull to die of thirst, are you?" McCormick demanded. Receiving a profane affirmative for an answer, he rode up to the miserable animal, dismounted, and cut the rope binding it. He was back in the saddle before the bull could scramble to its feet. "I have done you a favor," he icily remarked to his coworker. "I have not only prevented you from doing a cruel thing but also from destroying a bull belonging to the range." It was hard to tell which was worse: abusing an animal or trampling the property rights of its owner.[27]

The summer after his freshman year at Yale, McCormick hunted in Idaho. A year later he headed north instead of west, sailing into Arctic waters first charted three centuries earlier by Cartier and Frobisher. For two months he traversed the frozen wastes around Hudson Bay, a modern explorer living off caribou meat. The flat-faced Eskimos clutching their flint-sharpened spears held decidedly more charm for him than all the dandies of Vienna — or the scrub aristocracy of Lake Shore Drive, for that matter. Making the trip even more memorable was McCormick's first run-in with James Keeley, then a rising *Tribune* star. By intercepting Commodore Robert E. Peary on his return from the North Pole, he hoped to advance his own prospects at the paper. The idea held no charm for Keeley, already dealing with one McCormick and two Pattersons — three, counting Nellie.

By mid-July 1901, McCormick was taking the measure of fortified Quebec. His conclusions demonstrated that the spirit of manifest destiny had not died with the ferociously expansionist Joseph Medill. "It seems to me that Canada should be annexed and connected as soon as possible," the young American wrote in his diary. "Today it would be an easy undertaking. Her armed resistance could be no more than formal, and once she were annexed the flood of immigrants from this country would swallow the puny six million Canadian inhabitants."[28]

A few days later, having plied a Canadian customs officer with enough liquor to get his trunks passed, McCormick joined a dozen Yale classmates on board the *Algernine,* an ancient English gunboat with extra-thick sides designed to withstand the crushing force of Arctic ice. On July 21 he woke from his berth in good appetite, notwithstanding rough weather. Breakfast "went down like macaroni at a dago picnic." In the afternoon he climbed the ship's rigging for a view of the Newfoundland shore. The ship made harbor in the Bay of Islands, a scenic estuary surrounded by heavily timbered mountains. In a village store McCormick bought two toothbrushes for a quarter and tried, unsuccessfully, to purloin an oil can from under the eyes of the proprietor's wife, "a passionate looking female with hair down on her shoulders." After the ship dropped anchor on July 25 in a fishing port called Cutthroat, he spied another ship trapped in the ice. Huddled on the poopdeck was a forlorn group of women ranging in appearance "from wrinkled hags to beefy matrons and angular girls." None struck his fancy. That night the *Algernine* towed the hapless vessel to Turnavic, "the worst God-forsaken place I have ever struck," judged McCormick. "Deserted mining camps are heaven beside it."

On July 27 the ice was thicker than ever. A dispiriting series of accidents overtook the *Algernine.* A fireman caught his arm in the ship's engine. A crew member fell overboard and was nearly crushed between massive ice floes. A kerosene leak spoiled all the potatoes on board. When a second keg of beer was broached, "it was a little sour," noted McCormick, sourly. Tempers improved as the ship entered Hudson Strait. On August 2 Akpatoc Island was sighted in the pearl-tinted light of an Arctic dawn. For McCormick, the date represented a symbolic coming of age far more important than the drunken revels of his twenty-first birthday, three days earlier.

The morning's shoot yielded nearly one hundred birds. Bert had just climbed onto the forecastle of the *Algernine* after lunch when he heard an agitated cry from the captain: "Bear! Bear!! Bear!!!" Grabbing his rifle, the huntsman rushed to the port beam, from which he glimpsed two white bears perhaps a quarter-mile away. He began firing. A shipmate took up the fusillade, then two more. Suddenly the larger of the bears leaped halfway out of the water and began swimming for the ice. His companion followed suit. The ship maneuvered slowly through the icefield, its captain hoping to cut off any land escape route while pursuing the retreating animals as they lumbered across distant floes. A trail of blood half a mile long ended at an open stretch of water. The wounded bears, it appeared, had vanished. Then from the crow's nest came a shout: "Right ahead and about a mile away." The *Algernine* resumed its pursuit. The bleeding bears were quickly overtaken and killed. For McCormick, it was a contest of Hemingwayesque dimensions. Fifty years later, the bear he shot at Akpatok Island occupied a place of honor on the library floor at Cantigny, to the dismay of his fastidious wife.

The rest of the trip was anticlimatic. As the *Algernine* nosed its way among the barren islands of Hudson Bay, its stove gave out, forcing the crew to make a fire by pouring kerosene on kelp. "We had supper," runs a typical entry in McCormick's handwriting. "More s.o.b. stew. It is vile." Endless games of whiskey poker, played for champagne, enlivened the southern passage. "Hardly a pleasant word is spoken," McCormick noted primly, "and when it is, is generally taken out of the mouth of the speaker by one of the three others and turned into a cheap and malicious pun. This is especially noticeable at mealtime when all are brought together in a body."

Early on the evening of September 11, the *Algernine* made port at Turnavic. Mail was brought on board; McCormick was delighted to find three letters from his mother and one from his father, all postmarked Vienna. Neither senders nor recipient could yet know of an event in Buffalo, New York, that was destined to change their lives as surely as it altered the course of American development in the new century. An anarchist had shot President McKinley at the Pan American Exposition on September 6. After briefly rallying, the chief executive took a fatal turn on the night of the thirteenth. By the time Vice President Theodore Roosevelt could be summoned back from a hiking expedition in the Adirondack Mountains, there was little that he and nothing that McKinley's doctors could do. The president died early on the fourteenth. Two days later the *Algernine* sailed into Sydney Harbor on Nova Scotia's north shore. McCormick had missed Commodore Peary by hours. He was glad to return to Yale.

✧ 6

Although McCormick's Arctic diary evinces a more than passing interest in the opposite sex, his clinical assessments of the few women to cross his path seem as frigid as the surroundings. Since Yale was designed as a male bastion, McCormick would delicately recall, "the only young women seen in its vicinity were looking to increase their acquaintance." Some trod the floorboards rather than local streets; New Haven, an important way station on the theatrical tryout circuit, welcomed more than its share of chorus girls. One starstruck group of McCormick's classmates got themselves invited to tea with the female leads from *Floradora*.[29]

McCormick briefly romanced the daughter of a Supreme Court justice.

Emotionally and intellectually he was a late bloomer (his grandfather had called him a "winter apple"), with little of youth's biological exuberance. Upon returning from the Arctic, he talked of nothing but the glories of the frozen north, pausing just long enough "to pour hot air into six girls' ears," Medill revealed to his mother in Vienna. "I may say that his style has been cramped by the imminent arrival of another Wassal." 'Like her still?' said I. 'Ough!' 'Kiss her?' said I. 'Kiss THEM,' said he, 'HELL NO.' "[30]

"He is growing up now, much faster than before," added Medill, at once patronizing and shrewd, "and is quite as friendly with me as could be, much more so indeed than with any other member of the family." Calling his brother "very restless, uncivilized, and headstrong," Medill advised that he be led "with as long a line as possible. If I were you," he added, "I would make a cast iron agreement with him that he shall have two hundred dollars a month to pay for everything, summer and winter, traveling or resting; and require of him a promise that he will never ask for any more until he is thirty or a father. He will be much more tractable if he has the shadow of independence. He has got good sense when his wheels are not burning. The biggest wheel at present is 'liberty or death,' which is not serious. After he has had a bit of liberty he will see that he cannot do anything with it and cast about for a congenial form of slavery."[31]

Perhaps in response to this extraordinary document, McCormick's parents insisted that he spend the summer of 1902 with them in Vienna. He found much to feed his growing hostility toward the Old World and its stifling preoccupation with caste. His father cherished the latest drawing room banalities to fall from the lips of the All-Highest; Bert took a very different view of things, especially after being arrested for picking flowers in a park, then released on giving his name to the authorities. The next day an official from the Foreign Office arrived in a coach and four to deliver a formal apology to the American ambassador. Bert shook his head in amazement over the absurd deference shown an official's son.

Before the elder McCormick could assume his new responsibilities as U.S. ambassador to Russia, he and his son paid a visit to Constantinople, capital of the czar's traditional adversary, Turkey. For Bert, the ancient city, full of veiled women, wild dogs, Muslim rituals, and appalling filth, was hardly less astonishing than the snowy desolation of Labrador. Together with a young American diplomat, his Russian counterpart, and an English naval officer, he swam the Hellespont. On land he watched wide-eyed as a Japanese officer reviewed a Turkish infantry company to the strains of a Sousa march. He delayed his return home long enough to join friends in a fifty-mile balloon excursion from Paris to Tournon. "Navigation was simple," explained the newest member of the Aero Club of France. "The pilot threw cigarette papers overboard. When they fell we considered that we were going up; when they rose we knew we were falling." The surprised inhabitants of Tournon provided a feast for the Yankee daredevils and saddled McCormick with the bill. Less mercenary acquaintances obtained a permit from the Paris chief of police and staged an impromptu parade up the Champs-Elysées.[32]

Back in Chicago, Medill McCormick, worried that his astringent brother might fail to gain admission to Yale's Scroll and Key Society, enlisted the aid of Joe Patterson in some discreet electioneering. Their combined efforts paid off in the autumn of 1902. Bert filled another position warmed by his brother when the University Club, founded twenty years earlier for the ostensible purpose of "cultivating closer social relations between the faculty, graduates, and undergraduates of Yale," rewarded his labors as treasurer and bookkeeper by making him its president. The recognition of his peers ushered in the happiest year of his life.

"This club certainly is the place for a man who loves work," McCormick wrote to his parents in St. Petersburg. His diligence had won favorable notice from President Hadley, and none too soon, as the overextended senior had need of all the administrative sympathy he could muster. A record of fifty-four black marks and seven cuts briefly imperiled McCormick's academic future, but the threat was not enough to curtail his extracurricular activities. "I don't remember if I have told you that I have taken up squash," he told his parents. "Anyhow I have and it is doing me lots of good. I need plenty of exercise in these days of banquets. Lit banquet, News banquet, football banquet, etc., etc., all of which I attend ex officio. After-dinner speaking, once a matter of excitement for weeks beforehand, is almost an everyday occurrence and I have to read innumerable backfiles of *Life* to find jokes old enough to have been forgotten."[33]

Medill was right; his brother *was* growing up fast, cultivating a mordant humor that partially offset his starchy manner and emotional evasiveness. When a blizzard crippled New Haven, it made Bert long for Florida, "or any place but this. Medill had a spasm and begged me to clear out before I died which was considerate but I was afraid to try it on the dean." "Dear Parents," he began one letter. "Statistics have led me to believe that I have not stamped my individuality very strongly upon the University." A poll of his classmates had registered strong support for McCormick as "the newsiest man" in the class of 1903. More surprisingly, "a few (this will make Ma smile)" had voted him the hardest worker in the class. The only vote he received as "the man who had done most for Yale" was his own.[34]

Behind his jauntiness lurked feelings of abandonment. "During the interruptions of diplomacy," he teased his noncommunicative parents, "could you indite a short note?" "Your Excellencies!" he opened another letter. "Napoleon one used to complain that he had to get news of his dependent from the English Newspapers. His natural successor on Earth complains that he has to get news of those he depends upon through the

American newspapers!!" He voiced a similar lament to his cousin Cissy, then in the Russian capital as a guest of her uncle and aunt. "People who withdraw themselves from their relations in order to shine in foreign courts should at the very least recompense the deprived ones with accounts of their doings," he asserted, adding that he would consider it an honor if his flamboyant cousin took him into her confidence.[35]

That Cissy would bestow such recognition on Bertie the Swipe was unlikely, yet she was always willing to be amused. So Bert blithely recounted a college riot "that ought to be written up in heroic verse," touched off when a pair of inebriated football players planted themselves on a New Haven trolley track and blocked passage to streetcars. A battalion of motormen and conductors launched an assault. In the ensuing melee, trolleymen fell "thick as rain." Finally the offending athletes commandeered a snowplow and escaped into the night. At the end of this mock epic, McCormick's delight in his powers of expression spilled over. "I am beginning to believe that I am a wonderful person," he gushed, "in that I can write more words and say less than anyone living."[36]

Family ties were strengthened in November 1902 when Bert took his place as an usher at Joe Patterson's wedding to Alice Higginbotham, the socially ambitious daughter of Marshall Field's department store partner. A newspaper account gave prominent treatment to the Yale senior, whom it called "large for his age — for any age — 6'4" and built accordingly. When not at his studies he is hunting in the wilds or the mountains. He is a great admirer of President Roosevelt." A few months later another wedding afforded Bert an opportunity to meet his hero *and* to flirt with the bewitching Alice Roosevelt. On June 10, 1903, his twenty-sixth birthday, Medill McCormick married his childhood sweetheart, Ruth Hanna. Kate was conspicuously absent from the ceremony, for which the father of the bride had rescheduled the Ohio State Republican Convention. Few observers missed the political implications of a Medill-Hanna dynasty in the making. On the day of the wedding, TR predictably stole the show, his only competition for the spotlight coming from his irrepressible daughter. Bert was too engrossed in Princess Alice to pay much attention when his aunt introduced him to John D. Rockefeller.[37]

Devastated by the marriage of her elder son, Kate McCormick vented her unhappiness on her new daughter-in-law. Medill's protests were inevitably strangled by Kate's purse strings. Eager to demonstrate his managerial abilities away from the *Tribune*, Medill invested a quarter-million dollars of his mother's money in the *Cleveland Leader*. Bert, meanwhile, was left to confront his postgraduate future alone. "I have been writing abroad about every ten days," he pointedly reminded his parents. "It is a long interval, but not so long as the interval between the letters from St. Petersburg."[38]

McCormick took no prizes or medals to show for his years in New Haven. He delivered no commencement oration, turned in no dissertation, took part in no colloquies. His adventuring days seemed over. Stretching before him was a summer on North Shore polo fields and the lonely existence of a young bachelor without marriage prospects. He planned to enroll at Northwestern Law School in suburban Evanston, his father having vetoed an eastern school on the theory that he should study where he was mostly likely to practice law.

The graduating senior was more than able to contain his enthusiasm for the legal profession. "From all I am told," he wrote, "a knowledge of the principle of law would help me in the conduct of any work I may take up — and not least of all in running the *Trib*." Here, ironically, he hit upon the one course least likely to meet with family approval.[39]

Elsewhere in 1903 an obscure young Russian revolutionary named Ulyanov split with a handful of Social Democrats at a London party congress and organized a militant faction known as the Bolsheviks. Albert Einstein, a youthful examiner in the Swiss Patent Office, was probing deep into the mysteries of time, space, and the physical universe after having failed a schoolteacher's examination. In these same days of intellectual and political ferment, a Frenchman named Becquerel stumbled upon radioactivity; Planck, in Berlin, propounded his mystifying quantum theory; a lone scientist at Montreal's McGill University groped his way toward an understanding of the atom's structure; Henry Ford perfected his internal combustion engine; and the Wright brothers liberated mankind from an earthbound perspective. In Franz Joseph's Vienna, Sigmund Freud assayed the murky terrors of the unconscious, an emotional Arctic as yet barely penetrated by explorers.

All this and more remained largely shrouded from the class of 1903. "I had four enjoyable years at Yale," McCormick reminisced three decades later, "but none of my acquaintances proved of value in afterlife, and my education came later."[40]

PART II

Bulldog

1903–1918

"A kept newspaper is like a kept woman — no good."

ROBERT R. MCCORMICK

4

Silk Stockings

"Everybody here knows R. R., R. R. does things right,
Everybody here knows R. R., never dodged a fight.
Oh his arm is strong, his eye is keen,
and he will keep the 'District' clean.
Everybody here knows R. R., he'll trim the grafters right."

— campaign song, McCormick's 1905 race
for president of the Chicago Sanitary District

ROM YALE, McCormick returned home to find himself homeless. Unable to persuade Medill and Ruth to move into the old Joseph Medill house at 101 Cass Street, his mother put the place on the market. McCormick was forced to seek temporary shelter with a Yale classmate in an Erie Street mansion amply stocked with servants and other accouterments of gracious living. "It's great to be rich," he informed his Aunt Nellie. He was far from rich himself; his prospects for becoming so rested almost entirely with his mother, an unpredictable benefactor at best. Upon graduation from Yale he owned no *Tribune* stock. His employment opportunities at the paper were effectively foreclosed by the presence of his brother as business manager, reinforced by Joe Patterson's work on the editorial side.[1]

Before enrolling at Northwestern in September 1903, McCormick busied himself with social pursuits. Between rounds of polo he wooed Alice Roosevelt, then staying with friends on Bellevue Place. One afternoon the president's daughter looked outside and spotted her tall admirer astride a polo pony. Delighted at any opportunity to shock respectable opinion, Princess Alice motioned for man and beast to come in. McCormick, no less scornful of convention, prodded his mount up a dozen stone steps and through the front door. Whatever favorable impression he made was sadly transient. Before long he was expressing outrage that Miss Roosevelt should waste her charms on a "pusillanimous cur." That the young man in question happened to be the son of TR's attorney general mattered not a whit.[2]

From love, McCormick reluctantly turned his attention to the law. Each morning he boarded a 7:30 train for Evanston and such legal insights as the droning instructors at Northwestern might impart. Nearly suffocated by the school's wretched ventilation, he sought escape by volunteering his time at the prestigious downtown firm of Isham, Lincoln and Beale. More than an able attorney, William Beale was a natural diplomat and family counselor. It was he, after all, who had drawn Joseph Medill's will so as to prevent Kate and Nellie, in their increasingly bitter contest over the *Tribune*, from killing the goose that laid the golden eggs.

Now, thanks to Beale, McCormick was able to observe testament-making on a far greater scale. In his twilight years, Marshall Field was the largest taxpayer in America, his net worth estimated at $120 million. McCormick well remembered the old man from his regular visits to the Medill house, so it seemed only logical for him to greet the aging tycoon before whisking him into Beale's inner sanctum. The business transacted there came back to haunt McCormick, for the will published after Field's death in January 1906 left the bulk of his huge estate to his grandson, Marshall III. In time the younger Field would draw on this inheritance to wage a holy war against Colonel McCormick and his *Tribune.*

The wizened Beale was an unlikely mentor. One could scarcely envision this establishment lawyer riding a horse into a young lady's parlor. More improbable still was the thought of stolid, intractable William Beale fomenting a South American revolution in order to secure a transoceanic canal that would be built and operated to the glory of Uncle Sam. That is precisely what Roosevelt did in November 1903, abetted by the U.S. Navy gunboat *Nashville* and a Colombian colonel who, in return for $8,000 in gold, called off his government's feeble attempt to suppress Panamanian dissidents. Having humbled "those contemptible little creatures in Bogotá," TR rejoiced in his vassal regime in Panama City.

Early in 1904, Roosevelt's Chicago disciple McCormick, equally bored with legal niceties, decided to see the unfolding revolution with his own eyes. His journey, like nearly everything else associated with Panama's entry into the family of nations, was high adventure played as farce. For transportation he turned to Minor C. Keith, president of the United Fruit Company and "uncrowned king of Costa Rica." There was only one complication: when he arrived in Colón harbor on Panama's Caribbean coast, the revolution was over. Riding peacefully at anchor was a fleet of U.S. warships, their Marine contingents no longer needed to counter Colombian bushwhackers.

Undaunted by the specter of normality, McCormick headed inland. From the window of his train, the young American was astonished to find mile after mile of rusting machinery, the bleached bones of a heroic but mismanaged French effort to join two oceans across the spiny isthmus. One day McCormick walked three miles over refuse scooped out of the Culebra cut, an abandoned ditch now turned over to American engineers for completion. Precisely how such a transfer had come to pass sparked his journalistic curiosity. He quickly satisfied himself as to Roosevelt's controlling hand in the whole enterprise.

McCormick displayed some Rooseveltian hubris of his own when touring the area in the company of a former French superintendent and a United Fruit Company retainer who had hurried south "just to show the canal to me. He would have crawled if necessary. Now that we are to finish the work, it is touching and also amusing to see how anxious the Frenchmen are to get credit for what they have done."[3]

No viceroy ever addressed a subject race with kinder condescension.

McCormick's return voyage was made in a bathtub-size vessel under Norwegian flag, "loaded with bananas and cockroaches in about equal quantities." While still at sea he heard ominous reports of political currents dragging Russia and Japan into dangerous waters. Weeks of parental silence compelled him to follow the crisis through American newspapers. Unable to bear the suspense any longer, he rebuked his loved ones for keeping him in the dark about Russo-Japanese tensions and the looming prospects of conflict on a scale dwarfing Panama's comic opera.[4]

❖ 2

As war clouds gathered over St. Petersburg, the ambassador of the United States was embroiled in conflicts of his own making. Less weighty than the fate of Korea or czarist pretensions to Asian supremacy were the issues of Robert S. McCormick's wardrobe, his rent, and the romantic escapades of a rebellious niece who had fled to the Old World determined to be seduced. At a Winter Palace reception he attended in evening clothes, Ambassador McCormick was mistaken for a butler; the court chamberlain tactfully suggested that he return home under cover of feigned illness. He next appeared in public wearing a Ruritanian costume, replete with gold braid, knee breeches, and an admiral's chapeau topped by a white feather. Such peacock splendor, the *Chicago American* jibed, would cause a sensation at a charity ball on Lake Shore Drive. The *Washington Post* ran an editorial titled "Bob McCormick's Legs."

McCormick's sartorial habits were as nothing, however, compared to the controversy involving his sixty-five-room palace on the English Quay. The aristocratic owners of Kotchoubey House, reluctant to associate themselves with vulgar commerce, had nevertheless agreed to lease their vacant home to the sad-eyed American diplomat. The ink on the confirming documents had barely dried when McCormick was ordered to hand over the property to Grand Duke Vladimir, cousin of the czar, who wished to make a present of it to his son.[5]

In any other capital, duke and diplomat might have resolved their differences like gentlemen. But this was St. Petersburg, where divine right still prevailed and millions of illiterate Russians looked upon "the little father" in the Winter Palace as their intermediary before a capricious God and a repressive government. Unacquainted with Romanov absolutism, McCormick graciously offered to vacate Kotchoubey House — as soon as Vladimir found him a suitable replacement. He compounded his error by writing a letter to this effect and addressing it to "My dear Grand Duke." In the event, his royal correspondent showed no inclination to act as real estate agent for the interlopers from Chicago.

Kate McCormick displayed a firmer grasp of affairs. Innately regal in bearing, she was the kind of woman who could hold her head high even when humbling herself before the flighty czarina or the grave dowager empress, credited by court gossips with being the power behind Nicholas's throne. Cissy Patterson posed a sterner test to her aunt's unflappability. "If you leave Cissy in Austria with Aunt Kate," Joe Patterson had warned his mother, "she will certainly be courted by some foreign nobleman under delusions as to her money . . . As a rule marriages with foreigners, especially continentals, are unhappy."[6]

Sure enough, while in Vienna, Cissy had fallen under the spell of Josef Gizycki, a Polish count of distinguished lineage, military bearing, and appalling character. Less dazzled by foreign titles than his social-climbing wife, Robert Patterson made inquiries into the count's family and finances. Unfortunately, these were not pursued long enough to uncover Gizycki's illegitimate child, his gambling debts, or a bevy of mistresses repaid for their love with physical and mental cruelty. In April 1904, the twenty-two-year-old Cissy became the bride of an alcoholic, impoverished congenital liar nearly twice her age. The tone of their domestic life was set on her wedding night, when she was brutally raped by her new husband.

Family scandals aside, Ambassador McCormick notably failed to win the confidence of Theodore Roosevelt's White House. No worse than most diplomats — then or now — whose appointment rests on their financial or journalistic support for the party in power, Rob McCormick had the misfortune to have his inadequacies exposed by the glare of war and in-cipient revolution. On the brink of conflict between Japan and Russia, he predicted an amicable settlement of the crisis. Later, when the mikado's navy scored a decisive triumph at Port Arthur, on the Chinese coast, he picked this critical moment to consult a Vienna specialist about his gout. And in the aftermath of Port Arthur, as czarist military planners struggled to recover from their early mauling at the hands of a poorly regarded enemy, the American ambassador was reminding his government of an unpaid bill of 257 rubles on some band instruments used by John Philip Sousa during his Russian concert tour in the previous year.[7]

Helping to undermine McCormick was one of Roosevelt's most trusted intimates, Cecil Spring-Rice, first secretary of the British embassy in St. Petersburg, who had been best man at the 1886 wedding of TR and Edith Carow. During the intervening years their friendship had ripened to the point where Roosevelt let British officials know that by transfering "Springy" to Washington, they would be taking a gratifying step toward Anglo-American harmony. Whitehall, however, had good reason for delaying his reassignment. In St. Petersburg, Springy could advance British interests by flattering the American president and exaggerating Russian antipathy toward the Great Republic.

As evidence of the latter, Spring-Rice cited a McCormick dinner party attended by just two Russians. How unsporting, these snubs aimed at a true friend of the Russian cause — "indeed," sniffed Springy, "some of us thought, too friendly." With sweet malice he confided to TR that at a recent court reception, Ambassador McCormick had been seen clutch-ing the czar's hand with "too much effusion." "Very nice man" that he was, McCormick (like so many amateurs in the game of diplomacy) had showed himself a slave to the smile of royalty. The president really de-served better.[8]

In the fall of 1904, McCormick took an extended leave, ostensibly to attend to business affairs in Chicago. Sacrificing judgment to vanity, he gave a newspaper interview in which he professed astonishment over U.S. sympathy toward Japan and chided his ungrateful countrymen for their failure to remember Russian friendship for Lincoln's embattled govern-ment during the Civil War. In Washington, an angry Roosevelt wanted to sack his envoy on the spot. Only reluctantly did he yield to State Depart-ment pleas to switch the bumbling McCormick to a country where neither his feelings nor American foreign policy would suffer. McCormick learned of his subsequent transfer to Paris by reading of it in the press.

All this might be properly consigned to the archives but for one defining fact: the lifelong resentment that it bred in McCormick's son. Dismissing his father's blunders and indiscretions, young Robert McCormick came to see his parent as a victim of British snobbery and State Department treachery. For the rest of his days, he worked at his grievances like a black-smith at his bellows, with profound consequences for all who read or were influenced by the *Chicago Tribune*.

He might have done better to read one of his father's final reports from St. Petersburg, filed in the wake of Bloody Sunday, January 22, 1905, when a throng of disaffected workers and hungry peasants marched to the gates of the Winter Palace to petition Nicholas II for bread, peace, and the rudiments of parliamentary democracy. What they got instead from their little father was a deadly volley of Cossack bullets. Two weeks after the massacre, Ambassador McCormick wired news of a fresh atrocity, the assassination of the czar's uncle, Grand Duke Serge.

To the departing American, it was obvious that Russia had entered a new and perilous era. Unless demands made by responsible elements of Russian society were met and the nation was launched on a peaceful road to liberal democracy, "the people will at some time take by force what should have been granted them by a willing hand." As he had told court officials, if Peter the Great knocked a window into Europe, Alexander II knocked out the wall when he began construction of the railway and telegraph.[9]

Thanks to modern communications, newspapers included, the most repressive government is at a disadvantage when trying to block the free entry of ideas. As a result, McCormick predicted, official walls were destined to fall at the hands of the very people they were built to restrain.

Here Robert Sanderson McCormick was eighty years ahead of his time. However premature his forecast of human liberation, it remains his finest hour.

✧ 3

No czarist empire of multiple time zones and indigestible nationalities demanded more from its leaders than the ragtag collection of lakefront millionaires, Irish laborers, German farmers, Levee prostitutes, and flophouse derelicts residing in the twenty-first ward of Chicago. The breeze off Lake Michigan caressed the gold coast without dispelling the scent of corruption from the squalid badlands west of the Chicago River. Out of this unpromising soil came homegrown czars like the Republican boss Fred Busse. Busse, unprepossessing and ungrammatical, was the undisputed autocrat of the North Side, his Winter Palace a second-floor bachelor's flat over the coal company from which he nominally derived his living, his Duma John Murphy's saloon at the corner of Clark and Division streets.

Having North Side hoodlums for playmates had prepared young Busse to break into politics as loyal liegeman to the so-called Blond Boss, U.S. senator William J. Lorimer. Boon companion of the notorious Charles Yerkes, the Blond Boss was no favorite of the *Chicago Tribune*. He returned the paper's disdain with interest, taking particular exception to the *Tribune*'s demands for popular rather than legislative election of senators. Allied with the *Tribune* in its anti-Lorimer crusade were young, progressive Republicans in thrall to Theodore Roosevelt.

Busse's Democratic opposite was James Aloysius Quinn — "Hot Stove Jimmy" to those who believed that a hot stove was about the only thing Jimmy Quinn wouldn't steal. As Robert McCormick told it, Hot Stove Jimmy actually earned his nickname by making a sardonic proposal to heat Chicago's parks each winter. This was a dig at the earnest members of the Municipal Voters League, for whom Quinn (and Busse, for that matter) was a persistent obstacle to civic progress.* Quinn enjoyed an even bigger laugh at the expense of reformers in 1901, when he ran Honoré Palmer, son of the gold coast social lion and hotelier Potter Palmer, for an open seat in the twenty-first. What more effective rejoinder could there be to charges of political cronyism? The candidate's mother did her bit by campaigning from her carriage throughout the seedy boarding house district and by inviting a carefully screened delegation of Jimmy Quinn's clubhouse crowd to her home, a lakefront showplace afterward likened by the ward heelers to the Everleigh Club, Chicago's most elegant brothel.[10]

The unlikely success of Honoré Palmer demonstrated the willingness of voters who wore cotton stockings, or no stockings at all, to support a candidate in silk stockings. The lesson was not lost on Fred Busse. Behind his coarse exterior was an able, often farsighted leader, greatly superior to the system that produced him. The approach of municipal elections in April 1904 found the GOP boss scrambling for an aldermanic candidate to repossess the twenty-first for the party of Lincoln, McKinley, and Roosevelt. He approached Robert Patterson with an offer to nominate Bert McCormick.

What motivated Busse to embrace a political virgin who had faced no electorate larger than the membership of Yale's University Club? Of course there was all that *Tribune* coal to take into account, and the logical assumption that Honoré Palmer was not the last rich young man whose

---

*No less a public watchdog than the Chicago Civil Service Commission accused Quinn of providing police protection to criminals such as Big Jim O'Leary, son of the woman who had owned the incendiary cow of legend. At its peak, O'Leary's gambling enterprise offered odds on every horserace, prize fight, and football and baseball game in the United States and Canada. Scarcely less profitable was the *City of Traverse*, a floating casino that plied the waters of Lake Michigan each afternoon until eighteen detectives and seven reporters boarded the vessel in May 1907 for what turned out to be her final cruise.

family could be relied on to pay his campaign expenses. Beyond this, the ward was closely divided in its partisan loyalties. At the national level, Theodore Roosevelt was firing ambitious young men of his class with visions of public service. Why not take a chance on the youthful McCormick, son of TR's ambassador in St. Petersburg? Win or lose, by associating himself with yet another member of *Tribune* royalty, Busse could expect to earn chits useful to his own advance.

From McCormick's standpoint, the offer could not have come at a better time. Juggling law school with his unpaid duties as William Beale's errand boy had taxed his stamina without filling his pockets or leaving much time for polo and hunt riding. Not that such highbrow pursuits would be of assistance on the campaign trail; neither then nor later was McCormick accused of possessing the common touch. To win in 1904 he had to convince voters loyal to retiring alderman John Minwegen, "the Man with the Hoe," that he would fix their sidewalks and urge the cop on the beat to go easy on the constituent in a tight spot.

The magnitude of his challenge was made clear in the comments of disgruntled residents of the twenty-first as reported by the *Inter-Ocean*, a journal of impeccable Republican sympathies. "Who's going to get us jobs on de street cleanin crew?" fretted one elector excluded from the Social Register. "I goes to see me alderman and a big butler with brass buttons asks me for me card and wants to know what I want. Me who never had a card except one with pictures and spots on it. Will I get a job? Nah!"[11]

McCormick's platform was an unexceptional mélange promising cleaner streets, fairer taxes, more parks and bridges, and the honest expenditure of city funds. To lure disaffected Democrats, he contrasted the scrupulous incumbent mayor, Carter Harrison II, with the Gray Wolves, a feral pack of city councilors led by "Bathhouse John" Coughlin, Michael "Hinky Dink" Kenna, and others with larceny in their Irish souls.* On the decisive question of who was to own and operate local streetcars, McCormick assumed a dignified straddle, reminding audiences that years of extremist finger-pointing had produced neither a speedy nor a businesslike solution. "My wish is that the streets shall be used for the people to walk upon and not for the Democrats to talk about," he declared.[12]

The candidate himself walked local streets sixteen hours a day during the intense two-week canvass running up to the election. McCormick's

---

* "The Bath," who fancied himself a worthy rival to the Prince of Wales, had a mania for fashionable clothes. He also dabbled in musical composition and once held a premiere for a banal lyric, "Dear Midnight of Love," at the Chicago Opera House, with the assistance of the Cook County Democratic Marching Band and a chorus of fifty singers in evening clothes. As a collector, he numbered among his acquisitions a fleet of racehorses, a private zoo, and a Colorado castle that rivaled McCormick's cousin Harold McCormick's granite pile on Lake Shore Drive.

first day of campaigning set the pattern. At precisely eight o'clock he descended the granite steps of the Union League Club at Bughouse Square. He did not return until midnight. In between he shook a thousand hands, charmed Bohemian working girls in the steamy laundry of the Virginia Hotel ("My, isn't he a regular Gibson man," gushed one chambermaid), handed out cigars by the fistful, and ordered anyone crossing his path to call him Mac. Advised to pass up a Rush Street saloon, McCormick wouldn't hear of it. "Everyone step up and have a drink on me," he announced to startled patrons inside. "I am a candidate for alderman in this ward and want to know you all." After a quick lunch, he resumed his door-to-door campaigning, a nattily dressed scarecrow loping along Cass Street, pretending to a camaraderie with Joseph Medill's despised rabble. "I won't miss a man from Lake Shore Drive to the soap factories if I can help it," he vowed to an accompanying journalist. That evening he attended three meetings, one held at the 6 Tower Court residence of his cousin, Edward Adams, and Adams's dark-haired beauty of a wife, Amy. Win or lose, McCormick resolved to see more of the Adamses.[13]

On April 5, 1904, his strenuous courtship paid off. Voters in the twenty-first ward gave McCormick a 600-vote margin over his Irish Democratic opponent. That he owed his success to Fred Busse seems never to have crossed his mind. That it crossed a great many other minds may explain why the victorious candidate went out of his way to cultivate the appearance of one unbossed and unbeholden to any man. Medill McCormick was wrong when he dismissed his brother's overwrought attachment to "liberty or death" as the fancy of a college boy. As events would show, Bert wore no harness, fit no label. He held a libertarian distrust of any system or dogma that interfered with the pursuit of happiness on his terms.

This lack of deference extended to his political godfather. One evening at Murphy's, a patron infuriated Fred Busse with a tactless remark. Busse responded by calling into question the parentage of every aldermen, judge, and other hanger-on dependent on his favor. As he dressed down the line of cringing mediocrities assembled around the bar, the newest member of the club was openly disapproving. "Bert," explained Busse unapologetically, "discipline's got to be maintained."[14]

McCormick set out to disprove this valuable lesson at the earliest opportunity. Within weeks of his election, the most junior member of the council was taunting his uncle at the *Tribune*, as well as "Uncle Joe" Cannon, the Speaker of the House of Representatives in Washington, and other Republican potentates who hoped to derail the gubernatorial candidacy of Cook County state's attorney Charles S. Deneen. To McCormick, the old guard represented by Speaker Cannon and Senator Lorimer cast a dark and blighting shadow across GOP prospects. After twenty-two days of inconclusive balloting, youthful impertinence had its way as exhausted state convention delegates turned to Deneen. McCormick took an active part in the fall campaign, which ended in triumph for the Roosevelt-Deneen ticket.

In another move aimed at establishing his independence, McCormick bit the hand of that doughty champion of civic virtue, the Municipal Voters League, which he labeled the Lynch League. James Keeley printed this early example of McCormick's name-calling prowess in the *Tribune*, touching off a debate over the relative merit of gray wolves and lone wolves. In a 1904 cartoon book entitled *Chicagoans as We See Them*, the dandyish alderman was portrayed as a homegrown Oscar Wilde, holding a flower in one hand and a copy of *Pilgrim's Progress and Other Jokes* in the other. Adorning his stylish lapel was a ribbon marked *Emblem of Purity*.

Such caricatures did little to bolster his electability, even in the rarefied gold coast. Yet McCormick, a born contrarian, blithely went his own way, impervious to the ridicule his peculiarities excited. His wardrobe came in for special abuse. The young alderman sometimes appeared at council meetings dressed in polo togs. One night he fell through a coal hole on Dearborn Street, injuring his dignity and, far worse, tearing his elegant trousers. Repair the street within forty-eight hours, he ordered the hotel owners, or he would have the entire front of the building blockaded by the police. Hostile reporters delighted in the affair, rubbing their palms gleefully as the *rara avis* from the twenty-first ward expounded on the "afront to my society pants."[15]

Council contemporaries anticipated later students of McCormick's career in wondering how much of his famously "eccentric" behavior was spontaneous and how much was staged to provide an intrinsically shy man with a ready-made persona behind which to take shelter. By the 1930s, when McCormick's reflexive hostility to the New Deal had cast him as a Michigan Avenue Quixote forever tilting at collectivist windmills with his polo mallet, one of the kindest appraisals was that he was crazy like a fox. More perceptive observers detected emotional and psychological fissures deep within this seemingly monolithic symbol of reaction.

Symbols, needless to say, are rarely at war with themselves. In McCormick, however, blustery self-regard hid a fearsome struggle between the classic narcissist's egocentricity and crippling feelings of inadequacy that dated to his earliest years as an unwanted substitute for his mother's lost baby girl. Both qualities spilled over into the pages of the *Tribune*, which came to mirror not only the exaggerated pride felt by Chicagoans but also their inferiority complex as inhabitants of an overgrown prairie village, culturally and politically dwarfed by the hated, envied East. Thus a second son exemplified a second city. The Colonel wasn't Don Quixote but the Wizard of Oz.

❖ 4

Carter Harrison II rarely pulled his punches. In his memoirs, fittingly entitled *Stormy Years*, the five-time mayor lambasted his city's councilors as "lumpish louts, supinely agreeable to any proposition of enrichment that engendered no toil, led by a handful of nervy, keen-witted, unscrupulous schemers." This was the fraternity to which Bert McCormick pledged himself in April 1904. For the seventy aldermen (chosen from thirty-five districts), who formed a patchwork quilt of Chicago's ethnic and social diversity, the newcomer supplied more than comic relief. Those coming to laugh at the twenty-three-year-old political naif generally stayed to listen. Even Gray Wolves moved to snickers by his plummy Groton accent agreed that McCormick spoke with authority.

To a domineering personality McCormick added a vigorous pursuit of wrongdoing in all its forms — a full-time occupation in Chicago. During his first months in office, he led a well-publicized raid on a house of ill repute that was trying to establish itself in an affluent corner of the city's North Side. While the upscale inhabitants of McCormickville congratulated themselves on their deliverance from morality as practiced along Whiskey Row, other Chicagoans flooded the society alderman with appeals to help scour their neighborhoods. "What will you take to clean our ward?" asked one visitor to McCormick's office. "Will you give an illustrated lecture?" inquired another. "Did you use a disguise?" breathlessly demanded a third. When petitioners began paging him at his club, McCormick was forced to take refuge at his mother's Wheaton estate until the publicity generated by his crusade abated.[16]

Other entreaties were made each day by constituents, who streamed into McCormick's office in the Bush Temple of Music. Their individual tales of want, liberally salted with pathos, greed, and mendacity, supplied an important chapter in McCormick's education about how ordinary people lived. Few men could listen to such a catalogue of grievances day in and day out and not develop an enlarged outlook. One petitioner, desperate to transport his sick wife to a Kansas City specialist, got a promise of half fare for her and an attendant from the railroad; the other half was put up by Alderman McCormick. A precinct worker arrested for operating an unlicensed fruit stand obtained McCormick's help in getting the needed permit. A cigar-store owner complained of mistreatment at the hands of streetcorner rowdies. A member of the Alexander Hamilton Republican Club sought employment as a porter.[17]

And so it went, the meat and potatoes of urban politics. Every quid had its quo. A Chinese businessman, denied permission to erect an electric sign outside his establishment, resorted to crude means of persuasion. "Called and tried to bribe me with tea set, tea and fine cigars," McCormick recorded matter-of-factly in his diary. It didn't work. A family of ten loyal Republicans had greater success in selling their alderman a block of tickets to a church bazaar. These two transactions, each involving the barter of influence, each accompanied by fervent protestations of voter allegiance, were differentiated only by the size of the bribe and the audacity with which it was proffered.[18]

Monday evening council meetings were occupied with more public logrolling: antilynching resolutions, praise for Jane Addams of Hull House, extravagant recognition of the artistic contributions made by Chicago's huge German population. Then, in April 1905, a new mayor, Edward F. Dunne, took office, promising immediate municipal ownership (IMO) of all streetcar franchises. The issue was debated at immense and repetitive length. McCormick used his position on the Local Transportation Committee to present a counterproposal, one designed to retain private ownership within a system of stringent regulation. In this way he hoped to achieve low fares and an adequate return to the city without surrendering the holy writ of free enterprise.

For his efforts, the conservative reformer was assailed in the press as a tool of the traction interests. Mayor Dunne denounced McCormick for betraying the people of his own ward, who had supported IMO overwhelmingly in a nonbinding referendum. But McCormick, persuaded that neither the city's charter nor its financial condition justified radical action, held his ground. In attacking the abuses rather than the idea of modern industrial capitalism, he saw himself as governed by sense, not sentiment. As the fight escalated, however, emotions ran high on all sides. An alderman favorable to IMO implied disreputable motives to the opposition, prompting an angry McCormick to demand his censure by the full council. Ultimately he won something even more important, as a new traction law close to his original bill was passed over the veto of Mayor Dunne.

❖ 5

One afternoon at the height of the traction controversy, McCormick was called out of a committee meeting to receive some startling news from Fred Busse and two of his henchmen. Barely a year into his first term on the council, McCormick was being slated by Republican kingmakers to run for president of the Chicago Sanitary District. The district had been established in 1889 by Illinois legislators looking to safeguard the city's drinking water. Since then the Chicago Drainage Canal, an engineering marvel twenty-eight miles long and twenty feet deep, had effectively reversed the flow of the Chicago River, sweeping urban wastes southward into the Des Plaines River and thence to the Mississippi. More recently the legislature had voted to double the size of the district, until it stretched from Waukegan in the northern suburbs to the Indiana line. The same lawmakers had authorized construction of two new feeder canals, one through the leafy northern suburb of Evanston and a second, much larger one draining the Calumet region of South Chicago.

Busse's offer came just hours ahead of a letter from Kate McCormick inviting her son to come to Paris, where the senior McCormicks had embarked on their latest diplomatic adventures. With mercenary guile, Kate promised Bert $20,000 if he would place family before politics. He proved as deaf to maternal bribes as to the Chinese businessman's tea set and cigars. During his brief tenure on the council he had won the respect of his associates, he told his mother. Given two more years, he might inherit the chairmanship of the powerful Finance Committee. Down the road the mayor's office itself lay in his grasp.

Offsetting these cheerful prospects were some hard truths, above all a Democratic trend in the twenty-first ward, "as the respectable people move north and the bums come across the river." As a consequence of these unwelcome demographic changes, "I would have a hard campaign for reelection next spring and a trebly hard one two years from now. As it is," he went on, in slightly more hopeful vein, "I have about an even chance of election this fall" to the sanitation district presidency. Victory in November followed by a successful five-year term at the head of the fractious board of supervisors would establish McCormick at the age of thirty as "one of the foremost public men of the middle west."[19]

Motivated by visions of the Illinois governorship — for starters — McCormick threw himself into his second grueling canvass in as many years. The man his supporters called RR would never be mistaken for TR, whose essential class consciousness lay hidden beneath a snowcover of childlike enthusiasm. McCormick, by contrast, gave the impression of one who didn't need to be six-four to look down on his fellow creatures. That summer he found time to attend the Lake Forest Horse Show and to admire the ladies' champion, a Miss Lord, in her form-fitting blue crêpe de Chine riding habit. On July 4 he celebrated with a successful round of polo, waged as fiercely as he played the political games that absorbed most of his waking hours. He told Aunt Nellie that he had made an application for Cissy, now the unhappily married Countess Gizycki, to join the Daughters of the Polish Revolution. "It will help me with the Polish vote," he explained in a letter puckishly signed "Bertranski."[20]

Ironically, the *Chicago Journal* endorsed McCormick's candidacy on October 16 by contrasting his seriousness of purpose with those rich idlers "satisfied to fritter their lives away in the ballroom and on the polo field." McCormick was exactly the breath of fresh air Chicago needed, a practical, clear-headed reformer "placed by character and circumstances above temptation to betray his fellow citizens." Notwithstanding these sterling qualities, he went into the campaign trailing his Democratic opponent, Frank Wenter, an eighteen-year veteran of the district organization, whose undistinguished service included hiring his son at a higher salary than other clerks without caring much whether the young man ever showed up for work.

McCormick's opponents scavenged for mud with which to spatter the white knight of reform. Easily refuted was a whispering campaign alleging that the Republican alderman, not his cousin Harold, was a son-in-law of the odious John D. Rockefeller. (Harold McCormick's stone palace at 999 Lake Shore Drive was a garish blend of art and avarice, boasting a $185,000 Persian rug once owned by Peter the Great and gold-crested chairs from the court of the first Napoleon.) More serious was a charge in Hearst's *Examiner* that McCormick ran to save his rich relations $150,000 in dredging and dock work ordered by the district. Genuinely indignant over such campaign fodder, McCormick insisted that honesty alone was insufficient qualification for public office: "Without aggressiveness joined to his honesty — without the will and energy to enforce honest policy — his usefulness is as that of the stolid ox that responds only to the goad."[21]

His own aggressiveness did not extend to debating Wenter publicly. Such a confrontation, he claimed airily, would prove of little value; "live issues would be smothered by labored explanations of duty unperformed." The closing days of the campaign were a blur of street rallies, torchlights, and brass bands. McCormick invaded Democratic strongholds, turning up the rhetorical heat and sharply distinguishing between his muscular brand of reform and the policies of the whey-faced do-gooders of the Municipal Voters League. The silk stocking, so it seemed, was on the other foot. On election day the youngster defied the odds, winning by 8,000 votes out of more than 180,000 cast.

Before taking office a month later, McCormick treated himself to some violent exercise, herding cattle on a Texas ranch. Pondering the new avenues opening before him, he saw visions of glory in a drainage canal. Sewage, it appeared, was to be his political salvation. Well, why not? Hadn't Theodore Roosevelt launched his trajectory to the White House as a piping-voiced reformer in the New York state legislature, consolidating his reputation with a headline-making turn as police commissioner of New York City, a town affording much occasion for ambitious young foes of impurity to advertise themselves? Chicago offered targets no less alluring to those with crusading propensities.

Overlooked for most of his young life, McCormick now commanded the attention of millions. Yet even as he contemplated ways to purify his city's water and its politics, the incoming district president knew that he would have to share the local stage with a far more colorful apostle of reform. That this restless, mercurial, guilt-laden figure, so gifted in the arts of demagoguery and self-promotion, should happen to be his cousin only added to the drama for an audience long accustomed to politics as a blood sport.

✧ 6

Joe Patterson was not a simple man. A born skeptic given to fits of hero worship, Robert Patterson's son had the consistency of a weather-vane, the intensity of a blast furnace, and the attention span of a hum-mingbird. It would be tempting to describe him as the proverbial bundle of contradictions, except that even a bundle has form and therefore limits, while there seemed no end of paradox to Joe Patterson, a child of privilege who came to embody radical chic seventy years before it had a name.

At first blush, the youthful Republican legislator married to a depart-ment store heiress appeared an unlikely champion of the dispossessed. Tall and slender, Patterson had aristocratic features offset by an aggressive jaw and a wardrobe that ran to blue flannel shirts, corduroy trousers, and grease-spotted caps. His brown button eyes and down-turned mouth car-ried the hint of a sneer. Women found him boyishly irresistible. Men found him easy to disagree with and impossible to stay mad at for long. No one failed to notice his democratic instincts, his lack of pretense, and his Roman candle vitality.

No less than his outsize cousin Bert, Joe Patterson was a creature of vast appetites and churning enthusiasms. Unlike McCormick, however, he had charm to spare and a thirty-two-tooth grin to mask his contempt for the decent hypocrisies observed by lesser men. Gregarious when he chose to be, he showed no reluctance to put a foot upon the brass rail, for he had inherited his father's thirst, along with the restless temperament and deep reservoir of indignation from which both men drew their strength. There the similarities ended. Enjoying virtually every advantage save a set of par-ents fit for parenting, Joe spent most of his life trying to escape his origins. He was not so much a traitor to his class as a fugitive from it.

This frenzied quality, reminiscent of an animal caught in a trap, found expression in a string of autobiographical plays and novels with titles like *Dope, Rebellion,* and *Confessions of a Drone,* the last published in the *Hobo Review* and reprinted in pamphlet form as part of the Pocket Library of Socialism. At their best, these works advanced theatrical realism by dealing frankly with subjects such as divorce, drug abuse, and political corruption, once held taboo on the American stage. At their self-absorbed worst, they called attention to the author's alienation, much as a small child delights in shocking his elders through a precocious use of four-letter words.

As the people's friend, Patterson marched under bright banners of reform and progress. He went to the opera in muddy shoes and called it rebellion. For a bloodied taste of reality, he picked fights in North Side saloons. He had his grandfather's contempt for Europe, a decrepit continent filled with people who did not have the sense to come to America. Inspired by the *Tribune*'s renegade economic correspondent Henry D. Lloyd, his own friend Clarence Darrow, and Jack London's *War of the Classes* (Joe never could get beyond the first ninety pages of *Das Kapital*), he trilled the virtues of socialism. He demanded public ownership of Chicago's streetcars, docks, and utilities and denounced incorporated wealth with an unfailing knowledge of what it took to get his name in the papers.

At the same time, his promise to abide by the fraternal imperatives of socialism was conditioned by actual party success. Until socialism was a fact of life, Joe announced, "I do not intend to give any money or other property I have to less fortunate individuals." Much later, as a New York newspaper publisher, he would hire a famous architect to build him a country house overlooking the Hudson River at Ossining, stipulating only that it be so ugly that no one could possibly call it a showplace.[22]

Joseph Medill had kept his finger on the pulse of working-class Chicago by having his coachman regularly clip stories of interest to sweated laborers; Joseph Medill Patterson researched his first play, *Little Brother of the Rich*, by inviting his butler to dinner at Rector's. To his conventional wife, Joe was a source of embarrassment and, ultimately, scandal. One morning Alice Patterson took a call from the headmistress of the exclusive school attended by one of her three daughters. "I thought I ought to tell you," said the distraught caller, "that I saw your houseman kiss your little girl this morning." No one was more amused by this case of mistaken identity than the girl's rumpled father.[23]

Over time Patterson turned the lead of his limitations into the gold of legend. His flamboyant denial of his heritage began early, with harsh criticism of Robert and Nellie Patterson for subjecting him to "fashionable day school, fashionable boarding school, fashionable summer resorts, fashionable dancing class." At Groton, he was put down as a brooding individualist and dissenter. On the day of his arrival, he was teased because he wore an English blazer with brass buttons. At the end of his first year he was confronted by smug upperclassmen who ordered him to kneel before each of them and beg pardon. Patterson did as he was told until he came to Freddy Hale, a student he held in special contempt. "Damn you, Hale," he snapped. "I won't beg *your* pardon." For this insubordination he received a mass kicking; in later years Hale found it easier to win a Senate seat in Maine than to break down the antipathy of his former classmate.[24]

Joe impressed the Grotties with his formidable powers of concentration;

he could sit in a chaotic dorm room and devour Chicago newspapers, oblivious to the shouting adolescents all around him. On the athletic field he showed a flinty courage. In one baseball game, he was struck in the temple by a fly ball. Through sheer willpower, the dazed outfielder collected himself before hitting the ground, then straightened and stood erect as if nothing had happened. His reward was a rare ovation from his teammates.

Joe graduated from Groton in 1898. He continued his rebel ways at Yale. Following his junior year in New Haven, he went to work for Hearst's *New York Journal*, running dispatches for an American correspondent covering the Boxer Rebellion. While in China he nearly died of a fever. After graduation, he returned to Chicago and the *Tribune*, where he made it clear that he expected no favors because his father was editor-in-chief. So loudly did Joe protest his desire to be treated like everyone else that he immediately became the center of attention, as he had no doubt intended all along. One of his first assignments took him to the scene of a post office robbery near the lake shore. The robbers had used a tunnel under the building to carry out their crime, and Joe followed suit, crawling on his hands and knees at the risk of suffocation to experience the story for himself before communicating it to his readers.

In 1903 came his election to the Illinois House of Representatives, where his outspoken support of municipal ownership in Chicago quickly earned him the enmity of conservatives in both parties. From his father he learned, much to his dismay, that his legislative nomination had been engineered by GOP bosses. He got his revenge by lurching to the left. But when he tried taking the *Tribune* with him, in an editorial practically embracing the Socialist party, he ran into a brick wall with James Keeley's name on it. Finding the offending draft on its way to the composing room, Keeley telegraphed a copy to Joe's father in Washington.

March 4, 1905, was Inauguration Day in the nation's capital. At the *Tribune* bureau in the Wyatt building, a group of reporters clustered in an outer office were polishing stories about Theodore Roosevelt's day of triumph. They never penetrated the inner office, where Robert Patterson was on the phone, imploring his son not to ruin his career, disgrace his family, or otherwise make a damn fool of himself by embracing the campaign of Judge Edward F. Dunne, the Democratic reformer pledged to immediate municipal ownership. His appeal fell short; less than a week after Dunne's election, Joe resigned from the *Tribune* to become commissioner of public works in the new administration.[25]

Rob and Kate McCormick seized on Joe's abrupt departure to advertise the claims of their older son. "Medill is sane," Ambassador McCormick wrote to William Beale with what was, in light of subsequent events, cruel irony. "To whom else could you and I turn as trustees should Robert

Patterson be carried off or decide to absent himself as completely as he did last year and come abroad without notice?" To Patterson himself, Kate tactlessly declared her pleasure over the latest turn of events. Alas, she wrote, Joe was too radical in his convictions, too undisciplined in his habits. "On Medill's account I cannot but feel immensely relieved. His is a temperament so sensitive and high strung that the unhealable friction between him and Joe affected his health and work."[26]

As commissioner of public works, Joe Patterson indulged his capacity for moral outrage to the limit. Disregarding the position his father-in-law held with Marshall Field and Company, he fined Field's and other department stores $500,000 for extending their bargain basements under city sidewalks. He accused the same downtown merchants of paying sweatshop wages. The new commissioner insisted on open bidding for all public works projects. He infuriated Democratic bosses by removing an assistant street commissioner engaged in the time-honored practice of selling city hall jobs for campaign contributions. When not warning of dire consequences if J. P. Morgan got his hands on Chicago's streetcars, Patterson was busy alleging discrimination by the Water Bureau in favor of its largest users and denying a permit to the People's Gas Light and Coke Company on the grounds that the gas trust was imposing exorbitant prices on the city's poorest neighborhoods.

Gray Wolves on the city council who wished to add $194,000 to a proposed municipal garbage plant contract found Patterson an implacable foe. The newspaper scion went before a grand jury to tell of slugging tactics employed by rival newsboys, some of them selling the *Tribune*. His father fought back; the *Tribune* denounced Dunne's appointees as "freaks, cranks, monomaniacs, and boodlers." Dunne filed suit, winning damages and a retraction from the paper. But he was unable to revoke the ninety-nine-year lease of school department property at Madison and Dearborn on which the *Tribune* had erected a seventeen-story office building.

Even as Patterson risked a permanent rupture with the rest of his family, he made a cautious alliance with Bert McCormick, then in the final weeks of his campaign for president of the sanitary district. In September 1905 the two men joined the mayor on an inspection tour of harbor and dock facilities. The next day Patterson moved against Cyrus McCormick's International Harvester Company, closing part of the Chicago River to navigation in protest of the company's attempted land grab. He also prohibited the Chicago City Railway Company from carrying out repairs or laying down new track. Through such draconian methods he could pressure private interests, but he could not persuade a majority of the city council, Bert McCormick included, to accept Dunne's $25 million plan for immediate municipal ownership.

Following his election that fall, McCormick introduced an only slightly more decorous brand of reform to the sanitary district. The boyish president startled the political establishment by declaring that merit alone would govern his appointments. Such independence did not sit well with the factions pledged to Governor Deneen and Senator Lorimer. Who, they asked, was this frisky young colt now taking the bit in his mouth and threatening to run away from old warhorses such as Fred Busse? Hearst's *Examiner* thought it knew the answer. "R. R. McCormick, as president of the new Drainage Board, is to be a political Ramonoff [sic], with autocratic powers," the paper informed readers. "McCormick's little drainage machine" included just half the membership, but this was more than enough to prevail, given the president's veto power and his willingness to stack key committees with members sympathetic to his program.[27]

McCormick fed charges that a star chamber was in the making by holding secret meetings of the board. He caused offense among clubmen by assailing "plutocratic anarchists" such as Charles Yerkes before a student audience at the University of Chicago. As long ago as his Yale days, said McCormick, he had recognized the traction baron as "a scoundrel" and "jail-bird" seeking to corrupt the city council and state legislature. He did not stop with Yerkes. "Could Chauncey Depew come to New Haven now we might carry him home again, but this time it would be on a rail," he said of the old-guard Republican, who was also a Vanderbilt railroad lobbyist.[28]

He was no Socialist, McCormick hastened to add in a newspaper interview the next day. "I do not feel my conscience pricking me to any attack on wealthy men merely because of their wealth, any more than to attack the poor because some of them are bomb-throwers. I do not see any reason why the possession of wealth should interfere with a man's chances of passing through the pearly gates."[29]

RICH MAN TELLS HOW TO CRUSH RULE OF THE RICH bannered the *Chicago American*. One way to do this was to consolidate power in the hands of the able and disinterested. Here was an approach dear to the hearts of Progressive-era reformers, McCormick included. Before the end of March 1906, President McCormick, by a five-to-three vote of the board, was made district chief executive in the only way that mattered to Chicago's political class. In a sharp break from the past, when board members had divided patronage among themselves, the new president assumed sole responsibility for appointing all district employees. In just four months McCormick had dispelled the cozy climate around district headquarters. It remained to be seen to what ends he would employ his unprecedented authority.

That same month Joe Patterson was again dominating local headlines. For a year or more he had confidently predicted that a Socialist would be in the White House after the 1908 elections. Equally rash was his affair with

Mina Field Gibson, Marshall Field's niece, whose locally prominent husband achieved still greater fame after he challenged Joe to a fistfight on a downtown railway station platform. Inevitably, Joe's indiscretion crossed the desk of Andy Lawrence, Hearst's thuggish lieutenant at the *Chicago American*. Within the journalistic profession, Lawrence was best known for his blackmailing skills. He figured that Patterson, as commissioner of public works, was not just vulnerable but malleable as well. He was only half right.[30]

For Joe, the novelty of crusading had long since worn off. Typical of his targets was Charlie Martin, recalled by one contemporary as "a stupid-looking Gray Wolf from the fifth ward." Intellectually challenged he may have been, but Alderman Martin had a bookkeeping wife with enough ingenuity to siphon off $60,000 from coal contracts nominally overseen by Patterson's office. Early in March 1906, Patterson decided — with a not-so-gentle nudge from Andy Lawrence — that since all his efforts to restrain Charlie Martin had failed to keep the crooked alderman from crawling out of every city coal heap, it was time to go.

Joe being Joe, he draped his story in self-righteousness. "I realized soon after I took the office that to fight privilege under the present laws would be a jest," he wrote. "The cards were stacked in its favor from the start; the dice were loaded and are loaded against the community . . . It isn't because rich men are bad or a class apart. They are not. But when money possesses them (they practically never possess money) it alters their very souls without them realizing it, and it is simple to see why . . . Money is power and dominion. It is wine and women and song. It is art and poetry and music. It is idleness and activity. It is warmth in winter and coolness in summer. It is clothing and food. It is travel and sport. It is horses and automobiles, and silks and diamonds. It is books. It is education. It is self-respect and the respect of others."

Patterson weakened his indictment of capitalism by telling reporters that although he opposed inherited wealth on principle, he was willing to make an exception in individual cases, like his own. He confusingly dropped hints about returning to the *Tribune* — a course flatly rejected by his father — and volunteering for service in the Socialist cause nationally. Municipal ownership, he now concluded, was only "skin-deep socialism. I'm for the real brand, public ownership of all the sources of wealth . . . Not until we have removed all forms of ruinous competition, by having all the sources of wealth owned and operated by the people, shall we reach perfection. Then there will be a job for everybody."[31]

Asked if he might move to New York, Jack London's disciple showed himself to be every inch Joe Medill's grandson. "New York is the last place I'd settle in. It is too cynical and self-satisfied with present conditions. It isn't sufficiently American." No, on reflection, Patterson had decided that

Chicago was the best city in America "for the propagation of radical ideas." With that, he retired to a farm in rural Libertyville to write plays and novels, a trust fund radical living on $20,000 a year and aspiring to Broadway success, in blatant contradiction to his eloquent denials that money, power, and popularity were fair measures of human achievement. Joe Patterson was not a simple man.[32]

✧ 7

"As to my life since graduating from college," Bert McCormick notified his Yale class secretary in the spring of 1906, "if you were to say that I have felt obliged to spend 90 per cent of my time in saloons, and the remaining 10 per cent in barrooms, you would have it about correct." His dissatisfaction with Chicago politics was made even more explicit before a reform-minded audience at the YMCA. "I would advise no one to take to politics as a profession," he said. "The tenure of office is uncertain, and there are temptations. I don't mean money temptations, but the temptation that comes when you see your position in jeopardy."[33]

His discouragement was shared by other reformers for whom the prospect of a greater Chicago was clouded by an unholy alliance of suborned officeholders, venal businessmen, and professional cutthroats basking in the glow of their own notoriety. During a single twenty-four-hour period in January 1906, the city recorded four murders and seven suicides; another ten deaths were attributed to bombs or other acts of lawless brutality. An outraged *Tribune* declared that "no city in time of peace ever held so high a place on the crime-ridden, terrorized, murder-breeding" roll of urban degradation as did wide-open Chicago under the reform mayor Ed Dunne.

The crime wave added yeast to the general ferment of the 1907 mayoral contest between Dunne and Fred Busse. Dunne claimed credit for adding a thousand cops to the municipal payrolls; McCormick accused city hall of further politicizing a notoriously corrupt police force. "Save in strikes I never saw a man arrested in Chicago," he told voters. Making good on this deficiency, the president of the sanitary district instructed his Lilliputian constabulary, eleven members strong, to lock up any municipal employees who permitted industry to dump waste into the Chicago River.

Nineteen-six had seen publication of *The Jungle*, Upton Sinclair's scathing indictment of the meat-packing industry, which had long regarded the Chicago River as its private dumping ground. The author's all-too-vivid description of Bubbly Creek, so named for the carbonic acid, carbon dioxide, and methane gas rising to its surface from animal intestines and other body parts tossed into the stream, was justly famous. "A great open sewer, a hundred or two feet wide," Sinclair called the creek. "Here and there, the grease and filth have caked solid, and the creek looks like a bed of lava. Chickens walk about on it feeding, and many times an unwary stranger has started to stroll across, and vanished temporarily."

Sinclair's novel shocked consumers into demanding federal inspection of meat-packing houses. It also helped transform the role of government in the national economy, not always to the liking of incremental reformers like TR. Efficiency, professionalism, stewardship: these admirably bloodless qualities formed the rallying cry of most Progressive-era leaders, the best and brightest of their day, who dug ditches as they inspected meat: scientifically. It was in this spirit that Medill and Ruth Hanna McCormick left their apartment at 120 Lake Shore Drive in the fall of 1907 and moved to Packingtown, a squalid neighborhood of narrow rowhouses watered by Bubbly Creek and suffused with the stench of nearby slaughterhouses. For a brief time Ruth toiled in one of the area's Dickensian sausage works, alongside Poles, Slovaks, Bohemians, and Lithuanians recruited in place of upwardly mobile German and Irish laborers.

As an engineer, not a social worker, Bert McCormick was too busy trying to clean up Chicago to bleed for its masses. Less adroit than TR, he was no less "scientific" in his approach to Bubbly Creek than were the grimly cheerful agents of moral uplift who periodically invaded Packingtown. So he installed powerful pumps designed to shoot jets of fresh water into the creek's malodorous east branch twenty-four hours a day. Next he ordered experts at district headquarters to come up with screens that, lowered into place, might keep solid wastes from further polluting the river. Beyond this he wouldn't, or couldn't, go. To reach the source of the problem would require environmental controls alien to his generation and legal authority reserved to the state legislature.

Where McCormick possessed the requisite legal tools, he didn't hesitate to use them, often to breathtaking result. Battling what Carter Harrison liked to call the Order of Hungry Grafters, the district president discharged hundreds of political drones, replacing them with graduate engineers from Harvard, Yale, Michigan, and Wisconsin. He instituted a new system of accounting to bring order to the district's chaotic finances, insisted that the city of Chicago make good on long-deferred debt payments, and ended the costly, if politically rewarding, practice of farming out important legal work to nondistrict attorneys. Resolved that even a public agency could be operated with businesslike regard for the taxpayer, McCormick quadrupled income from the rental of docks and other district facilities. Hefty increases in the prices charged for dirt, fill, and stone removed from excavation sites kept the district books in black ink.

During the campaign, it will be recalled, McCormick had been tagged by his rivals as an errand boy for International Harvester, the family corporation, which possessed considerable acreage along the Chicago riverfront. In one instance in which water proved thicker than blood, McCormick exploited an obscure clause in Harvester's deed to force his cousins to make costly improvements to their property. Joe Patterson himself could not have executed a more satisfying measure of revenge against the monied classes.

His diligence equaled by his curiosity, McCormick made himself into an expert on electrical generation, sanitation, and hydraulics. His tall, shambling figure became a familiar sight in the field as he scaled piles of rock and gravel in hip boots. One night he discovered a construction crew playing cards on the people's time; the offending foreman was fired on the spot. On another occasion he walked into a fistfight pitting a hot-tempered foreman of Democratic sympathies named Ed Kelly against an insubordinate workman who loudly boasted of his pull with powerful Republicans, up to and including Fred Busse. Kelly knocked his tormentor to the ground, then spent a tortured weekend regretting his outburst and fearing for his job — understandably so, given the political sympathies of the district president and the partisan atmosphere pervading district headquarters in the past. On Monday morning the distraught Kelly hurried to McCormick's office in the hope of mending fences. His efforts to apologize were met with booming laughter. "I'm glad someone around here has some guts," McCormick said. He raised Kelly's monthly salary from $300 to $500.[34]

Kelly was later made chief engineer, with McCormick's blessing. Long afterward, when Mayor Edward J. Kelly was among the most vocal defenders of the New Deal, Chicagoans at a loss to explain the baffling cordiality between the *Tribune* and city hall wondered if McCormick had a weakness for engineers, particularly those whose subsequent achievements confirmed the Colonel's genius for spotting and rewarding executive talent.

As district president, McCormick initiated actions he would deplore as the *Tribune*'s publisher. Certainly his reverence for private property grew with the years. At the start of his term, one of his most cherished objectives was the North Shore Canal, an eight-mile offshoot of the main channel to be chiseled through the suburb of Evanston. Work got under way in April 1908. All went well until district steam shovels came up against a landowner who adamantly refused to sell two lots astride the proposed canal route. Spurning an offer of fair market value, the landowner instead rented his property to the Evanston Golf Club.

At this point McCormick's legal training came into play. Convinced that no court would assess damages higher than the book value of the property, he ordered his work crews to dig up the disputed parcel. Let the furious owner take him to court, and let a judge order the district to pay exactly what McCormick had offered in the first place. In the meantime, he would have right of way and the North Shore Canal would be on target for completion in the summer of 1910, in time to boost his reelection chances.

Meeting this deadline would require heroic efforts on the part of dilatory contractors, whose cost overruns and work delays had long been excused as a normal price of doing business with city hall and district headquarters. Here again the conservative President McCormick proved no respecter of tradition. At his orders, an insufficiently energetic contractor on the canal was directed to cease work within twenty-four hours and hand over to the district all his rock drills, steam shovels, concrete mixers, and rock crushers. McCormick then undertook to complete the project using less expensive and more reliable day laborers. Such rough justice sent shock waves through the political establishment. To his colleagues, he blandly justified his action by claiming that one in his position must occasionally behave "in a way almost socialistic . . . to preserve the public interest."

"You have seen that funds cannot be cared for to the best advantage when it is intended that they shall benefit a particular bank," McCormick had admonished the public in October 1906. "You have seen that printing cannot be done most economically when the profits are to go to a particular printer; that the police force cannot be really efficient when it is primarily the feeding trough for political henchmen; that the proper work cannot be gotten out of contracts when their political influence is taken into account in dealings with them."[35]

◇ 8

Medill McCormick was no businessman. His briskly executive wife made a joke out of her husband's absentminded ways, sometimes addressing him as Muddle. Early in their marriage, Ruth Hanna McCormick had encountered another, frightening side to Medill, whose abrupt mood swings from exhilaration to despair marked him as a manic-depressive. Today, as Ruth's granddaughter and biographer, Kristie Miller, has written, his condition would be treated with drugs. In those pre-lithium days, however, all too many victims of bipolar mood disorder turned to alcohol as a lethal form of self-medication. Medill was one of those who drank to feel better — or less bad — and wound up feeling worse.

The blessing of a loving and supportive wife was, in Medill's case, more than offset by the burden of a mother who made demands he could neither satisfy nor escape. Under the circumstances, it was tempting fate for him to double as treasurer of the *Tribune* and copublisher of his grandfather's Ohio daily, the *Cleveland Leader*. Early in 1906, the strain of these responsibilities, coupled with anxiety over having squandered a large chunk of his mother's fortune in the ill-starred *Leader*, brought on a nervous collapse. His doctors ordered him to take a three-month rest cure in California. Kate had a prescription of her own, and it wasn't California. "Take first ship over," she wired Medill from Paris; "give you $20,000 on arrival." (For once her appeal went unheeded.)[36]

At the *Tribune*, the sudden incapacitation of the heir apparent touched off a furious scrimmage over the paper's future. Medill's breakdown, coming on top of "Joe's latest eccentricity . . . puts a new face on my relations with the *Tribune*," Bert wrote to his parents. The family newspaper was no longer "a lass to be fought for but a lone woman who wants a helping hand." Bert's proposal that he join the board of directors was rejected out of hand. Rob and Kate were equally opposed to the possible return of Joe Patterson.[37]

They needn't have worried, for in embracing socialism Joe had sinned against the light. So Robert Patterson believed. Yet Patterson had no intention of allowing his in-laws to intervene in *Tribune* affairs. In a blistering letter to President Roosevelt, he denounced Rob McCormick as a diplomatic upstart who had grossly offended French sensibilities (in presenting his credentials to the republic's president, Ambassador McCormick had lectured his hosts on the unique status enjoyed by Great Britian as "the mother country of Americans") and made himself obnoxious to both Republican senators from Illinois.

Adding fuel to the fire, Parisian gossips reported that at a party to commemorate Washington's birthday, the American ambassador had replaced a portrait of Washington with his own likeness. Even if exaggerated, such stories lent credence to Kate's repeated warnings about "a weak spot on the McCormick brain." By the autumn of 1906, disquieting rumors of their impending recall were rustling the crystal chandeliers in the ambassadorial residence on the quai Debilley. Kate turned for help to her younger son, then in the thick of his fight to purge the sanitary district bureaucracy of time-serving hacks.

From Paris Kate issued instructions for "dearest Bertie" to go to Washington and alert western senators to the preponderance of choice embassies awarded to people from New York, Pennsylvania, and Rhode Island. After securing his father's position, he could cross the Atlantic and claim his reward. "Think how rich you will feel on your return trip!?" she wrote enticingly. "Forty thousand dollars is a lot of money! When I give it to you it will leave my cupboard bare!"[38]

Bert spared his mother this distressing prospect by staying put in Chicago. Kate spent her fury on the man in the White House, "an Eastern snob at heart [who] does not like the west for anything but its votes." Ambassador McCormick fired off a peremptory letter to his second son. "I hope that you can leave politics and canal work long enough to be in New York when I land," he wrote gruffly. "There is much for us to consult about for the conservation of interests, which fall naturally to Medill, now that others interested are out of the running." That Bert himself might be among those interested seems never to have occurred to the elder McCormick.[39]

On March 8, 1907, Rob sailed for home, a prematurely aged southern gentleman with a spade-fork beard, some minor foreign decorations on his chest, and a disaffected wife who chose to stay behind in London rather than face headlines like the one in the *Chicago American* that proclaimed MRS. MCCORMICK IS BLAMED FOR AMBASSADOR'S RECALL. Kate was still in the British capital six weeks later, when Rob reported that Medill was drinking too much and talking too freely, alienating potential supporters such as William Beale, without whose vote the McCormicks could never rid themselves of the hated Robert Patterson. Buried in his letter to Kate was a passing reference to "Bertie's shrewd observation" about the willingness of minority stockholders to pull some plums out of the pudding by exploiting an open breach between the McCormicks and the Pattersons. As he put it, "the vultures are gathering to feed on the carcasses of the combatants, leaving their well-picked bones to bleach on the shores of Lake Michigan." That same week it was announced that Medill McCormick was relinquishing his interest in the *Cleveland Leader* to concentrate his flickering powers exclusively on the *Tribune*.[40]

✧ 9

With the *Tribune* deaf to his claims, Bert McCormick burnished his reform credentials as a delegate to the 1907 convention by writing a new city charter. Voter rejection of the document that fall did not prevent Mayor Busse or his protégé at the sanitary district from embarking on an even more radical scheme, one intended to remake the face of Chicago. Suspicious of "theoretical city beautifiers" such as Daniel Burnham, Busse asked McCormick and more than two hundred other civic leaders, led by the Democratic businessman Charles Wacker, to implement Burnham's Chicago Plan, the most ambitious program of urban renewal since Baron Haussmann's brilliant reconstruction of Paris under Napoleon III. Along with numerous parks, a civic center, a subway system, and several downtown rail terminals, the Chicago Plan envisioned a great arterial boulevard — a corn-fed Champs-Elysées — connecting the city's north and south divisions across the Chicago River.

At the heart of Burnham's blueprint was the relationship between the city and the lake from which it derived much of its charm and prosperity.

McCormick and his fellow commissioners proposed to reclaim twenty-one miles of lakefront, bracketed by new harbors at the mouth of the Chicago River and, further south, at the convergence of the Calumet River and Lake Michigan. When corporate interests clamoring for the harbor improvements offered to construct them with private capital, McCormick smelled a rat. Investigation confirmed his suspicions: refusing to commit more than a fraction of the required $15 million, the private investors hoped to reap the benefits of improvements paid for by Uncle Sam.

To McCormick, the harbor project was inseparable from another great public works project essential to the health and economic development of South Chicago, the Calumet-Sag Canal. The same 1903 law that authorized construction of the canal also provided for the taking of 14,000 cubic feet of water per second from Lake Michigan. This was anathema to states bordering the lake and to cities such as Cleveland and Buffalo, which relied on Michigan's eastern sisters for their commercial livelihood. The Lake Shippers Association, fearing the impact of lower water levels, lodged a formal protest. So did the British government, on behalf of its Canadian subjects.

At the War Department, Secretary William Howard Taft came under heavy pressure from the Army Corps of Engineers and from diplomats to whom Chicago's water grab was an act of economic piracy directed against the British empire. In January 1907, the International Waterways Commission criticized the plan and recommended the sand dunes of northwestern Indiana as an alternative dumping ground for the city's waste. An inspection of the area left McCormick unconvinced and resentful of outside meddling. A later treaty with the British that guaranteed Canadian water rights only served to inflame his mistrust of the State Department, which had so abused his father.

A year passed. Federal officials obtained a court injunction halting the Calumet project in its tracks. Lengthy negotiations reduced the original allotment of 14,000 cubic feet to 2,000 feet. McCormick's frustrations over the glacial pace of construction drove him to establish an experimental sewage testing station at 39th Street. Here, in a facility still in use as late as the 1950s, scientists weighed sand filtration and aeration against sprinkling filters and other promising methods of waste treatment. Yet the march of technology was not fast enough to satisfy downriver rivals, led by St. Louis, which vowed to prevent the Windy City from discharging sewage into the Mississippi River. Residents of the Des Plaines and Illinois River floodplain were just as loud in condemning the unwelcome fertilization of their fields.

McCormick toured these rural areas on horseback, hoping to convince farmers that increased river traffic would more than compensate for any inconvenience caused by the construction of new dams. Often his temper got in the way of his arguments. One night in April 1907, he traveled to Joliet, at the southern terminus of the drainage canal, to address a banquet of the Joliet Commercial Club. Afterward, he heard a leading citizen quote the boast that Joseph Medill had rashly made, looking to the day when he might sail his yacht down the Illinois waterway. McCormick, furious that anyone would associate his grandfather with the idle classes, leaped to his feet. "I came here as an invited guest," he bellowed, "and I do not propose to listen to these insults." With that he bolted from the room.[41]

The same combative streak reasserted itself in the face of protests from the Illinois Manufacturers Association that he should be widening the Chicago River instead of building feeder canals through the suburbs. Returning the fire, McCormick condemned downtown real estate agents who had enriched themselves at taxpayers' expense by name. He forced corporate polluters to remove 90,000 cubic yards of refuse from the riverbed, assailed the Illinois Steel Company for illegally diverting water from the canal south of Lockport, and turned a spotlight on the cozy relationship between previous trustees and railroads, which had secured bridges at public expense and then failed to maintain their canal crossings.[42]

Psychological as well as political factors entered into McCormick's crusading. His friends on the polo circuit noticed a recklessness to his play. A similar quality marked his infatuation with early air travel; as a novice pilot, he walked away from two plane crashes and swam away from a third. As with horses and airplanes, so politics afforded him an outlet for his aggressive energies and a field on which to prove his manhood. McCormick needed enemies, it seemed, the way most men need friends.

❖ 10

Each day on the job brought fresh, disillusioning evidence of the distinction between free enterprise and monopoly capitalism. The greatest fight of McCormick's young life had its origins in the 1889 legislation by which the Illinois General Assembly had established the Chicago Sanitary District as a virtual state within a state, authorized to issue bonds and enforce sweeping police powers, subject only to legislative approval. The original drainage canal was carved from sheer rock and marshy prairie along a forty-mile route sloping downhill from the mouth of the Chicago River to the town of Lockport, where the waters of the Des Plaines River tumble through a mile-long valley gouged from sharply rising bluffs.

On the face of it, the canal was a sanitation project of unprecedented scope. Yet for a generation that had repealed the laws of geography by making a river flow backward, it was only a short step to a still more audacious goal — a vast inland waterway system knitting together the St. Lawrence River and the Great Lakes, the epic Mississippi and the warm-hearted Gulf of Mexico. More than two centuries had passed since Indians, missionaries, traders, and trappers had first made the narrow corridor separating the Chicago River from the Des Plaines into a heavily traveled portage for the products of French Canada and Spanish Louisiana. In 1673, the French explorer Louis Jolliet visualized a canal slashing across the Chicago watershed. A few years later, Jolliet's countryman Nicholas de La Salle paddled a canoe between the swollen Chicago and Des Plaines at floodtide. La Salle observed that the Des Plaines all but disappeared during the parched summer months.

Jolliet's vision remained just that. In the nineteenth century the Illinois and Michigan Canal, paralleling the Des Plaines for nearly a hundred miles, helped Chicago vault ahead of St. Louis as chief midwestern port and trading center. But while the iron horse rendered the canal obsolescent, it could not dull the enthusiasm of Chicagoans such as Joseph Medill for a Great-Lakes-to-the-Gulf waterway centered on the portage route first blazed by European explorers and soldiers of fortune.

By the time Medill's grandson took the helm of the sanitary district, the drainage canal, once valued for its commercial and hygienic possibilities, was coming to be seen as a source of abundant, inexpensive electrical power for a rapidly growing metropolitan area. One of McCormick's first moves as district president was to organize an electrical department, charged with an ambitious program of municipal power generation. At Lockport, thirty-two feet below the level of Lake Michigan, McCormick and his engineers constructed powerhouses to light Chicago and its suburbs, beginning in January 1907. Unlike his predecessors, McCormick proposed to sell this current at cost (approximately $15 per horsepower) as the generating capacity of the district blossomed. Since this was less than half what the city was then paying to produce its own power, he hoped to spur industrial development and achieve for the local economy what the Chicago Plan promised for urban aesthetics.

His enthusiasm proved contagious. After thorough investigation, the town of Morgan Park, the suburb of Cicero, and the West Chicago park commissioners cheerfully contracted for his electricity. Elected officials in Chicago, however, held back; worse, they tried to block the district from stringing wires or laying conduits by demanding so-called frontage consents from property owners, a requirement conspicuously waived for the giant Commonwealth Edison company. What an angry McCormick called "the Edison ordinance" was rushed through an eminently bribable city council.

Amid a storm of newspaper criticism of the deal, only the *Tribune* held its tongue. "Do you imagine that any well-informed person in Chicago is ignorant of the reason why?" wrote McCormick, painfully aware that his family's paper had been muzzled by the intimate friendship between its

chief trustee, William Beale, and Samuel Insull, the founder of Commonwealth Edison. It has been said of the predatory Insull that he did for
electricity what John D. Rockefeller did for oil, and with even less squeam-
ishness about the consequences for economic competition. "My experience
is that the greatest aid to the efficiency of labor is a long line of men waiting
at the gate," Insull once remarked, with chilling insensitivity.[43]

Like Jim Keeley, another *Tribune* power distrusted by McCormick,
Insull was a refugee from London, one of eight children reared in an atmosphere of strict piety. At the age of fourteen, ridiculed for delivering
temperance lectures on Oxford streetcorners, he walked out of a classroom
for the last time. Finding work as an office boy, he taught himself short-
hand and accounting, keeping a set of double-entry books for an imaginary business. These skills, added to his organizational abilities, led to his
appointment as personal secretary to the notoriously untidy Thomas
Edison. In February 1881, the twenty-two-year-old English immigrant
arrived in New York. Edison's biographer Robert Conot described Insull
as slight, "below average height, nearsighted, with slicked-down prematurely thinning hair and long sideburns. His voice was nasal and high-
pitched. He had the demeanor of a shop clerk."[44]

Appearances notwithstanding, the prim, teetotaling Insull rapidly made
himself indispensable. He impressed Edison with his encyclopedic knowledge of British industry and with the seemingly effortless way in which he
untangled the inventor's chaotic business affairs. In return, Insull gained
from Edison a priceless education in the budding electrical industry, "from
making deals in the boardrooms of Edison's financial backers to laying
cable under the street." In 1886 the great inventor asked his clerk to oversee
construction of a plant in Schenectady, New York, nucleus of the General
Electric Company. "Do it big," Edison advised his protégé. "Make it either
a big success or a big failure."[45]

Insull's success in Schenectady was sufficiently big to make him president of Chicago Edison in his mid-thirties. Joining the throng of fairgoers
who marveled at the incandescent bulbs and arc lamps adorning the White
City, the newcomer to Chicago saw only profits to be made. To his responsibilities he brought a vision of economic consolidation pursued with
ruthless efficiency. "Ours is a business that is a natural monopoly," he
explained bluntly. No restraining legislation or popular sentiment could
overcome that fact. "Eventually all the electrical energy for a given area
must be produced by one concern."

Yet Insull was more than a great consolidator. His innovations transformed the way electricity was produced and marketed to urban consumers. To make his product affordable to the masses, he authorized the
world's first steam turbine generators, vastly more powerful than existing
generators. Engineers, fearing a possible explosion, advised him to stay

away from tests of the risky new equipment. Insull refused. "If this thing doesn't work, I'm dead anyway," he said.

But it did work, spectacularly, and it laid the foundation for the nation's largest and most profitable electric utility. Since expensive copper circuitry was required to carry Edison's direct current (DC) around a one-way circuit, Insull turned to the rotary converter, which changed DC into AC, or alternating current, capable of traveling forward or in reverse. Thereafter high-voltage electricity was transmitted over noncopper wires to substations, where power levels were adjusted for local distribution.

Within three years of his arrival, Insull controlled all the central generating stations in Chicago. He convinced transit companies responsible for three fourths of local power usage to buy current from Edison rather than generate their own supplies. Where persuasion failed, he resorted to price wars, compensating for lost revenue by raising rates in his rapidly expanding service area (in time his Chicago companies supplied power across a 6,000-square-mile grid). By offering hotels, restaurants, and department stores a tungsten filament bulb that produced three times the illumination of its crude predecessor, Insull was able to supplant gas and kerosene as alternative power sources. His *Electric City Magazine* held out tantalizing glimpses of enhanced social status through sewing machines and hot plates. Door-to-door salesmen offered housewives free use of electric irons for six months. According to the historian Harold Platt, "After the household was hooked, or more properly, hooked up, the family's increasing use of lights and appliances would become profitable for the company."[46]

Insull averted the only real threat to his monopoly by obtaining exclusive patent rights to newly manufactured equipment. This enabled him to outsmart Gray Wolves on the city council who had established the phantom Commonwealth Electric Company to line their pockets. ("Hold out a piece of meat to them," said Insull at the time, "and they'll take your arm with it.") Shut out of the market, the economic blackmailers had no choice but to sell him an exclusive fifty-year franchise. In 1907 he consolidated his holdings under the corporate title of Commonwealth Edison.[47]

The future promised limitless wealth to the buccaneer who had a stranglehold on the commodity most essential to modern urban life. When suburban railroads teetered on the verge of bankruptcy, Insull took control, electrified the lines, and turned a profit while adding to his reputation as an economic mastermind. In due course he applied to the city council for permission to build the subway system called for in the Chicago Plan. His appeal was turned down. This came as a distinct shock; as a rule, elected officials were more accommodating.

One notable exception was the president of the sanitary district. The two men clashed over the future of electrical power, with McCormick arguing that taxpayers, having lavished $60 million on the drainage canal and related improvements, held rights to the water power generated with their money. Not for the first time, he found himself plowing a lonely furrow. "What we are fighting for is to establish unhampered and unrestrained competition with the Commonwealth Edison Company," he told reporters.[48]

⬦ 11

The ensuing contest appeared hopelessly unequal. Insull brought to the fray unparalleled experience, deep pockets, a publicly granted monopoly, and the momentum of industrial combination that defined the age. Blocking his way was a callow patrician less than half his age, disowned by his former associates on the city council, unsupported even by his family's newspaper. In his annual report for 1907, McCormick did not mention Insull by name, but the father of Commonwealth Edison was condemned in absentia as the type and symbol of unscrupulous forces "whose greed for gain is greater than their sense of propriety."

To bolster his case for publicly generated water power, McCormick first had to discredit the electric trust — not all that hard to do if one burrowed deep enough into sanitary district archives. Among the "startling and atrocious" deals McCormick uncovered was a lease arrangement between commissioners of the old Illinois and Michigan Canal and the Economy Power and Light Company of suburban Joliet. The resulting windfall for Economy Power and Light took the form of a dam and generating plant originally built with taxpayer dollars. For transferring valuable headwaters in and around Joliet to speculators at fire-sale prices, McCormick alleged, the canal commissioners had pocketed $75,000. These were no isolated transactions, he insisted, but part of an ongoing racket bilking Illinois taxpayers out of their right to cheap power.

Enter Sam Insull. Backed by the finest lawyers money could buy, the corporate pirate initiated condemnation proceedings against the remaining district properties in the region. He based his claims upon the novel theory that a private, wholly commercial enterprise had the same right as government to invoke eminent domain. The courts dismissed his arguments, but they could not prevent Economy Power and Light from falling into his clutches.

In February 1907, Economy began construction of a dam near the confluence of the Des Plaines and Kankakee rivers. About this same time, McCormick and some friends, oblivious to the barrier taking shape downstream, decided to test the navigability of the Des Plaines for themselves by rowing a boat from Joliet to Ottawa. As night fell, their fragile craft went over the cofferdam and was quickly swamped. Fortunately, its occupants were all good swimmers, able to reach shore unharmed.

Instead of apologizing, Economy Light and Power tried to have McCormick indicted for reducing water levels around its Joliet dam. "Why should a private corporation use the water flow in the canal to make power?" he retorted. Forming fists with words, the district president attacked the Joliet political ring, which, in league with private power interests, "made Tammany Hall look like a Sunday school class." Joliet's Republican congressman shot back that "the Chicago polo expert" had designs on the entire Des Plaines Valley. But McCormick had the last laugh, if not the last word, when voters at the next election discarded the offending congressman and three state legislators said to be receiving favors from the Insull machine.[49]

McCormick the engineer had no intention of stopping there. He would settle for nothing less than the lakes-to-gulf waterway first envisioned by his grandfather. Sam Insull was just as determined to thwart extension of the drainage canal south of Joliet and the deepening of the Des Plaines and other tributaries of the Mississippi. Commonwealth Edison lawyers redoubled their efforts to have the Des Plaines declared unnavigable. Their initial victory in state court was later overturned by the Supreme Court in Washington. And as the legal shadowboxing went on, McCormick kept up a withering verbal fire on the Insull juggernaut. The real obstacle to the proposed Illinois Waterway, he told reporters, was "graft, not gravel . . . rogues, not rocks."[50]

In August 1907, the fight shifted to the legislative arena as Insull sought in the back rooms of Springfield what he could not obtain openly from the bench. McCormick, meanwhile, placed himself squarely behind "the right of the people's ditch to develop and use this power for the people, against this private monopoly." When Insull's lobbyists bottled up McCormick's legislation in committee, the Illinois Waterway, like the idea of state-owned power, appeared stillborn. Yet the fruits of victory can hold the seeds of later defeat. Insull's brutish tactics within the general assembly produced an irresistible backlash. In the changed climate, lawmakers had no choice but to order the removal of all existing obstructions from the Des Plaines and Illinois rivers and a ban on construction of new ones. Stung by the public outcry, the Illinois house went a step further, launching an investigation of the hopelessly compromised canal commissioners.

Insull had hoped to sidetrack the river improvements by putting them to a statewide referendum. To his astonishment, voters in November 1908 approved a $20 million bond issue to fund work from Lockport to Utica. Hardly pausing to savor his unexpected triumph, McCormick moved to condemn not one but three Economy Light installations around Joliet. He even talked of cutting a new channel around the strategically located Dam Number One, thereby leaving Insull economically as well as physically marooned. Thrown on the defensive, the tycoon yielded grudgingly and only when he had to. City counselors friendly to Commonwealth Edison stalled McCormick's scheme to supply electric current to Chicago factories at 20 per cent below the going rate. District power lines were short-circuited. Transformers fell victim to sabotage.

Journalists, quick to see the dramatic possibilities of this modern David and Goliath tale, spread the name of McCormick far beyond the borders of Chicago. From a hectoring nuisance, the youthful district president had become Insull's most formidable adversary, hailed by his admirers as an incorruptible steward of the people's resources. Thus emboldened, McCormick signed contracts with the Busse administration to light city hall and other municipal buildings for a fraction of what Insull charged. Furthermore, he promised to save Chicagoans $1 million annually if they tapped into the excess generating capacity of the district.

As the crusade for public power made for curious alliances, so it triggered opposition in some normally friendly quarters. At the *Tribune,* William Beale was apoplectic over the assertion that water power latent in Illinois streams and rivers was anything but the exclusive property of corporate shareholders. McCormick was guilty of rank confiscation, said Beale. His arguments "would have horrified Mr. Medill." To prevent such indiscriminate assaults on private property in the future, Beale added menacingly, "some new editorial writers may be needed."[51]

Beale didn't know the half of it. When the *Tribune* finally parted company with Insull in 1909, its editorial condemning his monopoly was the work of two new writers named Patterson and McCormick. As for Insull, his pride suffered more than his profits. Besides retaining a dominant share of the Chicago market, Commonwealth Edison expanded operations to include 385 cities in eleven states. Insull himself chaired sixty-five firms and sat on the boards of at least eighty-five more. In November 1929, he threw open the doors of a cavernous new opera house, designed to seal his reputation as Chicago's first citizen and, not so coincidentally, to provide a fitting showcase for Mary Garden, a dubious diva with a knack for gaining bad reviews (so bad that she is credited with being the first public figure to declare, "I don't care what they write about me as long as they spell my name right").[52]*

No such wit leavened Sam Insull's later encounters with the press. No

---

*The Insull-Garden relationship was immortalized by Orson Welles, a Chicago native, whose character Charles Foster Kane was a composite of Insull, Colonel McCormick, and William Randolph Hearst. Like the film's Susan Alexander, Miss Garden showed herself to be ungracious in thanking her patron. Insull's latest monument to himself, she grumbled, was less opera house than convention hall.

sooner was the opera house dedicated than the stock market panic on Wall Street exposed the financier's overstretched resources. For three desperate years he chased his financial tail. By July 1932 he had drained half a million dollars in corporate funds to cover the margin on the brokerage account of his son Martin. Insull's reputation collapsed along with his fortune; 300,000 stockholders were trapped beneath the rubble. He fled to Europe to avoid charges of embezzlement but was brought back to stand trial before a jury, which, unwilling to personalize the systemic failings of the old order, acquitted him in recognition of his past services to Chicago.

Once free, Insull again abandoned the city, this time for good. Three years later his heart gave out on a Parisian subway platform. Gendarmes found his corpse, neatly dressed in a gray suit, its only identification the letters SI woven into his handkerchief and underwear. In the tycoon's pocket was eighty-five cents.

5

Into His Own

"If I can prevent the sale [of the *Tribune*] by any act which will not make it necessary for me to take charge of the property, I will do so with a cheerful heart. If the condition of retaining the property shall finally depend upon my taking charge of it, I will put the decision up to you and abide by your decision."

— Robert R. McCormick to his mother, May 1910

O NE AFTERNOON early in 1909, an agitated Bert McCormick barged into Robert Patterson's office with a bizarre tale of corporate embezzlement. While sitting in the steam room of the Chicago Athletic Club, he had learned of a *Tribune* accountant (and fellow club member) who was living beyond his means through the simple expedient of signing his name to company checks.

"Why don't you become treasurer?" Patterson replied airily. "Then you can sign the checks."[1]

The exchange was perfunctory, its implications profound. For McCormick, it was an unexpected ticket of admission to the newspaper from which he had so long been excluded. For Patterson, it was a chance to inflict the ultimate reprisal on his bitterly antagonistic sister-in-law. Just as Kate McCormick had wounded him by cultivating (some might say exploiting) his troubled daughter Cissy, so he would now wound Kate by upsetting her carefully laid plans to place the *Tribune* in the hands of her firstborn, Medill.

Actually, the position so casually bestowed on McCormick by his uncle was largely honorific. True, Patterson sold him a handful of shares in the Medill Trust. Beyond this, however, his new title, devoid of responsibilities and salary, promised little more than "the right to study the paper from the inside." Besides, warming the treasurer's chair was no guarantee of a seat on the *Tribune's* board of directors.[2]

On reflection, this was small loss to an active politician frequently mentioned as a potential successor to Mayor Busse, who was expected to retire at the end of his four-year term. In March 1909, McCormick went into legal partnership with Stuart G. Shepard, a Democratic contemporary whose credentials included a losing campaign for the superior court. Shepard and McCormick made up a ticket balanced in the hoariest Chicago tradition to generate broad political (that is, commercial) appeal. From his new office on the thirteenth floor of the Tribune building, the firm's junior partner had good reason to believe that his pro bono work as the paper's treasurer would be more than amply compensated by a healthy share of its legal business. This was doubly welcome news, for 1910 promised McCormick a costly and uncertain reelection battle at the sanitary district. Nearing his thirtieth birthday, he received most of his income from a $150,000 trust fund, sweetened by an annual allowance of $20,000 from his mother.

Cousin Joe Patterson's situation was even more precarious. After sinking $100,000 into his Libertyville farm (Sam Insull lived on an adjoining estate, raising pheasants, which Joe delighted in shooting when they flew over his property), Joe had been forced to mortgage the place to pay debts contracted by his extravagant wife. His playwriting career continued to generate more notoriety than cash. As his hopes of combining radical politics and commercial popularity faded, he found the literary muse elusive. "In the evening he had dinner alone," explained a friend familiar with Joe's creative process. "After dinner he had the butler remove the cloth from the table, bring a fresh cloth, candles, a quart of burgundy, and pen and ink. He confessed that he put his faith for inspiration in the fresh cloth and the candles."[3]

In due course an untitled script reached a New York producer, whose constructive criticism persuaded Joe that he would never attain in the theater the kind of success he had so blithely disregarded at the *Tribune*. There remained only the question of whether the family paper would have him back. Bolstering his prospects was the continuing decline of Medill McCormick. After suffering a second breakdown in the autumn of 1908, Medill had gone off to Europe to seek treatment at Carl Jung's psychiatric clinic near Zurich. Jung traced his patient's drinking to a crippling dependence on his mother. So long as he lived or worked under the debilitating influence of Kate McCormick, Medill was doomed.

For an entire week in February 1909, the *Tribune* led Americans in celebrating the centenary of Lincoln's birth. On the birthday itself, "the greatest issue of the world's greatest newspaper" included 194 pages crammed with Lincoln scholarship and rare photographs. The phrase "the world's greatest newspaper" struck a properly bombastic note in a city long in love with itself. Two years later it was copyrighted, and it remained a prominent part of the *Tribune* masthead until 1977. The same week the *Tribune* paid homage to its glorious past, trustees of the paper readmitted Joe Patterson to the fold as company secretary. Joe's response was to propose to Bert McCormick that they stage a coup, eliminating Robert Patterson once and for all from the *Tribune's* management.

McCormick rejected the idea as both dishonorable and unnecessary. More practical than Joe, he understood that for the House of Medill to retain its dominance within the *Tribune,* family solidarity was essential. His impulsive cousin, "so erratic as to be dangerous," appeared willing to ruin the paper in his quest to control it. "Joe will not walk along any line . . . Hell of a situation," McCormick observed in his diary early in April.[4]

The continuing turmoil made minority stockholders receptive to outside offers. In the summer of 1909, a rival publisher, Victor Lawson of the *Record-Herald*, intimated that because of Hearst competition in the crowded morning newspaper market, he might soon be compelled to halve the price of his paper to a penny, a move that would have devastating consequences for the *Tribune.* Of course, Lawson purred, by merging their journal with his own, *Tribune* shareholders could guarantee a combined circulation large enough to avoid the dreaded price reduction and resulting loss of income. Implicit in these promises was the threat of a brutal circulation war should his advances be rejected.

Transparent as it was, Lawson's scaremongering had its intended effect on the nervous descendants of Horace White and Alfred Cowles. Nellie Patterson likewise showed little stomach for a fight that, even if successful, might deplete her financial reserves and ultimately force her to hand the *Tribune* over to her sister. If Lawson erred, it was in underestimating the resourcefulness of Bert McCormick.

Following a secret visit from John Shaffer, the owner of the *Chicago Evening Post,* McCormick could scarcely contain his joy. Shaffer had expressed interest in buying a majority interest in the *Tribune.* As a result of this timely offer, Bert told his mother, "if the minority join any plan to sell the whole paper, we can say we will sell *our share* at a better figure!" His optimism was justified. Lawson was sixty years old; his best newspapering days were behind him, and he was notoriously cheap when it came to hiring or retaining top talent. His adversary, Jim Keeley, was in his forties, at the peak of his powers, and full of enthusiasm for the coming battle.[5]

Like a moth drawn to his own flame, Medill McCormick appeared firmly set on a course of self-destruction once back in Chicago. "All his talk is about enormous things," the journalist William Hard wrote to Bert. "He settles problems with his left hand, and without knowing any of the details. He loves to talk about Napoleon ... He refers to Roosevelt as 'a great sporad.' "[6]

Oblivious to his growing vulnerability, Medill demanded a hefty raise after claiming that an unnamed eastern publication had promised him $50,000 a year. His bitter quarrels with Keeley drove the managing editor to take a lengthy vacation, purportedly in Japan. In Keeley's absence, the *Tribune* joined forces with state's attorney John E. W. Waymen in a noisy war on vice. Never one to think small, Medill proposed to make this crusade different from earlier ones by revealing the identities of respectable Chicagoans who were profiting from commercialized wickedness. The result was a red leather book thickly padded with the names of some of Chicago's leading citizens.

Throughout February 1910 tensions mounted, as Lawson's $10 million merger package gained favor with exasperated stockholders and Medill make it clear that he did not intend to wait forever for the results of his vice probe to be splashed across the front page. Talk of an enlarged board of directors further strained relations between Bert and Medill McCormick. "We are too strong to work in one shop," said Medill. Bert disagreed. While a political career remained his preference, "I cannot but feel that my first duty is towards the Tribune Company and towards my mother." On February 21, the directors met and voted to pay Medill $30,000 a year, far less than his salary demands. The implied rebuke triggered a third and final breakdown.[7]

Simultaneously, Keeley reappeared on the scene. One of his first acts was to ask the city editor, Edward "Teddy" Beck, if he could examine the notorious red book. That night Keeley was in the composing room. Looking up, he saw Medill McCormick in formal dress advancing somewhat unsteadily in his direction. Silently Medill put down his opera hat and stick. He threw an arm around Keeley's shoulders and laughed until he shook. The next day he was gone. The red book vanished with him.*

In desperation, Kate McCormick appealed to her younger son for help.

---

*Medill's mother begged Jung to come to America and examine her son. When the two men met in New York a month later, Jung diagnosed Medill's condition as "mental fatigue" brought on by the strain of business. The real strain, he concluded privately, was Kate herself, a "real power devil" whose possessiveness had crushed her son's spirit and defeated all his efforts at independence. Deciding on what he called "an act of *force majeure*," Jung — without consulting Medill — concocted a medical certificate declaring Medill to be a hopeless alcoholic incapable of carrying out his present job. The powers at the *Tribune* accepted this diagnosis, Kate reluctantly, the others with a sense of relief. Medill's life was thus spared through an act of mercy for which Jung earned his patient's lasting resentment.

Robert Patterson "hates everything and everybody in our family," she wrote, "Nellie included. To sell he feels would be to dethrone our family forever . . . Remember his son has lost his birthright and you and Medill have still got yours." The future of the *Tribune* was hanging in the balance as Patterson went off to Atlantic City at the end of March to be close to his dying mother. Bert must seize the opportunity, said Kate, to write his Aunt Nellie a calm, judicious letter "pointing out all the families who went down in the world from giving up their family heritage . . . Now Bertie stir yourself!" she wrote. "You lost me a block of Reaper stock at 56 by your slowness," she reminded him. "Remember a woman's intuitions are to be respected. Get options on White and Cowles if possible." The letter was signed, "Your ever loving M."[8]

✧ 2

A few days later McCormick received a second message from his mother, confirming what family members had half expected of the unhappy Robert Patterson. "I've just heard R.W. is dead — alone of course," wrote Kate. "He died from an overdose of Veronal. I send this in case I do not go to Chicago. I don't want to!"[9]

Robert Patterson had ended his life in a Philadelphia hotel room a few hours after his mother died in the same city. Publicly, his death was blamed on a stroke of apoplexy following a cold. Bert McCormick had already been tipped off to the death by a *Tribune* telephone operator on the morning of April 2. He left immediately for Patterson's office. There an even greater shock awaited him. Assembled under the aegis of William Beale, a confused group of trustees and stockholders was intent on formalizing the sale of the paper to Victor Lawson.

Recovering from his surprise, McCormick pleaded with those in the room to reconsider the deal. Surely the death of one man could not justify killing Joseph Medill's legacy.* But it wasn't that simple, Beale's confederates replied. Patterson was gone. Medill McCormick appeared irretrievably broken in health. And with Kate and Nellie perpetually quarreling, the *Tribune* faced Lawson's threatened price war without a general to lead it.[10]

Later accounts may have exaggerated McCormick's powers of persua-

---

*Ironically, Beale, McCormick, and Joe Patterson had engaged as recently as March 24 in what Beale described as "a long and very satisfactory talk"; all three participants agreed on the need for Medill's removal. In a letter dated the same day, Joe Patterson made plain his and Bert's willingness to devote more time to *Tribune* affairs and to support Keeley as "the safest and ablest man" on the scene. In other words, the death of Robert Patterson merely hastened the cousins' formal moves toward control — a course they had been pondering for weeks, possibly months.

sion; the conspirators, after all, could hardly dispose of the paper before Patterson was given a decent burial. Still, it was a gutsy performance, the prelude to an even more impressive campaign aimed at rallying whatever forces might be brought to oppose Lawson and his Trojan horse, Beale.

McCormick began by securing pledges of support from his cousins Joe and Cissy. At a board meeting on April 6, Kate introduced a resolution granting Medill unlimited leave without salary. "Keeley naturally becomes the executive manager and will be retained there as long as he gives satisfaction," Bert wrote to his deposed brother the next day. In the same letter he held out hope that Medill might return to power once "you can convince your doctors and the directors that you are in condition to assume it."[11]

In contrast to her sister, Nellie Patterson frowned on the idea of "keeping the paper for the boys." The boys could do quite nicely for themselves, she declared. Besides, she wrote, "I feel no particular obligation to Joe." To be sure, selling the *Tribune* would be like parting with her heart's blood. But facts must be faced. *"The two owners are the weakness of the property,"* said Nellie, who believed that any attempt by the younger generation to control the *Tribune* was doomed by family rivalries.[12]

Joe Patterson disagreed with his mother. He and Bert were "too selfish" to quarrel, he contended; "we have too much at stake." Personalities aside, the *Tribune* was "the first newspaper in a growing city in the heart of the country." Why part with such a prize?[13]

Why indeed? In a chance encounter with McCormick two weeks after the death of Robert Patterson, Alfred Cowles reaffirmed his intention to sell out to Lawson, lacking "someone vitally interested" to fill Patterson's shoes. "What do you mean by someone vitally interested?" McCormick demanded. Would it make a difference, for example, if *he* were to take an active part in *Tribune* affairs? "It certainly would," said Cowles.[14]

Privately, McCormick accused minority stockholders of economic blackmail. A move to the *Tribune* would mean the "total abandonment of my prospects for a political career" a scant few days after he had been offered renomination at the sanitary district "practically by acclamation." Moreover, Victor Lawson's promise of support for any future McCormick campaign was conditional on the sale of the *Tribune* now. That he genuinely hoped the cup might pass him by was implicit in his vow to his mother to keep the *Tribune* in the family, whatever the personal cost. The conclusion is inescapable: McCormick hoped to win, if not Kate's love, then at least her grudging admiration by preserving family ownership of the *Tribune* — perhaps the only thing that coldly manipulative woman was truly capable of loving.[15]

First, however, he faced the unenviable task of informing Victor Lawson that the deal was off. In a tense confrontation, the glossy publisher with the quarterdeck manner and Prince Albert coat concluded that the *Tribune's* owners would never entrust their future prosperity to the nervous, chain-smoking figure before him. Pressing his advantage, Lawson warned that unless the sale went ahead, the *Tribune* would be destroyed in a circulation war for which it was laughably ill prepared. At his insistence, McCormick agreed to go to Europe and put the question of selling directly to his mother and other trustees then abroad.

Accustomed to being underestimated, McCormick carefully hid his personal feelings. He promised Lawson that in his self-created office as "ambassador from everybody to everybody," he would strive for consensus. Over the next few weeks he made an elaborate show of consulting Kate and Nellie. He pursued William Beale from one German village to another. In Manchester, England, he paused long enough to visit that city's famous ship canal. As further cover, he traveled to Berlin, where he examined a showcase sewage disposal plant.[16]

And all the while he bought time for Keeley to strengthen the *Tribune's* defenses. So thoroughly, in fact, did he disguise his true intentions that at one point Keeley himself expressed interest in buying the property if the McCormicks and Pattersons finally decided to sell. By the first week of August 1910, the empty-handed McCormick was preparing for his return journey on the *Lusitania*. From Chicago, the credulous Lawson pressed him to continue his phantom negotiations.

Not a word of maternal appreciation for his efforts reached Bert, only a businesslike listing of the suits and hats Kate had ordered for him from London tailors. "I hope you had a nice time in Ostend," she wrote. "Do give enough time to the fitting of your clothes!"[17]

❖ 3

On April 30, 1910, streamer headlines blazed the biggest scoop of Jim Keeley's eventful career: DEMOCRATIC LEGISLATOR CONFESSES THAT HE WAS BRIBED TO CAST VOTE FOR LORIMER FOR UNITED STATES SENATOR. The entire front page and most of pages two and three were devoted to the sordid revelations of a downstate representative named Charles A. White, a former streetcar conductor from East St. Louis. For $1,000, White, a Democrat, had sold his vote to the Republican William J. Lorimer, thereby aiding Lorimer's return to the Senate in May 1909. White had pocketed an additional $900 as his share of a general corruption or jackpot fund. As it happened, this was not enough to purchase his silence. By the time he approached Keeley, White had peddled his story to several publications, none of them willing to pay his $50,000 asking price. Keeley talked him down to $3,500, then spent $20,000 subjecting his narrative to an exhaustive review by *Tribune* reporters, private detectives, and investigators from the state's attorney's office.[18]

For weeks the Lorimer story dominated *Tribune* news coverage, yielding only to the spectacular appearance of Halley's comet. (COMET BUMPS US; WE'RE STILL HERE, read the headline concocted by Keeley.) Grand juries were convened in Chicago and Springfield. Lee Browne, the Democratic leader in the state legislature, was hauled before a judge and jury on bribery charges. Two of Browne's colleagues were indicted for perjury. On May 28, the Blond Boss broke his silence with a 12,000-word diatribe against the *Tribune* for conspiring to drive him from public life "because I will not do as other Republicans in Illinois have done — place myself under the absolute control and dictatorship of the *Tribune*." Diluting the impact of his performance was the confession that same day of yet another state senator, who had received $2,500 in return for his vote plus $700 from the now infamous jackpot and the promise of $1,500 on a statehouse desk contract.

Scenting blood, the *Tribune* offered a $5,000 reward leading to the identification of Lorimer's financial backers. Fresh indictments ensued. Springfield investigators seeking the source of Browne's slush fund learned that fishermen along the Illinois River had been contributing to the jackpot for years as the price of forestalling legislation hostile to their interests. This latest revelation cast a fishy odor over both parties. The stench reached as far as the nation's capital, where a Senate subcommittee aired the Lorimer allegations amid reports that old-guard Republicans were preparing a bathtub of whitewash with which to exonerate their colleague. Using its own brand of tortured logic, the committee found the testimony of Lorimer's accusers "of doubtful value."

After two months of heated debate, a motion to invalidate Lorimer's election was defeated, 46–40. Only the votes of ten lame-duck members of the old guard had saved the Blond Boss from explusion. "The Senate has vindicated Lorimer," declared Joseph Pulitzer's *New York World*. "Now who will vindicate the Senate?" Lorimer led a victory parade through the streets of Chicago, capped by a rally in front of the *Tribune* building. His celebration was premature, for in February 1911 the *Chicago Record-Herald* charged that he had purchased his seat with a $100,000 fund contributed for that purpose by business interests. As its authority the paper cited Clarence S. Funk, the general manager of the International Harvester Company, who in turn pointed a finger at a prominent lumberman named Edward Hines. (A prescient *Tribune* editorial had already inquired, "Was it Sawdust" that had bribed the legislators?)

The board of Chicago's Union League Club, displaying greater capacity for moral outrage than the U.S. Senate, took the unprecedented step of canceling Hines's membership. In Washington, the Lorimer case was reopened for a second round of hearings. Five million words later, on a Saturday afternoon in July 1912, William J. Lorimer's embarrassed colleagues retired him to private life. "A great deal has been done," said the *Tribune* the next day. "A great deal remains to be done."

By then Bert McCormick had himself been tossed out of office, a victim of the Democratic tidal wave that washed over the United States in the autumn of 1910. The two events were not unrelated. Although a shining chapter in *Tribune* history, the Lorimer case demonstrated anew the cost incurred by any candidate too closely associated with a newspaper whose penchant for making enemies was equaled by its usefulness as a punching bag. For sixty years the *Tribune* had remained faithful to the party of Lincoln and Joe Medill. Almost overnight, Jim Keeley, the Blond Boss, and William Howard Taft changed all that.

"Was there ever such a fool as Taft?" sighed Kate McCormick in the second year of that huge and hugely ineffective man's presidency. Taft's failures were so obvious, his ineptitude so universally derided, that many Republicans talked openly of a Roosevelt restoration in 1912. In the front of the pack yelping for the return of Theodore Rex was the *Chicago Tribune*. The cartoonist John McCutcheon drew a flattering series depicting Roosevelt on his famous African hunting trip. Another *Tribune* correspondent chartered a special steamer to pursue the ex-president up the White Nile. According to the paper's resident humorist, BLT, a fifth item now had to be added to the four "famous inevitables":

> The procession of the equinoxes
> The law of gravitation
> Death
> Love
> T.R.[19]

The GOP rift could not have come at a worse time for Bert McCormick, already saddled with the implacable hostility of Senator Lorimer and facing a revitalized Democratic party in his campaign for a second term as president of the sanitary district. Opposing him was T. A. Smythe, a former board president of no distinguishing merit, who accused McCormick of neglecting the Calumet-Sag Canal and of making excessive improvements everywhere else. Midway through the campaign, an unforgiving Cook County Real Estate Board got into the act, exacting revenge for McCormick's past highhandedness by announcing an investigation of district management.

Fighting back as best he could, McCormick reminded voters of the benefits accruing from his campaign for publicly generated water power. Yet it was far too early to declare final victory in the war against privilege. "The people of Illinois are being buncoed out of millions of dollars . . . by the greed of certain men who want to control the water power for their own private gain," he told a campaign rally in the third week of October. To the *Tribune*, hardly more objective than its Hearst-owned adversaries, the Republican candidate was "the kind of man you look at and like, boyish in appearance, offhand in manner, cleanblooded, an immensely vigorous, practically capable young man." In short, the very picture of a progressive-minded patrician.[20]

Not enough voters agreed with this assessment to keep McCormick from being crushed in a Democratic landslide on election day. His only consolation lay in running 25,000 votes ahead of the GOP ticket. Fortunately, he wrote a friend two days later, "I am not buried so deep that I may not some day come up again." Like his grandfather before him, he had performed creditably in a position of public trust, setting high standards for honesty and effectiveness, and the voters had booted him from office anyway. Such ingratitude went down hard. Defeat had toughened McCormick's skin, but it also had strengthened a latent distrust for the boss-led masses denounced as "rabble" by Joe Medill.[21]

"You are not one to mourn long, nor to remain inactive," Aunt Nettie McCormick wrote consolingly. True to her forecast, within weeks her nephew was organizing the Illinois Conservation Association, designed to guard the natural resources of the state from grasping politicians while providing a useful platform for at least one politician to keep his name before the electorate. "We have arrived at the point in this country where we realize that the old policy of destruction is wrong, and we must combine for the purpose of construction," McCormick told the National Irrigation Congress, meeting in Chicago the following summer. "We cannot follow our own paths, irrespective of the common welfare."[22]

For the moment McCormick himself hewed to a cautious path between the maladroit Taft — when backed into a corner by its enemies, said the unhappy president, "even a rat will fight" — and the noisy irregulars clamoring for Roosevelt redux. He had more than politics on his mind. In March 1911, the *Tribune* directors named him acting president, pending the recovery of his brother or the designation of a permanent replacement to fill the fourth-floor office once occupied by Robert Patterson.

McCormick's new position paid no more than his job as treasurer, but it did engage his legal skills in devising an expansive program of employee benefits. Over time these would grow to include generous annual bonuses and pensions, homeownership loans at favorable rates from a company credit union, free medical care and dental checkups, liberal vacations — even false teeth provided to loyal employees at no cost. Members of the *Tribune* family who were about to get married received a chest of silver, compliments of McCormick. For sleepy-eyed workers condemned to the dogwatch shift, there was plenty of free coffee to ease their labors. Such largesse went a long way toward cementing the allegiance of the paper's personnel.

Later critics would call McCormick inconsistent for showering benefits on his workforce while deriding the New Deal for attempting to provide for workers on a far smaller scale. But his actions were *voluntary*, the Colonel replied, sincere proof of his paternalistic regard for the *Tribune* fraternity. He, no less than Uncle Sam, would offer security to his dependents, but it would be on *his* terms. Anything else threatened not only his personal supremacy at the *Tribune* but his carefully nurtured image as a corporate patriarch.

Once, at the height of the Great Depression of the 1930s, the Colonel decided to eliminate the Christmas bonus, which had endeared him to employees for whom he otherwise seemed as remote as the Dalai Lama. Not economics but psychology dictated the move. The workers had come to take his annual gift for granted, said McCormick. Better to skip a year, he reasoned, thereby preserving dividends while reminding everyone who was founder of the feast.

✧ 4

Through his sledgehammer attacks in the Chicago press, William Randolph Hearst had helped to drive McCormick from public office. Beginning in the spring of 1911, the *Tribune* president got his revenge. The humorist BLT enjoyed a joke at Hearst's expense by rewriting the Doxology, not forgetting to include in his ironic hymn of praise the unsavory Hearst lieutenant Andy Lawrence:

> Praise Hearst, from whom all blessings flow!
> Praise Hearst, who runs things here below.
> Praise them who make him manifest —
> Praise Andy L. and all the rest.
>
> Praise Hearst, our nation's aim and end,
> Humanity's unselfish friend;
> And who remains, for all our debt,
> A modest sweet white violet.

Failing in bids for the presidency, the governorship of New York, and the mayoralty of New York City, Hearst was reduced to brandishing his fists in a Chicago circulation war that would claim twenty-seven lives over the next two years and leave his once dominant combination of the morning *Examiner* and the afternoon *American* eating the *Tribune*'s dust. As converts to the penny press, all four Chicago morning papers rang up impressive gains, the *Tribune* surging from 174,000 daily copies to 231,000, and the *Examiner* and *Record-Herald* both topping 200,000. Even the perennial doormat, Herman Kohlsaat's *Inter Ocean*, managed to increase its sales from 79,000 to 108,000.

But as the demand for paper soared with circulation, the *Tribune* and its competitors became victims of their own success. Hearst, wielding the clout that came with owning eight newspapers, was able to practice the economy of scale, and not a little restraint of trade on the side, by obtaining newsprint priced at $5 a ton less than what his rivals scrambled to purchase on the open market. McCormick knew that he could never beat Hearst at his monopolistic game. Instead, he hoped to level the field of competition by constructing a paper mill of his own. He wasn't the first to entertain such a scheme; Hearst had threatened to build a mill whenever his suppliers balked at renewing their contracts at rates favorable to his chain. The yellow journalist had gone so far as to carry on an intermittent courtship of the Warren Curtises, father and son, of International Falls, Minnesota, recognized authorities in the papermaking field.

In July 1911, McCormick cut in on the young Curtis, a short, chunky man with an engineer's precision and an encyclopedic knowledge of Canadian timberlands. Canada was the logical site for a *Tribune* mill, as it boasted an abundance of virgin forest and untapped water power. A new tariff law taking effect that summer slashed duties on Canadian newsprint imported to the United States. Still, the obstacles to success were daunting. Distances were vast and settlements sparse, increasing transportation costs and forcing McCormick to build whole towns to service his papermaking operations.

His first Canadian journey took him to Iroquois Falls in northern Ontario, whose natural advantages were more than outweighed by the cost of developing so remote a site. Much more to his liking was the Ontario village of Thorold, conveniently situated on the Welland Canal a mere ten miles from Niagara Falls. His experience with the sanitary district had taught him the benefits of water transport, and more than enough about electric power to appreciate the bargain rates that Warren Curtis was able to negotiate with the Ontario Power Company. Moreover, Thorold was as close to Chicago as any Canadian property was likely to be. An earlier mill there had established a local tradition of papermaking. Although the property lacked adjoining timber limits, nature itself seemed eager to make up the deficiency.

McCormick held fast to his plans, even after the Canadian government refused him a 300-square-mile timber concession; "pulpwood was as plentiful as hay," he insisted. Construction of the new mill got under way in the summer of 1912. For the next two years McCormick subjected Curtis to a barrage of advice, instructions, and anxious inquiries, supplemented by harsh words whenever men or machines fell short of his perfectionist standards. The tension in their relationship was predictable. McCormick was staking $1 million of *Tribune* money on a radical scheme to leapfrog the competition. At the same time, he was gambling on the success of the mill to dispel his lightweight image within his family and validate his claim as the natural heir of Joseph Medill.

Construction fell behind schedule, and skeptics had no shortage of explanations to validate their doubts. Industry veterans called the planned use of electricity to grind wood ruinously expensive. When the resourceful Curtis failed to locate 12,000-volt motors in North America, he found them in Sweden. (The motors were still running forty years later.) He also installed 202-inch paper machines, the largest ever built to that time. A nervous McCormick moved to Thorold and slept on a cot in the unfinished building dubbed "Curtis's Folly." His doubts persisted long after the startup of the first papermaking machine in September 1913. Curtis had rejected the usual steam engines in favor of steam turbines to power the operation. The theory made sense, but theories didn't heat the metal cylinders that carried wet paper. In practice the turbines ran unsteadily. McCormick's resulting criticism was only partly mitigated by compliments for the mill's halftone paper, a high-grade product reserved for illustrated sections of the Sunday *Tribune.*

By the end of the year, with production running far short of forecasts, McCormick was demanding "revolutionary improvements" and threatening a permanent return to Thorold. "This will mean to you what it will mean to me — failure," he wrote to Curtis. "The prospect is revolting. It has never happened to me before" — an interesting commentary on his defeat at the polls three years earlier. They might yet attain their common objective, he told Curtis, but only "if you will key yourselves up to a supreme effort."[23]

The combination of threats and exhortations produced the desired results. In its first year the mill turned a $100,000 profit. McCormick showed his appreciation by designating Curtis president for life of the Ontario Paper Company. After the start of World War I, when newspaper publishers everywhere — Hearst among them — were desperate for affordable newsprint, McCormick's gamble and Curtis's Folly looked prophetic indeed.

✧ 5

For all their achievements north of the border, McCormick and Curtis hardly surpassed the contributions of the *Trib*'s circulation manager, a junk peddler's son from Koenigsburg, East Prussia. Growing up in a tough, mostly Irish neighborhood on Chicago's West Side, Max Annenberg endured the taunts of an Irish gang leader who stood outside the

Annenberg family delicatessen and notion store and shouted, "Sheeney, get me a sausage." The bullying went on until the day that his father put in a stock of baseball bats. Instead of a sausage, young Annenberg's tormentor received a bone-crushing blow from Max's brother, Moe, who crept up on him from the rear.[24]

Standing at the corner of 12th and Wabash, Max learned that force, occasionally modified by discretion, held final sway in the brutal world of Chicago journalism. While still an adolescent he worked in the publicity department of the Columbian Exposition, quickly rising to become circulation manager of the fair's newspaper. As soon as the White City passed into history, he found employment as a home delivery canvasser for the *Tribune*, which under Robert Patterson bribed potential subscribers with atlases, clocks, lamps, and 200,000 Bibles. Gains in circulation were maintained by subsidizing successful carriers. The cost of the system was offset by its stability, at least until the arrival of William Randolph Hearst demolished the status quo.

Himself something of a one-man wrecking crew, Hearst knew the value of having on his payroll a few salesmen who were not above communicating the virtues of the *Chicago American* with their fists, blackjacks, or baseball bats. He took an immediate fancy to Max and Moe Annenberg. Then he took them away from the *Tribune*. In the first years of the new century, Max scaled the ladder from solicitor to verifier, branch manager, and finally circulation manager.

Along the way he heard Andy Lawrence boast of his intention to pour down Medill McCormick's back in hot lead every nickel earned by the hated *Tribune*. Lawrence tried to make good on his threat by enlisting other publishers in a 1907 campaign to prevent the McCormick paper forcibly from reaching the streets. Gunmen hijacked *Tribune* delivery trucks and dumped their contents into the Chicago River. Burly sluggers recruited by Max Annenberg intimidated newsstand dealers. Protesting carriers were beaten to a pulp. Medill McCormick responded by pressing charges of conspiracy against both Annenbergs, Lawrence, and the gravely respectable Victor Lawson. For a few years there was peace on the streets of Chicago.

Then came the great price war of October 1910, initiated by Lawson. This time the *Tribune* was more than ready. Even as Bert McCormick chased after the paper's trustees in Europe, Keeley snatched Max Annenberg back from the Hearst organization by promising him $20,000 a year and bonuses graduated to reflect increases in circulation. That Andy Lawrence should sue his former star for breach of contract came as no surprise. That he should lose was much less predictable. But lose he did; the court ruled that since the Annenbergs had originally been hired by Hearst to perform illegal acts, their contracts were invalid.

Lawrence speedily assembled a guerrilla army led by the Gentleman brothers, Gus, Dutch, and Pete, to replace the force Max took with him to the *Tribune.* Early casualties of the renewed fighting included Dutch Gentleman, shot to death in a saloon by an Annenberg lieutenant, Mossie Enright. Dutch was barely cold when Lawrence telephoned an unsubtle threat to run Keeley out of town, and the faithful Max was assigned to learn what Hearst's master blackmailer might have on him. (As Colonel McCormick told it, Keeley's vulnerability lay in his early, long-concealed marriage to a black woman.)

While the executive suite maneuverings played out, street warriors on both sides wrecked newsstands and busted heads. Among Chicago newspapers, only the *Daily Socialist* reported what everyone knew and the so-called press trust refused to admit — that the city was witnessing a dress rehearsal for the much larger gang wars of the 1920s. The violence escalated throughout 1911. Wayward gunfire riddled innocent bystanders, but since all major papers continued to observe a news blackout, public outrage was muffled. Speaking to a Senate committee looking into lawlessness as personified by Senator Lorimer, Jim Keeley casually acknowledged a violent confrontation inside the *Tribune* building itself; the exchange of shots continued even after one goon was tossed down an elevator shaft.

With a revolver in one hand and his commission as a deputy sheriff in the other, Max Annenberg roamed the battle zone dressed in his trademark red sweater and soft cap. He beat the rap in the kidnapping of a Hearst newsdriver. He won again, this time with the help of McCormick's law firm, after wounding a rival gunman who had tried to hijack his car. Hearst and Lawrence had confidently embarked on their campaign of intimidation under the jaunty slogan "Exit *Tribune,* Enter *Examiner.*" As the months went by, however, it was Keeley and not Lawrence who was winning the battle for Chicago readers.

He had no wish to invite trouble, McCormick told his mother, but having concluded that the fight against "Hearstism" must be made, he was pleased with the results. "Not only has the standing of the Hearst papers been affected, but these papers themselves have sued for peace. I believe this is the first time that has happened."[25]

❖ 6

In the long run, the strong-arm tactics of Max Annenberg proved less important than this systematic reorganization of the way the *Tribune* sold itself. Pre-Annenberg subscribers were still being wooed with floor rugs and illustrated histories of the Spanish American War. "We gave away everything from clocks to Kotex," recalled Louis Rose, Max's brother-in-law and his successor as the *Tribune*'s circulation manager. (A brilliant salesman, Rose was credited with the axiom that in street sales, what attracts readers is the news above the fold of the paper.) Annenberg overhauled the paper's distribution network, assigning exclusive territorial rights to the most competent dealers and subsidizing promising carriers until their routes turned a profit.

In another departure from industry norms, the *Tribune* touted the power of advertising and set forth its own claim to being the premier marketplace of the Midwest. "Some papers can sell toothpicks and some can sell flat buildings," said Annenberg. "We can sell anything." On McCormick's watch, the *Tribune* established new copy, art, and merchandising service departments to bolster its appeal to retailers. In 1912 it pioneered with the "Business Survey," an early attempt at market research designed to win over skeptical admen. An "Investor's Guide" followed two years later. During this same period the *Tribune* implemented strict codes governing financial advertising and the promotion of medical cures.*

Max Annenberg had definite theories about what attracted newspaper readers (his favorite headline: DOUBLE MURDER AND SUICIDE). Evening papers, he argued, with their additional features and regular helpings of fiction, enjoyed an advantage over their skimpier morning counterparts. Together with Keeley, he devised "Friend of the People," a column that took the role of ombudsman in holding those in public office accountable for their behavior. An Anti-Loan Shark Bureau was launched in 1911; soon the *Tribune* was drawing 3,500 letters a week from readers seeking help or information.

The success of such novelties inspired imitators — beginning with Joe Patterson. "Did you get my letter suggesting legal bureau?" he wrote to McCormick in December 1911 from London, where he had fallen under the spell of British tabloids. Untangling the legal problems of *Tribune* readers, Joe maintained, would be no more than a logical extension of Lillian Russell's beauty counseling or the "How to Keep Well" department entrusted to Dr. William Evans, a former Chicago medical commissioner. As ever alert to the commercial possibilities of public controversy, the "devilish restless" Patterson proposed that the *Tribune* hold a symposium on female suffrage. He also offered to introduce his bachelor cousin to "a peace suffragette" by the name of Inez Milholland the next time McCormick happened to be in New York. "You ought to take a good long look at her

---

*McCormick's assertion that he was instrumental in a national ad campaign might best be taken with a grain of salt, since he also claimed responsibility for the Lorimer fight while distancing himself from the roughhouse tactics employed in the 1910–12 circulation war. The latter he dismissed in a single sentence of his memoirs. In 1936 he admonished his former employee and frequent critic George Seldes that the street battles had occurred "before I was with the *Tribune.*" This overlooked the awkward fact that he was president of the Tribune Company throughout the fight, having attended directors' meetings as early as May 1910.

whether you listen to her or not," he concluded. For his part, McCormick took strong exception to "the tea party element" invading the masculine realm of politics. Bolstered by his recent slugging match with state's attorney Maclay Hoyne, he told Keeley in September 1913, "Government in the last analysis must be by force, and the feminist influence, however expressed, can only influence and never control."[26]

For less militant female readers, the *Tribune* distributed thousands of copies of booklets with titles like "How to Fight the Increased Cost of Living" and "One Hundred Ways to Earn Money at Home." Patterson assumed full control of the Sunday paper after its editor, William Handy, fled to South America to avoid alimony payments. Soon *Tribune* readers were being treated to serializations based on films running in local theaters. Amateur sleuths were offered prizes ranging from $50 to $5,000 for solving mysteries like *Adventures of Kathleen* and *Diamond from the Sky*. Within two years, the Sunday *Tribune* had left Hearst's *Examiner* in the dust.

McCormick's position with the *Tribune* had never been stronger. If his belatedly voted salary of $5,000 — doubled in the spring of 1913 as the Canadian mill project took off — was something less than princely, it was adequately presidential. William Beale's wings had been clipped. A vigorous new business manager, William H. Field, had been turned loose to work his promotional magic free of Keeley's oversight. As the dividend checks rolled in, even Kate McCormick began to see her sons in a different light.

Once the runt of the litter, Bert now became her "Dearest Lamb . . . a dear sweet boy," who must nevertheless remain vigilant against the cunning Pattersons. Under no circumstances, for example, should he hint at plans for a new *Tribune* building on Cass Street, since Nellie would oppose the scheme tooth and nail if she thought it advantageous to the McCormicks. "Don't tell that blab Medill either," Kate wrote. "We will just keep that idea to ourselves." In the end, more than a decade would pass before McCormick broke ground on "the world's most beautiful office building," at a location carefully chosen to dominate the sleek new Chicago born on Daniel Burnham's drawing table.[27]

✧ 7

The fact that 1912 was shaping up to be a Democratic year in no way discouraged the *Tribune* from its customary practice of anointing Republican presidents. The paper held a low opinion of Taft's political skills and reelection chances. In this it was hardly alone. "In Chicago, at least, the public is unanimous for Roosevelt," McCormick wrote to his

Aunt Nellie at the start of February. Of course, overwhelming popular support meant little so long as grassroots Republicans were shut out of the nominating process by party bosses.[28]

Hoping to short-circuit the Taft machine, the *Tribune* pressured Governor Deneen to call a special session of the Illinois legislature for the purpose of enacting the state's first presidential primary law. The wary Deneen conditioned his approval on public assurances of support from two thirds of the legislators. Rising to the challenge, the *Tribune* polled each lawmaker. On March 22 it published a front-page list containing the requisite number of state senators. Within forty-eight hours a similar majority in the lower house had been corralled. Thus reassured, Deneen signed the hastily prepared legislation, and on April 9 Illinois Republicans heartily endorsed the old Rough Rider.

Two months later, a thousand GOP delegates assembled in Chicago for a political bloodletting described by the *Tribune* humorist Mr. Dooley as a combination of the Chicago fire, Saint Bartholomew's massacre, the Battle of the Boyne, the life of Jesse James, "and the night iv th' big wind." Representing Illinois on the pivotal credentials committee, McCormick was called upon to help decide the fate of hundreds of contested delegates. The committee heard evidence in an atmosphere that was anything but judicious. For four tedious, frustrating days the debate raged, punctuated by a walkout of Roosevelt supporters who were furious over an attempted gag rule and other bullying tactics employed by the party establishment.

From first to last a Roosevelt man, McCormick could find little to distinguish Taft's managers from the heavy-handed Gray Wolves who dominated city hall or the jackpotters of Springfield. He joined thirteen other members of the minority in an unsuccessful appeal to the full convention. Taft's victory was sealed when he was awarded all but 19 of the 254 disputed delegates.

"To men of conservative thought and particularly men greatly interested in the present distribution of wealth, some of the Roosevelt leaders may have seemed radical," McCormick conceded afterward. "But to men whose moral sense had not been deadened, the extremists on the Taft side must have been sickening." As far as he was concerned, the old guard was guilty of nothing less than "a conspiracy to dominate the Republican party by fraudulent means for dishonest purposes."[29]

But that was in October 1912. His immediate response had been more equivocal. At first McCormick denied reports that he was considering bolting the party. Within ten days, however, convinced that the Progressive movement was rapidly gaining momentum, he stood upon TR's Sagamore Hill porch and declared flatly that Taft could not carry Illinois.

One week after his Sagamore pilgrimage, the reluctant rebel faced death in, of all places, a polo field in suburban Lake Forest. Five hundred onlookers saw McCormick suddenly break from a group of players in mid-field and dash after the ball. Attempting a quick turn, the oversize contestant was hurled from his mount. Briefly pinioned under his pony, his leg and ankle badly wrenched, he called for another horse and resumed play. Not until the start of the last quarter, unable to ride any longer, did he consent to leave the field. Soon after blood poisoning set in; for months McCormick walked with a noticeable limp.

That fall's campaign was fought on no less treacherous ground. In politics as in polo, events were in the saddle. McCormick became the chairman of a self-constituted Committee of One Hundred good-government Republicans torn between their party allegiance and Roosevelt's magic. As such, he walked a fine line between Progressives such as Charles Merriam, the Northwestern professor and alderman who had narrowly lost his 1911 bid for mayor, and Harold Ickes, a student agitator turned reporter, whose cranky passion for reform outstripped his loyalty to any candidate or party, and more orthodox Republicans, who hoped to elect the full GOP slate in Illinois notwithstanding the national party split. When Taft visited Chicago that September, McCormick was conspicuously absent from the welcoming committee. Instead, the president of the *Tribune* took the occasion to blast "corruptionists" in his party's high command whose brazen thievery had destroyed Taft's chances for a second term.

On election day, Roosevelt swept Chicago and its suburbs — *Tribune* country — only to be buried under heavy downstate majorities for Woodrow Wilson. Not all the news was depressing. Among the twenty-four Progressives elected to the Illinois legislature was Medill McCormick. By an odd turn of events, the McCormick brothers appeared to have swapped careers. That the *Tribune* had fully recovered from its flirtation with the Bull Moose became clear when Jim Keeley proposed to make TR the paper's new editor-in-chief. McCormick and Patterson rejected the notion, a clear signal of their own interest in running a newspaper hitherto viewed as Keeley's private domain.

With the money they saved by not hiring Roosevelt, the cousins bought a hugely successful new comic strip, "The Katzenjammer Kids," to add to their growing stable of popular Sunday features. In its first week, the heavily promoted strip produced a circulation gain of 24,000.

❖ 8

No less indentured to scandal than Hearst and his imitators, the *Tribune* grew fat on the social and political conflicts of the age. Little in the paper's news columns, however, could exceed the flamboyantly self-destructive behavior of its ruling families. One night in August 1913, Medill

McCormick stepped off a moving train as it chugged slowly across upstate New York; he was jailed on a charge of public intoxication. William Hale Thompson, a future mayor of Chicago whose hatred of the McCormick family was fully reciprocated, told an audience at the Chicago Athletic Club that the unfortunate Medill should not be censored for his "beastly habits," since "he got them honestly as a birthday present. *It's in the blood.*"[30]

Soon after this embarrassing episode, Kate McCormick demonstrated once and for all that she was beyond embarrassment. "I've got the most astonishing piece of news for you," she wrote to Bert from the Virginia countryside, where her invalid husband had taken temporary refuge from his Swiss doctors. The continuing decline of Ambassador McCormick, variously ascribed to sunstroke, hardening of the arteries, or alcoholic excess, had finally and conclusively been diagnosed as "softening of the brain caused by syphilis!" Kate confessed to "great relief" over the doctors' findings, believing they removed the congenital curse of insanity introduced to the McCormick blood by Bert's grandfather William. In her husband's shame was to be found her sons' freedom.[31]

Bert was less easily persuaded. Having listened since childhood to maternal warnings of incipient madness, he had come to view himself, subconsciously at least, as a loser in the tangled lottery of heredity. Reinforcing this conclusion was the reckless conduct of a family that lived ravenously and without caution. It was no accident that when McCormick, at the age of thirty-four, proposed marriage, it was to a childless divorcée of forty-two, unlikely to extend the McCormick line or to mother anyone besides a husband starved for maternal affection.

Putting aside dynastic ambitions, McCormick immersed himself in his work at the *Tribune*. After three years on the job, the stopgap president was beginning to cast a shadow. In May 1913, Secretary of State William Jennings Bryan came to seek his help at a time of grave peril for the untested Wilson administration. Elected on a platform of domestic reform, the first Democratic president since Grover Cleveland found himself unexpectedly wedged between the foreign millstones of Japanese immigration and the racist fears it stirred on the West Coast and seething unrest in Mexico which might at any moment spill over into the American Southwest. Adopting a statesmanlike tone that no doubt would have astonished later *Tribune* readers, McCormick assured Bryan that as far as he was concerned, partisanship stopped at the water's edge. (Of course, one could hardly expect Joe Medill's grandson to forgo entirely this first opportunity to lecture a president on the conduct of U.S. foreign policy. McCormick's demand, voiced privately to Secretary Bryan, for "a strong attitude" toward revolutionary Mexico foreshadowed forty years of editorial truculence.)[32]

McCormick denied to *Editor and Publisher,* the industry bible, that he held a controlling position at the *Tribune.* For humorous confirmation he cited the case of a Chicago meat packer named Ira Nelson Morris, recently designated as U.S. minister to Sweden. Morris was terrified that the American press, by revealing his common origins as a butcher, might scuttle his diplomatic career before it began. He took his problem to McCormick, who helpfully directed his managing editor to prepare a story extolling Morris's Harvard schooling, his more recent affiliation with the First National Bank, and his generous support of the Chicago Civic Opera and the Art Institute. The final text, carefully reviewed by McCormick and his editor, was pronounced admirable. Only one oversight marred their textbook collaboration — no one thought to alert the headline writers to the special circumstances surrounding the story, with the result that Morris and several hundred thousand other Chicagoans first read of his triumph via a front-page *Tribune* banner proclaiming PORK PACKER APPOINTED MINISTER.

Although McCormick still had much to learn about newspapering, no one questioned his energy or dedication. He developed early the habit of crowding two workdays into twenty-four hours. During the day he kept office hours, dictating editorials, issuing instructions to the *Tribune*'s papermakers and advertising force, discussing the intricacies of pressroom conveyors and wet presses with Max Annenberg. His evenings often began with a game of racquets followed by dinner or a visit to the theater with Joe Patterson. McCormick rarely saw a production through to completion; he once walked out during the first scene of *Romeo and Juliet* after declaring to his chauffeur in a booming voice, "Come on, Bill, I saw this play in college." Around midnight he returned to the *Tribune* to observe the birth pangs of the country edition. He ended his day on the loading platform at two in the morning, as thousands of freshly printed *Tribune*s were stacked on wagons for distribution throughout the sleeping city.

It was an exhausting, exhilarating, yet incomplete life for a thirty-two-year-old bachelor, alone and brooding over the ache and promise of his guttering youth. Home was an alien concept to McCormick, for whom childhood memories of Cass Street and Wheaton had long since been blotted out by a troubadour existence passed in the houses of friends and a dreary succession of clubs. In the summer of 1913, he found and furnished an apartment in the Pullman Hotel on Michigan Avenue. The reason behind this latest move says volumes about his stunted emotional life and a vacancy of the heart that no newspaper could fill.

It was too much to ask McCormick meekly to accept a loveless middle age, much less to repeat the mistake Joe Patterson had made of entering into a marriage as empty as it was respectable. Even so, few in his circle would have predicted the affair that was about to scandalize proper

Chicagoans and leave McCormick an outcast in the clubby, complacent North Shore society he frequented.

The charge had a long fuse. It wound back to the summer of 1905, when the newly elected alderman McCormick had begun paying visits to the Tower Court residence of his cousin Ed Adams. In short order he had made himself a more or less permanent houseguest, as much a part of the domestic routine as the corner chair in the living room that the Adamses set aside for him. Here each evening McCormick enjoyed a ritual whiskey and soda with Ed and his handsome, accomplished wife, Amy.

Behind their facade of compatability, Ed and Amy were strung on different wires. Unsuccessful in his brokerage business and fond of the grape, Ed Adams covered his failings as a provider by clinging to the tattered remnants of aristocratic pretense. Before long, McCormick was advancing his cousin regular sums of cash to help defray household expenses and to gratify the expensive tastes of Mrs. Adams.

"Amy liked to live high," recalled Ruth Roberts, a frequent visitor to the Adams household, "and they had a house in Lake Forest, and she rode." Indeed, Amy was considered one of the finest horsewomen on the North Shore by the discerning judges of the tony Onwentsia Club, where she was a stylish regular. In contrast to her husband, she came by her elitest claims naturally: as the daughter of General Bernard J. D. Irwin, a renowned Indian fighter and the first recipient of the Congressional Medal of Honor, she boasted the bluest of military blood. Much of her childhood had been spent in Europe, where she attended classes in Dresden and pressed flowers in the Swiss Alps. Later she studied painting under a Spanish master. Her portrait of her adored father, the "Fighting Doctor" who had made medical history by pitching a hospital tent on the field at Shiloh, later hung in the Washington office of the surgeon general.[33]

In 1893, Amy and her family moved to Chicago. Two years later she married Ed Adams. He was thirty-five on his wedding day, his bride just twenty-three. A decade passed. It became evident that the Adams marriage had been made somewhere other than heaven. By the time Bert McCormick first laid eyes on her, Amy was no longer the celebrated beauty of her youth, but she was far from dowdy. Still slender in her mid-thirties, she had an aura of quiet distinction, what a more colloquial generation would term *class*. This was enhanced by her pale ivory complexion, generous mouth, and a bell-like voice that some called musical and others thought affected. Eight years older than the houseguest she addressed as RR, Amy appeared more sympathetic than sensual.

To the casual observer she seemed an unlikely object of passion. Yet Amy's maternal qualities — qualities still attested to by family members and friends with long memories — may have sparked interest in a suitor whose coldly indifferent mother had left him forever seeking a substitute.

Above all, it was Amy's vulnerability as a woman held against her will in a failing and abusive marriage that appealed to the *gallant* in McCormick, for whom the tug of emotional need was both novel and flattering.

By this time noted chiefly for his ability to consume twelve cocktails before dinner, Ed Adams was unable to satisfy either his wife's emotional requirements or her material desires. He had to endure the hovering presence of his virile cousin, whose swashbuckling career in politics and journalism contrasted so sharply with his own alcoholic decline. Yet to outsiders, Bert, Ed, and Amy formed a seemingly contented ménage, dividing their time between the Tower Court apartment and a small farm in Lake Forest.

By the summer of 1909, both of the Adamses had become dependent on their guest; one had become romantically attached to him as well. According to court papers, Amy's relationship with McCormick turned adulterous in the first week of August. In fact, the cuckolded husband was late to acknowledge conduct that to more observant (or less bloodshot) eyes appeared flagrant. That July, for instance, found Kate McCormick wringing her hands over "poor poor Bertie! I can't get over his moral deterioration caused by a bad woman. A frank, candid soul has become sly, tricky, furtive and untruthful."[34]

Kate had in mind a vastly more suitable candidate when casting the role of her daughter-in-law: dignified, wealthy Marion Deering, whose father had sold his interest in Cyrus McCormick's International Harvester for $21 million. Bert, unimpressed by Miss Deering, her fortune, or her family connections, continued his high-risk affair with Mrs. Adams. Kate was furious. Her son was "clogging his life and his future," she wrote, "and bringing shame on me." Fearsome words these, hinting at the social ostracism and financial ruin sure to befall McCormick unless he broke off his relationship with Ed Adams's fortune-hunting wife.[35]*

Though jaundiced, Kate's assessment of Amy was not entirely fanciful. In addition to having undoubted charm, intelligence, and refinement, Amy was a determined woman who saw little future in being the wife of a hopeless drunkard. Ruth Roberts described a visit to Marshall Field's department store during which Aunt Amy fell in love with a toast-colored sailor's hat garnished with a white-and-black ribbon bow. "I'd like to buy

---

*So why not terminate the affair? As so often with McCormick, the most plausible explanation is implausible: while he had no intention of marrying Amy Adams (at least, not in 1910), he hoped with her help to create a domestic order, however unorthodox, in place of the misery and abandonment he had experienced under his parents' roof. Through the years the pattern would repeat itself with embarrassing frequency, a twentieth-century Restoration comedy starring McCormick and the various married women of impeccable social standing to whom he attached himself, all the while giving money or employment to his favorite's long-suffering spouse.

that," she told a store clerk, who apologetically explained that the hat was not for sale. "No," Amy persisted, "I have to have that hat." She carried her demand to the nearest floorwalker, and then to a buyer. Eventually she stood face to face with Field himself.

"How do you do, Amy?" said the courtly merchant. "What can I do for you?"

"Marshall, I want that hat."

"You shall have that hat."

Soon after, a smiling Mrs. Adams sailed home with her newest acquisition safely tucked away on the front seat of her victoria.[36]

Robert McCormick was less easily acquired, but if another story told by Ruth Roberts is to be credited, even he could not hold out forever against a protracted emotional siege. One evening at Tower Court, Amy interrupted a quiet dinner *en famille* by blurting out what had long been festering in her thoughts. "Edward, I want a divorce," she announced. "I am going to marry Robert." No one was more startled by this *cri de coeur* than the intended bridegroom, who nearly fell out of his chair. It would be hard to imagine a more effective — or crueler — way of forcing a reluctant lover's hand.[37]

In November 1913, Ed Adams moved out of his Lake Forest house. North Shore society pelted Bert and Amy with epithets like *home-wrecker* and *adventuress.* Nellie Patterson took a different tack. "Who could live with Ed Adams without trying to get away?" she asked, her sympathy for the beleaguered couple not unmixed with satisfaction over the latest humiliation visited upon her sister.[38]

Amy filed for divorce in February 1914. Her feckless husband, encouraged to expect a generous settlement in return for his silence, made no defense against courtroom allegations of habitual drunkenness. On March 6, after a hearing of less than an hour's length, Mrs. Adams gained her release. Under Illinois law she would be free to remarry within a year. McCormick hoped for a cooling-off period of up to two years, during which Amy might travel abroad while he finalized monetary arrangements with his cousin. Needless to say, so reasonable a plan was unlikely to pass muster with either of the two warring women in his life. With Amy between husbands, so to speak, and feeling more vulnerable than ever, Kate McCormick was willing to use any weapon, including the threat of disinheritence, to make her love-besotted son come to his senses. "That old tart shall never have a cent of mine," Kate stormed, "nor a *stick*, nor a *shred, living* or *dead.*"[39]

Coolly, McCormick took stock of his situation. His pursuit of Mrs. Adams might cause pained expressions among the *Tribune*'s shareholders, but their moral outrage was bound to be muted in the face of newfound corporate harmony and record profits. The board of directors would think twice before dissolving the paper's present winning team, he reasoned, particularly if it meant the return of his unstable brother as stage-managed by Kate. What he needed most was an ally, preferably one who needed him as well.

So he turned to Joe Patterson. The two men were as different as chalk and cheese, but their common interests outweighed their ideological divergences. As long as they maintained a united front and the *Tribune* continued to prosper under their joint leadership, both were safe. Kate McCormick might disown her son, but she could not unilaterally dismiss him from the *Tribune*. Nellie Patterson and the minority stockholders would see to that.

Traditionally, the so-called Iron-Bound Agreement drafted by Bert and Joe in the spring of 1914 has been portrayed as a simple act of friendship, impulsively drawn up on a scrap of newsprint and signed by two cousins, neither of whom imagined that in affixing his name with a grease pencil he was chartering the modern *Tribune*. The reality was more complicated. "The Iron Bound Agreement Lasts Until We Both Are Dead," McCormick scrawled at a time when his mother was threatening dire consequences if he married "his tender old tart." The compact served as a declaration of mutual loyalty at the same time it served as Bert's declaration of independence from the domineering Kate McCormick.

◆ 9

An Eden without Eve: so the uninhabited forests of Quebec must have seemed when McCormick, anxious to resolve the *Tribune*'s chronic paper supply problem, crossed into Canada in the first days of May 1914. Before returning to Chicago, he would inadvertently lay the foundation for an enduring *Tribune* legend, a combination of freakish coincidence and artfully edited truth meant to contrast his own cool-headed decisiveness with the treachery of Jim Keeley. Embellished through repetition, enshrined in official histories, and given a final gloss in McCormick's radio memoirs of the 1950s, the story of betrayal and quick-witted response says more about corporate myth-making than it does about either protagonist at a geniune turning point in *Tribune* history.

At the time, both McCormick and Keeley were practicing deception to gain a business advantage. Told of a promising timber limit in the remote countryside around Ha Ha Bay, some two hundred miles north of Quebec City, McCormick arranged to slip unannounced into the tract from a wayside freight station. To ensure secrecy he told no one but Keeley of his plans. His traveling party was restricted to the trustworthy Warren Curtis and one other companion. In the event, Curtis's loyalty surpassed his physical endurance; after a few days of trying to keep up with McCormick's long-legged strides across the crunching snowpack, his body rebelled.

Back in Chicago, meanwhile, Jim Keeley was preparing for a shorter but no less stealthy journey of his own. Late on the evening of May 7 he banged out the final scoop of his *Tribune* career, left the copy in his typewriter, and slipped out of the building that had been his professional home for two decades. Around midnight he strolled over to the nearby headquarters of the *Record-Herald*.

Cut to the Canadian woods, where Warren Curtis has collapsed in the snow and McCormick has sent for a doctor to treat his unathletic friend. The medical man brings with him a French-language newspaper containing the startling intelligence that Keeley, intending to merge the *Record-Herald* with the faltering *Inter-Ocean,* has that very day purchased the former with funds supplied by Sam Insull and other Chicago money men. The news momentarily staggers McCormick. Trapped in the woods a thousand miles from the scene of action, he fears, not illogically, that Keeley may inspire mass defections of *Tribune* men before he can return home to quell the revolt. Adding to his sense of panic — and betrayal — is the fact that Keeley's departure has been carefully timed to coincide with the absence of Joe Patterson, who is off with a contingent of U.S. Marines to occupy the Mexican city of Veracruz.

Visions of disaster spur McCormick to the nearest telegraph station, where he fires off a round of instructions. Leaving Curtis in the good hands of a local physician, he embarks upon a nail-biting return trip to Chicago, forty-eight hours that seem interminable at the time and will not grow noticeably shorter with recollection.

There is, however, another side to the story. For all his apparent dirty dealing, Keeley could claim extenuating circumstances. His financial backers had sworn him to secrecy until the last piece of the money puzzle fell into place. Not until the evening of May 7 did he have the requisite funding in hand. He then wired McCormick at the Château Frontenac in Quebec, revealing his intention to publish a consolidated paper as early as the following week. "Much as I regret to sever my connections with the *Tribune*," he asserted, "circumstances render no other course of action possible."

Only the timing of Keeley's departure could have come as a surprise to McCormick. As early as August 1910 he had warned his penurious mother that unless "liberal provision" were made for the talented editor, "he will inevitably be drawn into some competing publication." Kate had pooh-poohed the suggestion, stubbornly refusing to sell Keeley stock in the *Tribune* or take other steps which, by nailing down his allegiance, might block the eventual return of Medill McCormick. Now, almost four years later, the hens were coming home to roost.[40]

Nellie Patterson's diary tells a very different tale from the one Mc-Cormick unfurled when posing for posterity. In her version, the real heroes of May 7 were Stuart Shepard, McCormick's law partner, and the no-nonsense business manager of the *Tribune*, William Field. As it happened, Shepard was dining at the University Club that evening when he overheard from a fellow member that Keeley was about to jump ship. Hurrying to the corner of Madison and Dearborn, he found no trace of Keeley, save for the self-promoting valedictory still in his typewriter. The lawyer immediately suppressed the evidence, thereby assuring that the news would be released in a way favorable to the *Tribune*.[41]

Field described the atmosphere at the *Tribune* as "serene." If so, it was due in no small measure to his own foresight in obtaining prior pledges of loyalty from Teddy Beck, Max Annenberg, and others essential to the paper's continued success. (With considerable delicacy of expression, McCormick attributed Annenberg's decision to remain at his post to a feeling that "he had been well treated by the *Tribune* in a controversy in which he had been involved" — namely, the murder allegation arising out of the recent circulation war, for which he had been successfully defended by McCormick's law firm.) Marooned in the wilds of Quebec, McCormick was anything but serene. His first reaction to Keeley's treachery had been to obtain a court order prohibiting Keeley from going to work for another paper. Field, a hatchet-faced Yankee from Vermont, took a longer view of the situation: rather than restraining an obviously disenchanted employee from seeking his fortune elsewhere, McCormick should be strewing flowers in Keeley's path. "Any other course would be great . . . mistake and make public think we had received severe blow," Field told him bluntly. Keeley or no Keeley, the future of the *Tribune* had never looked brighter. "Glad to have you return," Field wired his impetuous boss, not wholly convincingly, "but set your mind at rest."[42]

Faced with unanimous opposition from those on the scene, McCormick dropped his injunction scheme. When the revamped *Herald* first appeared one week later, its rival gushed praise for Keeley's "many years of faithful and brilliant work." In a front-page statement, McCormick and Patterson assumed the roles of coeditors and promised that the *Tribune* would continue to be guided by the example of Joseph Medill. Privately, McCormick nursed a lifelong grudge against Keeley, whose contributions to the paper and American journalism generally were all but expunged from *Tribune* histories.

It quickly became apparent that far from crippling the *Tribune*, Kelley had actually strengthened the paper by leaving when he did. Six weeks after he jumped ship, McCormick told his mother, "By getting a lot of new blood in place of the old blood we are printing a better paper than before." The biggest circulation gains came on Sunday. Joe Patterson and his deputy, Mary King, breathed new life into the once stuffy *Tribune* flagship through specially commissioned "Blue Ribbon Fiction," lively features, and irresistible comic strips. Joe envisioned the Sunday *Tribune* as a magazine for the masses, stuffed with the latest movie news and gossip, four-color reproductions of notable paintings housed at the Art Institute of Chicago, and even a department devoted exclusively to "Bright Sayings of Children" (the *Tribune* paid a dollar for each precocious gem turned in by a proud parent).[43]

No Sunday *Tribune* went to press without at least one eye-catching map drawn to Joe's specifications, European battlefields competing for notice with short stories by F. Scott Fitzgerald and the latest adventures of Daddy Warbucks. Mary King, who would become Joe's second wife (but not soon enough to legitimize the birth of their son, James, in 1922), worked just as hard as her lover to dispel the journalistic fraternity's traditional disdain for women's news. At her urging, new departments were added to increase female readership. Fashion writers were encouraged to make their prose rival in snap and humor anything seen on the sports page.

Within the cooperative framework of the Iron-Bound Agreement, McCormick and Patterson followed a natural division of labor. Canadian operations, advertising, accounting, mechanical operations, and general production matters came under McCormick's supervision. This left Patterson free to concentrate his creative energies on news, features, and circulation. The unorthodox arrangement was put to its greatest test on the editorial page, with the cousins alternating control each month. Under McCormick the *Tribune* beat the drums for a deep waterway to the Gulf of Mexico and for military preparedness as the surest antidote to American involvement in wars outside the Western Hemisphere. After thirty days' worth of homage to the Monroe Doctrine and strident abuse of insufficiently patriotic easterners, the paper would veer off course, sometimes violently, to reflect Patterson's preoccupation with the alleged racial advantages enjoyed by German militarism and the need to redistribute American wealth and guard against the proliferation of unearned fortunes by enacting heavy inheritance taxes.

In time the cousins would discover that Chicago was too small to contain both of them, but at the moment the *Tribune* spoke no less authoritatively for having two voices. Despite occasional grumbling about Joe's "fool ideas," McCormick let himself be persuaded of the merits of those Progressive-era totems, the initiative and recall. "I did this to oblige him," he was careful to note, "not because I thought it was a good policy."[44]

Neither man believed the arrangement could last indefinitely. Joe, in particular, had a hankering to sell his wares in New York, that most un-American gateway to the land of *E Pluribus Unum.* In the spring of 1914, McCormick had traveled to Newport, Rhode Island, to sound out James

Gordon Bennett about selling his *New York Herald*. Negotiations were halted by the outbreak of war in Europe. "If war comes it will be the greatest tragedy in the history of the world," justifiable only if it led to the overthrow of continental monarchies, wrote McCormick. His mind was full of fears from another source. "If the yellow people should take the notion to rise against the white what hideous possibilities confront us!"[45]

In response to the June 28 assassination of Archduke Franz Ferdinand, heir to the throne of Austria-Hungary, by a Serbian nationalist, the *Tribune* ran an editorial called "The Twilight of the Kings." Reprinted in hundreds of American papers, it tolled the bell for Old World absolutism and predicted that a new Europe, cleansed of royal tyranny and churchly hypocrisy, would emerge from the crucible of war. "And now I commend you to God," it said, quoting Kaiser Wilhelm speaking on his Berlin balcony to a cheering crowd of subjects. "Go to church and kneel before God and pray for His help for our gallant army."

Other emperors, equally pious in their commands, had also invoked the divine right to send the flower of their nation's youth to do battle, a practice the *Tribune* found reprehensible. "Pray that a farmer dragged from a Saxon field shall be speedier with a bayonet thrust than a winemaker taken from his vines in the Aube; that a Berlin lawyer shall be steadier with a rifle than a Moscow merchant; that a machine gun manned by Heidelberg students shall not jam and that one worked by Paris carpenters shall." Go to church and pray for help, the potentates told their people, "that the hell shall be hotter in innocent Ardennes than it is in equally innocent Hesse; that . . . the name of Romanoff be greater than the name of Hohenzollern."

"The Twilight of the Kings" was McCormick's inspiration. So were colored battle pictures, war maps, and the early organization of a *Tribune* foreign news service. Disregarding these achievements, Kate McCormick chose to see the war as yet another opportunity to restore Medill to his rightful place. On August 5 she angrily wired Joe Patterson, denouncing him for even thinking of going abroad and leaving his cousin Bert in an editorial position for which he had no training. "In this situation, Bertie is much more easily spared than you," she added, lack of confidence in her younger son shading over into indifference as to the dangers he might confront on European battlefields.

Patterson responded that the *Tribune* had done very well under the joint management of himself and Bert, "and I don't hesitate to attribute the major part of this success to him." McCormick reminded his mother that by his actions in 1910, and through the continuing confidence of stockholders "in my ability and my scrupulous integrity," he had prevented the *Tribune*'s sale. "The obligation I then incurred is one of which I cannot divest myself," he added pointedly, notwithstanding the fact that "I am beginning to get a little tired of the beast of burden life." He hoped that events would clarify themselves in a month or two. "If that comes about I do want to get away and see one or more scenes of the great cataclysm."[46]

✧ 10

Late in September 1914, another kind of war exploded on what McCormick had assumed was a quiet front. Refusing to be shed quietly, Ed Adams without warning petitioned a court to reopen his wife's divorce case. He heightened the sensation by slapping his cousin with a $300,000 suit charging alienation of affection. McCormick made things worse, if possible, by countering with a suit of his own, calling in some $38,000 in personal loans made to his hapless cousin between 1907 and 1913. From then on scandalmongers could savor the case of *Adams* v. *McCormick*, Adams's separate application to reopen the pro forma divorce proceedings of March, and McCormick's retaliatory lunge at his cousin in bankruptcy court.

A mortified Kate McCormick accused "that old strumpet" of faking a pregnancy to entrap her son. If only she could separate the witch from the bewitched, perhaps time and distance would cool Bert's unseemly passion. Remembering his earlier, casual expression of interest in the European war, she cast a glance over the maps so prominently featured in the *Tribune.* The European tinderbox offered allurements that would dwarf conventional romance, particularly to an aspiring war correspondent who liked nothing better than dressing up in soldier's garb. Not pausing to consult Bert, she wangled from George Bakhmeteff, the Russian ambassador to the United States and a family friend since the McCormicks' days in Petrograd, an invitation for her son to tour the Russian battlefront "as a distinguished foreigner personally known" to the czar's cousin Grand Duke Nicholas.[47]

McCormick initially showed little enthusiasm for what his Aunt Nellie called "this dubious trip." In October 1914, dissatisfied with British censorship, he sent a protest to Cecil Spring-Rice, his father's old enemy, now the British ambassador in Washington. The American press was losing patience with the false news fed to Yankee reporters by His Majesty's government. "If this feeling on the part of newspapermen becomes fixed," he warned Spring-Rice, "it will result in their taking an antagonistic attitude." He proposed himself as a candidate to join the British army in France. "I was educated for several years in English schools and lived in England during my boyhood," he explained; "hence, I can comprehend the English viewpoint."[48]

Spring-Rice referred McCormick to the American embassy in London. Privately he urged his government to place *Tribune* correspondents James

O'Donnell Bennett and John McCutcheon under surveillance on their return from behind German lines. Beyond this, he continued, British authorities should be exceedingly cautious in their treatment of the Americans. Take Bennett, for example: Spring-Rice told the foreign minister, Sir Edward Grey, that the *Tribune* reporter was anxious to get arrested for publicity purposes. As far as King George's American representative was concerned, neither Bennett nor his *Tribune* employers should be gratified in their self-seeking purposes.[49]

While her son courted English officialdom, Kate McCormick continued pulling strings with the Russian embassy. In preparing for the journey, McCormick found that matters of dress held center stage. "Of course, in addition to my campaign outfit I will take all the clothes necessary to travel *en gentilhomme*," he told Kate. A few days before Christmas, he invited his mother to join him in a visit to the Naval Academy in Annapolis and a tour of the Gettysburg battlefield in Kate's Mercedes. "I want to see a good deal of the army men and learn at least enough to know when and how to salute in my toy soldier's uniform," he wrote.[50]

To enhance his stature in Russian eyes, McCormick sought an honorary commission in the Illinois National Guard. This meant placating Governor Edward F. Dunne, whose tempestuous relationship with the *Tribune* over the years made the Russian czar and the German kaiser resemble Damon and Pythias. "I'll give that bastard McCormick nothing," Dunne reportedly said when first approached on McCormick's behalf, "unless he runs an editorial completely repudiating everything the *Tribune* has said about me." Yet war has a way of recasting even the most intensely felt enmities; suffice it to say that the *Tribune* found previously undiscovered virtues in the Democratic governor, and Dunne showed himself as good as his word.

As his date of departure drew near, McCormick worried that he might disgrace himself on some foreign battlefield. Two years later, writing of his apprehensions at this moment, he turned a clinical eye on the culture that had produced him. Physical courage required training and practice, he claimed, and he was painfully aware that he was "steeped as fully as any other in the cult of cowardice which has been such a distinct feature of modern American thought." The fear never left him. Years later his lawyer and friend Weymouth Kirkland explained McCormick succinctly. "The only thing this guy is afraid of is being afraid," he said.[51]

Early in February 1915, mother and son had an awkward parting at Chicago's Blackstone Hotel. "I didn't cry as I am not the crying kind," Kate wrote of the encounter, "but I feel as if I shall never see him again." Turning her attention to the real enemy, she noted with sour contentment that " 'she' did not go. Because she didn't want to or because he didn't want her I don't know — but I think a separation of six months or a year may have the effect of bringing him to his senses." On February 10, McCormick left New York for London. No sooner had the liner *Adriatic* cleared U.S. waters than he received a wire from his mother notifying him of victory in the bankruptcy suit against Ed Adams.[52]

On February 15, McCormick sent Joe Patterson a message scrambled to conceal its meaning from prying eyes. "Under customary circumstances I would want to hear from you before congratulating you on your engagement," he told his cousin in words Patterson could easily decode. "But as I am beating it for the Russian army and will be short of facilities I will do it now." He arrived in London three days later. On the nineteenth he lunched with the press baron Lord Northcliffe and spent a fascinating hour with Winston Churchill at his Admiralty office. It was the start of a tumultuous relationship that would span forty years, with important consequences on both sides of the Atlantic.

McCormick was less impressed with Prime Minister Herbert Asquith ("political boss type," he wrote in his diary), even after Asquith promised to relax wartime censorship and introduce him to top British diplomats and frontline strategists. On February 27, McCormick crossed the channel to lunch with Asquith's representative in Paris. That same day, as her lover pulled strings for an interview at the French foreign ministry, Amy Adams boarded a ship in New York harbor destined for the British port of Southampton.

6

The Wine of Death

"What is the strange psychology that causes the mind depressed by the sight of wounded men to be cheered by the sound of the cannon that wounded them, the popping corks of the wine of death . . . Is it that, born to die, we have an affinity for what destroys and draw back only when too late?"

— Robert R. McCormick, *With the Russian Army*

FEW MEN exposed to random death in villages cratered by artillery shells would describe their experiences as "funny from beginning to end." Yet that is exactly how McCormick characterized his baptism by fire in the first week of March 1914. French foreign minister Theophile Delcasse, an old friend of his father's, had invited the fledgling war correspondent to visit the stalemated western front, where six months of mechanized terror had produced nearly a million French casualties. Delcasse hoped that by reporting German atrocities, McCormick might stir Americans to intercede before their sister republic was bled white.[1]

McCormick, however, had his own ideas about the war, and they bore little resemblance to official propaganda. Besides, his sense of the ridiculous kept getting in the way of his sense of outrage. By reminding him how quickly a little authority goes to the heads of little men, the war confirmed his harsh view of human nature and the corrupting tendency of power at all levels. Moreover, as a malignant outgrowth of Old World realpolitik, the conflict dispelled any doubts he may have entertained about America's moral and political superiority.

His misadventures began early. In Calais, he was arrested and briefly detained by a petty local official intent on enforcing the French government's ban on journalists visiting the front. After his release, McCormick showed up at the headquarters of British general Sir John French, where his bizarre costume of waistcoat grafted onto army breeches, topped off by an automobile cap, made him, in the wearer's words, "a fine likeness of a racehorse trainer." At dawn on Wednesday, March 3, he climbed into an enormous limousine provided for his comfort by the British commander. A cold drizzle was falling, and the driver of the car was soon coated in mud. At one point on the road to Arras the vehicle skidded, prompting an angry outburst from the general staff officer serving McCormick as tour guide. "It is impossible to control these chauffeurs," he said bristling. "Because they owned the automobiles before the war, they think they own them now."[2]

Sitting comfortably insulated from the elements to which the vehicle's rightful owner was exposed, McCormick laughed out loud at the ludicrousness of the situation. Later in the morning a tire popped, causing him to reflect on how the greatest war in history sounded exactly like the Battle of Gettysburg as reenacted at McVicker's Theater. But as McCormick approached Arras along a three-mile stretch of open highway within range of German artillery fire, his heart pounded, and he abandoned his breezy manner. On the outskirts of town the narrow road ended in a steep downhill plunge. Here the little motorcade halted, and its occupants were herded into a single vehicle — to provide a less conspicuous target for enemy gunners, he was told.

Feeling rather like ducks in a shooting range, McCormick and his party paused long enough for each passenger to put on "the expression I want to be found with." Then the chauffeur turned the car loose. "Hail Columbia," thought McCormick; "after the first half mile no shell could have overtaken us from behind, although we might have bumped into one going our way." "You will not be able to hear the shells coming," said a captain at his side. This was cold comfort to McCormick, for whom stray projectiles suddenly seemed less menacing than a flat tire or a jammed steering mechanism on a vehicle hurtling downhill at over eighty miles per hour.[3]

After the car and its rattled occupants arrived in town unharmed, McCormick was taken to see what remained of the local city hall and cathedral. "They certainly went at them with true German thoroughness," he observed drily. Standing outside a damaged hospital, he felt the shock of an explosion fifty yards away. The continuing bombardment did not preclude an excellent lunch at divisional headquarters nearby. As the visitors broke bread, bayonet-wielding Germans briefly succeeeded in capturing several hundred yards of French trenchworks to their immediate left.

That evening McCormick dined with General Sir John French, a knighted officer addressed by his title, as was customary among the English nobility, rather than his rank. More evidence of British class consciousness came the next day, on the road to Ypres. Neither French's aide nor the volunteer chauffeur knew what to do when McCormick's car broke down. No auto mechanic himself, McCormick nonetheless had the presence of mind to look under the hood and fasten a wire loosened in transit. His journey proceeded without further incident, marred only by the realization that in repairing the vehicle he had suffered a grievous loss of status in the eyes of his hosts, for whom manual labor was inconsistent with the social standing of a gentlemen.

A call on the First Army commander, General Sir Douglas Haig, preceded McCormick's inspection of an airfield crowded with flying machines far more sophisticated than anything known to Americans. What he saw on the improvised runway at Saint Omer inspired him to crusade for a higher state of military preparedness among his pacific countrymen. On a single stormy night, he informed stateside readers, the infant British Air Force had lost more planes than the entire American army possessed. To redress the inadequacy, Congress should fund an army air corps. Lawmakers should also establish a volunteer fleet of private aircraft owners, pledged to maintain their equipment and flying skills according to federally set standards. "Such scientific and patriotic activity would be better for rich men's sons than either adding to or spending father's fortune," he declared. Inevitably there would be fatalities, "but if the American people cannot screw up enough fortitude to face sacrifices of this kind it will before long come under the domination of a people less decadent."[4]

Under a hailstorm of explosives peppering the landscape around Ypres, his own nerve nearly deserted him. Only the fear of inviting ridicule from professional soldiers kept him from running for shelter. "This confession is not pleasant to make," he wrote afterward. "But it is put down with a hope that other boys will be instructed in courage as I never was." McCormick would never learn to enjoy the sound of crashing guns, much less develop urges "to rush into a shower bath of machine gun fire." After his epiphany at Ypres, however, "I never again approached the point of disgracing myself on the firing line."[5]

Or so he claimed. Not the first war correspondent to mask his fears with bravado, McCormick decided that physical courage was like piano playing or polite conversation, something best developed through constant practice. Apparently he was still practicing two and a half years later. In October 1917, as part of the vanguard of American forces who had belatedly answered the call to crush Teutonic militarism, he told a Chicago friend, "There is nothing particularly hard about war except control of fear."[6]

✧ 2

In contrast to the oddly lighthearted tone of his battlefield dispatches, McCormick's private correspondence reeked of melodrama. Coming under fire for the first time had cleared his mind, he informed his mother. "The danger of being killed was larger than I have dreamed of." Moreover, the experience had made him understand as never before "how really trivial were the gossip and scandalmongers" preoccupied by his affair with Amy. If guided by personal desires alone, said McCormick, he would not object to postponing his wedding. But he couldn't forget, nor was he likely to forgive his mother for, the fact "that you were rich and powerful and that in order to blackmail me, an innocent person had been used as a cat's paw and had suffered."[7]

Across the Atlantic, Kate dismissed her son's arguments as "casuistry — pure and simple." Bertie wanted to marry Mrs. Adams. Very well; he must accept the consequences. Kate filed the letter with other documents relating to her will. On March 10, exactly one week after his daredevil ride into Arras, Bert and Amy were married in a brief, nondescript ceremony at the registry office of St. George's Chapel, Hanover Square. In signing the register, McCormick listed his age, thirty-four, and put down his occupation as "journalist." "Amie de Houle Adams formerly Irwin, spinster," was recorded merely as being "of full age."[8]

"All over by 11," the bridegroom jotted in his diary, his mood reflective of the damp, cheerless weather outside. The press was less restrained. "R. R. McCormick Marries Divorcée," reported the *New York Times* in a page-eleven story rehashing the furor over Amy's divorce. Other papers emphasized the embarrassing truth that an Illinois appellate court had yet to rule on the legal challenge raised by Ed Adams to the original decree. (Another ten weeks passed before the suit was dismissed.)

What should have been the happiest event of McCormick's life had degenerated into a clandestine transaction uniting a pair of exiles. The long-term consequences were profound. By turns arrogant and shy, hearty and remote, McCormick concealed his insecurities behind a gruffly formal exterior. His Aunt Nellie thought him "sensitive as a woman." Marriage might have brought him out of his shell. Instead, the humiliations inflicted on him and Amy during their courtship had the paradoxical result of making each lonelier than before. From then on McCormick preferred the company of dogs to people and books to dogs. In later years he used unintentionally revealing words to justify his solitary habits, explaining that "the moment I become friendly with a man he wants me to keep his divorce out of the paper."[9]

✧ 3

In war the law of unintended consequences applies with deadly force. By the spring of 1915 it was obvious that Europe's agony was to be protracted; guessing that the carnage would continue another three years at least, McCormick sent home dispatches with headlines like WANTED: A GENERAL GRANT. Against all expectations, the age of mobility had produced a fixed line of trenchworks extending from the English Channel to the Swiss border. Inside crouched two million men, hollow-eyed victims of boredom, vermin, filth, and constant shelling from unseen batteries. In this terrain of death men and machines fought each other to a draw, yet both were hopelessly outmatched by the porridgelike mud that swallowed up wounded soldiers and starving animals.

British tommies dug in around Ypres sang a mocking tribute to the ghastly indecision of trench warfare:

> I've a little wet home in a trench,
> Where the rainstorms continually drench,
> There's a dead cow close by
> With her feet towards the sky
> And she gives off a terrible stench.

Such jests fell like sparks upon the combustible imagination of Winston Churchill. At their initial meeting in February, McCormick judged the first lord of the admiralty the most aggressive person he had ever met. Consistent with this appraisal, Churchill now hatched a daring scheme to break the military stalemate by sending a British fleet through the Dardanelles, the narrow strait dividing Europe from Asia Minor and leading into Russia's Black Sea. By so doing, Churchill hoped to kick in the door of the tottering Ottoman empire, knock Turkey out of the war, outflank Austria's armies in southeastern Europe, and open a desperately needed supply line to his Russian allies.

It was by a very odd turn of the wheel, therefore, that the anglophobic McCormick — who would later argue that all Rhodes scholars were British spies planted in Uncle Sam's bosom — should spend his honeymoon engaged in cloak-and-dagger activities at the behest of His Majesty's government. His venture into espionage began the day of his wedding. During a visit to the Russian embassy in London, McCormick was entrusted with a box "large enough to sit on." Inside were top-secret naval signal flags, intended to facilitate communications between the British and Russian navies once the allied fleets linked up in the Black Sea. The newlyweds left English waters at daybreak on Sunday, March 14. Torpedo boats escorted their steamer as far as the coast of Portugal. As non–British subjects, they were denied shore privileges at Gibraltar. McCormick retaliated by taking pictures of King George's warships in the harbor through a porthole.[10]

On March 21, the McCormicks docked at Malta, a cream-colored rock rising out of the Mediterranean. Amy attributed the "wonderful physical development" of Maltese beggars to their habit of turning handsprings alongside one-horse shays moving at breakneck speeds. In the Greek isles, she and her husband took up the trail of the mythical Jason and his Argonauts. Amy shuddered over a "horrid little boat" filled with "dirty Greek soldiers and red-bearded Greek priests, the menace of that decadent country." Their hotel in Salonika was redeemed only by an English-speaking porter calling himself Charlie, who had been to Chicago.[11]

Before boarding a train that would carry them across Serbia, where a typhus epidemic had claimed 70,000 victims around the city of Nish, Amy and her butler spent hours looking for alcohol and insect powder. The latter, poured into one's shoes and sprinkled under one's clothing, was supposed to kill the disease-carrying vermin. "Bug powder is one reason to wear khaki," McCormick notified *Tribune* readers with deadpan humor. "They are the same color." Covered from head to foot with the vile yellow substance, the newlyweds were warned by a traveling party of French doctors to sleep in their clothes and wash only in boiled water. Amy hung her head out of the train window to keep from suffocating from the fumes of formaldehyde, a locally favored disinfectant that caused red, burning eyes and aching throats. McCormick thought it discourteous of the Serbian crown prince, who was dining sumptuously in a private car, not to invite the American tourists into the royal quarters for lunch.[12]

A tense encounter pitted McCormick against customs officers in Sofia, the capital of pro-German Bulgaria. "I'm not going to open this box," he vowed, "and you can't open it." He was threatening to appeal to the American ambassador when a uniformed onlooker recognized him as a fellow Northwestern student. Through the timely intervention of his classmate, McCormick obtained permission to leave the quarantine train and spend a couple of days in the Bulgarian capital. The box remained shut. Elsewhere in the station, Amy was befriended by a French-speaking woman curious as to her destination. Grateful to hear a familiar tongue, the unsuspecting bride explained that her husband was to join the Russian army. Her inquisitor thanked her and flew to join a male companion.[13]

On learning of the incident, McCormick upbraided Amy for her loquaciousness. "From that moment forth until we reached the Russian frontier, our lives were made miserable," the new Mrs. McCormick recalled. "We were never able to lose our follower, and not for one moment, waking or sleeping, was that beastly box out of my sight. Changing trains I sat on it. At night I slept on it. If I drove it was placed in the motor or victoria beside me."[14]

At breakfast the next morning in the Hotel Bulgarie, Amy noticed a heavily scarred German occupying the next table. The same menacing figure appeared at luncheon and dinner, always arriving ahead of the McCormicks and waiting to depart until after they had finished their meal. On March 31 the couple left Sofia for Bucharest, Romania. Amy, to her horror, encountered the same blond German in the next stateroom. That night her husband slept with a loaded revolver under his pillow. Twice en route to Bucharest they changed trains in fruitless attempts to shake their pursuer. In Bucharest, officials at the Russian embassy told them that the man shadowing them was only one of 70,000 German spies working the Balkans.[15]

Not until April 2, when they were escorted to a Russian train, could Amy begin to relax. Free at last, she merrily chatted to the dining car waiters in German. A Russian officer advised her against repeating the gesture on penalty of imprisonment. Arriving in Petrograd on the morning of April 5, she was reminded of Chicago in December. No sooner had the couple checked into their hotel than they carted their precious box off to the foreign ministry, where it was handed over to grateful officials.[16]*

At a meeting with Foreign Minister Serge Sazonoff the next day, McCormick listened in amazement as the Russian diplomat knowledgeably analyzed the recent landslide election of Republican William "Big Bill" Thompson as mayor of Chicago. In another, rude reminder of the home front, he was notified that Kate planned to disinherit him because of his marriage to Amy. Only the intervention of Nellie Patterson had secured for him a token legacy of $5,000 a year. Nellie advised her sister to reflect on the melancholy examples of Rob and Medill McCormick before willfully destroying the child she had once called "my *good* boy . . . my *loving* boy."[17]

✧ 4

At one o'clock on the afternoon of April 10, wearing the full evening dress and white tie stipulated by court protocol, McCormick boarded a train for the fifteen-mile trip from Petrograd to Tsarsko Selo,

---

*The subsequent failure of the Gallipoli campaign cost thousands of lives among the Australian and New Zealand troops ordered to assault the beaches and slopes of heavily defended Cape Helles. As chief strategist of the invasion, Churchill was widely blamed for the disaster. Evicted from the war cabinet, his career in a shambles, the discredited first lord was in danger of becoming a historical curiosity, like McCormick's box and the unused signal flags it contained.

"the tsar's village." Here, in an eight-hundred-acre park rivaling Versailles in scale and grandeur, protected by five thousand hand-picked soldiers and Cossack cavalrymen in blood-red tunics, lived the heir to three hundred years of Romanov despotism. An unlikely autocrat, Nicholas II favored the dress and diet of the Russian peasantry (caviar gave him indigestion). Alone among the world's monarchs, he toiled without benefit of a private secretary. It was said that Nicholas avoided the grandiose Winter Palace in Petrograd out of fear of assassination. Just as likely an explanation for the present czar's absence from the capital built upon the Neva marshes by Peter the Great was his disdain for the unabashedly foreign tastes of his towering predecessor.

It was just before one-thirty when McCormick's train pulled into the station at Tsarsko Selo. A gaudy emissary of royalty picked "Mr. Cormick" out of the crowd by his silk hat and led him to a horse-drawn brougham. At the end of a broad tree-lined boulevard lay the imperial compound. Bypassing the two-hundred-room Catherine Palace, McCormick made for the much smaller Alexander Palace, built over a century earlier by Catherine the Great for her grandson, the future Alexander I. On hand to greet the American visitor at the entrance stood Nicholas's court chamberlain, who escorted McCormick through rooms perfumed by smoking pots of incense and brightened with flowers imported from the Crimea to offset the endless northern winter.

In the twenty minutes before his appointment, McCormick catalogued the contents of the royal waiting room: a painting depicting the boyhood of Louis XIV alongside a picture of peasants selling grain; books on hydraulic engineering and military aircraft sharing a tabletop with a jewel-encrusted Fabergé egg; a pair of horse's hooves, one conventionally shod, the other with a sliding joint, guessed by McCormick to be "a humane contrivance which the Czar was investigating." As the clock struck two, a matched set of scarlet-clad officers materialized at one door. McCormick imagined how Marco Polo must have felt at the exotic court of China.

On the far side of the room another door opened. "The emperor is waiting," whispered one of the attendants. McCormick strolled into a room much like the one he had just left. Standing before him was a slight, austerely garbed man of middle age, at five-foot-seven almost a foot shorter than his overdressed visitor. To McCormick he seemed a rather better-looking version of his English cousin, George V, with the largest eyes of any mortal he had ever seen.

"I'm very pleased to meet you, Mr. McCormick." Nicholas flashed a shy, oddly magnetic smile as he thrust out his hand.

The ensuing conversation was brief and entirely conventional. Nicholas inquired about McCormick's father. He expressed pleasure that an

American newspaperman should travel halfway around the world to uncover the truth about the war forced on Russia so unexpectedly. In response to McCormick's inquiry, he offered assurances that his cousin, Grand Duke Nicholas, would grant the foreign journalist access to the Russian battle lines arching 550 miles from the frigid Baltic on the north to the frothing warm waters of the Black Sea.

As they chatted, McCormick was struck by the czar's soft-spoken English, worthy of an Oxford don. The contrast between his baroque surroundings and the mild, unassuming monarch in his olive colonel's uniform, unadorned but for a single medal, did not escape the visitor's notice. Neither did the unpolished knee boots worn by his royal host. After a few minutes, a young girl popped her head into the room to summon her father to lunch. "I am very sorry," said Nicholas, without moving, "I must go now." McCormick, taking the hint, bowed his way out of the imperial presence. Outside, another functionary handed him his hat, coat, and cane. Departing as he came, McCormick did not neglect the substantial tip expected by any coachman who conveys the guest of majesty.

In the restaurant of the train station, unable to read the menu or make himself understood to the waiter, McCormick pointed to four randomly chosen items on the list. The waiter returned with two kinds of caviar, a cheese sandwich, and a bottle of Kvass, a Russian beer. However odd his table fare, McCormick reflected, it was no more improbable than a man wearing white tie and tails at three in the afternoon. A few minutes later he was on his way back to the capital, more amused than awed by his imperial encounter.[18]

✧ 5

Before leaving Petrograd for the front, McCormick wired Joe Patterson in Chicago, "I stick with you," thereby invoking the Iron-Bound Agreement against Kate McCormick. (Kate, distraught, decamped for the luxurious Greenbriar resort in West Virginia, excusing her indulgence by telling Medill, "I've got Bertie's $30,000 to spend!")[19]

Far less comfortable was Stavka, the main headquarters of Grand Duke Nicholas, which McCormick reached late on April 12. Assigned as guide and interpreter to the honorary colonel from Illinois was a hereditary prince of the Kalmuk race, revered as a god by his people. For the next month this youthful divinity would secure McCormick's train tickets, reserve his hotel rooms, and drag around heavy motion-picture equipment without complaint — in stark contrast to the unreliable slacker of a *Tribune* cameraman.

McCormick immediately came under the spell of the fiercely energetic commander-in-chief. Six feet, six inches tall, the fifty-eight-year-old Grand Duke Nikolai Nikolaievich was a whale among minnows. Combining the piety of a holy man with the ferocity of the Russian bear, the czar's cousin reminded McCormick of Henry of Navarre. A lifelong soldier who labored under multiple handicaps caused by his country's primitive rail system and chronic arms shortages, he had somehow managed in the first ten months of fighting to wreck forty years of strategic calculation by the German general staff. His aggressive tactics had forced the nervous Kaiser Wilhelm to divert troops from the western front even as Joffre was rallying his desperate army for a last stand outside the gates of Paris. At Tannenberg, the site of a fifteenth-century battle between Slav and Teuton, Nicholas had lost 110,000 men and declared, "We are happy to have made such sacrifices for our allies."

At this stage of the war he could afford extravagant gestures; in the third week of March 1915, Russian forces seized the Austrian fortress of Przemysl with 120,000 prisoners. More important to an army whose reserve troops were forced to pluck their weapons from the corpses of fallen comrades, the victorious Russians also captured seven hundred heavy guns to turn against the Central Powers. Thus McCormick joined Nicholas at a critical moment in the war. To be sure, Tannenberg had checked the Russian advance in the north. German armies barely twenty miles from Warsaw menaced the Russian center. Yet in the south the czarist forces continued their forward thrust into the Austrian province of Galicia.

McCormick was eager to join the human wave lapping against the craggy, densely forested Carpathian mountain range, which formed the eastern defenses of the Austro-Hungarian empire. The more closely he observed the affable, democratic grand duke, the firmer was his conviction that he had found his General Grant, and that the savage war of attrition being played out in the heart of Central Europe was the Wilderness Campaign of 1864 restaged on a continental scale.

Meanwhile, the object of his hero worship mapped out for his American visitor an itinerary that ran heavily toward German atrocity stories. On April 15, McCormick left headquarters for Warsaw. There he interviewed a Cossack warrior whose ear had been sliced off by his German captors. He also made the rounds of aristocratic houses converted into hospitals, some caring for as many as four hundred soldiers a night. In the skies over the Polish capital, a lone German pilot, formerly a resident of Chicago, conducted daily bombing raids; at night the city shuddered in anticipation of zeppelin attacks. The dull roar of German artillery could be heard above the bustle of Krakowskie Pryedmiescie Street.

The stoic heroism of the Poles moved both McCormicks deeply. In the teeth of the German war machine, elegantly dressed ladies gathered for "war dinners" and endless rounds of bridge, while patrons of the Sportsman's Club dined, heedless of the "baby-killers" dropped from the air. Amy, accompanying her husband on visits to hastily improvised hospital wards, never forgot an English-speaking patient who had once been employed in the steel mills of South Chicago. Assured of a warm welcome if he returned to the States after the war, the soldier replied, "Oh, I can never go back to America." Then he lifted his bedcovers to reveal two stumps in place of legs.[20]

Worse yet was a sheeted figure struggling to breathe. Amy inquired about his injuries, and a nurse rolled back the sheet. "What was a face was a mask of raw flesh with a hole where the nose should have been," wrote Amy, her horror still fresh. Yet the wretched creature was expected to live. McCormick himself nearly fainted while watching an operation being performed. That night he played poker at a fashionable club. The sixteen rubles he won he gave to some soldiers.[21]

With Warsaw as his base, McCormick made excursions to several fronts. (During his absence, Amy volunteered her services as a nurse.) He inspected trenches and rifle pits, interviewed front-line generals, and more than once came under fire. After climbing a stone wall for a closer look at the action, he received a reprimand from Grand Duke Nicholas himself. One "day of days" he traveled west on a road previously rutted by German vehicles. At a whitewashed corps hospital he met the former chairman of the Russian Duma, a grizzled survivor of the Boer War, and his wife, a veteran of Red Cross campaigns in the Balkans and Siberia. Observing a cavalry drill, the naive American forgot everything he had ever learned about the Cossacks from Buffalo Bill. "Nothing but international polo can equal it," he wrote of the wheeling, charging, countercharging lines of blond horsemen astride velvet-mouthed animals of incomparable grace and skill.[22]

In a trench cave, McCormick dined on sardines, canned lobster, and cake. A smattering of rifle fire competed for his attention with peasant tunes squeezed out of an accordion. Two mustachioed soldiers danced together, momentarily oblivious to the bursting shells all around them. "It is my great hour," McCormick told himself melodramatically, "to them only a break in the monotony of trench warfare." After lunch he tempted fate by raising a periscope and attracting fire from German sharpshooters fifty yards away. Thompson, his cameraman, displayed unwonted courage by grinding away at the action his impetuous employer had touched off. At the end of the day, there was water to drink, a welcome alternative to the tea poured down the visitor's throat ever since his arrival in Russia. A regimental band played "My Country 'Tis of Thee." McCormick, unable to convey his emotions verbally, fell back on a vigorous waving of his handkerchief.

On April 22 he left for the Carpathian front. Three days later he looked out on a valley carpeted with the bodies of Russian soldiers. Above him in the distance he could see exposed Austrian positions, vulnerable to artillery fire, yet all but impregnable to bayonet attacks from below. It soon became clear that the Russians lacked the guns to do the job. "Men and shells may be used interchangeably," a Russian corps commander told McCormick. "We have few shells but many men."[23]

That same week, visiting a dormant area of the battlefield, McCormick was surprised by a heavy German bombardment, the prelude to an infantry attack. The assault was halted by withering machine-gun fire a hundred yards in front of the Russian lines. Orders for a counterattack went out. McCormick, mindful of the grand duke's earlier displeasure, followed some distance behind the main advance. Suddenly a German soldier who had been playing dead rose up in his path. The unarmed McCormick froze in his tracks. It soon became apparent that the enemy soldier had no intention of killing him but wished to surrender to him. His Russian hosts found the encounter a source of vast amusement. They assigned their newest prisoner to be McCormick's personal servant.[24]

Returning to Petrograd, McCormick found waiting for him an ugly letter from his mother, their first communication since his wedding. "If a man lies to another, deceives him, betrays his confidence, obtains money under false pretenses — does this not constitute him in the eyes of the world a liar, a drunk and a swindler?" Kate wrote bitterly. "If the victim of such a man happens to be his mother, would it be a mitigating circumstance?"[25]

McCormick's reply was at once accusatory and abject. Had he received her letter while at the front, he told Kate, "I would never have remained alive. Death is very easy in that environment." So fascinated was he by the rhythm of battle that the grand duke had been forced to issue written orders keeping him out of the worst of the fighting "after I had been complimented for bravery." Having thus established his courage, he pointed a finger of blame at his parent, without confronting the gist of her allegations, much less apologizing for his conduct. He had been "sadly aware" of how his marriage to Amy would be received at home, "but you must bear in mind the visit to the front was not of my initiative. But I knew the chance I was taking, which you did not appreciate. If we attack again, draw the Germans from the other front, I will probably be assigned to the Guards corps which you know stopped the Prussians at Warsaw and Grodno." Otherwise, McCormick went on, by the time Kate got his letter he would be en route to England. "Please bear with me," he concluded pathetically, "I cannot live without my Mother's affection."[26]

Unsatisfied with this first effort, five days later he wrote a second appeal. "I am going back to the front again and as usual am feeling depressed. Thank heaven I get over that feeling when in action." Should he be killed in battle, McCormick urged Kate to let Joe run the *Tribune* without interference. "I am phlegmatic and can absorb a lot of jolts. Not so Joe. He would be thrown off his equilibrium and the consequences one way or another would be bad for you." On a more upbeat note, he expressed hope that his writings from the Russian front would help in establishing a national *Tribune* syndicate and that the motion pictures he brought back with him would provide stiff competition for Hearst's newsreel unit. "Anyway I will understand that coming phase of journalism, if" — and here he theatrically crossed out the qualifying word — "when I return."[27]

Such highly colored reminders of a child's mortality would melt most maternal hearts. Not Kate McCormick's. In Newport that summer, she ironically complimented the business acumen of Ed Adams, who "got $80,000 for a worthless antique already pawed over and cast aside by half a dozen very inferior men." In the absence of supporting documentation, the claim remains unproven. But it is clear that McCormick paid dearly for Amy Adams's freedom, both financially and in estrangement from his mother, who now closed her heart to her "poor wrongheaded goat" of a son. Henceforth Kate let it be known that anyone maintaining an acquaintance with "the former Mrs. Adams" would be unwelcome in her house. She took the step to restrict her son's circle of friends to "social outlaws and parasites . . . The proper place for him is the Pacific slope where everybody has a scandal of some kind. Puritan Presbyterian Chicago will 'chew Bertie up.' "[28]

In the end, imagining Bertie lying face down on the Russian earth and aware that his disappearance would open the door to a Patterson-dominated *Tribune*, Kate relented — to a point. Even so, for months she carried on as if there had been a death in the family.

It was all too much for Nellie Patterson. "Have you decided not to have paralysis on account of Amy?" Kate's sister inquired cuttingly. "Palsy, I hear, often develops from worry, and cancer *very* frequently."[29]

❖ 6

It had been McCormick's good fortune during the second half of April to witness the Russian advance at its highwater mark. On May 1 his luck ran out. In four hours that morning, 610 German guns lobbed 700,000 shells into Russian trenches — the opening salvo of a devastating counteroffensive that would chase the Russian army from Galician soil, cost the czar half his military might, and lead to the inglorious sacking of Grand Duke Nicholas. Only ten days earlier these same warriors had been the object of McCormick's lavish praise for their courage, their cavalry, and above all, their stalwart commander.

Denied access to a front that was suddenly anything but static, McCormick spent the first days of May holed up in Petrograd, toiling on his manuscript, which was published later in 1915 as *With the Russian Army*. Not until May 14 was he reunited with his military patron at Stavka. Although much reduced in force and physical vigor, the grand duke remained as considerate a host as ever. He attended a screening of McCormick's war movies and laughed along with everyone else when a Russian toastmaster whose hospitality exceeded his grasp of recent American politics raised a glass at dinner one evening in tribute to the president of the United States — Theodore Roosevelt. "The mistake is not yours but ours," McCormick assured him.[30]

Chafing at his exclusion from front-line action, McCormick persuaded a Russian pilot to fly him over German lines, an idea quickly scotched by higher-ups. By way of compensation he was permitted to visit the massive fortress of Ossowetz at the approach to East Prussia. He went to Ossowetz a skeptic, his doubts fed by the failure of similar installations in the Belgian cities of Liège and Namur to withstand German assault. He came away an enthusiast, so impressed with the location, design, and reinforcement of the fort that he devoted a full chapter of his book to arguing for a chain of Ossowetz-like bastions to protect the American interior should foreign invaders occupy one or both coasts.

McCormick's Russian stay was cut short by a nasty sinus condition, for which no immediate treatment was locally available. Before leaving at the end of May, he said his goodbyes to Grand Duke Nicholas (who told his cousin the czar that the American newspaperman had impressed him more than anyone he had met in months). In Stockholm, McCormick received medication for his inflamed sinuses and took steps toward establishing a *Tribune* bureau in the Swedish capital. Outside Paris he passed word of a desperate shortage of motor transport to Marshal Joffre. In response, Joffre sent a contingent of Belgian mechanics to assist his embattled ally.

McCormick deflected an invitation to see the French army with his own eyes to Joe Patterson, then in Europe making his own survey of the no man's land. Back home, it was apparent that four months of living on a war footing had only whetted his martial appetites. "Life is pretty strenuous in the little city," he wrote to Patterson on August 18. With his Russian war movies playing to full houses in Chicago, he envisioned national audiences being introduced to the World's Greatest Newspaper while thrilling to his personal exploits as the sole American correspondent to visit the eastern front. In practical terms, this meant invading the tough New York market. Unfortunately, he said, "the local producers are treating us in a way that makes me sympathize with the Russian pogram."[31]

His suspicion of New York as an alien place inhabited by hyphenated Americans was fast hardening into obsession. McCormick's frustration was commercial as well as cultural. As for competing with New York's existing journals, "the only way to break in would be with a stick of dynamite as Hearst did." McCormick railed against New York influence in suppressing war news unfavorable to the Wilson administration. He denounced the Associated Press as an eastern mouthpiece, and seemed almost pleased when J. P. Morgan and Company, a detested symbol of Manhattan's financial stranglehold, yanked its *Tribune* advertising to protest the paper's plague-on-both-your-houses attitude toward the European combatants.[32]

Early in September 1915, McCormick received encouragement from the most militant of hawks, Theodore Roosevelt, who praised his reports from England and Russia as "the strongest kind of missionary work . . . I hope you will fight as strongly as you know how for preparedness." TR needn't have worried; within days of his return from Europe, McCormick got himself elected a major in the First Illinois National Guard Cavalry, an elite outfit that supplied its own horses, uniforms, and weaponry. He owed his latest military title to Colonel Milton J. Foreman, in civilian life an obese Chicago alderman whose defective eyesight and impaired hearing inspired few comparisons with Sergeant York. Over the next few months McCormick and the *Tribune* waged a determined campaign to correct America's inadequate defenses, as well as the alleged deficiencies of a national character softened by indulgence and sapped by class and sectional hostility.[33]

McCormick appeared determined to make up in personal belligerence whatever was lacking in the supine Wilson administration and the complacent, unmilitary East. General Leonard Wood, then army chief of staff, invited the war observer to share his views with 12,000 would-be officers assembled at a Plattsburgh, New York, training camp. What McCormick saw at Plattsburgh left him unimpressed. "The one thing they learned," he said of Wood's college athletes, horsemen, and hard-puffing professionals, "was that they did not even know enough to be privates."[34]

With the Russian Army appeared in bookstores that October and received generally favorable notices for its realistic depiction of the Russian theater. It was, however, roundly panned by the *New York Evening Post*, "which seems to be equally hostile to Russia and to me," concluded the author. In his book McCormick adopted the protective stance of a lioness defending her cubs. Recalling his visit to Ossowetz, he urged the construction of massive fortifications at Albany, Buffalo, Pittsburgh, Atlanta, Vicksburg, and Houston, with additional installations guarding strategic mountain passes in the Rockies and Sierra Nevadas.[35]

McCormick's regional pride in the Midwest was easily matched by his prejudice against everything east of the Mississippi — or west of the Rockies. Thus, he was more than willing to leave the Atlantic littoral outside his defense perimeter. In 1917, a serialized novel cowritten with the *Tribune*'s Edwin Balmer, he fantasized a successful invasion of the United States in which the German army drove to the banks of the Mississippi

River, where it finally was halted by fervent patriots mobilized behind an Ossowetz-like defensive shield.

As McCormick saw it, the Midwest was itself a giant fortress. Here beat the heart of the nation, to a rhythm as old as the Northwest Ordinance of 1787, which had established a republic within the republic, divorced from southern slavery and home to a ruder brand of democracy than practiced in Illinois's parent state of Virginia. For McCormick, the Northwest Ordinance was more deserving of reverence than the Declaration of Independence or the Constitution, precisely because it made good on Jefferson's bold assertions of human equality in an American Eden.

In an article written for *The Century* magazine early in 1916, McCormick showed his disdain for the polyglot cities of the East, where recent immigrants of doubtful loyalties mingled with the sons of millionaires contemptuous of the Jeffersonian *demos*. "With what enthusiasm does anyone think that the American people would rush to arms to drive back an invader of the seaboard?" he inquired. "New York and the northeastern seacoast are to them nothing but the homes of dodging, obligation-shifting idle rich, in whose behalf they would certainly feel no call to die." With a dour fervency combining equal parts Paul Revere and Old Testament prophet, McCormick painted the United States as an unorganized, defenseless nation that offered plentiful reinforcements for any European invader able to establish a beachhead. "Mexico was no more ripe for the conquest of Cortez than we are," he asserted.[36]

The national ignorance of defense extended to relevant committees of Congress. "This statement, which would be hotly or contemptuously denied by the committees now," wrote McCormick, "will someday be urged for them in extenuation when a bitter and bereaved nation calls them thieves and murderers." Writing to Illinois senator Lawrence Sherman, a political ally, he urged preparedness-minded lawmakers in Washington to borrow a page from the European book by drafting municipal police to help keep order behind the lines. He wished to avoid a repeat of the comical neglect inflicted on the famed Rough Riders of '98, who, given wild horses by the War Department, were still trying to break their unruly mounts long after the cessation of hostilities. "You can imagine what chance our militia cavalry would have if they had to fight their horses with one hand and the enemy with the other," he concluded.[37]

✧ 7

In January 1916, tensions along the U.S.-Mexican border rose after followers of the rebel leader Pancho Villa murdered eighteen American mining officials and engineers working in their country. Two months later, Villa led a raid on the border town of Columbus, New Mexico, that left seventeen Americans dead. McCormick believed, not without reason, that "the row on the border" was being stirred up by German agents hoping to divert American attention and American arms desperately sought by European enemies of the kaiser. He began rethinking plans for a second summer of action on the Russian front.

For all his suspicion of German provocation, McCormick was careful to distinguish between the kaiser's agents and the vast rank and file of German-Americans, especially those of the younger generation, "more American than they know, more American than the rich young good-for-nothings who are accepted in English society on terms of *near* equality." Although content to shine in the reflected glory of German battlefield success, these descendants of militarism had not the slightest idea of bringing their adopted country under the Prussian yoke. In this they differed from "rich and powerful Easterners" bewitched by England and consequently indifferent "to anything west of the Allegheny Mountains."[38]

McCormick was no more favorably disposed toward the seemingly passive man in the White House. About the best that could be said of Wilson was that he had belatedly broken with his pacifist secretary of state, William Jennings Bryan — the Great Commoner of legend, who had dominated the Democratic party for twenty years simply "by having an asinine solution for every problem." Should his National Guard unit be called to the Mexican border, griped McCormick, "I have no doubt . . . it will be after the hot weather sets in and that we will be sent down without proper equipment or decent horses. Well," he concluded with a sigh, "we have only one more year of this president, thank heavens."[39]

After the Columbus massacre, Wilson changed course. From Mexican president Venustiano Carranza, he obtained permission for a "punitive expedition" of 6,600 men led by General John J. Pershing, a veteran of campaigns in Cuba and the Philippines. Pershing was to pursue Villa deep into the Mexican interior, capturing him if possible. McCormick made preparations to follow suit. In the first week of June 1916, he led 130,000 Chicagoans in a preparedness parade that filled local streets for thirteen hours.

A few days later McCormick took his place with the Illinois delegation to the Republican National Convention, also meeting in Chicago, scene of the party's fratricidal warfare in 1912.* Nominally pledged to Senator Lawrence Sherman, he astutely predicted the third-ballot nomination of Su-

---

*The journalist Walter Lippmann, whose heart belonged to TR but whose head was full of the Wilsonian gospel, papered over his divided loyalties with a unifying contempt for the convention, keynoted in sonorous voice by Ohio's less than noble Roman, Warren G. Harding. Wrote Lippmann of the ensuing spectacle, it was "the flag, red white and blue, all its stripes, all its stars, and the flag again a thousand times over, and Americanism till your ears ached and the slaves and the tariff, and Abraham Lincoln, mauled and dragged about and his name taken in vain and his spirit degraded, prostituted to every insincerity."

preme Court justice Charles Evans Hughes as the sole contender "around whom the entire Republican party would rally with relief, if not with enthusiasm." Having discharged his obligations to the national party, McCormick pulled strings to get his brother nominated for congressman-at-large.

Bearing out Jung's diagnoses, Medill McCormick had regained a measure of health by venturing onto the field of politics, where he and Ruth established themselves as more or less independent of Kate McCormick. Medill impressed his colleagues in the Illinois legislature with his diligence and commitment to practical reform. By 1916, after a single term in Springfield, he was ready to move on. His brother reminded him of an earlier president, Benjamin Harrison, who had served as congressman-at-large from his native Indiana. Medill was quickly persuaded.

In mid-June, McCormick interrupted his president-making long enough to return to the north shore of the St. Lawrence river, where he had finally closed a deal on 300 square miles of Quebec wilderness inhabited by traders, Indians, and a handful of fishermen scrounging an existence from the area's nameless lakes and vast stands of balsam trees. On an earlier trip to the region, he had tested to the limit his belief in the strenuous life. Finding himself stranded in the woods during a fierce snowstorm with nothing to guide him but a compass and a meticulously kept notebook recording his steps through the trackless forest, McCormick was able to retrace his route to an Indian cabin. Here he was given supper and invited to sleep on the floor with a dozen members of the Tibasse family.

Thus began a fruitful, if improbable, friendship between Tibasse, of the Saint Onge tribe, and the Ontario Paper Company, one marked by fair dealing and mutual trust rare between the races. On completing the company town of Shelter Bay (a name he proposed in place of the site's original name on the theory that "if we call this place Rocky River, no ship captain will come in here to get our wood"), McCormick made certain that the natives were charged the same prices for merchandise as everyone else, that their credit accounts were kept honestly, and that the company paid well for Indian moccasins, venison, and labor.[40]

In return the tribesmen reported fires, guided tenderfoot timber cruisers, and paddled canoes through whitewater with a skill that never ceased to amaze McCormick. With the head of the Tibasse clan he established a particular intimacy. It was entirely in character that McCormick, who once refused to leave the library of his townhouse to go downstairs and greet Queen Marie of Romania, should invite Tibasse to visit the 1933 Chicago World's Fair as his honored guest.

McCormick was drawn to the Quebec woods by more than their majestic isolation or sociological interest. By the fall of 1915, with the

Thorold mill producing 3,000 tons of paper a month, his Canadian gamble was paying off handsomely. If anything, he had been guilty of thinking too small. Lacking reliable supplies of northern timber to feed its paper-making machines, the *Tribune* was forced to import newsprint from the Pacific coast at $60 a ton. Worse, McCormick had to borrow the presses of his rival, the *Chicago Daily News*, to meet wartime demands for the *Tribune.*

In an effort to regain his independence and swell his profits, he allocated $125,000 for new presses to replace aging Linotype machines and another $300,000 to increase Thorold's papermaking capacity. Once realized, the combination would position the postwar *Tribune* and its New York spinoff, the *Daily News*, to steal a march on every other newspaper in America.

✧ 8

McCormick was deep in the Canadian forests on June 18, 1916, when President Wilson mobilized National Guard units to pacify the Mexican border and thereby lend support to the punitive expedition. McCormick returned to Chicago loaded to the muzzle with schemes to equip 11,000 Illinois volunteers temporarily housed at the state fairgrounds in Springfield. Tiffany Blake, the chief editorial writer of the *Tribune*, visited both his employers in the hastily erected tent city dubbed Camp Lincoln. He found Major McCormick sitting under an awning sipping lemonade prepared for him by the chef of the *Tribune's* executive dining room, who had been drafted to serve as his personal orderly. Nearby, Blake encountered Private Joe Patterson currying a horse under the broiling Illinois sun.

In retrospect, all three men might have been happier if McCormick had remained in Springfield, drilling his troops and dreaming of glory on a Mexican battlefield. On June 20 the *Tribune* announced that in their absence, McCormick and Patterson were entrusting editorial responsibilities to Bill Field and Teddy Beck. In the meantime McCormick converted his office into a quartermaster department for the ill-trained, ill-equipped First Cavalry. Long before mobilization orders came from the White House, he had sought to compensate through private subscription for the failure of the government to arm its fighting men properly. Early in May he had approached the Hartford, Connecticut, firearms maker Samuel Colt with a request for five machine guns. A month later he renewed his appeal, complaining to a deskbound general in Washington that "it is not only impossible to train a machine gun troop without machine guns but it is pretty hard to maintain their morale."[41]

On June 21, McCormick arrived in Chicago from Shelter Bay, to be met by Bill Field with news of a humiliating American defeat at Carrizal. Before the sun went down, he succeeded in obtaining funds from the meat packer Ogden Armour and the banker Charles Dawes with which to buy twenty machine guns. American weapons-makers were less cooperative. Told that the armies of Europe had first claim to their output, McCormick vented his wrath at businessmen who placed profits before patriotism.

June 22 was even more depressing. On page three of the morning *Tribune*, McCormick read a story headed "Flivver Patriotism." Based on information gleaned from Ford Motor Company officials by the paper's Detroit stringer, the article reported that no Ford employee answering the call to military service could expect to retain his job or have his family cared for while he was away. In fact, as Henry Ford's biographer, Carol Gelderman, has written, eighty-nine Ford workers heeded the presidential summons; each was issued a numbered badge identifying him as a member of the Michigan National Guard and entitling him to his old job when he returned from the border.

All this was lost in a haze of muddled reporting, emotional excess, and implacable deadlines. On the same day that "Flivver Patriotism" appeared, McCormick, self-commissioned hammer of American preparedness, was fuming over his inability to obtain machine guns from corporate malingerers. He was running late for a night train to Springfield when he encountered Tiffany Blake, "trembling with indignation" over Ford's obstructionist tactics. A stinging editorial rebuke had been prepared for the next day's paper. All it lacked was a title. "The man's an anarchist," said Blake. "Well," said McCormick, "call him one."[42]

Blake did that and more. "Henry Ford Is an Anarchist," although written by Blake's junior colleague, Clifford Raymond, gave 400,000 *Tribune* readers a full measure of the disgust McCormick felt over sunshine patriots like the famous industrialist. This was not the first *Tribune* blast directed at Ford. In December 1915 the automaker had launched his quixotic *Peace Ship* to Europe by urging reporters on the dock, "Tell the people to cry peace and fight preparedness." The resulting odyssey had sailed an uneven course between futility and ridicule, with the *Tribune* targeting the amateur diplomat in several roughly worded editorials. Nothing it had previously printed, however, came close to the semihysteria of "Henry Ford Is an Anarchist."

To the *Tribune*, it was self-evident that the rights of American citizenship carried with them obligations of service. Yet "Mr. Ford proves that he does not believe in service to the nation in the fashion a soldier must serve it." By his actions, the automaker had revealed himself as both "an ignorant idealist" and an "anarchistic enemy of the nation which protects him in his wealth." A man as ignorant as Henry Ford, declared the *Tribune*, "may not understand the fundamentals of the government under which he lives." This sad deficiency McCormick and his writers proposed to correct by reminding Ford that the government in Washington could lay its long arm upon his shoulder and forcibly command his services "as a soldier if necessary." That it had not done so they attributed to the facts that "it has not had the common sense to make its theoretical universal service practical," and that a large number of patriotic young men were willing to volunteer for a fighting force that protected Henry Ford *and* south Texas — "for which service he penalized them."

The only suitable place for so deluded an individual, the *Tribune* continued, "is a region where no government exists except such as he furnishes, where no protection is afforded except such as he affords, where nothing stands between him and the rules of life except such defenses as he puts there." The war-torn Mexican state of Chihuahua was just such a place. "Indeed, anywhere in Mexico would be a good location for the Ford factories."

Ford denied that he had threatened National Guardsmen in his employ with economic retaliation. His rebuttal was duly printed in the *Tribune*, which nevertheless stood by its inflammatory charges. Ten weeks later, goaded by corporate lawyers, Ford filed a $1 million libel suit against the paper. His action inaugurated a legal circus that dragged on for three years, culminating in the first of many "trials of the century," one richly documenting the plaintiff's ignorance of practically everything but the internal combustion engine.

Ironically, as McCormick fought a war of words with the pacifist Ford, he nearly despaired of the government whose omnipotence he extolled on the editorial page. To pressure Secretary of War Newton D. Baker into authorizing the sale of machine guns to his National Guard unit, he turned to Roger Sullivan, the Democratic boss of Illinois. Their unlikely alliance paid off when Colt agreed to ship five of the weapons to Brownsville, Texas, by July 1. For good measure the munitions-maker threw in 500,000 rounds of seven-millimeter ammunition.

This transaction formed the basis of McCormick's later inflated claim of responsibility for introducing machine guns *of any kind* to the American army. As with other McCormick boasts, a habit of exaggeration obscured genuine accomplishments. For instance, when the Colt machine guns finally arrived in Brownsville, there were no mules to haul munitions wagons, so McCormick personally paid for an automobile (a Ford, no less) to help transport the weapons and ammunition to the north bank of the Rio Grande. A few weeks earlier, in the first mechanized assault in U.S. military history, Lieutenant George S. Patton, Jr., had sent three Dodge touring cars against a group of Villa supporters holed up in a Mexican farmhouse. McCormick instantly embraced Patton's faith in motorized warfare. Few of the horses he shipped to the border region saw action off the polo field.

All that was in the future. On July 4, McCormick's regiment arrived in Brownsville with two rounds of ammunition per man and no horses. Grasping railroad officials had delayed their southern journey by side-tracking troop trains in favor of more profitable freight. Fresh indignities awaited the improvised army in the infernal heat of south Texas. Denied lumber to floor and frame tents, McCormick made fresh appeals to northern friends. The resulting accommodations were the only ones to withstand a fierce tropical downpour that left six feet of water in the poorly sited campgrounds.

Regimental housing shone by comparison with military equipment and intelligence. McCormick declared that army artillery pieces were fit only to decorate the parks of Washington, D.C. In preparing for a possible border crossing, the major and his men resorted to a dog-eared copy of Grant's *Memoirs* and an ancient Baedeker guide to Monterrey, the city occupied by American forces in the nineteenth century under General Zachary Taylor.

To justify an invasion, the Americans hugging their side of the Rio Grande needed an incident of Mexican aggression. McCormick the pro-vocateur rose to the occasion. On July 6, he accompanied a group of reg-ular soldiers on a riverbank reconnaissance. The major of volunteers rode ahead, his huge frame affording an irresistible target to Mexican sharp-shooters. An enemy soldier on the south bank duly fired at the tall Ameri-can, narrowly missing him. McCormick slid out of his saddle, pointed his Colt .45 at the Mexican astride his horse, and pulled the trigger. His at-tacker toppled from his mount. The Mexican's horse ran off. Neither were seen again.

Newspapers the next day reported conciliatory moves on the part of the Wilson administration. "Feel all let down," a dejected McCormick wrote in his diary. Hopes of battle rose briefly after reports that some members of the Fourth Infantry had been fired upon while cutting willows near the riverbank. These were soon disproved; the Mexicans seemed as pacific as the man in the White House.

Forsaking the primitive conditions of camp life, McCormick first rented a small house near the railroad tracks for $150 a month, then moved into larger quarters in San Antonio. He quartered polo ponies in a barn on the property. Each morning a Mexican gardener tended two hundred rose-bushes surrounding the place. With time on his hands, McCormick enter-tained regular army officers, General Pershing among them, for whom this mismanaged police action was a prelude to much greater things.

They were not his only guests, according to Walter Trohan, a close friend who later ran the *Tribune*'s Washington bureau. With characteristic frankness, McCormick told Trohan of a flamenco dancer whose sexual favors he had procured one night in San Antonio. "Imagine my surprise," said McCormick, "when I found out she wasn't Spanish but Mexican."[43]

"Amy arrived. Thank heavens," McCormick noted on July 21, his pleasure no doubt magnified by appreciation of his wife's nursing skills. A wave of dengue fever had swept through the camp, leaving him weak and groggy. His stiff neck and sore throat persisted for weeks. Less fortunate victims of the disease were housed in buildings reminiscent of Illinois chicken coops, while all around him Major McCormick saw modern hotels, large churches, and masonry garages ideal for conversion to infirmary use. He began to think that the unfeeling civilians of south Texas were as culpable for the plague as the mosquitoes infesting the waterlogged lowlands along the Rio Grande.

July 30 was his birthday. "Poor Bertie," wrote Kate McCormick. "Poor baby boy 36 with an old tart of 48 [sic] on his back. I suppose he is bored to death! Soldiering is not his profession and no fight to give zest to the hardship. I fancy he is sorry enough that he ever enlisted."[44]

Kate grazed the truth. McCormick's dissatisfaction grew with his boredom. The summer heat was debilitating, the mud bottomless. Incessant rains prevented him from giving his men much-needed riding instruction. "Our army spends more money for worse food than any other in the world," he complained, before purchasing a pair of field kitchens to redress the culinary crisis. Shortages continued to bedevil the expedition. McCormick had a single commissioned officer to help train nearly one hundred volunteers, few of whom had ever handled a rifle or mounted a horse prior to Wilson's mobilization order.[45]

At the end of August the frustrated McCormick reappeared in Chicago. "I'll get better soon, but right now I feel pretty punk," he informed friends. He was sufficiently healthy to go to New York City, where he paid a call on Charles Evans Hughes and purchased, at exorbitant rates, 20,000 tons of paper to keep the *Tribune*'s presses humming. Returning to Brownsville in September, he won a pistol competition, gave lectures on his Russian war experiences, and cultivated future generals on and off the polo field. He became fast friends with Major General Frederick Funston, whose democratic treatment of Joe Patterson left him puzzled ("After all, Joe was only an enlisted man").[46]

Convinced that no real fighting would be permitted to overshadow Woodrow Wilson's campaign for a second term, Patterson left camp early. McCormick, just as eager to close out his Mexican account, asked to have his regiment mustered out in Chicago rather than Springfield. Though not keen on sleeping in Grant Park, he considered it preferable to the multiple temptations of Springfield. Besides, he thought it would do the people of Chicago good to see real live soldiers in their midst, even strangers to combat like the First Illinois. In the end he and his men were sent to Fort Sheridan, just north of Chicago.

Their return coincided with the final days of a heated election campaign. McCormick and the *Tribune* viewed Wilson's domestic policies as bad, his record on preparedness worse, and his flirtation with internationalism as inexcusable. "Though fate offers us a golden apple in Mexico and bitter fruit in Flanders, Mr. Wilson, being for 'humanity' rather than for America, wishes us to taste the bitter one, and he will probably have his way," contended the *Tribune*.

Tuesday, November 7, 1916, came and went without a victor in the presidential contest. Not until two anxious days had passed did Charles Evans Hughes know for certain that California had slipped between his fingers; with it went the presidency. McCormick stamped his foot and published "Nobody Home in California," a classic example of *Tribune* invective.

"California is the state which every now and then causes the rest of the nation to wonder how the troubles it makes can be safely handled. California hates the Japanese. It offends and insults the Japanese. It pays no attention to the treaty obligations of the United States . . . Some day, when Japan is ready, a California offense will result in the seizure of the Philippines and Hawaii." Calling California "our junker state in all except willingness to strengthen the ability of the federal government to meet the trouble it may make," the *Tribune* pointed out the incongruity of Californians demanding federal protection for their long and vulnerable coastline while rejecting the party of preparedness. The state's residents claimed to favor a Pacific navy. Yet by endorsing Wilson over Hughes, they had voted "for a pacific navy . . . How a state which, when it is not scared to death itself, is scaring the rest of the nation to death could have given even two votes in a precinct to the administration which maintains Josephus Daniels as schoolmaster of the American navy is a question beyond normal intelligence." California, said McCormick, was "the champion boob state of the American republic," its voters "dead from the neck up."[47]

McCormick balanced his denunciations with advocacy when, in January 1917, he appeared before a congressional committee probing the state of national defense. Arguing the case for universal military training, commencing at age eighteen, he was careful to limit the United States to a purely defensive army. "All we want is to be so strong that nobody will attack us," he told the committee. He took equal pains to dispose of two "humbug" phrases — pacifism and militarism, the latter cynically employed by foes of national preparedness to justify the former. Physical cowardice explained the ardor of youthful pacifists, said McCormick, for "the helpless instinct of infancy to seek safety in flight and outcry does not readily yield in all of us to the higher principles of manhood when we come to man's estate . . . Having lost the mental and moral struggle which every individual must undergo to achieve physical courage," these timid souls took shelter behind the mystical word *pacifist* — a word coined by aging theorists hell-bent on enforcing their theories, even to the destruction of others.[48]

That McCormick should deride those not sharing his proclivity for attack or his need to submerge self-doubt in verbal or physical combat is hardly surprising. A December 1916 *Tribune* editorial, ostensibly favoring the legalization of prizefighting in Illinois, provides a window into the mind of a man at home in the ring: "Life is not a soft thing. It is not tender. It requires hardihood, endurance, courage, and fortitude. It demands physical as well as moral stamina." Unfortunately, said the *Tribune,* the most prominent aspect of modern American life was softness and the avoidance of shocks. Yet "Americans cannot afford to become ninnies and mollycoddles." Force was the iron law governing human existence. "When respectability sets its face against force it becomes decadent. It seeks feebleness and soft luxuries. It becomes unfit for life." In later years, resorting to a boxing analogy to convey his zest for journalistic conflict, McCormick claimed that the counterpunch was the most lethal weapon in a fighter's arsenal.[49]

His own fights were just beginning. In Russia he had been a mere observer of battle. The Mexican border campaign was hardly worthy of the name. As 1917 dawned, however, few informed Americans believed that their country could lead a permanently charmed life when it came to Europe's war. And McCormick, who never saw a fight he didn't want to get into, was determined to be part of the action.

7

Kaiser Bill, Kaiser Will

"Bob McCormick represents the trust press that would crush the life out of Chicago. He will smear any man that gets in his way . . . I'm gonna smash Bob McCormick!"

— Mayor William "Big Bill" Thompson

"Fighting is the primeval purpose of the male."

— Robert R. McCormick, "The Army of 1918"

To ADMIRERS he was Big Bill the Builder, a populist hero and the greatest showman since P. T. Barnum. Critics thought him a recessive gene in the body politic, combining the worst features of Huey Long, Elmer Gantry, and Boss Tweed. Everyone conceded his genius for publicity. "Throw away your hammer and get a horn," he exhorted Chicagoans with a flamboyance rare even by the hyperbolic standards of the Windy City. During three tumultuous terms as mayor, William Hale Thompson gave Chicago a badly needed facelift. Yet even as the city implemented Daniel Burnham's sweeping plan of urban renewal, it gained an international reputation for — in the carefully chosen words of the *Tribune* — "moronic buffoonery, barbaric crime, triumphant hoodlumism, unchecked graft, and a dejected citizenship."

Though both Thompson and McCormick claimed to speak for Chicago, it would be difficult to imagine another two men so fated by character and upbringing to be enemies. Ironically, each had entered the political arena at the turn of the century riding a wave of reform sentiment. Otherwise Thompson, garrulous and hotheaded, had practically nothing in common with the guarded, cold-blooded McCormick — except this: to mention the name of either man in Chicago between 1915 and 1940 was to start an argument.

Thompson was born in Boston in 1869 and taken to Chicago as an infant. His father, a New England blueblood, amassed extensive real estate holdings in the wake of the Great Fire. The Thompsons prospered with Chicago's reconstruction. As a boy, Bill skipped classes to chase fire engines. Later he passed up Yale to learn the cattle business under broad western skies. His decision to become a cowboy rather than a college man paid rich political dividends in an era bewitched by Teddy Roosevelt and his Rough Riders. Two generations of Chicagoans equated Thompson's trademark eight-gallon hat with the frontier vitality and direct, unpretentious style of its owner.

On the death of his father in 1891, the twenty-two-year-old Thompson forsook his Nebraska cattle ranch to return to Chicago and a congenial sportsman's existence made possible by inherited wealth. Packing 225 pounds of muscle on his sinewy six-foot, four-inch frame, Thompson won a legion of admirers — and the disarming nickname by which he was forever after known — as captain of the Chicago Athletic Association's national champion football team. Off the gridiron, Big Bill showed prowess as a boxer, sailor, and water polo star. Breezy and gregarious, his intellectual shortcomings blanketed by charm, he was a political natural. Though no Yale man, he proved a quick study in the gritty classroom of Chicago politics.

As befitting the mayor whose tenure is still remembered as the heyday of organized crime, Thompson's entry into politics came about as the result of a wager. A friend bet $50 that he wouldn't run for the city council. Thompson won the bet and much more. On the campaign trail, the former tackle showed a natural aptitude for personal confrontations. Indeed, when it came to name-calling, Thompson could teach the acerbic *Tribune* a thing or two. Then and always, he possessed a barker's flair for calling attention to himself. In the spring of 1900, with the help of a growing black population, he upset a Democratic alderman in the second ward. Working hard to justify his endorsement by the Municipal Voters League, he secured Chicago's first municipal playground and championed the regulation of boxing matches.

Anxious to move up the political ladder, Big Bill enlisted backing from real estate interests in a successful campaign for county commissioner. In 1904, he and McCormick, the latter himself a reform-minded Chicago alderman, met for the first and last time as political confederates. At the tumultuous Republican convention in Springfield, both men supported Charles Deneen for governor. At the behest of Mayor Carter Harrison, McCormick consulted Thompson about plans for Michigan Avenue, the great commercial artery first envisioned in the Chicago Plan. No friendship ripened from these passing contacts; the temperamental gulf between the back-slapping athlete and the introverted diplomat's son was too wide to breed trust, let alone intimacy.[1]

While McCormick ran the sanitary district, Thompson confined his office-holding to a stint as commodore of the Chicago Yacht Club. Itching for a comeback, he broke with Deneen and hitched his kite to the Blond Boss, William J. Lorimer. Following Lorimer's narrow escape in his first senatorial trial, it was Thompson who led Chicago celebrants in escorting the native son to his home on the West Side. A year later Thompson again played grand marshal to the now disgraced politician. Before a capacity crowd in Orchestra Hall, he reserved his most scathing words for "the trust press," which he blamed for martyring the noble Lorimer. A Catholic priest on the program was more explicit, denouncing the *Tribune* by name as "the greatest criminal in Illinois, a moral leper."

After July 1912, Lorimer might have been consigned to his political grave, but Lorimerism lived on in the form of the Lincoln Protective League, founded by diehard supporters of the Blond Boss and derided by a hostile press as the Lorimer-Lincoln League. Thompson served as the group's treasurer. (As its unsuccessful candidate for the Board of Review, a municipal agency charged with adjudicating tax disputes, he accused the *Tribune* of defaulting on $161,000 in taxes.) By whatever name it was known, the league swam against freshening currents of Progressive Republicanism. Lambasting the direct primary sought by the *Tribune* as "the dream of weaklings," Lorimer's friends endorsed Taft for renomination in 1912, "not because they love me," explained Taft, "[but] because they hate Roosevelt more."[2]

It was to thwart the league's "jackpot candidates" and block a Lorimer revival that Robert McCormick organized the rival Committee of One Hundred. He accepted Thompson's defeat in the GOP debacle that fall with a dry eye, but the brash charisma of the loser had a very different effect on a would-be Warwick named Fred Lundin. A Lorimer protégé esteemed for his organizational gifts and excused for his eccentricities, Lundin was a one-term congressman with a political base among his fellow Scandinavians. For archaeologists of political roguery, he is the fossil evidence that democracy and flim-flamming go hand in hand. A man of many poses, the diminutive, mop-haired Lundin referred to himself with contrived modesty as "the Poor Swede." Before entering politics, he had thrived as a patent medicine salesman peddling Juniper Ade, an all-purpose tonic concocted from juniper berries.[3]

The statesman's toga fit the Poor Swede badly. His wardrobe ran instead to ancient black frockcoats, unfashionable broad-brimmed hats, and flowing black ties, the sober effect of which he varied with amber-tinted glasses and a pink Japanese mink coat. As a salesman, he knew how to get a customer's attention; as a political string-puller, he operated best in the shadows. This was a good place for a Lorimer Republican to be at the start of 1913. Beginning with a core group of twenty Thompson adherents, Lundin furtively set about building a citywide organization capable of making Big Bill mayor in less than two years.

In December 1914, the Poor Swede outdid himself in formally unveiling his candidate before an overflow crowd at the Auditorium Theater. As bands serenaded the faithful, a curtain slowly drew back to reveal a huge Christmas tree festooned with pledge cards signed by 140,000 Chicago voters, imploring Thompson to make the race. It was an irresistible sales pitch for a product at least as dubious as Juniper Ade. Certainly Big Bill was sold.

But if Barkis was willing, few onlookers were inclined to take the Thompson campaign very seriously. In the weeks leading up to the March primary, circus parades and calliope music drowned out any serious discussion of issues. Under the banner "All for Chicago and Chicago for All," Thompson played the civic booster, promising to lure two million visitors a year to Chicago, drive the crooks out of town, and deliver a five-cent streetcar fare.

Hoping to mend fences, in January 1915 Big Bill paid a call on the coeditors of the *Tribune*. In separate interviews with McCormick and Patterson, he vowed to improve the business climate and insisted that he had outgrown his Lorimer past. Whatever the rationale for his candidacy, the *Tribune* wasn't buying. With McCormick away covering the Russian war front, the paper made no secret of its preference for Thompson's Republican primary opponent, a colorless municipal judge named Harry Olson. In the Democratic primary, it endorsed the incumbent, Mayor Carter Harrison.

Not for the last time, the voters of Chicago did precisely the opposite of what the lordly *Tribune* urged upon them. On primary day they narrowly chose Thompson over the listless Olson, while Harrison was upset by Robert Sweitzer, a Catholic of German ancestry closely associated with the Democratic boss Roger Sullivan. The ensuing runoff provided little reassurance to the friends of popular government. Accompanied by a fife and drum corps in all-American colonial garb, Thompson worked rich veins of religious and ethnic bigotry. The pope came in for his share of abuse. Big Bill vowed, with fist-pounding sincerity, to suppress crime and protect women from insult in public places. He regaled audiences with tales from his sagebrush days and with verbal broadsides directed at the trust press, whose downtown leases robbed Chicago schoolchildren of educational funding.

Confronted with so unpalatable a set of gamecocks as Thompson and Sweitzer, the *Tribune* was reduced to hoping for the best while preparing for doomsday, a stance that was to become more or less habitual whenever the paper contemplated Chicago under Thompson. In April, Thompson won a smashing victory, his 147,000-vote margin the largest registered in an American municipal contest until then. "Mr. Thompson enters the door of opportunity," conceded the *Tribune*, "and it will be his fault chiefly if he exits by the door of failure." The victor sent McCormick a graciously worded note of thanks for his evenhanded campaign coverage. It was virtually the last civil exchange between the two men.

With their champion sworn into office, Thompson's political allies turned to the serious business of looting the city treasury. Working out of a suite at the LaSalle Hotel, Fred Lundin distributed the spoils. More than 9,000 Thompson backers received ninety-day appointments, thereby avoiding civil service regulations. In time the Thompson-Lundin organization would place 30,000 political appointees on the city payroll. Few were hired for their professional abilities. Virtually all kicked back part of their salaries to grease the machine. The Poor Swede was unapologetic. "To hell with the public," he exalted, "we're at the feedbox now."[4]

Early in 1916, Dr. Theodore Sacks, the respected director of the municipal tuberculosis sanitorium, resigned in protest after Lundin packed the institutional staff with Thompson cronies. Dr. Sacks later committed suicide, but not before penning *To the People of Chicago*, an impassioned attack on unscrupulous politicians who appropriated for their own use money and facilities dedicated to the sick and impoverished. In rapid order corporation counsel Samuel Ettelson was denounced as an Insull mouthpiece, state's attorney Maclay Hoyne raided city hall looking for evidence in a vice probe, and Thompson's police chief was indicted for his part in a gambling conspiracy.

Local newspapers objected to official tolerance of police corruption. To counter the establishment press, Thompson and Lundin founded their own journal, *The Republican.* And a reconstituted school board dropped hints that it might condemn the *Tribune* building at Madison and Dearborn.

✧ 2

Local political wars were dwarfed by events in Europe, which reverberated with seismic force throughout Chicago's ethnic wards. On February 1, 1917, Germany announced the resumption of unrestricted submarine warfare. Overnight the *Tribune* jettisoned its longstanding opposition to U.S. involvement in the conflict and swung violently behind conscription, food and fuel conservation, and other measures designed to put the nation on a war footing.

Hoping for a commission in some future American Expeditionary Force, McCormick made cow eyes at the very policymakers on whom he had so recently trained his guns. "How can we do the most good?" he wrote to the hawkish undersecretary of the navy, Franklin D. Roosevelt, early in March. Reminding his fellow Grotonian that "the *Tribune* has been a great navy advocate since before we had a navy," he volunteered his services in mobilizing public support behind "the best expert opinion." Regrettably, such expertise was not always available — unless, of course, one had a personal pipeline to the Navy Department.[5]

"I do not know any more than do you," replied Roosevelt, not above engaging in shameless flattery of his own. FDR undercut his disavowal by sharing presumably well-informed opinions on navy training, recruiting, emergency preparedness, the relative merits of patrol boats, minesweepers, and scouts, and the regional impact of a Great Lakes naval reserve. "Strangely enough," his March 9 letter didn't reach McCormick until April 11, five days after Congress declared war on Germany and the *Tribune* carried a full-page advertisement inviting candidates for the Illinois cavalry and artillery to apply to Major McCormick and Captain Patterson at the *Tribune* building. Initial response to this trumpet blast was disappointing: in the war's first week, fewer than three hundred patriots came forward.[6]

Somewhat more encouraging was the reaction of the White House, where McCormick's olive branch was gratefully received. No less thankful was Secretary of War Newton Baker. On the slight chance that someone in the command structure had either missed his point or overlooked his availability for service, McCormick reiterated to Roosevelt his desire to help out "on enlistments and everything else." To spur lagging recruitment in his back yard, he promised to hold a place, at wages not less than their current level, for any *Tribune* employee wishing to follow him into uniform.[7]

In the ensuing mad scramble to possess the Stars and Stripes, accusations of disloyalty mingled indiscriminately with cries of warmonger. The *Tribune* demanded that school board members drop page 154 of a grammar school speller: "The Kaiser in the Making." The Bismarck School was renamed for General Frederick Funston. Illinois's governor, Frank Lowden, mobilized troops to suppress as "a treasonable conspiracy" the scheduled gathering of antidraft activists styling themselves the People's Council of America for Democracy and Terms of Peace.

Before the soldiers could carry out their orders, a most unlikely civil libertarian appeared from the wings. In September 1917, Big Bill Thompson threw a protective cordon of Chicago cops around the offending pacifists. Addressing a city council committee, Thompson went further, flaying both "an unholy war" and the humanitarian shipment of American foodstuffs to starving European populations. He discouraged liberty-bond salesmen from conducting drives at city hall, on the less than persuasive grounds that he opposed any coercion of city employees.

Simple mathematics dictated the mayor's uncompromising stance. "Chicago is the sixth largest German city in the world," he told reporters, who clamored to know why he refused to invite the venerable Marshall Joffre, custodian of French honor, to visit Chicago following a recent triumph in the nation's capital. Moreover, said Thompson, "It is the second largest Bohemian city, the second largest Swedish, the second largest Norwegian, and the second largest Polish." All those minorities added up to a majority, at least as calculated by Fred Lundin. Dreaming of a national political organization stretching from Chicago to the White House, Lundin found it easy to persuade Thompson that the war represented a losing hand among isolationist voters.

The Chicago city council, no slouch where political theater was concerned, harshly rebuked the mayor for his inhospitable behavior toward America's French allies. It was at this point that McCormick took it upon himself to travel to Washington and seek out Joffre, who warmly recalled their earlier meeting on the outskirts of besieged Paris. The old soldier just as graciously accepted McCormick's invitation to come to Chicago, Thompson or no Thompson. His May 4 appearance there touched off wild scenes of popular enthusiasm.

"Everybody cheered themselves hoarse," reminisced McCormick, "and I got very much excited and romantic, and dictated a letter to Pershing offering my services in any capacity. Well, after I dictated it I went to lunch or something, and cooled off. I thought, what the hell am I doing this for — if he wants me he can have me anyhow. I just slopped over. So I decided not to send the letter, but Miss Burke [McCormick's secretary], in her somewhat careless way, just sent it unsigned."[8]

Within days McCormick received an acknowledgment from Pershing's chief of staff, Lieutenant General James Harbord, with whom he enjoyed a friendship dating to the Mexican campaign. Acting on orders from the commanding general, Harbord directed McCormick to embark immediately for France. Or so McCormick claimed. The story became one of the most cherished in his extensive repertoire of the improbable. And it may well be that, caught up in the emotional riptide, he "slopped over" and impulsively tendered his services to Black Jack Pershing.

Yet he didn't stop there. Of what use was a brother in Congress, seemingly recovered from his earlier illness and widely mentioned as a potential president, if he couldn't or wouldn't pull a few strings with the capital's military establishment? Which is exactly what Medill McCormick did, approaching Pershing at his Washington club to reinforce an appeal already lodged with Secretary Baker. So determined was Medill's brother to experience the war firsthand — if only from the vantage point of Pershing's general staff — that he now went hat in hand to Franklin Roosevelt at the Navy Department. (In later years McCormick liked to tell how a "bumptious" Roosevelt had condescended to a senior admiral who was present.)[9]

Success crowned these lobbying efforts when Pershing included McCormick's name on a list of potential liaison officers. Secretary Baker returned the document, authorizing the general to select "anyone you like." Before sailing for France on June 30, McCormick received a wistful sendoff from Theodore Roosevelt. Denied a soldier's part in the contest he had done so much to agitate, Roosevelt joined his disciple for lunch at the Harvard Club. The former president's parting words were blatantly envious: "Lord, how I wish I were going with you!"[10]

The French passenger liner that carried Major McCormick and his wife across the treacherous Atlantic sailed without convoy protection. At night, fearing that lights on board the ship might invite submarine attack, the captain prohibited the use of matches and ordered all portholes covered. One evening at the dinner table, McCormick confided an irrational terror of being wounded and unable to move from the battlefield. The next day a female passenger suffering from inoperable cancer slipped him a package containing a handful of morphine capsules. The grateful McCormick had them sewn into his uniform.[11]

❖ 3

McCormick reached Paris on the morning of July 11. His first act was decidedly unwarlike: he checked into the Ritz Hotel. After a civilized breakfast and bath, he reported to Pershing's nearby headquarters. The newcomer had already insured that Pershing had his calling card, in the form of the *Chicago Tribune Army Edition*, a well-timed innovation hatched by a stateside employee named John Pierson. The office of the *Army Tribune*, near the Place de la Concorde, possessed all the solemnity of a frat house on the eve of a big game. Its exuberant regulars included the Texan Peggy Hull, whom McCormick hired as the first female war correspondent; sports writer Ring Lardner, assigned, so he said, to report on "the funny side of the war"; and Charlie MacArthur, the future Broadway playwright, who nearly wrecked his car in a mad dash across the French countryside.[12]

McCormick did not check his vigorous commercial spirit with French customs. Since winter clothing and boots were all but unobtainable in the battle zone, he expected the *Army Tribune* to be "a gold mine" for mail-order houses and other merchants who shared his desire to make a profit while making war. By selling the paper for two cents (later raised to four) and charging a dollar per ad line, he figured that it could afford to pay stiff cable tolls, employ a zany crew of correspondents, and still break even.[13]

His sights, however, were fixed far beyond the current balance sheet. Anticipating a rush of Yankees to Paris after the war, McCormick argued the necessity of having an American journalistic presence in the French capital. "We are the only paper capable of conducting one," he said. "The other big papers very largely follow the lead of the English — due to social aspirations of their owners and lack of self-respect, perspective, American feeling and capacity on the part of their editors." England's day was past, he insisted, its once formidable might neutered by the submarine. "She can rule the world from now on only by an intellectual and moral ascendancy over us — such a one as usually is seen when an American and an Englishman meet. IT IS OUR MISSION TO BUILD UP THE AMERICAN CONSCIOUSNESS, THE AMERICAN PRIDE."[14]

Thanks to the *Army Tribune*, then, McCormick arrived in Europe considerably better armed than the rest of the American Expeditionary Force, which began trickling into French ports in the summer of 1917. Pershing, assured that his visitor was fluent in French, assigned him as an intelligence officer to work with the French war department. For the next few weeks McCormick spent more time spying on America's allies than on her enemies. He had no alternative, given French determination to withhold vital information concerning Allied strength and deployment.

To find this out, McCormick employed methods worthy of a vaudeville skit. Upon learning where a secretive French contact kept an organization table, McCormick had a subordinate start an argument next door. Once the Frenchman scurried down the hall to investigate the ruckus, McCormick stepped into his room and was able to retrieve the list from his desk and copy it for American military planners. (In later years the document occupied a prominent place in his Tribune Tower office.)

U.S. relations with the other chief Allied power were scarcely warmer. Whereas the French patronized, the British tried to coopt the unsophisticated doughboys they called Sammies. Fueling their hopes were certain members of the American diplomatic set. At a dinner hosted by an embassy friend of McCormick's father, a disparaging British major general straight out of *Pinafore* conceded that while Pershing's soldiers might compare with the finest colonial troops, present circumstances required that they be placed under British command. McCormick hotly disputed the idea of American inferiority. For this he was chastised by his hostess, who was imbued, in his opinion, with "the State Department view" and therefore quick to make unfavorable comparisons between the flower of His Majesty's armed legions and her own country's Mexico- and Philippine-trained generals.[15]

On hearing of this teapot tempest, Pershing turned brick red with anger. He commended McCormick for behaving "exactly right" in the face of British provocation. The AEF would, of necessity, rely on French artillery and airplanes for much of its firepower. Its battlefield tactics had been perfected a century earlier by the first Napoleon. But it remained the *American* Expeditionary Force, and Pershing was adamant that it must answer to American officers. His reasoning, however infuriating to Old World statesmen who looked to the United States to replenish their decimated ranks, went beyond national pride. Only by maintaining a separate identity would American fighting men and the diplomats to whom they gave the sanction of force be in a position to disregard secret treaties and selfish war aims pursued by continental powers.

A month after his arrival, still ensconced at the Ritz, McCormick observed that food was more plentiful in Parisian markets than at home. To be sure, coal supplies were running low in the French capital, but this was a temporary shortfall. "The real shortage is men. They are being killed off too fast. We will have to figure on sacrificing 500,000 a year as long as the war may last, several years perhaps, or face defeat," McCormick wrote to friends back in Chicago. Veiling his loneliness in gruff, schoolboy humor, he informed Emory Thomason, a recent addition to his law firm, "I have got a trained trenchdog. I will name him after the first guy that writes me."[16] With time on his hands, he went back to school, poring over English and French artillery textbooks. A deprecatory McCormick explained his regimen to Joe Patterson:

> Small mastery of the)
> subject, plus weak)   = (Tiresome
> comprehension of the)   (Job
> language.)[17]

In mid-August, French agents, at last persuaded that their American allies had no intention of truckling to the British, alerted McCormick to peace feelers coming out of the Vatican. The possibility that fighting might cease before Pershing secured his place in the history books caused dismay at American headquarters. As it happened, the general worried needlessly; the papal initiative died at birth. Of more immediate concern were fifth columnists in their midst. For example, the ability of France to eavesdrop on the most sensitive German communications was one of the most tightly guarded secrets of the war, shrouded even from the French navy. Yet when French operators deciphered radio signals beamed from neutral Spain to Germany, and later picked up suspicious communications identifying American ships in the French harbor at Le Havre, the information found its way to McCormick.

The intelligence scoop presented him with a conundrum. In 1917, coordination among the American armed forces was virtually nonexistent. Messages between the services, even those deployed on European battlefields, had to be routed through Washington. Fearful of compromising himself, yet unwilling to brook delay when American lives were in jeopardy, McCormick made a social call on the American naval attaché in Paris. In the middle of an otherwise innocuous conversation, he asked nonchalantly, "Isn't it extraordinary how the French decoded that German message?" This thinly veiled warning produced a naval inquiry that culminated in the arrest of a Frenchwoman, a small-bore Mata Hari accused of monitoring and reporting Allied shipping movements to the enemy. At her trial she insisted that she would never betray a French secret. Toward the Americans she felt no such responsibility. The French tribunal that heard the case was less inclined to make distinctions and ordered her executed as a spy.[18]

Notwithstanding these modest triumphs, McCormick was unhappy with intelligence work. Combativeness, not finesse, was the keystone of his personality. No general staff could long contain one of his inventiveness, authoritarian tendencies, and self-dramatizing flair. Cloak-and-dagger work required anonymity, and McCormick had not come to Europe to hide his light under a French hedgerow.

His first and longest-running battle was with a military establishment that was disdainful of civilian soldiers. Far more than he let on in his rose-tinted memoirs, McCormick fell between the stools. Through the intercession of Major General Peyton March, himself something of a maverick among Pershing's Chaumont set (so named for the village to which the American commander removed his headquarters in September 1917), McCormick gained entry to the artillery training school at Valdahon. Here the National Guardsman of francophile sympathies was ostracized by army regulars, for whom his presence violated the natural order of things. Forced to bunk with his Gallic instructors, McCormick put his exile to good use by translating French training manuals. Over the strenuous objections of an infantry officer with the euphonious name of Beaumont Buck, the upstart was given command of two batteries in the Fifth Field Artillery (an assignment he received, McCormick candidly acknowledged later, "because I had to be attached to something.")[19]

His new outfit was part of the vanguard of American soldiers destined for glory as "the Big Red One." Living up to its name, the First Division established precedents with every mile it tramped, every headline it won. During McCormick's relatively brief career within its ranks, the division achieved fame as the first U.S. contingent in Europe to enter a hostile sector, fire a shot in battle, capture German prisoners, and be singled out for praise by the high command. Drawn from every state in the Union, the men of the First exhibited a tolerance for idiosyncrasy missing from more established units. Even so, Major McCormick cut an exotic figure, at once more zealous and less orthodox than the sneering professionals for whom he would always be an intruder.

It was in France that McCormick first grew the toothbrush mustache that, along with his unnatural height, spaniel eyes, and clipped, world-weary demeanor, put one in mind of a lankier, less languid William Powell. Whatever he did carried a highly personal stamp. Near the command post known simply as McCormick was a lake in which he showed his men how to kill fish with hand grenades. He was a hard man to regiment, beginning with his decidedly nonregulation monocle and walking stick — the latter justified, he said, by an old football injury. Here Major McCormick flouted the military code of honor as well as the dress code. His leg had been hurt, all right — in his serious polo accident of July 1912. Perhaps he thought a football injury sounded more virile, more respectable among a brotherhood for whom modern war was the ultimate contact sport.

He was "painfully thin," McCormick informed Bill Field back in Chicago. "My ribs close together like broken band staves. As Happy Hooligan says, 'My bones hoits.' " Joking aside, he gave the impression of a man who had seen too much in his relatively brief existence. His cool skepticism surfaced during a camp visit by General Henri Philippe Pétain. McCormick concluded that the victor of Verdun, a future marshal of France, was "intelligent but nothing wonderful."[20]

More to his liking was Captain Billy Mitchell, a born rebel whose fervent advocacy of air power made him a bone in the throat of less visionary offices. The two men became friends, united in their passion for the airplane and their contempt for the fossilized hierarchy. Mitchell even offered to make McCormick chief of the air intelligence section, a gesture as quixotic as McCormick's proposal that he accompany Mitchell on an aerial inspection of German positions. The military establishment was quick to reject both ideas. McCormick consoled himself by taking to the skies whenever possible. He pronounced high-altitude flight delightful, in contrast to the "psychologically distressing" effects produced by a spiraling descent.[21]

Writing to his brother in mid-September, McCormick lavished praise on his French instructors as soldiers of distinction, blessed with abundant tact and charm. "I have no idea when we are going in the line," he continued. "If peace comes by spring, we will probably be the only Americans to see fighting." His question was answered in the third week of October, when elements of the First Division occupied a quiet sector of the Allied front in Lorraine. "The first American shell fired into the German lines went over my head," McCormick boasted in a letter home; "it took a little effort, but less than to get a desk job somewhere."[22]

He had little else to crow about. In a country inn one evening, he enjoyed a simple meal of raw oysters served up by "a pulchritudinous if not immaculate damsel who kisses all the officers for a franc" — all, that is, except himself. For McCormick, cold, soaked, and heartily tired of fresh-killed beef and boiled potatoes, the Ritz was a taunting memory. Some canned meat laid him low with food poisoning. A severe attack of hemorrhoids caused him pained embarrassment. Autumn rains flooded the trenchworks, canceling badly needed gunnery practice. During fitful breaks in the clouds, he rambled over the countryside, map in hand, teaching himself the topography of north-central France. To frustrate Germans listening in on his telephone exchanges, he fell back on American slang, a language impenetrable to the orderly Teutonic mind.[23]

"The Heinies dropped a shell about 50 yards from my Ford yesterday," McCormick wrote home in a display of almost British phlegm. A doctor in his party detected a whiff of gas in the air, "whereupon Henry was vigorously cranked and took us away *vite.*" Not long afterward a seventy-five-millimeter gun burst in his vicinity, carrying off a gunner's leg. To his brother, McCormick described "a funny dream. I was in the Willy McCormick house on Rush Street when the Germans began to bomb the tower . . . I woke up and found that all the guns hereabouts were firing. I don't know whether it is a trench raid or a bombing expedition."[24]

McCormick told his brother that a martial pecking order had spontaneously developed: "A battery commander addresses a quartermaster as a Lord would a banker or shipowner." So much for the vaunted Wilsonian war for democracy. Fortunately, few American enlisted men had adopted Old World notions of deference. "One sergeant blacked an interpreter's eye for preceding him through a door and said at his trial that the man was trying to act like an officer."[25]

McCormick readily chose French *liberté* over *egalité.* Writing from Valdahon late in the summer of 1917, he reminded Chicago friends that people with ability were rare, in or out of uniform, and that it was neither sensible nor heroic to condemn "competent men" to "insignificant positions." He openly scorned the elderly functionaries infesting the army command structure. "They have been trying to polish off a lot of bricks and call them diamonds," he said. "I am off these summer cream lady guys. I want boys who can deliver per cents."[26]

❖ 4

The soldier in McCormick never crowded out the newspaperman. Accepting random death with equanimity, he angrily damned military censorship as "government by man without jurisprudence . . .

Over here there is no longer any claim that it is to keep news from the enemy." Rather, the blue pencil of the censor was wielded indiscriminately in order to cloak defeat in misguided patriotism and shield incompetents from exposure and removal. Writing of the British and French censors, McCormick called the former "a lie factory," the latter "part of a political conspiracy."[27]

Late in October, as the First Division filed into trenchworks near Luneville, McCormick obtained leave to visit Paris whenever *Tribune* business called him there. After three months in Europe, the major was eager to take on the world, or at least as much of it as an elite corps of hand-picked foreign correspondents could make sensible for midwestern news-paper readers. Taking Paris for a hub, McCormick envisaged a news ser-vice with bureaus in London, Stockholm, Petrograd, Athens, Rome, Berne, Madrid, and The Hague.

As befitted the World's Greatest Newspaper, this was to be no ordinary newsgathering organization. "Why must American newspapers send a lot of bums on the most important assignment in history?" he growled after seeing a group of drunken reporters, the ragpickers of their trade, raising hell in Dijon. Decorum aside, *Tribune* correspondents were to address more than the latest follies of continental statesmen or the most outré fashions to set Parisian tongues wagging. As ambassadors from the House of Medill/McCormick, they must communicate the patriotic American viewpoint to European opinion-makers.[28]

McCormick's design took on added urgency after November 1917, when well-drilled Bolshevik cadres overthrew the provisional Russian govern-ment headed by Alexander Kerensky. Suddenly Allied military prospects were overshadowed by the specter of Slavic communism extending a bloody hand to European workers in their charred cities and shriveled economies. "Either we control the destinies of Europe or Europe controls ours," McCormick darkly prophesied.[29]

To get his news service off the ground, he turned to Floyd Gibbons, a daredevil in the rankish tradition of Richard Harding Davis and Nellie Bly. During the Mexican campaign, Gibbons had scored a coup by interview-ing Pancho Villa in a railroad boxcar. At the urging of the *Tribune* corre-spondent, the bandit leader had postponed a planned attack until the American World Series ended and baseball-crazy gringos might again focus their attention on the border. Early in 1917, in search of new thrills, Gibbons booked passage on the 18,000-ton Cunard liner *Laconia*. When the ship was torpedoed by German U-boats, he found himself handed the story of a lifetime. His evocative reporting of the *Laconia*'s final hours and of his own rescue from the Irish Sea made him a global celebrity before his clothes were dry.

Four months later he returned to Europe to record the arrival of

American soldiers in France and to attribute to Pershing, wrongly, the electrifying greeting — "Lafayette, we are here!" — with which the Great Republic stepped forward to redeem her wayward Old World cousins. Pershing, being only a man, raised no objection to becoming a myth. He praised Gibbons to McCormick as "a warm personal friend" ideally qualified to run the *Army Tribune*. This came as unwelcome news to the current editor, John Pierson. On November 24, McCormick bluntly informed Pierson that his management was "rotten" and his staff badly in need of pruning.[30]

Not content to change the music, McCormick wanted to shoot the piano player. So charged Farmer Murphy, a veteran *Tribune* reporter with roots set deep in the Robert Patterson–Jim Keeley era. Murphy's brief acquaintance with McCormick never risked developing into friendship. With a fondness for the personal pronoun rivaling that of his employer, Murphy claimed responsibility for saving the *Army Tribune* from Chicago bean-counters reluctant to compete with the official service newspaper, *Stars and Stripes*. (This overlooked McCormick's personal commitment to the *Army Tribune* as the nucleus of his postwar European news service.) Murphy also quoted McCormick as saying, "I'll be a bigger man in the Army with the paper going on in Paris."[31]*

McCormick was big enough to be a frequent visitor to Pershing's headquarters, where he conveyed French demands, depressingly familiar through repetition, for at least 800,000 Americans with which to reinforce the western front by August 1918. In the presence of the commanding general, McCormick urged an aggressive press campaign, calling attention to the inadequacies of U.S. shipping and the resulting shortages, which hampered the war effort. Pershing, having no wish to antagonize either his commander-in-chief or the federal shipping board he had appointed, silkenly changed the subject.[32]

Not all McCormick's suggestions were so easily deflected. General Fox Conner credited the self-taught artillery expert with the idea, belatedly adopted by the AEF, of adding eight automatic rifles to each battery. McCormick's adaptation of the standard-issue trenching tool into a protective headpiece for doughboys peering over trenchtops earned its inventor the first of his seven patents. Monocle or no monocle, it is fair to say that McCormick's vision extended beyond the status quo; certainly it exceeded that of Farmer Murphy.[33]

Murphy's greatest skill was for rewriting history. To anyone who would

---

*That the egocentric publisher might entertain such thoughts is not difficult to imagine. But it strains credibility to believe that this crafty, self-protective businessman, who had successfully concealed his past intentions from the likes of Victor Lawson and William Beale, should now open his heart to a "windy and not effective" reporter he neither liked nor trusted.

listen in later years, the erstwhile *Tribune* correspondent blamed Mc-
Cormick for his abrupt firing. As Murphy told it, his severance came
without warning or the slightest opportunity for him to defend his twenty
years of faithful service.[34]

McCormick's diary says otherwise. "Saw Murphy and read his correspondence with Field," reads an entry dated March 8, 1918, almost four
months after McCormick's original order to John Pierson to reduce his
bloated staff. "Told him could have another month's trial." In fact McCormick did much better than that, employing Murphy at the Versailles Peace
Conference and still later sending him to Vienna, notwithstanding Murphy's
habit of filing copy "too editorial" for McCormick's taste. (From McCormick's standpoint, Murphy's greatest crime may have been geographical.
His entire *Tribune* career, prior to 1917, had been passed in New York City.
And as long as McCormick lived, the New York office of the paper was
regarded, only half in jest, as a foreign bureau.)

In return, Murphy related a series of anecdotes depicting McCormick's
love of battle as strictly platonic. The reporter claimed that McCormick
was derided by those unfortunate enough to fall under his command as
Dugout Mac, and that on one occasion he had left an active front and
rushed back to Paris in search of his runaway trench dog, Sweeney (which
may or may not have been poisoned by his resentful subordinates). Actually, Sweeney *did* briefly disappear, but in a rural village, not Paris. Local
gendarmes returned the animal to its distraught owner, who happened to
be in town as part of a group of officers on their way to the front. Indeed, if
one is to credit Murphy, McCormick may be said to have given a whole
new meaning to "the dogs of war." He was accused of ordering his batman,
in the event of gas attack, to slip a protective mask over Sweeney's nose
before attending to his own safety.[35]

But by far the most damaging of Murphy's stories belittled the part
McCormick played in the May 1918 battle of Cantigny, at which the First
Division proved its mettle by storming a German-held village barely
sixty miles from Paris. By this account, McCormick fled the American
staging area before a hostile shot was fired, then hightailed it back to
Paris with the complacent observation, "That was doing pretty well,
wasn't it?"[36]

To be fair, the man who liked to be known simply as the Colonel had
invited scrutiny by donning a cloak of papal infallibility where military
subjects were concerned. That McCormick could be an unreliable narrator
of his exploits will come as no surprise. Fortunately, we do not have to rely
on his admittedly imperfect memory to render a verdict on Murphy's
shameful charges; there is no shortage of independent, contemporary evidence attesting to McCormick's presence and conduct at Cantigny.
Murphy succeeded anyway in wounding his target more seriously than any

battlefield adversary could hope to. Dishonor, even if the product of common gossip, is not a stain easily removed.

For the rest of his days McCormick was dogged by intimations of cowardice and hypocrisy on a prodigous scale. The effect of Murphy's malicious tongue was to increase the burden of proof on a sensitive man already plagued by self-doubt and the deeply felt need of the outsider to justify his existence.

❖ 5

The road to Cantigny was littered with improvised strategies and broken reputations. McCormick shed no tears over the departure, late in 1917, of the First Division's commander, Major General William Sibert. He held a considerably higher opinion of Sibert's replacement, a slender, aristocratic Alabamian named Robert Lee Bullard. The new commander reciprocated, having been impressed by McCormick's persistence in equipping Americans along the Mexican border with machine guns. Offered a place at the general staff school, McCormick begged off with the remark that "the competition for jobs at the rear is a trifle uninspiring." Not for him the derisive label *embusqué*, applied by front-line soldiers to those well-fed officers whose valor increased in direct proportion to their distance from combat.[37]

A notable exception to this rule was his immediate supervisor, Colonel Dwight Aultman. The two men hit it off from the start. They formed an alliance to counter the disorganization and chronic supply shortages that continued to sap divisional strength. "No tallow, no gun oil. Short spare parts, caissons, feed, damn near everything," McCormick complained early in January 1918. Soldiers' pay was two months in arrears when, later in the month, the Big Red One was assigned to the Ansauville sector, north of Toul. Roads under water or frozen solid slowed movement to a crawl. An outbreak of trenchfoot, blamed on a lack of protective footwear, added to the misery. McCormick advised a National Guardsman embarking for Europe to be sure and bring as much warm clothing, blankets, boots, and galoshes as he could pack. "Sears, Roebuck does not deliver over here!" he scribbled with cold-stiffened fingers.[38]

This was no idle jest. McCormick was hard-pressed to find tools, cement, lumber, or concrete posts with which to fortify his position along a low, marshy line nearly five miles long. Without engineers to build gas shelters for his men, he was forced to rely on ill-fitting gas masks of English or French design. Offsetting the scarcity of talent and materiel was a surfeit of orders, many confusing or contradictory, issued by competing American, French, divisional, and brigade-level warlords. The AEF was not the first army to make war on common sense. At the start of 1918, it had little ammunition on hand. Moreover, availability did not always equal reliability (McCormick one morning counted fifty-two powderless shells in his daily allotment).

Disregarding such practicalities, the Fifth Field Artillery was directed to commence a harassing fire against enemy strongholds on and around Mont Sec, a 400-foot ridge affording German defenders views of the entire Ansauville sector. Within days a second set of orders sharply restricted shelling, unless sanctioned in advance by divisional headquarters. McCormick, never one to accept bureaucratic idiocies with a crisp salute, wrote Colonel Aultman a long letter protesting the use and placement of heavy guns. Some of his ideas were eventually adopted. Yet too many American gunners continued shooting at targets beyond their range, succeeding only in revealing their positions to the other side.[39]

Unsuccessful in stemming the flow of "querulous and unreasonable" commands from GHQ, McCormick busied himself devising methods for defending his batteries, camouflaging 155-millimeter cannons, and neutralizing German trench mortars. It was exhausting work. His diary falls silent for a full week early in February; its author was too "dog tired" to record his actions. There were compensations: on an inspection tour of the Ansauville sector, Pershing sought out his former intelligence officer and expressed satisfaction at finding him flourishing in his new role.

McCormick's relationship toward those under his command foreshadowed his paternalistic administration of the *Tribune*. Drunkards could expect to have their pay docked by a third. On investigating the source of a persistent disagreeable odor in his room, he learned that his striker hadn't taken a bath in two months. He promptly ordered every man in the battalion to bathe. Rigorous daily inspections of barracks and batteries were instituted. His perfectionism landed him in another kind of hot water after he instructed sentries to fire on a Red Cross vehicle attempting to evade a military checkpoint. Luckily for him, the divisional artillery commander, Brigadier General Charles P. "Sitting Bull" Summerall, wrote off the affair to the overzealousness of a young officer.[40]

During the early morning hours of March 1, Major McCormick detected firing on the American right. He repositioned his guns to provide cover for the Eighteenth Infantry Regiment, the object of a recent German gas attack, whose exposed position in the Bois de Remières left it vulnerable to fresh assaults. With aggressive movements boiling up on the right flanks, McCormick requested permission from brigade headquarters to lay down a protective barrage. His warnings were dismissed by an inexperienced reserve officer on duty, who reminded him of French unhappiness over the prodigal use of powder and shot by trigger-happy Americans.

Forced to chose between the military code of unquestioning obedience and the possible sacrifice of American lives, McCormick by his own admission went "berserk . . . I knew it was an attack and opened fire. As soon as I opened fire everybody else thought the order had been given and the whole brigade opened fire." For the next hour guns on both sides blazed away. German aggression was foiled, and McCormick's gamble was vindicated. He had little time for self-congratulation; no sooner had quiet returned to the front than he received a telephone call demanding his presence at General Summerall's headquarters.[41]

Anticipating the worst, McCormick glumly covered the distance on horseback. By the time he arrived at his destination, lunch was being served. This assured that his humiliation would be all the more public. But he was in for a surprise. Instead of reprimanding him, Summerall theatrically rose from the table, extended his hand in friendship, and declared, "Thank God there is one man in this outfit who knows when to disobey an order."[42]

Summerall was not always so forgiving. On another occasion, told that his shells were falling on advancing American forces, McCormick went to investigate the report for himself. While he was away, a call came in from divisional headquarters. For his absence he was hauled before Summerall and given a brutal dressing-down. All attempts to explain or justify his behavior were coldly rejected.

In later years McCormick developed a profound admiration for Summerall, going so far as to present the old soldier, then serving as commandant of the Citadel military academy in Charleston, South Carolina, with an estate in nearby Aiken. All this, however, was the fruit of mature reflection and McCormick's nostalgia; his war diary is peppered with slighting references to Summerall's alleged deficiencies as an artilleryman and a leader.

Two days after the aborted German raid, McCormick learned of an American counterthrust set for March 4. At one o'clock that morning, the Fifth Field Artillery joined other units in a thundering wake-up call delivered to the German lines. It soon became apparent, however, that it was the Americans who had been caught sleeping. The raid had been called off after a group of engineers appeared too late to blast an avenue of attack through no man's land. Embarrassingly, no one in the infantry had bothered to inform the artillery. The resulting thirty-five-minute demonstration did little more than waste Allied ammunition.

With this comedy of blunders the First Division neared the end of its apprenticeship. Rumors of a huge German offensive taking shape just a few miles to the east kept McCormick in suspense. "I don't sleep any more," he confided to Tiffany Blake on March 16. "I hear every shot. The first buzz of the telephone wakes me." Artfully wording his letter to evade "41,144 rules of censorship," he acknowledged that "the cockiness of the artillery is very visible in us." Meanwhile, he organized a musical entertainment for those with nerves frayed by constant shelling from eight-inch German howitzers. The terrors of war were momentarily forgotten amid the jaunty sounds of Irish dance tunes, the heady aroma of coffee and oranges, and the steadying pleasure of that greatest of dugout luxuries, cigarettes.

As the German army, its ranks swelled by sixty divisions released from service on the Russian front, prepared to deliver a crushing blow in the west, McCormick found diversion in a two-day Parisian furlough. In the French capital he encountered evidence of cultural rot far more offensive to his nostrils than an unwashed battalion. "I didn't mind the pleasure-seekers. I was one," he told Blake. "I got mad at the business community. Damn sordid!"[43]

✧ 6

Allied strategists feared the coming onslaught as a burned child dreads fire. Operation Michael, launched early on the morning of March 21, was backed by three hundred planes and six thousand field guns. Within two days, British and French armies along a fifty-mile front were in full retreat and the British Fifth Army was virtually annihilated. Paris came under bombardment from three gigantic Krupp cannon installed seventy miles from the city gates. A numbing sense of déjà vu gripped war-weary populations for whom the clock had suddenly been turned back to the summer of 1914.

The comparison worked to the kaiser's advantage, for with Russia immobilized by revolution, he no longer had to worry about a two-front war. And few military experts, in Berlin or any other European capital, expected green American soldiers to redress the imbalance created by the Russian abdication. On the evening of March 23, Kaiser Wilhelm pronounced the war all but over. At virtually the same hour, British prime minister David Lloyd George sent an emergency plea for American assistance through his ambassador in Washington. With their backs to the wall, the Allied powers were driven for the first time to practice coalition warfare, without thought of national jealousies or competing objectives. Out of the crisis came a unified command, under the leadership of Ferdinand Foch. It emerged not a moment too soon, for the Germans were knocking at an open door.

On March 25, McCormick learned that advance elements of the invading force were crossing the Somme River. That evening his batteries came under heavy fire, which he returned after painstakingly calibrating the location of enemy artillery guns. Trigonometry had its uses after all. At the start of April, amid scenes of wild confusion, the First Division was pulled from Ansauville and sent to Gisors, north of Paris, for a crash course in open-field combat. Passing up the "nasty, dirty, 3rd class coach" set aside for officers, McCormick made the hundred-mile journey in one of the forty-foot-by-eight-foot boxcars christened "Side Door Pullmans" by their overcrowded passengers. For the next week, under the close supervision of American and French officers, the division took part in simulated attacks and other field maneuvers.[44]

On April 13, Pershing appeared before a group of officers to deliver what army historians immortalized as his farewell address to the First and McCormick dismissed as "a weak speech saying we were to go in line." The latest turn of events had forced Pershing to soft-peddle his demands for an independent American army. He now ordered the First Division to the Montdidier section of Picardy, where the First French Army was struggling to contain the advancing Germans. Three miles west of Montdidier lay the tiny, half-ruined village of Cantigny. This melancholy cluster of slate-roofed houses, guarded by the inevitable château and church tower, had been overrun by the Germans in the first days of Operation Michael. Soon it formed the westernmost point of a German salient, lodged knifelike in the Allies' vitals. Its elevated position provided not only a prime observation post but a natural staging ground for further German attacks on the key river town of Amiens and on Paris itself.[45]

For the Americans, the importance of Cantigny was less strategic than psychological. Retaking the fortified village would demonstrate their combat readiness and bolster Pershing's case for military autonomy. No one thought it would be easy. En route to Cantigny, McCormick left a platoon to guard the crossroads of Seicheprey. As if anticipating the savagery to come, he bade the group an emotional farewell, declaring that "the nearer you are to the enemy, the nearer you are to God." His theology was put to the test early on the morning of April 20. Under cover of fog, three columns of crack German troops mauled the U.S. Twenty-sixth (Yankee) Division, made up mostly of National Guardsmen from Connecticut. In the close fighting that raged most of the day, eighty-one Americans were killed; nearly two hundred more were taken prisoner or reported missing.

The sobering lesson of Seicheprey was not lost on Major McCormick. Four days later, his First Battalion reached the outskirts of Cantigny. While waiting for the infantry to catch up and dig in, McCormick resorted to deception in order to conceal his weakness from enemy eyes. He placed antiaircraft machine guns along his lightly defended front and deployed reserves in precisely those areas likeliest to come under surveillance from German patrols probing for enemy strengths and vulnerabilities.

As the departing French readily acknowledged, this was not a sector in the usual sense. Unorganized until now, the area lacked entrenchments and barbed wire defenses. The original American line consisted of little more than a broken arc of occupied shellholes, separated from Cantigny by seven hundred yards of unplanted wheat fields. For the Americans, the first order of business was to scratch out emplacement dugouts for their 155-millimeter field weapons. No less important were ammunition shelters for the two million shells stockpiled in anticipation of a furious artillery duel. These expectations were more than realized over the next month, as 90 German batteries lobbed an average of 3,500 shells a day into the American positions.

The metal rainstorm forced the besieging army to live a molelike existence in damp wine cellars or rat-infested barns well behind the lines. (McCormick and Floyd Gibbons spent one harrowing night cowering in a filthy cellar while German shells pounded the ground around them.) Food and medical attention could be supplied only under cover of darkness, so close was the opposing army, so constant the threat of daytime detection by spy balloons and observer planes.

As unpredictable as the army's provisions was the liaison between Allied forces. Once, upon concluding a predawn reconnaissance mission, McCormick made his way to French divisional headquarters in hopes of finding some breakfast. On his arrival he was given a paltry demitasse of coffee and brandy by an ancient chief of staff in a soiled dress uniform. "It is better to have an empty stomach if you are shot through it," explained his bedraggled host.[46]

The epicure turned stoic accepted his lot with surprising equanimity. "There is a certain class to this life," McCormick wrote to Tiffany Blake at the beginning of May. "You get up after a sound sleep — some nights — you find that the supply service has sent some eggs, so you breakfast grandly with three cups of the excellent coffee furnished in the French ration, put on your Christmas tree belt with compass, field glass, map case, pistol and gas mask and order, 'Send the instrument corporal at once' . . . You go to your batteries, then out to your O.P.'s [observation posts]. You change your route to avoid terrain under fire, you wait for a barrage to lift, you hole up quickly in a shell crater. Time passes rapidly. You see you must miss lunch, as you decide to search for new and better points for observation or to visit the doughboys. A late hour in the afternoon brings you back to your P.C. saying wearily, 'I wish this damn war had come ten years ago.' You are overtired; you take a needed tonic in the form of a scotch whiskey and water which gives you energy for the evening's work. But no — the people who make a living out of prohibition have prevented that and the Germans' task is rendered easier."[47]

General Bullard arrived one afternoon in the midst of a withering barrage. McCormick tried to wave him away. "If you come here several times a day, I can stop here once," said Bullard. McCormick responded that the divisional commander was too valuable to throw his life away. Besides, he told Bullard, "you are keeping me here."[48]

He didn't exaggerate the peril in a zone where life expectancy was measured in days. Knocked unconscious by an exploding shell, McCormick counted himself luckier than the motorcycle messenger he saw wrapped around a tree by a German whizzbang. "All day long the opposing artilleries fired to destroy each other," he later recalled. "All night they fired on roads, paths and stream crossings, to impede the advance of supplies, ammunition, and reinforcements; day and night they poured their shells upon trenches, villages, and woods, to rob the enemy of sleep, shatter his nerves, and kill him."[49]

✦ 7

Laconic as a Hemingway hero, McCormick recorded the gallows humor with which young Americans under fire gave vent to their fears and feelings. "One of our captains was buried by a shell yesterday," he wrote in mid–May 1918. "The story is related as though it were a joke. He has a flaming red mustache. Eyewitnesses describe him with nothing but his face appearing. Everybody roars. A rather unpopular officer was wounded in the leg and lost a tooth and was rolled some distance. This also passes as funny."[50]

In an army still "pretty constabularyish" McCormick frequently skated over the thin ice of insubordination. "You have to *interpret* them," he said of orders from above, "which often means *change them* . . . Some men agonize over it. I rejoice in a safe nest in private life in case of downfall."[51]

In truth, McCormick was seeking promotion and a transfer even as the relentless American shelling softened up Cantigny's defenses. Early in May, Colonel Aultman gained a brigadier's star, and with it reassignment to the Fifty-first Field Artillery Brigade of the Twenty-sixth Infantry Division. He asked McCormick to be his adjutant. "Ran into General Pershing," McCormick wrote on May 2, "who complimented me on my appearance, saying I looked the part! Gosh!"

Appearances were deceiving. Aultman could obtain the services of his friend only with the permission of General Summerall, and Sitting Bull was not inclined to surrender an experienced artilleryman on the brink of an offensive. On May 5, McCormick left the front for Paris and three days of strenuous self-promotion. The Germans weren't the only adversary to occupy his thoughts. Jim Keeley had just sold the fading *Chicago Herald* to Hearst and was rumored to be crossing the Atlantic. Was Keeley angling for his old job at the *Tribune*? Or did he hope to ingratiate himself with Lord Northcliffe, the London tabloid king whose phenomenally successful picture–paper, the *Daily Mirror*, McCormick and Joe Patterson hoped to duplicate in postwar New York?

While in Paris, McCormick gave a dinner party for General Aultman and turned down a job offer from his old Chicago friend Charles Dawes, who since August 1917 had been the AEF's general purchasing agent. Who else he may have seen and what strings he may have pulled in his jockeying for a reassignment are hinted at in a postwar First Division document affirming that on May 7, 1918, the last day of his Parisian furlough, he was officially relieved of his duties with the Fifth Field Artillery.[52]

A further clue to his activities in the French capital is contained in a diary entry coinciding with his return to the Cantigny front at dawn on May 8. During his brief absence, two of McCormick's trusted subordinates had been transferred out of his battalion. "The little circle is breaking up," he wrote resignedly. "I will not be sorry to leave."[53]

But he didn't leave. Not then. He got sick instead, falling victim to the Spanish influenza. On May 13 he managed, with difficulty, to conduct his regular morning inspections. Before nightfall he was so debilitated that he was forced to lie down in a clearing, heedless of deadly shrapnel slicing the air above him. His condition, at first misdiagnosed as trench fever, worsened over the next few days. It was aggravated by a flareup of the painful sinus ailment he had experienced during his Russian trip.

On May 20 McCormick picked up rumors of a *second* promotion, no doubt engineered during his recent visit to Paris, to a vacant lieutenant colonelcy in his former National Guard regiment, since renamed the 122nd Field Artillery. He sent off for champagne and pork for a celebration. His car was hit five times by enemy bullets, leading him to decorate its iron mudguards with wound and service stripes.

The next day, adopting a deliberately ironic tone to mask his eagerness, McCormick sought confirmation of the news from Pershing's headquarters. He claimed that no heroine of the silver screen had ever been so torn between rival suitors. "Now, I ask you," he said with clumsy wit, "how can I beat the Germans with all these uncertainties harassing me and taking my mind off hate?" His arch prose did not conceal his transparent self-interest at a time of supreme anxiety for the American war effort.[54]

Preoccupation with the coming battle combined with Charles Summerall's unyielding opposition to thwart McCormick's desire for immediate promotion. Still weak from the flu, he took up residence in a hillside dugout after a German shell destroyed his former command post. At the entrance to these improvised quarters he hung a cowbell as a primitive warning system, to be activated at first sight of lethal gas clouds drifting toward American lines. On the morning of May 26, rejecting the advice of doctors who wanted him hospitalized, he hobbled to a final briefing on the battle plan, now scheduled for execution within forty-eight hours.[55]

The next night was anything but still as American infantrymen, machine gunners, engineers, and carrying parties filed into position. Under a blanket of darkness, 200,000 artillery rounds were delivered to Allied gunners. McCormick, near the end of his rope, undertook a final survey of his position. He upbraided a negligent lieutenant for abandoning his gas mask. He returned to his sickbed. At 4:45 on the morning of May 28, Allied artillerymen seeking their ranges unloosed the first tentative volley of the day. An hour later a full-throated cannonade erupted from nearly four hundred guns. McCormick concentrated the fire of his batteries on the German trenchworks. He laid down a rolling barrage, sheltering four hundred members of the Twenty-eighth Infantry as they traversed a mile of open country at twenty-five yards per minute. On reaching the advanced German trenches, the attackers found no signs of life — grisly tribute to the accuracy of McCormick and his gunners.[56]

Three times that morning McCormick ordered his batteries to shift their fire in line with the changing fortunes of the combatants. "He seemed to sense where his shells would stop the Germans the quickest," recalled one aged Cantigny veteran long afterward, "and he personally observed his own fire to see for himself that all was being done to support the doughboys." (The same observer, Charles Bourcier by name, also said that he "hated" to report the latest combat developments to McCormick, "because it always meant that I would have to seek [him] out in the places where the most furious fighting and shelling was going on.")[57]

Luck was with the Twenty-eighth that morning. The German garrison protecting Cantigny had been replaced during the night with less experienced troops. Adding to the woes of the defenders, a mixup in communications prevented German pilots from sending warning messages to their comrades on the ground. Assisted by a dozen French tanks and 150 flamethrowers, the Americans seized the battered village in just thirty-five minutes. By 7:30 A.M. elements of the attacking force had pushed beyond Cantigny and were digging in along a ridge to the north. Taking their objective had been relatively easy. Holding it against seven ferocious German counterattacks over the next three days cost the division nearly two hundred lives; there were over a thousand casualties in all.

Among those evacuated for medical reasons was Robert McCormick. At 11:30 on the morning of the twenty-eighth, he turned over command to his adjutant, second lieutenant Arthur Schmon. Two hours later he was helped into an ambulance for the trip to the American hospital at Neuilly, on the outskirts of Paris. Here he remained for a week, receiving treatment for frontal sinusitis and getting belated confirmation of his reassignment to the 122nd Field Artillery. While hospitalized, McCormick asked a young doughboy with a broken ankle how he had sustained his injury. "Kicking the wounded Germans," the soldier replied.[58]

On June 5, impatient to return to the front, McCormick wrote to Major General George Bell, his newest commanding officer. Later that day, after learning of a bloody encounter between the U.S. Third Division and a German force attempting to drive the Americans into the Marne River at Château Thierry, McCormick called for his car and driver and made his way to the battle zone. Given his weakened state, his services were unlikely to be of much value, but that didn't prevent him from offering them, unsuccessfully, to the divisional commander.[59]

❖ 8

The ten weeks McCormick spent with the 122nd Field Artillery were enough to convince Milton Foreman, his original National Guard sponsor, that he had outgrown his old unit. "He has become a big man," Foreman wrote to Amy McCormick in July 1918, "tremendously improved, stabilized, broadened." The recuperating McCormick drew up an instructional manual for troops about to enter the line. Based on his experiences at the front, the twenty-six-page guide offered advice on how to conduct a march, select gun emplacements, and make the most of unappetizing army cuisine ("The cook . . . should be encouraged to prepare soup, which will use up his bones and furnish valuable heat in the winter and liquid in a palatable form.")[60]

Equally thrifty with words, McCormick inserted his primer into his second book, *The Army of 1918*, published early in 1920. Before sailing for home at the start of August, he learned that he had been recommended for promotion to full colonel. In a celebratory mood he set off to find Joe Patterson, a captain of artillery with the famous Forty-second, or Rainbow, Division. Borrowing a helmet and gas mask from the flamboyant Colonel Douglas MacArthur, McCormick tracked Patterson to a regimental command post in the village of Mareuil-en-Dole, near the Ourcq River. The two men climbed out a back window to escape the noise inside. They found a quiet spot for conversation atop a barnyard manure pile. Amid these earthy surroundings, went the oft-told story, was born the *New York Daily News*, the picture-filled offspring of Joe Patterson's gritty imagination, *Tribune* capital, and the urban populism of the cockney-flavored Northcliffe gazettes.

In Paris, McCormick met disappointment when his Groton classmate Edward ("son of a bitch") Bowditch refused to announce his presence to General Pershing. Just at that moment, an explosion shook the neighborhood and brought the general running to investigate the source of the blast. Spotting McCormick, Pershing invited him into his office, where the younger man revealed that he had been offered regimental commands by both Dwight Aultman and General Malin Craig of the Second Army.

Instead of congratulations, Pershing administered the verbal equivalent of a slap in the face. He reminded McCormick that recently promoted colonels were being sent home to help train the vast new army expected to tip the scales in favor of the Allies no later (and no earlier) than the summer of 1919.

"I don't care about the colonelcy if I can have a regiment," said McCormick.

"The war is over for the summer," Pershing reiterated, in an exchange no doubt colored by wishful thinking on McCormick's part. "We may have a little scrap here and there, but we don't expect any more fighting until next spring." By going home and sharing with fresh recruits what he had learned in the trenches and on the training grounds, McCormick could assure himself a bright future. Indeed, said Pershing (as McCormick recounted the exchange), the next time he set foot in Europe, it would be as a brigadier general.[61]

Visions of glory went glimmering before McCormick reached New York. "While I was on the ocean the Germans broke," he recalled with an injured pride still tender after three decades. "They had been fighting, fighting like hell until that time. Something went wrong with them. Then [the Allies] pushed it right to the end. I never got back." On such melancholy occasions he sounded as if the kaiser had perversely capitulated in November 1918 for the express purpose of denying Colonel McCormick the honors that might easily have come to General McCormick.

He hid his disappointment from friends who greeted him in the flower-bedecked offices of the *Tribune* during the third week of August. A reporter for the *Herald-Examiner* detected an unmistakable "aura of capacity" in "Chicago's fighting writing man." With his planed physique and stentorian voice, McCormick seemed a natural commander. Admiration for the plucky doughboys he had left behind overcame his normal reticence. "If only our parents could see," he gushed — and one could picture Kate and Rob, the latter, his mind irretrievably wasted, dying by inches in a suburban Chicago nursing home — "how astonished the Allies are to see the Yanks fight, and if only they could see the grey terror that the sight of a yelling, wild-eyed Yank puts upon the face of a Hun when they leap at them with bayonets flashing! Oh boy!"[62]

McCormick's ardor was severely tested by his next assignment, with the Sixty-first Field Artillery at nearby Fort Sheridan. Here he found himself supervising a regiment of artillery, an infantry battalion, a motor transport school, and a post hospital teeming with victims of the same Spanish influenza that had threatened his life in France. As an army unit in the making, it was, he thought, "a joke." At the moment, however, no one around Fort Sheridan was laughing. Schooled as McCormick was in hardship, the horrors of that summer haunted him to the end of his life. "A man who attended officers' call in the morning would turn black and die before night," he remembered with a shudder.

To contain the spread of the plague, McCormick boarded up congested barracks and moved his men into well-ventilated tents. Against another epidemic, this one manmade, he was virtually powerless. As he phrased it, with unaccustomed tact, "Girls in the neighborhood were overcareless in going out with strange men." He appointed investigative boards to examine each allegation of rape that crossed his desk. He assigned wives of regular army officers living on base to interrogate the alleged victims. For the most part he accepted their verdicts, protesting just once, on behalf of a young lady who, in defending her honor with a hatpin, had poked her assailant full of holes.

In October 1918, McCormick was ordered to accompany the Sixty-first Field Artillery on a training mission to Camp Jackson, outside the South Carolina capital of Columbia. Unreconstructed southerners studiously avoided social, or any other, intercourse with their Yankee oppressors. It was during his "imprisonment" at Fort Jackson that McCormick received a letter from Pershing, dated November 1, expressing a strong desire to see the Colonel return to France at the head of a regiment — an invitation superseded by news of the armistice, which took effect on November 11.

Even before peace broke out, McCormick struggled to come to terms with what might have been. "I feel keenly my absence from all that is going on," he wrote to Joe Patterson, who was far more eager to put the war behind him. Patterson's greatest source of anxiety, however, had nothing to do with the cumbersome process of demobilization. Not made for renunciation, he dreaded the experiment in self-denial about to be launched by his puritanical countrymen. "If the country is going dry," he told Bert, "buy me up a lot of sherry and red and white wine — good quality. You can spend 2 or 3 thousand or up to 5 or 10 . . . I want to average a quart a day for 20 years."[63]

This was fine by McCormick, whose reverence for the American Constitution never prevented him from cheerfully violating its Eighteenth Amendment. In preparation for a long siege of enforced sobriety, he had been careful to stash an "ample supply" of spirits at Amy's Lake Forest house, a few miles from Fort Sheridan, thereby provisioning himself for the long march across the desert of Prohibition.

✧ 9

A week after the armistice, still chafing against his involuntary confinement at Camp Jackson, McCormick penned instructions for Floyd Gibbons, who was about to leave for Europe to take charge of the *Tribune* foreign news service. "By and large foreign correspondents don't get news," McCormick warned him. "They get propaganda, they get hot gossip, they get the stories brought to them by people with axes to grind. I am sorry to say that I read each piece of foreign cable with all the skepticism of a newspaper hater." Ideally, the Paris edition should afford Americans "a direct entrance into French political, economic, social and military life. We have not availed ourselves of it yet. You and yours must get to *know* the editors of the papers with which we are associated."[64]

A successful publication would give the *Tribune* a prestige unmatched by anyone else. A "reasonably good management" ought to be able to run the enterprise without loss. "Be on the lookout for features that can be bought," McCormick went on. "Pictures for roto or color section. Authentic stories of the true military history both this summer and before . . . I differentiate this from the flag-waving stuff which is coming over now. The army edition should have all army news, demobilization plans, reorganization plans. A good cable a day, including politics and wages."

McCormick contrasted the superb war coverage of the *Saturday Evening Post* with the slapdash reporting filling the regular press. "Many men think that in writing for newspapers they are not required to write as well as for magazines. Except for rush cables, this idea must be eradicated." In wishing Gibbons godspeed, McCormick also entrusted him with a message to spread across the masthead of the *Army Tribune*: SEND THE BOYS HOME — TOOTS SWEET.

❖ 10

Even at a distance of eighty years, it is difficult to find anything redeeming in Big Bill Thompson's cynical manipulation of antiwar sentiment to advance his political aspirations. Cruder still were his attempts to intimidate critics in the press. In September 1917 he filed the first of five libel suits against the *Tribune*, seeking cumulative damages of $1.3 million. As with so much of his behavior, it is unclear whether the suits were serious or a campaign device intended to dramatize the gulf between Big Bill the Builder and the dark forces of privilege and greed represented by the trust press. Exploiting the feud to maximum advantage, Thompson accused his journalistic enemies, led by "that pipsqueak Bob McCormick," of tapping his phones and boring holes in the walls of his apartment. (In fact, state's attorney Maclay Hoyne employed almost 1,500 phone-tap conversations in his unsuccessful prosecution of Thompson's police chief, Charles Healy, and black alderman Oscar DePriest, another Thompson ally. According to the historian Douglas Bukowski, the Justice Department also bugged a mayoral strategy session held at the LaSalle Hotel.)

Had the *Tribune* not existed, Thompson would have invented it to serve as both a foil for and a diversion from Chicago's deteriorating finances. In his first term, his free-spending habits had converted a municipal surplus of $2.5 million into a deficit nearly twice as large. Much of the red ink was spilled by the burgeoning political machine assembled to replace the crumbling Lorimer organization. Acting apparently on the theory that a politican who is poor is a poor politician, Lundin had chartered the William Hale Thompson Republican Club with an initial capitalization of $100,000. This proved more than enough to fund, among other adventures, a cross-country caravan of Thompson partisans in the summer of 1915, the opening gambit in a long-shot campaign to place Big Bill in the White House.

The early demise of Thompson's presidential boomlet in no way dulled his appetite for higher office. As Republican national committeeman, he hoped to extend his influence statewide. Late in 1917 he let it be known that he had designs on the U.S. Senate seat occupied by Democrat J. Hamilton Lewis, an Edwardian dandy with pink whiskers and a florid oratorical style that looked back to Daniel Webster and forward to Everett Dirksen. Opposing Thompson in the March 1918 Republican primary was Congressman Medill McCormick, freshly returned from a well-publicized tour of European battlefields.

The Thompson–McCormick race was conducted with slanderous ingenuity on both sides. The mayor called his rival a stooge of war profiteers and a stalkinghorse for the hated *Tribune*. The master of invective got a taste of his own medicine, however, as the war-roused electorate vented its anger on "Kaiser Bill." Hecklers followed Thompson wherever he went. Stones were tossed at his motorcades. In the downstate community of Edwardsville, a theater manager canceled a Thompson appearance at the last minute, declaring that his stage was reserved for unadulterated patriots. Medill beat Thompson in the primary by 60,000 votes. The *Tribune*, less than magnanimous in victory, noted Big Bill's conspicuous absence from a GOP unity dinner whose "sturdy Americanism" was equaled by its disdain for "pandering to any element whose loyalty is not 100% pure." Medill went on to narrowly defeat the foppish Lewis in November.

No one took greater encouragement from the midterm elections, with their implied rebuke of Wilsonian diplomacy, than Bert McCormick. Having earlier compared Wilson to Alexander Kerensky, he now decided that the president was the reincarnation of Andrew Johnson. "I think we are going through a period no less involved than . . . Reconstruction," he told his brother days after the election. "Your next six years will be interesting if not easy."[65]

Shared animosities can be a powerful cement. Despising Thompson in

Chicago as much as they distrusted Wilson in the White House, the McCormick brothers enjoyed a measure of harmony for the first time in years. Each was ideally positioned to perform useful favors for the other. The *Tribune*, for its part, supplied a ready platform for Medill's hard-shell nationalism. It also reported favorably on the enlightened campaigns waged by Senator McCormick for a federal budget law and a constitutional amendment outlawing the use of child labor.

Medill reciprocated by lobbying Franklin Roosevelt and the Navy Department to approve a *Tribune* application for use of a radio receiving station at Halifax, Nova Scotia, forerunner of its Press Wireless system of international news transmission. He intervened as well in the delicate matter of his brother's war record. Tired of whispered disparagement, Bert sought aid in obtaining "some official recognition" of his wartime contributions. Within months, Pershing came through with the Distinguished Service Medal. The accompanying citation praised McCormick's "rare leadership and organizing ability, unusual executive ability, and sound technical judgment."[66]

These carefully chosen words did not overstate the case. Coming five years after the armistice, however, the award conspicuously failed to silence McCormick's detractors, many of whom conveniently overlooked the fact that artillerymen were not supposed to go over the top, at Cantigny or on any other field of battle. Burton Rascoe, an iconoclastic *Tribune* book reviewer, never forgot the sight of McCormick striding through the newsroom "attired in whipcord breeches, English officer's jacket, boots, spurs, Sam Browne belt and officer's cap, a polo stick in one hand and three yelping German police dogs on a leash." Rascoe wore a blank expression as McCormick, practicing polo shots astride a mechanical horse, expounded on the strengths and shortcomings of German warlords.[67]

McCormick's admission to the First Division had been grudging. His service in the Big Red One had lasted barely nine months. Yet its importance can scarcely be exaggerated. The division had taken him in, however reluctantly. In testing his abilities and validating his courage, it had helped dispel his deepest fears about himself. Small wonder, then, that over time the division would rank just behind the *Tribune* as a surrogate family and lifelong source of pride.

Each June, McCormick, wearing a blue sportcoat emblazoned with a red number 1, happily presided over a divisional reunion on the grounds of the Wheaton estate he renamed Cantigny. At Christmas, veterans down on their luck could expect a holiday package replete with razor blades, cigarettes, and a $5 bill, compliments of the Colonel. To commute the thirty miles from his country home to his downtown office, McCormick relied on "the world's only bullet-proof khaki-colored Rolls Royce coupe." Alighting from his car, he clutched a briefcase striped with the red and khaki of the First Division. The same colors were reproduced on his luggage and the funnels of Tribune Company ships.[68]

His devotion to the Big Red One was more than sentimental. It reflected a fascination with nearly everything military. A voracious reader, McCormick could discourse knowledgeably about thirteenth–century artillery pieces and the role played by Union gunboats in the American Civil War. As the author of a quirky biography of Ulysses S. Grant, the self-taught historian stoutly denied the well-documented insobriety of his hero. Invited by General Pershing to speak at the dedication of the First Division monument outside Cantigny, France, in 1937, he was so pleased with his memorial address that he had portions of the text carved on the exterior walls of Tribune Tower and incised in gold letters in the floor of his library at Cantigny's American namesake.

Yet long before he went to his grave, dressed in his faded World War I uniform, to the triumphant strains of "Onward, Christian Soldiers," McCormick had become the leading advocate of American diplomatic isolation and military retrenchment. He justified his *volte face* by harkening back to the closing days of the Great War, when a European peace had seemed less desirable than his own promotion to brigadier general. If military ambition could so sway his values, reasoned McCormick, think of its calamitous effect on vote-seeking politicians and combat shirkers (like FDR) who sought vicarious glory without regard for the cost in soldiers' lives. After 1918, he never again supported American involvement in a foreign war.

His military experience shaped him in other ways. To many, he appeared to run the *Tribune* like an army camp. It would be more accurate to say that he resembled a feudal lord. (Describing her husband, clad in formal morning wear and mechanically pumping the hands of *Tribune* workers at the paper's annual New Year's Day reception, Amy McCormick waspishly remarked, "Bertie likes to crack the whip and watch the serfs march by" — a remark widely, and incorrectly, attributed to the Colonel's unpretentious cousin, Joe Patterson.)[69]

As with his feelings toward England, McCormick's attitude toward the military establishment was deeply conflicted, reflecting warm nostalgia for the part he had played as an individual balanced by a fear and distrust he reserved for anything threatening his fragile sense of self. He confessed as much when informing his mother, in October 1919, that he had been offered a colonel's commission in the Army Reserve Corps, "but as there are a number of limitations on my independence I may not be able to accept it." (In the end he relented, spending the next ten years as a reserve officer.)[70]

Most important of all, the army bestowed a title behind which McCormick could take permanent shelter, thereby eliminating the tiresome and emotionally taxing demands of meeting strangers on grounds not to his liking. "I am commonly known now as 'the Colonel,' " he wrote late in life to the aged widow of his Ludgrove schoolmaster, "a very useful moniker, as it can be either familiar or formal."[71]

Delayed it may have been, but Colonel McCormick had finally mastered the British art of understatement.

PART III

The World's Greatest Newspaperman

1919–1932

"As circulation is to the air, so is
agitation and plentiful degree of speculative
license to political and moral sanity.
Vive, the attack — the perennial assault!"

WALT WHITMAN

8

"We Seem to Be Fighting All the Time"

"When I came home from Europe it was with the psychology of a man born again. All former enmities and hostilities of whatever nature had been burned out. I was not interested in the Ford controversy, but Ford insisted upon a fight and we gave him one."

— Robert R. McCormick, April 1920

"Bertie, don't you know the war is over?"

— attributed to Joe Patterson

COLONEL MCCORMICK was in and out of Paris in the spring of 1919, keeping a weather eye on the peace conference headquartered at the Hotel Crillon, just a block from the *Tribune* offices. As the diplomats wrangled over the spoils of victory, the Colonel interviewed prospective correspondents. One of these was a recent graduate of the Army Air Corps named John Clayton.

"Gibbons tells me you have a good war record, Clayton," remarked McCormick as he plopped himself down beside the younger man's desk.

"If you call a year as a flying inspector a good record."

"In the service we do what we are ordered to do," said McCormick. "I'd be willing to wager you risked your life many times." He gave Clayton a wintry smile. "I didn't like some of the things I had to do, either. But now we are here and it's a different kind of job. Mr. Wilson in November spoke of open covenants openly arrived at. In January he found that he had to agree to a closed and secret peace conference bound by still unpublished agreements among allies, with the newspapers given exactly what the conferees want us to have. That we don't buy," McCormick announced magisterially, as if spurning overripe fruit at Les Halles. "It's our job to find out the things we are forbidden to know. All of us must be alert to every opportunity to penetrate the peace conference and disclose its secrets. A diplomat, even a president, can be muzzled, but not a free press."

McCormick concluded his monologue with a lament wrapped around a call to battle. He and Clayton inhabited "a sorry world ... everywhere unrest, revolution, bolshevism. We are the ones who must be constantly on watch to see that it does not take over our own land. The leftists will try. We are the ones," he reiterated, "who must expose and defeat them."[1]

✧   2

On April 16, 1919, the tormented life of Robert Sanderson McCormick flickered out, three months shy of his seventieth birthday. His son and namesake signed the certificate listing pneumonia as the cause of death. Rob's widow made little pretense of bereavement; writing on the obligatory black-bordered stationery, Kate complained of the $18,000 a year in medical bills caused by her husband's insanity. Now she feared for her own mind. "No woman could have the shocks I have had without going down," she moaned.[2]

According to Nellie Patterson, Kate wasn't the only McCormick showing signs of mental instability. The social ostracism occasioned by his scandalous marriage to Amy Adams had driven Bert to spend two months in the Paris Ritz, she claimed, where he had been observed crying uncontrollably. Picking up the thread, the gossip sheet *Town Topics* reported that Bert and Amy would escape their continuing isolation by taking up permanent residence in the French capital.

Not so, Kate told Medill McCormick. The unhappy couple were actually debating between Paris and New York. "And he is going to experiment in newspapers at our expense before he makes up his mind," Kate wrote caustically. "Isn't he the longheaded sly one ... He has no Medill about him — all McCormick. That is the reason your father loved him best, although you were far the most dutiful son."[3]

Less jaundiced observers readily discerned the audacious spirit of Joe Medill in the chest-beating headline that greeted Chicagoans as they rubbed sleep from their eyes on the morning of June 9, 1919: TRIBUNE HAS TREATY. Thus far withheld from the U.S. Senate, which had to pass ultimate judgment on its merits, the treaty in question assessed blame and reparations in equally crushing terms on the defeated German Reich. The release of an official summary early in May had done little to allay suspicions back home that Woodrow Wilson, acclaimed by European throngs as a modern-day Prince of Peace, might unilaterally discard American sovereignty in favor of collective security as enforced by his proposed League of Nations. More immediately, by acquiescing to Japanese claims to the Shantung Peninsula, the American president had sent shock waves of anger and disgust through the Chinese delegation in Paris.

Fearing the dismemberment of his nation at western hands, an indignant Chinese diplomat named Eugene Chen nervously entered the *Tribune*'s Paris office shortly before noon on June 1. He found it deserted, by careful prearrangement with Spearman Lewis, Floyd Gibbons's deputy. When Lewis returned from an early martini at Maxim's, he discovered a bulky envelope resting on Gibbons's desk. Inside the envelope was a complete, numbered copy of the unsigned peace treaty. Lewis entrusted the precious document to Frazier Hunt, another *Tribune* correspondent, who had earned Wilson's contempt by piercing the curtain of secrecy surrounding U.S. intervention in the Russian civil war. Hunt wrapped the treaty in a copy of the *Petit Journal*, hid it in his luggage, and caught a train for Cherbourg. When he reached Washington on June 8, he personally delivered the 75,000-word document to the antileague senators Henry Cabot Lodge and William Borah.[4]

The next day, using typeface big enough to be read from Paris, the *Tribune* trumpeted its windfall.*

"Hunt all right. Stop. Lewis gets bonus. Stop. Congratulations," the Chicago editors wired their Paris bureau. Following the formal signing of the treaty on June 28, the *Tribune* delivered an uncharacteristically low-keyed appraisal of its contents, contrasting the soaring Wilsonian vision of a new world order with the incontestable existence of "a very old order, the order of Adam, which under many appearances and mutations will continue to rule the affairs of the world long after Mr. Wilson has taken his place in history."[5]

Three months later, Wilson's voice was tragically silenced. From her Washington doctor, Kate McCormick learned that "that villain W. W." had been felled by a massive stroke. "The old wretch is completely finished," she rejoiced. Only the *Tribune*'s moderation on the subject of

---

*The *Tribune*'s feat was actually surpassed by the *New York Times*, which printed the entire text, while *Tribune* readers were forced to settle for just 25,000 words — all that could be transmitted over the available wires in a limited amount of time. The *Tribune* conceded that the full text contained little not already revealed in the official summary. But the melodramatic sequence of events surrounding the treaty's improbable appearance before the Senate magnified the paper's scoop, much as the unauthorized publication of the Pentagon Papers in May 1971 lent extra weight to that ponderous official history of U.S. military involvement in southeast Asia.

the league marred her pleasure. "Wobbling on the fence was not the way your grandfather made the *Trib* the great western voice for good that it was," she admonished her thirty-nine-year-old son, "but he was a man of stern morality and immovable convictions, and you and Joe are neither and the reading public knows it."[6]

❖ 3

Disproving the adage that crowing cocks lay no eggs, on June 26, 1919, less than three weeks after flaunting its treaty exploit, the *Tribune* gave birth to the *New York Illustrated Daily News*. It was a complicated delivery. The previous December, McCormick had deputized Bill Field to survey the New York market and gauge the prospects for a new kind of newspaper, one in which the camera became the reporter and the photograph a story in itself. Citing his childlessness and sharing Amy's disaffection with haughty Lake Forest, he volunteered to serve as midwife to the New York venture — a startling concession, given his low opinion of the city and its inhabitants.[7]

He had formidable competition in Joe Patterson, who saw New York as a way out of his own personal and professional blind alleys. From its inception, the *Daily News* embodied the Patterson formula for success, combining enough sex, mayhem, and violence to gratify the taste of working-class New Yorkers. Inseparable from its winged camera logo was the stated determination of the *News* to be "aggressively for America and for the people of New York." Dominating the first issue were photographs of the playboy Prince of Wales and the announcement of a $10,000 beauty contest to be judged by George M. Cohan and D. W. Griffith. Along with five pages of "peppy news pictures," readers found a smattering of United Press bulletins, popular features such as "Embarrassing Moments" and "Real Life Stories" lifted intact from the *Tribune*, and individual pages devoted to sports, society news, and original fiction.

Conspicuous by its absence was local advertising; there wasn't so much as a line. The mood in the *News*'s rented quarters at City Hall Place was bullish nevertheless, as curious New Yorkers snapped up the initial run of 200,000 copies. Before the sun went down on June 26, Hearst dispatched Arthur Brisbane, the editor of his *New York Evening Journal*, to City Hall Place with a $50,000 inducement for Patterson to abandon the field. The bribe was scornfully rejected. It was renewed at year's end, with no greater success, even though by then the *News* was widely thought to be on its last legs. On some days circulation dipped as low as 24,000; advertisers continued to stay away in droves.

A member of the *Tribune*'s promotional staff sent out from Chicago to turn things around quickly identified the source of the trouble. Because of *Tribune* involvement, he found, New York merchants had expected the *New* to be "rotogravure in nine colors on super fine vellum." Patterson apologized for the poor printing in a front-page box. Then he fired the press foreman, borrowed, as were the presses themselves, from the *Evening Mail.* Living up to his army nickname of Sloppy Joe, he became a familiar sight on the New York subway system, where he counted the number of commuters reading the *News* and craned his neck to make out which features or news stories drew the most interest. He dragged sleepy-eyed editors along on dawn excursions to size up their clientele in Brooklyn and Queens, telling them that he did so "to make sure you fellows realize that every line you put in the paper ought to be aimed directly at these people. You can't publish a successful paper by ear."[8]

Ever the cultural tuning fork, throughout the hedonistic twenties "the Captain" filled his pages with short, breezy stories about showgirls, street-sweepers, flamboyantly crooked politicians, judges on the take and gangsters on the loose, sports celebrities, ax murderers, flagpole-sitters, and proletariat heroes. Scoffers professed bewilderment over a newspaper designed for people who moved their lips as they read.* The upscale *New Yorker*, product of a radically different urban sensibility, sniffed that the *Daily News* was edited to appeal to the truck driver in everyone. Eventually a *Tribune* ad genius named Leo McGivena crystalized the blue-collar appeal of the paper with an irresistible slogan: "Tell it to Sweeney (the Stuyvesants will understand)."

✧ 4

By the time the *Daily News* turned its first profit, in October 1920, McCormick had poured over $1 million into the venture. Yet as his money was being siphoned off to New York, his thoughts were focused on a frowzy little Michigan health resort twenty-five miles from Detroit. In normal times the streets of Mount Clemens, population 10,000, were clogged with sufferers of rheumatism, eczema, and gout. They were drawn to the self-styled Bath City on the banks of the Clinton River by the promise of its health-giving, foul-smelling sulfur springs. Beginning early in May 1919, however, cure-seekers in bathrobes jostled for space in local hotels with a small army of attorneys, journalists, witnesses, public rela-

---

*To overcome resistance from advertisers who protested that only vulgar New Yorkers read, or rather looked at, the picture newspaper, Joe added a movie cameraman to his early morning rambles. Thereafter corporate executives visiting his office were treated to a film show depicting *Daily News* readers who wore coats and ties.

tions men and their image-conscious clients, rubbernecking tourists, and dozens of spies employed by both sides in a courtroom spectacle without precedent in American history.

"I want to look back upon the summer I spent in Mount Clemens as one of the happiest seasons of my life," said Henry Ford, displaying a naiveté more criminal than anything he had charged against the supposedly libelous *Tribune*. Ford was no stranger to controversy. In the three years since the editorial "Henry Ford Is an Anarchist" had first roused his ire, he had been much in the headlines — first attacking President Wilson for playing politics over Mexico, then campaigning for the Senate in 1918 as the administration candidate, more recently flirting with a run for the White House in 1920.

Part folk hero, part publicity hound, Ford challenged Washington's conventional politicians with a brashness equaled only by Ross Perot in modern times. "I am the only businessman in the country that can afford to talk on any subject that I please," he boasted. Drawing on his enormous personal fortune, the crusading industrialist had run full-page ads in dozens of major-city newspapers decrying military preparedness as wasteful and immoral. (The *Tribune* readily accepted one of these screeds, but donated his payment to the Navy League.)*

Fed up with press criticism of his zigzag diplomacy, Ford hired a *Detroit Free Press* reporter named Theodore Delavigne to be his "peace secretary." Delavigne produced a gusher of antiwar brochures and articles, to which Ford contributed little besides his name. Whatever its provenance, Delavigne's output faithfully presented the maverick side of his employer. Ford claimed that every soldier and sailor ought to have the word *murderer* embroidered upon his breast. "All the soldiers are either lazy or crazy," he said. As far as he was concerned, war was a conspiracy between munitions-makers, professional militarists, and corrupt politicians who waved the flag to whip up mass emotions. Personally, said Ford, "I do not believe in the flag; it is something to rally around. I don't believe in boundaries . . . Boundaries are silly things; nations are ridiculous things." Once the present conflict had spent its malignant fury, he continued, he fully intended to pull down the American flag and never raise another.[9]

To McCormick and the *Tribune*, these were fighting words, unmitigated by Ford's abrupt shift to military production once the United States

*Early in 1919 Ford took his own turn at the newspaper business, purchasing the *Dearborn Independent* and turning it into a distasteful mélange of pacifism, anti-Semitism, and cracker-barrel posturing of the sort that endeared the paper's owner to millions of rural Americans. That Ford himself had done more than anyone else to destroy this imagined Arcadia, simply by giving his dissatisfied countrymen the mobility to flee from their drab origins, hardly registered with the carmaker. Irony was wasted on Ford, with his cold, shrewd mind.

actually entered the war. In 1918, fearing the loss of a Democratic majority in the Senate, President Wilson implored Ford, his erstwhile critic, to run for the Michigan seat being contested by Truman Newberry, a wealthy Republican and secretary of the navy under Theodore Roosevelt. The race became a referendum on Ford's antiwar activities and on the draft defer- ment granted under suspicious circumstances to his twenty-four-year-old son Edsel. Newberry tucked into his deep pockets to finance full-page newspaper ads lambasting Ford the Hun-lover. The tone of the campaign grew nastier still when TR invited himself into the state and contrasted the heroic service of his own sons with the contemptible skulking of the privi- leged Edsel Ford.

Whether such sledgehammer blows won Newberry more votes than they cost him is debatable. Incensed over the personal attacks, Ford refused to concede his narrow loss in November. Instead he filed suit against Newberry, alleging that his rival had violated campaign spending limits. He hounded Newberry relentlessly, until the object of his wrath finally resigned from the Senate in 1922. "I tried to put some fight into Newberry," McCormick grumbled the following year, "but Newberry wouldn't fight."[10]

It was a mistake McCormick had no intention of repeating. Ford's paci- fism, he soon discovered, was strictly theoretical. When his personal inter- ests were at stake, the carmaker was a ferocious competitor, one who never went into battle unless armed to the teeth. In anticipation of the *Tribune* case, Ford induced the silver-tongued judge Alfred Murphy to leave the bench and lend his oratorical gifts to the prosecution. He also flooded the press with articles lauding his wartime production efforts. Less successful was a projected series of critical pamphlets under the general title, "The War Record of the *Chicago Tribune*." Only two issues came off the press; hoping to nail the *Tribune* for its alleged pro-German leanings, Ford was unable to convict the newspaper of anything worse than inconsistency.

By naming the *Tribune*'s Detroit distributor, the Solomon News Com- pany, as a codefendant in the case, Ford and his attorneys were able to win a change of venue from Chicago to the Motor City. The *Tribune* counter- attacked, and both sides compromised on sleepy Mount Clemens. With opening arguments set for May 12, 1919, Ford dropped hints that he was considering building a large factory in the area. (According to McCormick, still seething with anger four years later, these moves did not exhaust Ford's ingenuity when it came to influencing potential jurors. The automaker secretly employed the brother of one juror, he alleged. Ford agents also tried unsuccessfully to suborn witnesses friendly to the *Tribune*. A press agent later confessed to hiring women in the hope of sexually compromising people important to McCormick's case, "even the judge.")[11]

McCormick's preparations for the coming showdown were hardly less elaborate. To supplement the work of his own firm, he enlisted a second Chicago law firm to impersonate the Ford legal team, a gambit that culminated in a mock trial before a hired judge. Howard Ellis, a youthful attorney assigned the task of coaching *Tribune* witnesses, pressed McCormick hard.

"Suppose they ask you if Christ was an anarchist?" demanded Ellis.

"If they ask me that," replied McCormick, "I'm going to yell 'Blasphemy' at them!"[12]

He did more than that. To trip up the chief Ford counsel, Alfred Lucking, McCormick recruited Lucking's courtroom nemesis, Elliott Stevenson, a leader of the Detroit bar whose previous run-ins with Ford had only whetted his desire to inflict maximum public humiliation on "the Sage of Dearborn." Spearheading McCormick's defense team was a dapper forty-two-year-old Mayflower descendant named Weymouth Kirkland. As counsel to the North Shore Electric Company, Kirkland had caught the notice of Bert McCormick, who was then jousting with Sam Insull and Commonwealth Edison. Intent on adding him to the firm, McCormick resorted to a shrewdly calculated act of presumption. Without ever discussing the matter with Kirkland, he simply introduced him to friends as his latest legal acquisition. In doing so, he established his personal supremacy at the start of a forty-year relationship that would leave a lasting mark on American press freedoms.[13]

A wily strategist, Kirkland had no intention of fighting the coming showdown on Ford's terms. The death of Theodore Roosevelt in January 1919 had deprived the *Tribune* of a star witness, one who might have been counted on to mesmerize a jury of Michigan farmers while supplying a helpfully expansive definition of what constituted anarchy. Yet to the opportunistic Kirkland, Roosevelt's death was a blessing in disguise. With an almost clairvoyant instinct for sizing up the weakness of his enemy, he chose to make Ford's ignorance, not the *Tribune's* arrogance, the central issue of the trial. By turning the tables on McCormick's accuser, he would cast the aggrieved Ford as the agent of his own undoing.

✧ 5

Before leaving for Mount Clemens the second week of May, McCormick gave some orders to Philip Kinsley, the *Tribune* correspondent who had been assigned to the coming showdown. "I want you to cover that trial as if you were a reporter for the *New York World*," he told Kinsley.[14]

Henry Ford had his own ideas about the press, and they followed somewhat different lines. To guarantee that his side of the proceedings reached the public, he established the Mount Clemens News Bureau under the supervision of his personal secretary, Ernest G. Liebold. In the first of its daily dispatches to nearly 3,000 papers, the bureau portrayed Ford as a victim of "speculative capitalists" who resented his prolabor attitudes and his outspoken commitment to social justice.

"If you spit on the floor of your own house, do it here," read a welcoming sign over the entrance of the Clinton County Courthouse. "We want you to feel at home." Inside the remodeled courtroom, space was set aside for representatives from fifty of the nation's leading news outlets. Most closely watched was Floyd Gibbons. Merely by appearing each day, immaculate in his khaki uniform, with a black eyepatch covering the socket emptied by a German machine-gun bullet, the dashing Gibbons served to remind everyone present that he, like the publishers of the *Tribune*, had fought the kaiser with more than words.

In a display of efficiency that would not be repeated, a jury of eleven farmers and one road inspector was impaneled in less than four days. For the next week lawyers on both sides engaged in furious debate over the scope of evidence to be presented. Ford's attorneys hoped to limit testimony to the accuracy and motivation of the *Tribune* in describing their client as an anarchist — an especially hateful term in Chicago, they hastened to point out, ever since the infamous Haymarket riots of 1886. Insisting that they had not come to Mount Clemens to "wander all over the world like a lot of fishwives," they proceeded to do exactly that, seeking to prove that the *Tribune*, its chief stockholders, and its youthful coeditors were engaged in a vast conspiracy to plunder Mexico and increase the already staggering wealth of John D. Rockefeller's Standard Oil and the International Harvester Company of Cyrus McCormick and his descendants.

As Ford looked on, his advocates charged that both McCormick and his mother had a direct and lucrative stake in Mexican conquest — or at least in Mexican sisal, $14 million worth of which Harvester purchased each year for conversion into binder twine. Alfred Lucking drew an unflattering picture of a family whose newspaper embodied the greed and bloodlust of its owners. To him, it was simple. Ford had dared to oppose the *Tribune*'s aggressive designs on revolutionary Mexico. He had spoken out against the exploitation of that unhappy land by the Rockefellers and McCormicks. For this he was targeted for editorial abuse. (Lucking's contentions were factually flimsy. McCormick owned just 165 shares of International Harvester, and Weymouth Kirkland did not exaggerate when he said it was highly unlikely that Kate McCormick knew what sisal was.)

Not surprisingly, the *Tribune*'s lawyers pressed Judge James G. Tucker to adopt a much broader view of the case. Preparedness itself was on trial, argued Weymouth Kirkland, and there could be no just verdict without a full understanding of conditions along the Mexican border *and* in the *Tribune*'s editorial offices during the tense spring of 1916. Aware that the case pivoted on his ruling, Tucker decided not to decide.

Over the next several weeks, it was not unusual for the door of Kirkland's hotel room to be flung open and the lights snapped on at three in the morning. "Here are some suggestions I've typed up," the Colonel would declare, tossing a thick sheaf of papers on the nearest table. "I want them to go into the case tomorrow."[15]

On May 26 the evidentiary phase of the trial got under way. Frank Klingensmith, the Ford spokesman credited as the source of the original *Tribune* story, denied making the statements attributed to him. A parade of Ford assembly-line workers who had served in the National Guard without repercussions followed Klingensmith to the stand. Family members who had been cared for during the absence of their breadwinners paid tribute to Ford's famed "sociological department." Other witnesses heaped praise on the automaker for instituting the five-dollar day and hiring disabled workers.

Ford's lawyers rested their case on June 6. The dithering Judge Tucker had yet to issue his ruling on the admissibility of evidence. In the resulting vacuum, the defense proceeded to recreate with melodramatic flourishes the desperate conditions prevailing along the U.S.-Mexico border at the very moment when Henry Ford was most loudly discouraging his employees from taking up arms. A colorful lineup of Texas Rangers in silver-buckled belts and high-heeled boots were trotted out, reinforced by border sheriffs and piteous women robbed of their husbands and sons by Mexican bandits.

On June 17, five weeks after the start of the trial, Judge Tucker dealt the plaintiff a crushing blow by declaring that "anything that indicates Mr. Ford's anarchist tendencies is material. I don't care where it comes from." Granted this judicial license for a fishing expedition, Stevenson and Kirkland hauled in a rich catch of red herring. Ford's earlier statements disparaging military preparedness and flag worship were unearthed and paraded before the jury. A political scientist from the University of Michigan claimed to find in Ford's writings disturbing parallels with such "recognized anarchists" as Proudhon, Tolstoy, and Emma Goldman. (In cross-examination, Lucking compared his client to Emerson, Thoreau, Saint Paul, and Jesus Christ.)

Colonel McCormick took the stand on July 7. He impressed most onlookers with his memory and bland self-assurance. The *Tribune*'s commitment to a strong national defense long predated his tenure, he contended. As proof, he entertained the courtroom audience by recounting how his grandfather had once dragged the ponderous Tom Reed, Speaker of the House of Representatives, to the top of the Washington Monument for an impromptu lecture on the vulnerability to enemy attack of the nation's capital.[16]

Of somewhat greater relevance was his vivid description of events leading up to June 23, 1916. Returning from Canada by train, said McCormick, he had read a newspaper interview that threw doubt on Henry Ford's patriotism. He had spent most of the next few days trying to secure needed machine guns for his National Guard unit and had approved the offending editorial just before leaving for Springfield. At that moment, McCormick told the court, "it was uncertain whether the United States government had the right to compel the militia to respond to this call. Some of the Texas militia had already refused to respond to an earlier call. There was a terrible crisis confronting us. A Mexican invasion was expected hourly."

The *Tribune* had argued that employers ought to ease the financial burden on National Guard members who were called away. According to the best information available to him at the time, McCormick cautiously noted, the pacifist Ford had done just the opposite. "I thought if this stand became in any way common, it might be a serious deterrent to getting the troops out; and that in turn would make the question of protecting our border, or even of winning such battles as I expected we would go into, extremely hazardous. The idea of the editorial," he concluded, "was to deter other employers from following his example, and to encourage Mr. Ford to modify his stand." Under the circumstances, to call Henry Ford an anarchist was to act in the national interest.[17]

✧ 6

Next it was Edsel Ford's turn. A whiff of hypocrisy scented the courtroom as the younger Ford strained to reconcile the wartime profits of the Ford Motor Company with his father's verbal rejection of "blood money" earned from government military contracts. The witness was rescued from his discomfort by events outside the courtroom. On July 11, it was revealed that Edsel's father, at a cost of $105 million, had regained sole authority over the company he and a handful of other investors had started in 1903 to produce and market the Model A. In his suite at the Medea Hotel in Mount Clemens, the ecstatic Henry Ford celebrated his stunning buyout by dancing a jig.

He should have been going to school. In a fatal misjudgment, Alfred Lucking had not confined his suit to the *Tribune*'s offending headline but had challenged the full editorial, which alleged, among other things, that Ford was "an ignorant idealist." Now, anticipating a brutal grilling of his client at the hands of Elliott Stevenson, Lucking belatedly embarked on a crash course of historical instruction. But the job of educating Henry Ford had been neglected forty years too long; at fifty-six, a would-be president basking in his favorite role of America's conscience, Ford was unteachable.

Ford's ordeal commenced on the afternoon of July 14, when Stevenson showed him a series of antiwar publications printed under his signature but actually composed by Theodore Delavigne. Ford confessed that he had not bothered to read a good deal of what was attributed to him; "When you ask me what I meant by this," he said, referring to one of Delavigne's pamphlets, "you are asking for what goes beyond my knowledge." Neither did he read much beyond newspaper headlines. Nevertheless, he added brightly, his chief purpose in bringing suit against the *Tribune* was to foster among the press a greater truthfulness "behind their headlines."

The next day a threat of subpoena produced a Ford company flag, a white globe in a blue field meant to represent the triumph of international brotherhood. Ford said he had discarded it on aesthetic grounds as "a pretty poor flag." In response to Stevenson's jabbing questions, he conceded that in August 1915 he had advocated "absolute disarmament." Yes, he had called General Pershing a murderer. Yes, one might say that his extensive campaign of publications had as its purpose the discouragement of military recruitment.

"You call yourself an educator," Stevenson continued in an insinuating tone. "Now I shall inquire whether you were a well-informed man, competent to educate people." He replayed for Ford his remark (ironically, made to a *Tribune* reporter) that "history is more or less bunk."

"I did not say it was bunk," Ford shot back. "It was bunk to me . . . I did not need it very bad." Admitting that "I am ignorant about most things," he professed an enjoyment of banjo music. Of art, he said that he was "coming to like it a little better than I did."

From popular culture, Stevenson maneuvered the examination onto still more treacherous ground. Ford's horror of overpreparedness was mentioned in the same breath as "the old flintlock guns" relied on by an earlier generation of Americans to defend themselves.

"Isn't that in history?" Stevenson asked Ford.

"I suppose so."

Alfred Lucking popped up like an indignant jack-in-the-box. "Do you mean at the Revolution or what time?" he demanded of Stevenson.

Stevenson pounced. "Do you know anything about the Revolution, Mr. Ford?"

"What . . . what do you want to know about it?"

Amid a flurry of objections from his lawyers, Ford allowed as to how there had been one revolution — back in 1812.

"Don't you know there wasn't any revolution in 1812?" said Stevenson.

"I don't know that. I didn't pay much attention to it," Ford replied. He "guessed" that he had forgotten about events transpiring in 1776. He was equally hazy about the Civil War. The rattled witness confused "chili con carne" with "a large mobile army," equated "ballyhoo" with "blackguard," and defined "an idealist" as "anyone who helps another to make a profit." He did remember Benedict Arnold, but as a writer, not a traitor. Unable to identify anything significant within the Declaration of Independence, Ford had a clear and fixed definition of anarchy: "overthrowing the government — throwing bombs."[18]

Invariably Lucking's objections to all this were overruled by Judge Tucker. "When a man is charged with being an ignorant idealist," said the judge, completing the role reversal involving defendant and plaintiff, "mustn't he submit to an inquiry as to all things that would go to make an ignorant idealist?"

In Judge Tucker's court, ignorance was no defense, but a crime. As Ford continued his astonishing performance, the court stenographer began selling mimeographed copies of each day's testimony at twenty-five cents a page. He earned enough to buy a house.

Eight days after Lucking's client first climbed into the witness box, he at last had a chance to repair some of his self-inflicted damage. The lawyer elicited a strong defense of Edsel Ford's wartime contributions. Beyond this the senior Ford would not go. He had been on the stand long enough, he informed Lucking on the morning of June 23. With that he stalked out of the courtroom. Later that day he left town for good, bound for a camping trip in upstate New York with his friends Thomas Edison, Harvey Firestone, and John Burroughs.

It is accepted history that the unequal battle of wits between Ford and Stevenson left the automaker permanently diminished in the eyes of the public. Whatever hopes Ford may have entertained of succeeding Woodrow Wilson in the presidency almost certainly died in the Clinton County courthouse. Far less attention has been given to the impact the trial may have had on McCormick and his newspaper. The Colonel later made much of the fact that he had spent $300,000 to defend a million-dollar libel suit. However, no one ever attempted to put a price tag on the free national publicity generated during the ninety-eight-day trial, much less the increased circulation and ad revenue accruing to the *Tribune* as a result, for they were literally priceless.

Less dramatic than the crackling exchanges between Ford and Stevenson but ultimately more important to the making of the *Chicago Tribune* was the testimony of Ford advertising men such as Charles Brownell. In arguing the destructive powers of a single *Tribune* editorial, Brownell unintentionally advanced the paper's claims to national influence. "We never put out a campaign of advertising that did not include the *Chicago Tribune*," said Brownell. Besides dominating its home turf, he went on, the newspaper was influential in Illinois, Iowa, Michigan, Minnesota, and Wisconsin. Another Ford agent claimed that the *Tribune* exercised a hold over "a very excellent class of people" in as many as fifteen states. Needless to say, every such testimonial enhanced the visibility and prestige of a newspaper notably lacking in self-effacement.[19]

McCormick got another windfall in Judge Tucker's 10,000 word charge to the jury, delivered to a rapt courtroom early on the morning of August 14. Casually discarding the preparedness issue, which he had allowed through his earlier rulings to dominate the trial, the judge showed more care in delineating the rule of fair comment, which governed the right of a newspaper to pass judgment on the conduct and statements of a public figure. When at last the jury foreman, Orvy Hulett, a thirty-eight-year-old farmer sympathetic to the *Tribune*, asked his fellow jurors behind closed doors whether any of them regarded Henry Ford as an anarchist, there was a brief moment of silence. "Well, I don't know," volunteered one juror, summarizing the feelings of most. "I think he is a damn fool."[20]

Over the next ten hours a consensus emerged. Ford, it was agreed, was no anarchist in the generally accepted sense of the term. Neither, however, could he pass himself off as merely a well-intentioned crusader trying to educate his countrymen about the immoral and hazardous course advocated by the generals and their friends in the press. Although jurors concluded that the *Tribune* had been careless in its choice of words, its publishers were adjudged "fine young men" who had acquitted themselves nobly in the war, particularly in contrast to Edsel Ford. Orvy Hulett voiced a near universal conviction when he said that the case ought never to have been brought in the first place.[21]

The final verdict held no comfort for the plaintiff. The jurors decided that Ford had been libeled. But they also absolved the *Tribune* of malicious intent. Damages were assessed at a humiliating six cents, a sum McCormick refused to pay, thus daring Ford to take the case to a higher court. The award went uncollected. Ford, furious at all lawyers and angriest with himself for ever initiating the Mount Clemens travesty, had no intention of providing the *Tribune* with still another promotional platform.*

Unsatisfied with his moral victory, McCormick spent years pursuing the full story of Edsel Ford's draft exemption. In time he traced the deferment

---

*Three weeks later, a disgruntled juror named Paul Puls sent a note to Captain Patterson and Colonel McCormick. "I just thought if I would write and let you know that I was the means of saving you five hundred thousand dollars," wrote Puls, "that you would not be the kind of people to let me, a poor farmer, to be the loser." The crude shakedown elicited no response from the victorious cousins. In reality, a single member of the panel had argued for such an award, and he had been overwhelmingly outvoted.

to an order overruling the local draft board, typed on President Wilson's personal typewriter. Even then he wasn't finished. In 1923, McCormick voiced strident opposition to the automaker's bid to acquire government nitrate plants and an unfinished hydroelectric dam along a section of the Tennessee River called Muscle Shoals. His letter to Secretary of War John W. Weeks did not lack for point.

"My excuse for writing you is that I believe Henry Ford is an unscrupulous, rapacious hypocrite and that I think I have his number," McCormick told Weeks. Remembering the fate that had befallen the passive Senator Newberry a year earlier, he urged the secretary to take on the industrialist and defeat him at his own game. Specifically, Weeks should publicize the millions of dollars in wartime profits that Ford had solemnly vowed to return to the treasury and had instead kept for himself. "Show how he solicited contracts to build the unseaworthy Eagle boats which capsized at anchor. Show how he used his political influence to have the Government condemn a right of way for a canal up to his factory ... Expose the petty larceny whereby he deprived the country of the puny services of Edsel by forcing Wilson to violate the spirit, if not the letter, of the draft law."[22]

Frustrated and angry, Ford eventually withdrew his offer to purchase Muscle Shoals. This cleared the way in the 1930s for the Tennessee Valley Authority, to McCormick a prime example of government willingness to encroach on the traditional prerogatives of free enterprise. By then the bitter antagonists of Mount Clemens had found in Franklin D. Roosevelt someone they despised more than each other. McCormick in particular came to appreciate just how much he owed the litigious carmaker from Dearborn, for if the fourteen weeks he had spent in Mount Clemens shattered the myth of Henry Ford, they laid the foundation for a myth of his own.

Their relationship came full circle when, in December 1943, McCormick visited Detroit and staged a very public reconciliation with his former antagonist. Before photographs could be taken of the meeting, the diminutive Ford had to be propped up on several pillows in order to appear in the same frame as McCormick. Afterward McCormick couldn't conceal his delight.

"Ford's a great little guy," he remarked to Harry King, the *Tribune*'s customer relations manager. "Do you know what he said?"

"No."

"He wants me to run for president of the United States ... and furthermore he'd back me with every penny — every cent he has he'd put on me if I'd run for president."[23]

Flattered though he might be, McCormick refused to take the idea seriously. Employing a rarely glimpsed gift for self-mockery, he told one gushy admirer that although a Rolls-Royce, his car of choice, could take a man many places, the White House was not one of them.

✧ 7

McCormick didn't need the White House to conduct his own characteristically blunt foreign policy. The Colonel singled out for abuse the British empire, full of threadbare aristocrats selling old titles for new American dollars. Writing from London in November 1919, he likened the U.S. relationship to the infant League of Nations to that of an American heiress contemplating marriage to an impoverished duke. Unless the Senate adopted an unyielding position toward the league, McCormick feared that his naive countrymen would be drawn into a loveless foreign union "like a rube to a shell game, or a reformer to a county convention."[24]

Paris was "amusing," McCormick informed his mother, "but I have been cutting expenses and firing people" at the *Tribune* bureau there, "never pleasant." Still he had managed to reduce costs by $15,000 a month, "which is something." From the French capital he denied an allegation by Lloyd George that the European edition of the *Tribune* was biased in favor of Irish nationalists belonging to Sinn Fein. The Colonel contrasted the ingenuity of the rebels in cultivating the press ("Indeed, a gentleman styling himself Minister of the Irish Republic has been good enough to invite me to lunch") with the self-defeating secrecy of Whitehall.[25]

Lloyd George was both prompt and gracious in his response. "We have allowed judgment to go against us not merely on the Irish Question, but on many others, by default," he acknowledged. He thanked his American correspondent for calling attention to "a conspicuous defect" in his government's organization, and promised in the future to take Yankee newspapermen into his confidence. The door thus opened led to events unimaginable in 1919, as John Steele, the elegant, Irish-born head of the *Tribune*'s London bureau, was pressed into service as a go-between for Irish revolutionaries hoping to negotiate a peaceful separation from Great Britain.[26]

While in Galway covering the long-simmering revolt, Steele had been introduced by the rebel leader Arthur Griffith to a grocer named Patrick Moylett, who stood high in Sinn Fein councils. Within days Moylett appeared at Steele's London quarters. In the course of their conversation it became apparent that Moylett was looking for a way to contact the British government through Steele. Unable to engage Downing Street in the scheme, Steele turned to C. N. Phillips, director of the government news office. Out of this initial, seemingly casual encounter grew prolonged secret discussions, some held under *Tribune* auspices, others in the British

Foreign Office. Through his confidential secretary, Geoffrey "Red" Shakespeare, Lloyd George was kept abreast of developments.[27]

Late in 1921, negotiations reached a critical stage. Eamon De Valera, a fugitive from English justice, was summoned from his American sanctuary to confer directly with the British prime minister. Yet even as Moylett and Shakespeare were hammering out an Irish treaty in a back room of the *Tribune* office, McCormick, from a distance of 5,000 miles, was demanding changes in the European edition. Fueling his anger was a vicious lampoon of the Prince of Wales, the work of a Sinn Fein propagandist on the *Tribune* payroll. No doubt reminded of an earlier outrage against French pride,* McCormick ordered John Clayton to "clean out that lot of Irish rebels" and, not so coincidentally, prevent a wave of red ink from swamping the whole enterprise.[28]

Exhausted by his diplomatic labors and still more by the strain of keeping them secret from Chicago, which periodically demanded to know why the *Tribune*'s coverage of the Irish situation differed so radically from every other newspaper's, Steele sought a few weeks' respite. McCormick told Clayton to replace him. Clayton instead traveled to London, where he was let in on the Irish negotiations for the first time. On his return to Paris, Floyd Gibbons showed him two cables. The first, signed "McCormick," read: "Steele has been constantly scooped on Ireland. Clayton didn't do any better. Fire them both." Clayton, dejected, slumped in his chair. When he looked up, he saw Gibbons grinning maniacally. "Aren't you going to read my reply?" Gibbons said. He held out a cable containing just four words: "Keep your shirt on."[29]

On December 6, 1921, the British and Free Irish representatives affixed their signatures to a treaty. Steele, belatedly recognized for his role in achieving a settlement that had long eluded professional diplomats, was called home to be lionized at a Chicago banquet. By January 1922 the European edition was in the black. The next year McCormick was able to forecast a profit of $50,000 to $100,000, "unless war comes." Clayton was rewarded with a long-coveted posting to India; the Colonel had a hunch that the civil disobedience campaign led by Mohandas K. Gandhi might yet lead to dominion status, the first way station on the road to full independence.

As early as 1920, McCormick was able to boast that 70 percent of all foreign dispatches quoted in the European press were credited to the *Tribune*. Such dominance was not achieved risk-free. The *Tribune* correspondent

---

*On Bastille Day, 1917, a drunken group of *Tribune* employees had celebrated France's national holiday by hoisting a pair of women's panties to the top of the *Tribune* flagpole on the rue Royale. McCormick was forced to apologize to the French foreign ministry over the insult to Gallic pride.

Richard Henry Little was seriously wounded near Petrograd while covering the conflict between Lenin's Bolsheviks and White Russian forces loyal to czarist tradition. Floyd Gibbons, officially accredited to Herbert Hoover's famine relief mission, slipped into Russia about the same time another *Tribune* man, Larry Rue, crossed the Black Sea from Constantinople and journeyed up the Volga River into the heart of the district suffering from famine.

In the autumn of 1920, Clayton himself caused a sensation by unearthing a plot by Indian nationalists to assassinate the Prince of Wales. A royal visit to the subcontinent was postponed. Two years later, the American high commissioner at Constantinople credited an exclusive *Tribune* interview of the Turkish leader Mustafa Kemal with averting war between Turkey and Britain. Thousands of miles to the east, McCormick's man in China, Charles Dailey, supplied graphic accounts of the devastating Yellow River floods and resulting famine. Other *Tribune* reporters described or analyzed the rise of Mussolini in Italy, the Primo de Rivera dictatorship fastening its grip on Spain, an uprising of Georgian peasants against their Soviet masters, and a revolt in the Riff section of Morocco. In 1923 a *Tribune* photographer obtained the first pictures taken inside the newly discovered burial chamber of Egypt's King Tut.

Like a proud but stern Victorian father, McCormick made regular trips to Europe to check up on his offspring. In Paris he invariably stayed at the Ritz, which is where correspondent Hank Wales discovered him one morning, in a room whose glass door panel had been smashed to pieces.

"I put my shoes outside to be shined last night, and while I was doing it the door blew shut," explained McCormick. "So I punched in the glass, opened the door from the inside and went to bed."

Why not simply call someone to fetch a passkey? asked Wales.

"I was in my pajamas and bare feet," the Colonel replied indignantly. "I wasn't going to traipse up and down the corridor like that looking for someone to open the door."[30]

At a dinner for the Paris *Tribune* staff, the sports editor Herol Egan, a self-professed military expert, rashly grabbed a place at the table immediately to the Colonel's left. Egan launched into a rambling discourse on the inadequacies of the American high command, culminating in the supreme idiocy of those in the artillery who had shelled their own infantry ranks at Cantigny.

McCormick rose from the table like a rocket. "That man has spoiled my evening."

The next day he gave explicit instructions to Egan's superior: "Never fire that man, and never give him a raise."[31]

In his charming memoir, *The Paris Edition*, correspondent Waverly Root recalled his initial encounter with McCormick in London, where the publisher had invited Root and his colleagues to join him for dinner. The house gourmet, an English cable editor named Sidney Cave, was not alone in imagining the lavish meal and superb wines to be enjoyed at *Tribune* expense. When at last the Colonel appeared, an hour and a half late, he quickly dashed such expectations by announcing that he had passed a little place around the corner that didn't look bad. "Let's eat there," he said.

Worse lay in store.

"What would *you* like to drink?" McCormick inquired. Cave cleared his throat to speak, only to be cut off by the knowing John Steele.

"What are *you* drinking, Colonel?"

"Beer." The order was enthusiastically seconded by everyone around the table.[32]

The next morning McCormick let it be known that he wanted Root's companionship on a stroll about the city. For Root, this meant shouting upward at his much taller boss while maintaining a half-trot through neighborhoods familiar to McCormick since his boyhood. Given that the Colonel, like royalty, never carried money on his person, the bureau thoughtfully supplied Root with enough cash to act as disburser.

"Best hatter in London, Root," McCormick observed complacently outside one venerable, and very costly, Mayfair shop. "Buy all my hats here. Advise you to do the same."

Back at his hotel, McCormick's hospitality took a perverse turn as he invited Root to join him and Steele for lunch. Neither guest had to worry about making conversation; the Colonel did the talking for all three of them. As the dessert cart rolled into sight, he pulled out his watch.

"Root," he said, "I understand things are pretty bad in the Welsh coal mines. There's a train for Cardiff at three o'clock. I want you to hop aboard it and give us seven or eight good stories on the situation there."

"Cable, Colonel?" asked Root.

"No, no. Mail will do."

Root suggested, as gently as possible, that by taking a later train he could notify his wife, away from home just then, of his need to be gone on business for a few days.

"I think that you should take the first train available," said McCormick, in the voice of one unaccustomed to repeating himself.

Fifteen minutes after Root checked into his Cardiff hotel, the phone rang in his room. On the other end was the Colonel's secretary, verifying that he had done as told.[33]

✧ 8

In 1920, *Editor and Publisher* polled leading newspapers, asking them to identify the "most influential editorial page in the country." The *Chicago Tribune* finished in a three-way tie for first place with the *New*

York Times and the *Boston Post.* The postwar *Tribune* was admired for more than its editorial pugnacity. Under Patterson and McCormick, it had a national reputation for mechanical innovation and enlightened labor policies. One of McCormick's first actions when he returned from the war had been to investigate and redress complaints from *Tribune* compositors over working conditions. Early in 1919 he established the Medill Council, to solicit worker input on safety and health concerns and to promote greater opportunities for study, athletics, even music appreciation within the *Tribune* family. McCormick offered his employees free evening classes in English and a liberal bonus plan.

By the early twenties, the *Tribune* was distributing over $300,000 in annual bonuses, justified by McCormick as "a cheap way to buy profits" by ensuring worker loyalty. "The greatness of Marshall Field and Carnegie," he reminded Patterson in November 1921, "lay in their willingness to let their associates become rich while they became billionaires." Between them, McCormick and Patterson had already rewarded Max Annenberg with a $10,000 bonus for his circulation-building prowess. Now the Colonel dangled the sum of $1 million, to be divided equally among Annenberg, business manager Emory Thomason, managing editor Teddy Beck, and advertising manager Eugene Parsons, if the quartet managed to double the *Tribune*'s advertising. The goal was realized and the handsome prize awarded.[34]

Looking to the future, McCormick anticipated bidding wars for scarce talent as papers such as the *Chicago Daily News* and the *New York Times* passed into the hands of trustees who were businessmen first and newspapermen second. He had no intention of practicing the self-defeating thrift of publishers like Victor Lawson, who had valued immediate return over long-term loyalty and had wound up sacrificing both.

McCormick had long been critical of ill-trained or irresponsible reporters. In 1921 he donated *Tribune* funds to Northwestern University to establish the Joseph Medill School of Journalism, which opened its doors that summer to an inaugural class of sixty students. The idea of training office boys and other entry-level workers for better jobs in the field had originated with a *Tribune* reporter named Eddie Doherty. Warmly approved by McCormick and Patterson, the concept was broadened to include non-*Tribune* personnel by Northwestern's dynamic president, Walter Dill Scott. At the Medill School, journalism rubbed elbows with the more established professions of law, medicine, and business. This was in accordance with McCormick's wishes. Newspapermen and -women belonged to a "priesthood," he told an audience at the school in June 1921, "servants of an institution which scorns all service less than the public welfare and which leads or drives individual factions, even political parties, in that direction."[35]

McCormick displayed shrewdness as well as vision in September 1919, when he paid $185,000 for a quarter-acre of land just north of the Chicago River, in a scruffy neighborhood of soap and malt factories. To a group of workers summoned to the top of the *Tribune* building at Madison and Dearborn, the Colonel supplied a rationale for his action: "If I look to the west, I can see my farm in Wheaton. If I look to the south, I see the stock-yards . . . to the east I see . . . Lake Michigan. Then I look to the north and I say, 'There's opportunity.' "[36]

The thought of abandoning Newspaper Row was beyond the comprehension of *Tribune* veterans accustomed to working in the Loop. But McCormick was convinced that the future of Chicago lay north of the river, in an area made newly accessible with the May 1920 opening of the Michigan Avenue Bridge. In dedicating the double-deck span, Big Bill Thompson had some harsh words for newspaper proprietors who would reap handsome profits by raising skyscrapers in the area. On June 7, McCormick and Patterson bore out his prophecy by laying the corner-stone for a printing plant. Built to McCormick's specifications, the facility was carefully designed to take full advantage of water, rail, and highway transportation. It could be easily expanded to accommodate future growth.

Reflecting the vertically integrated business envisaged by McCormick, docks and warehouses were built to receive tons of Canadian newsprint delivered by a fleet of *Tribune* ships. After arrival, the paper was carried by gravity feed to a storage area beneath the subterranean press room. Here, sixty feet below street level, McCormick revolutionized the way news-papers were printed. Discarding the conventional grouping of five or six presses, he formed a continuous line of twenty-five high-speed Goss printers, each weighing thirty tons, interspersed for greater efficiency with half a dozen folding machines. To keep all those presses running, he required 1,900 tons of newsprint and 77 tons of ink a week.

The war had sent the *Tribune*'s circulation skyrocketing at the same time it caused work in the Canadian woodlands to be suspended. The resulting paper shortage — at one point, barely five days' supply sat on the Chicago docks — forced reductions in news columns and the loss of advertising dollars. So it was with a sense of urgency bordering on panic that McCormick, on the final day of 1918, invited his wartime adjutant, Arthur Schmon, to oversee development of the *Tribune* properties in eastern Quebec. The Princeton-educated Schmon compensated for his lack of engineering experience with a pioneer's hearty disdain for obstacles. Given the brutal climate of the region, there was to be no shortage of these; for six months of the year Shelter Bay was accessible only by dogsled. A log cabin sheltered Schmon and his adventurous bride, Celeste, when they moved to the north shore of the St. Lawrence in August 1919.

The most pressing need of the Ontario Paper Company was for a wharf capable of withstanding the gulf's treacherous tides and lashing winter gales. McCormick had a brainstorm. To lay the foundation for an all-weather dock at Shelter Bay, he filled an old barge with worn-out grindstones from the Thorold paper mill, then scuttled the vessel. That night a howling wind pounded the sunken hull to pieces. It fell to an illiterate Frenchman named Ouilette, working without blueprints, to succeed where McCormick and professional engineers had failed.

McCormick found other ways to employ the engineering skills he had first displayed at the Chicago Sanitary District. He dammed a waterfall to obtain electric power for the remote settlement. A more daunting challenge was posed by a series of rapids, waterfalls, and small islands that impeded the flow of traffic near the mouth of the Rocky River. McCormick designed a series of dams to convert the natural obstacle course into a liquid highway to carry millions of logs, shortened to four-foot sections for their passage down the Rocky. When asked how he was able to move such vast quantities of pulpwood, McCormick said it was simple: "We pull the chain and flush the logs down the river." His offhand comment understated the dangers involved. He narrowly escaped death when the powerful river current ruptured a fragile wooden boom on which he was standing. Luckily for him, the section beneath his feet swung toward the riverbank; otherwise he would almost certainly have been swept over a nearby dam. The incident led him to insist that wooden booms be replaced with hollowed steel ones.

When in residence at Shelter Bay, McCormick avoided the murderous black flies endemic to the region by living aboard a *Tribune* ship. (He also scandalized thirsty loggers by disinfecting one insect bite with fine, fiery Scotch whisky.) His days began with a dip in the heart-stopping St. Lawrence. In bad weather he stood on deck in shorts while crewmen doused him with buckets of icy river water.

But he took seriously his grand seigneurial responsibilities to the "primitive and domestic" Québecois, whose conservatism and love of tradition had their roots in three centuries of authoritarian Catholicism. He encouraged local inhabitants to render unto God what was rightfully his while never forgetting their American Caesar. At Shelter Bay, McCormick built a hospital to care for the population's physical needs and a church to address their spiritual needs. A company-raised school educated the next generation of loggers and stevedores. Arthur Schmon offered finished lumber and other building materials at cost to anyone willing to erect permanent dwellings more pleasing to the Colonel's eye than the crude log houses of the sort Schmon himself knew all too well.

To move his pulpwood from Shelter Bay to Thorold, a four-day boat ride in those days, the Colonel formed the Quebec and Ontario Transportation Company. From a little wooden steamer battling upstream against the swift current, McCormick's navy grew to include an American submarine chaser decommissioned after the war and renamed the *Mareuilendole* in honor of the French village where Joe Patterson's New York tabloid had been incubated. Later the *Chicago Tribune* and the *New York Daily News*, sleek steel vessels over 250 feet in length, joined the fleet.

When the American economy went slack in 1920 and paper prices headed south, McCormick refused to trim his sails. To counter pessimistic forecasts, the *Tribune* unfurled a defiant new slogan — "1921 Will Reward Fighters." Backing his words with deeds, McCormick expanded his Canadian holdings by purchasing seventy-two square miles of Quebec timberland on the Franquelin River southwest of Shelter Bay. In the spring of 1921, a new paper machine came on line at Thorold, increasing the capacity of the mill by 20 percent. The additional newsprint made possible a Sunday edition of the *Daily News* — by 1926 the largest-selling newspaper in America — as well as *Liberty*, a glossily unprofitable national magazine conceived as a showcase for the parent company's work in color printing.

Eager as always to beat the competition, McCormick authorized construction of an experimental four-color press in 1920. Two years later, notwithstanding imperfections in the printing process, which tended to limit its use to various shades of red, the *Tribune* introduced the novelty to the Sunday paper. *Liberty* followed. McCormick proposed to call the new magazine *Coloroto*, an idea to which Patterson took strenuous objection. An international contest was staged to pick a more suitable name, with Queen Marie of Romania, the evangelist Billy Sunday, and Chief Buffalo of the Cherokees among 1.4 million entrants from thirty-one countries. All this took time, and the publication was still unnamed when its first issue went to press. Adding to the embarrassment, the color presses fell short of their promise. Over half the initial run of 500,000 copies had to be destroyed.

It was an appropriately madcap launch for *Liberty*, which broke virtually every journalistic rule and paid heavily for its originality, showing a profit in just three of its twenty-six years. Technology crowded out a consistent editorial viewpoint in the magazine, which was designed to lure middle-brow readers away from the *Saturday Evening Post* and *Collier's*. Whereas those publications had distinctive personalities, *Liberty* seemed unable to decide whether it would reflect Patterson's gift for the sensational or McCormick's religion of color. It wound up being one more twenties stunt. Undaunted, McCormick as late as 1930 dreamed of a full-color newspaper printed at the rate of 50,000 copies an hour. Less visionary advertisers shied away from the added cost of $720 a page daily and $800 on Sunday.

Probably the first man in Chicago to wear pink shirts to the office,

McCormick publicly regretted that he couldn't print the entire *Tribune* on paper of the same hue. Unfortunately, he concluded, readers might confuse a pink *Tribune* with the lurid *Police Gazette*. Innovation had its limits.

✧ 9

July 30, 1920, was McCormick's fortieth birthday. He had given up trying to stay thin, he told his brother, to the great improvement of his health and nerves. If nothing else, Big Bill Thompson could always be counted on to keep him in fighting trim. As Chicago slid toward bankruptcy, the *Tribune* stalked Thompson with the grim tenacity of Ahab chasing his great white whale. It was a pursuit McCormick had hoped to leave to others, as he made clear to Weymouth Kirkland in the spring of 1920. The *Tribune* had first claim on his time and organizational abilities. Frankly, the identity of the latest bosses to run Cook County mattered less to him than strengthening the paper's foreign service, local circulation, advertising, artistic features, mechanical equipment, and paper supply.[37]

Nevertheless, McCormick continued, "if the guiding spirits of the Thompson machine think they have collected enough power to overawe, dominate or injure the *Tribune*, the scene changeth." If the fight were brought to him, "I know only one way to conduct it, and that is with every resource I can command and with every ingenuity of assault." Bearing this out, McCormick asked Floyd Gibbons to obtain from the French Foreign Ministry proof of Thompson's wartime contacts with German sympathizers. Such tactics were born of desperation, as "the Thompson–Lundin Ring" rode a wave of postwar reaction to extend its control far beyond the borders of Chicago.[38]

In the April 1920 Republican primary, Thompson supporters swept all but one of the city's thirty-five wards. In the same contest, the mayor embarrassed Governor Frank Lowden by delivering Chicago to General Leonard Wood, Lowden's chief rival for the GOP presidential nomination. That July a thousand Republican delegates packed the steaming Coliseum, whose temperature rose higher still when Thompson resigned from the Illinois delegation in feigned outrage over Lowden's lavish campaign expenditures. The mayor recruited a beautiful woman, dressed entirely in pink, to walk down the center aisle and distribute hundreds of copies of Hearst's *Chicago American*, the entire front page of which was devoted to his well-timed bolt. Stopping the convention in its tracks, the lady in pink took her place in Chicago political folklore.

Thompson completed his demolition of Lowden by undercutting the governor's hand-picked successor, Lieutenant Governor John G. Oglesby, in the September primary. He threw his support to Len Small, a ferret-

faced Kankakee banker and former state treasurer who had run unsuccessfully for governor as a Lorimerite in 1912. "I never did understand the
damned politics of that town," said Lowden on learning of his latest
humiliation at the hands of Big Bill.

With Harding in the White House and Small in the statehouse, the
Chicago machine had at its disposal an estimated 30,000 jobs. At their
apogee, Thompson and his allies claimed a hammerlock on the board of
education, the library board, the sanitary district, and the state's attorney's
office. Big Bill owned Cook County's electoral machinery. With assistance
from Governor Small, he was able to grab the patronage-laden west parks
and Lincoln Park. Only the south parks eluded his grasp. Thirty million
dollars had been set aside for reclamation of the south shore of Lake
Michigan. To obtain this glittering prize, the mayor had to overrun the
South Park Commission, whose members were appointed by local circuit
judges.

Drunk with success, Thompson and Lundin now cast a bleary eye at the
judiciary. Before raiding the courts, the mayor decided once and for all to
silence his enemies in the press. As usual, he reserved his harshest blows for
the *Tribune*, and not without reason. Throughout 1920, McCormick's
readers had been treated to a dismal series of exposés. City workers entrusted with the maintenance of bridges were being paid instead to work
at Thompson–Lundin headquarters. The paper revealed the names of
politically favored lawyers who had pocketed tens of thousands of dollars
for drafting the mayor's latest traction scheme. Editors accused Thompson
of diverting transit funds to cover basic operating expenses and exhausting
the borrowing authority of the city.

On December 10, 1920, Thompson struck back. On behalf of the city of
Chicago, he filed a $10 million libel suit against the *Tribune* and Victor
Lawson's *Daily News*, charging both papers with impairing municipal
credit through their relentlessly negative coverage of his administration.
Not since 1798 had the ancient doctrine of "libel upon government" been
recognized in American jurisprudence. On the face of it, Big Bill was
inviting legal humiliation. McCormick was less sure. Privately, he feared a
jury trial, "as the jurors might argue that taking money from the *Tribune*
and *Daily News* would save taxes."[39]

It is hard to imagine a greater threat to popular liberties than ceding
control of the courts to those intent on crushing the press through confiscatory litigation. Yet that is exactly what Thompson hoped to achieve
through the largest libel action ever filed in the United States at that time.
All this made the June 1921 judicial elections a defining moment. If the
machine could defeat a *Tribune*-backed coalition slate at the polls, it would
gain sovereignty over the trial judges, the commissioners who picked
juries, and the appellate courts. Lundin would enjoy additional control of

at least two of the seven supreme court judges, said McCormick, "with unlimited power to coerce the rest." Under the circumstances, Thompson's "faked-up ten million dollar libel suit" would become "an overwhelming menace."[40]

Six weeks before the June 6 voting, the *Tribune* filed a suit of its own, based on the legwork of city hall reporter Oscar Hewitt, alleging that the Thompson administration had bilked taxpayers out of more than $1 million (a figure later raised to $2.7 million) in "expert's fees" paid to appraisers who earned as much as $1,900 a day in condemnation proceedings stemming from Big Bill's ambitious program of civic improvements. So long as the electorate approved bond issues to support its implementation, the Chicago Plan originally devised by the forces of good government as a means of beautifying the city offered the machine limitless possibilities to reward its friends and perpetuate its grip on the levers of power. For example, a single Thompson project — widening Michigan Avenue from Randolph Street across the new bridge to Lincoln Park — would require the assessment of more than 8,700 pieces of property.

What the *Tribune* called Big Billism crested and broke in the first week of June. More than 600,000 Chicagoans, three times the usual number, voted in the judicial elections. The Thompson slate went down to defeat by a three-to-two margin. Fearing ruin in the expert fees suit, the mayor appealed to his friends in Washington. He reminded President Harding of a post-election conversation in which he had portrayed Medill McCormick, the *Tribune*, and a U.S. district attorney allied with both as mortal enemies of the state's regular Republicans. Harding, as regular as they come, had promised Thompson that he would restrain federal officials intent on making trouble for the mayor. He now honored this pledge by refusing to provide tax returns or other information that might aid the *Tribune* in its suit.

On June 22, the Chicago congressman Martin B. Madden obtained the desired assurances from the president. Harding, he informed a Lundin associate, "had definitely arranged the matter in connection with which you called on me, and . . . was sure there would be no further reason to complain." As it happened, this was premature. Unaware of White House interest in the case, John Cannon, a collector of internal revenue, had already instructed the Chicago district attorney to file contempt proceedings against Frank Masce, one of the "building experts" charged by the *Tribune* with enriching himself at taxpayer expense.[41]

On June 29, Congressman Madden had a second meeting with Harding. Afterward he wired Masce directly: "Wright's Friend saw his man this morning. Two very strong letters written by the P ordering proceedings stopped at once by both Departments (Justice and Treasury). Results should be satisfactory. The P kept your telegram for reference. Keep me posted." That same day Masce formally refused to turn over papers sought by Cannon or submit to oral interrogation by federal agents. Attorney General Harry Daugherty, professing warm friendship for Thompson, prohibited Justice Department employees from giving testimony concerning Thompson's wartime activities.

While the legal skirmishing played itself out in Chicago and Washington, Governor Small borrowed a page out of Big Bill's playbook. Thanks to a $60 million bond issue enacted during the Lowden administration, Small was able to build 7,000 miles of hard roads during his governorship. It cannot be said that these new highways were laid out according to the strictest engineering principles. LaSalle County, for instance, was notably overlooked in the road-building boom after its state senator, one Thurlow G. Essington, made the mistake of opposing Small in the Republican primary.

Another factional quarrel erupted between the governor and state Attorney General Edward J. Brundage, a *Tribune* favorite. It began when Governor Small vetoed part of the regular appropriations bill for the attorney general's office. Brundage retaliated by indicting Small on charges of conspiracy and embezzlement dating to his earlier service as state treasurer. Small's criminal trial ended with an acquittal amid rumors of jury fixing. Several jurors were subsequently appointed to state jobs. Prospective witnesses, including a racketeer whose habit of collecting graft in an umbrella had won him the nickname "Umbrella Mike" Boyle, received contempt citations for their refusal to testify — and pardons from Governor Small.

Brundage, egged on by the *Tribune,* filed and won a civil suit against the governor, who raised his $650,000 penalty by dunning state employees as much as 80 percent of one month's salary and twisting the arms of roadbuilders and other state contractors. "It is a great fight we are making," McCormick told his mother in the fall of 1921, "perhaps the greatest in *Tribune* history . . . Last June only the *Tribune* stood between Thompson and complete control of government and the courts. Today he is beaten and disgraced. All his crowd face the penitentiary."[42]

On October 15, 1921, Judge Henry M. Fisher of the Cook County Superior Court dismissed Thompson's libel suit against the *Tribune* with a ringing affirmation of a free press as "the eyes and ears of the world . . . the advocate constantly pleading before the altar of public opinion. It holds up for review the acts of our officials and those men in high places who have it in their power to advance peace or endanger it." Editorial pages throughout the country hailed the ruling, which was upheld by the Illinois Supreme Court in April 1923.

For McCormick, the taste of victory was especially sweet. "I have been threatened with assassination as well as everything else," he confided to his mother as the war on Thompson reached fever pitch. "For a month I have never gone out alone. I have an armed guard at the house. Beginning tonight I am also to be followed by a gunman." The organization would only assure its ruin by killing the publisher of the *Tribune*. McCormick doubted they would try. Still, he intended to take every precaution "to protect myself and to get any would-be assassins."[43]

In 1922, Fred Lundin was indicted on charges of defrauding the Chicago school system of over $1 million. The *Tribune* had done its part by publicizing the fact that a pliant school board had bought $133 potato peelers. Even as Clarence Darrow successfully defended Lundin, the scandals in Springfield proliferated. Governor Small's superintendent of paroles and pardons, accused by two grand juries of abusing his position, resigned and went on the payroll of the state commerce commission. Small appointed the commission chairman, Frank L. Smith, to a vacant place in the U.S. Senate, but senators refused to seat the newcomer after the *Tribune* exposed a $125,000 contribution to Smith's war chest from Sam Insull.

Under the rain of press attacks, Thompson had no choice but to drop out of the 1923 mayoral race. Desperate to keep his name before the voters, he announced his intention to lead an expedition to the South Seas in search of tree-climbing fish. He had it on the best of scientific authority, he declared with a straight face, that lurking in distant waters were fish that could not only climb trees but had been known to leap three feet into the air to catch grasshoppers. In July 1923, the yacht *Big Bill* sailed down the Chicago River en route to the South Pacific. Thompson abandoned ship before reaching New Orleans. The former mayor also organized the Fish Fan's Club, ostensibly to promote the eating of fish but actually as a springboard to a third term in city hall once Chicagoans wearied of reform as personified by his colorless successor, Judge William E. Dever.

Governor Small was luckier than his Chicago ally. Aided by his campaign manager, Fred Lundin, Small coasted to a second term on the strength of the 1924 Coolidge landslide. The next day the *Tribune* ran an editorial under the heading GOV. SMALL ELECTED. The rest of the column was blank. Words were unnecessary.

More dismal news awaited Thompson. Not until March 1926 did the *Tribune's* real estate expert suit come before Judge Hugo M. Friend of the circuit court. The plaintiff's opening statement alone consumed three weeks. In all, the trial lasted two years. Finally, on June 20, 1928, Judge Friend ordered Thompson, city controller George F. Harding, Michael J. Faherty, president of the Board of Local Improvements, and four others to pay the city of Chicago $1,732,279.23 of public money, a sum that grew with interest to $2,245,604.

Protracted as it was, the fight had yet to run its course. In October 1930 the Illinois Supreme Court unanimously reversed Judge Friend. Although harshly critical of the Thompson administration, the court found no evidence of a deliberate conspiracy to defraud the city. But by then even Fred Lundin, angered over Thompson's decision to make his personal secretary police commissioner, had severed his ties to Big Bill.

✧　10

"We seem to be fighting all the time," McCormick acknowledged to a downstate editor. "Although we sometimes wonder if this does not tire our readers, we do not seem to be able to keep away from it. I suppose it is part of the duty of a newspaper."[44]

McCormick was the last publisher to pursue duty at the sacrifice of profit. He had every reason to believe he could have both, especially as the *Tribune* continued to put distance between itself and its morning competitor, the *Herald and Examiner*. Since the war the rival sheet had played the sympathy racket, hiring ex-servicemen to sell papers by promising customers that a portion of their subscription fee would go to assist crippled veterans. The results had been disappointing. Early in November 1921, Hearst dropped pity for greed as a more reliable sales ploy. The *Herald and Examiner* launched a daily lottery worth $500 to lucky holders of correctly numbered tickets, ingeniously dubbed Smile Coupons.

The public response to Hearst's easy money quickly wiped the smile off McCormick's face. On November 25 the *Tribune* announced a lottery of its own devising, with $20,000 in daily winnings. Mass panic ensued as 25 million *Tribune*-printed Cheer Checks were dumped on money-mad Chicagoans. In the Loop, crowds swarmed *Tribune* delivery trucks; some of the vehicles were overturned in the rush for instant wealth. Churches and Sunday schools clamored for their share of the action. Bakeries delivered Cheer Checks with wrapped bread. Banks slipped them inside depositors' passbooks. Overnight, the *Tribune*'s circulation shot up by 250,000. Rival papers cried foul over a cheap stunt carried out at their expense. A stunt it was, most assuredly, but hardly a cheap one, and McCormick was secretly delighted when, eight days after the madness began, Postmaster General Will Hayes stepped in and declared that both lotteries violated federal law.

Looking ahead to the *Tribune*'s diamond anniversary in June 1922, McCormick had much to celebrate. He informed his mother that her share of annual profits was likely to reach $2 million. The company had $1.4 million in cash reserves, no debts, and at least 80,000 cords of wood, worth $1 million or more, floating in Canadian rivers. "I go up next week to see [the surplus]," he told Kate. "I have bought an airplane, the only way to travel!"[45]

This latest indulgence provoked harsh maternal laughter. Bertie was nearly forty-two, the head of a great and growing business, she complained, but he was "still hearing the call of the wild." To Medill McCormick she observed that his "hard, cold, clear" brother was given to periodic seizures of childlike enthusiasm. Oswald Garrison Villard, writing in *The Nation* in February 1922, echoed her assessment, noting McCormick's "many boyish traits" and impulsive decisions. More generously, Villard called McCormick "well educated, well read and much traveled . . . genial and democratic." This did not prevent him from making obvious, unflattering parallels between the *Tribune* and its "inconsistent, shifty, generally reactionary, extremely prejudiced, arrogant, intensely nationalistic" editor.[46]

One McCormick passion was to alter the local skyline, glorifying the *Tribune* and publicizing Chicago's claims to world-class status. On the paper's seventy-fifth birthday, the Colonel threw out an unprecedented challenge to architects across the globe — to design for the *Tribune* a new office tower that might justifiably be regarded as the most beautiful building on the planet, and pocket $100,000 in prize money as well as incalculable prestige accruing from the most lucrative design competition ever staged. By the end of the year nearly three hundred entries had been received from twenty-three countries.

William Randolph Hearst had a somewhat different anniversary present in mind. Hearst proposed to buy the *New York Daily News* for $1 million and to employ Patterson and McCormick at annual salaries of $100,000, with a five-year guarantee to both men. The yellow journalist was spurned by both men. He had no greater success in spiriting away Arthur Sears Henning, the *Tribune*'s respected Washington bureau chief. If Hearst grabbed Henning, Patterson vowed, "we'll grab Damon Runyon." With much the same cockiness, he rebuked a *Daily News* executive who had questioned his treatment of a story. "The fact that I decide against you is no proof that I'm right and you're wrong," Joe conceded. "It's purely because of an accident of birth that I happen to be in a position to get my way. But I *do* get my way, and don't ever forget that," and Patterson struck a desktop to drive home his point.[47]

As late as 1924, McCormick and Patterson continued to alternate editorial-page responsibilities for each month's *Tribune*. But their partnership was fraying badly. According to Kate McCormick, the cousins were "no longer Siamese twins." Henning, too, recalled "hot and heavy" editorial conferences, concluding with Joe's stinging rejoinder to "write it any damn way you want." Clearly, the restive Patterson didn't plan to spend much time in the massive new building under construction on North Michigan Avenue. He seemed indifferent when his cousin bought a thousand-watt radio station perched atop the Drake Hotel. McCormick changed its call letters from WDAP to WGN (for World's Greatest Newspaper) and scooped the competition with live broadcasts of Big Ten football games. In 1925 he aired the sensational trial of the Tennessee schoolteacher John T. Scopes, in which Clarence Darrow and William Jennings Bryan crossed swords over the state's right to limit the teaching of Darwinian theories of evolution in the public schools.[48]

In October 1925, Patterson moved permanently to New York, where he mingled happily with the masses, for whom he presumed to speak *ex cathedra*. "He was a great guy for the man on the street," remembered the cartoonist Chester Gould, whose fictional detective Dick Tracy was a mainstay in both the *Tribune* and the *Daily News* for nearly half a century.[49]

Gould was twenty-one years old in 1921, an Oklahoma native with a dream to draw for the *Tribune* and, if he was lucky, to win a national audience for his creations via the *Tribune* Syndicate, which under Patterson's supervision sold cartoons and features to over two hundred American newspapers. To put food on his table, he sketched canned corn and Oriental rugs for a Chicago commercial studio. A short-lived job with the *Tribune* advertising department preceded stints at the *Chicago Daily Journal* and the *Herald and Examiner*. For Hearst's *Evening American*, Gould created a pair of strips, "Fillium Fables" and "Radio Cats." Through it all, never losing sight of his original motive for leaving the *Daily Oklahoman*, he regularly took ideas to Patterson at the *Tribune*.

When Joe went to New York, Gould subscribed to the *Daily News* for three weeks. Over the next month he worked up a daily editorial cartoon and placed it on the Twentieth Century bound for New York, "so that when Patterson opened his mail each morning there would be a cartoon by Gould in front of him." Gould had become convinced that the increasingly violent gangster wars rocking Chicago had the makings of a great strip. He invented an undercover detective named Plainclothes Tracy and sent off a week's worth of his adventures to Patterson.

"I believe Plainclothes Tracy has possibilities," Patterson wired back. "See me on the 20th when I'm in Chicago. Call my secretary for an appointment."

Gould went out and bought a stylish new suit, shoes, and hat. On the appointed morning he strode down Michigan Avenue looking "like the little *Esquire* fellow." He found Joe, casual as ever, tieless, in shirtsleeves and wearing old army shoes.

"Hi, how are you?" said Patterson.

"Awfully glad to be here, Captain."

Patterson picked up the sample strips Gould had sent him. "This name is too long." Joe paced the room, deep in thought. "Charlie, Harry, Harry Tracy, Buck Tracy, Dick Tracy. Let's call this man Dick Tracy. They call cops Dicks."

Gould voiced no objection.

"Now, for the beginning," said Patterson. "Have this young man, not a detective, calling on his girl. Call her Tess Trueheart — that sounds like a good heartthrob name. Her old man runs a delicatessen, and each night he takes the money upstairs after he closes the shop. They live upstairs and he takes the money up there and puts it under the bed. Have crooks on another roof looking over after dark and seeing what's going on. Have them break in through a window while the family is eating dinner. Tracy is there — it's the night he's going to ask the old man for his daughter's hand. The old man puts up a tussle and the hoodlums shoot him and kill him right in front of Tracy and go down the hall with blazing guns. Then have Tracy stand looking to heaven over the prostrate form of his future father-in-law saying, 'I swear I'll find the killers — I'll find the doers of this deed.' That's the beginning," said Patterson, pausing in his staccato delivery. "Can you have two weeks of that ready by the first?"[50]

At the urging of Patterson, Gould steeped himself in criminal detective procedures. He enrolled in classes at the Northwestern University crime laboratory and studied blood analysis, lie detectors, and the science of fingerprinting. Patterson wanted authenticity and more, as he made clear at monthly script meetings, for which he returned to Chicago.

Patterson's story sessions were in every sense a hands-on collaboration between cartoonist and editor. "What's your latest play?" he asked Frank Willard, the artist behind "Moon Mullins." Laughter filled the room as Willard and Patterson traded gags like a vaudeville team. Next it was on to Sidney Smith and "The Gumps," so named because that was what Joe's mother called stupid people. Knowing that urban automobile owners liked to spend Sunday mornings tinkering with their vehicles in the nearest alley, Patterson gave the title "Gasoline Alley" to a strip featuring the popular Skeezix characters. "Winnie Winkle, the Breadwinner" grew out of Joe's observations of New York stenographers and his belief that there was a large audience for a strip dealing with the problems faced by working women.

Those were the days of full-page strips, when readers chose their newspaper not for its editorial policy but for its familiar gallery of cartoon characters. Long before today's multimedia merchandising, a single strip like "Little Orphan Annie," running in six hundred papers, adapted for weekly radio broadcast, and spinning off lucrative dolls, books, and Ovaltine mugs, could bring millions of dollars into the Tribune Syndicate coffers. To Chester Gould, the comic strip was "the television of the newspaper" and Patterson a genius of visual entertainment. "I want an interesting picture," the Captain told his assembled cartoonists. "Make it as funny as you can. If I wanted an author with a lot of words and no picture, I would have hired an author, but God gave you fellows the ability to draw. Now let's see you draw some stuff."

Reminiscing about his friend and employer in 1977, Gould described Patterson as "a gritty man. He didn't want the worn-out hackneyed sort of thing. He wanted something that was extremely new, that fired the blood vessels and the imagination." When he got what he sought, Patterson was capable of extraordinary generosity to his stable of artists. Sidney Smith earned $120,000 a year, with a Rolls-Royce thrown in as a signing bonus. But Patterson was an autocrat as well, not above pulling a strip when he disagreed with its contents.

Rarely did his sense of popular entertainment fail him; when it did, it only added to his larger-than-life persona. Patterson got into a dispute with Harold Gray over the cartoonist's plan to have Little Orphan Annie adopted by Daddy Warbucks, her fabulously wealthy patron. Patterson said it would ruin the strip — who would care about the plight of a wealthy orphan? Gray stood his ground. "Little Orphan Annie" did not appear in the next morning's *Tribune*. Panic-stricken readers flooded the paper's switchboards with more anxious inquiries than had been received on Armistice Day. Annie was reinstated immediately, as Gray had pictured her.

Not even Gray, however, was prepared for the crush of national interest when Annie's beloved dog, Sandy, ran away from home. Among the thousands of messages of concern received by the *Tribune* in the wake of the dog's disappearance was one from a real-life Daddy Warbucks. "Please do all you can to help Annie find Sandy," it implored. "We are all interested. Henry Ford."

9

The Man in the Tower

"Newspapers are the most familiar objects of the present day, newspapermen the most mysterious."

— Robert R. McCormick

O UT OF OFFICE, Big Bill Thompson lost no time in avenging himself on the McCormicks. The unlikely instrument of his revenge
was the former object of his loathing, the onetime Progressive
Republican governor Charles S. Deneen, now running for the U.S. Senate.
In the spring of 1924, Big Bill leagued with Deneen, the incumbent governor, Len Small, and the Ku Klux Klan, then at the height of its influence
in rural Illinois, to deny Medill McCormick a second term in the Senate.
So confident was Medill of his chances against Deneen in the April GOP
primary that he skipped the final week of campaigning and went back to
the nation's capital.

It was a fatal miscalculation. On primary day, Deneen won by fewer
than 5,000 votes out of more than 700,000 cast. Medill's unexpected loss
shattered his hopes of one day inhabiting the White House. It also
reopened old family wounds, as the loser blamed his defeat on the *Tribune*
and its strident opposition to Prohibition. Rumors that President Coolidge
might give him a prestigious ambassadorship or a place in the cabinet
proved groundless. Medill returned to Washington late in February 1925,
his future in doubt. Ruth remained in Chicago, awaiting the birth of her
friend Alice Roosevelt Longworth's first child.

On the morning of February 24, a friendly journalist knocking on
the door of the senator's suite failed to rouse him. The hotel carpenter
was summoned to remove the door from its hinges. Inside the suite

the visitors found Medill's lifeless form, still in bed. Ruth hastened to Washington. In the hotel room where her husband had been pronounced dead of a heart attack, she came across several empty vials of barbiturates in a trunk only she could open. Instantly she understood: this was Medill's way of communicating his despair to a woman well versed in political discretion. For years the suicide remained a tightly guarded family secret.[1]

The death of his favored brother haunted Robert McCormick until the day of his own. A friend visiting him at his Palm Beach retreat in the final weeks of his life found the old man sitting in front of a fireplace, staring wordlessly into the flames. The years fell away, and for a moment the dying publisher reverted to his youthful status as a plodding, emotionally deprived second son. At length he broke his silence. "He was brilliant," mused the Colonel about the long-dead Medill. "I was never brilliant."[2]

❖ 2

Within days of Senator McCormick's Chicago funeral, employees of the *Tribune* began moving into their new home at 431 North Michigan Avenue. Built to the specifications of the New York architects John H. Howells and Raymond M. Hood, Tribune Tower was a thirty-six-story confection of Indiana limestone loosely patterned after the Butter Tower at Rouen Cathedral in France.

It was designed to call attention to itself. In this it perfectly reflected the man most responsible for its creation. Indeed, some observers began speaking of McCormick BT or AT — Before Tower or After Tower. Prior to 1925, overshadowed by his gifted brother and his dynamic cousin, the Colonel had had to serve as his own tower. Now, for $8.5 million, he had achieved the majesty and inaccessibility that would set him apart from the common run of men.

To critics, the massive Gothic shaft was a *folie de grandeur*, as misplaced on Michigan Avenue as Xanadu in an Illinois cornfield. Especially acerbic was Louis Sullivan, the dean of Chicago architects, who expressed horror over "the monster on top," as he characterized the flying buttresses and heavy masonry piers that formed the tower's distinctive crown. (Hood had special cause to feel gratitude for winning the *Tribune*'s international design competition: until recently employed as a designer of radiator covers, he had to borrow money to buy a decent coat for the Chicago award ceremony. But he partially recanted in later years, excusing the ornate historicity of his design as the byproduct of an era infatuated with architectural "embroidery.")[3]

From a distance, the building appeared hopelessly traditional. Only on closer examination was it revealed to be a composite, like McCormick himself, of the modern and the medieval, its uncompromising bulk leavened by a playful wit. High above Michigan Avenue, leering gargoyles kept watch over Chicago, their stony ranks reinforced by fanciful grotesques, including an owl clutching a photographer's camera and a scandal-mongering elephant holding its nose. McCormick and Patterson were memorialized in a magnificent carved screen above the main entrance. In the exterior walls, lodged like so many stones of truth, were fragments from the Parthenon, St. Peter's, Independence Hall, and over a hundred other historic structures assembled by the globe-straddling network of *Tribune* foreign correspondents.

McCormick meant to ground his newspaper of the future upon the received wisdom of past civilizations. From the day it opened, Tribune Tower was the presbytery of midwestern conservatism. In the grandly conceived Hall of Inscriptions, the Colonel indulged his taste for the monumental by covering every available space with quotations testifying to the glories of a free press. On the south wall, beside the words of Thomas Jefferson, a nineteenth-century lord chancellor of England, and the Gospel of Saint John, McCormick chiseled his 1924 definition of a newspaper as "an institution developed by modern civilization to present the news of the day, to foster commerce and industry, to inform and lead public opinion, and to furnish that check upon government which no constitution has ever been able to provide."

Off the main lobby, richly inlaid with English oak and Italian marble, the Colonel had installed the fastest elevators in Chicago, which were somehow never fast enough to suit his demanding nature. His tightly coiled restlessness was captured in a 1929 magazine profile:

"Get me our Paris office!" he instructed a telephone operator.

Fifteen minutes elapsed, during which the girl made increasingly frantic efforts to establish a wireless connection.

Presently her employer re-emerged from his lair. "Where is that Paris call?"

"I'm trying sir — haven't been able to get the call through."

"Then cancel it! Cancel it!" McCormick bellowed. "*I* can't waste any more time." And with that he withdrew to his office.[4]

McCormick cut an imposing figure stalking around the executive suite, his fifty-two-inch chest and thirty-six-inch arms draped in Savile Row suits, replaced on the hottest days with elegantly tailored khaki shorts. At forty-five, the Colonel still managed to give his polo ponies an honest week's work. His physical stamina exhausted men half his age. "Let's get out where we can talk" was an alarmingly familiar phrase to *Tribune* executives, whose feet throbbed after a ninety-minute "conference" conducted over six miles of Chicago pavement. McCormick refused to buy a yacht, obligatory among his class, for the simple reason that "you can't get off a yacht and walk."[5]

According to *Tribune* lore, Joseph Medill had once said to his friend Lincoln, "Take your goddamned feet off my desk, Abe." Medill's grandson adopted an equally dim view of workplace informality. Nicknames, like other forms of intimacy, repelled him. Hearing a Palm Beach houseguest address an acquaintance by his first name, he reproached his friend for undue familiarity. "After all," he observed, "you've met the fellow only a few times." He frowned on off-color stories, women who wore rouge, and anyone who lit up in defiance of the NO SMOKING signs he had posted throughout Tribune Tower. A prudish streak prompted orders to the art department to paint more clothes on an offending model and to conceal feet, because "feet are ugly."[6]

Hypersensitive to noise, McCormick found the sound of whistling as grating as the cooing of the mourning doves he shot from his bedroom window at Cantigny. He personally ordered the firing of the legendary police reporter Shadow Brown, whose frayed sweaters and caps he regarded as a crime against fashion. (Brown's superiors responded by telling him to lay low for a while, taking special care to avoid the fourth-floor newsroom, where McCormick appeared as fancy dictated.)[7]

Few penetrated McCormick's inner sanctum on the twenty-fourth floor. Here, amid the smell of freshly printed paper, the Colonel toiled behind a protective cordon of feuding secretaries and armed guards — the latter hired after some goons answering to Big Bill Thompson chased him down a dark alley one night. Endless speculation swirled about the floor. It was rumored that secret passageways afforded escape from any gangsters who managed to slip past McCormick's driver/bodyguard, a tough ex-cop named Bill Bockelman. McCormick was also said to keep an ax handy with which to dispatch assailants and a machine gun secreted in the ceiling of his walnut-paneled suite.

The truth was more prosaic. The gun was purely ornamental, part of an elaborate plaster depiction of highlights from an eventful life. At the southern end of his thirty-five-foot-long office, reverently placed upon a raised platform, a seven-foot slab of red-and-white Italian marble purchased by Amy on their honeymoon served McCormick as a desk. Here he sat, framed by sunlight streaming through a lacy Gothic window; if visitors gazing up at him felt a bit as if they were staring into the face of God, the effect was purely intentional. Adding to the atmosphere of studied intimidation was a concealed door, which McCormick controlled by a buzzer on his desk. First-time callers, on bowing themselves out, were invariably discomforted to find no apparent exit. It was the Colonel's little joke, one he never tired of playing.

Accompanied by one of the menacing-looking Alsatians or slobbering English bulldogs that were his constant companions, McCormick was able to leave the cloistered setting without ever breaking stride, thanks to a small brass plate that triggered the latch, installed for his convenience at floor level. Trained to obey their master exclusively, the dogs were no respecters of other persons. The chief offender was Lottapups, whose fecundity made her the bane of *Tribune* staffers and police officials in three counties assigned to locate and return the Colonel's runaway bitch when she was in heat.

The whereabouts of Lotta's owner were never in doubt. "I'm here six days a week and I think you should be too," he bluntly informed a managing editor who had the temerity to ask for two days off. In similar spirit, he avoided fashionable clubs and the wastrels who frequented them. "You can't edit a newspaper from the Pump Room," he exclaimed.[8]

On a rare evening out, McCormick could dampen the spirits of those around his table by putting down a half-empty wineglass and extracting his grandfather's ancient watch. One time, declaring it to be nearly eight o'clock, he rose and announced his intention to catch the next train for Wheaton. "Anybody else going?" he asked.

"I think I'll wait and catch the nine o'clock," said editorial writer Cliff Raymond.

"Well," replied McCormick in his most pontifical manner, "the man who says he'll wait for the nine o'clock usually misses the twelve o'clock." He disappeared into the night.[9]

McCormick's workday began long before his morning arrival on the twenty-fourth floor. During the commute from Lake Forest or Cantigny, he shredded the *Tribune*, tearing out clippings and stuffing his pockets with notes scrawled in an all but illegible hand. These mutilated scraps of paper occasioned much head-scratching among editors and reporters, who were forced to enlist the aid of McCormick's secretaries, neither of whom displayed the slightest command of current events.

Adding to the problem, McCormick spewed story ideas as a volcano spews rocks. In the words of Don Maxwell, his last managing editor, the Colonel was "a great day city editor." (One of Maxwell's predecessors received so much editorial guidance from the publisher that he vowed to write a book about his *Tribune* experiences entitled *The Colonel Told Me*.) More than a few crusades had their origins in McCormick's thirty-mile drive from home to work. "There are too many stray dogs on the street," he announced one day after his car narrowly missed several dogs on Roosevelt Road. The next day the *Tribune* launched a vigorous campaign to rid Chicagoland of the canine menace.[10]

"Too many garden hoses being stolen in Chicago," read another decree from the twenty-fourth floor. As no one around the Colonel was anxious to dispute this insight, an inquiry was made. It revealed a single hose stolen during the previous six weeks. "Please see that our radial highways into Chicago are widened to forty feet," the Colonel directed managing editor J. Loy "Pat" Maloney, and Illinois legislators duly authorized a $30 million bond issue in compliance with his wishes. Chicago parks commissioner Ed Kelly was even more accommodating. On learning secondhand of a McCormick remark about the paucity of trees in Grant Park, Kelly didn't wait to hear it for himself. "If the Colonel wants trees," he said, hastening to plant hundreds of elms in the lakefront park, "he gets trees."[11]

Kelly had a special reason to take McCormick's suggestions as commands. Before his 1933 election as mayor — a selection engineered in the wake of incumbent Anton Cermak's murder, without resort to the voters and with maximum backstage prompting by the Colonel — Kelly was indicted for income tax evasion, an event that left his career hanging in the balance. In time he was able to negotiate a settlement with the Internal Revenue Service, under which he paid $105,000 on income for 1926–28. Yet as long as he faced a possible jail term, his friends made themselves scarce. Just when his spirits were at their lowest ebb, the commissioner received a call from Colonel McCormick.

"Ed, would you have lunch with me?"

Kelly was delighted to accept the invitation. Where did the Colonel suggest they meet for lunch?

"At the Chicago Club."[12]

The significance of this gesture was not lost on Kelly. Ostracized by his nominal allies, the controversial official was being given the most public of blessings in a setting favored by Chicago's power elite.

No other publisher would presume to reinvent the English language, as McCormick attempted to, beginning in 1934. Thereafter two generations of Chicagoans struggled to make sense of *iland* for *island*, *frate* in place of *freight*, and *jaz* shorn of its final consonant. Not until 1975, twenty years after his death, did the *Tribune* throw in the orthographic towel, conceding in a wryly worded editorial that "thru is through and so is tho." (Even then, however, the paper stubbornly clung to such words of its own making as *dialog* and *synagog*.)

McCormick's whims were a reporter's hard work. Sometimes they led to a fool's errand, as when a *Tribune* correspondent was dispatched to the liberal hotbed of Madison, Wisconsin, to investigate the Colonel's theory that University of Wisconsin men wore lace underwear. Other journalists were ordered to find out for *Tribune* readers how hard a lobster pinches, the difference between the horse chestnut and the buckeye, what makes the sap rise in a tree (the Colonel contended that wind action was the cause), and why New Yorkers seemed especially prone to spitting on their city's sidewalks.[13]

Such oddball requests masked a ranging curiosity, the hallmark of any great editor. "Do sunflowers turn with the sun or against it?" McCormick asked the farm editor Richard Orr. From the same source the Colonel wished to know whether it was practical to breed chickens that would double their market value by laying double-yoked eggs. "The big fish are eating the little fish," read one cryptic McCormick memo in its entirety, leaving Orr to fathom the mysteries of aquatic cannibalism. "Write Greer Garson" — unknown to either of them — McCormick instructed, "and ask how she is getting on with her White Shorthorns." Orr hoped the Colonel might in time forget this curious assignment, but he should not have been surprised two months later to receive an inevitable sequel from the twenty-fourth floor: "Have you heard from Greer Garson about those white Shorthorns?"[14]

The first time Don Maxwell visited the twenty-fourth floor, he was stopped in his tracks. "Don," asked McCormick, "how far is it from Vladivostok to Shanghai?" Odder still was the experience of *Tribune* correspondent Willard Edwards. One Sunday in 1925, Edwards took a transatlantic telephone call from the Colonel in Paris. "Which way is the river flowing?" McCormick shouted into the phone. It developed that the Colonel, sitting in his hotel room, had come to the conclusion that recent heavy rains in the Midwest might reverse the flow of the Chicago River and carry raw sewage into Lake Michigan. The quick-thinking Edwards sent a reporter down to the Michigan Avenue Bridge, from which he gauged the flow of the water by tossing scraps of white paper into the foaming current.[15]

McCormick was probably the most widely traveled man in Chicago. On one storm-tossed flight from London to Paris, a frightened *Tribune* correspondent closed his eyes, gripped his armrest, and mentally prepared for the worst. Outside the wind shrieked and lightning danced around the wings. A tap on his shoulder interrupted these terrifying reveries. "When you translate an editorial from a French paper," bellowed McCormick, oblivious to everything but the point he was making, "you oughtn't to follow the grammatical structure of the original. Break it up into smaller sentences."[16]

Wherever he went, McCormick traveled in state. He spent one ocean voyage holed up in his suite reading every non-trade journal then published in the United States. "Just wanted to find out what's going on in the magazine field," he remarked to a companion who discovered him in his littered stateroom. (Still more startled was a reporter who found his employer sleeping in the bathtub of his cabin. McCormick explained his choice of accommodations by saying that the woodwork in his bedroom creaked.) In the late twenties, the Colonel frequented the Twentieth Century Limited between Chicago and New York, occupying a freshly aired drawing room with "an armload of newspapers from all over. As he would read these papers," recalled a *Tribune* colleague, "he'd open up the drawing room door and throw them out in the aisle." Porters came by every hour or so to clear away the paper mountain blocking the passage.[17]

Whether the Colonel was brilliantly inventive or merely unhinged was a much debated topic around the *Tribune*. Was a Baha'i temple in suburban Wilmette really the architectural equal of the Taj Mahal? The Colonel said so, with the same dogmatic conviction that made him ascribe the perfection of Illinois singing voices to a geographical quirk of nature. Out of his experience, Don Maxwell evolved a practical method of humoring his eccentric boss. "If you really thought something he proposed wasn't valid, you didn't say, 'I think that's goofy,'" said Maxwell. "You said, 'That's interesting. But I'd like to have twenty-four hours to go into both sides of it.'"[18]

On more than one occasion, McCormick's fruitful brain produced innovations lost to more conventional thinkers. "I don't see why they bring these suburban trains into Chicago and then turn them around," he told J. Howard Wood, a North Shore reporter turned financial writer, in March 1927. "Why don't they leave the engine at one end of the train and run it back and forth?" Railroad officials confronted with this notion scoffed at "another one of McCormick's crazy ideas." Not long after, they were doing precisely what the Colonel had urged.[19]

McCormick moved on to glass milk bottles. He thought it absurd for consumers to put out these heavy containers or haul them back for the bottlers to disinfect before washing and reusing them over and over. "Why don't they put milk in paper cartons?" he wondered. Again, dairy companies knowingly shook their heads, full of good reasons why it couldn't be done — until they started doing it.

"I have drifted on an idea which I think is very good," McCormick wrote to Joe Patterson in September 1929. "I think that available parking space in an office building would be a big seller of office space. It so happens that the height of our storage paper floors is just about right for storing automobiles." With this in mind, he had ordered his building manager "to figure out some way of getting automobiles in and out . . . I believe a building with such space to rent will have a decisive edge on [the] competitor."[20]

✧ 3

McCormick filled his mornings meeting with *Tribune* department heads, placing calls, and answering his voluminous mail. His administrative style was "sort of military," concluded the advertising director Paul

Fulton, "in that each division was in charge of its own operation, and only if there was a problem would he step in ... But never would he allow one division to criticize or question another division." The Sunday editor A.M. "Mike" Kennedy agreed with this assessment. "He kept an eye on everything," said Kennedy, citing a flowery story turned in by a society reporter named India Moffett (later Edwards). McCormick tore the piece out of the paper, scrawled "This is bullshit" across Miss Moffett's mannered prose, and sent it on to Kennedy. Much to his embarrassment, Kennedy hadn't bothered to read the story before it ran, a mistake he never repeated.[21]

Ernest Fuller, low man on the financial section staff, experienced McCormick's attention to detail firsthand when he received a Delphic note from the twenty-fourth floor saying, "Get rabbit quote daily." On investigation, he found that the Colonel had been sold a rabbit for dinner at what he considered an inflated price. Compounding the offense, he had been unable to find hares listed in the *Tribune* livestock price tables. Hence the memo.

It wasn't easy, but Fuller eventually located a dealer in rabbits, to whom he thereafter placed a daily call, being careful to distinguish between November jacks and March hares. As the price of rabbits took off, Fuller concluded that his prized dealer was using the *Tribune* to engage in price fixing. He took his predicament to the financial editor. Perhaps they should simply inform the Colonel that no market in rabbits existed.

Fuller's superior had a better idea. "Take the rabbit quotes out of Sunday's paper and put them back in on Monday," he told Fuller.

After a week's silence, the editor went a step further. "Now take them out Monday, Wednesday, and Friday."

Still no word from the twenty-fourth floor.

"Now put them in once a week on Friday," Fuller was instructed. After several more weeks, he received permission to drop the rabbit quotes altogether.[22]

Among the greatest drawbacks of newspapering, McCormick once wrote, was that "sooner or later the paper steps on the toes of everyone we know. Little by little we draw into a shell and lose those many friendships that make life so pleasant." In truth, he had few friends to lose; his almost pathological shyness made him a social misfit. A hardworking aristocrat resolved to be under obligation to no man, he instinctively returned season football tickets sent to him as a courtesy by George Halas, owner of the Chicago Bears. He expected *Tribune* employees to practice the same monkish restraint. If they traveled first-class, stayed at the finest hotels, and turned in ample expense accounts, they were to thank Colonel McCormick and no one else.[23]

Few screwed up the courage to try.

"The Colonel was a difficult man to talk to," said Don Maxwell. "You couldn't sit on a sofa with him and do anything except to ask questions you thought that he would like to answer" — which typically resulted in a ten- or fifteen-minute monologue contrasting the battlefield strengths of Grant and Sherman. Those who knew him best found his silences eloquent. On visits to Washington, McCormick regularly dropped by the home of his bureau chief, Arthur Sears Henning. The house, situated in Rock Creek Park, had a huge living room with Palladian windows overlooking the sluggish stream. Here McCormick and Henning sat wordlessly, the only sound the tinny syncopation of a grandfather clock. After half an hour had passed, the Colonel got up from his chair: "Well Arthur, nice to see you."[24]

However remote he appeared, McCormick was capable of spontaneous generosity. Maxwell was abruptly promoted from the sports desk to news after the previous editor foolishly told the Colonel that a map he wanted run in the *Tribune* had already appeared three days earlier. The new editor confirmed McCormick's judgment by engineering the switch of a charity football game between Notre Dame and Northwestern from Dyche Stadium in Evanston to the much larger Soldier Field in downtown Chicago. A week after the game, Maxwell was called to the twenty-fourth floor. "Don," McCormick told him, "we're going to cut down on bonuses this year and I'm going to issue you one now and I don't want you to talk about it." He presented Maxwell a check for $11,000, $2,000 more than his annual salary at the time.[25]

The Colonel showed similar appreciation to Arch Ward, Maxwell's successor as sports editor, who, along with Maxwell's brother Phil, helped organize such signature *Tribune* promotions as the Golden Gloves Boxing Tournament, the Chicagoland Music Festival, and baseball and football all-star games pitting the best college and professional players against each other. Told that Ward earned $15,000 a year, McCormick issued a crisp order: "Pay him twenty-five and put him under a five-year contract."[26]

A *Tribune* book editor felled by pneumonia drew her full salary during a six-month absence, a policy later extended to other workers and sweetened by the offer of half-pay for a second six months if necessary. Alcoholic executives were quietly and repeatedly sent to Wisconsin or Canada to dry out. A pressman who had been discharged for accidentally inserting a rival's ad in the middle of a twelve-page section trumpeting the glories of the Fair Store chain found an unlikely champion on the twenty-fourth floor. "Bring him back to work," McCormick told the production manager, John Park. "Any man can make a mistake."[27]

Toward the venerable Pulitzer Prize-winning cartoonist John McCutcheon, McCormick displayed special consideration, excusing McCutcheon from drawing the unsubtle front-page images with which the *Tribune* brayed its opposition to Prohibition. Along with the courtly Tiffany Blake and the outspoken Cliff Raymond, McCutcheon was a mainstay of McCormick's daily lunch circle, which assembled in the Overset Club (named for the type left over after the newspaper was put to bed) of Tribune Tower. Table conversation at the Overset was lively and often heated. The cartoonist Carey Orr, a former pitcher for the Seattle Seals, once told a skeptical Emory Thomason, the *Tribune's* business manager, that he could hurl a baseball across a plate at sixty miles per hour. On hearing Orr's boast, McCormick happily piled the entire group of writers, cartoonists, financial managers, and editors into two Cadillacs and drove to a vacant lot on the lakefront. Orr spent the rest of the afternoon tossing balls while McCormick and John Park served as judges of the impromptu competition.

In later years a crippling protocol inhibited such rowdiness. No visitor to the Overset could begin eating before the Colonel's arrival or precede him in leaving the table. As a practical concern, this imposed scant hardship, since McCormick ate in haste, rarely lingering more than half an hour, save for the rare instance when he might be entertaining a guest such as Herbert Hoover or Winston Churchill (who welcomed a proffered Scotch only after the ice was removed). Before this captive audience McCormick was able to relax and indulge his poky sense of humor. On one memorable Friday he invited George Cardinal Mundelein and one of Chicago's leading rabbis to join him for lunch. As the two men sat down, McCormick, with a poker face, enthusiastically sliced into a platter of ham. The clerics pleaded a lack of appetite. Their host, barely able to suppress a snicker, motioned to a waitress, who returned with a freshly cooked salmon. "I guess they got their appetites back again," said the Colonel, chuckling to himself as the cardinal and the rabbi polished off their lunch.[28]

Another day, on the stroke of one, McCormick declared his colleagues in for a culinary treat. Thick steaks appeared from the kitchen. Those around the table competed in praise for the mouthwatering dish. They were still buttering the apple the next day when McCormick asked whether any of them had experienced indigestion. On the contrary, said the diners; they could not recall a more enjoyable meal. He was glad to hear it, said McCormick, before explaining that the steaks had been carved from one of his best mares at Cantigny, shot after breaking a leg. Nor was he above serving crow bagged at his estate to employees in need of a little comeuppance.[29]

After lunch the editorial team would reassemble in his office to hear McCormick rattle off his causes of the moment. With Medill dead and Joe Patterson exiled to New York, the Colonel's authority to set the *Tribune* agenda for Chicago, the Midwest, and the United States went unchallenged. The newspaper became a megaphone to amplify the publisher's caprices. In the fullest sense, McCormick's editorial meetings never ended; a telephone equipped with an extra-loud bell linked the Colonel with his city editor on the fourth floor. Along this line flowed an unending stream of orders to attack, expose, and investigate.

The balance of the afternoon was taken up with additional conferences, daily reports from circulation and other departments, preparation of a speech or radio broadcast, and far-ranging explorations of his realm. "He kept his own finger on the newsroom without appearing to do so," said Eleanor Page, a society editor whom the Colonel insisted on calling Front Page. (With the same persistence, he had the *Tribune* invariably refer to "W. R. Hearst, California publisher," and "Henry Luce, who was born in China but is not a Chinaman.") "You'd walk out on the fourth floor hall and you'd hear this voice booming out, 'Well, I've got a couple of bitches here that are going to do something or other.' "[30]

Unexpected visits from the Colonel could produce unintended consequences. Once he discovered a *Tribune* executive and his secretary cavorting on an office divan. The scene led McCormick to impose a ban on full-size sofas throughout Tribune Tower, a self-denying ordinance he modified only slightly in later years, when a carpenter put hinges on the arms of his favorite red leather couch. Visitors to the twenty-fourth floor grew accustomed to seeing the aging Colonel giving dictation while lying down, his long legs protruding from one end of his sawed-off sofa.[31]

Late in the day McCormick would retrace his morning route through the high-vaulted lobby of the building, past the branch station of the *Tribune*'s Public Service Office. Here war veterans came to apply for government benefits, confused taxpayers obtained expert guidance in filling out their tax forms, and aspiring college students perused catalogues from every American university and business or trade school. Local residents made use of the *Tribune*'s borrowing library while tourists picked up road maps and garnered sightseeing tips.

It was only a short ride from the tower to 1519 Astor Street, an elegant four-story townhouse built of brick and limestone, which McCormick purchased in 1926 to serve as his town residence.* The house, a recent addition to Chicago's toniest neighborhood, boasted a formal garden with orange trees and marble busts surrounded by a high, ivy-draped wall to protect the security-conscious newspaper publisher and his wife. Outside, Amy could show off her gardening talents. Inside, she held benefits for

---

*Not until the 1930s was his Cantigny estate in Wheaton winterized. In the meantime, the Colonel used the place sparingly during cold-weather months. With the same thrift that prevented him from wearing a hat — he said he hated to be dunned by hatcheck girls — he complained that it cost him $40 to heat the old farmhouse for a family Thanksgiving.

groups such as Orphans of the Storm, an animal rights charity she founded in 1928 to protest the wanton killing of hundreds of dogs by the Anti-Cruelty Society. Halley's Comet was more frequently seen than Amy's husband at these altruistic events.

McCormick's limited tolerance for society in any form was matched by a boyish impulsiveness. One evening in the 1930s, he decided to visit the house in which he was born. Located a few blocks north of Tribune Tower, the modest structure had long since been converted into a posh, members-only establishment called the Key Club. (Taking a perverse pride in this, McCormick boasted that more people visited his birthplace than Abraham Lincoln's.) The most famous man in Chicago decided to go incognito, his disguise consisting of a pair of dark glasses. For good measure he fitted his German shepherd with the collar of a Seeing Eye dog. Together they set off up Michigan Avenue. Inside the club at 150 Ontario Street, McCormick spent several hours surrounded by solicitous strangers, or so he claimed later. Finally he left, unable to tolerate the excessive sympathy shown to the "blind man."[32]

Whatever their address — and by the end of the twenties, Bert and Amy owned a hunting lodge in Aiken, South Carolina, as well as homes in Palm Beach, Lake Forest, Chicago, and Wheaton — husband and wife operated in separate spheres, pursued separate diversions, occupied separate bedrooms. Amy displayed little interest in *Tribune* operations beyond reminding the man she called RR to bring home the superior radio page of the rival *American*. More maternal-looking than ever, Amy was happiest leading her pack of forty hounds across the open fields of Cantigny. Painting ranked close behind the chase of foxes as a source of pleasure; one Chicago reporter noted in 1932 that "she works Sundays like an unknown struggling to make a few dollars to eat." By then Amy had gratified a decade old wish to own a Degas pastel of ballet dancers. This latest acquisition joined an impressive collection of canvases signed by Cezanne, Matisse, Renoir, Picasso, and Modigliani.

The master of the house was indifferent to the artistic genius animating Rousseau's landscapes and Gauguin's sunflowers. He much preferred immersing himself in Civil War tactics in the solitude of his library. Direct lines there and in his bedroom connected him with the *Tribune*'s managing editor, who could expect to hear from the Colonel several times a night before the final edition went to press, carrying late-breaking reports of fires, train wrecks, gangster shootings, and the latest resignation of a French premier. The tenor of these communications inevitably warmed as the evening advanced and the Colonel's alcohol consumption mounted.

At length a heavy set of chimes would announce eleven o'clock. Satisfied that he had done all in his considerable power that day to promote his friends and discomfit his adversaries, McCormick donned red silk pajamas and peeled off two Cartier wristwatches, worn face inward, one of which was always set to Chicago time. Then he settled down for the night in a huge, rough-hewn bed made, he insisted, from rails split a century earlier by Abraham Lincoln.[33]

✧ 4

In December 1925, McCormick addressed those attending the annual dinner of the *Tribune*'s advertising department. Before this audience of salesmen he did some selling of his own, acknowledging that he had not reached his current position via the traditional editorial route and taking pains to associate himself not merely with Joe Patterson but with the advertising and sales functions derided by "tea party magazine writers."

His view of their common enterprise, he said, was far more robust: "Ours is a great life. We are the most vital single force at the center of the world." Sounding like a Manchu emperor persuaded that the Middle Kingdom lay at the heart of the universe, McCormick likened the *Tribune* to Standard Oil, the Roman empire, and the German general staff. He boasted of home-grown features enthusiastically read in dozens of other American cities, and of modern reporters "no longer confined to young men with silk hats and tall canes, riding on a street car to endeavor to put more color in a story," but rather recognized experts in their individual fields. Under McCormick, nearly thirty enterprising correspondents, scattered from Buenos Aires to Manila, cabled intelligence "such as no other generation could even contemplate, and . . . no other newspaper can have except by agreement of the *Chicago Tribune*." A business employing 1,400 people in 1914, when the abrupt departure of Jim Keeley had pitchforked McCormick and Patterson into the executive suite, now provided work for 6,000. Thanks to McCormick's initiative, the Tribune Company owned paper mills at Thorold, Ontario, and Tonawanda, New York, the latter facility annually turning out 40,000 tons of magazine and rotogravure paper to sustain the two biggest-selling newspapers in America as well as the weekly magazine *Liberty*.

In 1923, McCormick had added 2,000 square miles of spruce and balsam timberland in the basin of Quebec's Manicouagan River to his holdings at Shelter Bay. Two thriving towns housed *Tribune* workers in the Canadian woods. A growing fleet of ships transported raw materials and finished paper to docks on the Chicago River. Beginning in May 1923, passengers on fifteen ships plying the Atlantic between the United States and Europe were never at a loss for news of home, thanks to the Oceanic Edition of the *Tribune*. The moment travelers walked down a gangplank at Southampton or Cherbourg, they could obtain fresh word of the home front in the same paper's European edition. The Paris bureau was careful to maintain a supply of caps worn by newspaper vendors, each blazoned with *The Chicago Tribune.* These were prominently displayed, if only for a few minutes, by salesmen hawking the Paris edition — "*La Liberté, La Presse, La Chicago Tribune*" — wherever the Colonel might alight.[34]

The period of expansion that coincided with the McCormick–Patterson management could be measured in daily circulation — up from 299,000 in 1914 to 658,000 twelve years later — or by the 700,000 letters addressed to feature departments in 1925 alone, or by the six million telephone calls handled each year by the *Tribune's* switchboard operators. (Liberal with praise, especially when it reinforced his exalted view of everything connected with the *Tribune*, McCormick insisted that his chief telephone operator was the greatest in the business.) The Colonel's habit of viewing the world through long-range spectacles had paid off most handsomely on the business side of the *Tribune*. Net annual earnings, pegged at $1 million under Keeley, had multiplied tenfold. Dividends had gone from $500,000 in 1910 to nearly $7 million in 1925. McCormick attributed much of the *Tribune's* fabulous growth to his own guiding principle — "that a man should be paid as much as he can earn."

Yet for all his achievements, McCormick was acutely aware that the success of the modern *Tribune* largely reflected the circulation-building genius of Joe Patterson. Nowhere had the Patterson magic been more profitably employed than in the Sunday *Tribune*, which tipped the scales at two and a half pounds and reached over a million homes each week. Readers couldn't get enough of such features as "Isn't It Odd?" wherein they learned how a single ounce of moth eggs could result in ten pounds of silk; "Home Harmonious," a column devoted to furnishing and decorating tips; the self-explanatory "My Greatest Thrill" and "The Cheekiest Person I Ever Met"; the evergreen "Love Problems Department" ("When walking north on Main Street, is it proper to walk on the inside or the outside of a lady?"); and "Maiden Meditations," a weekly half-page of drawings and verse evoking "the real spirit of the modern girl."

Eager to show that the *Tribune* could flourish in the post–Patterson era, in 1926 McCormick launched a Better Homes Competition, attracting nearly a thousand designs for affordable middle-class housing. He unveiled an Investors' Guide and the *Chicago Tribune Business Survey*, a monthly compendium of statistics covering everything from railcar loadings to consumer savings accounts, which served as a business barometer in the days before the federal government supplied regular snapshots of national economic output.

His most radical break with the past came in February 1927, however, when the Sunday *Tribune* was distinguished by a new metropolitan section, in reality five separate publications tailored to reflect the interests of diverse city neighborhoods as well as the burgeoning suburbs. The advantages of this "split circulation" were immediate and lasting. In localizing news coverage, the *Tribune* strengthened its hold over the loyalty of readers throughout metropolitan Chicago; by the end of the decade, the paper was a staple in three quarters of area households. For retailers targeting scarce promotion dollars, the deliberately fragmented audience offered rich prospects. Many a small business originally lured to the metropolitan section by the copy and art, merchandising service, or business survey department went on to advertise in the full run of the *Tribune*.

As McCormick moved aggressively to put his imprint on the paper, relations with his cousin in New York became strained. Jurisdictional disputes broke out involving the Tribune Syndicate. Patterson was unhappy over the elimination of some features and the treatment of cartoonists. Carl Ed, ordered to drop the word *sheik* from the adventures of "Harold Teen," protested to Patterson, who was already miffed over a Little Orphan Annie contest that had been staged without his knowledge and the removal of the trademark "Blue Ribbon" seal from *Tribune* fiction (McCormick complained that the symbol resembled a beer sign).

McCormick widened the gulf by demanding more detective stories, more war stories, and more stories with a Chicago angle. By complying with his requests, Patterson countered, the syndicate wouldn't have any room left for romance and love stories, "the essentials of successful fiction." The quarrel escalated. The cousins disagreed over features and paper contracts, even over a deal Patterson struck with the swimmer Gertrude Ederle, famous as the first woman to swim the English Channel, to appear in the pages of the *Daily News*. Yet somehow their differences were patched over. McCormick agreed to let Max Annenberg move to New York as the general manager of *Liberty*, and Patterson assured his cousin that "you can depend on me to keep the old machine going" when McCormick contracted a severe case of jaundice in the autumn of 1926.[35]*

The two men soldiered on, mindful of their Iron-Bound Agreement. While the Colonel withdrew to the splendid isolation of his Tribune Tower eyrie, Patterson dropped into Manhattan moviehouses and tramped from door to door helping to conduct the *Daily News*'s famous straw polls. He once canceled a yacht race sponsored by the paper after observing the riverbank crowd cheering on the majestic sailing vessels: not a *News* reader among them.

It wasn't as if Patterson deliberately spurned the respectability that came with commercial success. "The *Daily News* was built on legs," he liked to explain, "but when we got enough circulation we dropped them."[36]

---

*The Colonel credited his recovery to a doctor who was unafraid to break the anti-narcotic laws. He told Patterson, "He filled me full of opium last night. I have had some very strange sensations but the effect on my intestines has been remarkable and I am almost white today."

The paper's photographs might no longer resemble French postcards, but no one was likely to confuse Sloppy Joe with his aristocratic Chicago cousin. In 1930, flush with cash, Patterson built a shimmering skyscraper on East Forty-second Street. Like Tribune Tower, the new building rose thirty-six stories above the city for which it claimed to speak, but there the similarities ended. Sleek and boxy, the Daily News building was totally contemporary, belligerently impersonal, and devoid of historical flourishes, except for the words of Lincoln that Patterson had inscribed across the front of the $10 million edifice: "The Lord must have loved the common people, he made so many of them."

Unfortunately for both Patterson and McCormick, not enough of these divinely favored readers purchased *Liberty* to make it profitable. Quality was never an issue. The magazine offered prose from F. Scott Fitzgerald, Ring Lardner, Ben Hecht, Stephen Vincent Benét, Elmer Davis, Heywood Broun, and Rupert Hughes. Its roster of illustrators included James Montgomery Flagg, Neysa McMein, Rollin Kirby, and John McCutcheon. Designed for a fast-paced age, *Liberty* specialized in the one-page short story, alerting readers with a trademark clock to precisely how much time they would need to complete "Please May I Bob My Hair?" by Mary Pickford or Kathleen Norris's wry investigation of flappers as prospective daughters-in-law.

Readers liked *Liberty* better than advertisers did. Scanning the horizon for elusive profits from their stylish magazine, the cousins marched toward a national media empire like lemmings to the sea. Patterson, the cultural blotter, hoped to run a Los Angeles tabloid. McCormick, the frustrated politician, craved influence in the nation's capital. "I might find Washington a nice town to grow old in," the Colonel confided to Max Annenberg in December 1927. But to do so he must first get his hands on the "rotten" *Washington Post*, which under the erratic ownership of Ned McLean consisted of little more than Associated Press dispatches. McCormick envisioned a quick and inexpensive makeover of the *Post* in which he would simply add the *Tribune*'s Foreign News Service and "one or two brilliant political writers" to bolster its appeal.[37]

As it happened, the *Post* was not for sale. No matter. At the behest of Emory Thomason, McCormick considered buying papers in Cleveland, Boston, Minneapolis, and Detroit. Not until April 1931, however, did he and Patterson actually close a deal for a newspaper property outside their existing markets. Then they swapped *Liberty* for the *Daily Mirror*, an ailing tabloid owned by the Detroit publisher Bernarr MacFadden. As long as *Liberty* hemorrhaged red ink, the cousins were stymied in their diversification plans. Now, ironically, they were trading one sick property for another. The *Mirror* limped along for two years, never flirting with prosperity, until it expired, unmourned, in the trough of the Great Depression.

By then McCormick was conducting a cautious courtship of the newest instrument of mass communication. At the start of 1925, radio station WGN was one of 530 stations nationwide beaming election returns, bad poetry, and worse music to a few thousand homes equipped with primitive "cat's whisker" sets. Those crude receivers soon gave way to oversized cabinets that became part of twenties decor. Before the year ended, WGN presented the Chicago Symphony Orchestra and several Gilbert and Sullivan operettas. It offered piano lessons, gave air time to Gloria Swanson and Benito Mussolini, broadcast Jewish New Year services, and featured four U.S. senators in two nights of debate, live from the Capitol in Washington, over U.S. membership in the World Court. It will come as no surprise that 86 percent of the WGN audience polled agreed with the *Tribune*'s opposition to further involvement with the European cardsharps who had bilked Woodrow Wilson and tarnished America's wartime sacrifice.

Between 1924 and 1930, the Tribune Company lost nearly $1.5 million on commercial-free radio broadcasts. Even after WGN changed its policy to allow for paid sponsorship of professional football games, soap operas, and the widely popular dramatization of *Tribune* comic strips, including "Little Orphan Annie" and "Dick Tracy," the station spent lavishly to cover national political conventions. Only three broadcasters were present at the 1928 Democratic conclave in Houston that nominated Al Smith: CBS, NBC, and WGN. That same year the *Tribune* station, at its own expense, installed the first police radio system in Chicago, an innovation that did little to stem the city's organized crime wave but did earn WGN favorable publicity.

As for McCormick, he had mixed feelings about the new medium. Content to exploit its newspaper-selling possibilities (he liked to say that WGN should become the *Chicago Tribune* of the air), he was less comfortable with the technological demands radio made on its listeners. On at least one occasion the Colonel angrily telephoned Carl Meyers, the head engineer of WGN, from his Astor Street house. "The damn radio won't work. Fix it!" he barked. Meyers soon determined that McCormick's set wasn't plugged into a wall socket. He said as much to the Colonel. "Now it's working," replied McCormick, with no trace of embarrassment.[38]

McCormick's pride cost him much more than inconvenience when the door of his office slid open to reveal Freeman Gosden and Charles Correll, a pair of Chicago singers reborn in January 1926 as Sam n' Henry, whose specialty was Negro dialect comedy. Overnight the team became the hottest property on the airwaves. They were worth vastly more to the *Tribune* than the $100 a week McCormick was paying them, and they knew it. Early in 1928 they took their case for a 50 percent raise to the twenty-fourth floor, where they ran into a stone wall of imperial resistance. "When you leave this office you enter oblivion," McCormick told the unhappy performers. Instead Gosden and Correll walked over to NBC, which signed them to a $100,000 contract on the spot. Sam n' Henry became Amos n' Andy, blackface proprietors of the Fresh Air Taxi Company, whose popularity compelled movie theaters to schedule film showings around their nightly broadcast at seven o'clock and department stores to carry the pair's comic adventures over loudspeakers so that shoppers wouldn't miss an episode.[39]

McCormick had better luck with aviation, a personal passion ever since the day almost twenty years earlier when he had witnessed a demonstration flight by the Wright brothers outside Washington, D.C. He had closely followed developments in the air during World War I. After the war he bought a De Havilland flying boat for timber-cruising and fire-patrol duties on the St. Lawrence River. The *Tribune* also leased two Curtiss planes to beat the competition to major news stories and prime photographs. In May 1929, the foreign correspondent Larry Rue took delivery of a De Havilland Gipsy Moth coupe, the name of his newspaper inscribed on its fuselage in Gothic script, and became the first European journalist to chase the news by air.

Closer to home, McCormick tirelessly promoted a lakefront airport for Chicago, a vision belatedly realized with the 1946 opening of Meigs Field. Determined to make Chicago a hub of international commerce and culture, he set out to prove the feasibility of a northern, over-the-pole route from the American Midwest to Europe. To further his designs, the Colonel in 1928 acquired a twin-engine Sikorsky amphibian, which he christened in classic McCormick fashion. Even Joe Patterson, accustomed to his cousin's peculiarities, shook his head over the plane's name, *'Untin' Bowler.* "When I was in London I asked the clerk in a hat store for a strong hat to wear riding," McCormick explained. "He replied, 'You will be wantin' a 'untin' bowler.'" Originally the plane was to have blazed a new route between New York and Chicago. But a feckless pilot, disregarding instructions, ran out of gas and made a forced landing at Cleveland. This was hardly the sort of advertising for the *Tribune* or air travel that McCormick had in mind.[40]

Ignoring the setback, at the start of July 1929 he authorized a far more daring adventure. "It is a great experiment we are making," he wrote to his mother on July 3, "sending a flying boat from Chicago to Berlin over Greenland." By that evening the *'Untin' Bowler* rested on the frozen surface of Ontario's Remi Lake, over six hundred miles from Chicago. Later, thick fog sweeping south from the Arctic icefields marooned the plane at a remote station of the Hudson's Bay Company. On July 9 the fragile craft threaded its way between high cliffs and alighted in a fjord running into the Hudson Straits, off Labrador. Soon ice floes jammed the waterway, crushing a rudder and tearing away both pontoons. Early on the fifteenth, the plane was engulfed in a shrieking gale, and its three-man crew, after scrambling to safety, was unable to prevent the battered airship from going to the bottom.

McCormick's promotional stunt had ended in disaster, and his northern air route seemed as star-crossed as the *'Untin' Bowler* itself. Yet the Colonel appeared almost nonchalant to Pat Maloney, whose melancholy duty it was to report the humiliating disappearance of the airplane. "Up like the rocket, down like the stick," said McCormick in response to the news. He quickly ordered a second Sikorsky amphibian to replace the *Bowler* and gave it the name *'Arf Pint*.[41]

✧ 5

Make Chicago the first city in the world. Throughout the feverish twenties, this Burnhamesque injunction held a place of honor at the top of the *Tribune*'s "Platform for Chicago," a regular daily feature on the editorial page. From the vantage point of the Tribune Tower's heavily visited observatory, it was easy to believe with McCormick that his hometown, already the most representative city in America, might shortly surpass New York in cultural influence and commercial productivity. Still following the steep trajectory of growth that predated the Civil War, Jazz Age Chicago saw its population top 3 million and its annual economic output reach $4 billion.

While McCormick preached the glories of superhighways, electrified railroads, a beautified lakefront, and a long-delayed subway, other builders transformed the local skyline with towers sleekly functional or gaudily overdressed. Across North Michigan Avenue from Tribune Tower rose the Wrigley Building, a white terra-cotta monument to a chewing gum magnate. The Moorish dome and minaret of the Medinah Club, the gathering place for companionable Shriners, earned instant landmark status among the smart shops and conventional office buildings lining the Magnificent Mile, at the portal of which stood Tribune Tower. Urban boosters let nothing deter them from erecting the biggest, tallest, or least indigenous of structures heralding the new Chicago. In 1926 they completed a tower at 100 West Monroe Street, bisected by a cowpath to nowhere. Ten feet wide and eighteen feet high, the functionless route was maintained in accordance with a nineteenth–century compact between the city and a property owner who had been indignant over efforts to ban cows and pigs from Chicago streets.

That same year motorists breathed sighs of relief over Wacker Drive, a double-deck boulevard with a lower-level expressway set aside for freight traffic. With 3,000 rooms, the Stevens Hotel announced itself as the world's largest when its many doors opened in 1927. Three years later the

Merchandise Mart, housing 25,000 workers in 93 acres of floor space, staked its claim as the biggest building on the planet. Meanwhile the vast new Union Station reaffirmed the long-standing importance of Chicago as a transport hub. Adjoining Grant Park — itself saved from developers in the 1890s after A. Montgomery Ward discovered a forgotten clause in the municipal code ensuring that the lakefront must remain "forever free and clear" — Soldier Field was dedicated in 1922. Before the decade ended, the 80,000-seat stadium played host to spectacles ranging from the international Eucharistic Congress to a rematch between boxers Jack Dempsey and Gene Tunney (the latter broadcast nationally by WGN radio). The same lakefront district contained a greatly expanded Field Museum of Natural History, the John G. Shedd Aquarium, and the spectacular Buckingham Fountain, which shot multicolored jets of water 135 feet into the air.

The *Tribune* meanwhile campaigned vigorously to preserve the crumbling Fine Arts Building in Jackson Park, a legacy of the Columbian Exposition, reborn through the generosity of philanthropist Julius Rosenwald as the Museum of Science and Industry. Secure in his Gothic fortress, McCormick feigned unconcern as the *Daily News* and the *Daily Times* erected modern structures on the other side of the Loop. Among the "budding Balzacs" apprenticed at the *Daily News* to the legendary editor Henry Justin Smith was Carl Sandburg, the prairie poet whose exuberant characterization of Chicago as "Hog Butcher for the World, Tool Maker, Stacker of Wheat, Player with Railroads and the Nation's Freight Handler" perfectly captured the swagger of McCormick and other destiny-minded Chicagoans.

Yet for much of the twenties, Sandburg's City of Big Shoulders was slumped in shame and helplessness. Overshadowing physical renewal along the lakefront was a corrupt cartel involving the political class and organized crime, an alliance founded on the thirst-quenching possibilities spawned by Prohibition. From December 1917, when Congress approved the Eighteenth Amendment, outlawing the manufacture or sale of spirituous liquors, until repeal of the amendment sixteen years later, the *Tribune* ran more than 1,100 editorials chastising those who would use the awesome powers of the federal government to regulate private conduct. "Abolish the Bootleg Law" became McCormick's mantra, his all-purpose condemnation of legislative busybodies out to convert the Constitution from a charter of inalienable rights to a moral straitjacket. "We do not like statutory prohibition as a substitute for character," fumed the *Tribune*.

McCormick's personal habits were far from abstemious. Told that a friend had died from cirrhosis of the liver, he was flippant. "Well, he had a good time anyway," he said. The Colonel trusted an iron will to save him from a similar fate. "If you don't drink before luncheon, or you don't drink after dinner," he declared, "you'll never be a drunkard."[42]

He felt less confidence in the common run of humanity. By lending an air of adventure to an otherwise unattractive habit, he editorialized in March 1927, "Prohibition has done everything to make drinking both attractive and disgusting." In place of the saloon, the sociable anchor of community life, antiliquor laws had given rise to the disreputable speak-easy, of which Chicago alone counted 20,000 in 1926. Worst of all, by driving the production, distribution, and consumption of spirits underground, the forces of purity had unwillingly extended the hand of friendship to bootleggers, racketeers, and pimps, who were responsible for the deadliest crime wave in the nation's violent history.

Nowhere in the twenties was human life so cheapened or legal codes so widely flouted as in Chicago under the dual reign of Big Bill Thompson and Al Capone. Each man had reason to cultivate the other, Thompson out of eagerness to prove that he could regain city hall in 1927 without help from the turncoat Fred Lundin, and Capone (also known as Scarface Al) because the fumbling attempts of Mayor Dever to promote civic morality, while effectively uniting local teachers and police against his own reelection, had also inconvenienced the mob into moving its base of operations to suburban Cicero.

A former speakeasy bouncer from Brooklyn, Capone was identified on his business card as a used-furniture dealer. Yet his annual income exceeded $100 million. His fortunes had risen with those of his patron, Johnny Torrio, whose uncle, Big Jim Colosimo, had dominated crime in Chicago until his murder in May 1920. In the wake of his uncle's death, Torrio moved quickly, with little resistance from the Thompson administration, to expand his share of the bootleg market. This unavoidably brought him into conflict with a rival gangster, Dion O'Banion, whose hegemony north of the Chicago River was rudely terminated in November 1924 when Capone's agents gunned him down in his State Street flower shop.

O'Banion went to his grave in a $10,000 casket, attended by a covey of judges, city aldermen, and state legislators. Their presence was duly noted by a streetwise *Tribune* reporter named Jake Lingle, whose extensive underworld contacts were more than enough to make his editors overlook his meager literary skills. The beer wars escalated dramatically. North Side gangsters out to avenge O'Banion seriously wounded Torrio, who fled to New York and left Scarface Al, at the age of twenty-six, in charge of a sprawling criminal empire. Mob violence in 1926 took at least sixty-four lives — sixty-five if we include Assistant State's Attorney William H. McSwiggin, rumored to be hot on the trail of Capone when he was shot down outside Cicero's Pony Inn one mild April night.

Six grand juries failed to prove anything in the McSwiggin case except that the Cook County jury system was hopelessly compromised. Capone, a physical coward so fearful of needles that he refused treatment for the syphilis that led to his agonizing death in 1947, surrounded himself with a protective army of bodyguards. He traveled in a seven-ton, custom-built limousine with thick plates of armor off which machine-gun bullets bounced harmlessly. For another kind of protection, Capone turned to politicians of both parties, including McSwiggin's boss, State's Attorney Robert Crowe.

As bootlegging operations branched out into extortion, gambling, labor racketeering, prostitution, and other forms of vice, political corruption became an accepted price of doing business in Chicago. By 1928, Capone was shelling out $30 million a year to purchase legal immunity. Exactly how much he contributed to Thompson's 1927 mayoral campaign is a matter of guesswork, but a conservative estimate runs to $260,000, generously supplemented by the loan of burly sluggers and triggermen pressed into service as election day "poll watchers."

Big Bill earned mob support by proclaiming himself "wetter than the middle of the Atlantic Ocean" and by promising a wide-open town, in stark contrast to Mayor Dever's chilly embrace of reform. Thompson polished his populist credentials by addressing a campaign audience of society women as "my hoodlum friends." To the *Tribune* he was "a buffoon in a tommyrot factory," variously posing as Napoleon, Billy Sunday, Buffalo Bill, Thaddeus Stevens, George Washington, Oliver Cromwell, the vaudeville team of Weber and Fields, and Balaam's Ass.[43]

Between choruses of his campaign anthem, "America First and Last and Always," Thompson threatened to punch England's King George V on the royal snoot if His Majesty ever set foot on the shores of Lake Michigan. He also sprayed verbal abuse over the superintendent of schools, a fumblingly earnest reformer named William McAndrew. Citing McAndrew's Scottish ancestry as proof of his intellectual treachery, Big Bill alleged a conspiracy to adulterate American history textbooks used in the Chicago schools. He first advanced this ludicrous charge in a pamphlet entitled "Shall Your Taxes Be Spent to Make Your Child Hate George Washington and Love the King?"

The *Tribune* reminded voters that it wasn't the king of England who bore responsibility for looting the city treasury through exorbitant payoffs to real estate "experts." Nor could Thompson expect proclamations of his own 100 percent Americanism to make voters forget "the fifty percent collections his fellows levied on everything they could reach in city hall." But McCormick's starchy protestations were drowned out by the roar of laughter and applause that Thompson's antics stirred. The former mayor lambasted one Republican primary opponent for playing handball "in the semi-nude. That's right, with only a little pair of pants on." Another rival, the former city health commissioner John Dill Robertson, a Thompson defector backed by Fred Lundin, was blasted as "Dill Pickle Robertson . . . so dry he never even takes a bath."[44]

Thompson overwhelmed his primary opposition, then went on to defeat the hapless Dever by 83,000 votes in the general election. He celebrated his comeback before a delirious throng at the Hotel Sherman. "Tell 'em, cowboys, tell 'em," he yelled above the beery jubilation of the crowd, "I told you I'd ride 'em high and wide."

Within weeks of Thompson's third inaugural, Chicagoans had reason to wonder just who occupied the municipal saddle. Was it the mayor, once again advertising his interest in the White House? Or was it Thompson's criminal ally, Al Capone? Forsaking Cicero, Capone and his entourage took over most of the Lexington Hotel on South Michigan Avenue. The hotel management installed a fourth-floor kitchen for their exclusive use. The gangster's vast office featured likenesses of his chief American heroes: George Washington, Abraham Lincoln, and William Hale Thompson. Capone quickly reestablished the heart of his gambling operations in a building one block from city hall — where his loyal agent Daniel Serritella looked out for his interests as city sealer.

❖ 6

Four years later, with federal tax investigators closing in on Capone, Mayor Thompson fighting for his political survival, and Serritella under indictment for defrauding Chicago consumers out of $54 million through short weights and measures, Capone's friend came forth with a startling tale linking the mobster and McCormick. "A little over two years ago," claimed Serritella, he had been approached by Max Annenberg and asked to intervene with Joe Duello, then the business agent of the union representing Chicago's chauffeurs and drivers. In a meeting with *Tribune* circulation manager Louis Rose, Duello had demanded $25,000 as the price of labor peace.

"Annenberg said he wanted to treat the boys right and that he wanted to reach someone who could get the executive committee to fix the strike up," asserted Serritella. In short, he wanted Capone's help. To get it, he was said to have telephoned the gangster, invited him to Tribune Tower, obtained his pledge of cooperation, and introduced him to Colonel McCormick, who had graciously thanked Capone before observing, "You know, you are famous like Babe Ruth. We can't help printing things about you, but I will see that the *Tribune* gives you a square deal."[45]

This eye-popping story, duly reprinted in numerous books and articles dealing with the period, proves on investigation to be a pastiche of truth, half-truth, and cynical invention. There *had* been a threatened strike, not in 1929, as Serritella remembered in February 1931, but in the summer of 1927. On September 29 of that year Joe Duello and six other union representatives *had* met with the publishers of five newspapers, McCormick included — not at Tribune Tower but in the Dearborn Street offices of the Chicago Publishers Association. McCormick, as the association's president, took his seat across the negotiating table from Duello. Annenberg, accompanied by the *Tribune's* John Park, called Duello out of the room and into a brief conference with Al Brown (one of Capone's aliases), who was there ostensibly because of his clout with the newsboys' union. Back in the main meeting, agreement was quickly reached on a new contract, after which "Brown" was brought into the room and introduced to those in attendance. Whatever McCormick may have said to the most renowned lawbreaker of the age, he almost certainly did not compare Capone to Babe Ruth.[46]

Yet another gangster threat involved a tough Irish labor leader and Capone adversary named Big Tim Murphy. One afternoon Murphy telephoned McCormick with word that he was on his way over to kill him. McCormick put down the receiver, then ordered his secretary and uniformed guard downstairs. Concealing a forty-five-caliber Colt automatic behind a pile of encyclopedias on his desk, he propped open his office door and sat for an unknown period of time, daring Murphy to show his face. "If he had come through that door I would have shot him," McCormick said afterward. "I wouldn't have had any conversation with him at all. But he didn't come. He was killed later, but he killed a lot of people first." Some of these, the Colonel broadly hinted, were murdered at the instigation of Samuel Insull.[47]

✧ 7

Hardly more welcome than Big Tim Murphy's call was an invitation from Mayor Thompson to join a committee of Chicago businessmen advising him on public issues. McCormick begged off politely, reminding Thompson, "It is impossible to separate the individual from the editor." With rather more courtesy than the occasion required, he reassured the mayor that "in view of our former relations," the past was indeed past. As for the present and future, "I wish you nothing but success in this administration."[48]

McCormick, of all people, must have known that this was a vain hope. The same month that Big Bill solicited the Colonel's views, he appointed Capone to an official delegation to welcome the Italian aviator Francesco de Pinedo on his round-the-world flight. Later that year he pricked up his ears and detected a ghostly popular clamor for himself to succeed Calvin

Coolidge in the White House. In the spring of 1927, the Mississippi River overflowed its banks; Big Bill seized the opportunity to present himself as a humanitarian in competition with Secretary of Commerce Herbert Hoover, a global hero lionized for his wartime feeding of Belgium and his postwar ministering to shattered European nations.

Hoover, himself a strong contender for the 1928 Republican presidential nomination, added further luster to his reputation by organizing vast tent cities in the flooded Mississippi Valley and channeling millions of tons of relief supplies to the stricken area. Thompson, by contrast, was sued by Illinois's attorney general and ordered to remit to the Red Cross $73,000, plus interest, in funds allegedly earmarked for victims of the flood. The mayor compensated for this embarrassment by making good on his pledge to evict school superintendent William McAndrew. In pursuing his vendetta against McAndrew, the *Tribune* concluded, Thompson had "gained a name for lunacy and lost a distinguished superintendent of schools." Undaunted, Big Bill appointed his yachting crony Urbine "Sport" Herrmann to sanitize the Chicago Public Library of pro-British books. Herrmann envisioned a grand book-burning on the lakefront. In the end, however, he settled for removing from circulation four works by eminent American historians, each condemned on hearsay. "A feller tipped me off. I don't have time to read 'em myself," he explained.[49]

On March 21, 1928, the same day Superintendent McAndrew was discharged, Capone gunmen fired fifty-eight bullets into Diamond Jim Esposito, a political power in the Italian community and long-time associate of Senator Charles Deneen. In the next few days, bombs were tossed at Deneen's Chicago residence and at the home of his candidate for state's attorney, John A. Swanson. The explosive devices, of a kind popularly known as pineapples, unleashed an avalanche of popular indignation against Capone, Thompson, and their allies Governor Small and State's Attorney Crowe. In Washington, Senator George Norris urged President Coolidge to withdraw Marines from Nicaragua and send them to fight domestic insurrectionists in the streets of Chicago.

Short of that, the *Tribune* led a popular uprising. April 10, 1928, was the date of the so-called Pineapple Primary. Capone's troops were out in force, intimidating election officials, stuffing ballot boxes, fabricating vote totals, and destroying tally sheets not to their liking. Police did nothing, on orders from mob-controlled ward bosses or Capone himself. But the voters did. Eight hundred thousand Chicagoans — twice the number predicted by preelection forecasts — turned out to register their disgust with the status quo. They buried Small and Crowe, smashed the Thompson machine, and brought about the mayor's nervous breakdown.

McCormick rejoiced in the disgrace of his enemies. "Chicago can again walk proudly among the cities. Illinois has purged herself of her shame," the *Tribune* boasted in a full-page ad in the *New York Times*. As for Thompson and Small, "they have given a greater testimony to *Chicago Tribune* influence than any friend of the *Chicago Tribune* could give. They have acknowledged only one Chicago newspaper their enemy . . . In years to come, cunning hands may build other political engines of corruption in Chicago. The World's Greatest Newspaper will be on the job to smash them, too."[50]

Shades of the Henry Ford trial: in virtue was to be found profit. A well-chosen enemy could sell more papers than Little Orphan Annie.*

Turning his attention to the national political scene, McCormick didn't like what he saw. Hoover was far too activist for his taste. Still, the Colonel did what he could to coopt the likely Republican presidential nominee. In August 1928, he warned Hoover to keep his distance from the Cook County Republican Committee, "a criminal organization conducted to . . . the protection of crime for profit." Things were hardly better among the party faithful in Ohio or in neighboring Indiana, "the last governor being a penitentiary convict." Most alarming of all was the threat posed by prohibitionists who had gone to the nation's capital "from the backwoods of illiteracy," determined to make the Republican party "the lay arm of their new inquisition."[51]

Hoover tactfully replied that he was in agreement "with nearly all of your rough words." He received a *Tribune* endorsement in the fall campaign, notwithstanding his straddle on the liquor question and an internationalist outlook developed as the "Great Humanitarian" of wartime legend. "You will have an inspiring time," McCormick predicted one day after Hoover's landslide victory over New York's governor, Alfred E. Smith, "and yet, I think, will sometimes regret your quieter days in Belgium." Writing to his mother (who had been made sick by Hoover's nomination), McCormick was less circumspect. He praised Coolidge for his shrewd timing in leaving office at the peak of his popularity and the top of a bull market. "This crazy stock market must come to an end some day," he wrote at the end of November 1928, "and after that I imagine it will be a long slide downhill . . . I think Hoover can look forward to quite a disagreeable time in the White House."[52]

On March 4, 1929, the *Tribune*'s chief Washington correspondent, Arthur Sears Henning, observed the formal transfer of power from

*McCormick was notably less aggressive in pursuing his protégé Edward J. Kelly, chief engineer of the scandal-plagued sanitary district, where investigators had uncovered grossly padded payrolls, exorbitant legal fees, and boondoggles, including $1,400 lampposts and a million-dollar cinder path. Seven district trustees were indicted, but Kelly escaped prosecution, retained McCormick's loyalty, and went on to become mayor in 1933 with *Tribune* backing.

Coolidge to Hoover. As a cold rain drenched the inaugural participants, Henning didn't linger. The new president outlined an ambitious reform program reminiscent of the ideas of his political hero, Theodore Roosevelt. At the *Tribune* bureau, Henning had just completed the lead of his story when he was handed a telegram from McCormick: "THIS MAN WON'T DO." Less than an hour old, the Hoover presidency had already been placed under the ban of the Colonel's disapproval.[53]

McCormick followed up with some tartly worded criticism of Hoover's attempt to remake the Republican party in the South, where a skeletal organization living off crumbs of federal patronage afforded otherwise disenfranchised black voters the semblance of influence at national conventions. Hoping to build on his strong showing in the region in 1928, Hoover wanted to end the trafficking in offices and dissolve the rotten boroughs that had long wielded disproportionate power in the GOP nominating process.

As would so often be the case with an ill-fated Hoover administration, good intentions were submerged in maladroit public relations. To McCormick, the president seemed intent on establishing a personal organization south of the Mason-Dixon line, one bound inextricably to support of Prohibition. Hoover complained that the *Tribune* was grossly distorting his position to black Chicagoans. He invited McCormick to the White House for a discussion "of this and many public matters of importance, upon which I should like to have your views." McCormick accepted the offer of presidential hospitality, but not before making it understood that "my Mother will never consent to my staying with anybody but her when I am in Washington."[54]

Among the subjects Hoover wished to take up was Al Capone. In his memoirs, McCormick, characteristically vague about dates and stingy with context, nevertheless left a vivid portrait of his encounter with the president. As he described their meeting, Hoover listened intently as he explained Capone's criminal stranglehood. The president made a point of writing down Capone's name, as if hearing it for the first time.

Once again McCormick's habit of putting himself at the center of any drama he was narrating placed him at variance with the facts. As president-elect, Hoover had met with the *Tribune* editorial writers Tiffany Blake and Cliff Raymond on February 18, 1929, just four days after Capone gunmen slaughtered seven members of the rival Bugs Moran gang in a North Side garage. For Chicagoans tired of having gangsters shoot each other in the streets, the St. Valentine Day Massacre was the final straw. "The butchering of seven men by open daylight raises this question for Chicago: Is it helpless?" demanded an outraged *Tribune*.

A month after the massacre, Hoover spent another grim afternoon with a group of Chicago's leading citizens, chaired by Walter Strong, the publisher of the *Chicago Daily News*. McCormick was not present as Strong and his delegation portrayed the horrors of their gang-infested city and sought Washington's help. Hoover, clearly sympathetic, protested that he had few legal tools with which to do a job traditionally entrusted to state and local officials. Like it or not, federal jurisdiction was limited to infractions of Prohibition and income tax laws.

On Sunday, April 14, McCormick joined the Hoovers and three White House guests for lunch. Three days later he returned to tell the president that Capone's enormous income made him vulnerable to prosecution by the Internal Revenue Service. (Unknown to McCormick, the chief of the IRS Enforcement Branch, Elmer Irey, was already examining fraudulent returns filed by several Chicago gang lords, including Capone's brother Ralph.) Thereafter, at sessions of Hoover's medicine-ball cabinet, an early morning workout at which presidential intimates tossed an eight-pound ball over a net on the south lawn of the White House, Hoover inquired of treasury secretary Andrew Mellon, "Have you got that fellow Capone yet?"[55]

Judging from his correspondence with Hoover, McCormick's chief interest lay in smashing the Prohibition enforcement mechanisms put in place by assistant attorney general Mabel Willebrandt, a militant prohibitionist and leading Hoover partisan in her native South. *Tribune* reporters preparing an exposé of the controversial Willebrandt uncovered an extensive prison spy system operating out of the Justice Department. In addition, Willebrandt had reassigned reliably dry judges from the South to try Prohibition cases in New York and other wet strongholds. With all this fresh in his mind, McCormick again took up his pen in June 1929 to warn Hoover against "fanatically minded professional zealots" who would bring the president nothing but failure and unhappiness.[56]

Hoover replied testily that he was under greater pressure from ardent wets in his administration than from drys. But he also concluded, after a decent interval, that his administration could do without the services of Mrs. Willebrandt, whose departure from office disheartened few outside the Anti-Saloon League.

✧ 8

Thanks to the well-stocked cellars at Cantigny, Prohibition presented no personal hardship for McCormick. It did, however, give rise to one of his more mystifying acts of generosity. On discovering that some of his finest champagne had been ruined through improper handling, he made presents of the sour liquid to his *Tribune* associates, who were left to pour the stuff down their drains and scratch their heads over the Colonel's latest joke.

His attitude toward Prohibition was anything but mirthful. For McCormick, Al Capone held less terror than the officially sanctioned crusaders of the Anti-Saloon League. Capone was merely a symptom of evil; the genuine article was embodied in malleable lawmakers eager to substitute for the limited-government doctrines enshrined in the Constitution their own sweeping desire to police the private behavior of average Americans. Put another way, the threat that Scarface Al and his bootlegging army posed to American livers was nothing compared to the menace that the Anti-Saloon League and its friends in Washington presented to American liberties.

McCormick, as suspicious of concentrated power as the founders he deified, saw in Prohibition confirmation of his worst fear: an overreaching government enacting laws that resulted in unprecedented lawlessness. If allowed to stand, the Eighteenth Amendment would permanently alter the relationship between individual Americans and their government. Seen in this light, McCormick's campaign to undo the ban on liquor sales and consumption was inseparable from his role as constitutional watchdog.

In 1928 he gained a national platform, as the American Newspaper Publishers Association asked him to chair its newly established Committee on Freedom of the Press. The timing was no accident. Dwindling support for Prohibition had not deterred lawmakers, including many allied with corrupt business or gangster elements, from urging legislative panaceas to remedy their private grievances. Most notorious of these was Minnesota's Public Nuisance Bill of 1925, popularly known as Lommen's Gag Law after its sponsor, state senator George H. Lommen.

Lommen had been angered by highly personal attacks on him and his political associates in the *Duluth Ripsaw*, a brash weekly whose lurid reports of official corruption in the wide-open Mesabi Iron Range district had generated physical threats and libel actions in roughly equal measure. Lommen was unappeased by a printed apology coerced out of the editor, John L. Morrison, and declared ominously that "there ought to be a law against such scandalous sheets." Aided by postwar cynicism and an apathetic establishment press, he was able to implement his threat. When formally approved by Governor Theodore Christiansen, the Public Nuisance Law empowered any Minnesota judge to suppress, without recourse to jury trial, any publication deemed "lewd and lascivious" or "malicious, scandalous and defamatory." In practice, this implemented the doctrine of prior restraint, anathema to newspapermen, whose journals might be silenced by judicial injunction and whose editors were subject to contempt-of-court proceedings and heavy fines or imprisonment if convicted.

Outside Minnesota the new law was met with outrage. Any legislation that hampered newspapers in placing facts before the people, warned the *Philadelphia Record*, "is pie for crooked politicians." McCormick took time out from fighting Big Bill Thompson in the courts to heap scorn on the Gag Law as "an ideal weapon in the hands of a corrupt administration which could use it effectually to prevent criticism of itself." Minnesota, jibed the *Tribune*, had become a "monkey state," no better than ridiculous Tennessee.[57]

This was familiar ground to McCormick. For more than a decade he and Weymouth Kirkland had studied the evolution of a free press since Magna Carta. Their efforts would stand him in good stead if and when the Gag Law faced a challenge in the courts. Yet any attempt to overturn the law would come too late for John L. Morrison and his *Duluth Ripsaw*. In May 1926, Morrison died of a stroke in the Superior, Wisconsin, hospital to which he had been rushed the previous night, one step ahead of an avenging Minneapolis sheriff. DEATH DEFEATS WARRANT FOR DULUTH EDITOR bannered the *Minneapolis Tribune*.

Others willing to take up the martyr's cross included Jay M. Near and Howard A. Guilford, copublishers of the *Twin City Reporter*. As described by Fred W. Friendly, whose *Minnesota Rag* is the definitive history of what followed, Near and Guilford practiced "a brand of journalism that teetered on the edge of legality and often toppled over the limits of propriety." On September 26, 1927, frontier justice caught up with frontier journalism. Tipped off to an upcoming exposé of local gambling rings and of the close relationship between the mob leader Mose Barnett and Minneapolis police chief Frank Brunskill, Barnett's hitmen critically wounded Guilford as the editor drove to his office.

Guilford recovered sufficiently to rail in the pages of the *Saturday Press*, the gamy successor to the *Twin City Reporter*, against county attorney and "Jew lover" Floyd B. Olson. Olson, accustomed to turning a blind eye to much of the gambling and corruption that thrived in Minnesota's largest city, showed less tolerance of the yellow press. Acting under the Public Nuisance Law, he secured a court injunction to halt publication of the *Saturday Press*. The action won unanimous approval by the Minnesota Supreme Court. Distinguishing between liberty and licentiousness, the justices ruled in December 1927 that the state constitution afforded "a shield for the honest, careful and conscientious press"; it was never intended to protect purveyors of scandal or defamation "when untrue or published with bad motives."

The ruling set off alarms at the New York offices of the American Civil Liberties Union. Roger Baldwin, the group's pacifistic founder, had little but the First Amendment in common with Jay Near. (Guilford, wearying of the struggle and fearing for his life, had by this time sold his interest in the *Saturday Press* to his partner.) Yet this was enough for Baldwin to commit $150 to Near's defense. In search of deeper pockets, Near appealed to Colonel McCormick, whose confrontations with Henry Ford and Big Bill Thompson had made him the foremost champion of First Amendment rights in cases where those in power tried to repress legally what they could not control personally.

As McCormick recounted his actions, "I immediately realized that that principle [of prior restraint by injunction] would put every newspaper at the mercy of any corruptible judge and I carried the appeal to the Supreme Court of the United States." This was the truth, but hardly the whole truth, for it overlooked the part played by Weymouth Kirkland in convincing McCormick to proceed with the case. The mere existence of the Gag Law "makes my blood boil," Kirkland told McCormick. To allow prior restraint of a newspaper, accurate or not, by a judge acting on his sole authority was "unthinkable." To Kirkland this was just the latest step on an ominous trail, first blazed by the Volstead Act, that led unavoidably to the extinction of jury trials in America.[58]

Kirkland also reminded McCormick of the havoc that could result if a future Illinois governor as hostile as the discredited Len Small succeeded in ramming his own gag law through a docile state legislature. "I wonder if there is some way we could get in touch with the people appealing to see that their briefs are properly prepared," Kirkland mused. McCormick took the hint. Shouldering aside the ACLU, he committed himself to a fight without quarter.[59]

Seeing links among the moral perfectionists responsible for Prohibition, the gangsters who had fouled Chicago's nest even as they slaked its thirst, and judges free to act as censors without deigning to consult a jury, McCormick was in high dudgeon. As chairman of the ANPA Committee on Freedom of the Press, he fancied himself a latter-day Paul Revere, rousing his fellow journalists to the grave peril they faced.* But he received a setback when the Minnesota Supreme Court in December 1929 grimly reaffirmed the constitutionality of the Gag Law.

Having torn at his enemies with a fierce joy, Jay Near now turned on his friends. Hardly the first litigant to feel dismay over the dawdling pace of justice, Near sent McCormick a blistering denunciation of Howard Ellis, Kirkland's hard-drinking subordinate, who had been entrusted with

---

*Both his frustration and his delight in combat spilled over into a November 1929 *Tribune* editorial hailing the recent felony conviction of Albert B. Fall, Warren Harding's secretary of the interior, whose malfeasance in the Teapot Dome scandal barely hinted at the hypocrisy and greed of Harding's Ohio Gang. "Ohio," claimed the *Tribune*, "with the headquarters of the Anti-Saloon League at Westerville, had produced a school of politics whose perfumed rascality with the odor of sanctity and which found protection in the political pew [sic]. This scheme of combining the lip service of religion with the expertise of burglar tools had the approval of Ohio's moralists and prohibitionists, because it enabled them to use the politicians for the one purpose they had in mind, the coercion of government."

Near's defense before the Minnesota court. "Mr. Ellis might be a Daniel Webster," raged the ungrateful client, "but Daniel never sampled our Minnesota brand of moonshine." McCormick dismissed the screed as a renewal of Near's earlier, unsuccessful attempt to shake down the *Tribune* for financial support. What Near couldn't know was that the Colonel was resolved to fight all the way to the Supreme Court.[60]

Before opening his checkbook, he hoped to enlist unanimous backing from the members of the ANPA. At the end of December, he tested the waters by contacting his colleagues on the Committee on Freedom of the Press. He made no attempt to conceal the risks, whatever their course of action. Defeat at the hands of the Supreme Court would almost certainly lead other legislatures to emulate the repressive example of Minnesota, secure in the knowledge that no judges would intervene to save the disreputable likes of the *Saturday Press*. Doing nothing, warned McCormick, entailed even greater dangers, robbing newspapers of both their independence and their financial value. He gave the latter argument special emphasis with Harry Chandler, the reactionary owner of the *Los Angeles Times*, who responded by urging his publishing brethren to "let sleeping dogs lie." To get around such graybeards, McCormick boldly urged that the cart be placed before the horse. Let the board of directors go on record as favoring a court test at the earliest possible date, and only *then* poll the entire ANPA membership by mail for confirmation of the board's fait accompli. "In this way I think you will put practically every newspaper in America actively behind our movement," McCormick contended.[61]

His strategy was vindicated when all but five of the ANPA's 259 members endorsed his stand. But if American publishers wanted to see the Near case appealed to the Supreme Court, they were just as sure they wanted McCormick to pay for the appeal. The ANPA made a token contribution of $5,000 toward the $25,000 Kirkland's law firm received to carry the case to the nation's highest court.[62]

The retirement of the conservative chief justice, William Howard Taft, in February 1930 gave McCormick grounds for hope, as did the continuing presence on the bench of such civil libertarians as Louis Brandeis and Oliver Wendell Holmes. Muting his optimism was his reading of history. "It is to be borne in mind that the Courts were never favorable to the Freedom of the Press," he wrote to Emory Thomason two weeks after Taft's resignation. "The press attained its freedom by legislative action." On February 18, McCormick instructed Kirkland to perfect arguments for a case that might not land on the court docket for a year. In the interim he showered his lawyers with advice. Learning from the editorial writer Leon Stolz, himself Jewish, that "Brandeis is . . . a fairly orthodox Jew," McCormick wrote to Kirkland that when preparing his arguments "it may not be wise to greatly emphasize the crucifixion." Kirkland should instead point to Russia, Spain, and Italy as doleful instances of what happens when government muzzles the press. The Colonel quoted James Madison: "To the press alone, checkered as it is with abuses, the world is indebted for all the triumphs which have been gained by reason and humanity over error and oppression." He recounted ancient battles between Federalists and Jeffersonians over the character of the young American republic, and the narrow triumph of first constitutional principles in contrast with the harshly restrictive Sedition Act embraced by John Adams and repealed by Jefferson.[63]

At least the Alien and Sedition Acts had provided trial by jury for past censure of official acts, Kirkland argued in his brief. In its rush to impose prior restraints on the press, the Minnesota Public Nuisance Act had eliminated the essential right to be judged by one's peers. Under such a law, the notorious Boss Tweed might have squelched revelations of corruption in the *New York Times* and *Harper's Weekly*. Told that the Constitution was never intended to safeguard malicious, scandalous, or defamatory untruths, Kirkland maintained exactly the opposite: "Every person does have a constitutional right to publish malicious, scandalous, and defamatory matter though untrue, and with bad motives, and for unjustifiable ends, in the first instance, though he is subject to responsibility therefore afterwards." Since no sane government would undertake to suppress "harmless and colorless statements," no constitutional protection was recognized for such bland content. Yet there was, argued Kirkland, an overwhelming need to protect offensive publications.

Newspapers were by their nature defamatory, never more so than when uncovering illegal or unethical conduct on the part of public officials. To defame both the government and its officers was "an inalienable privilege of national citizenship," not requiring the special protection of the Fourteenth Amendment. Kirkland came to the crux of the case when he said, "The control of the press is not given to the legislature but is reserved to the people. If there is an abuse of the liberty it is for the people to decide so in the persons of the jurymen, not for the legislature to restrain it in advance."

On January 30, 1931, Kirkland distilled his sixty-seven-page brief into a fifty-four-minute oral presentation before Chief Justice Charles Evans Hughes, Taft's less predictable successor, and his brethren. Four days later, encouraged by reports from his lawyer, Jay Near again solicited McCormick for funds with which to take the *Saturday Press* national. "No other paper in the United States has been given so many inches of free advertising," he wrote, stunningly oblivious to the role played by the *Tribune* in generating all that notoriety. Victory in the Supreme Court would result in a bonanza of additional publicity. This "golden opportunity" Near now generously offered for McCormick's taking, if only the Colonel would agree to underwrite, "to a reasonable extent," the *Saturday Press* for a few months.[64]

Near's letter went unanswered. On June 1, 1931, the last day of its 1930–31 term, a badly divided Supreme Court ruled Minnesota's Gag Law unconstitutional. Chief Justice Hughes, writing for the majority, five justices, declared the law in violation of the due process clause of the Fourteenth Amendment. "The fact that liberty of the press may be abused by miscreant purveyors of scandal," he wrote, "does not make any the less necessary the immunity of the press from previous restraint in dealing with official conduct."

McCormick, jubilant, wrote to the chief justice effusively praising his ruling, which he predicted would "forever remain one of the buttresses of free government." Acknowledging mistakes by sensationalistic journals, he told Hughes that he welcomed "well studied measures" to protect the public from such abuses. Yet "the method proposed in Minnesota would have destroyed the only check we have upon corrupt government." Privately, he took less encouragement from his narrow escape. "If Taft were still occupying Hughes' place," he confessed to a Seattle publisher, "we would have been beaten."[65]

For Roger Baldwin, his unlikely ally from the American Civil Liberties Union, McCormick placed the controversy in a larger perspective: "I have felt from the beginning that the Minnesota legislation was merely another step in the demolition of private rights and in view of all the other successes in that direction a logical one." The slap at Prohibition was unmistakable. McCormick hoped that the decision would serve as a warning "to crooked politicians and legislators," he told Harry Chandler on June 15. As for his own role, it was akin to "somebody who sees a fire, turns in an alarm, and carries out the furniture."[66]

In October 1931, McCormick organized a victory party at Monticello. Ostensibly there to dedicate Thomas Jefferson's study as the Hall of Famous Ideals — a classic McCormick touch — the Chicago publisher celebrated his spiritual kinship with America's third president. Sounding very much like his hero, he declared that "the State has no power to put the human mind in shackles." Yet the battle for free expression, he argued, must be refought by every generation, and with special vigilance to guard against "the invincible pragmatism . . . at war with the spirit of constitutionalism."[67]

With a nationwide radio audience listening in, McCormick delivered an impassioned appeal to save his result-oriented countrymen from a practicality that "deals with the ponderables of a problem and measures the value of any action by its immediate, practical consequences." The constitutionalist, by contrast, "asserts that there are underlying principles of government, the great verities of liberty, which must be vindicated, even though the exercise of given liberties will at times result in evil or injustice. In other words," said McCormick in the most eloquent speech of his life, "the eternal principle must never be sacrificed to present considerations of expediency."

McCormick's Monticello address hinted at his fears for the future of the republic. "No thief in the night moves so silently as oppression," he told his listeners. What else was Prohibition, he might have added, but an unholy alliance of moral utopians and political pragmatists, led by the incumbent president of the United States? "Hoover is to be the great victim of Prohibition," McCormick had written early in 1930. The name of the chief executive promised to "go down in history as one of the leading tyrants," his domestic policy ruled by the Anti-Saloon League, his international stance dictated by the English.[68]

The indictment is worth remembering, if for nothing more than McCormick's consistency. It didn't take the Great Depression to alert McCormick to the fragility of his idealized constitutional republic. Long before the advent of Franklin Roosevelt, the man in the tower was warning of an erosion of personal liberties and upholding the rugged individualism required to sustain them in the face of government encroachment. Here, then, are to be found the roots of a paranoia that sprouted strange blossoms as McCormick and Roosevelt, the patriot and the pragmatist, fought a duel over the American way of life.

Whatever course the Colonel followed, he was unlikely to be distracted from his ultimate objective. Early in 1930 he displayed his single-mindedness before a writer sent to interview him on the value of color printing in newspapers. Having developed his story sufficiently, the reporter tried to solicit McCormick's views on freedom of the press, a subject with which the Colonel was identified by millions of Americans who had never seen a copy of the *Chicago Tribune*. "Young man," snapped McCormick, "I like my whiskey straight. Let's stick to color."[69]

10

Hard Times

"It does not do the poor any good to take the rich man's money and dissipate it. It merely makes it impossible for the rich man to hire anybody."

— Colonel McCormick, June 1932

THE STOCK MARKET CRASH of October 1929 did not take McCormick by surprise. Having predicted an end to the bull market for over a year, he initially saw Wall Street's tumble as "a godsend" to newspaper proprietors like himself. Besides discouraging wildcat speculators from invading the field, the crash dramatically reduced the capital value of all companies for taxation purposes. As a shrewd investor — his elderly mother paid him $30,000 annually to oversee her portfolio — McCormick survived the market meltdown with minimal losses. His annual salary of $50,000, although dwarfed by what other top *Tribune* executives were paid, was generously supplemented by bonuses and dividends. These brought his Depression-era income to more than $300,000 a year.[1]

As the post-crash economy deteriorated, so did McCormick's early optimism. Those prattling on about "better business conditions," he told his mother early in 1930, were merely expressing nervous relief that a bad situation was not even worse. He sang a different tune in the pages of the *Tribune*. "The period of recession is about over," he announced blithely in a March 1930 editorial entitled "Let's Go." Saying it did not make it so. Between 1930 and 1933, Chicago payrolls were slashed by 75 percent. Foreclosures quintupled. A hastily erected camp of cardboard shanties, christened Hooverville, sprang up on the edge of the Loop.[2]

"You can ride across the lovely Michigan Avenue bridge at midnight," wrote a visiting journalist in the winter of 1930–31, "with the 2,000,000 candlepower Lindbergh Beacon flaming above you and the lights all about making a dream city of incomparable beauty, while twenty feet below you, on the lower level of the same bridge, are 2,000 homeless, decrepit, shivering and starving men, wrapping themselves in old newspapers to keep from freezing." In August 1931 the Urban League reported that the dispossessed occupied every available bench and dry spot of ground in Washington Park for ten blocks.

Thanks to a steep decline in the price of paper, the *Tribune* never lost money. Yet it hardly escaped the Depression unscathed. Not until 1938 would daily circulation return to precrash levels; the Sunday paper took until 1941 to regain its lost ground. Wherever possible, McCormick pared operating expenses. He shed the unprofitable *Liberty* magazine and rejected as too costly the daily syndicated column written by former president Calvin Coolidge. With the money he saved, he installed sixteen new press units to speed production and added two color sections to the Sunday paper. Half a million dollars was spent on seventy delivery trucks, a garage, and other machinery for the circulation department.

Recognizing "the changed habits of our people," vast numbers of whom were on the streets, McCormick advanced the first edition from nine to eight o'clock in the evening. He continued to decry hopelessness and defeatism in the expressions of public officials. "If prices are down, so is the cost of living," he told his editorial writers in May 1931. "Courage, enterprise and effort will bring back generous prosperity and bring the principal rewards to the individuals developing these qualities."[3]

Whether these sentiments provided consolation to the unemployed of Chicago, whose courage, enterprise, and effort were invested in the daily struggle to survive, may be doubted. Still, no one ever questioned McCormick's faith in Tribune Town (renamed Chicagoland in 1934) or the capitalistic system that, he boasted in the dreary autumn of 1930, "has provided more goods and a wider distribution of goods than the world has ever known." In this spirit, the *Tribune* blasted the English government for providing a dole to the destitute, warning of "demoralization and waste" sure to follow the weakening of individual character by the state.[4]

McCormick's eyes weren't entirely shut to the squalor and misery of the masses. Every morning the farm manager at Cantigny sent a truck to the nearest depot to pick up laborers, for whom work was found throughout the harshest days of winter. The experiment was repeated in 1931. At the same time, the estate owner argued that in view of the heavy burden carried by "the productive people" of society, dispensers of charity faced even greater pressure to guard against sympathy-exploiting "malingerers."[5]

This McCormick had little in common with the doughty battler for abstractions like freedom of the press. Understandably so, for the First Amendment was more real, more immediate to the Colonel than the armies of vacant-eyed, defeated men who cared nothing that (to quote a *Tribune* promotional piece) "concentration of wealth in Tribune Town makes it especially inviting to the financial advertiser." As the economic crisis deepened, the editorial page endorsed birth control, a cure for snoring, and an end to unsightly billboards. McCormick urged the removal of the nation's capital from Washington, D.C., to a more representative city (he thought Grand Rapids, Michigan, an ideal site).[6]

Life remained adversarial. The sportswriter Westbrook Pegler, reporting on the Army-Navy game, was told to refer to "two Eastern teams," for the reason that both "always want to play in New York and not out West." Others might seek out financial scapegoats; McCormick reserved his indignation for young Katharine Hepburn, the subject of a *Tribune* article on "Progressive Polygamy in Hollywood"; the Federal Trade Commission, "a propaganda agency for the Socialists"; and purported royalists in the White House. "At all Anglo-American dinners I have attended a toast is given 'the King and the President of the United States,' " McCormick wrote to Tiffany Blake at the end of November 1930. "Why King first ... This is another indication that where Englishmen and Americans get together the first are intensely nationalistic and the second flunkies."[7]

Consistency would never be McCormick's hobgoblin. The same expansionist who wanted the United States to purchase the Galapagos Islands from Ecuador for conversion into a national wildlife park deplored a federal deficit of $800 million incurred as a result of economic pump-priming in Washington. McCormick excoriated Hoover for pursuing the St. Lawrence Seaway at the expense of the long-delayed Illinois Waterway. Secretary of State Henry Stimson was a favorite *Tribune* target, combining as he did eastern hauteur and an unmanly deference to Europe. McCormick reserved his harshest invective, however, for American friends of the Soviet Union. Leading the drive for recognition of Stalin's regime, said the Colonel, were "a few selfish moneyed interests supported by individuals whose international altruism never takes account of actualities."[8]

Wherever one looked in these locust years, altruism was in short supply. Adding to Chicago's hardship was the profligacy and mismanagement of the Thompson administration. A taxpayer strike depleted municipal coffers just as the Depression strained private philanthropy to its limit. By the autumn of 1930, Thompson was the figurehead leader of an exhausted, bankrupt city. Around him huddled a motley collection of placemen serving out their allotted time in the condemned cell while waiting for the voters to sign the order for their execution.

Fearing that the expert-fee case then under appeal before the state's highest court might leave him a pauper, Thompson dispatched Sam Ettelson, his ethically challenged corporation counsel, as a dove of peace to Tribune Tower. McCormick, enjoying the mayor's discomfiture, refused to see Ettelson except in the presence of editorial writer Cliff Raymond. With Raymond looking on, Ettelson discussed the weather, the Cubs' pennant chances, practically everything except his reason for coming. Finally he played his hand. Thompson would support Congresswoman Ruth Hanna McCormick in her bid to gain the U.S. Senate seat formerly occupied by her husband, Medill. In return the mayor wanted an armistice in his long-running war with the *Tribune*.[9]

No deal, said McCormick. Ettelson was sent packing. Ruth won the GOP primary on her own. The fall campaign was another story. With the contest between Medill's widow and Democrat J. Hamilton Lewis in its closing days, the Illinois Supreme Court unanimously reversed a lower court finding that Thompson and his cronies were liable for nearly $3 million in taxpayer funds squandered by the city hall machine. As fear evaporated, vengeance took its place. "I hope this is the beginning of the end of the *Chicago Tribune*," Thompson exalted.

Certainly it was the beginning of the end of Ruth McCormick's senatorial hopes, already harmed by allegations of excessive campaign spending and the onus of being a dry Republican in a wet, Democratic year. Within hours of the court decision, anonymous handbills addressed "To the Negroes of Illinois," linking Mrs. McCormick to racist remarks made by her late husband and recounting the unsympathetic attitude of the *Tribune* at the time of the 1919 Chicago race riots, flooded Chicago's South Side. They didn't stay anonymous for long. "I got it out," boasted Thompson. Not satisfied with a whispering campaign, he chose the most public of settings, a mass rally of Lewis partisans at the Apollo Theater, to air still more *Tribune* dirty laundry.

On the morning he was to speak, Thompson fell ill with what appeared to be acute appendicitis. Ignoring demands for his immediate hospitalization, he called for a secretary and dictated a blistering "deathbed statement" to be read for him by his commissioner of public works, Richard Wolfe. Two hours later, as his employer went under the surgeon's knife, Wolfe employed a verbal scalpel to tear open eighty years' worth of *Tribune* misdeeds. Rambling and reckless, Thompson's speech linked old Joe Medill to the assassinations of Abraham Lincoln and Mayor Carter Harrison, accused the nineteenth-century editor of debasing half a dozen prepubescent girls, and blamed the death of Governor Len Small's wife on the paper's relentless hounding of "the greatest constructive governor the state of Illinois ever had." Thompson also dredged up the affair between "the moral pervert" Joe Patterson and the wife of a friend, leading to Patterson's fervent embrace of Socialist doctrine and his abrupt resignation from Mayor Dunne's cabinet.[10]

Big Bill saved his heaviest blows for Colonel McCormick, "who, while he was a bachelor, followed in the footsteps of his cousin Patterson" by seducing Ed Adams's wife while living under Adams's roof. A messy divorce had preceded the obliteration of all court records and a large out-of-court settlement. Threatening to turn over everything he had compiled on "this rotten outfit" to a Senate committee looking into Ruth McCormick's campaign expenditures, Thompson concluded with the hope that some courageous citizen might step forward to administer suitable punishment to "the present editor of the *Chicago Tribune.*"

A few days later, Mrs. McCormick was overwhelmed at the polls. Yet in ways unintended by its author, the "deathbed message" turned out to be just that — politically. In February 1931, the mayor's supporters celebrating their hero's cowboy image rode a pair of horses into the city council chambers. Grinning from the podium was Thompson, whom his Republican primary opponent, Judge John H. Lyle, had called "Jumbo, the flood relief quack." But a city squeezed between organized crime and economic depression was less inclined than in the sassy past to laugh at such antics. Running for his fourth term, Big Bill had little to talk about except the "tax-dodging, Loop-protecting" *Tribune* and its cowardly publisher, who rode to work each day in "a steel-lined closed car."

In a split Republican field, Thompson came out on top, demonstrating once more that the *Tribune* lacked the muscle to defeat him; only he himself could accomplish that feat. In the runoff against Anton J. Cermak, president of the Cook County board, Big Bill and his dwindling army of loyalists traveled the low road. "Only lazy precinct captains steal votes," claimed Cermak, a Czech immigrant and onetime beer-truck driver whose organizational gifts had welded fractious Jewish, Irish, Polish, and Bohemian elements into a formidable political machine. The *Tribune* gave unqualified backing to the Democratic candidate. McCormick filled hundreds of columns with pro-Cermak stories. Thompson was reduced to assailing "Tony the Pushcart Peddler" and making crude ethnic appeals (in one Polish neighborhood he promised to "load the city hall up with Poles" if reelected, a performance repeated in Irish, Jewish, and black communities).[11]

On April 7, 1931, voters added the name of William Hale Thompson to the growing ranks of the unemployed. Cermak won forty-five of the city's fifty wards. An exultant *Tribune* called the result a New Deal for Chicago.*

*A suitable epitaph for the Thompson era comes from George Reedy, Lyndon Johnson's White House press secretary, whose father was a *Tribune* reporter during Big Bill's heyday. Of Thompson, Reedy observed, "He'd steal a hot stove and come back for the ashes."

✧ 2

Of all the calculated insults in Thompson's Apollo Theater diatribe, none had struck a rawer nerve than his damning of "the Lingle-
Tribune wrecking crew." Big Bill liked the phrase so much that he kept on
using it throughout his doomed reelection campaign. With good reason.
Around Tribune Tower, it would be hard to imagine a more sensitive
subject than the fate of Alfred "Jake" Lingle, a tainted journalist whose
violent downfall called into question much more than his personal ethics. Asked to define a newspaper's most important function, McCormick
was quick to respond: exposing corruption. But what if the press itself was corruptible? What if individual reporters, subject to the same
weaknesses and appetites as other mortals, could be infected by the virus
of greed and illicit power released into the American bloodstream by
Prohibition?

For twenty years McCormick had ridden his high horse, targeting for
destruction Senator Lorimer, the Thompson-Lundin ring, opportunistic
politicians out to muzzle press criticism, and Prohibition itself. All the
while he had crusaded from a position of moral superiority, a position he
now asked the Supreme Court of the United States to codify in *Near* v.
Minnesota. By the spring of 1930 he was riding for a fall.

On June 8, McCormick met in his *Tribune* office with Frank J. Wilson,
chief of the Secret Service, then hot on the trail of Al Capone. Wilson had
learned that a *Tribune* reporter named Jake Lingle was often seen accompanying Capone in Miami, the luxurious safe haven from which the gang
leader supervised half a dozen breweries, fifteen gambling houses, a string
of lucrative brothels, a thousand speakeasies and as many bookie joints.
The government would appreciate any assistance Lingle might be able to
provide, Wilson told McCormick.

The Colonel was eager to help. "I'll get word to Lingle to go all the way
with you," he assured Wilson. An appointment was arranged for noon,
two days later.[12]

The reporter never kept it. Shortly after one o'clock on June 9, the off-
duty Lingle descended into a pedestrian tunnel leading from Grant Park to
a station of the Illinois Central Railroad. His destination was a familiar
one, the Washington Park racetrack in suburban Homewood. Lingle was
not too engrossed in his copy of the *Daily Racing Form* to remark to a
friendly policeman he spotted near the underpass, "I'm being tailed."
Despite that knowledge, apparently neither noticed a tall blond man
dressed in a light suit who approached Lingle from behind, stuck a thirty-
eight-caliber snub-nosed Colt revolver just above his collar, and fired a
single bullet upward, execution style. Lingle fell forward, still clutching his
Racing Form in his hand and a lit cigar between his teeth. His murderer

tossed away his gun before fleeing up the stairs leading to Michigan and Randolph streets. He quickly lost himself in a maze of nearby alleys.

A few minutes later, the distraught Colonel McCormick appeared in the *Tribune* local room: "Jake Lingle has been shot. We have got to find the man who did it and find out why."[13]

McCormick remained just long enough to post a $25,000 reward for information leading to the arrest and conviction of Lingle's killer. Then he returned to the twenty-fourth floor. Managing editor Teddy Beck and Weymouth Kirkland were there to help him map plans for an all-out investigation. Based on information gleaned from his meeting with Frank Wilson, McCormick jumped to the conclusion that Lingle was the victim of gangsters whose criminal activities he was about to expose. This helps to explain his almost hysterical reaction to the slaying, conveyed in a June 11 editorial entitled "The Challenge." "It is war," thundered the *Tribune*, not without a certain grim satisfaction at fighting yet another crusade. "There will be casualties, but that is to be expected."

Lingle's byline had never graced the *Tribune* in his eighteen years as a legman gathering information about the underworld. "He murdered the king's English," recalled India Edwards, a society reporter whom Lingle often took to lunch, paying the check with a hundred-dollar bill peeled off a huge bankroll. His editors valued his connections, however, which he had first developed as the playmate of future cops — among them chief of police William H. Russell — and future gangsters. Since coming to the *Tribune* on the recommendation of the West Side political boss John J. McLaughlin in 1912, the stocky, affable Lingle had befriended the likes of Big Jim Colosimo and Johnny Torrio. He had also won the trust of Al Capone, who formalized their relationship by presenting his new friend with a diamond-studded belt buckle.

Lingle visited Capone in jail, and his exclusive interviews with Scarface Al made the *Tribune* bosses all the more inclined to overlook his sumptuous lifestyle. If asked, Lingle variously attributed his three homes, Cuban vacations, and tailor-made suits to killings in the bull market, a $50,000 inheritance from his father, and an extended lucky streak with the ponies. Newsroom colleagues from whom he occasionally bummed $50 or $100 nicknamed him Lucky.

Lingle's luck ran out in the Michigan Avenue underpass. The journalistic fraternity closed ranks around the slain reporter. Hearst's *Herald and Examiner* matched McCormick's $25,000. The *Evening Post* sweetened the pot with another $5,000. At a June 11 meeting of Chicago publishers, McCormick obtained unanimous approval of actions he had already set in motion. At his request, State's Attorney John A. Swanson named Charles Rathbun, a well-regarded member of the *Tribune* law firm, to conduct the Lingle inquiry. The noted private investigator Patrick

Roche would assist Rathbun. The *Tribune* would assume all costs of the probe.

From Emory Thompson, now publisher of the tabloid *Chicago Times*, McCormick learned of a case in which Philadelphia bankers had furnished documentary evidence to break the back of organized crime in their city. The next day he appealed to the Chicago Clearing House Association for help in tracing the intricate web of gang finance. The chairman of the Lake Shore Bank supplied him with records detailing Lingle's banking and brokerage transactions for the past three years. These made for interesting reading. During the past eighteen months, Lingle, who earned $65 a week as a crime reporter, had deposited over $63,000. In addition, he had lost $85,000 in the market collapse that began with Black Tuesday. Among his investment partners was none other than Police Chief Russell, a lifelong friend who had often lent his official car to the reporter, whom Russell likened to a son.[14]

The dead man's halo was beginning to slip. On June 14, McCormick attended a second meeting of the local publishing fraternity in a radically changed atmosphere. Herman Black, of Hearst's *American*, who hadn't attended the earlier session, questioned the portrayal of Lingle as an honest journalist rubbed out by mobsters who feared his wrath. McCormick tried to distance himself from the fallen reporter. Black, refusing to be put off, repeated gossip linking at least one *Tribune* executive to the mob. By handpicking Rathbun and Roche, Black went on, McCormick risked the appearance, if not the substance, of a coverup.[15]

"Mr. Black, you have not been in Chicago very long," interrupted McCormick, visibly struggling to restrain himself. Otherwise, "you would know that the *Tribune* cannot be under suspicion. It is a preposterous thing even to discuss." Black's request for two additional lawyers to assist Rathbun was flatly rejected. To the insinuation of corrupt dealings in the *Tribune*'s circulation department, the Colonel replied frostily that he could run his newspaper very well without outside interference. On this note the conference concluded. The rattled McCormick picked up Black's Panama hat by mistake. Feigning courtesy, the two men smilingly exchanged hats; soon they would be exchanging blows.[16]

❖ 3

As the *Tribune*'s rivals scoffed at the "Board of Strategy" made up of Rathbun and his team, stories about Lingle's reputed mob ties proliferated. It was said that he had once boasted of setting the price of beer in Chicago. He had quarreled with boss John McLaughlin, his original sponsor, over a gambling resort to which he had faithlessly promised legal protection. Eyewitnesses to a heated confrontation in the lobby of the Sherman Hotel swore that they heard McLaughlin tell his former protégé, "I'll catch up with you, mister."

Others pointed the finger of blame squarely at Scarface Al, who was reportedly furious over million-dollar losses at his unprotected dogtracks after Lingle had pocketed a $100,000 payoff. Still other newspaper accounts claimed that Lingle, in his capacity as "unofficial police chief of Chicago," had leaned hard on Capone's enemies in the Bugs Moran–Joey Aiello gang, going so far as to threaten to cancel the opening of the Sheridan Wave Tournament Club, a plushly appointed gambling joint on the North Side, unless he received $15,000. Lingle's palm went ungreased. Instead, on the very day the new club was to have welcomed its first high rollers, he was gunned down by the mysterious blond man in the underpass.[17]

Early in July, Herman Black escalated the newspaper war by demanding, in 120-point type, WHO KILLED JAKE LINGLE AND WHY? After the same headline appeared a second time, alongside a demand that *Tribune* executives go before a grand jury, McCormick convened a general staff meeting. He asked the sole female reporter present to leave the room. Then, sitting atop a city room desk, idly fingering a riding crop, he professed ignorance of Lingle's extralegal activities and vowed to let the legal chips fall where they might. To those inquiring into his paper's moral standing, the Colonel said he would emulate the reply of a British duchess to a common gossip: "Nothing a streetwalker may say about a woman can slander her, if she is a lady."[18]

McCormick's language was decidedly unladylike when the *Herald-Examiner* implicated *Tribune* city editor Bob Lee in the growing scandal. Lee sued Herman Black and his paper for $250,000 and won a grudging apology for his troubles. In the meantime, McCormick instructed his corporate auditor, Daniel Deininger, to conduct an exhaustive review of Lee's personal finances, as well as those of his day city editor, Pat Maloney, who had been Lingle's immediate boss. Maloney emerged from the probe as clean as a hound's tooth. Lee's status was more equivocal; Deininger reported that while his documented expenditures were "extravagant," they did not appear to outstrip his legitimate financial resources. "The Colonel knew nothing" about Lingle's criminal activities, recalled Pat Maloney in old age, "and Lee knew everything . . . He was Lee's fellow, and while he never exactly brushed me off, yet I knew that he never told me all the truth that he knew."[19]

Reports compiled by outside detectives were just as ambivalent. Lee and Lingle had been close friends and frequent traveling companions. In the immediate aftermath of Lingle's death, Lee had impulsively sent for the chauffeur of his Lincoln and advised him to keep his mouth shut. Lee sur-

vived this damning revelation, but with diminished authority, as Mc-
Cormick established himself in a rarely used office near the city room.[20]

As his eyes and ears around the fourth-floor newsroom, McCormick
designated a West Point graduate and polo-playing crony named Maxwell
Corpening, whose sole qualification for the job was slavish loyalty to his
boss. If the Colonel hoped that an outsider might penetrate the cozy city
room culture and explain to him how Lingle's treachery had for so long
escaped detection, he could hardly have chosen worse. Corpening's inadequacies as a spy were equaled by his journalistic shortcomings. Lee
gained revenge of sorts several years later when McCormick sent Corpening on a fact-finding trip to South America. Unable to carry out the
simplest of assignments, Corpening copied whole pages of the *Encyclopedia Britannica* to cable back to Chicago under his byline. Tipped off to
the scam, a sardonic Bob Lee observed, "At least it proves the son of a
bitch can read."[21]

By the middle of July 1930, the vow of Chicago publishers to battle
criminal and political "viciousness" wherever it existed was long since forgotten. In its place local newspapers reverted to an old-fashioned donny-
brook reminiscent of the deadly circulation wars fought twenty years
earlier. The present struggle, conducted with words in place of bullets, was
scarcely less brutal than its fabled predecessor, in part because the stakes
were even higher. The economic holocaust of the 1930s had left *Tribune*
competitors awash in red ink. Even McCormick was forced to cut advertising rates in 1932, the same year he suspended his annual employee
bonus.

The arrest of a Bugs Moran lieutenant named Frank Foster provided
little to advance the Lingle inquiry, but the story of his capture, leaked to
the *Herald and Examiner,* did ignite a wild scrimmage among rival newspapers. With the competition daily exploiting the Lingle crime at his
expense, McCormick decided to give his peers a dose of their own medicine. On July 2, he granted an extended interview to Harry Brundige of the
St. Louis Star. McCormick enthusiastically seconded Brundige's proposal
to impanel a grand jury to explore the murky relationship between local
gangsters and the press.

Suddenly the *Tribune's* pursuers became the pursued. On a visit to
Capone in Florida, Brundige heard the boastful mob leader assert that his
payroll included "plenty" of reporters. Why, McCormick wondered, had
Herman Black been so insistent that additional investigators be hired,
using Hearst funds if necessary, to assist the Rathbun probe? What could
Black have to hide?

It was a question Harry Brundige was also asking, to devastating effect.
Tribune readers were soon introduced to Harry Read, the city editor of the
Evening American and a frequent visitor at Capone's Miami retreat. They

encountered Matt Foley, the *Herald and Examiner*'s assistant circulation manager, who in his spare time helped promote a bogus lottery that swindled thousands of Chicagoans. The same paper's Ted Tod, when not pursuing his nominal calling as a criminal reporter, had moonlighted as a press agent for the Fairview Kennel Club, a dog track operated by the Moran-Aiello gang.

Nor was the *Daily News* spared Brundige's investigative fervor. After a *News* crime reporter named Leland Reese was run off the road and nearly killed by gangsters, Reese disclosed the name of the late Julius Rosenheim, an informant with the dangerous habit of blackmailing gamblers and whoremeisters by threatening to expose them in the pages of the *News*. Harry Brundige's articles, thoughtfully carried by the *Tribune* alone among Chicago papers, turned a spotlight on one reporter who received five cents for every sack of cement sold to local builders, an editor who unapologetically observed to Brundige that he saw no reason for journalists to go poor while the gangs "pass around filthy lucre like rainchecks at a ballpark," and yet another reporter whose connections at the graft-ridden County Building enhanced his regular income by $200 a week.[22]

Given that none of these offending newsmen were employed by the *Tribune*, it should come as no surprise that McCormick's enemies viewed the Brundige series as a put-up job. This was a matter of supreme indifferene to the Colonel. "Newspaper fights do not benefit any newspapers," he acknowledged on August 12 to Emory Thomason, who had been cast in the thankless role of peacemaker, "but I am inclined to think it is less damaging for a newspaper that has been attacked to fight back occasionally than to maintain a continuous silence."

In time Thomason was able to engineer a compromise, leaving Rathbun free to pursue promising leads in the Lingle case. Frank Foster may not have panned out, but Foster's North Side gang connections led Rathbun straight to Jack Zuta. As business manager for Bugs Moran, Zuta had good reason to hate Lingle for demanding a cut from the ill-fated Sheridan Wave Tournament Club. But Zuta was unable to satisfy Rathbun's curiosity, having absorbed sixteen bullets on August 1, courtesy of mob associates who wished him permanently silenced. He enjoyed a posthumous revenge by secreting in locations where Rathbun was sure to find them hundreds of incriminating documents, including canceled checks payable to two sitting judges, two state senators, one city editor, and the William Hale Thompson Republican Club. The most jaded Chicagoans were left gasping at the extent of official corruption. Both Police Chief Russell and his chief deputy resigned. Mayor Thompson, oblivious to the shame of his police department, happily accepted Russell's head and got on with the business of denouncing the "Lingle-Tribune Evangelistic Institute."

Joseph Medill in 1855, around the time he purchased a part
interest in the *Chicago Daily Tribune*, a struggling paper
in a raw lakeside settlement.

Cissy Patterson, the Colonel's cousin and sparring partner, was the flamboyant publisher of the *Washington Times-Herald* in the decade before her death, in 1948.

McCormick appointed his favorite niece, Ruth "Bazy" Miller, to run the *Times-Herald* in 1949. He fired her in 1951, before selling the paper to the *Washington Post*.

Robert R. McCormick, the last of his kind, in 1954.

✧ 4

"We always get our man." That phrase, given a sinister twist and repeated for emphasis, had formed the heart of Thompson's ferocious "deathbed statement" read out by his surrogate at the Apollo Theater. Yet Jake Lingle's killer proved elusive. Then, four days before Christmas 1930, a former bank robber turned informant named John Hagan led Rathbun, Roche, four detectives, and *Tribune* reporter John Boettiger in a raid on the Lake Crest Drive Apartments.

Utilizing the services of a woman who lived across the hall, the *Tribune* men lured a tall blond man with smoky blue eyes, known to Hagan simply as Buster, to accept an imaginary phone call. Once taken into custody, Buster was identified as Leo Brothers, alias Leo Bader, a down-on-his-luck graduate of a St. Louis gang called Egan's Rats. Three weeks elapsed between Brothers's "kidnapping" (his word) and his indictment on murder charges. During this time the suspect was held incommunicado in a Loop hotel, where he was subjected to an interrogation brutal even by the standards of that pre-*Miranda* era. Being hung over a door by his captors and burned with glowing cigars didn't shake his claim of innocence. He was guilty of nothing worse, he said, than trusting Hagan, with whom he had planned a bank robbery to replenish his funds. (If Brothers went free, Boettiger reportedly told Pat Roche, he would "own the *Tribune*.")[23]

Charges of a frameup began circulating the moment the beaming Roche presented his catch to a skeptical press corps. Brothers portrayed himself as a card-carrying member of the motion picture operators' union, working the spotlights for Tex Guinan's show at the Green Mill Gardens nightclub. Clearly that is not all he was; his disingenuousness was on a par with that of his general counsel, a legal volunteer named Louis Piquet, who was subsequently disbarred and sent to Leavenworth on charges unrelated to the Brothers case.

At his March 1931 trial, Brothers certainly *acted* like a guilty man, remaining mute (on the advice of counsel, he said afterward, to avoid questions about a long criminal record that included robbery, arson, bombing, and murder charges). As the trial unfolded, seven witnesses, among them an investigator for the state's attorney, a plumber under indictment for robbery, and a transient worker paid a few hundred dollars in "expense money" for his testimony, fingered Brothers as the man they had observed running from the murder scene. An equal number of bystanders disputed their claims.

McCormick, already furious at *Time* for insinuating that Brothers was "a man we have picked up to muddy the water," threatened to sue the magazine, in blatant contradiction of his earlier defense of a free press. He pointedly reminded prosecutors that the outcome of the trial would depend on their ability to make jurors understand Brothers's place in a much larger conspiracy. "It is he who knows the higher-up that hired him and he can tell," said McCormick. By his stolid silence at the trial, Brothers lent credence to this theory. (He was no more forthcoming when visited in his cell four years later by Big Bill Thompson. Conceding that "a North Side man" had killed Lingle, Brothers was extremely reluctant to be any more specific. Finally he spoke of "a Dago," since dead, who had changed his name and, in Thompson's words, "lived off the hides of women.") Not for a moment did McCormick believe that Brothers had acted alone. Neither, apparently, did the jury, which deliberated twenty-seven hours before finding the defendent guilty and imposing the minimum sentence under Illinois law.[24]

With good behavior, Leo Brothers would be eligible for parole in a little over eight years. "Eight years!" he muttered as he was led from the courtroom. "I'll serve that standing on my head."

Who killed Jake Lingle? The victim's friend and coworker George Reedy, who was to have accompanied Lingle to the racetrack on the day he was killed, attributed the crime to Al Capone, angry over a Lingle doublecross. McCormick held the same view. In August 1932, Louis Piquet confirmed to McCormick that Brothers had indeed been the hit man responsible for Lingle's murder and that he was one of a gang of five, whose members split $3,000 as payment for the crime. According to Piquet, Jake Lingle was the sixth man Brothers had killed in his criminal career. The Colonel never regretted his part in the arrest and trial of Leo Brothers. Addressing a gathering of the *Tribune*'s advertising department in June 1931, he said, in effect, I told you so. Whatever Lingle's moral shortcomings, his death had been part of a conspiracy to frustrate any serious move against Chicago gangs. Indeed, claimed McCormick, much of the dirt thrown at Lingle after his bloody demise was a deliberate effort by the killers to divert investigators "into the wrong channels."[25]

This was preposterous. It ignored McCormick's own role in documenting Lingle's dishonesty, and it obscured his suspicions about Bob Lee and others on the *Tribune* payroll. The whole sordid affair demonstrated nothing so much as Joe Patterson's indispensability. Far closer to his employees than McCormick, Patterson might easily have seen through Lingle and would never have praised the dead man so lavishly without knowing all the facts. Moreover, as long as he had shared management responsibilities with his impulsive cousin, Patterson had acted as a restraining influence.

Now the brake was lifted. There was no one to oppose McCormick's growing tendency to confuse himself not merely with the *Tribune* but with Chicago and all the "real" Americans who inhabited Tribune Town.

Having stood alone in defending the press from its enemies, McCormick regarded himself as divinely chosen to purify it from the human weaknesses personified by Jake Lingle. High-mindedness was inseparable in McCormick's character from highhandedness.

So was loyalty to those who shared his agenda or served his purposes. The Brothers case proved to be the making of its successful prosecutor, C. Wayland "Curley" Brooks, whom McCormick and the *Tribune* promoted into a seat in the Senate in 1940. (A similar buildup was accorded to the prosecutor Dwight H. Green after he sent Capone to prison in October 1931 on charges of income tax evasion. Green eventually rode a *Tribune*-generated updraft into the Illinois governor's mansion.)

Jake Lingle's betrayal left McCormick feeling more suspicious than ever about human nature. Once burned, twice shy: having made himself look ridiculous by rushing to defend a political fixer and influence-peddler, he would think long and hard before extending his trust to any man. Learning exactly the wrong lesson from the debacle, the Colonel became more, not less, reclusive. His office came to resemble the jail cell in which Leo Brothers served his sentence, but with one critical exception. When his time was up, Lingle's convicted killer walked out of prison for good. McCormick remained incarcerated by his own wish for as long as he lived.

❖ 5

"It is the duty of the city editor to know the reporters, not mine," McCormick once asserted imperiously. Much as the inhabitants of the city room might resent his spasmodic interest in their work, they considered themselves lucky by comparison with the *Tribune* Foreign News Service. In McCormick's office there hung a large world map bristling with colored pins, each of which represented an overseas correspondent. These were forever being adjusted, as a field marshal deploys his troops on the eve of battle. The men so cavalierly moved about were expected to produce a weekly letter apprising the Colonel of activities within their sphere. In addition, they were called on to attend biannual conferences, usually at the Ritz Hotel in Paris.

Notwithstanding the chic surroundings, McCormick played the role of hayseed philosopher at these assemblies, unfooled by the rich, the sophisticated, and foreigners of any description. To the Ritz he and his men repaired in 1927 to find a replacement for Floyd Gibbons, the chief roving correspondent of the *Tribune* ("probably the best newspaper job in the world," according to Gibbons's envious colleague George Seldes), who had been fired after socking Chicago with a $20,000 expense account run up during a safari to Timbuktu. (Gibbons justified his conduct by describing a lifelong ambition to send his aged mother a postcard marked Timbuktu. "And I did," he cheerfully remarked to Seldes.)[26]

McCormick opened the conclave by asking how many in attendance spoke French. All but one in the room raised his hand.

"How many speak German?" inquired the Colonel. This time three hands pierced the air.

"Italian?" A single hand rose, somewhat shakily.

McCormick paused only a moment before announcing that Larry Rue would become his designated globetrotter.

"But Colonel," a brave soul piped up, "Larry is the only one here who does not speak any foreign language."

"That is exactly what I want," said McCormick. "I don't want my fine young American boys ruined by these damn foreigners."[27]

In truth, McCormick was more a man of the world than either he or the world cared to admit. To the end of his days he ordered his footwear from the venerable London firm of John Lobb and his personalized luggage from Hermès of Paris. His distrust of an entire continent was colored by the resentment of a suitor scorned. For years both the *Paris Tribune* and the Foreign News Service had waged unsuccessful campaigns to obtain for McCormick the French Legion of Honor, in recognition of his wartime contributions. In retaliation for Gallic ingratitude, the Colonel demanded a complete list of Americans holding decorations of any kind from the French government. As it happened, thousands of his countrymen had been so honored — too many for McCormick to humiliate publicly by printing their names in the pages of the *Tribune*.[28]

The Colonel's men, not unexpectedly, dreaded his European inspection tours. "Root," he said, greeting young Waverly Root on their first encounter in London, "what was the population of Patagonia when Charles Darwin visited it in the *Beagle*?" In time Root came to be flattered by the assumption that he and his peers were human encyclopedias. Yet he never became wholly reconciled to McCormick's turns of fancy.[29]

These could be sharp and disagreeable, as Root discovered one morning outside the Ritz while he and McCormick waited impatiently for a car and driver. When at last the vehicle pulled up, an obsequious gold-braided doorman opened the car door. McCormick waved Root onto the back seat. He then folded his own long frame inside the car. Without warning he began shouting, in a voice that stopped traffic in the Place Vendôme, "Get out, Root! Get out at once! This is an outrage! This is intolerable!" Cringing hotel employees poured out onto the sidewalk, begging the pardon of their distinguished guest as Root, mystified, looked on. When at last the Colonel regained his composure, he pointed to an offending ashtray used by the prior occupant of the vehicle.[30]

Toward the *Paris Tribune* the Colonel adopted an attitude that was only slightly less demanding. He treated the paper much as one might a favorite naughty pet, harmless if not entirely housebroken. Unlike the rival *Paris Herald*, McCormick bragged, his Parisian mouthpiece was not edited for effete "lobster palace" Americans who had the misfortune or bad taste to live on the wrong side of the Seine. His smug characterization of the *Paris Tribune* as "an exponent in Europe of everything American" came as news to Henry Miller, F. Scott Fitzgerald, and James Thurber, among other employees of that rakish journal. (Thurber's special genius was to concoct, relying on nothing more than ten words cabled from the other side of the Atlantic, fictitious addresses of astonishing banality, which he then attributed to President Coolidge. "A man who does not pray is not a praying man," Thurber imagined Coolidge telling a convention of Protestant churchmen.)[31]

Ford Madox Ford, Ernest Hemingway, and Gertrude Stein were but a few of the literary and cultural refugees from Coolidge's America who found shelter in Montparnasse and a ready platform in the *Paris Tribune*. "I'll give you a lesson in American history," Stein breezily informed a *Tribune* correspondent over tea. "America made the twentieth century just as England made the nineteenth. We have given Europe everything." Her artistic judgments were just as sweeping. "The natural line of descent is the big four," she announced, "Poe to Whitman to James to myself. I am the last."[32]

Such pronouncements shared space with "Is Sex Necessary in America?" and the latest unorthodoxies from the pens of Kafka, Rilke, and Mauriac. Colonel McCormick frowned on lengthy think pieces, remembered a colleague, "unless he did the writing and thinking himself." This hardly endeared him to independent-minded journalists like George Seldes. A $20-a-week graduate of the *Army Tribune*, Seldes had been named chief of the Berlin bureau in 1920. He shared McCormick's tendency to view the world through the glass of ideology. But the two men differed radically in their politics. They clashed when McCormick, eager to repeal Woodrow Wilson's wartime nationalization of American railroads, proposed a series of articles critical of socialized rail systems in Europe. Together with his stalwart assistant, Sigrid Schultz, Seldes prepared a carefully researched cable of three hundred words testifying to the efficiency of publicly held railroads in Weimar Germany.

This provoked a heated McCormick rejoinder, so detailed that Miss Schultz was moved to tell Seldes that "the Colonel has written your story for you." All Seldes had to do was change the tenses, sign his name, and cable the report back to its author. He did nothing of the kind. Redoubling his investigative efforts, he transmitted to Chicago a 1,200-word cable, at a dollar a word, effusively lauding socialist transport in Germany. He heard nothing more from the Colonel on the subject of railroads.[33]

Although his sympathies lay with the left, Seldes's cheekiness boxed the ideological compass. For revealing the brutal tactics of state intimidation practiced by the Bolshevik Cheka, he was expelled from Russia in 1921. McCormick presented him a $500 bonus and a gold pin admitting him to the exclusive fraternity known as McCormick's Eagles. This stood the journalistic troublemaker in good stead when he was again ejected, this time from Mussolini's fascist paradise in 1925. McCormick printed every word of a dozen Seldes articles maligning the Italian dictator and his jackbooted followers. He brought the correspondent home to brief an inquisitive Coolidge at the White House on developments in Soviet Russia. (Seldes had less success with Sigmund Freud, whom McCormick hoped to lure to Chicago for $25,000 to psychoanalyze the defendants in the notorious Leopold-Loeb murder trial.)

In 1927, his health impaired by the grind of daily journalism, Seldes sought escape via magazine work. McCormick warmly recommended him for a job with *Liberty*, but when the desired position failed to materialize, he refused to take Seldes back. Seldes thanked the Colonel anyway, calling his association with the *Tribune* "the happiest part of my life."[34]*

John Clayton was more sincerely appreciative when, in April 1928, he informed McCormick that he was leaving the *Tribune* after nine years to take a job with Sam Insull and the Chicago Opera. The Colonel wished Clayton success and gave him a $1,000 bonus in recognition of some recent work in South America. "The door of this office always will be open to you whenever you wish my counsel or just a friendly chat," remarked McCormick as he shook the departing reporter's hand.[35]

McCormick sent his foreign correspondents to cover wars, revolutions, and palace coups the way local reporters covered fires and gangland shootings. In the mid-1930s, Will Barber of the London bureau was ordered to Addis Ababa, the Ethiopian capital, which was thought to be in peril from Italian invasion. Barber sensibly inquired as to the inoculations he would need to ward off African diseases. These would delay his departure by two weeks, information he duly cabled to Chicago. Back came McCormick's testy response: "Are you a historian or a newspaperman?" The chastened Barber left England without obtaining all the recommended shots. He died of breakwater fever on the day Mussolini's forces belatedly crossed the Ethiopian frontier.[36]

---

*Seldes expanded on this a decade later, describing McCormick as "modest, friendly, easy to get along with ... one of the few press lords who had escaped the Napoleon-Northcliffe power obsession." World War II and the postwar Red scare at home caused him to change his views radically. In a bitter eulogy printed two weeks after McCormick's death in April 1955, he called his late boss "one of the most stupid leaders of men I have ever known." Seldes claimed that his fellow correspondents had spoken to McCormick as they would to "a rather retarded child."

Other correspondents drew even stranger, if less life-threatening, assignments. William L. Shirer, a balding, bespectacled Iowan from Cedar Rapids, freshly graduated from the copy desk of the *Paris Tribune*, was sent to Cantigny, France. His mission: to locate a pair of binoculars McCormick had left in a barn nine years earlier. In his memoirs, three panoramic volumes collectively published as *Twentieth Century Journey*, Shirer enjoyed sweet literary revenge at the expense of "the terrible Colonel McCormick," beginning with the Colonel's overreaction to his coverage of a routine speech delivered at Oxford by the U.S. ambassador to Great Britain, Charles Dawes. "Stop toadying to British. Be American," McCormick angrily cabled to his man in London. "Do you think British are going to give you a tablet in Westminster Abbey?"[37]

No such communication has been preserved in McCormick's papers. There *is* a McCormick telegram to Shirer dated August 24, 1929. Without mentioning any speech by Dawes, it cautions Shirer against taking the British side in an ongoing debate over major-power naval strength. "No *Tribune* correspondents will be given tablets in Westminster Abbey," McCormick told Shirer, adding that such tributes were reserved for foreign ambassadors. The tone was lightly mocking, even self-mocking.

In *The Start*, the first volume of his autobiographical trilogy, Shirer paints his only direct encounter with McCormick in comical terms. It occurred during a brief American furlough in the winter of 1929–30. Following lunch in the Overset Club, the two men repaired to the twenty-fourth floor, where Shirer nervously lit a cigarette. "Put that thing out!" barked McCormick. "Didn't anyone tell you? No one smokes here."

Shirer sat mute as McCormick busied himself with paperwork. Tense minutes crawled by. Unexpectedly, McCormick rose to his feet and stalked across the room to the opposite wall. He beckoned to Shirer to join him before a large wall map of Europe.

"You did a pretty good job there," said the Colonel, pointing to a spot on the map obscured from Shirer's view by the broad back of his host. "Some of your stuff was pretty good." Shirer craned his neck, but it was no good. He was unable to see through, or around, the massive publisher.

"I want you to go there," stated McCormick, theatrically stepping aside to allow Shirer a peek at his new assignment. "I want you to take over the bureau." At the end of his fingertip was the city of Vienna. Shirer, elated, wore a respectful gaze as McCormick dispensed advice based on his own youthful residence in the Austrian capital. "Don't fall for all these Communists and Socialists there. And don't let all the counts and countesses take you in."

Shirer was not too dazed by his good fortune to pay bogus tribute to the late Ambassador McCormick, still fondly remembered in Vienna thirty years after his tour of duty there. The Colonel expected as much. "They liked us," he remarked to Shirer, notwithstanding his family's evident disdain for "all that Hapsburg stuff."

If McCormick entertained doubts about the twenty-five-year-old Shirer's qualifications, he quickly swallowed them. Age mattered little around the *Tribune*, he observed complacently. "If you're good enough to make the paper, however young, you're good enough to take on any assignment."

Shirer could hardly wait to assume his new duties. First, however, he must find a way out of the Colonel's office. This was no simple task; the entrance through which he had come was nowhere to be seen. "Excuse me, sir," he blurted out. "I don't seem to remember where the door is."

McCormick's eyes remained stapled to his desk. "It's right behind you, Shirer."

Suddenly a panel slid open. Shirer made a hasty exit. Over his shoulder he thought he could hear the sound of McCormick's low chuckle. His employer was a queer duck, he thought as he left the tower and turned down Michigan Avenue. *But he gave me Vienna!* The realization warmed him against an icy gale sweeping the Magnificent Mile.[38]

✧ 6

Shirer was wrong. As events would prove, McCormick hadn't given him Vienna, merely offered to share the old city for as long as the young reporter's interpretation of events in the bubbling cauldron of Central Europe conformed to his own view of the region. At the outset, McCormick advised Shirer to pay special heed to the restless minorities herded into a series of artificial states by the diplomats of Versailles. "The American people are still very sympathetic to the oppressed," he wrote, with one eye on Chicago's huge ethnic populations, "although their government is under the intellectual dominance of the oppressor."[39]

With the American economy shriveling by the month, the Colonel had no choice but to cut two pages form the daily *Tribune.* This led him in turn to urge his foreign correspondents to send shorter stories. He instructed his Vienna bureau chief to rely less on costly cables and more on the mail. Before long the Foreign News Service itself came to be seen as a luxury McCormick could ill afford. First to go was Vincent Sheean, a gifted writer made famous after he slipped behind French lines in Morocco and landed an interview with a charismatic leader of anti-French rebels named Abd-el-Krim. Sheean attributed his dismissal to a prolonged Parisian dinner one evening in 1925. The Colonel took a different tack, pronouncing Sheean "a liar, disloyal and dishonorable," and accusing the correspondent of perverse conduct while on assignment in Italy.[40]

Floyd Gibbons and George Seldes filed their last *Tribune* stories in 1927. Gibbons's successor as chief roving corespondent, Larry Rue, lasted barely two years in the job. McCormick fired him in November 1929, professing disappointment over his failure to exploit the *Tribune*'s recently purchased European airplane for its news-gathering possibilities.[41]

When the health of reporter Jay Allen prevented him from going to India in the fall of 1930, Bill Shirer was sent in his place. His new post allowed him to stoke his employer's anglophobia at regular intervals. Minimizing the importance of an upcoming round-table conference in London, for example, Shirer told the Colonel that delegates purporting to represent India were actually titled defenders of the raj who cared more for preserving their privileges than for installing a democratic government representative of the Indian masses. In October 1930 Shirer gained permission to visit Afghanistan, the remote mountainous kingdom that served as a buffer between Soviet Russia and British interests on the subcontinent. He filed an impressive string of exclusives describing the enthronement of the youthful Afghan king, Nadir Khan. He also took the occasion to appeal yet again to McCormick's distaste for the British, twice writing to ascertain whether his Afghan scoops had arrived safely at the *Tribune*, as "you can never be very sure about letters from police-ridden India these days."[42]

The Colonel praised Shirer for his "very interesting" Afghan reports, which were heavily promoted in the *Tribune*. In addition, he offered verbal encouragement when Shirer and his bride were laid low by dysentery and malaria. Shirer, said the Colonel, must never forget that he occupied the single most interesting listening post on earth, a front-row seat from which to observe the epic political movement led by the shrewd saint Mahatma Gandhi.[43]

His own curiosity about India was boundless. He asked Shirer how "wild and woolly" were the Indian principalities, and how outrageous the conduct of princes "who are being trotted out as the savior of the British empire. To what extent do they starve their peasants and do they tyrannize over all their subjects? Are their harems enormous and extravagant?" Were India's minor royalties "with their Oxford education" becoming modernized, or did they cling to the ways of their ancestors? It was all grist for McCormick's mill.[44]

By mid-1931, deteriorating health made Shirer's return to a more temperate climate a matter of urgency. Mindful of his employer's prejudices, he continued to sink harpoons into His Majesty's imperial hide. "Did I ever write you that the *Tribune* was the most frequently quoted foreign paper in India — and the most hated by the governing bureaucracy?" he asked McCormick. In refusing to grant him an interview, the British viceroy confirmed the *Tribune*'s unique self-importance. "All the other American newspapers, either through their proprietors or through their correspondents, are reached in one way or another," maintained Mc-Cormick. Shirer needn't hesitate to insert in his reports, "whenever the occasion presents itself," information testifying to the ease with which foreign officials gulled impressionable Americans.[45]

Shirer instead raised questions about his own gullibility. In writing about Viennese housing conditions, he employed harsh language to describe the lot of prewar workers in the Austrian capital. McCormick exploded. He gathered from Shirer's article that his Vienna correspondent was either reading the New York papers "pretty assiduously" or else associating with New York newspapermen, a disreputable clique wedded to "parlor socialism" (defined by the Colonel as "nothing but a form of mental laziness somehow translated into dreamy egotism"). Writers so infected rarely sought out facts, settling instead for "lazy ecstasy."[46]

In his memoirs, Shirer reproduced his impudent response to this stinging epistle while leaving out the barb he tossed at "Englishmen who, however brilliant they may be, must see Europe from a different slant and background than we do." In other words, after more than a year abroad, he was still working hard to cultivate his prickly patron in Chicago. In this spirit he reassured McCormick that "since college days I have been completely cured of quack routes that promised to lead to Utopia." Shirer subtly shifted ground, blaming the oppression of Viennese workers on the Hapsburgs and a feudal aristocracy "greatly sought after by visiting Americans, easily impressed by titles."[47]

One day in May 1932, Shirer received from the Colonel a newspaper clipping showing a ruined bridge over a small river. "Shirer — go there," read the accompanying message. Was this some sort of crazy parlor game? Was Shirer again being tested, two years after he had groped his way out of the Colonel's office in Tribune Tower? Whatever the motive behind his latest assignment, he accepted the challenge with brio. Using his wits and the services of a Russian-speaking friend, he managed to locate the bridge, at the very doorstep of Soviet Russia. For a full week he interviewed desperate refugees slipping across the Dniester River, carrying with them heartrending tales of inhuman treatment at the hands of Red guards.[48]

Was McCormick conducting a long-distance tutorial in the evils of European collectivism? If so, his efforts were academic, for the ax was about to fall on Shirer's career with the *Tribune*. In his memoirs, Shirer portrays his firing in October 1932 as a bolt out of the blue, unanticipated, unjustified, and, for five excruciating weeks, unexplained. Eventually Teddy Beck wrote to him and referred to a "routine dispatch" (Shirer's words) in which the reporter had mistakenly identified Hollywood film star Anna May Wong as the "May Wong" involved in a traffic accident outside Vienna. Miss Wong had taken strenuous objection to the resulting article, leading McCormick to settle the matter with a printed retraction and $1,000 to salve the actress's wounded feelings.

In fact, the story printed in the September 12, 1932, *Tribune* was more serious than Shirer let on. He had portrayed Miss Wong as spending the night in jail with her traveling companion, the songwriter Rudolf Friml, after the couple ran over and gravely injured a child. Both had left the scene of the accident, he wrote, in an "expensive car with an American license number." If the child died, Shirer concluded, the film star would be charged with manslaughter. On review, almost nothing about the piece checked out. Wong objected as much to the implication of sexual impropriety with the songwriter (whom she had never met) as to the alleged reckless driving. To McCormick, Shirer bore responsibility for "a hell of a libelous story" and an "utterly indefensible libel suit."

But there was another reason behind Shirer's termination, unreported until now. Several months earlier, an unscrupulous Hearst double agent in Athens had scooped Shirer by landing an exclusive interview with Samuel Insull, then a refugee from American justice. No one involved in the matter, it appears, had entirely clean hands. McCormick told Shirer's superior, Edmond Taylor, that he was to use his judgment in deciding the reporter's future, as "I never met the man." This was plainly untrue — unless Shirer fabricated his account of meeting McCormick in Tribune Tower in 1929, a tall order indeed. Ironically, in light of subsequent events, McCormick stated to Taylor that he had leaned over backward trying to give Shirer "a square deal" after Shirer had been double-crossed over the Insull exclusive.[49]

Writing to Beck on October 19, 1932, Shirer argued that he was a victim of circumstances. "I am not trying to wiggle back into a job," he asserted, less persuasively. In an angry rejoinder to the Colonel, Shirer reminded McCormick that on the very day he was fired, the *Tribune* was readying a full-page ad hailing his latest scoop, in the form of a cabled message from the fasting Mahatma Gandhi. Shirer's letter crossed in the mail with a communication from McCormick, who, seemingly oblivious to what had happened, mildly wondered why his man in Vienna had all but disappeared from the scene. "Is it that your health is so bad," he asked, "or do you think that your field is non-productive? We might transfer you elsewhere, if that is so."[50]

In his memoirs, Shirer describes himself as "dumbfounded" by this apparent reprieve. Putting aside his hurt feelings, he thanked the Colonel in writing for his "sympathetic inquiries and criticism." The reason he had nearly vanished from the Central European scene, Shirer remembered, "was that on October 16 last he had fired me." But his memory played him false. What he had actually sent McCormick was a *tour d'horizon* of a continent pregnant with conflict and a promise to make the region "interesting, if you give me the chance. At 28, and just when I've really got to know Europe, its languages and its curious ways, which are notorious, why should I fade out as a European correspondent? I don't want to. I won't. And I can prove it to you, if you want me to."[51]

McCormick rendered this appeal moot, and himself ridiculous, by having his secretary send Shirer instructions on January 11, 1933, to disregard his earlier, friendly message, written when the Colonel hadn't known that Shirer was already off the *Tribune* payroll. "What a contemptible son of a bitch!" Shirer the memoirist sputters in disbelief that McCormick could be as ignorant — or innocent — as he claimed.

Later Shirer came to see himself as one more casualty of the Depression, a conclusion rooted in McCormick's 1934 sale of the *Paris Tribune*, for a rumored $50,000, to the rival *New York Herald*. By then Henry Wales, lionized for his "exclusive interview" with Charles Lindbergh the night he landed in Paris after his historic transatlantic flight in May 1927 — in truth a pastiche of comments the Lone Eagle made to several reporters at the American embassy — had fatally offended the Colonel by refusing to accompany Secretary of State Stimson to a European disarmament conference. Wales made matters worse by jumping ship in Hawaii for a drunken spree. Jay Allen, too, would be cut adrift after he wrote a fierce anti-Franco polemic during the Spanish Civil War, putting at risk a *Tribune* correspondent assigned to the Nationalist armies.

None of these professional separations, however unpleasant, caused a fraction of the harm to McCormick's historical reputation as his maladroit firing of William L. Shirer. At the time, no one anticipated Shirer's enormous success in chronicling Hitler's Germany or the moral and intellectual prestige accruing to the author of *The Rise and Fall of the Third Reich*. So great was his standing, so authoritative his literary craftsmanship, that few readers of *Twentieth Century Journey* paused to ask whether Shirer had taken more than the usual memoirist's pains to settle old scores while casting himself in a flattering light.

✧ 7

Among the diverse tasks performed by the Colonel's European staff was scouting for polo ponies and buying ships for the *Tribune*'s Canadian fleet. Neither of these functions was as distasteful as overseeing Kate McCormick, whose declining years were largely spent in luxurious exile. Her loud protests over hotel food had made her unwelcome at Palm Beach resorts and a dreaded figure on board the *Île de France* and the other ocean liners that her solicitous son was always meeting (after making certain that the "necessary stimulants" requisitioned by Mrs. McCormick would be available on her arrival in dry New York).

Kate's tongue grew sharper as her mind weakened. George Seldes learned this for himself one day in 1924. Sent to greet Mrs. McCormick as her ship nosed into the French port of Le Havre, the *Tribune* emissary found himself being eyed by the old lady with unnerving intensity.

"Mr. Seldes," said Kate.

"Yes, Mrs. McCormick."

"Jew, aren't you?"

"Yes, Mrs. McCormick."

"Mr. Seldes, I hate the Jews. I hate the British. I hate the French. God damn them all."[52]

Exchanging the restless flapper culture of the twenties for a more heroic past, Kate imagined herself once more a girl sitting on General Grant's lap. She ordered Bill Shirer, assigned one afternoon to keep her company at the Ritz, to take a memo for President Lincoln. ("Forget it," Henry Wales dryly informed Shirer on his return to the office. "Mr. Lincoln, I believe, is dead.")[53]

The Colonel gave Kate his Distinguished Service Medal to wear. He introduced her to the abstemious Charles Summerall — too good, she concluded, to be a general in the mold of Grant or Sheridan. Although McCormick couldn't gratify his mother's wish for a private audience with Charles Lindbergh or a concert recital in her Paris hotel suite by the famed Polish artist Ignace Paderewski, he never missed Christmas in her big stone house on Massachusetts Avenue in Washington. Year round he indulged her tart-tongued instructions. In 1930 she told him not to go too hard on Big Bill Thompson, so long as there was any chance the roguish mayor might endorse Ruth's candidacy for the Senate. She never mellowed toward "that white trash Patterson blood" into which her sister Nellie had so treacherously married; she had given up reading "Joe's *Liberty*," she wrote her son. "It's so dull."[54]

Kate acknowledged that Bertie was more of a fighter than his late brother had ever been. Making amends for past slights, in old age she revised her will in belated recognition of his attentiveness.[55] This presented another set of problems, for Kate's love could be as cloying as her neglect had been casual. "If you don't come and see me soon," she wrote to the Colonel ominously in November 1931, "I will go to Chicago myself." Painfully alone, she briefly considered selling her Washington mansion and returning to the city of her girlhood. But she had no wish to spend her final years in the same time zone as her reviled sister. Besides, Chicago held too many memories.

And so, in the spring of 1932, Kate resumed the comfortable life abroad made possible by monthly dividend checks of $105,000. Taking rooms at the Trianon Palace Hotel near Versailles, she seemed invigorated by drives through the French countryside and the private piano recitals regularly staged for her enjoyment. Mrs. McCormick was well, her companion informed the Colonel at the end of June, if undecided about her next destination. It was a decision made for her a few minutes after midnight on July 5, when her heart gave out.[56]

"It seems to have been brought about by the excitement of the 4th of July celebration," McCormick explained to a friend. "Her end had to come some time," he crisply told Kate's doctor, "and I am sure that nothing was left undone which could have been done to lengthen her days." For $3,500, he ordered "the best casket in Paris," thanked his mother's attendants for their devotion, and rescheduled a board of directors meeting to avoid conflict with the Chicago funeral.[57]

Whatever emotions the death of his mother may have churned up were hidden behind a stolid exterior. When, long after, McCormick destroyed much of Kate's correspondence, he carefully preserved one of her final letters, enjoining "my dearest possession" to guard his health. In his later years, he liked to revisit Washington landmarks to which his mother had introduced him sixty years earlier. One of these was the resting place of Henry and Clover Adams in Rock Creek Cemetery, memorialized by Saint-Gaudens's haunting figure of a young woman shrouded in grief. The sculpture paid ambivalent tribute to a difficult relationship.[58]

McCormick's feelings toward Kate would challenge an artist of Saint-Gaudens's subtlety. One thing was clear, however: with Kate McCormick at last reunited with her husband in Chicago's Graceland Cemetery, her son was left richer, more powerful, and more alone than at any time in his fifty-two years.

❖ 8

For McCormick and other hard-shell conservatives, the 1932 presidential campaign posed an unappealing choice. Neither Herbert Hoover nor Franklin Roosevelt shared their view that the nation's economic paralysis was the inevitable result of excessive taxation and government profligacy.

"We have reached the extraordinary situation where the ownership of property has become a liability, not an asset," McCormick argued over CBS radio in April. In a series of addresses that spring, he blamed the dislocation and extravagance of the Great War for unhinging the traditional arm's-length relationship between American citizens and their government. Foreign conflict had bred domestic organizations with no purpose other than collecting and spending money on a scale unimaginable prior to 1917.

When the soldiers had demobilized, said McCormick, "the slacker armies . . . accustomed to the easy existence and regular pay of public office" had remained in the field. So had propaganda artists skilled at promoting government activism. At the same time, a national antipathy toward war profiteers had been perverted, he claimed, by "tax thieves" who scorned all profit-making. So-called progressive taxation was in fact punitive, yet necessary to sustain a 1931 federal budget of $14 billion (five times prewar levels) and a locust army of three million public employees.

Under the grinding load of taxation, which McCormick estimated at $400 for every American family, industry had faltered and jobs melted away. These were fearsome numbers to McCormick's generation. (As recently as 1894 the Supreme Court had ruled the income tax unconstitutional. Even wartime taxes had been modestly scaled, starting at 2 percent on incomes greater than $5,000 and rising to 50 percent on those in excess of $2 million.)

"Our government was established on principles of simplicity and economy," McCormick asserted before another audience that spring. From the ratification of the Constitution, it had taken Washington sixty years to invent a new cabinet department (Interior) "so continuously laced with corruption and scandal that someone said its only hours of good reputation were when it was not found out." Requiring forest lands for his paper mills, he had visited this "organization of genteel parasites" for himself. For his troubles he had received polite murmurings and nothing else remotely useful. Nor had Farmer McCormick obtained any greater satisfaction when forced to deal with Hoover's Federal Farm Board.[59]

From such unhappy experiences McCormick generalized a historical indictment condemning virtually every expansion of federal authority since the Civil War. Among his bureaucratic targets was the Civil Service Commission, formed in 1883, "the constitutional officers of government being no longer considered honest enough to employ their own assistants"; the Interstate Commerce Commission (1887), "which does not move a pound of freight or a passenger, but costs the astounding sum of ten million dollars a year to maintain," and which had succeeded in a little over four decades in bringing America's railroads to the verge of bankruptcy; and the Department of Commerce and Labor, created in 1903 by "some ingenious spoilsman . . . to direct the commerce of the country," then divided, a decade later, when "some political demagogue produced the Department of Labor to handle the foreign vote."

And on it went, a roll call of Wilsonian meddling that included the Federal Reserve Board, established "to dominate the banks and bring on the panic of 1929," the Federal Trade Commission, the National Advisory Commission for Aeronautics, and "a racket called the Employers' Compensation Commission." More recently, government had begun to license broadcasting stations "just as four hundred years ago Henry VIII licensed printing presses." McCormick railed against Washington's "Arabian night activities . . . operations to put water on land, and to take water off land; to tax farmers who own their farms in order to subsidize other farmers to compete with them; to build harbors where there is no shipping, and dredge waters where there is no commerce." And this did not begin to include state, county, and local expenditures for roads paved and unpaved, for school courses "in ballet dancing and lipstick" and "palatial college buildings which turn schoolboys into drones before they have ever worked."

McCormick worked himself into a lather over a spendthrift Congress "dominated and driven by the Red members who are working to destroy our government and civilization, and who in turn are supported by that group of scholastic morons calling themselves Progressives and Liberals, whose principal concern is to make private enterprise unprofitable." Everywhere citizens cried for relief, he said, not from economic hardship but from federal tax collectors. "If you are to exist you must tear these weasels from the throat of the nation," he melodramatically told his CBS audience.*

Speaking three months later on NBC, he sounded a slightly more optimistic note. Appearing under the auspices of the National Organization to Reduce Public Expenditures, he took comfort from the recent primary defeat of Iowa senator Smith Brookhart, "whose pilgrimages to Moscow expose the path that all his crowd propose to follow." Meanwhile, Louisiana patriots were organizing to combat "the unspeakable Huey Long" and all his works. The Colonel was not without hope that in New York City, the enemy heartland, a leader might yet emerge to challenge "the alien-minded Fiorello La Guardia, who would destroy the government which American George Washington there set up."[60]

Still, McCormick saw squalls ahead: savings squandered, future earnings mortgaged, an inflationary debt run up by "office-holding tyrants." National survival required a U-turn in the form of a 50 percent reduction in government spending. Slash bloated taxes, he proposed, and business would be emancipated to generate a prosperity beyond the restorative capacity of any federal agency or big-city political machine.

✦ 9

The most conspicious of McCormick's targets was the Republican president, locked in a forlorn campaign for reelection. "Off hand I do

---

*If McCormick's black cloud had any silver lining, it was to be found in the downfall of England, halted in its tracks by the same overtaxation that now threatened the United States. Thus, "while in Chicago we are now building an industrial museum, every factory in England *is* an industrial museum filled with antique machinery fit for the junk shop."

not think of a single question upon which I hold the same views as Mr. Hoover," McCormick confessed to an associate in August 1932. He entertained no higher an opinion of Hoover's Democratic opponent, New York governor Franklin D. Roosevelt. As early as December 1929 Mc-Cormick had predicted a Roosevelt presidency if Hoover continued to make mistakes and his onetime Groton schoolmate was able to reform his party along Jeffersonian lines. In the years since, the politically inept Hoover had done his part. Roosevelt, however, had remained stubbornly resistant to the siren song of state's rights.[61]

In the spring of 1932, out of patience with the incumbent, McCormick tried to draft former president Calvin Coolidge. Both the Colonel and his Washington bureau chief, Arthur Sears Henning, paid calls at the Coolidge residence in Northampton, Massachusetts. Both came away empty-handed. McCormick simultaneously criticized Roosevelt for warning the International Society for Crippled Children that in "the mad scramble to cut" federal expenditures, care must be taken to protect the most vulnerable members of society. "The best hope of crippled children," pronounced the *Tribune* with misplaced outrage, "is in the restoration of public and private solvency and prosperity." Cut taxes, it implied, and the lame would grow limber.[62]

As of July 1, 1932, McCormick reluctantly instituted "interim quantity discounts" — a wordy euphemism for price cuts — in *Tribune* ad rates. "Four banks failed yesterday and three have failed so far today," he notified Joe Patterson. "Anything may happen." He invested heavily in gold. At the bottom of the trough, he received encouragement from an unlikely source. "For your personal information and not for publication," wrote Franklin Roosevelt, he wished to share the results of a "preliminary survey" of federal expenditures, which led him to believe that a 20 percent reduction in spending could be achieved through elimination of nonessential functions and reorganization of existing departments. He had been giving the matter "deep study," said FDR, and would like to discuss it with McCormick.[63]

McCormick remained mired in gloom. He rejected Roosevelt's solicitation for a private school gift, saying that as long as government took half of all private income and a 40 percent share of inherited wealth, he could see no margin for philanthropy. One week after making this sour observation, he learned of his mother's death. In her will, Kate McCormick gave her surviving son *Tribune* stock conservatively valued at $4 million, left in trust to elude Uncle Sam's grasping fingers. As a result, McCormick's annual income more than doubled. At a time of mass economic misery, the publisher of the *Chicago Tribune* earned three quarters of a million dollars, mostly in dividends, each year.[64]

Neither the death of Kate nor the economic gain accruing to him as a result were enough to push politics to the back of McCormick's mind. At the end of June, Roosevelt's sons, in town for the Democratic convention, pitched their tent at the Colonel's Astor Street house. McCormick assigned John Boettiger, the somewhat equivocal hero of the Lingle affair, to cover the Roosevelt campaign. Boettinger quickly won the candidate's confidence. It took him only slightly more time to establish intimate relations with Roosevelt's unhappily married daughter Anna.

At the start of August, Boettiger arranged for McCormick and Roosevelt to meet at Hyde Park. He had enjoyed "every minute" of the visit, McCormick informed his host on August 6, not least of all a frantic dash to the Peekskill train station. As for Roosevelt's driver, he said, "I told him he ought to become a racing car chauffeur."[65]

Besides displaying his famous charm, FDR had made vaguely empathetic remarks disparaging those who would tax corporate profits to force their distribution. McCormick responded with a veiled warning of the consequences sure to ensue if Roosevelt emulated Hoover by intruding into the private affairs of businessmen. "Whatever my successes or failures, or those of anybody else running a business," he informed Roosevelt tartly, "I am sure I can do it better than any outsider, whether his motives be good, theoretical, or hostile to our form of government."[66]

The *Tribune*, believing that Hoover had dangerously expanded government power, nevertheless endorsed him as the only viable alternative to those on the left who criticized the president for not expanding it further. Forced to choose between the truly radical and the merely bureaucratic, McCormick held his nose and voted for the doomed incumbent. But Hoover's crushing defeat in November did not cause excessive grief around Tribune Tower. Quite the contrary. A few days after the election, using Boettiger as his back channel, the Colonel alerted the president-elect that the outgoing administration hoped to commit him to the reduction of war debts owed to the United States by its refractory allies. He would watch Roosevelt's efforts with sympathy and a willingness to help whenever possible, McCormick told his old classmate on November 12. "Party considerations will not weigh with me when I think you are doing the correct thing."

Belying this expression of post-election goodwill was a *Tribune* inquiry into a $500,000 insurance policy listing Roosevelt's Warm Springs Foundation as beneficiary. "The question occurs to me whether Roosevelt paid the regular premium on this or whether it is partly an advertising stunt. We might query our correspondent for the facts," McCormick instructed Teddy Beck, "without printing a story of it." To a Michigan correspondent who had urged the new president to make McCormick secretary of state, the Colonel responded that he saw two obstacles to such a plan: "The first is that Mr. Roosevelt will not make the appointment, and the second is that the Senate will not confirm it." Nevertheless, the proposal was not without value, if only for the pressure it exerted on Roosevelt to appoint "an American-minded" secretary of state, "which is a thing his past and his surroundings will not influence him to do."[67]

✧ 10

By the first week of January 1933, McCormick's fears were rising. "Is Mrs. Franklin Roosevelt cuckoo?" he asked a *Tribune* reporter in New York after hearing that she was writing a 40,000-word book for publication that spring. "She seems to be perniciously active," he went on, "as though she had been kept quiet during the campaign and is now uncontrollable." Still more alarming were reports that the new administration, persuaded that expenses could not be reduced nor taxes raised further, was likely to pursue inflationary policies. On January 6, the *Tribune* called for reductions in Illinois's relief expenditures; six days later, the paper condemned the dole for encouraging men "to think that the world owes them a living."[68]

In the weeks leading up to Inauguration Day, McCormick's editorial writers poured scorn on the Federal Council of Churches, demanded an end to Hoover's Reconstruction Finance Corporation, and opposed an economic boycott of Japan as "a logical prelude to war." Most pointedly, they adjured the president-elect to follow the path of Thomas Jefferson, not Karl Marx. Through John Boettiger, Roosevelt gave private assurances of his soundness on the inflation issue. FDR reaffirmed his intention to slash government expenditures and credited McCormick with being the first to advocate 25 percent across-the-board cuts, an idea Roosevelt had appropriated for use in a Pittsburgh campaign speech (much to his later regret).[69]

The president-elect indicated his desire for a second meeting with McCormick before his inauguration. Lunch at Hyde Park was arranged for February 24. "I feel that you are going over the top," McCormick wrote on the eve of his visit, "and the least I can do is to wish you well." In the event, the encounter was almost purely social. Afterward, McCormick remembered an atmosphere of messianic self-regard. Equally shocking had been Roosevelt's *sotto voce* revelation that he intended to call in gold.[70]

At the time, however, the Colonel seemed as willing as most Americans to accept radical measures as the price of restoring public faith in capitalism. As the nation's banking system neared collapse, he conceded that only a government guarantee of deposits would meet the crisis. Others, led by Raymond Moley, a conservative member of Roosevelt's Brain Trust and an economic thinker of impeccable orthodoxy, thought of McCormick and Roosevelt as prospective allies. Determined to block any reduction of

European war debts to the United States, Moley hoped that the Colonel might play a useful role in counteracting British propaganda. More discreetly, he sought McCormick's help in "stiffening [FDR's] spine" against internationalists who were trying to sway the president-elect to their viewpoint.[71]

March 3, 1933, was Hoover's last night in office. As the sands ran out on the old, discredited administration, *Tribune* reporters were monitoring the White House and the Mayflower Hotel, where Roosevelt and his advisers discussed the plight of America's banks in a crisis atmosphere. In a hotel bathroom, James Simpson, then head of Marshall Field and Company, tipped off correspondent Tom Furlong that financial institutions in New York and Chicago would not open the next day. Inauguration Day found banks in nearly two dozen states shut tight. The financial heart of America had ceased to beat.[72]

The *Tribune* decried the situation as the inevitable consequence of excessive taxation "to meet fantastic government expenses." From Aiken, where he had gone to coddle a severe cold, McCormick hailed the new president's boldness in declaring a nationwide bank holiday and slapping an embargo on gold shipments. He hoped Congress would be equally decisive in slashing federal spending. On March 6, he confessed to Joe Patterson that he hadn't the foggiest idea what the future held. To weather the storm, he had cut the *Tribune* to the bone and placed Canadian operations on a day-to-day basis. Easing his worries was $1 million in cash sequestered in the *Tribune's* vaults. Yet the new order in Washington remained an enigma. "I want to avoid signing any blank checks," the wary McCormick told his editorial writers on March 9. Since he had blamed government extravagance for causing the crisis, the last thing he desired was to "admit that the government is a mere rescuer of the country from itself."

Out of the White House came the first muffled notes of unhappiness over the *Tribune's* coverage of the young administration. "We have never had a cartoon of Roosevelt carrying a red flag," McCormick blandly informed John Boettiger on March 20. "He must have been thinking of the Huey Long cartoon."[73]

In private McCormick was less circumspect, writing to Joe Patterson that "Roosevelt has been a leader in all that . . . has brought this upon us." Lumping together the recent victory of Adolf Hitler's Nazis in Germany, "the dictatorial powers given to Roosevelt," and a concentration of legislative authority in the British cabinet, he concluded mournfully that "it looks as though representative institutions are in a decline."[74]

PART IV

The Fox
and the Crow

1933–1945

"I think he must be a little touched in his head."

FRANKLIN D. ROOSEVELT,
on Colonel McCormick,
March 1942

11

The Duel

"Frank Roosevelt and the NRA have taken the place of love nests."

— Joe Patterson, summer 1933

"We must win this election or submit to dictatorship."

— Colonel McCormick, October 1936

I N THE LAST WEEK of March 1933, the countryside around Aiken, South Carolina, was ablaze with fragrant dogwood and wisteria. From his Whitehall estate, built on twenty-six acres sold to him by Marshall Field III, McCormick drank in the beauties of the season. Other big houses might be empty, he commented, "but as they are set among trees, that fact is not noticeable." More alarming was a shortage of polo players among the horsy set. In this fourth spring of economic sickness, he counted no fewer than five abandoned Aiken polo fields.[1]

Grudgingly, McCormick conceded that a five-day work week was a Depression-fighting necessity. "I would rather see it come in as a matter of custom than of statute," he told his editorial writers. His personal faith in the capitalist future, reflecting the early thirties rage for technocracy, was unshaken. McCormick looked to aviation, new passenger engines and cars, metal alloys, chemicals, and newspapers to duplicate for the modern world the kind of revolutionary advances once attributed to iron and steel. Qualifying his optimism was the danger of "government interference" that might discourage individual genius and visionary investment.[2]

That McCormick could remain hopeful about the new regime in Washington for much of 1933 is both a measure of his relief over the departure of

Herbert Hoover and a tribute to Franklin Roosevelt's uncanny ability to be all things to all people. Torn between reform and recovery, inflation and deflation, the early New Deal seemed an extension of the 1932 campaign, in which Roosevelt had championed "the forgotten man" victimized by Wall Street and an uncaring government while he attacked Hoover's "novel, radical, and unorthodox economic theories."

From the outset, McCormick strongly seconded Roosevelt's demand for half a billion dollars in spending cuts. He praised the Civilian Conservation Corps as "relief at its best." Moreover, as an economic and political nationalist, the Colonel had no grounds to complain in July when Roosevelt torpedoed a London conference called to renegotiate European war debts and lower the formidable tariff walls erected around the United States and other trading nations by frightened, insular politicians. Best of all, the advent of Roosevelt meant the end of Prohibition. At one of his first press conferences — when he had already scored points by promising to serve White House reporters the first batch of legalized beer — the president likened himself to a quarterback making up his game plan as he went along. "Future plays will depend on how the next one works," he said.

With improvisation came contradiction. Roosevelt's action in taking the United States off the prevailing gold standard was as deflationary as the Agricultural Adjustment Administration, established to restrict farm output, was profoundly inflationary. Initially, the AAA and its policy of organized scarcity provoked only a muted cry from Tribune Tower. "We hope it may do good," McCormick informed his editorial writers in mid-April, "but there is opportunity for almost unlimited ill."[3]

Even Roosevelt's call for $3.3 million in public works spending failed to get a rise out of McCormick. The *Tribune* mildly urged the White House to finance any jobs program by issuing greenbacks rather than sending "tax collectors once more and yet again into the breach." On April 26, the paper voiced sharper criticism of the Tennessee Valley Authority, a vast public works project envisioning federal purchase or construction of two dozen dams to supply electricity and flood protection to 40,000 square miles of Appalachia. Flood victims, argued McCormick, like the poor, would always be with us. Since floods were normal for rivers, "people who take advantage of the richness of river bottoms can expect to pay for their luxury." (The *New York Times* was no more enamored of the TVA, predicting that its establishment would "mark the 'low' of Congressional folly.")[4]

Behind this seeming acquiescence in the new order was the public demand for action and the president's lip service to the gods of fiscal austerity. More important than either factor in the unlikely alliance between McCormick and Roosevelt was their mutual antipathy for FDR's predecessor. Each man had reason to cast Hoover in the worst light possible. And in John Boettiger, his trusted emissary to the Roosevelt White House, McCormick had the perfect go-between. At the start of May, McCormick confided to Boettiger his hunch that Roosevelt was cagily "letting the radicals push out all their plans" as so many lightning rods. This spared FDR the unpleasant duty of openly opposing the more extreme measures generated by his administration. It also absolved him of personal responsibility for questionable legislation.[5]

Roosevelt's method of dealing with his more impractical associates was "to kid them along," Boettiger replied on May 8. "He told me the other night, confidentially of course, that he has to call them in every once in a while and hold their hands." Boettiger saw the president as "a practical radical," opposed to "violent reds" yet determined to pursue old-age pensions, unemployment insurance, and other socially advanced ideas just as soon as he got the country back on its feet. Boettiger closed his letter to McCormick with the kind of scoop a publisher lives for. "We are working on the misdeeds of the old farm board," he confided. "With some secret help from Roosevelt," the *Tribune*'s White House correspondent hoped to expose corruption in Hoover's Federal Farm Board, for McCormick a hated symbol of Washington's tendency to meddle in the free market.

A grateful McCormick invited Roosevelt to stay with him and Amy in their Astor Street townhouse when FDR visited Chicago at the end of May to open the Century of Progress Exposition. "It seems to me you are making very good weather of it in the storm," he told the president. Ten days later, he received a reply addressed "Dear Bert." Changes in his schedule had precluded Roosevelt from accepting his classmate's hospitality but not from reciprocating his generous offer. "Do let me know when you are coming to Washington," wrote FDR.[6]

✧ 2

Opening honors for the Century of Progress fell to the star Arcturus instead of the president. The fair was inaugurated using energy that had left a distant galaxy at the exact moment an earlier generation of Chicago boosters had thrown open the gates of the Columbian Exposition. The new fair, housed in a futuristic cluster of brightly colored pavilions ranged along the lakefront, celebrated the wonders of applied science. Toward William Beebe's ocean-diving bathysphere and R. Buckminster Fuller's three-wheel Dymaxion automobile, capable of covering 40 miles to the gallon at speeds up to 120 miles per hour, fair planners showed an enthusiasm akin to McCormick's unquestioning embrace of technocracy.

The May 27, 1933, opening of the Rainbow City was still two weeks off when McCormick began to have second thoughts, if not about his class-mate in the White House, then about the top-heavy Democratic majorities whooping to early passage whatever legislation Roosevelt sent up to Capi-tol Hill. All true friends of the administration, he said, would join in wishing for Congress's speedy adjournment. "Its continuance . . . is an injury to business recovery, and none of the measures it is likely to pass will help." For McCormick, the Hundred Days could not end fast enough. At the White House, however, the legislative blitz remained incomplete pending action to stimulate industrial recovery. In a May 7 fireside chat, Roosevelt had spoken vaguely of a "partnership in planning" between gov-ernment, industry, and labor. Out of this seed would grow the National Industrial Recovery Act (NIRA), hastily conceived to forestall Senator Hugo Black's "ridiculously unworkable" legislation — the description was FDR's, used in a conversation with John Boettiger — mandating a thirty-hour work week to help alleviate mass unemployment.[7]

In his May 8 letter, Boettiger had alerted McCormick that the president intended to move against "throat-cutting" competitors in private industry. As subsequently developed, the NIRA suspended the Sherman Antitrust Act in pursuit of what the historian Arthur Schlesinger has called "in-dustrial self-government through codes of fair competition." The same measure would enforce minimum wage standards, abolish child labor, establish the right of workers to organize, and authorize an enormous public works program. The bill's Senate sponsor, Robert Wagner of New York, hailed it as an essential first step toward national economic planning.

It was for precisely this reason that the *Tribune* opposed the scheme. After reading an analysis of the legislation that stressed executive authority to license business enterprises — including, quite possibly, newspapers — McCormick put a simple question to Tiffany Blake: "Is not the Industrial Law fascism?"[8]

A flurry of nervous communications among publishers preceded a June 9 meeting in New York. At first it seemed like a repeat of *Near v. Min-nesota*, with McCormick denouncing "the Industries Control Bill" and more cautious newspaperman, such as Joseph Ridder of the *New York Journal of Commerce*, dismissing his fears as exaggerated. The NIRA was an emergency measure, argued Ridder, reminiscent of Woodrow Wilson's old War Industries Board. In his opinion, the papers' response should be one of "watchful waiting." McCormick, however, pressed for a harder line. His peers came down somewhere in between. Acknowledging the futility of opposing the NIRA per se, the publishers vowed to resist any attempt to bring them under its licensing provisions "because giving the power to license gives the power to control, and such power potentially completely abridges the freedom of the press." In other words, the only code they would accept must incorporate an explicit declaration of their First Amendment rights.[9]

Four days later, lawmakers passed what Roosevelt pronounced "the most important and far-reaching legislation ever enacted by Congress." Hoping to placate his administration's warring camps, the president divided the public works section of the newly established National Recovery Administration (NRA) from the writing and enforcement of industrial codes. The former he entrusted to Harold Ickes, soon to be among the *Tribune*'s bitterest foes. For now the paper hailed Ickes, an old Chicago Progressive, as an administrator of unquestioned integrity, "well equipped to turn down the pork spoilsmen on the one hand and the contractor spoilsmen on the other." Ickes thanked the Colonel for his unexpected endorsement. "It is only right," replied McCormick, "that we should lend as much support as we can to the administration. I thoroughly believe in a party of the opposition, but I do not believe in captious criticism."[10]

Congress adjourned on June 16 after passing all fifteen major legislative proposals crafted by the White House for its review. Two days later the *Tribune* added a new demand to its daily Platform for America: "Elect Better Men to Congress." To John Boettiger, McCormick wired a half-serious inquiry: "Any chance of getting some of this easy money to put pneumatic tires on the mail trucks that are gouging up Chicago's streets without paying either licenses or gas tax?"[11]

Ickes's colorful counterpart at the NRA, General Hugh S. "Ironpants" Johnson, rushed to draft codes affecting millions of business establishments. Consequently Washington regulated the number of strips in burlesque houses and, under Code 427, promulgated guidelines for the "Curled Hair Manufacturing Industry and Horse Hair Dressing Industry." The pugnacious general sent millions of Americans into the streets under the heartlifting slogan "We Do Our Part." His genius for publicity was equaled by an alcoholic penchant for making threats. To recalcitrant employers who shunned the NRA's trademark Blue Eagle, Johnson promised "a sock right on the nose."

What he lacked in tact, Johnson more than made up for in passionate sincerity. By midsummer, industries employing nearly ten million workers had joined his crusade. Still the newspaper profession held back. Industry representatives did submit a draft code, including a passage written by McCormick that reaffirmed First Amendment freedom of expression. This was rejected by Johnson, who believed that newspapers had no special rights exempting them from NRA regulations. Off the record, he took a less belligerent tone, contenting himself with the hope that publishers might voluntarily agree to federal provisions limiting wages and hours. (He had good reason to forget his threat to use military force to enforce compliance with the new codes. The Blue Eagle took flight on strong gusts of publicity, so Johnson needed America's newspapers and advertising associations more than they needed him.)[12]

"There may be an important distinction between complying with Roosevelt's hours and wages scale and signing the [code] agreement," McCormick notified Joe Patterson on July 24. If forced to accept some measure of government oversight, he would at least try "to avoid signing on the dotted line." Weymouth Kirkland offered additional reassurance. Nothing in the NRA's "code of fair competition" should be confused with press licensing, Kirkland told McCormick. "The whole thing is nothing more or less than a boycott . . . approved by the Government."[13]

Hoping that he might yet avoid a nasty confrontation with the White House, McCormick left for a European pleasure trip at the end of July. In London he discussed politics and finance with Winston Churchill, attended a play "so vulgar as to be in bad form," and blamed extortionate taxation of the pound for choking British roads with automobiles "of the road lice variety." After a brief excursion to the Netherlands ("perhaps the most modern country in the world"), he boarded a train for Germany, another benighted land wherein democracy appeared to be a casualty of economic depression.

❖ 3

On an earlier visit to Weimar Germany, McCormick had worn a jacket with four patch pockets; nothing less would do for travelers forced to carry huge amounts of paper currency in a time of hyperinflation. The collapse of German prosperity had discredited Weimar-style liberalism and opened the door to Hitler and his National Socialist movement.

Within days of Hitler's designation as chancellor in January 1933, the *Tribune* had denounced Nazi persecution of German Jews as a hateful reminder of the Dark Ages. Yet when pressed by his editorial writers to strike fresh blows at the regime, McCormick held back. Claiming to be "very much concerned" about anti-Semitism in the United States, he feared the scapegoating of Jews, who were widely believed, as a class, to be "much better off than the average run of people." This bred feelings of envy, he explained, which grew ugly in periods of economic distress. Indeed, said McCormick, "I don't see how the next election can avoid the Hebrew issue. With governors of the two principal states both Democrats and both Jews, with two judges of the United States Supreme Court both Democrats and both Jews, political expediency will point the Republicans towards a Ku Klux movement." The less drum-beating by the press, he hinted broadly, the less chance that America would succumb to the racial and religious divisions then poisoning Europe. "I feel . . . a very great sense of duty to protect the Jews in this country," he concluded, "but not abroad."[14]

In giving instructions to Sigrid Schultz, now the *Tribune*'s Berlin bureau chief, however, McCormick sounded more like a Nazi apologist. It had always been difficult for Americans, he said, bound together by loyalty to republican institutions, to understand how the Germans saw themselves "as a race rather than a nation" — with a corresponding intolerance for Jews and anyone else deemed to be an alien influence.[15]

Schultz, a forty-year-old Chicago native who had been raised in Europe by artist parents, found Hitler's mass appeal incomprehensible. Before the Colonel arrived in Berlin on August 7, she told him that the Nazi leader inspired comparisons with "a cheap hysterical actor." McCormick, too, professed to be amused by the more outlandish trappings of the regime, beginning with the Nazi salute, a gesture "which only the fanaticism of the givers can save from the ridiculous." In the course of their travels through the Reich, Schultz introduced her employer to the intricacies of German wines. Much less welcome was some intelligence she imparted during a mass review of 150,000 storm troopers.[16]

"I was sitting beside the Colonel and I could see his soldier's heart throbbing," recalled Schultz almost half a century later. "The way they marched was just absolutely beautiful." Afraid that McCormick might be swept off his feet by the spectacle, she drew his attention to Ernst Rohm, a Hitler confidant who was to pay dearly for his command of the burgeoning SA, or Storm Section, of the Nazi movement. "Colonel," Schultz explained above the din of the crowd, "the little man there right beside Rohm is his former lover, and his other lover, the new one, is standing right behind."[17]

At an American embassy luncheon later in the day, the scandalized McCormick denounced his own correspondent. "That Schultz is terrible," he muttered to embassy staffers, who assured their guest that Miss Schultz had only rippled the surface of Nazi sexual depravity. In a later commentary, McCormick himself repeated whispered allegations linking Captain Rohm to the crime "that no man can live down." He suggested that even greater names in the Reich were grist for the salacious rumor mill.[18]

Gossip aside, the *Tribune* described Nazism as "a passing insanity, caused by fear and temporarily powerful fallacies." While Hitler played at being a Teutonic Julius Caesar, wrote McCormick, "the gangsters who surround him" conducted their reign of terror. Suspected Communists, members of opposition parties banned under the regime's organic Law for Removing the Distress of the People and Reich, and all Jews faced constant threats of violence and imprisonment. No business office was without government agents, observed McCormick, mindful of Roosevelt's accelerating campaign to bring American enterprise within the long arm of the

National Recovery Administration. Some of these were mere busybodies, others industrial spies enlisted by the Nazi state to make off with American secrets. Not only were German newspapers censored; "they are told exactly what to say on any subject that any high up Nazi is interested in."[19]

A defender of the regime, aware of McCormick's ongoing crusade to keep American newspapers out of the clutches of Hugh Johnson and his Blue Eagle, couldn't resist drawing parallels between "Herr Johnson" and Hermann Goering, another military hero turned political revolutionary. The comparison struck uncomfortably close to home for McCormick, fresh from observing brownshirted censors wielding blue pencils on the German press. "Poor Jews, poor Germans," he concluded. "A bitter road lies ahead of both."

McCormick was sufficiently alarmed by what he had seen — and its implications for his own country — that he cut short his European jaunt and sailed for home on August 12. The blinkers of class had not been entirely discarded, as Sigrid Schultz learned after questioning the reliability of an aristocratic former army officer named Alexander von Schimpf, with whom McCormick had had several conversations before he left Germany. Although von Schimpf was not yet enrolled in the Nazi party, Schultz warned her employer that it was only a matter of time before he joined its ranks, thereby rendering himself useless as a *Tribune* source. "He's a gentleman," McCormick protested. "You can rely on him whether he's a Nazi or not."[20]

❖ 4

Another factor spurring McCormick to leave Germany was economic self-interest. In his absence, *Tribune* representatives had challenged a proposed NRA code governing the manufacture of newsprint. Under section 3-e of the National Industrial Recovery Act, the president was authorized to restrict imports of any foreign product threatening the delicate balance of prices and supply mandated by Congress. Mindful of the *Tribune*'s vulnerability, McCormick oscillated in the weeks following his return between friendly criticism of the Blue Eagle, to which he acknowledged a "patriotic duty" to lend all possible assistance, and reminders of newspapermen's obligation "to publish the truth as they see it, without fear and despite all threats."

When Roosevelt came to Chicago early in October 1933 to address the convention of the American Legion, the *Tribune* led the chorus of cheers for a leader whose "buoyant confidence and undismayed optimism" were proving contagious. The pendulum swung violently a few days later, as it became known that Roosevelt intended to extend formal recognition to the Soviet Union. The president was sadly mistaken, the

Tribune contended on October 25, if he thought the Russian bear had been domesticated.

Two days after this salvo, John Boettiger put a question to Roosevelt at a White House press conference. "There has been noted in various parts of the world increasing curtailment of the freedom of the press," he said, using the exact words urged on him by the Colonel. "Will you give your views on this question?"

"You can say to Bert McCormick that he has been seeing things under the bed," said Roosevelt, plainly annoyed.[21]

Early in November, McCormick teamed up with Pathe Movie News to deliver a warning about the NRA to millions of filmgoers. His wooden speaking style posed no threat to FDR's mastery of the airwaves, but it was enough to provoke the excitable Hugh Johnson on a Chicago visit into a verbal broadside aimed at "gentlemen of the fourth estate" who were guilty, in Johnson's words, of "primitive witch doctor dancing." Roosevelt directed his press secretary, Steve Early, to keep a scrapbook of *Tribune* clippings demonstrating animus toward the New Deal. McCormick moved to fill it quickly. In response to a delegation of Chicago merchants pleading for a halt to his attacks on the Blue Eagle, the Colonel ordered a brutal front-page cartoon from the caustic pen of Carey Orr. It showed a group of desperate people separated from tantalizing piles of food, clothing, and fuel by a barbed wire fence and the looming letters NRA. Orr's title, "No Recovery Anywhere," said it all.[22]

On the evening of Sunday, November 12, Roosevelt enlivened a White House scrambled-egg supper with complaints of McCormick's continuing hostility. Soon after, John Boettiger discovered Steve Early in his office on a Saturday morning, "getting up the material for the president's broadcast" denouncing the *Tribune* and the *New York Herald Tribune* as enemies of national recovery. The planned speech never came off; Roosevelt evidently thought better of giving his critics confirming evidence of press intimidation.[23]

At the end of December, Arthur Sears Henning, the Washington bureau chief, regaled his boss with an account of FDR's tasteless performance at a recent Gridiron Dinner. Before this elite audience, the president had observed that as proof that his political honeymoon was over, he only had to look at the number of sore brides plaguing him. If FDR became too "disagreeable," McCormick replied irrelevantly, the *Tribune* could always report the number of occasions on which he had had himself painted or sculpted since entering the White House: "I bet it is an all-time record."[24]

That Christmas, McCormick gave John Boettiger $1,000 on top of his usual bonus. In the next breath he instructed Boettiger to tell the president that he shouldn't listen to White House tattlers who had tagged the Colonel as "a sweatshopper." And he sent along a front-page story dedicating the *Tribune*'s New Year's open house to "a busy 1933." There was more to the gesture than empty flattery. Whatever the shortcomings of the NRA — and the left distrusted its domination by big business as fully as conservatives resented government control of the marketplace — it had lifted the national mood. More modestly, the program had also raised the indices of economic output.[25]

Part of the growth in purchasing power claimed by the Blue Eagle found its way into the *Tribune*'s coffers. Profits, which had bottomed out at $3 million in 1932, climbed to $3.7 million in the first Roosevelt year (a figure that did not include over $5 million in black ink run up by the *New York Daily News*). Ironically, it was the passing of the crisis atmosphere that made the Blue Eagle an endangered species. Early in February 1934, the administration declared its intention to modify the newspaper draft code in ways objectionable to the publishers. McCormick called for a national meeting of industry leaders to weigh their next step. Before he could implement his strategy, General Johnson invited a new round of talks aimed at breaking the impasse. On February 17, Roosevelt reluctantly gave way. Determined to have the last word nevertheless, the president called the resulting guarantee of press freedom "pure surplusage," having no more place in the code than the Ten Commandments.

McCormick was hardly more gracious in victory. "There has never been a spending orgy with less intelligent thought of the future since Louis XVI," he grumbled. The time had come, he told his editorial staff, to organize America's property owners. "They are the forgotten people."[26]

A few weeks earlier McCormick had accepted "with pleasure" an invitation from the March of Dimes to lend his name to a nationwide series of fund-raising balls coinciding with Roosevelt's fifty-second birthday. All proceeds were to be earmarked for the Warm Springs Foundation, organized by FDR to help carry on the war against polio. Last-minute preparations for the festivities were under way on the afternoon of January 30, 1934, when the Colonel asked the financial writer Howard Wood to come to his office.

"Howard, I know you collect unusual headlines. This is one you cannot have."

McCormick slid a piece of paper across the smooth marble surface to a spot where Wood could make out the words: PRESIDENT'S BALLS TO COME OFF TONIGHT.

"I suppose," sighed McCormick, "that is rather too much to hope for."[27]

✦ 5

"I am certainly not looking for a quarrel," McCormick told John Boettiger at the beginning of March 1934. Squelching rumors that he might be calling on Roosevelt at the White House, he recalled earlier visits he had paid to Taft and Hoover. Both presidents had felt betrayed when the Colonel had assailed their policies after enjoying their hospitality. He had no desire to repeat the experience with Roosevelt. Besides, if he crossed the presidential threshold just then, "the conversation would have to veer around to unpleasant topics."[28]

This was an understatement. Before April 1, the *Tribune* would take issue with FDR's latest attempt to regulate the barons of Wall Street, hinting darkly that some around the president wanted nothing less than "a proletarian dictatorship." McCormick bristled over federal restrictions on cotton growers "worse than the fugitive slave law" of the nineteenth century. At least the slaves, whatever their other mistreatment, hadn't been starved to death. Under the new policy, he claimed, "men will be sent to the penitentiary for trying to earn the price of a loaf of bread, and the landowners will turn their unfortunate tenants and employees out to starve in order to raise the price of clothing to working people."[29]

The lack of military credentials among Roosevelt's inner circle also disturbed McCormick. "Are we ruled by a cabal of slackers?" he asked his editorial staff. In April, the *Tribune* ran a week-long parade of articles purporting to expose the foreign origins and outlook of those who had Roosevelt's ear. Three classes made up the new order in Washington, wrote Boettiger. By far the most powerful were the collectivists, led by agricultural utopians such as Secretary Henry Wallace and his youthful undersecretary, the former Columbia professor Rexford G. Tugwell. "If the New Deal means anything," Boettiger quoted Wallace as saying, "it means the subordination of capital rights and property rights to human rights." Of somewhat greater embarrassment to the administration was Wallace's assertion, made in his book, *Statesmanship and Religion*, that Lenin, Mussolini, and Hitler were comparable in their "tremendous earnestness" to those sixteenth-century Protestant revolutionaries Luther, Calvin, and Knox.[30]

Another collectivist was Donald Richburg, general counsel to the NRA. When not ridiculing traditionalist members of the League of Stuffed Shirts, Richburg assailed the daily press for "playing upon the taut nerves and raw prejudices of our bewildered and long-suffering victims of economic ill health" — in short, for criticizing the NRA. As seen by the *Tribune*, the collectivists, not content to subvert the cabinet or neuter Congress, wished to exploit the economic emergency in order to place government in direct competition with the private sector. Thus Hoover's old Reconstruction Finance Corporation, now reorganized by the professoriat of the Brain Trust, held in its grip virtually the entire banking and credit system of the country. Likewise, TVA planners, turning a deaf ear to complaints that they were driving private power companies out of existence, pushed ahead with what the *Tribune* called "the socialization of the Columbia River and Missouri River valleys."

Second in importance to the collectivists, wrote Boettiger, were the legalists, most recruited for the New Deal by the Harvard Law School professor Felix Frankfurter. Their radicalism was of a different hue. "The Legalists want to regulate society," following in the footsteps of their Wilsonian hero, Justice Louis Brandeis, "while the Collectivists want to control it." A third group, as subject to fluctuating influence as the currency to which they gave their undivided allegiance, was the monetarists. Typical of this school was the Yale economist who espoused "a commodity dollar, the value of which would be altered from month to month by presidential edict, according to the rise or fall of commodity prices."

Unabashedly experimental, the early New Deal found consistency in the centralization of economic power and the personalization of the presidency. To many conservatives, Roosevelt encouraged a cult of personality reminiscent of Europe's dictators. "The shadow of Hitler is on the government walls," charged the *Tribune* in May 1934. Such accusations did not go unnoticed, or unpunished. Boettiger urged the White House to designate Chicago's proposed lakefront airport, long advocated by McCormick, as a worthy recipient of public works money. Roosevelt said that he would have to take the matter up with Secretary Ickes. Yet Ickes wasn't talking — not, at least, to the *Tribune*. "The *Tribune* is so vicious," he explained while declining to be interviewed.

In his autobiography, the combative Ickes reproduced a bit of doggerel composed at the Colonel's expense.

> There is a news fellow named Bert,
> To whom Ickes is just a hair shirt;
> Like a pig to his sty,
> He runs straight as a die
> To get him more handfuls of dirt.[31]

This was both harsh and more than a little foolish, yet also understandable, given the tendency even of solid journalists like Boettiger to slant their reporting in line with McCormick's prejudices. The *Tribune* alumnus Greer Williams wrote scathingly of a corporate culture that sacrificed accuracy to curry favor with the twenty-fourth floor, from which all blessings flowed, along with the "RRMC assignments" accorded priority treatment. These required careful translation. For instance, a reporter asked for the number of musicians of military age employed by the Works Progress Administration was actually, by Williams's account, being ordered to unmask the WPA's musicians project as a haven for young pacifists and Communists.

It took Williams six months to gratify the Colonel's curiosity over the relationship between unemployment and syphilis. "I first tried writing a story giving the known facts," Williams said afterward, "but this was not what was wanted. I was expected to prove that syphilis was more prevalent among Chicago relief clients than among the employed, which I finally did, after hounding four government agencies into making a joint survey." During the summer of 1934, McCormick demanded a fresh round of stories about New Deal graft, "such as use of government steamers as private yachts; putting the children on the payroll, like the Ickes children; the use of government airplanes by Johnson and . . . not excluding the marvelous Mr. Farley." The Washington bureau was ordered to examine the first lady's use of a special train from Miami to Washington.[32]

Looking ahead to the fall elections, the *Tribune* proposed creation of a third political force, the American party, to provide more effective opposition to the New Deal than shell-shocked Republicans were able to muster. Riots in half a dozen cities were on McCormick's mind when he celebrated his fifty-fourth birthday on July 30 by delivering, via NBC radio, his highly personal take on "The Rising Red Tide in America." He blamed the pitched battles between militant union men and the forces of law and order on addled Brain Trusters who hoped to color urban pavements "a little red." What further outrages lay in store? That, said McCormick, could only be guessed at, pending the election of another rubber-stamp Congress "willing to pass without reading it further legislation written in the little red house in Georgetown in the spirit of the big red square in Moscow."

One week after his broadcast, McCormick raised a new and urgent concern with John Boettiger: "I am constantly receiving rumors that Trotsky is in this country directing a revolution. What can you get from the Immigration and State Departments?"[33]*

✧ 6

To modern ears, McCormick's fears sound absurd. Seen against the context of his times, his class, and his growing isolation, however, his fulminations lose some of their paranoid tinge. If 1933 was the year when the emperor exposed his nakedness, 1934 witnessed a spontaneous movement by the dispossessed to ransack what remained of the royal wardrobe and overturn kingly authority wherever it oppressed the commons. That January, Huey Long went national with his Share Our Wealth crusade,

*FDR was not adverse to pursuing rumors of his own. In August 1934, an angry president obtained from the War Department an accounting of McCormick's military service.

aimed at redistributing the national bounty by dissolving private fortunes and legislating a universal minimum wage. Within a year Long had a mailing list of 7.5 million names. Roosevelt tacked left in an attempt to steal his rival's thunder and prevent the bayou populist from seeking the White House on a third-party ticket in 1936.

From his Shrine of the Little Flower outside Detroit, Father Charles Coughlin preached the virtues of inflation and decried the pagan god of gold to a weekly radio audience conservatively estimated at thirty million listeners. Once a Roosevelt supporter who had not hesitated to proclaim that "the New Deal is Christ's deal," the radio priest had recently parted company with FDR over his economic policies. McCormick editorialized on behalf of Father Coughlin's right to speak at Soldier Field (just as he denounced the small-town censors of Taylorville, Illinois, who wanted to prevent the Socialist leader Norman Thomas from addressing an audience there). Otherwise the *Tribune* was no friend of the priest's. To one insistent Coughlinite demanding to know why the *Tribune* failed to share Coughlin's view of bankers as worse criminals than Capone or John Dillinger, McCormick replied, "We do not write at the dictation of agitators."[34]

Class warfare threatened to give way to military action when textile workers in twenty states took advantage of the Labor Day holiday to stage the biggest single strike in U.S. history. In targeting the NRA's restrictive Cotton Code Authority for much of their wrath, the strikers reaffirmed McCormick in his conviction that government should stay out of the cotton fields. Farm blood flowed through McCormick's veins. His grandfather had helped to organize the first Farmer's Club in Illinois. For many years Medill had written a *Tribune* column devoted to plow handles and crop rotation. Carrying on in this tradition, McCormick risked the displeasure of his cousins at International Harvester by campaigning in the pages of the *Tribune* to bring back the horse. In motorizing American agriculture, he argued, farmers had denied themselves a market for their oats. Besides, horses were cheaper than tractors.

Eager to offer an alternative to the killing of pigs and plowing up of crops sanctioned by the AAA, McCormick in the spring of 1934 established an experimental farm on 1,300 acres of rich prairie earth in Yorkville, Illinois, less than a two-hour drive from Chicago. Here he conducted tests involving eighty-five plant varieties, many imported from exotic foreign locales. He planted twenty-two kinds of soybeans and five strains of millet. He pursued a new barley crop containing more starch and less nitrogen than the barley Americans were used to. Visitors to the Tribune Farm were shown how to improve pasturelands without resorting to lime or other forms of soil doctoring. They were introduced to shrubs and seedling trees as agents in the war against erosion. Barnyard raids by hungry brown hawks shared column space in the *Tribune* with attacks on German Jews by Hitler's brownshirts.*

In 1935 McCormick opened a second experimental farm, at his Cantigny estate in Wheaton. That June, 8,000 sunburned onlookers, many of them pasty-faced urbanites getting their first whiff of clover and new-mown hay, attended an old-fashioned horse pulling contest in the Colonel's back yard. Amid the bucolic surroundings, it was easy to forget that the apostle of technocracy had just announced plans to spend $400,000 to make Tribune Tower one of the world's largest fully air-conditioned office buildings.

In September 1934, radio station WGN joined hands with sister stations in Newark, Detroit, and Cincinnati to form the Mutual Broadcasting System. The president of the new network, William McFarlane, had polished his skills as the *Tribune*'s business manager. By the end of the decade, Mutual counted 109 affiliates in 29 states. Long before then McCormick broke ground on a $500,000 radio complex adjoining Tribune Tower. Tower office space was 80 percent occupied in the summer of 1934, a sharp increase over recent years. Since Roosevelt's inauguration, the daily *Tribune* had nearly doubled in size. Monthly income was up some $200,000.

This and more about the internal workings of the paper was known to the White House thanks to a deputy collector of internal revenue who found time, after pursuing delinquent income taxes, to forward to IRS headquarters in Washington a daily pastiche of Chicago newspaper clippings critical of the administration. The same informant wrote directly to Roosevelt's alter ego, Louis Howe, who gratefully responded that his correspondent should "always feel free to write me at any time regarding such matters." (Howe shared his findings with Steve Early. He also sent to the Justice Department a letter from a Chicagoan claiming to possess information about the *Tribune* which, "if followed to conclusion, would cause them to cease their attacks upon the President.")[35]

Taking Howe at his word, in August 1934 the tax collector reported a funereal atmosphere at Republican headquarters on North Michigan Avenue. With his friend Ed Kelly in city hall and several *Tribune* alumni holding important positions in the Kelly administration, the Colonel hoped to cut a deal with the Democratic crowd that had dominated Chicago politics ever since the demise of Big Bill Thompson. The *Tribune*, it was whispered, would go easy on the local Democratic ticket in return

---

*The summer of 1934 was a tense one for Sigrid Schultz, forced to telephone some of her more "dynamite" stories on the Nazi regime via Paris or London — and to plead with the Colonel to have "the Paris boys" tone down the more explosive portions for European consumption. "There is no use getting the tiger madder than he is — and is he mad!" Still, said the gutsy Miss Schultz, "I don't think I've held back on a single story I firmly believed was true and I don't intend to."

for tacit support of GOP congressional candidates. "In a life filled with mis-takes," McCormick told Kelly late in 1934, "I look upon you as one of my great successes." It was a welcome change, he added, for Chicago to have a mayor "we can put on exhibition." Yet Kelly never forgot that his first alle-giance was to Roosevelt. As another sign of the Colonel's diminished clout, Republican voters in the tenth congressional district repudiated his protégé James Simpson in favor of a rival endorsed by Harold Ickes.[36]

On July 4, 1934, McCormick combined his passion for color printing with his spread-eagle patriotism by publishing a special pull-out of the Constitution, with each line pertaining to individual liberties set off in blue ink. He waved the flag still more conspicuously by sponsoring a Constitu-tion Day extravaganza that drew nearly 400,000 visitors to the Century of Progress on September 17. "You cannot have it both ways," he told the crowd via radio hookup. "There is no way station between democracy and tyranny; between honesty and anarchy." In the despotism of Russia, Italy, and Germany, where "everyone rises in terror and lies down in dread," McCormick glimpsed the shadows of the NRA and AAA. He credited a century and a half of American progress to the Constitution, a document more notable for the limits it placed on government than for the authority it bestowed on republican rulers. "Do not let men coming in a Trojan horse with pretended gifts take it away from you," he concluded.

As the fall campaign entered its final days, the *Tribune* took heart from historical trends that favored the "out" party in nonpresidential years. His-tory was repealed in November 1934. Republican membership fell to less than a third of the Senate and under a quarter of the House. Among the rare survivors poking their heads above the New Deal tidal wave was the wry, middle-of-the-road governor of Kansas, Alfred M. Landon. He had precious little company.

The *Tribune* responded in character to the electoral rout. It charged the victorious Democrats with converting the entire U.S. Treasury into a cam-paign fund with which to bribe the electorate. McCormick found what consolation he could in the past. In this he emulated his British friend Winston Churchill, whose autobiography the *Tribune* purchased for syn-dication in the autumn of 1934. "What a disappointment the Twentieth Century has been," lamented Churchill. "Leadership of the privileged has passed; but it has not been succeeded by that of the eminent."

Much as the two men might share an elegiac longing for dying stan-dards, they disagreed over Churchill's Victorian elite. McCormick said as much in the preface to his biography of Ulysses Grant, published in time for Christmas. "There are two groups of people," declared the author, employing his gift for sweeping generalization. The first was "those whose sympathy, instinct, tradition guide them toward everything that may be construed as democratic, liberal, and idealistic." In the opposing camp was to be found everyone "whose hopes and feelings exalt whatever points toward royalist and aristocratic conceptions of life." Grant's reputation had suffered grievously at the hands of the second group, whose membership included far too many "servile Americans" overawed by foreign generals.

McCormick persuaded few reviewers that Grant deserved to rank above Lee, Napoleon, and Alexander in the military pantheon. *Time* dismissed the book as "an avowedly partisan attempt to paint Grant with whitewash bright and glistening." Henry Steele Commager, writing in the *New York Herald Tribune*, was more generous, balancing praise of McCormick's "lively description and lucid analysis" with disparagement of his dogmatism and rhetorical overkill. As one might expect, the book revealed more about McCormick than about Grant. The Colonel considered himself qualified to rescue Grant's historical reputation, he remarked to a friend, "because I am not required to accept the dictates of society, civil or military."[37]

It was that disdain for convention, that willingness to operate outside the rutted channels of conservative thought, that prompted no less a New Dealer than Henry Wallace to observe privately that Colonel McCormick was himself something of a prairie populist.[38]

❖ 7

Reviews of his Grant book were just beginning to appear when McCormick learned, on Christmas Eve 1934, that the IRS had disallowed a $512,242.12 loss claimed by the Tribune company on its sale of *Liberty* two years earlier. He sustained another setback that month when John Boettiger left the *Tribune* to marry Anna Roosevelt. McCormick offered Boettiger an executive position with the paper in Chicago. When that proved impractical, he wished the couple a long and joyous life together, suspended judgment on Social Security legislation newly proposed by Boettiger's father-in-law, and turned his attention to events beyond American shores.

The trouble with his country's foreign policy, McCormick declared in February 1935, was its domination by "Tory-Colonial-minded" leaders who wished to return the United States to its former position of inferiority. For his part, he was more inclined than ever to keep his distance from the Old World, whose dictators showed every day how promises of economic security could lead to one-man rule. He doubted the survival prospects of the Spanish republic, increasingly dominated by left-wing elements. "What began as a justifiable effort to do away with ancient tyrannies" in feudal Spain, said the *Tribune*, "has been turned into the greatest of all tyrannies, anarchy."

Regarding Asia, the old fear of yellow domination resurfaced. "Japan is apparently determined to find an excuse for war with the United States," McCormick wrote early in 1935. "They have driven us out of the Philippines, the Yop and the Aleutian Islands. They now attempt to prevent our fortifying Hawaii, and they have objected to our even keeping a navy in the Pacific. I can see no other possible conclusion to draw." To counter such threats, the Colonel supported army mechanization and the consolidation of services. "I get so tired of people trying to frighten us out of preparedness," he complained to Tiffany Blake. "It is the losers who do most of the suffering in war. The savage countries, Japan, Russia, Germany and Italy, are all arming and organizing to the limit. They are the ones who will not hesitate at any brutality. Our only protection is to be stronger than they are."[39]

If the world refused to do his bidding, then he would fashion a world of his own at Cantigny. Notwithstanding his strictures on the high-born critics of General Grant, McCormick was an aristocrat to his fingertips. Hadn't his father told him so? Now, at a time of economic desperation, when the scales of history appeared to be decisively tipped against the landed classes with their pillared homes and social carelessness, the Colonel would spend his mother's money to realize belatedly his father's fantasies. In doing so, he would also proclaim his own status as the ideological descendant of Thomas Jefferson.

The idea of transforming Joseph Medill's graceful frame dwelling into something much grander first came to McCormick in the late twenties. "Now I know why architects are insane," he confessed to Raymond Hood in September 1929, after spending several frustrating hours on a train trying to sketch the perfect floor plan. "It's quite simple to get a general idea, but how to fit the skeleton and the blood vessels, to say nothing of the lungs and the liver, into the carcass, is something else again." Initially, he envisioned "a comfortable flat for Mrs. McCormick and me to live in and three or four very effective living rooms." Bedrooms should be placed at the opposite end of the house from the public rooms "so that the somnolent ones will be away from the traditional, if imaginary, whoopee." The windows of his dream house must be big enough to be impressive, and spaced "to look like Mount Vernon plus Hampton Court."[40]

In the end Hood was too busy with other projects to supply more than preliminary guidance. McCormick then engaged the services of Willis Irwin, the Georgia architect responsible for Whitehall, his traditional southern brick mansion in Aiken. "I am as ambitious for the new house as I was for Tribune Tower," the Colonel excitedly told Irwin. Amy took a different view of things. She had no desire to live in a public building, much less a shrine to her husband's ancestors. The existing house, she believed, was more than adequate for the needs of a childless middle-aged couple.[41]

Here, perhaps unwittingly, she struck a raw nerve, for McCormick's phobias about fire and noise, developed as an artilleryman in the war (in later years he moved out of one Washington house because he could hear servants walking past his third-floor bedroom door), were as nothing compared to his fear of being forgotten. He said as much in a 1935 pamphlet entitled "Why So Much House." "If the efforts of the designers and builders shall prove successful," he wrote, "the bricks piled here will remain a while, a fitting monument at the western portal of the city." One did not have to be clairvoyant — or married to the homeowner — to see who was being memorialized.

Irwin proposed a relatively modest residence west of Medill's farmhouse and beyond the sounds of traffic on busy Roosevelt Road. McCormick vetoed the idea, saying that a hilltop house of one story would resemble a lump of butter on a stack of buckwheat cakes. Fearing the visual effect of Virginia brick on Illinois eyes a century in the future, he wondered whether it might not be wiser to use native stone. The issue was mooted when early estimates placed the cost of the new house, brick or stone, at more than $300,000. The Depression curtailed McCormick's plans until the death of his mother in 1932 and the explosive success of the *New York Daily News* made him a wealthy man in his own right.[42]

In 1934 the project was revived, on a bigger scale than ever. "I suppose that the Villa d'Este and the Taj Mahal were designed and landscaped at the same time," McCormick breezily informed Irwin that spring. A recent stable fire had killed a dozen of his finest Irish hunters, blue-ribbon winners with names like Fan Tan, Silverheels, and Grand Duke. With the memory of charred horseflesh all too vivid, McCormick demanded that the new house be fireproof. At his age, he had no desire to sleep on the second floor, he said. Every ground-floor room must have its own fire escape route. Double-thick steel plates recessed into the walls would guarantee that family books, pictures, and documents wouldn't be at risk from a careless cigarette — assuming that any guest dared to light up in the Colonel's presence.[43]

To solve the noise problem, Irwin turned the existing house around, facing it away from the congested highway. The architect sheathed the 1896 dwelling in brick, being careful to preserve its New England portico. On each side he constructed enormous wings, the one to the west containing bedrooms and servants' quarters and the one to the east housing McCormick's 5,000 books and family memorabilia. McCormick was adamant that the house should complement the natural terrain. He preserved oaks and chestnuts originally planted by Joseph Medill even if they intruded on an otherwise perfect vista. "They were here first," he said.[44]*

McCormick's original vision of a simple flat and a few substantial public rooms underwent a radical transformation, one having more to do with politics than with architecture. By the time he actually broke ground on the project, late in 1934, the Colonel had nailed his anti-Roosevelt colors to the mast of constitutionalism. It was only logical for the new house, whose construction coincided with "the opening of the fight to destroy the American Constitution," to become, in McCormick's words, "a shrine to human liberty." So wedded to the wisdom of the founders that he inserted their names into the exterior walls of his house, the squire of Cantigny took his homage a step further by reproducing the look of Jefferson's Monticello and Madison's Montpelier (in the Madison Porch, he wedged in bricks from Lincoln's tomb, Fort Sumter, and Boston's Old North Church). Adding to the theme of house as history lesson, niches were left for statues of Washington and Patrick Henry, both "looking into the morning," said McCormick, "in token that we will not allow their work to be destroyed." Amy disliked the idea in theory and the completed figures in practice. She won a rare victory when the toga-clad Washington was banished to the cellar and wrought-iron standards took the place of Revolutionary heroes.

Few construction projects are without their surprises, and Cantigny was no exception. While enjoying the view from the Madison Porch one day, the Colonel was stung by a bee. This necessitated wrapping the huge terrace in glass and a fine-mesh netting originally used to strain pulp in a Canadian paper mill. Of far greater consequence was the decision to paint the vast house — all 160 feet of it — white. McCormick and Irwin instantly regretted their action. Crews were put to work chipping and sandblasting the freshly coated brick. Quite by accident, the operation produced a soft rose patina pleasing to all.

Inside, the house was filled with Amy's favorite French Provincial furnishings and delicate Aubusson carpets. British hunting prints adorned the walls of a sitting room that had once been Joseph Medill's library. In the basement, Irwin placed a private movie theater, with walls of shimmering silver leaf. Bedrooms wore plaques commemorating visits by Charles Lindbergh and Charles Summerall. To reach McCormick's library, formally christened Liberty Hall but universally identified as the Big Room,

---

*It was the trees and their precarious long-term prospects that drove McCormick to Otto Kerner, then Illinois's attorney general, in hopes of guaranteeing Cantigny for the enjoyment of future generations. "We have ample parks and playgrounds," he said, "and very little preservation of nature." Might there be a way for people to experience Cantigny while safeguarding the beauties of the estate against "unlimited public trampling?" This foreshadowed his decision to bequeath the estate in trust for the enjoyment of the people of Illinois.

guests walked through a hallway lined with swords and souvenirs acquired in the Colonel's travels. Stepping down, they found themselves in a stunning space, forty-four feet long, with twenty-two-foot-high walls paneled in Brazilian butternut. Overhead, hundreds of tiny recessed bulbs supplied an early form of indirect lighting.

The room boasted two large fireplaces and a device inspired by Jefferson's dumbwaiter at Monticello, which, when activated by a key in the mantelpiece, brought up four-foot logs from the basement. A portrait of Joseph Medill hung above the south mantel, while the north wall was dominated by an oil likeness of the Colonel in his World War I uniform, painted by Amy. Without comment, McCormick placed his mother's picture above the art deco bar. The furnishings, in common with everything else about the Big Room, were built to the outsize expectations of their owner. "I want the new house to last a very long time," McCormick instructed his architect, "and possibly become one of the showplaces of Chicagoland because of its sheer beauty."

Willis Irwin served his patron too well. For all its elephantine dignity, his design never resolved the fundamental contradiction between a livable house and a monument to family self-importance. Cantigny was built for posterity, not for the humans who temporarily sojourned under its roof before McCormick's will declared it public property. Today's house exudes a chill deeper than the constant sixty degrees McCormick insisted upon in his rooms.

❖ 8

While her husband rebuilt Medill's 15,000-square-foot residence to reflect his self-image as the scion of Virginia aristocrats, Amy found shelter in a small cottage cum artist's studio she called Bois de Madame. Located almost a mile south of the main house, her getaway symbolized the lengths to which she would go in search of a separate existence. Her days were spent reading, walking her dogs, visiting her purebred Guernsey cattle (each one identified by its own brass nameplate in Cantigny's model dairy), and working in the estate gardens.

Sixty years old in 1932, "a little on the dumpy side" as recalled by a young visitor to Cantigny, Amy excelled at bridge and hostess duties. She organized a women's guild to distribute lilacs to Chicago's sick and shut-in. On visits to Palm Beach, she exchanged her riding togs for rod and reel with which to catch pompano, tarpon, and sailfish. Only the sporty two-door Packard she drove around Aiken and the nasty, protracted legal fight she waged against a Long Island banker who had sold her a lame setter, which eventually divided the Aiken polo colony into pro- and anti-

McCormick camps, set her apart from the company of utterly conventional society matrons.[45]

Beginning in May 1931, Amy served as master of foxhounds for the DuPage Hunt Club, organized by her husband's cousin and Wheaton neighbor, Chauncey McCormick. It was their shared interest in the hunt that led Bert and Amy to join Grasslands, a new club laid out in the undulating landscape of western Tennessee, not far from Nashville. The development was the brainchild of Joseph Thomas, a Yale classmate of McCormick's, who since leaving New Haven had distinguished himself as a builder of New York apartments and the author of the definitive *Hounds and Hunting Through the Ages*. In 1930, hoping to spur business at his resort, Thomas founded the Grasslands International Steeplechase, patterned after England's Grand National.

McCormick paid his first visit to the area in 1929. Clambering down from his amphibious plane, he seemed "an amiable gentleman in British costume" to Frank Waldrop, then a young reporter from the *Nashville Tennessean* sent by his editor to interview "the shocking editor of the awful *Chicago Tribune*." Among southerners, the *Tribune* was about as popular as General Sherman, yet McCormick gave Waldrop a surprisingly empathetic assessment of the region as seen from the air. He even offered the services of the newspaper in promoting reforestation of the area.[46]

On subsequent trips to Grasslands, McCormick took Amy, for whom the club promised a welcome alternative to the sudden chill besetting Aiken. She did not linger once it became obvious that her husband was having an affair with Joe Thomas's wife. Clara Fargo Thomas had been born to wealth; her father, James, was the guiding force behind the American Express traveler's check. Accustomed to rarefied social settings, Clara made a most presentable mistress. Like Amy, she was an artist; her murals graced the homes and offices of Vincent Astor and Percy Rockefeller. A onetime Broadway set designer, she thrived in the fast lane of New York. Her vitality and sex appeal only exacerbated the nineteen-year difference between her and Mrs. McCormick.

The affair seemed eerily reminiscent of the Colonel's raid a generation before on the Adams household. Once again there was a cuckolded friend, unable to compete with his rival's power and wealth; a straying wife, blinded by McCormick's status; and a disapproving old woman, the Kate McCormick role now cruelly assigned to Amy. Something about McCormick required the ego gratification that came from stealing another man's wife. Yet something else shrank from repeating the scandal of his marriage.

Whether wooing a mistress or building a house, McCormick would have what he wanted and damn the cost. To the end of his days he carried a small scar on his lip as evidence of the price incurred by his passion for Clara Thomas. He got it one night when the Ford in which he and Clara were riding missed a bridge in a torrential rainstorm and plunged into Pilot Knob Creek. Clara's classic profile was split from hairline to nose tip. A country doctor stitched her up. Two days passed before McCormick, embarrassed yet stoical, returned to seek attention for an inch-and-a-half gash across the floor of his mouth.[47]

It was only a matter of time before Clara was commissioned to adorn her lover's office in New York with a mural celebrating the glories of a free press. The sixteen-by-twenty-four-foot painting, later displayed in the lobby of Tribune Tower, depicted heroes from Socrates to Tom Paine. Its most indelible image was of a man biting a dog.

By then Clara was willing to leave her husband and three children to marry the Colonel. Yet McCormick, having precipitated one scandal by hijacking the wife of his cousin, had no wish to fuel fresh gossip by divorcing Amy.* His affair with Clara Thomas ended as abruptly as it had begun. In July 1934, the *Tribune*'s Sunday editor, A. M. "Mike" Kennedy, was ordered to pick up some paintings Clara had sent for possible inclusion in the coloroto section. Kennedy heard nothing more until one day in November, when the Colonel summoned him to the twenty-fourth floor. "Mrs. Thomas hasn't got her sketches here . . . get up some pages and let me look at them," McCormick said. Forced to improvise, Kennedy produced a dummy cover that won quick approval. "Tell Mrs. Thomas we don't need her services anymore," McCormick told his editor.[48]

His amorous exploits overdrew more than his emotional accounts. In 1931, McCormick was forced to pacify Amy by purchasing a Goya for her private collection. The next year Grasslands went bankrupt, and Amy bought Joe Thomas's hounds. Transported to Cantigny, the dogs were set on the trail of Illinois foxes.

❖ 9

To save capitalism, FDR told a Hearst emissary in the spring of 1935, it must be modernized. In practical terms, this meant a more equitable distribution of wealth, achieved in part through a steeply graded tax code. Such proposals led the comedian Will Rogers to hail the New Deal as the first time in history that "the fellow with money is worrying more than the one without it." (Hearst, unamused, began referring in print to Stalin Delano Roosevelt.) Although Roosevelt's tax package was watered down by congressional conservatives, McCormick found it noxious all the same.

Stung by the Supreme Court's 1934 invalidation of the NRA, Roosevelt

*Informed that her first husband, whom she hadn't seen in years, was suffering from cancer, Amy asked a dinner companion for news of his condition. On being told that Ed Adams was in great pain, she rose and left the room. Adams died soon after.

demanded and got from Congress a Social Security act, sweeping changes in labor law favorable to union organizers, a banking bill strengthening federal control over credit and currency, and legislation drastically curtailing the power of public utility holding companies.*

Like a modern-day King Canute, the Colonel tried to hold back the second wave of New Deal reforms. "Business cannot prosper when the President of the United States embarks upon a campaign to destroy the Constitution," he told *Business Week* at the beginning of June 1935. Tipped off by his intrepid Berlin correspondent, Sigrid Schultz, to Hitler's reliance on astrologers and his secret income of $2 million a year in royalties from *Mein Kampf*, McCormick decided that Roosevelt was an American dictator whose personal finances would not stand up to critical scrutiny. To test his theory, he sent the political correspondent Willard Edwards to Schenectady, New York, to investigate rumors that the president and other New Dealers were profiting from their actions through heavy investments in General Electric. When Edwards discovered that FDR held a substantial block of GE stock as a trustee for his mother, McCormick was ecstatic. "This is the biggest story the *Tribune* has ever had," he exclaimed. Few other papers shared his assessment, or reprinted his accusations.[49]

Instead of sanctioning modern egalitarianism, McCormick's reading of history — especially military history — taught him to see life as a meritocracy wherein men of exceptional gifts were encouraged to test the limits of their genius, unimpeded by the restraining hand of government. "Is not Roosevelt's partiality for the unemployed, his coldness to the soldiers, and his hostility to the industrious," the Colonel inquired in October 1935, "accounted for by his having been unemployed when out of office, never having fought for his country, and never having earned his living?"[50]

As of January 1, 1936, the *Tribune*'s Platform for America carried a new and insistent demand: TURN THE RASCALS OUT. Just who would implement this agenda became a subject of considerable speculation. McCormick told the Kansas editor William Allen White that it should be "a man under fifty, a front-rank soldier not drawing a bonus and not running a newspaper." If this did not amount to an outright endorsement of White's forty-eight-year-old governor, Alf Landon, it most assuredly eliminated *Chicago Daily News* publisher Frank Knox, at sixty-two a vigorous expo-

---

*Curiously, McCormick held his tongue on Social Security long after other conservatives denounced the old age and unemployment insurance program, to be financed by employee contributions and an employer's tax (1 percent the first year, rising to 2 percent thereafter). The *Tribune* estimated the corporate cost of Social Security at $152,000 in 1936, a figure that would grow, along with projected incomes, to nearly $600,000 within a decade. Even so, the Colonel continued to pay annual bonuses and pensions for his employees, in sharp contrast to Roosevelt supporter Joe Patterson, for whom the advent of Social Security led to the dropping of the *Daily News* pension plan.

nent of the first Roosevelt, with whom he had fought at San Juan Hill. Like McCormick, Knox was a former World War I artilleryman with a continuing interest in military matters and a passionate nationalistic faith. In 1912, the year of the Bull Moose, Knox, then a successful Michigan newspaper editor, had stood with his hero at Armageddon. Later he had created the Manchester, New Hampshire, *Union Leader* and overseen Hearst's Boston properties.[51]

Following the death of Walter Strong in 1931, Knox had enlisted the potent financial support of Charles Dawes to snare Strong's *Chicago Daily News*. The two Pulitzer Prizes won by the *Daily News* in the 1930s left McCormick unimpressed. He regarded the Pulitzers, he told his New York cousin, as the work of "a mutual admiration society" of cultural gatekeepers in the east. As for himself, he maintained, there were only two standards of excellence, "individual taste and public acceptance." Nothing else mattered.[52]

An intermittently courageous publisher whose political aspirations colored his journalism, Knox displayed TR's vehemence without his thoughtfulness. Among his most conspicuous deficiencies was a sense of humor. With Walter Trohan as their willing accomplice, the *Tribune* editors Teddy Beck and Bob Lee decided to give their ponderous competitor a hotfoot. Trohan, well aware that Knox was intimate with a female editor named Leola Allard, to whom he was not married, persuaded a telephone operator to call up the *News* and pose as a long-distance operator from Palo Alto, California. Knox, assuming that the call was from Palo Alto's most famous citizen, Herbert Hoover, fell for the ruse.

"Hello," said the publisher.

"Is Leola there?"

"Hello! Who is it?"

"Never mind who it is. Is Leola there?"

"Who wants her? Hello! Hello! Who is it?"

"This is your conscience, Frank," said Trohan in his most sepulchral voice. Then he hung up. Beck and Lee were redfaced with laughter.[53]

McCormick, angered by Knox's courtship of Len Small and the remnants of the Thompson machine, saw less to laugh about. Leaving aside presidential politics, the Morning Colonel and the Evening Colonel, as Chicagoans referred to McCormick and Knox, were engaged in a skirmish testing each man's clout. Beginning in October 1935, the *Tribune* pressed local officials to extend summer daylight time to a year-round basis, in effect placing Chicago in the eastern time zone and thereby depriving the *Daily News* of an hour's advantage in publishing news from Wall Street. According to Lloyd Wendt, in his authoritative 1979 history of the *Tribune*, a deal was arranged whereby McCormick would acquiesce in a GOP ticket with Knox's name on it and the voters of Chicago could decide for themselves their preferred time zone. Although the Morning Colonel had Mayor Kelly in his pocket, the Kelly organization failed to deliver, and McCormick's crusade ended ignominiously.

Early in 1936, the *Tribune* published an admiring series of articles on Landon of Kansas. A formal endorsement of the governor followed on January 26. McCormick was confident of victory in the fall, notwithstanding the economic bribery perpetuated by postmaster general Jim Farley and his lavishly funded patronage machine. To the Democrats, McCormick readily conceded "all the lazy, all the worthless, all the larcenously inclined, all the muddle-heads, all who hope to profit from disorder including the gangsters, and all whose vote can be bought by the four billion dollar corruption fund." To one of the Colonel's outlook, this came perilously close to an electoral majority.[54]

Under the circumstances, he found it easy to rationalize his own journalistic bias. "When Roosevelt came into power he immediately tried to control the correspondents and overawe the newspapers," McCormick told Teddy Beck in June. "We reacted against him and have led the fight ever since ... Our demonstrated independence and courage did us more good than our bias did us harm." Convinced that Republican success would depend on support from conservative, anti–New Deal Democrats, he attended a New York strategy session in the Empire State Building office of former governor Al Smith. Among those present were Bainbridge Colby, Woodrow Wilson's final secretary of state, former Massachusetts governor Joseph Ely, and Missouri senator James Reed. A week after the Republican delegates meeting in Cleveland dutifully nominated Landon and Knox, the New York conspirators sprang their surprise. They issued a manifesto urging Democratic convention delegates to reject Roosevelt and reassert the ancient faith of Jefferson, Jackson, and Cleveland.[55]

THE SOVIETS GATHER AT PHILADELPHIA, proclaimed the *Tribune.* In the event, Smith's intervention fell flat. McCormick, undeterred, contributed generously to a splinter group styling itself the National Jeffersonian Democrats. In Chicago, meanwhile, he tried to impress on Landon the need to court Jewish voters, many of whom regarded the Kansan as an unsympathetic figure of "the narrow Protestant type." (In truth, Landon had been an outspoken opponent of the Ku Klux Klan at a time of maximum Klan influence, in Kansas and nationally.) Even before Landon could deliver his acceptance speech on July 23, McCormick was warning the candidate that his advisers reflected "too much Long Island and Lake Forest to appeal to real Americans."[56]

No such veneer of sophistication was permitted to interfere with the acceptance ceremonies, staged before 100,000 people on the grounds of the statehouse in Topeka. Cecil B. De Mille helped organize the day's pageantry. An almost painfully sincere Republican nominee paid tribute to government efficiency and constitutional balance. He criticized "the slap-dash, jazzy methods" followed by the Roosevelt White House, without condemning New Deal objectives root and branch. Landon enthusiasts raised their voices in song, setting their philosophy to the tune of "Oh, Susanna!":

> Landon, oh Landon
> Will lead to victory —
> With the dear old Constitution
> And it's good enough for me.

✧ 10

BE A VOLUNTEER IN GREAT FIGHT TO SAVE NATION! blared the *Tribune* at the end of July. "Only 97 days left to save your country!" This shrill warning, solemnly intoned by every telephone operator at the *Tribune* switchboard, ushered in a fall campaign of unparalleled venom. Through the alchemy of words, McCormick hoped to transform the political frog Landon into a prince capable of evicting "the playboy of the White House."

This would not be easy. More progressive than many of his nominal supporters, Landon detested being packaged and sold as a Kansas Coolidge. His brand of constitutionalism did not blind him to the need for change or the irrelevance of documentary ancestor worship for millions of downtrodden Americans who scorned the moneychangers so recently driven from their temples. Still, he was not about to turn down offers of assistance, whatever their source.

Neither was Colonel McCormick. Before July ended he struck an unlikely alliance with May Preston Davie, a New York socialite whose organizational skills inspired him to finance Landon partisans who called themselves the Volunteers. A hundred members of the group worked phone banks on the seventeenth floor of Tribune Tower. Nationwide, as many as 50,000 citizen activists rang doorbells, licked envelopes, and made streetcorner orations extolling the virtues of Landon and Knox and warning of the degeneracy of American liberties sure to accompany a second Roosevelt term.

Mrs. Davie did little to bolster their cause by declaring before an audience of Chicago women that she had given up a European vacation to work for the Republican ticket. "No sacrifice is too great to make to defeat Roosevelt," she observed righteously, clutching her mink coat against the chill of an autumn evening. A wicked parody of Landon's tone-deaf society patrons, and of the Colonel's aristocratic radio persona, was offered by a *Chicago Times* columnist named Gail Borden:

> There was a young man from Topeka
> Whose campaign grew weaka and weaka
> Till the Volunteers came
> And made every old dame
> A bellringa, singa, or speaka.

By paying the Volunteers' expenses, McCormick became the single biggest contributor to the Landon campaign, his generosity easily surpassing the $50,000 donated by advertising magnate Albert D. Lasker. His greatest sacrifice, however, was not money but journalistic integrity. As the campaign intensified, the *Tribune* abandoned even the pretense of impartiality. The slashing tone of coverage had actually been set a full year before by Carey Orr, a favorite McCormick hatchet man, who drew Roosevelt, Hitler, Stalin, and Mussolini as the Four Horsemen of the Apocalypse.

Toxic as they were, Orr's front-page cartoons were hardly distinguishable from the news columns. For correspondent Willard Edwards, 1936 was his first year in Washington, and very nearly his last. In filing a story on a railroad investigation being spearheaded by Montana senator Burton J. Wheeler, he overlooked Wheeler's status as "a radical Democrat of notorious ill fame." The next day Arthur Sears Henning handed his naive colleague a chastising message. "Has Edwards hired out to be a press agent for Wheeler?" it read. "McCormick."[57]

Edwards was careful not to repeat his mistake. His job was made harder by the fact that Alf Landon offered poor material for the kind of social reconstruction favored by McCormick. In compensation, the *Tribune* assailed Roosevelt's patriotism and the greedy antics of his personal and official families. "Fat Jim" Farley was regularly abused, especially after McCormick heard reports that the postmaster general kept a card file on every recipient of federal relief or administration patronage. Just before Labor Day and the traditional start of the fall campaign, the Colonel stirred the pot by instructing his editorial writers to puncture Roosevelt's image as a Hudson Valley farmer: "What he has is a large suburban estate on the Hudson River. His so-called farm is nothing but suburban acreage . . . held for speculation."[58]

McCormick teamed up with investigators from the Republican National Committee who were probing the insurance business run by Roosevelt's son James. Nor was Jimmy Roosevelt the only member of his illustrious family whose taste for wealth exceeded his scruples in obtaining it. In September, McCormick learned of a potentially explosive story involving Jimmy's brother Elliott. In the last week of January 1934,

Elliott and the aircraft manufacturer Donald Douglas had called at the White House. Within days of their visit, FDR moved to cancel existing airmail contracts with American, United, and Transcontinental and Western airlines. Simultaneously, a friend of Elliott's named Herbert Reed conceived the idea of merging the three into a single company, in a stroke realizing the president's stated objectives of wiping out the airmail deficit then plaguing the post office and paying off existing stockholders. Better yet, Reed would enrich his partner to the tune of $750,000 a year (a figure representing Elliott's 5 percent cut of the new aviation monopoly).[59]

Reed shared his vision with the celebrated German warplane builder Anthony Fokker. Both men saw the wisdom of hiring Elliott to help further their plans. With the White House hinting at substantial changes in the airmail delivery system, Fokker sent the president's son $5,000 as a down payment sealing their business partnership.

On February 9, the same day FDR's cancellation order was made public, Reed was informed of this in a letter, almost certainly typed on Elliott's typewriter. The same message contained a code to be used in all future communications among the participants. In it, the president was referred to as Rochelle; Elliott was New Rochelle. On February 28, Elliott made a second agreement with Fokker, this time promising assistance in arranging the sale of fifty Lockheed military aircraft, disguised as commercial planes, to Soviet Russia — a deal expected to put $500,000 in Elliott's bank account.

Herbert Reed was sent to New York in an effort to enlist Al Smith as chairman of the consolidated airline. Smith, valuing his political independence and probably more than a little suspicious of the deal, spurned Reed's offer. Then, on March 9, 1934, five army pilots died in an airmail crash, the latest in a series of disasters that spurred criticism of the administration for entrusting airmail delivery to the army. Elliott's hand, already weakened by the public backlash, was now trumped by none other than Jim Farley. The postmaster general had compelling reasons to look charitably on the disenfranchised American Airways, a generous contributor to past Democratic campaigns.

At Farley's urging, the aviation lobby employed former North Carolina governor O. Max Gardner, at a salary of $75,000, to press the White House for restoration of the old contractors. The president agreed to reinstate the private carriers pending a permanent solution. This was the end of Reed's monopolistic fantasies. Soon after, the Russian plane deal fell through as well. At the urging of his father, Elliott accepted a $10,000-a-year sinecure with the Aeronautical Chamber of Commerce — the same industry group responsible for hiring Gardner. Called before a Senate committee chaired by North Dakota's Gerald P. Nye, Elliott denied receiving $5,000 from

Fokker and knowing anything about plans to sell military planes to the Soviet government to which his father had so recently extended official recognition.

There the matter might have rested if not for a New York publisher named Frank Tichenor. It was Tichenor who, at Herbert Reed's behest, had tried unsuccessfully to obtain Al Smith's services in the spring of 1934. Since then, he had emulated Smith in turning against the New Deal. Now, at the height of the 1936 campaign, he took the story to the *Tribune.* His evidence included copies of the initial contract between Elliott and Fokker, of the $5,000 payment from the German manufacturer to the president's son, and of the code worked out between Elliott, Fokker, and Reed. He also had in his possession telephone records linking the three men.

McCormick set his legal and aviation experts to work examining Tichenor's documentation. Pat Maloney, the managing editor, voiced the resulting consensus when he told the Colonel that Elliott "was either in a plot with his father, or is a crooked son of a gun who imposed terribly on the old man's name." Maloney hastened to add that nothing existed to link the president directly to Elliott's attempt to trade on his name.[60]

Modern editors would be less restrained in their judgment. So would independent counsels faced with issues of national security, the misuse of federal agencies (including the IRS; Elliott appears to have evaded taxes on the $5,000 he received from Fokker), and the blatant sale of official favors by the postmaster general, among others. A different climate prevailed in 1936. Presidential offspring were less vulnerable to press inquiry, if only because they were less likely to exploit their White House connections for personal gain.

The *Tribune* and Frank Tichenor's *Aeronautical Digest* went public with their allegations in the first week of October. The Associated Press refused to disseminate any charges about the aborted Russian plane sales. A lengthy exposé carried by the McClure Syndicate later that month failed to generate more than a ripple of public interest. Election-year skepticism was heightened in this case by the story's source. For millions of readers accustomed to Colonel McCormick's vendetta against Roosevelt, this was only the latest attempt by the *Tribune* to throw mud in the president's eye.

Quite simply, McCormick had cried wolf too often — especially where Soviet Russia was concerned — to have credibility when reporting wrongdoing by the Roosevelt White House. Few readers and even fewer reporters were able to distinguish between the Colonel's brand of investigative journalism and the scurrilous character imputed to his paper's 1936 election coverage. What would be a prized — or prizewinning — scoop in the *New York Times* was discounted as just another *Tribune* smear.

✧ 11

"I have coming over in the mails a copy of the official Communist publication, calling upon American Communists to vote for Roosevelt," McCormick notified Landon on August 13. Printing the document might help the GOP with the large Polish vote in many American cities, and with "the American vote" everywhere. Left unmentioned was his own need to buttress the *Tribune*'s credibility following a disputed story that correspondent Donald Day had filed from Riga, Latvia, headlined MOSCOW ORDERS REDS IN U.S. TO BACK ROOSEVELT. The *Chicago Times* offered $5,000 to anyone able to substantiate Day's claims. The prize money went uncollected.

Seemingly unfazed, McCormick continued to challenge Roosevelt's policies by questioning his patriotism. He passed on rumors that likenesses of the president and his left-wing adviser Rex Tugwell were displayed in Moscow's Lenin Museum. He quoted Earl Browder, head of the American Communist party, as being "100 percent opposed to Landon" (which was not the same thing as implied in the Day piece). An angry Roosevelt denounced "a certain notorious newspaper owner" for impugning his loyalties. McCormick dismissed the statement as tantamount to a confession.

He shifted tactics anyway. "The Communist alliance is being pretty well proved," McCormick wrote Landon in mid-September. "In the current exchange of hostilities, is not there room for a note of idealism, love of country and its people?" For this belated attempt to raise the level of the campaign, Landon gave pro forma thanks. Privately, the Republican candidate wished that McCormick would emulate Hearst, who had left the country a few weeks earlier and was not expected to return before election day.[61]

Others expressed openly what Landon was inhibited from saying. "I am beginning to think they do not want me in California," McCormick mused after the editor of the *San Francisco Chronicle* joined GOP leaders in making plain how dispensable the Colonel's presence was in the Golden State. Closer to home, the *Tribune* waged an uphill campaign to win over traditional Democrats supposedly alienated by New Deal corruption and Communist influence. By the start of October, McCormick was predicting that Landon would carry Chicago. If he failed to do so, it certainly wouldn't be for lack of press support. During the last month of the campaign, FDR received less attention in the pages of the *Tribune* than did Mrs. Ernest Simpson, soon to achieve notoriety as the American divorcée for whom Britain's King Edward VIII would abdicate his throne.[62]

When the president did appear on the front page, it was invariably in an unflattering light. RECORDS SHOW ROOSEVELT AIM A REVOLUTION, declared the October 6, 1936, *Tribune*. MR. ROOSEVELT REFUSES, THEN

SEEKS RED AID, the paper announced three days later. On another day, readers curious as to the president's activities had to turn to page thirteen for the desired information. Here they were informed that Roosevelt had canceled a White House press conference, "presumably to avoid embarrassing questions about recent campaign developments." Among these, presumably, was an October poll in the *Literary Digest* forecasting a Landon triumph. Stung by criticism of its methodology, the *Digest* conducted another, secret survey, McCormick told Landon on October 13, with identical results. By further way of encouragement, McCormick promised his reluctant ally that the *Tribune* would soon publish a 15,000- to 20,000-word history of the New Deal that was "positively annihilating."[63]

Twenty-four hours later, the Colonel again put pen to paper, this time to alert Landon that Nazi officials in Berlin expected him to win the election and were looking forward to obtaining economic credits from the new American administration. McCormick warned Landon that such a course would only strengthen the Nazi dictatorship. Hitler's name surfaced under very different circumstances on October 14, when Roosevelt visited Chicago and received a delirious welcome from half a million supporters. Many in the throng shouted their disapproval of Hearst and of *Tribune* reporters accompanying the presidential motorcade. For its part, the *Tribune* churlishly likened the huge turnout to the artificially stimulated mass enthusiasm of Europe's fascist regimes.[64]

However flagrant, this latest instance of guilt by association paled beside the conduct of a *Tribune* photographer who paid a city street cleaner to strew Roosevelt buttons on the pavement, then sweep them up for the benefit of McCormick's readers. The resulting picture was intended to demonstrate popular indifference to Roosevelt, but it backfired when the pesky *Chicago Times* gleefully exposed the hoax, complete with an affidavit signed by the suborned municipal worker.

On October 16, the *Tribune* struck back with the oddest charge yet in the escalating war of headlines: ROOSEVELT AREA IN WISCONSIN IS HOTBED OF VICE. On examination, the story, about petty crime in a couple of Wisconsin communities, had almost nothing to do with the Roosevelt-Landon contest — except as it illustrated the extremes to which FDR's enemies would go to blacken his name. McCormick boasted that "eighty per cent of the nation's newspapers" and a similar proportion of clergymen were "now more or less openly for Landon." To be sure, *Time* magazine did its best to rain on the Republican parade by contrasting the positions of McCormick's *Tribune* and Joe Patterson's *Daily News*. (The latter had dismissed Landon as "either a dumb bell or a hypocrite.") McCormick, snarling that "*Time* is always crooked," refused to pose for a cover picture with his liberal cousin.[65]

But it wasn't only eastern establishment types who protested the

Colonel's sledgehammer tactics. A group of Chicagoans canceled their *Tribune* subscriptions, complaining to McCormick that his "genius for distorting political news can only equal the low regard in which you hold the intelligence of your reader." Others joined suit. As the campaign neared its climax and partisan emotions boiled over, *Tribune* sales tumbled by nearly 100,000. Yet even as the paper's reporting became more rancid, the Landon-*Tribune* marriage of convenience grew closer. On October 21, Roy Roberts, the respected publisher of the *Kansas City Star* and a Landon intimate, telephoned Teddy Beck with a request for speechwriting assistance from Beck's take-no-prisoners editorial staff. McCormick's response was to urge Landon to smoke out Roosevelt on his plans for a second term. "What is the planned society he has in mind?" the Colonel demanded. "What does he intend to do with NRA, AAA, the control of securities, the extension of the TVA, the taxation of industrial reserves?"[66]

Self-delusion afflicted many Roosevelt haters that fall. Ruth Hanna McCormick, now married to a Republican congressman from New Mexico named Albert Simms, confidently predicted a GOP landslide. In Washington, Arthur Sears Henning was placing bets on Roosevelt's defeat. As for the Colonel, he was positively giddy with anticipation. "Next Tuesday will be the most momentous day in American history," he wrote one week before the election. He assured Landon that his final campaign address, delivered at New York's Madison Square Garden, would rank alongside the immortal Cooper Union address given in the same city by Abraham Lincoln. McCormick professed horror over Roosevelt's concluding appeal in the same arena, wrinkling his nose as the president taunted "the forces of selfishness and of lust for power" arrayed against his reelection. When FDR vowed to master his adversaries after January 1937, it was too much for the *Tribune* publisher to bear. "The President of the U.S. has no authority under the Constitution to make himself master of any part of the people not duly convicted of crime," McCormick responded. "He is elected to be their servant."[67]

While McCormick and the *Tribune* were conducting their seminar in constitutional theory, Roosevelt was remaking America. Beyond endorsing the president and his policies, the 1936 contest witnessed a radical shift in the center of political gravity. The old idea that government must remain a neutral bystander in the economic and social struggle was yielding to a much more activist view, one that argued for government intervention on behalf of the weak, the exploited, and the oppressed. In burying Landon, Roosevelt also buried laissez-faire notions linked to the discredited wizards of Wall Street.

McCormick could hardly acknowledge it at the time — he had too much emotionally invested in the chimera of a Landon victory — but 1936 marked the passing of the culture of deference, in which dictators of public opinion such as himself could hurl their thunderbolts and imagine themselves on a par with the president of the United States. Words took on new meaning as Roosevelt arraigned all those who used the sacred concept of liberty to justify individual and corporate greed. McCormick, oblivious to the ground shifting beneath him, rejected Ed Kelly's warning that the Roosevelt juggernaut was unstoppable. Loyally, Kelly accepted an invitation to McCormick's election night victory party, a dismal affair made worse when jubilant Roosevelt partisans surrounded Tribune Tower and tossed bricks through a ground-floor window.

The morning after exposed the hollowness of the *Tribune's* claims to speak for America. Sweeping all but two states, FDR could savor the greatest Electoral College triumph since a single elector in 1820 had held out against James Monroe on the grounds that no American should repeat George Washington's two victories by acclamation. Nationwide, Roosevelt crushed Landon by 11 million votes; in Chicago, the president racked up a stunning 2-to-1 margin over his Republican challenger. Amid the rubble of defeat, McCormick showed flashes of humor. He had always loved his country, he remarked. With the pain of rejection fresh in his soul, he couldn't help but add, "I hope I never love another country."[68]

His discomfiture gave joy to many. Wrote one irate Chicagoan, "You know what you can do with Tribune Tower." The *Chicago Times* blithely reminded readers on the morning of November 4 that they had only fifty-two days left . . . to shop before Christmas.[69]

Swallowing his humiliation, McCormick complimented Landon on running the strongest campaign possible under the circumstances. "The majority vote was made up of many discordant elements," he wrote bitterly. These ranged "from the Communists in New York to the would-be slave drivers in the South; from the beneficiaries of inside tips on the stock market to the penniless creatures supported by the dole." The most sterling of candidates had found it difficult to overcome Tammany Hall; the New Deal was merely Tammany on a continental scale. "It is just possible that if we had named a Democrat for Vice President, he could have brought the Democrats with him, as Colby, Smith, etc. so signally failed to do." McCormick could think of nothing else that might have altered the results.[70]

Still, Landon could hold his head high. Seventeen million voters had rallied to his standard. A less vigorous campaign might have left republican institutions prostrate in the dust. "As it is," McCormick concluded hopefully, "we have enough of an army left to continue the battle."[71]

12

Undominated

"All successful newspapers are ceaselessly querulous and bellicose. They never defend anyone or anything if they can help it; if the job is forced upon them, they tackle it by denouncing someone or something else."

— H. L. Mencken

CCORMICK LOVED GOSSIP, all the more so when it confirmed his worst suspicions about New Dealers, latter-day Tories inhabiting the Atlantic seaboard, or anyone remotely connected to royalty. As for the scandalous romance between King Edward VIII and "Wally" Simpson, his mannish-looking courtesan from Baltimore, it raised "possibilities of a repulsive nature," he wrote with lip-smacking relish.[1]

Determined to pierce the curtain of discretion drawn around the royal affair, McCormick shifted Alex Small, a correspondent accompanying the Nationalist army in Spain, to the French Riviera in hopes of securing an interview with the most famous woman in the world. Small stalked his quarry to the Hotel Carlton in Cannes where, two days before Christmas 1936 (by which time the king had abdicated), he invited Mrs. Simpson to name her price. Wallis merely smiled. Repeated efforts to elicit her story produced nothing more than assurances that the future Duchess of Windsor held no grudge against the *Chicago Tribune*.[2]

The Colonel instructed Sigrid Schultz to crash the household of "David Windsor" — so called in line with a short-lived campaign to eliminate titles of nobility from the pages of his newspaper — and nab the reclusive ex-king before he could rejoin his mistress in the south of France. Again foiled, McCormick traveled to England in August 1937 to plumb the mysteries of the abdication for himself. He spent several days with Winston Churchill at Churchill's country house in Kent, listening intently as the statesman talked of preparations for war. The submarine menace had been solved, Churchill said, while acknowledging British concern about growing Nazi superiority in the air.[3]

It may well have been from Churchill, then languishing in the political wilderness, that McCormick got the idea that King Edward hadn't jumped but had been pushed from his throne after drawing unwanted attention to the plight of his most impoverished subjects in ways which "even a well censored press could not ignore." More improbable still was McCormick's belief that England had embraced fascism, a theory he picked up from a London banker who observed that the government of Stanley Baldwin hoped to get the benefits of Nazism without its penalties. In support of his assertion, the American visitor cited the petty tyrannies of "the milk control board, the bacon marketing board, the wheat commission . . . the herring industry board, the textile commission, the hops marketing board . . . the coal mines reorganization commission, the fishery board for Scotland," and other tentacles of the state that were squeezing the life out of a free marketplace.[4]

British fascists, it would appear, bore more than a passing resemblance to New Deal functionaries.

Toward Roosevelt, McCormick continued to harbor feelings as raw as meat in a butcher's window. FDR's second inaugural address was relegated to an inside page of the *Tribune*. The arrest of a local cop-killer was judged more important than the president's acknowledgment that fully one third of his countrymen remained ill housed, ill nourished, and ill clad.

The *Tribune* quickly made up its election-year circulation losses. By the end of the decade, daily sales topped 930,000, with over a million households taking the Sunday paper. By no means all of these sympathized with McCormick's shrill nationalism, his disdain for Europe, or his distrust of labor unions and Washington "burocrats" (the latter dictated by the Colonel's simplified spelling). One 1937 poll in the heavily Democratic West Side of Chicago revealed that 72 percent of those asked read the *Tribune* in spite of its editorial page.

Yet another reader survey showed how formidable a journalistic arsenal the Colonel had assembled. By substantial margins, Chicagoans voted the *Tribune* the paper they could least do without. Men said it had the best sports and radio coverage. Women awarded it first place in features and society reporting. And both sexes thought it lapped the field when it came to pictures, comic strips, and movie news. "It is the housewife's guide," conceded *Time* in an extensive analysis coinciding with the *Tribune*'s 1947 centennial, "the politician's breakfast food, a bible to hundreds of small-town editorial writers."[5]

Under McCormick's leadership, the *Tribune* had a superb physical plant, typographical vigor, splashes of color, the finest presses money could buy. It belonged to virtually every available news, feature, and trade organization. Where existing operations fell short, the *Tribune* did not hesitate to spend lavishly to create services of its own. With a local staff of eighty-three reporters, generously supplemented by bureaus in four American and a dozen foreign cities, the *Tribune* outwrote, outreported, and outhustled the opposition.

It did staff morale no harm that McCormick assumed that anyone good enough to pass muster with him must, *ipso facto*, be the best in the field. His invariable practice of promoting from within the *Tribune* organization bred a tightly knit fraternity. So did the knowledge that no *Tribune* reporter ever went into battle alone. For example, it was a fairly minor scandal when an employee of Marshall Field's department store absconded with company funds — at least it was until a Field executive tried to suppress a *Tribune* inquiry into the theft. Thereafter Pat Maloney gave the story three columns on page one, and McCormick backed him to the hilt.*

In February 1939, a Cleveland ad man named McCabe, retained by Greyhound Bus Lines, objected to a depressing portrayal of bus travel in the comic strip "Winnie Winkle." Unless the *Tribune* let up, he hinted, Greyhound might have no alternative but to withhold future advertising. The *Tribune*'s response was pure McCormick. As for the choice posed by the unhappy advertiser, "That's easy. We're going to edit the *Tribune* and Mr. McCabe is going to continue not to edit it. If Mr. McCabe thinks his client isn't getting his money's worth from advertising in the *Tribune* it is Mr. McCabe's duty to cancel the contract."[6]

In other, more tangible ways, McCormick inspired staff loyalty. As early as June 1936, he told Joe Patterson that he favored employee ownership of the *Tribune* after both men were gone. Two years later he made good on this vow by offering executives the chance to own stock in the privately held company. More impulsively, he awarded $70,000, a full year's salary, to the widow of an advertising manager who had cultivated a profitable association with the big State Street department stores.[7]

In the spring of 1939, Hearst's bedraggled *Herald and Examiner* finally gave up the ghost, and *Tribune* domination of the morning market was

---

*Every year, Maloney, a Dartmouth Phi Beta Kappa who had flown with Eddie Rickenbacker in World War I, augmented the news department by hiring up to eighteen bright young men from the City News Bureau, a sort of homegrown Associated Press. McCormick looked on approvingly. Excellence of the *Tribune* variety, he contended, could not be produced at will by a board of directors representing shareholders, "as in the case of banks and railroads." True superiority came from pride of service in an enterprise where passion and profit were inseparable.

absolute. As an extension of McCormick, the paper was an object of fascination to many readers, whether or not they agreed with its eccentric owner. The Colonel might be a son of a bitch, as the old saw had it, but at least he was *their* son of a bitch. Certainly no one ever questioned his allegiance to Chicago, even if some doubted his loyalty to the United States during the overwrought period leading up to World War II.

Tens of thousands bought the *Tribune* just to learn about McCormick's latest target of abuse. Giving offense was the least of his concerns. Invited by the president of Goldblatt Brothers to donate to a memorial honoring the Revolutionary War hero Haym Solomon, McCormick said that he agreed with Moses that "there should be no graven images of any kind." While declining to join in the erection of another Chicago monument, he would gladly contribute his share "to tearing down those already in existence."[8]

Around Tribune Tower it was an article of faith that whatever McCormick endorsed was sure to be opposed by Frank Knox and the *Daily News.* McCormick was not blind to the comic possibilities of their feud, as he demonstrated one afternoon in November 1936. "Ho, ho, ho!" boomed the Morning Colonel as he strode into the city room. "He'll be at a disadvantage next week when we come out against syphilis!" A few weeks later McCormick prodded Mayor Kelly into convening a meeting of three hundred civic and public health officials to combat the disease, which until then had been kept out of polite conversation. The campaign took an unexpected twist when a reader casually inquired as to how many *Tribune* employees had the loathsome ailment. Without hesitation, McCormick ordered staff-wide blood tests.[9]

As such incidents suggest, Tribune Tower was run like a feudal baron's castle. It was just one of McCormick's many contradictions that he expected submission from those he paid generously to disseminate his views, yet he rewarded handsomely the rare subordinate who displayed genuine independence. Even a baron grows weary of the company of vassals.

"He had a devilish sense of humor," said Walter Trohan, a free spirit who passed an important character test the first time he was called to the twenty-fourth floor. Also present was the Colonel's English bulldog, Tribby, whose unattractive habit it was to slobber over the shoes of *Tribune* executives before systematically tearing their footwear to shreds. Pat Maloney, among others, had suffered in silence as the dog chewed up his shoes while McCormick pretended to be ignorant of the little drama being enacted under his nose. Trohan was made of sterner stuff. On hearing that he had been sent for, he didn't bother to don a tie or jacket. He wanted the Colonel to know he was working. "The dog, of course, came over and started on my shoes, and I stepped on his toes," Trohan recalled. "And the dog came back and I stepped on him again. And the dog came a third time and I stepped harder, and he left me alone." Only much later did Trohan learn that in fending off Tribby, he had distinguished himself from the all too pliable lieutenants surrounding McCormick.[10]

To Trohan, McCormick was a bulldog among spaniels. Trohan observed the publisher at his Palm Beach estate, "the most ridiculous house I've ever been in," with living and dining rooms separated by the great outdoors and a fountain into which late-night celebrants were forever tumbling. Although he owned a mile of shoreline, McCormick reserved less than one hundred feet of beach for his private use. The rest was open to the public. "I'm not using it," he explained to Trohan. "Let them come and enjoy themselves."

On the same oceanfront expanse, McCormick built a house as a present for his friend Kent Cooper, who for many years was the executive director of the Associated Press. He took secret delight in seeing Tribby drool all over Mrs. Cooper's coffee table and paw her immaculate rugs. "She's too fussy," he said. "Tribby does her good."

"A lot of his amusements weren't out loud," Trohan commented in a 1990 interview. "If you were . . . fool enough to take this seriously, you had it coming to you. I think that was his attitude in many things."

Too tall to notice most people, too shy to respond gracefully when greeted by a stranger, with age McCormick became too deaf to invite conversation. Though burdened with a heavy sense of his own dignity, he was capable of surprising gallantries. Spotting an elderly Polish woman weighed down with packages one morning on Roosevelt Road, McCormick commanded his driver to stop. Alighting from the vehicle, he bowed low before offering her assistance. He displayed the same Old World formality toward a WGN child star and her mother, who were caught in a rainstorm outside Tribune Tower: they were driven home, snug in the warmth of a fur throw, by the Colonel's chauffeur.[11]

McCormick's fumbling attempts to befriend reporters illustrated just how far he would go to assert his patriarchal control. One night the managing editor dispatched a member of his staff to the Colonel's Astor Street townhouse. In his hands the emissary clutched an editorial, studded with errors, marking the death of German general Erich von Ludendorff. The reporter came upon McCormick still dressed in the tweeds he had worn while spending the day at Cantigny. Much to his surprise, he found his boss in an expansive, even jovial, frame of mind.

McCormick offered the visitor a drink while he perused the editorial copy. He had one himself, then another. As the reporter rose to leave, the Colonel asked whether he had transportation back to work. Indeed he did, said the reporter; a staff photographer had brought him over.

"Take the photographer some cigars," said McCormick, thrusting a fistful at him.

The visitor eyed the door anxiously.

"I believe we are the same height," observed the Colonel. "How tall are you?"

The reporter agreed, with more tact than truthfulness, that they were of identical stature.

"Let's measure," said McCormick. A butler was sent for. As the Colonel and his guest stood awkwardly back to back, the servant climbed atop a chair and placed a silver salver across the heads of both men. Suddenly the reporter felt a hand pressing down on his scalp. Involuntarily he bent his knees.

"Exactly the same, sir," announced the butler.

McCormick beamed. "I thought so." The reporter was excused.[12]

✧ 2

By 1937, however tall McCormick stood in his own imagination, he was dwarfed, even in Chicagoland, by the man in the White House. Around Tribune Tower it was no secret that most employees had supported Roosevelt against Landon. Not every soldier in the *Tribune* army was assigned to combat duty, however. The society editor, India Moffett, for one, was a conscientious objector. Even so, said McCormick, "if she can stand me, I can stand her."

The only serious threat to Moffett's autonomy came early in World War II, when she gave prominent coverage to British War Relief activities in Chicago. The ink was barely dry on these offending articles when she received a scrawled rebuke from the twenty-fourth floor. Was it the custom of the women's page, the Colonel wished to know, to pursue an editorial course at variance with the rest of the *Tribune?* "We have the policy of reporting the news as faithfully and fully as possible," Moffett replied. "If you want us to do otherwise, please notify me." She heard nothing further on the matter.[13]

At a heated moment in the 1936 campaign, FDR had brusquely informed advisers that the election would pivot on a single issue — "myself." His overwhelming victory in November affirmed his sense of personal mastery. But the eminence from which he dominated the American landscape was to prove unexpectedly thorny, and his descent brutally swift. In February 1937, Roosevelt sent Congress a controversial plan to remake the federal judiciary. Under its terms, he and his successors would be empowered to appoint one new federal judge or Supreme Court justice for every incumbent who refused to step aside on reaching the age of seventy. Theoretically, the Supreme Court could be expanded to include as many as fifteen justices — and FDR would at last have a majority sympathetic to his thinking.

Designed ostensibly to relieve an overburdened judiciary, what quickly became known as the Court-packing bill fooled no one. To the *Tribune* it was a boldfaced attempt to rob the Supreme Court of its independence. Yet while Herbert Hoover and other conservative Republicans sprang to their battle stations, McCormick held his fire. The fight should be led by those who had not been active in the Landon campaign, he told an Indiana reader, "which cuts me out." With unusual adroitness, he deferred to Democrats (led by the irascible Burton J. Wheeler) whose veneration for the Supreme Court outweighed their loyalty to the White House. The strategy paid unexpected dividends. As the Court struggle dragged on through the spring of 1937, Roosevelt's usually faultless instincts deserted him. With a conviction, and a hubris, reminiscent of his messianic wartime chief Woodrow Wilson, the president showed contempt for his enemies and disregard for his friends. "The people are with me," he maintained in the face of mounting evidence to the contrary. "I know it."[14]

McCormick fed ravenously on rumors of White House disarray and presidential illness (speculation over Roosevelt's condition ranged from "bladder trouble to paranoia"). Actually, the biggest pain around the White House was Chief Justice Charles Evans Hughes, who had shrewdly demolished FDR's arguments for expansion of the Court in a carefully timed letter to Senator Wheeler.[15]

As the air went out of his judicial sails, Roosevelt found himself contending with a wave of sit-down strikes by militant workers in the steel and auto industries. "I have nothing to criticize about labor unions," McCormick told an audience at the Naval War College in Newport, Rhode Island, on May 12, 1937. "They are no more selfish and grasping than anybody else. You can live with them." This reasonable attitude went by the boards less than three weeks later, when police, acting on orders from Mayor Kelly, fired indiscriminately into a fleeing group of strikers outside the South Chicago plant of Republic Steel, killing ten and wounding thirty others.

McCormick's voice trembled with rage as he directed his editors to label the disaffected steel workers "rioters." The *Tribune* headline for June 1, 1937 didn't mince words: RIOTS BLAMED ON RED CHIEFS. "Working men, as we call them, are not aggressive men," McCormick had confidently told his Naval War College audience. The Memorial Day Massacre, as it came to be known, burst his patronizing attitude like a skyrocket.

And it wasn't only men who were taking up the cudgels of union organizing. Virginia Gardner was a *Tribune* investigative reporter whose success in nailing medical quacks failed to compensate in McCormick's eyes for her radical politics and emotional instability. (Pat Maloney once talked the distraught Gardner out of jumping into the Chicago River, and she ended her journalistic career as the Washington correspondent for the Communist *New Masses*.)[16]

Gardner drew the wrath of the Colonel for walking a picket line outside the *Herald and Examiner*. For this infraction of the code that forebade "professionals," including reporters, photographers, and compositors, from joining a labor union, he terminated her employment. The National Labor Relations Board ordered him to take her back. McCormick exacted revenge by denying her a byline. Undaunted, in September 1938, the union activist organized a short-lived *Tribune* chapter of the Newspaper Guild. On learning that the guild would demand at least $60 a week for experienced workers, McCormick raised *all* his employees' wages to that level. The guild was in any case hopelessly mismatched in going up against an organization so paternalistic that it ran a so-called drunk bank for employees who woke up penniless after a binge.*

As the controversy swirled around her, Virginia Gardner toiled in obscurity. Then, out of the blue, she was handed a spectacular scoop by the liberal prelate George Cardinal Mundelein. His Eminence quietly passed along word of proceedings that anticipated the canonization of Chicago's first saint. Under the circumstances, not even Colonel McCormick dared to withhold Virginia Gardner's byline. Thus was Mother Cabrini, the founder of Columbus Hospital, credited with one of the miracles necessary to join the company of saints.[17]

✧ 3

In the autumn of 1937, a severe economic recession added to Roosevelt's woes. As unemployment surged past ten million, his foes lost no opportunity to pin blame for "the Roosevelt recession" on White House hostility toward business.** The renewal of hard times struck with special force in Chicago. Even before the bubble burst nationally, it was clear that Carl Sandburg's city "with lifted head singing, so proud to be

---

*"It is my observation that labor unions, once they get established in an industry, gradually strangle it," McCormick wrote in October 1939. Granted, "the tragedy in the newspaper world has not yet affected us, because we have fallen heir to the business of newspapers that have died. However, if the trend continues, we will become the only newspapers in Chicago and New York. There will be no more business to get."

**According to Ickes's choleric diary, FDR had evidence that McCormick had avoided paying taxes by setting up "a personal trust." In fact the Colonel paid $523,065.72 that year on income of $794,786.04. An IRS audit of the Tribune Company turned up no evidence of wrongdoing.

alive and coarse and strong and cunning," had failed in its bid for grandeur. No longer did the *Tribune*'s editorial page feature the daily admonition "Make Chicago the First City of the World." A huge sign above Michigan Boulevard still welcomed out-of-towners to the Magnificent Mile, "lined with the most beautiful buildings and the finest and most luxurious shops in the world." But such hyperbole rang increasingly hollow as the thirties slipped away.

After the slapdash Thompson years, Ed Kelly won plaudits from McCormick and others in the business community for providing basic services and opposing tax increases sought by Democratic governor Henry Horner. "He has to go his way and I have to go mine sometimes," said Kelly of McCormick. "On the other hand, I don't think he could write anything in his paper that could make me dislike him." For scandal-weary Chicagoans, the smoothly functioning political organization named for Kelly and his *consigliere*, Pat Nash, foreshadowed the claim made by a later machine Democrat, Richard J. Daley, that Chicago was a city that worked.

Efficiency came at a price. McCormick let his friendship for the mayor blind him to continuing police corruption, fueled by gambling interests who spent $20 million a year to purchase protection from ward leaders aligned with the Kelly-Nash machine. When Chicago relief authorities, acting on orders from the mayor, halted cash payments to drunks, McCormick was unmollified. Kelly's action was a step in the right direction, he wrote, but it didn't go nearly far enough in separating those "who cannot get work from those who do not want to work. The unemployed are slowly starving the country to death."[18]

By 1937, Chicago's heedless optimism about a Panglossian future was as dead and discredited as Sam Insull. The city's cultural star was descending, its economy reliant on handouts from a friendly administration in Washington. "Roosevelt is my religion," Ed Kelly boasted, and with good reason. Federal money was the mother's milk of modern urban politics, and Chicago was well suckled. Thanks to Roosevelt and the federal relief administrator, Harry Hopkins, Kelly was able to obtain millions of dollars with which to build a long-postponed subway and expand the pitifully small municipal airport. The New Deal also funded extensive improvements to Chicago's highway and transport grid.

Among these was the Outer Drive Bridge, built within the shadow of Tribune Tower. Harold Ickes had little difficulty in persuading Roosevelt to attend the dedication of the bridge, set for October 5, 1937. To the president, the ceremony was too good to pass up, both as an opportunity to showcase a great construction project carried out by the Public Works Administration and as a chance to humble Colonel McCormick in his own bailiwick. En route to Chicago, FDR made a western swing. At Yellowstone

Park, swapping good-natured jokes with Walter Trohan, the president said that Old Faithful reminded him of the *Tribune*'s fulminations. Trohan saw the same natural wonder and thought of Harold Ickes "on one of his happier days."[19]

McCormick took a grimmer view of the world. While Roosevelt and Landon had been pummeling each other and the *Tribune* was imagining an American soviet in the making, real Communists were lending assistance to the Spanish republic in its bloody civil war with nationalists led by General Francisco Franco. Hitler's Germany, already an imperialist power solving its problems in other people's countries, was marshaling heavy air support for Franco's rebels. Mussolini, wearing a jackel smile on his lips after his armies overran Ethiopia, provided additional aid to the fascist cause in Spain.

These were the locust years, in Churchill's unforgettable phrase, when Hitler reoccupied the Rhineland unopposed by France or England and the United States took shelter behind two oceans, neutrality legislation that precluded arms sales to either side in Spain, and an isolationist tradition first sanctified in George Washington's Farewell Address (wrongly, as it turned out, since Washington never used the expression "entangling alliances," famously attributed to him by isolationists ever since. That stern warning against European snares was issued by Thomas Jefferson, the most cosmopolitan man ever to occupy the presidency).

When looking east, McCormick adopted a fatalistic stance. "Japan is in the hands of the military," he wrote in February 1937, as Japanese forces pressed their advantage against poorly equipped Chinese defenders, "and the military when in power always wants war. I am afraid we will have it, no matter what we do."[20]

Against the backdrop of a scorched and gloomy world, Roosevelt contemplated offering his peacemaking services to fifty-five nations. Neville Chamberlain, newly installed at 10 Downing Street, had no desire to leave it to come to Washington and coordinate strategy with his American cousins. Roosevelt's advisers were no better disposed toward his mediation efforts. It would be far wiser, they urged, to educate the American people to foreign dangers by dramatically bearding the isolationist lion in his midwestern den. Harold Ickes supplied the venue and the organizing metaphor for what would become known as Roosevelt's quarantine speech, wherein the spread of dictatorship in Europe was likened to a contagious disease against which the democratic community had the right to quarantine itself.

Three quarters of a million Chicagoans cheered the president as his motorcade crept along Lake Shore Drive on a perfect October morning. McCormick was prepared. Well aware that the speaker's platform lay directly across from a sprawling *Tribune* warehouse on the north bank of the Chicago River, the Colonel had ordered workmen to paint in five-foot-high letters both a greeting and a challenge:

UNDOMINATED. CHICAGO TRIBUNE.
"THE WORLD'S GREATEST NEWSPAPER"

Roosevelt seemed oblivious to the studied insult as he rose to deliver the most provocative speech of his presidency. After some commonplace remarks dedicating the bridge, he invited his listeners to survey with him a continent sliding toward the abyss. With violence and tyranny engulfing much of Europe, said the president, the United States could no longer hope to exist in splendid isolation. "Let no one imagine that America will escape" the triumph of barbarism overseas, he warned; neither should his countrymen indulge the naive belief that in such an eventuality, the Western Hemisphere would be permitted "to carry on the ethics and arts of civilization" unmolested by the new masters of Europe.

Roosevelt used powerful phrases to cloak actions that were, even by his enigmatic standards, models of inexactitude. To counter the foreign threat, he urged that "the peace-loving nations" join in a quarantine to check the spread of lawlessness by aggressors "sick" with war lust. At a post-dedication lunch at the residence of Cardinal Mundelein, he hastened to explain himself in ways that rendered his bold proposal virtually meaningless. He envisioned no military action to buttress his words, he told the churchman, nor sanctions as generally understood. Instead, Roosevelt said he would rely on moral force to make his quarantine stick, up to and including the ostracism of nations whose militaristic conduct offended the international conscience.

To McCormick, the speech was a curious mix of benevolence and fraud. Hardly the first time FDR had worn more than one face, the president's deft performance nevertheless reminded McCormick that Janus was a war god. In a biting editorial entitled "He Too Would Keep Us Out of War," the *Tribune* resurrected the ghost of Woodrow Wilson, another moralist who had started out preaching the sanctity of international treaties and wound up leading a reluctant nation into battle. "We are to associate ourselves with the powers that abide by their word," that is to say, with Britain, France, Russia, and, by implication, China. But what about faithless nations like Japan? An economic boycott of Japan might or might not bring that imperialistic power to its senses; it almost certainly would not bring it to its knees. What would Roosevelt do, demanded the *Tribune*, if moral suasion failed to halt the Japanese occupation of north China? "The moment came when Mr. Wilson found himself with no alternative but war . . . It would be difficult today to obtain a declaration of war from Congress, but after months of propaganda the task may be simplified. It was so in 1917; it may be so again in 1938."

Roosevelt had taken pains to reassure his Chicago audience that he hated war. The crowd's response had been all the speaker could hope for. Woodrow Wilson had won similar cheers during the 1916 campaign, then turned around and committed U.S. troops to battle a month after his second inauguration. McCormick could only hope that history would not repeat itself.

✧ 4

It would be a mistake to conclude that McCormick squandered all his energies in regretting the past or dreading the future. A month after the quarantine speech, he indulged his sense of whimsy in thanking Winston Churchill for sending his biography of his distinguished ancestor, the Duke of Marlborough. To Churchill, "the only man I know who drinks bourbon before breakfast," McCormick painted an improbable word picture of himself in an armchair by the fire, digging into the new volume "with a glass of gingerale and orange juice on the table." "I hope the Christmas season will bring you what cheer and comfort it can in this lunatic world," he told Churchill.[21]

For McCormick, there was precious little in recent years to raise his spirits or instill faith in human relationships. The passage of time had exacted a heavy personal and professional toll. After forty-two years with the *Tribune*, Teddy Beck retired as managing editor on January 1, 1937. His place was taken by Bob Lee, for whom the job proved to be literally a mankiller. After Lee died of a heart attack in January 1939, his title passed in the normal order of succession to Pat Maloney. Along with the promotion, McCormick gave Maloney a bit of advice, no doubt rooted in bitter memories of the ostracism visited on him and Amy by their snooty North Shore neighbors. "Don't ever move to Lake Forest," he remarked.[22]

Examination of genealogical research into McCormick's ancestors convinced him, as he waggishly told his niece Katrina (Triny to her relations), that they were "a pretty inbred lot." Triny posed a different set of problems for her uncle. Following her 1935 marriage to a New York blueblood named Courtlandt Barnes, Jr., Triny, the eldest daughter of Medill and Ruth McCormick, became a regular in the city's fashionably liberal circles. She informed Uncle Bert that she wished to dispose of her *Tribune* inheritance.[23]

McCormick, already overextended through a new mill and company town at Baie Comeau, sixty miles upriver from Shelter Bay, borrowed $2.2 million to gratify her request. "I think you have done about the right thing," he told her. His niece could not live in the past, as she would be forced to do if dependent on a newspaper "which you have left behind . . . You have acted like an officer and a gentleman. I am very fond of you."[24]

As the publisher of *Common Sense,* a liberal magazine promoting racial equality and international cooperation, Triny lived in a converted coach-house with her husband and their young son, Medill. Over time she became more eager than ever to sever residual ties to the *Chicago Tribune.* Giving away — anonymously — the bulk of her fortune to left-wing causes released her from feelings "of being in bondage," she told her uncle. For her six remaining shares of *Tribune* stock, the family rebel wanted a higher price than what she had originally received. This time McCormick's expressions of regret were pro forma. The most he had ever paid for the stock had been $35,000 a share, to Triny's mother. "As long as the excess profit tax exists — and that will probably be indefinitely — the stock cannot become more valuable," he concluded, in a pointed reminder that New Deal beggers could hardly expect to be too choosy when liquidating their ill-gotten assets.[25]

With Triny cashing in her chips, those curious about the future of the McCormick-Patterson dynasty turned their sights on her younger brother, a twenty-one-year-old Columbia dropout named Medill McCormick, known within the family as Johnny. Any hopes they might have nurtured were snuffed out late in June 1938, when a search party organized by his mother found the young man's broken body at the foot of a 2,000-foot cliff in the Sandia Mountains, not far from Albuquerque. Johnny had been mountain climbing when a bolt of lightning sent him hurtling to his death. The news stunned Colonel McCormick, who had grown comfortable with the idea of his nephew as uncrowned heir to the *Tribune.*

Adding to his disappointment was a widening gulf between himself and Joe Patterson. Mercurial as ever, Joe had set McCormick back on his heels by calling for a breakup of the Tribune Company and an equitable division of spoils between Chicago and New York. Patiently, the Colonel tried to explain the tax consequences of such a divorce, as well as the complications sure to attend future dealings for Canadian paper and anything else tied up in joint ownership. "I want to meet your wishes and your interests now as always during the past twenty-five years," he informed his cousin. "I don't want even a coolness between us in the twilight of life."[26]

The corporate partnership remained intact, although relations were often strained. One week after receiving word of young Medill McCormick's death, the Colonel traveled to New York for a quiet family ceremony uniting Joe Patterson, at last released by his fiercely Catholic wife, Alice, and Mary King, the mother of his sixteen-year-old son, Jimmy. Looking on was the waspish sister of the groom, Cissy Patterson. To her admirers, Cissy appeared to reincarnate Elizabeth I, sharing with the great queen flame-red hair and a pronounced streak of misfortune where men were concerned. To her enemies, in whose ranks were to be found many former admirers, Cissy was a viper with a $20,000-a-year clothes habit, still costlier tastes for alcohol and cocaine, and the sharpest tongue in Washington.

Cissy's storied career as America's first female big-city newspaper publisher is to be recommended to connoisseurs of invective as much as to students of journalism. Of her former son-in-law Drew Pearson, Cissy once wrote, "Ah, Drew, rose-sniffing, child-loving, child-cheater, sentimental Drew," before adding that "Robespierre [too] loved flowers ... canary buds and little children." The otherworldly Henry Wallace was a "crystal-gazing crackpot." As for the radio commentator Walter Winchell, it was "hard to tell what's biting this middle-aged ex-chorus boy," speculated Cissy for her 200,000 daily readers, although she did allow that Winchell suffered from "a chronic state of wild excitement, venom and perpetual motion of the jaw."27

Alice Roosevelt Longworth, Cissy's only rival for social supremacy in the nation's capital, summed up her outrageous contemporary by declaring, "I said a lot of things, but Cissy *did* them." Born in Chicago in 1884, Cissy weathered her disastrous first marriage, to the philandering Polish count Josef Gizycki. In 1917 she bought her freedom and that of her daughter Felicia, whom Gizycki had kidnapped in London and refused to relinquish until Nellie Patterson paid him $200,000 in ransom money. "She grew up to be very beautiful," boasted Cissy of the daughter she eventually disowned, "which I never was, God knows."

In 1925, Cissy married Elmer Schlesinger, a Chicago attorney and former counsel to the Federal Shipping Board. For a few years her turbulent spirit seemed tamed. Of course, Cissy being Cissy, no one really expected her to stifle her genius for self-advertisement. Her 1926 novel, *Glass Houses*, had Washington in an uproar over its thinly disguised portraits of Alice Roosevelt Longworth and Senator William Borah, the man many suspected was Alice's lover. In 1929, Elmer Schlesinger dropped dead on a South Carolina golf course. With admirable prescience for the economic rainy days that lay in store, the grieving widow took her late husband's children to court and emerged $600,000 richer.

Cissy had need of such reserves. She had decided to enter the Washington newspaper market, but only after obtaining assurances from her Chicago cousin that he had abandoned all thought of buying the *Washington Post*. If she really wanted to take on the established *Post* and *Star*, McCormick advised her, she should exploit the local angle. "Washington contains more personalities than any city in America," he reminded her. Cissy herself did not lack for personality. Given her flair for making news as well as reporting it, McCormick thought she needed little more to launch her new venture than "two or three bright writers, several part-time cartoonists, a good photographer or two, an advertising manager from *Vogue* or *Vanity Fair*, a contract with a Philadelphia or Baltimore printer," and an Associated Press membership. He couldn't promise her that her paper would achieve instant success, "but I can assure you it won't cost you much if it doesn't succeed."[28]

In 1930, William Randolph Hearst hired Cissy for $10,000 a year as the editor of his failing *Washington Herald*, circulation 61,000. On a sweltering August day the tyro met her staff for the first time. They had donned coats and ties for the occasion, which were insufficient to conceal their doubts about the society woman whose previous journalistic career had been limited to sporting articles in *Field and Stream* and the *Chicago Herald and Examiner.* "Suppose you say my being editor is just a stunt," said Cissy breezily, "but even so, let's all try to put it over." She examined more closely the sweaty masculinity herded into a back room of the *Herald*'s barnlike building on H Street. "And you don't have to wear coats while I'm around either."[29]

Over the next seven years, Cissy transformed the pallid *Herald* into a lively journal that was conservative in its politics and nothing else. As McCormick had forecast, success was not instantly gained. "My first year I was really too stupid for words," she acknowledged, with the frankness that disarmed — and often misled — her adversaries. "For instance, I refused to run the story of the Kentucky Derby on the front page. A horse race — how vulgar! Can you imagine?"

Cissy had printer's ink in her veins and her family's gift for making enemies. An early issue of the *Herald* disparaged Alice Roosevelt Longworth for her alleged inadequacies as a campaigner and declared that any assistance she might provide to the Senate campaign of her friend Ruth Hanna McCormick would "resolve itself, as usual, into posing for photographs." A more serious, and therefore profitable, feud erupted with Eugene Meyer, the publisher of the *Washington Post.* First Cissy raided Meyer's staff. She nabbed the best society editor in partygoing Washington. She also made off with Bob Considine, an ace sports writer.* When the *Post* ran a trademark rooster on its masthead, the *Herald* countered with its own symbolic greeting of the day, a dead chicken with its feet in the air and the caption, "You asked for it, Eugene." The warring publishers went to court over rights to "Andy Gump" and other popular comics syndicated by the *Tribune.* Cissy's family connections did not avail her with the judge, but she enjoyed a public relations victory anyway, sending Meyer a lump of raw meat with a card reading, "Here's your pound of flesh."

Theatrical as ever, Cissy boldly walked through the gates of Al Capone's

---

*The tables were turned when Hearst pirated Considine away from his protégé. As he recalled the scene in his 1967 book, *It's All News to Me*, Considine squirmed through a long, mock-friendly telephone conversation between Cissy and the squeaky-voiced W. R. After thirty minutes of extravagant praise for Considine, Cissy's voice lost its girlish simper. There was one final thing W. R. ought to know about young Mr. Considine, she snarled: "He's my illegitimate son by Calvin Coolidge!"

Miami mansion and talked her way past eight menacing bodyguards to obtain a newsmaking interview with the mobster. Her nerve temporarily failed her on another occasion: finding the famous physicist Albert Einstein sunbathing in the nude, Cissy modestly retreated, and was furious with herself for days afterward. Denied a systematic schooling, she brought to the *Herald* instincts rather than anything resembling a coherent philosophy. "A steady middle-of-the-road policy is the way to be popular and prosperous," she conceded. "But what fun is there in that?"

Accompanied by a photographer, Cissy visited southern sharecroppers and conveyed the full horror of their existence. Playing the role of Lady Bountiful, she campaigned for hot lunches for schoolchildren. Her "Suffer Little Children" feature took readers inside some of the capital's most desperate households.

Photos rarely appeared on Cissy's front page. "I was forever quarreling with the managing editor's choice of pictures, poor man," she explained. "I try to have a clean paper."

"Clean typography," she was asked, "or in content also?"

"Clean in typography only," she shot back.[30]

Her most celebrated adventure unfolded throughout the demoralizing winter of 1931. Borrowing some old clothes from a maid, Cissy sailed forth as Maude Martin, a destitute actress taken in by the Salvation Army and subsequently employed as a $5-a-week cook. Given that she arrived at her place of shelter in a sixteen-cylinder chauffeur-driven Cadillac, one may safely doubt the completeness of her disguise.

During the early years of the New Deal, Cissy accepted entirely too many White House invitations for the liking of her Chicago cousin. Roosevelt himself said it was a pity that Mrs. Patterson didn't write more, her pen being so "trenchant." He didn't know the half of it. On the front page of the *Times-Herald*, the journal she had cobbled together from the morning *Herald* and the evening *Times*, she declared in 1938 that the chief priority of the Roosevelt White House must be the restoration of confidence. The president alone could achieve this, but only if he forsook "hate and vanity" and resumed "the patience with which you so nobly and courageously conquered an illness that would have broken the spirit of most of us. You have been a great leader and a great man," Cissy lectured FDR. "You can be again."[31]

Thereafter the White House invitations dried up. By 1941, charging that Roosevelt had "lied us into war," Cissy was joining McCormick in bitter condemnation of the president she had admired so extravagantly. Toward her brother Joe she displayed unwavering hero worship, forgetting the divergence between her champagne tastes and his loudly proclaimed affinity for the common man. Her relations with Cousin Bertie ran hot and cold. Cissy ridiculed his military pretensions and pontifical manner, comparing him to a Bourbon king in exile and spurning his gift of "a serious-minded lady police dog," which appeared unlikely to get along with her covey of nervous, inbred, and highly jealous French poodles.

Yet Cissy was never reluctant to employ her catlike femininity or assume a stance of womanly helplessness to enlist McCormick's sympathy and aid. Declaring "my business office is in a bad way," in September 1939 she asked to borrow McCormick's lieutenant Bill McFarlane to review her entire operation. (A *Tribune* circulation expert was already advising her on how to improve home delivery.) She hesitated to make such a request, she wrote unconvincingly, "ashamed to admit that I'm a flop in business." McCormick lent McFarlane and then some. He urged Cissy to unload the *American Weekly*, a tired Hearst supplement, and to eliminate her least profitable editions.[32]

What he meant as encouragement, or at least as an expression of cousinly sympathy, Cissy took as a slap at her leadership. When they were together, the two fought like cats and dogs, recalled Maryland Hooper, a Wheaton neighbor who chanced to observe the argumentative cousins together. Yet the nature of the McCormick-Patterson Trust and the thin margin of control it gave the three cousins over their respective properties enforced an uneasy coexistence.[33]

✧ 5

Living for and through the *Tribune*, McCormick found it easy to think in terms of generations and even centuries. His vision had led him to plant his flag in Canadian soil. Canada held less allure for Joe Patterson, who was already contemplating retirement and who had four children and two wives to further concentrate his thoughts. The two cousins had long chafed in their unlikely partnership. Now, in the late 1930s, Joe was being asked, or rather told, to invest millions in a *Tribune* subsidiary at Baie Comeau, in a desolate backwater inhabited by servile French Canadians, with their hierarchies and their bleeding hearts of Jesus.

To one of Patterson's aggressively populist outlook, the new town represented a costly attempt by his seigneurial kinsman to carve out a wilderness domain in compensation for the rejection he suffered at the hands of his own countrymen. The ensuing struggle tested each man's will. The advantage lay with McCormick, long accustomed to playing the turtle against more charismatic hares. Still, Joe Patterson was not alone in accusing the Colonel of economic and cultural imperialism. As a result, McCormick's Canadian empire seemed fated for extinction almost before it could be proclaimed.

That Joe Patterson should entertain doubts about the most audacious building project in *Tribune* history was not without irony, for it was the runaway success of the *New York Daily News* that led to negotiations with the province of Quebec for a second paper mill to complement the overtaxed facility at Thorold, Ontario. Under terms of a pact signed in 1923, McCormick was obliged to construct a Quebec mill no later than 1930. Over the next few years he invested $5 million in docks, dams, and other improvements along the rugged Manicouagan and Outardes rivers. Overexpansion in the Canadian paper industry and the ravages of economic depression forced several postponements in the projected starting date for the mill.

These delays encouraged rivals of the Ontario Paper Company to demand mandatory limits on commercial papermaking north of the border. Prorating, as it was formally called, was designed to equalize Depression-era hardship. McCormick, uninterested in easing the distress of his competitors, argued that because the Ontario Paper Company sold its product exclusively to the *Tribune* and the *Daily News*, it did not meet the definition of a commercial establishment. As a result he was able to stave off the paralyzing hand of government control. But the threat of prorating remained, a serpent coiled under the negotiating table where McCormick and the Liberal provincial government of Premier Louis Alexandre Taschereau dickered over interpretation of the 1923 agreement.

McCormick was given an ultimatum: start work on the new mill by July 1, 1937, or purchase an existing facility — ideally in the premier's home district of St. Anne de Beaupré, where half the papermaking workforce was idle. Overriding Arthur Schmon, McCormick set out to build not just a mill but an entire community to go with it. The town of Baie Comeau, two hundred miles east of Quebec, represented the single largest Canadian construction project in the 1930s. The rigorous climate of the area and its virtual inaccessability during much of the year strongly argued against such a risky undertaking. So did the premier of neighboring Ontario, who shook his fist and talked of legal action to block any *Tribune* expansion outside the borders of his economically famished province.

Legislation to establish the new town site was introduced in the Quebec parliament in May 1936. It did not enjoy smooth sailing. Opponents of the Taschereau ministry, quick to exploit any vulnerability in the closely divided legislature, denounced the premier as an agent of foreign exploitation. Nationalists led by Maurice Duplessis, a fiery lawyer from the Montreal suburb of Trois Rivières, accused Taschereau of complicity in a $10 million giveaway to the Ontario Paper Company. In fact, the premier was guilty of far worse, as a most inconveniently timed corruption scandal implicated several members of his cabinet. Preliminary site work at Baie Comeau was well under way and contracts totaling $12 million were about to be let when the voters of Quebec went to the polls in August and turned the keys of power over to Duplessis.

Confronted with a "radical and possibly revolutionary" new government in Quebec, McCormick ordered the postponement of work pending clarification of the Nationalist party's intentions. He needn't have worried. After a rocky start, he and Duplessis established a surprising rapport. "They were the same type of man," according to Terrence Flahiff, a long-time *Tribune* correspondent in Ottawa. Duplessis, a bachelor, was married to Quebec with the same ardent fidelity that characterized McCormick's devotion to his newspaper. Both men had sacrificed friendship and trust to the pursuit and exercise of power. Patriotic to a fault, they were fated to be partners in developing Jacques Cartier's "land that God gave to Cain."[34]

Each morning Duplessis left his eleventh-floor suite in the Château Frontenac to attend mass in a basilica a stone's throw from the grand old railroad hotel. By seven-thirty the premier was back at the château barber-shop. Provincial law prohibited barbers from cutting hair before eight in the morning but was silent on the practice of shaving. As his chin was scraped, Duplessis read three morning papers and held court with favor-seekers like Arthur Schmon.

"You are one of those Taschereau lovers," Duplessis told Schmon, an offense for which Schmon was never entirely forgiven. Worse, the plodding Schmon bored the quick-thinking premier with tedious details. Once, Schmon paused in the middle of a lengthy monologue about timber limits on the Outardes River. "Do you follow me, Mr. Prime Minister?" he asked. "Follow you? Goddamnit, I'm thirty minutes ahead of you," the premier replied.[35]

Duplessis was perfectly capable of accepting the *Tribune*'s hospitality, including an excellent meal and fine cigars, then plunking himself in a comfortable chair and looking at Schmon with studied indifference. "Now Arthur," he would remark condescendingly, "take a couple of trots around the track."[36]

In short, Maurice Duplessis was the sort of man with whom McCormick could do business. The stocky politician with the slicked-back hair, undisputed master of the National Union, proved to be the Colonel's equal in anti-Communist fervor and his superior in authoritarian rule. Favoring free speech more than he feared subversives, McCormick took exception to a Quebec statute under which Duplessis, in his dual roles as premier and attorney general, was authorized to close any establishment suspected of being used for "subversive activities."

"You know, Mr. Prime Minister, I don't like your padlock law," McCormick observed at their first meeting. Although the ensuing debate changed no minds, it was never less than civil. Neither man was anxious to offend the other: McCormick had a huge investment to protect, while Duplessis hoped to solidify his corporate power base and spur economic development at minimal cost to the provincial government. In return for special treatment by Quebec City, McCormick agreed to charter a new firm, the Quebec North Shore Paper Company, and to pay into the provincial treasury a $50 fee for every square mile transferred from the preexisting Ontario Paper Company to its French Canadian offspring. Even before Duplessis came to power, McCormick had accepted without protest an 8 percent provincial sales tax, which promised to add half a million dollars to the Baie Comeau construction budget. In a further concession to Canadian nationalism, he rejected lower bids from German manufacturers and bought papermaking machines of Canadian design. He did so, he told Patterson, out of concern that Germany might soon be at war. Left unsaid was the need to placate his northern neighbors, who were feeling none too hospitable in the summer of 1936.[37]

McCormick's mostly polite sparring with Duplessis showed how unrealistic his desire to escape government controls by fleeing New Deal America was. Less than a week after Roosevelt's triumphant reelection, Joe Patterson received an effusive expression of presidential gratitude ("I do not need to tell you how very splendid you have been throughout . . . I only wish you had been able to get the *Literary Digest* to back their crazy poll with a million dollars"). McCormick didn't wait around to be reminded of the special relationship his cousin enjoyed with the Roosevelt White House. On November 8, he left Chicago for his Canadian colony in the making.[38]

He quickly learned that not everyone along the St. Lawrence wished to be colonized. More jarring discoveries awaited him in Baie Comeau, where the unyielding terrain had forced workman to bore through as much as eighteen feet of rock in order to lay out sewer and water lines. At a time when finished houses cost $5,000, McCormick's crews were spending that much to blast a single foundation from the granite hillsides. "He thought he was going broke," recalled Arthur "Froggy" Sewell, the first mayor of Baie Comeau. "And he just stood there and shivered" in exasperation. All work was halted for three weeks. By the time engineers persuaded McCormick to go forward, construction was slowed by the brutal northern winter. Workers found shelter in long structures like barracks, built to replace an earlier tent city. (A handful of women passed the desolate season in asphalt-shingled houses rushed to completion before the first snows.) As temperatures fell to fifty below zero, shivering homeowners burned six tons of coal between November and March.[39]

All fuel, not to mention food, building materials, and construction equipment, had to be transported to the work site by water. At the time, few shared McCormick's vision of the temperamental St. Lawrence as a commercial avenue. Yet by the summer of 1937 the logistical puzzle seemed well on its way to solution. Five thousand laborers, woodsmen, road builders, drill operators, riveters, and locomotive drivers toiled from daybreak to evening star. They laid thirty-two miles of highway and moved tons of rock and steel on virgin rail tracks. They completed the world's longest flume, a fourteen-mile marvel of design fashioned from Douglas fir. They constructed an electric plant at Outardes Falls, then strung thirteen miles of cable to power the $8 million red-brick paper mill rising in the raw village of Baie Comeau.

McCormick returned to the area in October 1937. "I've visited the job and I find it's going very well," he remarked at a meeting of department and construction heads. Nevertheless, he continued, "if you work a little harder you could do better. For every day that you bring the mill into production before the scheduled date I'll give you $5,000." Rising from his chair, he slapped on a hat. "Good morning, gentlemen."[40]

The gambit paid off handsomely. Originally scheduled to take two years, the mill was completed in twenty months. Maurice Duplessis joined McCormick in dedicating the new community on June 11, 1938. Before the hard-drinking premier's arrival, company officials secreted bottles of Holland's gin behind practically every tree in town. McCormick took the occasion to praise English- and French-speaking Québecois for their cooperation and express the hope that Baie Comeau might one day supply the province with a bishop or premier. (Not long afterwards, Duplessis, a diabetic who required a daily shot of insulin to maintain his health, went cold turkey. The man who ran Quebec as his personal fiefdom explained that he couldn't afford to play tricks with his memory. "I have people come to me and say, 'You know, last night you promised you'd build us a bridge and give us money for a school,' " said Duplessis. "Now I remember what I promised.")[41]

For once he was guilty of thinking too small. On visits to Baie Comeau, McCormick generally stayed in Long House, a rustic log fishing camp perched on a hill overlooking the salmon-filled English River. In the living room of Long House was a piano, atop which a small boy of precocious charm and vocal skills earned $50 for performing jaunty melodies like "The Wreck of the *Julie Plante*." The boy had a standing invitation to return whenever the Colonel was in residence. Fifty years later, the child prodigy from Baie Comeau was prime minister of Canada. Not the least of Brian Mulroney's political assets was his voice, an instrument of astonishing range and silken sincerity.

The town in which Mulroney honed his stage presence grew into a thriving settlement of more than 3,000 inhabitants, nearly all dependent on McCormick for their livelihood. The Colonel paid wages better than the prevailing standard and was not stingy with overtime. Taxes and rents in Baie Comeau were deliberately kept low. The Tribune Company shouldered 90 percent of municipal operating costs and absorbed losses of $15,000 a year in running the local hospital. McCormick built an ice rink, community hall, and arcade. He furnished the land for a Catholic cathedral and embellished the building with stained glass windows and bells imported from France.

With profits from the sale of beer to thirsty loggers, Baie Comeau got a library. "Alice, it looks to me like you need some furniture," McCormick said to the town librarian. Thus encouraged, she compiled a list of everything required to create a first-class library, not excluding solid brass paste pots. Her itemized wish list exceeded $5,000 worth of goods. With more than a little trepidation she presented it to McCormick, who merely noted that she had left off a traveling ladder with which to gain access to books near the ceiling. "You'd better get one," he said before scribbling 'O.K. McC" at the bottom of her list.[42]

At the same time, the Colonel was perfectly capable of making a scene over the price of cotton gloves in the village store — a retail outlet he owned. The gloves were a practical necessity, given his dread of insect bites. On excursions into the woods he donned a specially designed hat and protective screen. During his early visits to the region, he lived in a remote camp, sparsely furnished with an oversize bed and bath, and at his insistence, with no telephone. He took dinner at the Manoir, a five-star company guesthouse, before retiring for the evening with a book and a bottle of scotch.[43]

His energy seemed inexhaustible. Before lunch one day, Arthur Sewell called his wife and asked her to retrieve the carefully planned itinerary drawn up in anticipation of McCormick's visit. "Tear out the first five days," he told her. "We've done them."

Once a week, McCormick had a loaf of bush bread, cooked in the lumber camp, wrapped airtight and flown to him wherever he was. As often as not, he celebrated his birthdays in Quebec. Days in advance, woodsmen would be dispatched to make a clearing and build rough tables ten miles upriver from Baie Comeau. The actual dinner was overseen by the head chef of the Ritz Hotel in Montreal, brought in for the occasion. Guests were transported to the party by barge, along with a vast walnut chair, set up for the Colonel's use, that reminded his niece Bazy of a throne. Swaying happily to French Canadian folk songs, his mood elevated by copious amounts of champagne, McCormick played his role to the hilt, even addressing his subjects in French as "mes enfants."[44]

He was not always so amenable to local custom. At a dinner attended by two self-important political figures, McCormick shocked Arthur Schmon by announcing that he wanted to sit beside Alice Lane, the local librarian. Schmon reminded him of the power wielded by the official guests. "I don't care," said McCormick. "I'm not having those trumps on both sides of me. I'll take one of them, but I won't have both."[45]

At another function, the wife of the Anglican bishop of Quebec turned to her dinner partner and said, "Well, Colonel McCormick, what do you think of the president of the United States?"

"I never discuss politics at a social gathering."[46]

In private, his tongue loosened. McCormick enjoyed hearing of Alice Lane's father, who despised Roosevelt as much as he admired good English. Unfortunately, said the old man, nobody in public life spoke decent English "except that bastard in the White House."[47]

In September 1938, McCormick had the satisfaction of showing off Baie Comeau to Joe and Cissy Patterson. Joe made no effort to hide his boredom. Cissy at least feigned enthusiasm. "Your vision and force have created a working empire out of the wilderness," she wrote after returning to civilization. "It's an astonishing accomplishment."[48]

❖ 6

McCormick's Canadian foray was intended to secure his economic and political independence, whatever might come to pass in New Deal America. Instead it ensnared him in multiple layers of domestic bureaucracy and foreign intrigue. Looking over his shoulder — and implicitly standing in judgment of the *Tribune*'s editorial policies toward Great Britain — were proprietary officials in Quebec City, Ottawa, and London. Under the system of crown rental, the *Tribune* owned the land on which its mill at Baie Comeau stood, as well as the actual town site and some adjoining territory, but it leased most of its timberlands.

This left McCormick vulnerable to British displeasure. Mortally offend the dominion's London overseers, said Froggy Sewell, and "you've got a big mill and no wood." Even within French-speaking Quebec, twisting the lion's tail carried political risks, as Maurice Duplessis learned to his sorrow just after World War II broke out in September 1939. Overestimating his strength, Duplessis fought an election over the War Measures Act passed by Ottawa, which he attacked as an intrusion on provincial autonomy. His defeat at the polls was a rare British victory in the war's early rounds.

From his vantage point in Montreal, Arthur Schmon warned McCormick that retribution was inevitable unless he moderated his anglophobic editorials. With their mother country at war, few Canadian patriots relished the thought of supplying newsprint for the Colonel to vent his hostility against an empire fighting for its life. Beyond proposing a U.S.-Canadian military alliance at a juncture when Britain's survival appeared in doubt, McCormick seemed impervious to economic pressures. The *Tribune* clung to the view that it was the refusal of Great Britain and France to return German territory wrongly claimed by the victorious Allied powers at Versailles, not naked aggression by Hitler, that had sparked the latest round of European war fever.

In fact McCormick knew better, thanks to the remarkable work of Sigrid Schultz. At the end of March 1938, his Berlin correspondent had forwarded an uncanny assessment of Hitler's future military intentions. Barely pausing to digest Austria, said Schultz, which he had bloodlessly annexed a few days earlier, the Führer would next turn his attention to Czechoslovakia. Agitation of German-speaking inhabitants of the Sudeten region was the necessary prelude to Nazi occupation. The combined strength of these newly acquired lands would swell the German army by 800,000 men. This was not an unmixed blessing, for rapid expansion of his domain would also mean more mouths to feed. Schultz wrote that Hitler coveted the French provinces of Alsace and Lorraine for their vital minerals, which he needed to sustain the German war machine. Yet "there is only one territory that can provide the food needed for this great conglomeration of Germans," she went on, predicting over three years before it happened the Nazi invasion of the Ukraine, Europe's granary and the Soviet Union's indispensable breadbasket. Schultz had read *Mein Kampf.* She took seriously its author's shrill assertion that a German master race could realize its destiny only by expanding to the east at the expense of inferior Slavic populations.[49]

Schultz was a student of history, McCormick its prisoner. Seeking parallels where none existed, McCormick made the further mistake of defining Hitler in evolutionary, not revolutionary, terms. "Just how like Bismarck is Hitler?" he asked Schultz. The Iron Chancellor had not come from the German nobility. "Was he, perhaps, from the same class as Cromwell? Hitler comes from the same class." As McCormick saw things, the Nazi dictator's comparatively lowly origins gave him special insight into mass opinion. Regrettably, however, Hitler's modest record in the Great War had also instilled in him the brutal habits of the European noncommissioned officer.[50]

Odd as this analysis is, it is harder still to explain how McCormick persuaded himself that Britain under George VI was a fascist redoubt and that British imperialism was indistinguishable from Nazi aggression against Germany's neighbors. Trapped in his conventional balance-of-power theories, McCormick came under scrutiny by British intelligence officers in the United States. At the start of January 1938, King George's ambassador in Washington, Sir Ronald Lindsay, described the *Tribune* publisher for his government in London as "stubborn, slow thinking and bellicose." The Colonel's anti-British attitudes were thought to stem from canings he had received as a schoolboy at Eton — a school he never attended — or possibly from the refusal of British authorities during World War I to permit him access to enemy territory. "For some reason he has always found some difficulty in getting himself taken seriously," concluded Sir Ronald, exhibiting the patronizing air so offensive to McCormick and millions of his fellow Americans.[51]*

The Colonel revealed perhaps more than he intended by recounting his visit to the home of one English nabob, where he had introduced himself as McCormick of the *Chicago Tribune,* only to be told by an officious majordomo that members of the press were to use the back door. Others blamed his anti-British mania on the royal refusal to receive Amy McCormick as a divorcée.[52]

Whatever snubs may have been inflicted on him or his wife, they mattered less than McCormick's reading of history and his repeated encounters with an English mindset as insular as it was insufferable. "I have never been able to discuss the monarchical form of government with an Englishman," he once observed. He found incomprehensible a social climate wherein dukes were to be contemplated but not criticized. He thought English courts "haughty, harsh and arbitrary," cloaking their imperfections in absurd pageantry and costumes worthy of Little Lord Fauntleroy. Worse, British newspapers did the bidding of the establishment, whether censoring a royal affair or downplaying Communist demonstrations within earshot of Buckingham Palace.

In covering the British royal family, the *Tribune* practiced a *lèse majesté* scarcely removed from the petty disrespect earlier shown by Big Bill Thompson. The paper ungallantly theorized that Queen Elizabeth's resentment of her more attractive sister-in-law, the Duchess of Kent, had led her to banish the Kents to Australia. The announcement that George and Elizabeth would pay a visit to the United States in 1939 brought out the paranoid worst in McCormick. The timing of the news, just prior to the 1938 midterm elections, made him suspect political skulduggery. To David Darrah, then his London bureau chief, the Colonel fired off a message inquiring whether the White House had sought the royal visit in the belief that it would help Roosevelt "with the snobbish East."[53]

McCormick repeatedly denied that he was anti-British. With considerably more credibility, he portrayed himself as being exclusively proAmerican. If so, he was not the first nationalist to love his country more than the people who inhabited it. In this as in so much else, he emulated his xenophobic grandfather, whose disdain for Queen Victoria's far-flung emissaries was no greater than his contempt for those Chicagoans whose devotion to "gambling sports and sensuous personal interests" unfitted them for the privilege of voting. On the eve of the crucial McKinley-Bryan

---

*Sir Ronald was hardly more generous in assessing Franklin Roosevelt, whom he accused of being obstinate and of surrounding himself with yes men. Moreover, wrote the undiplomatic British diplomat, "his intellectual powers are only moderate and his knowledge of certain subjects, particularly finance and economics, is superficial."

race in 1896, Joseph Medill had denounced welfare state advocates for preaching the gospel of "pamperism, where the worthless, the drunkards, the loafers, the lazy vagabonds, the fellows who hate to work" expected the industrious, the self-respecting, and the efficient to support them "in pauper homes."[54]

Now, looking to the 1938 elections as a referendum on the stalled Roosevelt revolution, Medill's grandson delivered some equally astringent comments. The concept of government-built housing for those with the lowest earning power struck McCormick as "insane." Builders had no respect for other people's money. On the contrary, they had "a riot of pleasure" in filling new houses with unnecessary gadgets. "People of good earning power, and even of great wealth, are often found living in houses half a century old. Why then brand-new construction for the least competent of our citizens?"[55]

From time to time his editorial instructions invited head-scratching. "Let us say that through the instrumentability of the *Tribune*, it is gradually dawning upon the nation that weeds are among our principal evils," McCormick notified his writers. "We do not feel that the time is ripe yet to put it in our platform, but we hope to do so fairly soon." As he warned of weeds in the garden, the Colonel pointed an accusing finger at another kind of noxious growth. "Anybody who suggests that we have a foreign policy, because of his nationality, other than American" should be deported. This anathema on disloyal Americans, pronounced against the backdrop of feverish diplomatic efforts to avert a war over Czechoslovakia, preceded by hours a draft editorial on the European crisis entitled "If War Comes."[56]

McCormick was confident that a superior British fleet, in partnership with its French ally, could swiftly blockade Germany and the Mediterranean. Doubtless, Nazi bombers would kill people and destroy property, he wrote, "but there is nothing to indicate that they can be at all decisive in the war." Moreover, no known weapons had the capacity to pierce existing French or German fortifications. Thus, whatever the fate of the Czechs, McCormick anticipated a replay of the stalement of 1914–17, with a disproportionate share of the war's burden falling on "the central powers." "If we are able to maintain our sanity and resist our communists," he concluded, none too hopefully, "we will be the only solvent and civilized power left on earth."[57]

At the start of September, McCormick reminded Winston Churchill that he was expected to stay with Bert and Amy during his forthcoming trip to the United States. "I hope you will be here for the pleasure of seeing you," wrote the Colonel, "and also because it will mean there is no war." These hopes were soon crushed. Unwilling to be out of his country at a moment of supreme peril — and high drama — Churchill was to experience great mortification over the eleventh-hour deal between Hitler and Chamberlain that averted war and sacrificed Czech honor. The *Tribune* shed no tears over the demise of the "Jig Saw Nation," which had been cobbled together by the men of Versailles in defiance of ethnic and geographical realities. Most Americans agreed, with 52 percent of those interviewed by George Gallup voicing support for Chamberlain's "peace in our time."[58]

McCormick turned his attention to the closing weeks of the American political campaign. To a reader who was fearful that his harsh attacks on Roosevelt as a Communist might boomerang, he was unapologetic. "The trouble is that Mr. Roosevelt *is* a Communist," he wrote, "and there are those who will be against him for that reason, once they can be persuaded of the fact." Four days later, Republicans scored major gains at the expense of the becalmed administration. Overnight the GOP doubled its membership in the House of Representatives. The rejuvenated party also welcomed to the national stage attractive newcomers such as Thomas E. Dewey, the gangbusting New York district attorney who had come within a whisker of upsetting governor Herbert Lehman; Ohioans Robert Taft and John Bricker; and the thirty-three-year-old governor-elect of Minnesota, Harold Stassen.[59]

In New York, McCormick invited the conservative Democrat Bainbridge Colby to join him for a celebratory cocktail. "If it had not been for us," he told Colby, thinking back to the abortive Republican–Jeffersonian Democrat coalition of 1936, "there might not have been any election."[60]

Roosevelt recalled his ambassador to Berlin in protest of Jewish persecution. McCormick dismissed the gesture as a post-election sop to public opinion. "I would like to see anything done that would ameliorate the conditions of the Jews in Germany," he claimed, "but it does not look as though it can be accomplished by coercion." On the side he took a poke at Joseph P. Kennedy, Roosevelt's man in London, as "the most royalist of American ambassadors." He had already clashed with Kennedy, who had threatened to sue the *Tribune* over an article that questioned his White House standing following the leak of sensitive diplomatic information and Kennedy's presidential aspirations for 1940. (In fact, Roosevelt's press secretary, Steve Early, had personally supplied Walter Trohan with the evidence of Kennedy's treachery. Kennedy's friend Arthur Krock, thinking the president might find Kennedy's reports of interest, innocently sent FDR copies of them; they differed dramatically from the official assessments Kennedy was providing the State Department and the White House.)[61]

"You are the victim, not of the reporter, but of your political associates," McCormick told Kennedy. "We are living in a troubled world, and if we suffer from nothing worse than the most savage abuse, we will be fortunate."[62]

In the first week of January 1939, Roosevelt proposed a $2 billion re-armament program, which was strongly endorsed by the *Tribune*. McCor-mick was unable to confirm reports that FDR, supposedly in financial straits, was negotiating to write a newspaper column after leaving the White House in 1941. But he did uncover credible evidence from former employees of the Interior Department indicating that Honest Harold Ickes had employed departmental investigators to harass a rival in a love affair, that he had obtained the man's income tax return, and that gov-ernment agents had followed Ickes at his request to make certain that he was not being shadowed en route to trysts in Baltimore and Atlantic City.[63]

The paranoid Ickes had also used federal gumshoes to examine the origins of the Landon campaign, possible payoffs to Jim Farley by gov-ernment truck contractors — even Mrs. Roosevelt's new town project, Arthurdale, in the Maryland suburbs not far from Washington. When the *Tribune* hinted at graft in the secretary's purchase of a Maryland farm, Ickes reacted explosively. He drafted a withering nine-page letter ques-tioning McCormick's mental health and challenging his hated rival to a public debate. For unknown reasons, the letter was never sent. Ickes con-tented himself with helping other McCormick critics secure radio time and with muttered complaints against the "World's Gutter Newspaper."[64]

A different kind of threat to the *Tribune* emerged in April 1939, when McCormick picked up unsubstantiated rumors that Marshall Field III might invest part of his hundred-million-dollar fortune to buy Hearst's dying *Chicago Herald and Examiner* and make University of Chicago presi-dent Robert Maynard Hutchins his editor-in-chief.

✧ 7

Electing a Republican president in 1940 afforded McCormick a more pleasing prospect. He settled early on Thomas E. Dewey. Dewey's preconvention campaign manager, Ruth Simms, excitedly told Joe Pat-terson that the New York gangbuster was exactly the needed antidote to old fogy Republicanism — "young, vigorous, someone who isn't afraid to take on the corrupt forces in society." (Dewey reciprocated her praise, calling Mark Hanna's daughter "the ablest woman I have ever known.")

A fresh wave of enthusiasm for Dewey swept the country after his Feb-ruary 1939 conviction of Tammany chieftain Jimmy Hines. The *Tribune* happily noted Dewey's triumph over "Roosevelt job giver . . . Boss Hines." Overnight, the thirty-seven-year-old prosecutor became the most glam-orous young man since Charles Lindbergh. By the spring of 1939, Dewey led FDR in a mythical matchup, 58 percent to 42 percent. He was even further ahead of a Republican field that included the isolationist senators Robert Taft and Arthur Vandenberg.

If uncertain of Dewey's attitude toward the rest of the world, McCormick was fully convinced of his electoral appeal. In May the *Tribune* ran a flattering profile of the DA, complete with a color portrait that Dewey pronounced "the best anyone has done." The two men lunched together in New York on May 23, after which the Colonel invited Dewey to commit himself to "a real republican form of government" at the *Tribune*'s annual Constitution Day observance in September. Dewey proved elusive, blaming the crush of business for his decision to forgo the rally, "although I have a tremendous urge to discuss with some vigor the very subject which would be appropriate for that meeting."[65]

McCormick, desperate to win in 1940, made allowances for his reluctant champion. Overseas events made him fearful of a second European war — and a third term for Roosevelt. Reporting from Berlin in May 1939, Sigrid Schultz noted a cocky, almost unshakable conviction among Nazi officials that Hitler was destined to prevail, "whether through peace or war seems immaterial to them." Of late the Führer had passed his leisure time drawing maps, copies of which had fallen into Schultz's hands. These redrew the boundaries of central Europe, reducing Poland to a small province around Warsaw, splitting Yugoslavia with Mussolini, and bringing Romania, the Baltic states, and Scandinavia under German domination.[66]

Bluster was an important part of Nazi diplomacy. "We have 24,000 planes," crowed Hitler. "The minute I hear that the English have mobilised their fleet against us, the German and Italian airplanes will start from Germany and Spain." London would be leveled by Nazi bombing raids. "It may cost us 15,000 planes, but it will be worth it." Merely by threatening mass destruction, Hitler hoped to overawe the flabby regime of Neville Chamberlain, exactly as similar boasts had crippled Czech resistance earlier in the year.[67]

Adding to the mood of impending conflict, Schultz informed McCormick that thirty-two antiaircraft guns had secretly been installed on the roof and top floor of the chancellery in Berlin. At the end of June she reported scenes of SS officers toasting Moscow and raising glasses of champagne to the approaching day "when Germany divides Poland with her ally Russia." Astonishing as it appeared, this confirmed a *Tribune* forecast, made a month earlier, that the two dictators might reach an accommodation. Schultz predicted a Nazi offensive against the Polish port city of Danzig, unless the encircled Poland disintegrated before any shots were fired. According to her sources, Hitler was prepared to sacrifice 15,000 soldiers to achieve the partition of Poland. France was to be kept off guard and on the sidelines through intimidation and assurances that "little protest notes" from Paris would be sufficient to save French face.[68]

McCormick scheduled an August visit to the Nazi capital, by which time Schultz promised him "a good chunk of tense atmosphere." In the meantime, the intrepid correspondent fended off Nazi officials, who had learned of the impending visit by opening Schultz's mail and who complained that during the Colonel's earlier stay in the Reich, he had not been "properly guided." McCormick, skeptical of Hitler's military claims, thought that "the bombing bunk" was part of British propaganda efforts to lure the United States into a European war. In the last war, thousands of Americans had experienced bombardments "at least one hundred times as intense as could be laid down on London" by the present German air force. Undoubtedly such raids would inflict casualties and cause damage, "but the cost to the Germans, both in lives and money, will be greater than to the Londoners."[69]

Before an audience at the University of Notre Dame on July 29, McCormick professed indifference to the fate of "the German city of Danzig." As the possible flashpoint of a new world war, Danzig starkly illustrated the need for Americans to shun foreign entanglements. European instability, claimed McCormick, was rooted in the insoluble conflict between racial and economic aspirations. "Racial states were and are economically unsound," he declared. "Economic states are racially unstable." In contrast to the United States, whose union had been made comparatively simple through ethnic and political consensus, Europe was doomed by the multiplicity of resentful races, incompatible languages, and clashing religious beliefs. The most that American intervention could achieve, said McCormick, was a repetition of what had occurred in 1918 — "the use of our power to strengthen one side of a quarrel — at our expense."

Before going to Notre Dame, McCormick informed Sigrid Schultz that his planned Berlin trip, for unspecified reasons, was off. Schultz pretended to regrets she could hardly have felt, given the accelerating pace of military activities in the Nazi capital. Two million soldiers awaited orders to march against Poland, their aggression momentarily stalled pending successful completion of Hitler's Russian talks and some last-minute strengthening of Germany's western fortifications. Schultz noted the increasing scarcity of high-grade petrol in Berlin as the Führer and his generals hoarded precious fuel, further proof of "the excitement we expect in August."[70]

✦ 8

McCormick's travel plans had been aborted by a personal crisis in his household. Amy was dying, and her husband was as helpless to prolong her life as he was to avert a European war. In an era when the word *cancer* rarely entered polite conversation, Amy had been hospitalized with "chronic appendicitis" in October 1937. Thereafter the sick woman was twice victimized, first by the disease and second by the drawing room reticence that kept news of her true condition from her. The Colonel, as inventive as ever, pursued home remedies for her illness. He asked Joe Patterson to scour New York for windowpanes of fused quartz, which admitted ultraviolet sun rays as a primitive form of radiation therapy.

A Passavant Hospital nurse named Margaret Lacey moved into Cantigny, and the formal "Miss Lacey" was soon changed to "Slacey," a form of intimacy denied to other McCormick retainers. The newcomer observed the divergent lives led by her employers. Amy spent mornings on the telephone and afternoons inspecting the estate or occasionally visiting a nearby racetrack. Late in the day the Colonel joined his wife and her attendant for a tall scotch in the Big Room. Husband and wife ate a sparse dinner, separated by an eight-foot table. When through, McCormick retired with the early edition of the *Tribune*, delivered to the house by a local boy who was paid fifty cents to meet the evening express train out of Chicago. Amy played backgammon in her upstairs sitting room with guests such as Max Corpening and an impecunious family friend named Ed Pendergast. A lifelong bachelor known to the Colonel since childhood, Pendergast received a monthly stipend of $100, in return for which he accompanied McCormick on wordless excursions around the estate, pulling up dandelions in the summer and grubbing stumps for winter amusement.[71]*

Life at Cantigny mixed punctilio and farce. Houseguests Gloria Swanson, Charles Lindbergh, and Lillian Gish were told that breakfast was served at their convenience. Dinner was promptly at seven. "Don't mind being late," announced the management, "we won't wait for you." McCormick's idiosyncratic ways of telling time caused embarrassment to a pair of prominent Chicagoans invited to dine with him. The two men arrived in the mood for a predinner cocktail, only to be greeted coldly by a butler, who informed them that their host had already finished his meal: "The Colonel dines on Eastern Standard Time."[72]

During the Yuletide season, McCormick enjoyed recreating English holiday traditions, lighting the Yule log and presiding over wassail parties in his favorite pink hunting coat. Those in violation of his strict dress code could expect to be reprimanded. "If he didn't like something, Uncle Bertie would chew out your ass," said Brooks McCormick, son of the Colonel's

---

*Neither man wholly escaped McCormick's sometimes petty wrath. Before the Colonel made Corpening president of the Lake Shore Bank, he used his polo-playing crony as a buffer between himself and Amy. In a fit of pique one day, he reduced Corpening to selling farm vegetables at a roadside stand outside the gates of Cantigny. Pendergast was luckier; his humiliation consisted of the docking of ten cents from his regular monthly pension — the price of a razor blade the permanent houseguest had stolen from his host.

Wheaton neighbor (and cousin) Chauncey McCormick. However, said the younger McCormick, "if you didn't try to take advantage of him or ask for favors, he could be your friend."[73]

This was a privilege severely rationed. McCormick's closest friend was Ed Hurley, a washing machine manufacturer with whom he contended unsuccessfully, as a matter of pride, for the telephone number Wheaton 1. After an incompetent contractor installed a swimming pool that could be emptied only through the use of buckets, McCormick had it filled with trout — until Hurley, a practical joker, invited Brooks McCormick along on an impromptu fishing expedition "to catch a couple of trout for the Colonel's breakfast."[74]

"Hardly anyone ever got fired by the Colonel," explained Don Maxwell, a rule impartially applied to inept builders, second-rate farm managers, inebriated domestics, and out-of-favor managing editors. Cantigny featured an English butler named Emil Hawkenson, who hid ninety-seven empty gin bottles in the shrubbery and who nearly decapitated himself one evening when he leaned back into the electric dumbwaiter. "Emil used to get a little tight," acknowledged Howard Wood, recounting one disastrous meal during which the tipsy butler tripped on the rug, sending the main course, sliced roast beef on a silver platter, flying through the air. "Good God," said McCormick. Then he rose from the table and, without another word, stalked off to bed. (Yet McCormick insisted on paying Emil's hospital bills when the alcoholic butler was operated on for cancer.)[75]

Even on more decorous occasions, it was not unusual for the Colonel to get up after a course or two and walk out of the room without bothering to say goodnight to his guests. And when a young dinner companion made the mistake of feeding bits of meat to the Colonel's beloved Alsatian, she touched off a minor explosion. "Don't do that!" McCormick told the young woman. "Lotta is *my* dog."[76]

As his ability to shape external events waned, McCormick withdrew to a series of enclaves, including Tribune Tower and his Canadian properties, where his word remained law. Cantigny was his Xanadu, a self-sufficient world producing its own milk, honey, fresh vegetables, ice cream — even frog's legs, from a pond grandly dubbed Swan Lake. Guests were treated to squirrel and raccoon shot on the estate. The Colonel tramped through the woods on snowshoes in the winter; on his birthday each year he handed out $10 and $20 bills to farmworkers. Beneath his austere front beat the heart of a lonely man, who carried candy in his pockets and shared cookies and milk with neighborhood children who cut across the estate on their way to a nearby swimming hole.

His isolation increased in the spring of 1938, when Amy went to Palm Beach. McCormick joined her there for a few days at a time, always taking along a briefcase full of work to do as she fished in the blood-warm waters of the Gulf Stream. As a rule, he disliked the Florida resort patronized by wealthy northerners such as his next-door neighbor, Joe Kennedy. He thought the place snobbish and shallow. Amy, who had once confessed her ambition to be rich enough to have fresh sheets on her bed every night, enjoyed the climate and reveled in the angling.[77]

Back at Cantigny, Amy kept up appearances, riding as long as her health permitted. The Colonel had given up polo in 1935 but chased foxes well into his sixties. As his wife's condition worsened, he sometimes slipped away from a party and lost himself astride one of his favorite Irish jumpers, bounding over obstacles on his private hunt course.

In August 1939, Amy entered Passavant Hospital for a minor operation, ostensibly to correct a bowel stoppage. But when doctors opened her abdomen on the morning of August 13, they found her body riddled with cancer. "As she will never regain consciousness, it is an ideal end," McCormick wrote to Max Corpening from her hospital room. "Kindly do not mention this. There is no sense in having it gossiped around the country." Over the next few hours a blizzard of memos and telegrams went out from Passavant: to Ruth Simms, excusing her from a long, fatiguing journey to attend Amy's funeral; to his secretary, Genevieve Burke, instructing her to put both the Aiken and the Astor Street house on the market ("china and silver are not for sale"); to his farm manager, ordering him to stake out a private cemetery at Cantigny; to the *Tribune*'s religion edition and a local Wheaton pastor, asking them to pull whatever strings were necessary to consecrate the plot — under Presbyterian auspices if possible, Episcopalian or Catholic if necessary.[78]

"Amy can only live a few days. She is unconscious and not suffering," McCormick wired Joe Patterson the next day. She died at four o'clock that afternoon. Always sensitive about the discrepancy in their ages, Mc-Cormick shaved two years off her date of birth in filling out the death certificate. (He told a much greater fib on her tombstone, advancing her birth from 1872 to 1880, the year of his own.) Ceremony offered its consolations. A full-dress military funeral was conducted at Cantigny around a horseshoe-shaped altar banked with dahlias. The *Tribune* family turned out en masse. A string quartet from WGN radio played Amy's favorite hymns while an honor guard from Fort Sheridan fired a volley over the grave. The Colonel's plane scattered rose petals from above.[79]

McCormick engaged the architect Andrew Rebori to design a tomb on the same monumental scale as the rest of Cantigny. Rebori looked for inspiration to the ancient Athenian gathering place known as the exedra; his final vision owed as much to the granite backdrop of Saint Gaudens's brooding figure of Lincoln in Chicago's Lincoln Park. A preliminary rendering was shown to the Colonel early in 1940, but distaste for the subject of his own mortality precluded construction of the memorial for as long as he lived.

He may have buried a wife, but not his business acumen. Amy had been in her grave less than four months when the widower shared his latest brainstorm with Howard Ellis of the *Tribune* law firm. "If I deed the burial lot to the Episcopal Church," inquired McCormick, "won't the mausoleum be a gift to the Episcopal Church and tax exempt?"[80]

13

America First

"I suppose if I were twenty years younger I would want to get into the excitement, but at my present age my only wish is to end this disaster."

— Colonel McCormick, January 5, 1940

"I think it's time that someone speak up for the Republican Party. We have been battling for eight years now to preserve the democratic processes that are vital to the life of the republic. Battling against a President who seems to have no conception of them, and has repeatedly taken 'short cuts' in the name of 'emergency.' And now, because we refuse to go along on the lend and lease program, we are accused of petty partisan spirit. But I'll tell the world, the *Tribune* has always been in the forefront of the fight."

— Alf Landon to McCormick, January 25, 1941

LESS THAN TWO WEEKS after burying Amy at Cantigny, McCormick saw Europe engulfed in conflict for the second time in as many generations. Henry Stimson, putting aside their past disagreements, reminded his frequent critic that his useful work was far from complete. Conjuring up the ghost of an earlier Roosevelt, Stimson conceded that "the leaders whom you and I used to follow a quarter century ago are gone." New ones appeared to be in short supply. Yet, according to Hoover's secretary of state, there was a desperate need to rouse Americans to a fuller understanding of their obligations in a broken and dangerous world.[1]

Brushing aside the condolences of his First Division colleague General George Marshall, McCormick offered some advice to the newly promoted army chief of staff. "There are thousands upon thousands of game and trapshooters in this country who could easily knock down any of the low-flying airplanes with your new automatic rifles," he told Marshall. Why not have the army recruit civilian marksmen for this purpose, to be held in reserve pending the outbreak of hostilities? Nothing came of the proposal, or of McCormick's offer to organize a military police force made up of 10,000 volunteers aged thirty to forty-five.[2]

On September 1, 1939, Hitler's army and air force brutally thrust into Poland. Time alone would disclose the full cost and consequences of a second European war, said the *Tribune*. Already, however, memory and bitter experience should put Americans on guard. Exactly twenty-five years had elapsed since the last time "imperialistic programs had clashed in a corner of Europe," resulting in carnage and betrayal on a sickening scale. The hideousness of World War I had produced a hope, "nowhere stronger than in the United States," that humanity might somehow be purified by suffering and that slaughter would give way to universal peace and free-dom. America had entered the conflict of 1917–18 cherishing such hopes. In light of all that had since happened, asked the *Tribune*, "how can we have that illusion again?"

Caring little whom he offended, McCormick in the natural order of things offended a great many. Two weeks after the German blitz-krieg knifed Poland, a *Tribune* cartoonist depicted FDR as an aspiring dictator, trying on costumes variously associated with Hitler, Stalin, Mus-solini, and Napoleon — the last getup "always becoming to the plump man." A local beautician, who also happened to belong to the American Legion, took the Colonel to task for disloyalty. McCormick dismissed his complaint as "the kind of letter we would expect from a man in the beautyshop business."[3]

As events overseas spun out of control, McCormick exercised an even tighter rein on those he employed to report and interpret foreign develop-ments. In the autumn of 1939 he received a long, overwrought, and thinly documented cable from Edmond Taylor, his Paris bureau chief. Taylor claimed knowledge of a recent meeting at which Hitler and Stalin had jointly plotted strategy for world conquest. "Send no more of your bed-time story," McCormick replied. Taylor was thus goaded into making still more fantastic claims, including a prediction that the dictators would move in concert against Romania.[4]

Since Taylor was so obviously hell-bent on dragging a reluctant United States into war, McCormick suggested to the reporter that he set an example by enlisting in the French Foreign Legion. Either that, said the publisher, or check into a sanitarium until his war fever abated. He reas-signed Paris to Larry Rue, a black sheep who was readmitted to the *Tribune* flock under the shadow of European war clouds. Taylor resigned, and enjoyed a measure of revenge by denouncing his former boss at prowar rallies in Chicago.

McCormick sided with Colonel Charles Lindbergh, who reassured a national radio audience that "an ocean is a formidable barrier, even for modern aircraft." McCormick praised Lindbergh for his "patriotic speech," then reiterated his own view that the Atlantic and Pacific formed secure frontiers, if patrolled by a navy "so strong that an enemy cannot attack it" and strategically dispersed to provide an impregnable shield for both coasts. Hawaii, amply garrisoned, promised just such protection. Unfortunately, there were no Hawaiis off the eastern seaboard of the United States. The closest models were the British possessions of Bermuda and Trinidad and French-owned Martinique in the deep turquoise waters of the Caribbean.

When, late in September 1939, Roosevelt proposed an ingenious "cash-and-carry" scheme to evade existing neutrality laws and rush military assistance to the outgunned Allies, McCormick had in mind another kind of transaction. "The owners of these islands owe us vast sums of money and propose to owe us more," he said. Located thousands of miles from their embattled colonizers, the lonely outposts of European sovereignty held no value to their landlords "except for the purposes of attacking the United States." Their purchase, for a generous price, should be the immediate priority of the American State Department. The subsequent trade of Britain's Atlantic bases for fifty aging U.S. naval destroyers, announced at a moment of supreme peril for the beleaguered British government, took most Americans by surprise. To McCormick, the deal merely reaffirmed his claims to strategic omniscience.[5]

No arguments of sentiment or self-interest could shake his belief in American isolation (a corollary to American superiority). Among the "overexcited easterners trying to get us into war to improve their social position," McCormick counted Gifford Pinchot, an old Bull Moose Republican later elected governor of Pennsylvania. Pinchot appealed to the Colonel to endorse FDR's cash-and-carry program as the surest way to avert Allied collapse and a future war between Hitler and the United States.[6]

"Twenty years ago, after the French and English had been defeated by the Germans, we defeated the Germans," replied McCormick. "England and France then imposed the beastly treaty of Versailles ... welshed on their war debts and postwar debts ... bungled everything in the intervening time ... and are at war again." If Poland and its European allies were unable to lick the Nazi war machine, "that is their misfortune." As for a transatlantic invasion, McCormick found the notion laughable. Hitler and his armies "will not come over here," he lectured Pinchot, "because they had a taste of Americans twenty years ago."[7]

To McCormick, the present German demand for *Lebensraum*, or living space, was merely a repetition of the World War I drive to the east and its battle cry, *Drang Nach Osten*. He forgot that the German kaiser, a blustering throwback to the age of divine right, had been a conservative autocrat. The German Führer, armed with the murderous ingenuity of modern science, was no garden variety imperialist but a mutation of past hatreds and a harbinger of the soulless state. In confusing the Nazi push for expansion — and racial extermination — with long-standing territorial rivalries, McCormick viewed the present war as a clash of armies rather than ideologies. His contempt for decadent parliamentarians blinded him to the far greater crimes of the Third Reich. At the least, it dulled his capacity for moral outrage.

As early as February 10, 1940, Sigrid Schultz, alias John Dickson, supplied McCormick with credible evidence that Hitler was prepared to annex Scandinavia, Holland, Belgium, the Burgundy region of France, and southeastern Europe. So the dictator had informed his *gauleiters*, in rambling harangues verified by a trio of Schultz's most trusted informants. That was not all she reported to the Colonel. She described concentration camps where Czech students were subjected to medical experiments that caused a form of epilepsy and the loss of intellectual function. At least one SS man had begged a friend of Schultz's to supply him with enough poison to end his own life should he be caught trying to alleviate the suffering of prisoners. Another German army officer returned from an inspection tour of occupied Poland in a state of emotional collapse. In one small city he had looked on helplessly as six hundred Poles and Jews were herded into a cellar and "the death's head boys" hurled grenades into their massed ranks.[8]

A Nazified Europe. Concentration camps. Systematic killing of the Jews. The evidence was solid, the sources reliable. Schultz had earned a reputation among the most clear-eyed and dispassionate of *Tribune* reporters. Her courage in staying on in Berlin was as undeniable as the trustworthiness of what she was able, against great odds, to smuggle out of the Nazi capital. Yet the Colonel was unmoved. One can well imagine the resources he would have committed to following up any rumor casting unflattering light on members of the mercenary Roosevelt family, but when it came to allegations of state-sponsored murder, he didn't want to hear what Schultz had to tell him.

As he had with Edmond Taylor, McCormick now decided that Schultz was behaving oddly, perhaps on account of ill health. "John Dickson" would remain at his post a while longer, but with diminished clout. The reason that McCormick turned a deaf ear to such reports became clear in a testy exchange of letters with William Allen White, the pro-interventionist editor of the Emporia, Kansas, *Gazette*. White wrote to the Colonel seeking favorable publicity for the Children's Crusade for Children, a grassroots campaign to benefit the youngest victims of the fighting. "I believe I sympathize with homeless people as much as anybody," McCormick replied on February 24, 1940, "but there is so much effort made to get us into the European war that I am loath to back up organized sentimentalism, which may be used to that end."

In a sharply worded retort, White compared McCormick to the priest and Levite who had distinguished themselves throughout history at the expense of the Good Samaritan. Angrily, McCormick denied the accusation. He noted to White the 60,000 men of the First Division who had been killed, wounded, or maimed for life as a result of World War I. "For twenty years I have kept in touch with those whose existence has been a living death." Had White experienced such horrors for himself, he too might look with suspicion on a movement — "however noble some people consider it" — that could ultimately subject young Americans of 1940 to the same bloody futility that haunted McCormick's memories.[9]

◈ 2

Toward the faltering government of British prime minister Neville Chamberlain, McCormick showed even less sympathy than for the childish refugees fleeing the German blitzkrieg. "Chamberlain," he said, "ought to die of old age." In April 1940, the Colonel was in New York for the annual meeting of the Associated Press board of directors. Following a heated discussion of U.S. foreign policy, two questions were put to a vote. First, according to McCormick, was whether the United States should go to war to help out the British. A bare majority responded in the affirmative. The second debate asked whether Americans were inevitably going to be drawn into the conflict. This time, the positive vote was overwhelming. As the *Tribune* correspondent Bill Fulton looked on, McCormick lapsed into a long, thoughtful silence. "Maybe we're wrong," he muttered.[10]

The spell of uncertainty passed quickly. The war news turned blacker than ever. "So the Germans have got the jump on them again," McCormick told his old friend Charles Dawes on the morning of May 10, as Nazi columns sliced into Holland, Belgium, and France. "I believe it will all be over one way or another inside of two weeks." He thought the bombing of French cities showed yet again "the supreme imbecility" of locating arms and aviation factories along the coastlines of his own country. On May 14, with Allied prospects increasingly grim, McCormick demanded an editorial on "the paradox of Roosevelt" — how his "parlor pinkishness" made the president consort with Earl Browder and other domestic Communists even as his "intensive seaside snobbishness" inspired him to rush pell-mell and unprepared into the war on England's side.[11]

In London, Winston Churchill replaced the discredited Chamberlain at 10 Downing Street. McCormick listened raptly to the prime minister's fighting words, then wired praise to his friend. The Battle of France had not only doomed the ineffectual Chamberlain; it had also reshuffled the deck of American politics. With each passing day, the renomination of Roosevelt became more likely. The air began to go out of the Dewey campaign. In the crisis atmosphere of May 1940, youth and glamour were seen as liabilities, not assets. The Gangbuster shriveled into plain Buster, an untested, essentially local figure whose courtroom experiences left him ill prepared to contend with international gangsters such as Hitler and Stalin.

McCormick never wavered in his support of the DA. Rumors of a Stop Dewey movement spurred him to declare his allegiance publicly and exert pressure on Illinois delegates to follow suit. By the start of June, anti-Dewey forces were rallying behind a New York utilities executive and darling of the Luce press named Wendell Willkie. Such a course held no attraction for McCormick. On June 5 he confided to Arthur Sears Henning that he was considering his own run for the White House. "I am demonstrably the best qualified man to be a war president . . . in either party," he declared. As proof, he cited his command and staff experience, wartime record, and Grant biography — "a textbook in the war college." Moreover, said McCormick, "my executive capacity is unquestionable, and my labor relations the best." Although it would undoubtedly be difficult for the loyal Henning to discourage him from running, "it will be harder for you to give me bad advice, so I know you will tell me exactly what you think."*

The thought of McCormick in the White House did nothing to gladden the hearts of *Tribune* staffers, least of all in the Washington bureau. They found comfort in knowing just how unlikely it was that the Colonel's electoral fantasies would be realized. Henning's reply to McCormick's proposal is lost, but the Colonel's faith in his objectivity was apparently well placed, for when McCormick next addressed Henning, on June 14, he dis-

---

*On one occasion McCormick urged his readers to invest funds in a bond issue producing an annual income of $3,000. Or he would have, had not chief editorial writer Leon Stolz gone to the twenty-fourth floor and told his boss point-blank that he couldn't run such a piece.

"Colonel," said Stolz, "do you realize that 75 percent of your readers haven't got $3,000 today to live on?"

"Well, how do they live?" responded McCormick, genuinely surprised.

claimed all interest in the presidency. "Whoever succeeds Roosevelt must kill himself in office and then very likely fail to prevent catastrophe," he said. Although still prepared in theory to make the sacrifice, he saw that the situation had radically changed over the past ten days. "I have had to go on the Illinois delegation to keep Knox from dominating it," he told Henning. In his new position he would be forced to take an uncompromising stand against American intervention, one sure to destroy his already slender chances. In the end, he predicted, "the nomination will probably go to some master straddler, or some genuine dark horse who has no occasion to commit himself."

As the convention approached, the European situation grew desperate. In a Mutual radio broadcast on June 9, McCormick appealed for calm and took solace in what he called the world's strongest navy. Reluctantly, he sold *Tribune* ad space to the newly formed Committee to Defend America by Aiding the Allies, a pressure group chaired by the "certainly honest, and equally certainly simple," William Allen White. On June 13, defying State Department attempts to quash the story, the *Tribune* reported that France was on the verge of making peace with Hitler, a scoop confirmed by the resignation of premier Paul Reynauld and his replacement by the venerable Marshal Henri Philippe Pétain. Instead of criticizing the new puppet regime based in Vichy, McCormick blamed the former Socialist premier Léon Blum for the collapse of the Third Republic. It was Blum, he maintained, who had denuded France by sending its best arms to Spanish Communists. In his own hemisphere, McCormick detected a threat to American security in Mexico, which was allegedly in thrall to Russian agents.

A more immediate danger, to the *Tribune* at least, bubbled up north of the border, where the *Ottawa Journal* spoke for many patriotic Canadians enraged by the Chicago newspaper whose anti-British diatribes were printed on paper harvested in Ontario and Quebec. The Canadian Senate debated the possible closing of McCormick's mills, while editors from Halifax to Vancouver demanded a halt to newsprint exports and the belated enforcement of prorating against the American firm. Secretly, the *Tribune* employed public relations experts to remind Canadians of the importance of outside investment and of the need to stay in the good graces of their southern neighbor. Tensions eased somewhat after McCormick editorialized in favor of a formal military alliance between the United States and Canada, taking into account the obligation of each Canadian citizen to the British Commonwealth.

No one was happier over this turn of events than Arthur Schmon. "As one of our men phoned me today from Montreal," he wrote on June 20, "he does not now have to sneak home up an alley."

Fresh challenges awaited McCormick on the eve of the Republican convention in Philadelphia. Shortly before the delegates were to assemble, the Colonel took an agitated phone call from the party's 1936 nominee, Alf Landon. In Chicago en route to Washington and a meeting with Roosevelt at the White House, Landon was seeking McCormick's counsel. "Colonel," he said, "if he does run for a third term, should I go into a cabinet of national unity?" "Yes," said McCormick without hesitation.[12]

Landon, convinced that he was being used to blunt GOP attacks on the administration's defense record, shared his fears with his 1936 running mate, Frank Knox, who had also been asked to the White House. On Roosevelt's doorstep the two men exchanged vows to have no part in the developing conspiracy. Landon kept his word. Knox recanted. On June 20, the publisher of the *Chicago Daily News* joined the Roosevelt administration as secretary of the navy. The same day, it was announced that former secretary of state Henry Stimson would take over the War Department. Henceforth, McCormick notified his editorial writers, Stimson and Knox were to be treated as nonpersons. "If the issue should be forced upon us," he continued, "we should call them two old men who deserted their party and sent young men to die before they do."[13]

In Philadelphia, McCormick resisted the Willkie juggernaut to the last, voting for Dewey on each of six ballots. Later investigation cast doubt on the spontaneity of Willkie's popular uprising, dubbed by one cynic the Charge of the Electric Light Brigade. At the time, McCormick attributed the outcome to the war scare and a widespread feeling that "a great industrialist" could do a better job than a prosecutor of building up the country's neglected defenses. In thanking McCormick for his support, Dewey spoke warmly of the *Tribune*'s power and influence. McCormick, "more conscious of the blows I receive than those I deliver," demurred. He hoped the convention had acted wisely. "Four more years of Roosevelt and the country will be through," he told Dewey. It was a lament growing familiar with repetition.[14]

❖ 3

In the months following Amy's death, McCormick spent more time in New York than he had before or would again. He lived like a maharaja in a large suite at the Ritz Hotel. *Tribune* reporters found themselves invited there, in the days leading up to Christmas 1939, because the Colonel had no one else to talk to. He would never feel at home in Manhattan. He confined his theatergoing to musicals and other productions that made few demands on their audience. He saved his art criticism for Diego Rivera's "Communist cartoons" in Rockefeller Center, which he found offensive but hardly surprising. "Public opinion in New York is so unbalanced," claimed the Colonel, "that naturally the Communists can dominate."[15]

His opinion of America's largest city did not improve with concentrated exposure to "phony Easterners" suffering from "England envy." In July 1940, he was railing against the feminine dominance of Park Avenue dowagers, Broadway, and the New York literary set. At a luncheon in his honor, he listened perfunctorily as publishing types urged him to start a *Tribune* book section to compete with the distinguished *New York Times Book Review.* "Readers of the *Tribune* don't read books," announced McCormick, glad to act the philistine if it would shock his sophisticated hosts.[16]

Admittedly chary of the "toot, toot, toot stuff" of grand opera — there had to be something wrong with any form of entertainment unable to make itself commercially viable, he said — the Colonel nonetheless imported the singer Grace Moore to perform a Christmas night concert on WGN radio in 1939. Apparently Miss Moore liked what she saw, for she soon embarked on a campaign to succeed Amy as mistress of Cantigny. She found McCormick an elusive quarry. (Some time later, when asked by Joe Patterson whether he intended to marry a rumored love interest, the Colonel was dismissive: "I got away from Grace Moore, didn't I?")[17]

Perhaps Miss Moore's problem was that she was a miss. "The Colonel likes women," explained his confidant Weymouth Kirkland, "but only if they are married to other men." Given his behavior toward Amy Adams and Clara Thomas, this was only a slight exaggeration. Over the years, McCormick's name was linked in gossip to a number of women, including such Hollywood luminaries as Hedda Hopper and Arlene Dahl. Among *Tribune* executives it was a tightly guarded secret that McCormick had a New York mistress who received monthly payments approved by the business manager, Elbert Antrim — payments that reportedly continued long after the Colonel's death. She was Grace Parker Pickering, a fashion consultant to the rich — including, at one time, Amy McCormick.[18]

With the fall of France in the spring of 1940, Sunday *Tribune* editor Mike Kennedy was left with a yawning hole where Parisian fashion photos traditionally went. Not to worry, said McCormick. He intended to make Chicago the new hub of international fashion, and he had just the woman to give Coco Chanel a run for her francs. That July the *Tribune* revealed plans for a nationwide design contest "to develop American fashions for American women." The competition was the brainchild of Mrs. Pickering, formerly affiliated with Lucille's, a Michigan Avenue shop patronized by the wealthiest women in Chicago. Pickering was a woman of mystery, divorced from a still more shadowy husband. In New York she lived at the Biltmore Hotel, to which McCormick was a frequent visitor. When in Chicago she held court at the Drake, whose proprietors received lengthy instructions several days before her arrival. For example, stoves were required to warm her bath, since Mrs. Pickering refused to bathe in anything but bottled water.[19]

Small in stature, peremptory in manner, with brightly dyed orange hair and custom-made platform shoes, "Gracious" Pickering chose the sketches, hired the models, and supervised the production of more than 40 dresses (from some 12,000 designs submitted) for the production. The 1940 show wound up costing the paper nearly $40,000. McCormick didn't care. He was interested in publicizing himself and promoting Chicago. The competition became an annual event, and after the war he expanded the shows to New York, assuring Mrs. Pickering that her additional labors would be handsomely compensated. The true nature of their relationship was confirmed shortly before his death in 1994 by Harold Hutchings, for sixteen years McCormick's trusted deputy in the New York office of the Tribune News Service.

A more ambiguous intrigue involved McCormick with still another married woman whose husband relied for his livelihood on the good will of the Colonel. Henry Weber was conductor of the WGN Orchestra, a logical sequel to his career with the Chicago Civic Opera, to whose podium he had been called at the age of twenty-three. On a European scouting trip, Weber had heard and recruited a vivacious blond soprano named Marion Claire, "so ordinary you wouldn't hire her if you had an audition," according to one member of the WGN family. Miss Claire's ambition more than compensated for her limited musical gifts. In 1929 she married Weber. Later she earned modest fame in a Broadway production of *The Great Waltz.*[20]

Seeking new fields to conquer, Marion wrote to McCormick in October 1939 soliciting his direct involvement in WGN, "which in my humble thought still awaits the strong benefit of your attentions." The timing of her appeal, less than two months after Amy's death, may not have been accidental. In truth, McCormick had been giving considerable thought to radio and its potential for selling newspapers in a cluttered market where movies, electric signs, Sunday golf, and automobiles competed for reader interest and advertising dollars. Prodded by Marion, he challenged his advertising department to make WGN the most outstanding (that is, profitable) radio station in America before he retired from the *Tribune.*[21]

Thanks to the Webers, he had a ready vehicle with which to realize his aspirations. Commencing in April 1940, WGN and the Mutual network broadcast a weekly series of light operas in a program known as *The Chicago Theater of the Air.* McCormick commissioned new librettos with patriotic and historical themes to supplement the usual repertoire of Sigmund Romberg and the Strauss family. He promised that during intermission, each broadcast would also feature "an outstanding speaker," a euphemism that fooled no one. Addressing an audience of several million fed his ego, as McCormick was the first to acknowledge. (Asked late in life what led him to occupy his electronic pulpit, he replied with refreshing candor, "Vanity, I guess.")

Every Saturday night, McCormick stood before the WGN microphone in formal wear; as he finished each page of his homily, generally confined to long-forgotten American heroes or unsought military advice, he let it flutter to the floor. One evening he was so moved by his tale of the scalping of a pioneer mother at the hands of an Indian made drunk on rum sold him by an English nobleman that he burst into sobs before the studio audience. Periodically, he repeated his 1937 tribute to the First Division, originally delivered at Cantigny, France. Like all his weekly addresses, this one was printed in full in the Sunday *Tribune.*

Occasionally his observations needed decoding, as Walter Trohan discovered when he received a telegram from his employer reading, "This is a paragraph from my radio broadcast. What do I mean?" No amount of scripting could suppress the spontaneity of live radio, especially given McCormick's habit of bringing his dogs to the studio. One evening Buster Boo, his English bulldog, slobbered over the microphone as his master paid homage to Nathan Hale. Listeners from across the country wrote in to express concern about the Colonel's respiratory problems. Another McCormick pet became so excited on hearing the voice of his owner that he ran up Marion Claire's skirts, prompting the diva to let out a very undignified scream.[22]

Few of her performances were so entertaining. *The Chicago Theater of the Air* was an instant success anyway, drawing 200,000 letters in its first season. Around the *Tribune* this was seen as a mixed blessing, as it fed the operatic temperament of its star. McCormick seemed oblivious to the gossip generated by his weekend visits to the Weber household in Lake Bluff. Many assumed that it was a replay of the Adams-McCormick ménage, an impression Marion only furthered through her high-handed behavior. In a crowded field, she was her own worst enemy. Approached for a donation to the Red Cross, she haughtily refused, asserting that Colonel McCormick had no use for the organization. When stopped for running a red light in June 1941, the prima donna did what came naturally: she telephoned Pat Maloney, who wasted no time in paying her bail. Later Weymouth Kirkland was pressed into duty to obtain a dismissal of the case. "It's hell what power I have with women," cracked Kirkland, to whom Miss Claire dedicated a Grant Park concert. (Both Kirkland and Maloney believed the singer to be McCormick's mistress, a viewpoint that gained greater credence, through no fault of the principals, with the 1941 release of *Citizen Kane,* in which an aging newspaper tycoon promotes the opera career of a singularly untalented young woman.)[23]

In 1947 Marion was retired to the role of "production supervisor." *The Chicago Theater of the Air* continued for as long as its founder and biggest fan lived. In keeping with McCormick's wishes, the show was broadcast without commercials, thus costing the *Tribune* $1 million a year. For their swan song, staged one month after the Colonel died in April 1955, the WGN company presented Noel Coward's *Bittersweet,* the same production that had marked their debut fifteen years earlier. For all concerned, it was a sentimental gesture, rare in a business rapidly becoming too impersonal and too competitive for sentiment.

❖ 4

Sunday, July 14, 1940. On the eve of the Democratic convention in Chicago, *Tribune* readers found a new, overarching set of demands crowding out the familiar platforms for America and the Midwest:

1. Adopt an American foreign policy
2. Adopt an American domestic policy.

In his welcoming address to the delegates, Mayor Ed Kelly proclaimed that the salvation of the world rested on one man. To draft Roosevelt for the third term the president professed not to want, Kelly turned to his superintendent of sewers. By careful prearrangement, this disembodied cheerleader, secreted in a basement room of the convention hall and hooked up to the amplifying system, stirred sluggish Democrats with his deafening chants of "Illinois wants Roosevelt," "America wants Roosevelt," "The world wants Roosevelt."

The voice from the sewer was soon drowned out, in Chicagoland at least, by the voice from the tower. In handwritten instructions to his editorial staff, McCormick framed the fall campaign in stark terms: *Are you for Willkie, Preparedness, and Peace, or Roosevelt, Confusion, and War?*

For McCormick, the 1940 campaign differed markedly from that of 1936. His relationship with Alf Landon, although sometimes strained, had never been adversarial. In recent months the two men had drawn closer than ever, bonded by distrust of FDR and his less than candid approach to possible U.S. involvement in Europe's widening war. With Wendell Willkie, by contrast, McCormick shared little but midwestern roots and antipathy to the economic intrusiveness of the New Deal. His first encounter with the rumpled, bearlike candidate, at Willkie's post-convention retreat in Colorado Springs, left the Colonel both impressed and mildly disturbed. Willkie was "fascinating," he concluded, "too fascinating." So charming was the nominee that before leaving, McCormick counted his ideological spoons, just to be certain he hadn't been robbed of his deepest convictions.[24]

Until recently a lifelong Democrat, Willkie suddenly found himself leading a Republican crusade. He was a Wilsonian internationalist grafted onto an essentially isolationist party, whose fissures over selective service and aid to Britain were sure to be exposed by the coming campaign. An amateur forced to work in tandem with professional politicians, a critic of New Deal defeatism shouting into the wind of a massive defense buildup, Willkie wrote his own speeches and could never quite shoehorn himself into the conventions of presidential politics. He talked too much, ate too much, was incautious in his romantic life.* In journalist Roscoe Drummond's phrase, he did not know how to play it safe.

All this made Willkie the most exciting political newcomer since Theodore Roosevelt at his bulliest. But it also made him a high-risk contender for a party torn between accommodating the New Deal and denouncing it as the bastard progeny of *Das Kapital* and other Socialist tracts that Willkie had devoured as a student at Indiana University. In his acceptance speech, delivered on August 17 before a throng of 200,000 admirers at his Indiana birthplace of Elwood, Willkie sought to paper over his contradictions. "Only the productive can be strong," he cried, using a line that would become his mantra, "and only the strong can be free."

After eight years in power, Roosevelt presided over ten million unemployed Americans and a power-hungry Washington elite running up the national debt while practicing the politics of class division. The true test of reform, said Willkie, was simple. Did it lead to increased industrial output, expanded opportunities for the young, and a universally high standard of living? The New Deal flunked all three tests, he charged. By contrast, his criticism of Roosevelt's foreign policy was muted. Willkie refused to exploit fears of a peacetime draft, much to the dismay of the *Tribune.* McCormick denounced the Selective Service Act passed on September 16 as a threat to every American male aged twenty-one through thirty-five. "Roosevelt has not the executive skill to administer it," he grumbled, "nor the conservative judgment to resist the temptation of military adventure."[25]

Willkie also made clear his solidarity with the British, whose survival was being tested nightly in the skies over London. Adlai Stevenson, writing as chairman of the Chicago Committee to Defend America by Aiding the Allies, eloquently disposed of the *Tribune* argument that by lending assistance to the hard-pressed British, the United States would inevitably

---

*Willkie had a mistress, Irita Van Doren, the book review editor of the *New York Herald Tribune.* In White House tape recordings that surfaced nearly half a century later, FDR can be heard plotting ways to use this fact against his 1940 opponent if the Republicans tried to exploit damaging correspondence between Democratic vice presidential candidate Henry Wallace and a Russian mystic cum philosophical adviser named Nicholas Roerick. In the end, both parties observed a truce, burying their most explosive allegations.

become embroiled in a combat role. McCormick dismissed Stevenson and his group as "cookie pushers" and "bleeding hearts" who impeded American rearmament and exaggerated the German menace. "We can beat the Germans any time we have to," claimed the swaggering *Tribune.*

In September came the Roosevelt-Churchill bases-for-destroyers deal. Reminding readers that it had campaigned since 1922 for the cession of foreign naval and air bases in "the American defense zone," the *Tribune* labeled the Anglo-American swap "the greatest contribution of this newspaper to the country's history since the nomination of Lincoln." On September 8, McCormick unspooled for his radio audience a scenario involving Nazi landings in Newfoundland and Nova Scotia. North America had nothing to fear, said the Colonel; any invading force was certain to bog down in the wilds of Quebec. An amphibious assault on the New England coast was even less likely to succeed.

McCormick had little other comforting news that fall. Roosevelt's masterly performance as commander-in-chief overshadowed the Willkie campaign. What had appeared refreshingly spontaneous in June now seemed bumbling and amateurish. The Republican candidate turned down an invitation to attend the *Tribune*-sponsored Chicago Music Festival as the Colonel's guest. "It looks as though we were right and that Dewey should have been nominated," McCormick confided to a friend late in September. Still, "we must try to elect this man if we can, or else!"[26]

As the Battle of Britain raged, McCormick delivered a radio account of the last genuine invasion threat posed to the United States — by redcoated veterans of Wellington's armies during the War of 1812. At a time when Londoners were bracing themselves against nightly bombardment from the German Luftwaffe, he described the resulting damage as more than annoying yet less than decisive. Besides, he claimed in a September 22 broadcast, "people whose houses have been destroyed can be moved into the unused buildings — of which there are many — as soon as machinery for this new form of real estate transaction has been devised."

McCormick blamed Roosevelt for driving Japan into the arms of Germany and Italy. He minimized the likelihood of an attack on Hawaii as long as the U.S. navy was safely ensconced at Pearl Harbor, "looking at the hula dancers." Convinced that his country enjoyed an overwhelming advantage in naval and air power, he told his Mutual audience, "Let us be of good cheer. If we can avoid bankruptcy and bolshevism, we will see again the age of manifest destiny." Sigrid Schultz was less confidant. Hitler wanted to burn London like ancient Carthage, she told McCormick in an October 8 dispatch, because the British capital symbolized bourgeois resistence to regimentation. Nazi war planners, assuming that the United States would join the fighting, had drawn up blueprints to stir internal American dissent and cripple trade between the Americas.[27]

Overseas events conspired to knock Willkie from the lofty perch he had occupied at the start of the campaign. On October 11, he flatly told a Boston audience that if elected, he would see to it that "our boys shall stay out of European wars." Roosevelt was driving to make his own pledge of noninvolvement in the same city. "I have said this before, but I shall say it again and again and again," vowed the president on October 30. "Your boys are not going to be sent into any foreign wars." For McCormick, who estimated the cost of American combat involvement at one million casualties and $400 billion, there was only one way to make FDR honor his peace commitment, and that was to retire him to private life.

He drew encouragement from an unlikely source. According to Walter Trohan, Jim Farley was calling the election in the bag for Willkie. Luckily for Farley's reputation as a seer, his home-stretch assessment went unpublished. After a brief scare early on election night, FDR pulled away from his challenger. He went on to win 442 electoral votes to Willkie's 82. McCormick chose to accentuate the positive. Despite a campaign spent blurring the distinctions between himself and the New Deal, Willkie had reduced Roosevelt's 1936 margin by almost seven million votes. "The opinion here is that he did not oppose Roosevelt strongly enough," the Colonel wrote one week after the election; "therefore, a lot of Republican voters did not vote the presidential ballot."[28]

As proof of this theory, he cited his own success in electing Dwight Green governor of Illinois and in landing the shopworn C. Wayland "Curley" Brooks in the U.S. Senate on his fifth try for electoral office. Willkie, concluded McCormick, was an attractive aberration, a bogus Republican with even less right to speak for his party than Alf Landon or Herbert Hoover.[29]

✧ 5

"Never before since Jamestown and Plymouth Rock has our American civilization been in such danger," FDR declared in a December fireside chat. The president reminded his countrymen that there was less distance between German-held North Africa and vulnerable Brazil than between Washington, D.C., and Denver. "If Great Britain goes down," he said, "all of us would be living at the point of a gun."

To avert such a fate, on January 10, 1941, the administration introduced in Congress H.R. 1776, "the Dictator Bill" to the *Tribune*, more popularly known as lend-lease. Beginning with its patriotic bill number, lend-lease combined shrewd White House packaging with more than a touch of the surreal. Under its terms, the president would be given broad powers, including the unilateral right to transfer U.S. arms and other war supplies to any nation engaged in fighting considered vital to American interests. Roosevelt likened the idea of lending weapons, then repossessing them when hostilities ended, to what a good neighbor would do with his garden hose when fire broke out next door. Senator Robert Taft thought the analogy strained. To him, it was more like lending chewing gum, not a commodity you were eager to take back after it had been used.

To all eyes, lend-lease was a blatantly unneutral act. Supporters of the legislation argued that the best way to keep America at peace was to keep Britain at war. Nonsense, said McCormick, for whom U.S. assistance to the British stood in the way of a negotiated peace. Foreign policy was not to be confused with social work.

Congressional hearings on lend-lease were scheduled for early February. On the sixth, McCormick appeared before the Senate Foreign Relations Committee. He was there not to offer comment on the presidential plan to aid Britain, he told the senators, but to refute hysterical reports of an impending Nazi invasion of the Western Hemisphere. No army in history was capable of traversing the rugged Spanish landscape before crossing the African desert, navigating the South Atlantic, and hacking its way through Brazilian rain forests, all the while dodging British bombers based in the Cape Verde Islands and American air attacks launched from the Caribbean. Hitler's 8,000-mile-long supply lines would be untenable. Scarcely less absurd was the thought of a German thrust across the North Atlantic via Iceland, Labrador, and the Cabot Strait. "The experience of the Athenians at Syracuse, the Romans in Germany, Napoleon in Egypt, and the Russians in Manchuria," said McCormick, showed that nations that embarked on distant military adventures invited disaster.

With history on his side, the Colonel held his own against the tough questioning of hawks such as Tom Connally of Texas and Florida's Claude Pepper. Pressed on what he would do if the Germans managed to acquire the British fleet, the witness recited the promise made by Churchill ("A more thoroughly honorable man never lived") to retain his naval forces whatever the cost.

"What would be your attitude," asked Senator Pepper, "as to the policy of this country if Hitler should conquer England and proceed to take over and occupy the British bases . . . in this hemisphere?"

"I would not let him do it," said McCormick.

What if the Nazi leader sought the French fleet and military installations in the West Indies? demanded Pepper.

"I would not let him."

Well then, what about Bermuda?

The United States already had a base there, McCormick reminded his questioner. He predicted (correctly, as it turned out) that England and the United States would reach an accommodation over the Portugese-held Azores. And if Hitler were to overcome both England and Portugal, said Pepper, more than slightly annoyed, and were to establish a Nazi base in the islands, what would the Colonel do about it?

"I would go right in and take them," replied McCormick. "That is how we got Florida."

The panel turned to British prospects and requirements. McCormick minimized the danger, citing Churchill's recent assignment of a large motorized army corps to fight in Libya. A nation teetering on the brink of collapse does not redistribute its meager firepower, he contended. He was careful to distinguish between the resources necessary to invade occupied Europe and the far more modest requirements of Britain's home defense. As for the latter, "she should have whatever she needs for defense," said the Colonel, "and I do not think she needs anything."

University of Chicago chancellor Robert Maynard Hutchens congratulated McCormick for making an "absolutely impregnable" case before the committee. The experience had reminded him of a staff officer spending a day on the firing line, McCormick confessed to Arthur Vandenberg. In the end, however, it was another witness, playing his part with a melodramatic flair once reserved for schoolboy productions of *Hamlet*, who galvanized public support behind lend-lease. On February 10, Wendell Willkie went to Capitol Hill straight from the Washington airport to describe what he had seen in London as a special emissary from the Roosevelt White House. With flashing eyes and powerful sincerity, he warned Republicans that unless they renounced isolationism, they might never again hold the levers of power in America.[30]

One day after this spellbinding performance, McCormick launched an investigation into Willkie's "secret history." His faith in their cause remained unshaken, he told Senator Vandenberg. So did his conviction that most Americans shared their views, save for "plutocrats, who are closer to Europe than to America, and the Jews, who have been injured and insulted beyond their self-control." He took additional encouragement from the unexpected resignation of William Allen White from the preparedness committee to which he had lent his name and credibility. Before quitting in protest of lend-lease, White suggested that the group adopt a motto McCormick would gladly have made his own: "The Yanks Are Not Coming."[31]

Scarcely less astonishing was the reconciliation of Bert McCormick and Joe Patterson, the latter breaking with the White House over what he perceived as a deliberate, if disingenuous, policy leading to war. While the Colonel in Chicago concentrated his fire on "the Republican Quisling" Willkie, the Captain in New York published cartoons featuring a pair of skeleton-faced harlots named World War II ("Uncle Sap's New Girl Friend") and her ghoulish mother, World War I. Joined by Cissy Patterson and her *Washington Times-Herald*, the reunited publishers were dubbed the Three Furies of Isolation by Henry Luce. FDR called them the McCormick-Patterson Axis.

On March 11, 1941, Roosevelt signed lend-lease into law. Churchill took the occasion to offer public thanks for "the most unsordid act in the history of any nation." The next morning the *Tribune* editorial page sported an urgent banner: SAVE OUR REPUBLIC. This was a bit much for the *Chicago Times*, a financially precarious tabloid run by Emory Thomason, formerly the general manager of the *Tribune*. Thomason and McCormick had been friends since their days as Northwestern law students. As recently as June 1938, when a fire had threatened to keep the *Times* from publishing, McCormick had lent his presses to Thomason. "There is no profit in doing a contemporary a dirty trick," he observed.[32]

McCormick could afford to be gracious, for the struggling *Times* presented scant challenge to the *Tribune*'s dominance. But the intense debate over lend-lease and broader disagreements over U.S. foreign policy wrecked the civilized rivalry as it spurred each paper to rhetorical excess. Thomason landed the first blow. The *Times* cited German and Italian news reports containing praise for the *Tribune* and its stand against American warmongers. McCormick, feeling his patriotism impugned, struck back with a scorching editorial, "These Jackals Grow Too Bold!"

Hitherto the *Tribune* had regarded its "two little evening contemporaries," as the *Times* and Frank Knox's *Daily News* were categorized, with a silence born of contempt. But it could hardly let pass a deliberate distortion of its attitude toward the Third Reich, based upon "a garbled story from Berlin." Because Hitler's system of government oppression promoted war and fostered both racial and religious persecution, the *Tribune* detested it. "We hate it in Germany, we hate it in Italy, we hate it in Russia, and we hate it in the United States." Having tasted the horrors of combat firsthand, the *Tribune*'s owners understood firsthand that war breeds dictatorship and intolerance. Thus McCormick looked reproachfully on those "fat old men who sit in comfortable offices fanning hysteria while a million young Americans are plodding thru the mud of unfinished training camps."

This was hitting below the belt. A livid Thomason denied that he was fat. Then he composed a blistering rejoinder to his erstwhile friend in Tribune Tower. "Bertie McCormick is yapping like a feisty dog," he wrote. The *Times* repeated its charge that Hitler and the *Tribune* were mutual admirers. And the paper took a slap at "certain people," most notably successful newspaper owners, who mistakenly equated their wealth and power with greatness.

As if to compensate for the loss of his thirty-five-year friendship with Thomason, McCormick became even closer to Charles Lindbergh. The famed aviator had been McCormick's houseguest in August 1940, when 40,000 antiwar activists cheered him at Soldier Field. Returning east, the Lone Eagle contrasted the "emotional stability" of the Mississippi Valley with excitable New Yorkers, who he thought were governed by sentiment. McCormick agreed that New York was a victim of war lust, a condition he attributed to commercial factors, ties of blood and social ambition, and the understandable loathing of the Nazi regime by the city's large Jewish population. He hoped, McCormick told Lindbergh, that they might unite "to oppose the combination of hysteria and foreign propaganda which is trying to get us into war."33

As evidence, McCormick cited Roosevelt's 1937 quarantine speech in Chicago and his own conversation with Churchill that summer in England. He recalled for Lindbergh a New York dinner at which he had listened as Lord Lothian, the British ambassador to the United States, Morgan banker Thomas Lamont, Arthur Krock of the *New York Times*, and other establishmentarians contemplated a war they regarded as unavoidable. In April 1939, McCormick's annual Associated Press luncheon in the same city had been enlivened by an impassioned call from Arthur Sulzberger of the *New York Times* for direct U.S. assistance to England and France if those countries fell victim to German aggression. Once fighting broke out, McCormick learned of a Washington meeting attended by Lord Lothian at which the chief topic of discussion was how to punish the *Tribune* for its isolationist sins. (Before his death in 1940, the British ambassador gave McCormick private assurances that neither he nor his government was out to harm the *Tribune*.)34

The litany of grievances did not end there. Early in 1941, the *Tribune*'s Canadian operations came under renewed pressure. Hostile petitions were filed with the governments of Ontario and Quebec. McCormick subscribed $3 million to a Canadian victory loan. Privately, he complained of foreign persecution — and propaganda. Lindbergh agree that behind "the agitation for war" lay an orchestrated campaign.35

That this wasn't wholly fanciful became clear with the 1976 publication of *A Man Called Intrepid*. Based on the records and recollections of Sir William Stephenson, Churchill's hand-picked chief of British intelligence services, the book described an espionage ring that penetrated the highest levels of the American government. Working under the innocuous-sounding umbrella of British Security Coordination (BSC), Sir William oversaw at least 30,000 agents worldwide. Not all of them were on his payroll. Roosevelt did not exaggerate when he told the British spymaster, "I'm your biggest undercover agent." British operatives exploited the president's love of intrigue. They provided him with forged maps, purportedly taken from captured Germans, which detailed Nazi plans to seize Latin America and conduct bombing raids on New York and Washington. They also set out to discredit the defeatist Joe Kennedy — admittedly, not a difficult task — and to undermine other prominent isolationist spokesmen.

At a Detroit labor convention, members of the left-wing Fight for Freedom Committee, an offshoot of the BSC, falsified a poll naming Senator Burton Wheeler, Lindbergh, and McCormick as America's leading fascists. Sir William got considerable help from domestic agencies of the United States government, especially the IRS and FBI. Lindbergh and likeminded shapers of opinion were subjected to tax audits and wiretaps. Also bugged was the Washington bureau of the *Tribune*, where Walter Trohan in particular remained a burr under Roosevelt's saddle. Trohan got the official cold shoulder for his dogged attempts to report on the close friendship between the president and Crown Princess Martha of Norway. The royal refugee was in residence at the White House and a frequent weekend visitor to the Roosevelt home at Hyde Park.

Trohan refused to be put off the trail of a possible dalliance. The exasperated White House press secretary, Steve Early, sought to reason with him. "My God," said Early, "after Eleanor, isn't he entitled to a bit of femininity?"[36]

For all his enjoyment of Washington gossip, McCormick refused to print Trohan's findings about the old affair involving FDR and Lucy Mercer Rutherford. (Told that the *Tribune* didn't fight that way, Trohan turned his files over to Westbrook Pegler, the bitter New Deal critic and columnist, who knew no other way to fight.) Neither would the Colonel touch the story peddled to him by Sewell Avery, Montgomery Ward's Roosevelt-hating chairman, concerning a homosexual advance made by Undersecretary of State Sumner Welles to a black porter on a train returning from the Alabama funeral of House Speaker William Bankhead in November 1940.

Somehow Roosevelt maintained his sense of the ridiculous, a winning trait demonstrated anew on Inauguration Day, 1941. Just before the swearing-in was to take place, Trohan left the press stands outside the Capitol in search of a friend. He had no trouble making his way past familiar Secret Service agents. He was a few feet from the podium when the president came forward to recite his oath of office for the third time.

"What in hell are you doing here?" snapped FDR.

"Looking for a friend," said Trohan, irreverent as ever. "I have one, even though you may doubt it."[37]

Roosevelt couldn't keep from laughing. As much as he despised Trohan's boss, he could never stay mad for long at the sardonic Irishman, who entertained as he enraged.

✧ 6

    McCormick never formally joined America First, the 800,000-member isolationist flagship berthed in Chicago and captained by his friend General Robert Wood. But the *Tribune* gave extensive favorable coverage to the group and its leading spokesmen, especially Lindbergh and Wheeler. In addition, the New York bureau of the paper enlisted the conservative writer Victor Lasky to furnish negative information on prominent internationalists. (By 1970, Lasky was taking money from Nelson Rockefeller to write an unflattering biography of Arthur Goldberg, Rockefeller's opponent for governor of New York.)[38]

McCormick found space to print the isolationist creed of Lillian Gish as delivered to a Chicago rally in March 1941. "But for you and a few others like you," Miss Gish told him, "it would seem that these are the last days of a government called Democracy." The Colonel thanked the actress profusely. "Few professional people dare antagonize the organized forces of the Colonials," he observed, cracking wise at the expense of Tory-minded easterners. He traced Gish's courage to her Ohio forebears. In crossing the Alleghenies, this hardy stock had become thoroughly nationalized, unlike those who had remained behind on the coast to be "diluted in their Americanism by other hordes of immigrants."[39]

This was strong stuff, even by *Tribune* standards. The paper had no choice but to administer the equivalent of a public spanking, however, when Lindbergh, addressing a Des Moines audience in September 1941, suggested that American Jews were divided in their loyalties. The *Tribune* moved to distance itself from the tarnished hero, whose medals it had photographed for a singularly ill-timed display coinciding with the furor caused by his harsh words about the Jews. Yet McCormick refused to disown Lindbergh, or America First, to which he was a generous contributor.

He was less favorably inclined to the newly chartered United Services Organization (USO), a private effort aimed at improving the lives and easing the loneliness of American servicemen by providing them with recreational opportunities. McCormick accused Tom Dewey, his 1940 stalking horse, then traveling the country to raise funds for USO programs, of taking on "a slacker job." Marshall Field's chairman, Hughston McBain, himself active in the USO, protested to Chesser Campbell, the *Tribune*'s advertising manager.

"This is the damnedest thing I've ever heard of," McBain told Campbell, a long-time friend.

"Well," said Campbell, "the Colonel is pretty hard to control."

He didn't want to control McCormick, McBain answered, just prevent the USO from being strangled in its crib. Both men worked on the Colonel, persuading him of the merits of a nongovernmental agency ministering to servicemen away from home for the first time.

"After all," McCormick finally told McBain, in an admission belied by each issue of the *Tribune*, "I'm not omniscient."[40]

The extent to which McCormick really believed such protestations may be doubted. Certainly he showed little modesty when directing his countrymen to avoid the snares of European involvement. The continent would survive the present war, he maintained, but seething with age-old rivalries, addicted to balance-of-power politics. American democracy was a more fragile plant, easily trampled underfoot in the rush to take up arms. Fearing regimentation at home more than the loss of freedom overseas, he pursued what the historian James C. Schneider calls "a strategy of deterrence" marked by U.S. preparedness and passivity.

Many readers found it understandably difficult to reconcile the Colonel's restraint toward foreign dictators with his constant harping on domestic tyranny. General Robert Wood, the dynamic chairman of Sears, Roebuck, saw no contradiction in these views. Wood, who chewed cigarettes so incessantly that his doctor finally prescribed a rubber cigarette for him to chomp on, read census reports the way most of his customers devoured pulp novels. "I'm just looking at the trends," he explained to a curious R. Douglas Stuart, the youthful national director of America First. The tough-talking businessman spoke the same language as McCormick, distrusted the same adversaries, revered the same heroes. Both men had been traumatized by World War I, in which Wood had performed impressively as Pershing's quartermaster general. Each had his Churchill anecdotes to buttress a conviction that the United States was being railroaded into a war it didn't want, to shield an anachronistic British empire from the winds of change. On a 1936 visit to England, Wood had listened in amazement as Churchill declared, "Germany is getting too strong. We must smash her."[41]

McCormick, like Wood, took a grandfatherly shine to young Doug Stuart, whose antiwar activities at Yale Law School had set the pattern for America First to become the leading voice of isolation in 1940–41. On visits to the twenty-fourth floor, Stuart encountered a figure less intimidating than his public image. "I knew that God wasn't present," he later recalled. (Actually, his first reaction on being ushered into the big room was that he "had better make pals with a very large police dog" standing guard over McCormick.) The Colonel showed Stuart historic memorabilia cluttering the office. He shared his wartime experiences with the young activist, whose generation was facing another European conflagration. He also put Stuart in touch with Joe Patterson at the *Daily News*.[42]

A long list of luminaries rallied to America First. These included Joe

Kennedy, Chester Bowles, Oswald Garrison Villard, Frank Lloyd Wright, and Alice Roosevelt Longworth ("She was fun to be with," remembered Stuart, "if you were on her side"). Lending the group intellectual cachet was the iconoclastic chancellor of the University of Chicago, Robert Hutchens.[43]

One student for whom Hutchens most definitely did not speak was Katharine Meyer, daughter of the *Washington Post*'s owner, Eugene Meyer. As Katharine Graham, she would far outstrip her father's contributions to American journalism. She would also have occasion to rethink her youthful opinion of McCormick and a newspaper she had once regarded as "the devil incarnated." In the tradition of Hearst, Pulitzer, and the Scripps family, "mad geniuses" all, McCormick had succeeded in building "an extraordinary newspaper in the middle of the country. With all his strangeness," said Graham in a 1992 interview, "he really did have integrity and professionalism of his own kind." She readily understood how the Colonel and his contemporaries could inspire nostalgia for a more colorful past. Modern journalism was undeniably fairer, more accurate, and more reliable, she asserted. But in accepting its obligation to be responsible, it had also become blander and, one suspects, less fun.[44]

✧ 7

Hitler's invasion of the Soviet Union in June 1941 transformed the war. For McCormick, it supplied the most compelling reason yet for the United States to shun military involvement. "Are we to send an army to reestablish atheism in Russia and the slaughter of the priests?" he asked Joe Patterson. His longing for the defeat of Soviet communism was undisguised, tempered only by the hope that Hitler's victory would leave him "incapable of further offensive effort for a generation."[45]

In August, as the Nazis advanced in the face of stiff Russian resistance, Roosevelt and Churchill convened a floating summit off the coast of Newfoundland. Their talks produced the Atlantic Charter, dismissed by the *Tribune* as a rehash of "Wilsonian futilities" endorsed by "the fighting prime minister" for a single reason: "He wants soldiers." Buried in the lofty prose pledging self-determination and the equitable use of raw materials was a joint vow by the leaders to pursue these and other postwar objectives "after final destruction of Nazi tyranny." This, said the *Tribune*, stretched presidential powers beyond their constitutional limit. When making his promise to Churchill, FDR "was more than outside the country. He was outside his office."[46]

McCormick threw his support behind legislation to forestall lend-lease assistance from reaching Stalin. As aid to Soviet Russia became a test of American resolve, its opponents were held up to scorn. Writing from

Topeka, Alf Landon tried to reassure McCormick that "this copperhead business" was merely the latest attempt by the Roosevelt White House to equate criticism of its policies with treachery to the nation.[47]

McCormick's objections were smothered by sympathy for the latest victim of unprovoked Nazi aggression. At the end of July, an overflow crowd meeting under the auspices of the Chicago Fight for Freedom Committee cheered Edmond Taylor, formerly the *Tribune*'s Paris correspondent, as he denounced the "criminal nonsense" emanating from Tribune Tower. Shouts of approval greeted the rallying cry, "Millions for defense, but not two cents for the *Tribune*." The audience filling Orchestra Hall adopted a resolution calling for a new morning newspaper to combat the McCormick monopoly. Then its members filed out onto Michigan Avenue to make bonfires of the hated *Tribune*.

Emory Thomason, still smarting from his vituperative exchange with McCormick over lend-lease, went to New York to discuss a possible alliance with Marshall Field III, the department store heir, whose enormous personal fortune was matched by his willingness to bankroll liberal causes. For almost a year, Field had been the financial angel behind *PM*, a visionary New York journal whose refusal to carry paid advertising was in keeping with its radical editorial page. Undaunted by his losses, Field wanted to invade the Chicago market. He hoped to purchase both the *Chicago Times* and Frank Knox's *Daily News*, he confided to Thomason, and merge the two papers into a *Tribune* rival, inevitably dubbed *AM*.[48]

Thomason, reluctant to sell, tried to cool Field's ardor by assuring him that he could expect to lose over $1 million in his first year of operations. But Field was a difficult man to dissuade. He turned his sights on the *Daily News*. Under Frank Knox, the *News* had surrendered two thirds of its market value and been forced to omit 1941 dividends on common stock. Shrewdly, Knox concealed from Field the parlous state of his finances. By playing hard to get, he only inflamed his suitor. Field pursued his quarry to Washington, where he was taken out on the official yacht used as a residence by the secretary of the navy. Then he was taken.[49]

According to John S. Knight, who purchased the *Daily News* from the Knox estate in 1944, Roosevelt was the guiding force behind the sweetheart contract by which Knox agreed, for the princely sum of $400,000 a year, to lease Field three vacant floors of the Daily News Building, along with the use of presses idle during the overnight hours. Knox could not restrain his glee. "Well," he told members of the Chicago Club, "we have got the *Tribune* fixed now. Marshall Field is going to start a morning paper with the backing of everyone from the President down."[50]

This opened the door to an epic contest pitting the grandson of Joseph Medill against the grandson of the first Marshall Field, each a Chicago legend. It had been Field to whom a reluctant Medill had appealed in 1874, seeking funds with which to reassert his undisputed control over the *Tribune*; Field whose unsolicited advice had led Medill to celebrate the day he finally paid off his loan as the happiest of his life. Marshall Field's billed itself as the world's largest department store, the *Tribune* as the World's Greatest Newspaper. Adding to the drama was the flamboyant reputation of the combatants, their violent political differences, and the prospect of two great fortunes colliding in the most savage street brawl since McCormick and Hearst had gone at it early in the century.

Journalists hyped the coming showdown at sunrise. "Ink will flow. Checkbooks will open. Millions will battle millions," breathlessly predicted the *Chicago Times*, the bruised evening warrior that was no doubt glad to have someone else step into the ring and absorb the Colonel's punishing blows. Thirteen times the *Tribune* had pronounced funeral rites over a fallen adversary. Yet Field had advantages beyond awesome personal wealth. He possessed gilt-edged White House connections, the sympathy of organized labor, and a Chicago electorate in tune with his message. If anyone could humble the *Tribune*, Field was the man.

✧ 8

Before crossing swords, Field and McCormick had often crossed paths. Both were born in Chicago and educated in England. Both returned home to assume active roles in the family business and married before making war on Germany in 1917. That spring Field went to McCormick, then busy recruiting men for the First Illinois Cavalry. He asked what part he should play in the great drama unfolding overseas. McCormick didn't mince words. Since Field's male ancestors had been slackers in the Civil and Spanish-American wars, he bluntly informed his guest, he "had better get into this one if he wanted to stay in the country." Field joined the McCormick regiment expecting to redress its social deficiencies. Once the shooting started, however, the private recruited for his Cambridge patina distinguished himself for his courage at St. Michel and the Meuse-Argonne.[51]

Field returned to the States wearing a captain's stripes. For a while he was content to sell bonds and help other vets find jobs in the shriveled postwar economy. But in 1921 he left Chicago for New York and the baronial splendor of a 1,700-acre Long Island estate. Within a decade he divorced the mother of his three children and remarried, this time an English blueblood who shared his adventurous tastes in big game hunting, aviation, and racing boats. He courted danger as an alternative to boredom. Yet however fast or high he went, Field seemed unable to outdistance his atrophy of spirit. The midlife collision of passion and propriety wrecked his second marriage within three years.

Then, one day in 1935, he walked into the Park Avenue office of Dr. Gregory Zilboorg, psychiatrist to the stars, whose mental probing inspired his patient Moss Hart to write *Lady in the Dark* for Gertrude Lawrence. Falling under Zilboorg's spell, Field submitted to analysis five times a week for over a year. He felt his spiritual emptiness lift, to be replaced by a driving sense of purpose. Field took pains to deny that his therapist exercised undue influence over him. "He frees you," he told a reporter curious about the Zilboorg connection. Forsaking investment banking, Field became a zealous philanthropist, advancing the causes of child welfare, slum clearance, and civil rights. He established the Committee for the Study of Suicide, with Dr. Zilboorg as director of research. He found belated personal happiness in his 1936 marriage to Ruth Phipps.[52]

As a staunch New Dealer, Field was inclined to be generous when approached by Ralph Ingersoll, an idealistic refugee from Henry Luce's publishing empire, who dreamed of starting an unapologetically liberal newspaper for New Yorkers, free of advertising and free to oppose the social and political status quo.* Field invested $200,000 in the venture, dubbed *PM*. When sales tumbled after an initial burst of enthusiasm, the reformed playboy with a social conscience bought out panicky investors at twenty cents on the dollar. Critics raked *PM* as an uptown edition of the Communist *Daily Worker*, a perception Field strengthened by rededicating the paper under his ownership to the fight against "the internal Fascist forces in America."

In search of fresh challenges, Field launched *Parade* as a Sunday supplement, incorporating features from *PM* for national distribution. He invited Silliman Evans, the combative editor of the *Nashville Tennessean*, to come to New York. Over lunch at the Recess Club, Field recounted for Evans his failed attempt to combine the *Chicago Times* and the *Chicago Daily News* into a single pro-Roosevelt paper in competition with the insolent *Tribune*. Snagged in the net of Field's enthusiasm, Evans agreed to take a leave of absence from the *Tennessean* and report to Chicago by September 1.

This allowed Evans just three months in which to recruit a staff, find presses, establish his local credibility — and rattle McCormick. Evans was a throwback to earlier Chicago newspapermen, who had cared less about remaking society than about scooping the competition — and making certain that someone else's papers wound up floating in the Chicago River.

---

*McCormick lumped Ingersoll and Luce together as the most loathsome publishers in the business. "For a while they used to print attacks on me and the *Tribune*," he wrote to Charles Lindbergh in the summer of 1940, "and then send an advertising solicitor around. One day we published that fact and we have not been bothered since."

Whereas Field was a fighting liberal, Evans was merely looking for a good fight. More than anything else, he was drawn to Chicago by the alluring prospect of giving Colonel McCormick unsheeted hell. He hoped in the process to embellish his own journalistic legend and advance the interests of his political godfather, Jesse H. Jones, a Houston financier.

Jones's methods of acquiring riches and denying them to competitors had raised eyebrows even in Texas. In 1928 he had helped bankroll the Democratic national convention in his city in the forlorn hope that weary delegates might be stampeded to a hometown favorite. Named to the board of the Reconstruction Finance Corporation, he had used his power to rescue his faltering banks and mortgage companies. Roosevelt justifiably distrusted the ambitious Texan, whose pontifical manner won him mockery as Jesus H. Jones. Yet FDR raised Jones to the chairmanship of the RFC, and he didn't hesitate to ask his appointee, "as a special favor," to liquidate substantial debts run up by Elliott Roosevelt in a bankrupt Texas radio network.[53]

Now, as part of a disinformation campaign, Silliman Evans spread stories through the Chicago grapevine that Field was prepared to sink at least $9 million into his as yet unnamed paper, with Jesus H. Jones and the full resources of the federal government ready to assist the venture if and when the liberal philanthropist flagged in his commitment. Frank Knox fed McCormick's paranoia by renting facilities to Field and bragging that the Morning Colonel had at last met his match. The war of nerves escalated throughout the autumn of 1941. A $10,000 contest to name the embryonic paper attracted 220,000 entries. Evans hired former *Newsweek* editor Rex Smith to oversee the newly christened *Chicago Sun*. To run the Washington bureau, he chose Bascom Timmons, a veteran capital reporter with close ties to Jesse Jones. Most spectacularly, he raided the *New York Times*, making off with the distinguished Turner Catledge as a roving "world correspondent."[54]

Evans was racing against the holiday season, when advertisers spent heavily to attract Christmas business. This was not the only factor heightening his sense of urgency. After a typically frenetic day on the job, he would raise a highball glass and exclaim, "Here's hoping we beat the war." In Washington, Knox told Ickes that the *Sun* would start with a solid circulation base of 250,000. On September 18, FDR instructed Steve Early to reply "in confidence" to a recent correspondent and "tell him about the possibility of a new paper" in Chicago.[55]

Early's deputy, William Hassett, went a step further. "You know," Hassett said to Walter Trohan, "the president likes you, and you and he could go back to your old relationship if you were on another paper, a friendly paper."

"Hold it, Bill," interrupted Trohan. "You can go back and tell him I hate war, a phrase he may recognize, more than I hate the New Deal, and that he can't buy me with someone else's money."[56]

McCormick warned his troops against cockiness. "We're tops in Chicago," he told a hastily convened meeting in the *Tribune* newsroom, "but I don't want you to act like top dogs. Be sporting. I want every one of you to remember that in your work you are to be a gentleman or a lady. You are not to swagger."[57]

Outwardly unruffled, behind his facade of icy belligerence McCormick seethed over a breach of etiquette for which he never forgave Field. On returning to Chicago, Field had given a cocktail party at which he planned to announce his entry into the newspaper wars. By mistake, McCormick's name was added to the guest list. Rather than embarrass the Colonel under his roof, Field kept mum about his plans. Neither did he consult McCormick before making formal application for membership in the Associated Press. The Colonel, already angered over this latest attempt by Washington to punish the *Tribune*, thought Field was guilty of bad form in trying to force his way into the AP club.

Under bylaws last upheld by the federal government in 1915, the AP could withhold membership from any applicant in a market that was already being served by a member paper. Since the demise of the *Herald and Examiner* in 1939, Hearst had retained a phantom membership, theoretically revivable anytime he wished to reenter the morning battle zone. McCormick, believing that Chicago was capable of sustaining only one morning paper, naturally preferred a hypothetical competitor like Hearst to a real and present danger, which is what Field and his millions posed at the beginning of December 1941. The cocktail party snafu gave him the rationalization he sought in order to blackball Field's application. A gentleman might overlook many effronteries, but not so flagrant a violation of club rules by another gentleman.

Besides, McCormick was furious with the mercenary Frank Knox, whose profitable collaboration with Field promised to reward both himself and the administration he served. *Tribune* correspondents accused Knox of enforcing a double standard, leaking naval secrets to his own paper and applying strict rules of censorship to everyone else. As the December 4 debut of the *Sun* drew near, the combat ravaging the Russian steppes was locally overshadowed by what journalists around the world were calling the Battle of Chicago. Field's audacious challenge to McCormick, said the *London Daily Mail*, represented "the last great drive to torpedo isolationism" in the United States.

McCormick, equally portentous, let his judgment be clouded by hatred of Roosevelt. This led him to reenact the fable of the fox and the crow, which he had had carved into the side of Tribune Tower, never imagining that the crumbs he gathered in hopes of eclipsing the *Sun* might have been deliberately placed within his reach by the fox in the White House.

✧ 9

What happened next remains, more than half a century later, the subject of controversy and conjecture. Any attempt to render a verdict on precisely who did what to whom, his motive for doing it, and the impact of his actions on the course of World War II must ultimately rest on circumstantial evidence and informed guesswork. Asked once to justify the *Tribune*'s methods, McCormick acknowledged that the paper made use of every available weapon. "My one rule is never to print anything obviously untrue," he said.[58]

These broad parameters posed no hardship for Pat Maloney, the managing editor, whose job it was to make Chicagoans forget the rival *Sun* before they could ever really notice it. Long before December 4, Maloney instructed his bureaus to troll for scoops big enough to deflect attention from the new kid in town. Both he and the Colonel got more than they bargained for when, late in November, Capitol Hill correspondent Chesly Manly alerted his colleagues in the Washington bureau to the existence of detailed plans for a U.S. invasion of Nazi-occupied Europe — plans authorized by Roosevelt at a time when he was publicly maintaining his peaceful intentions.[59]

Manly did not exaggerate. On July 9, 1941, the president had written to the secretaries of war and the navy requesting a joint service report outlining the production and strategic requirements needed "to defeat our potential enemies." Two months later, a draft of the so-called Victory Program was ready. Five copies were made, only to be recalled because the plans failed to include the defense of Hawaii. A revised 350-page document, codenamed Rainbow Five, was delivered to Roosevelt on the afternoon of September 25. Thirty-five additional copies, each clearly stamped *Top Secret*, were distributed among the military brass, including General H. H. "Hap'" Arnold, a skilled leaker ("second only to Roosevelt," as recalled by Walter Trohan) and bureaucratic infighter. Resenting the short rations allocated to his Army Air Corps, Arnold blamed lend-lease for leaving the United States virtually defenseless.

At least ten other copies of the Victory Program found their way to air corps officers. One of these, an unnamed colonel, offered late in November to leave a complete copy of the war plans for the overnight perusal of Senator Burton Wheeler. An excited Wheeler relayed the tantalizing proposal to Ches Manly. Both men had cause to rejoice over the unexpected windfall. Wheeler had enraged FDR during the lend-lease debate by predicting that the administration would "plow under every fourth American boy" in a perverse application of its domestic farm policies to foreign battlefields. Manly, too, had offended the White House with a string of stories portraying an Anglo-American alliance promoting a joint invasion of Hitler's Europe.

The full extent of the president's rearmament program emerged in a Manly piece dated October 2, 1941: "War Planners Envision Army of 10,000,000, Aim at 500 Divisions and 80,000 Planes." His figures, said Manly, were based on funding already authorized by Congress. Then came Wheeler's phone call offering documentary evidence to confirm McCormick's worst suspicions.

The first fruits of the Wheeler-Manly partnership appeared in the November 27 *Tribune*. Readers were told of the existence of military blueprints for an American expeditionary force (AEF) of five million men. In addition, U.S. funds were earmarked to construct a $15 million base in British-held Eritrea.

The *Tribune* was swimming in deep waters, as Walter Trohan, clearly uncomfortable, pointed out. To reveal highly sensitive military plans seemed incompatible with McCormick's martial background and continuing associations. Moreover, said Trohan, if Wheeler felt so strongly about sharing the information, he should do so on the floor of the Senate and not through a friendly reporter. Contingency planning was a staple of military life, often nothing more than an intelligence-gathering exercise. If McCormick doubted this last argument, all he had to do was read his own newspaper following an October 27 Navy Day speech in which Roosevelt had alluded to secret maps in his possession, said to prove the determination of Hitler to add South America to the Nazi empire.[60] The *Tribune* had scoffed at the president's claim. "Anyone familiar with such matters knows that every general staff in the world has studied every conceivable problem of military action," it said. "If Mr. Roosevelt were to go into the files of the War or Navy Department, he no doubt could find documents which indicate how we would attack and seize and govern Canada. The mere presence of such papers proves nothing beyond the desire of military men to prepare for contingencies, however remote, which might arise."

Spies, the *Tribune* might have added, were not alone in uncovering such plans. Disgruntled army officers were perfectly capable of ferreting out national secrets. So were crusading senators and opportunistic journalists. Still, Trohan had a point. What could possibly lead McCormick, the soldier's soldier, barely a month after making light of alleged Nazi war plans, to splash his own country's most jealously guarded secrets across the front page of the *Tribune*? The simplest answer is that competitive pressures colored his judgment. The urge to say "I told you so" in 144-point type was irresistible. Most of all, McCormick welcomed the chance to expose presidential duplicity and ruin Field's debut.

Shortly after midnight on Thursday, December 4, delivery trucks bearing the first of 900,000 copies of the *Chicago Sun* pulled away from the Daily News Building. "We're here! We're here!" newsboys shouted at expectant knots of customers gathered around newsstands. "Have just seen Field's paper," McCormick wired Joe Patterson. "It's ridiculous."[61]

McCormick was not wide of the mark. In its premier issue, the *Sun* gave prominent play to an obscure conflict in the Balkans. Even those hoping to avoid the *Tribune* could hardly ignore its electrifying front-page streamer:

FDR'S WAR PLANS!
GOAL IS 10 MILLION ARMED MEN;
HALF TO FIGHT IN AEF

Citing "a confidential report prepared by the joint Army and Navy high command by direction of President Roosevelt," the *Tribune* revealed plans for total war on two oceans and three continents. An extensive air campaign against the German Reich, accompanied by offensive ground action in North Africa and the Near East, would theoretically culminate in a massive U.S.-led invasion of Fortress Europe no later than July 1, 1943. Forgetting his earlier disregard of contingency planning, McCormick extravagantly praised his Washington bureau for "the greatest scoop in the history of journalism." (In fact, the war plans story, as it came to be known, merely embroidered Manly's November 27 description of a new AEF, based on whatever documentation had come his way thanks to Wheeler.) A telegram conveying these sentiments was framed and hung in Arthur Sears Henning's office.[62]

The Manly story caused an uproar in the military hierarchy, where fingers of suspicion were pointed at nearly everyone in the War Plans Division. Singled out as the most likely culprit was Lieutenant Colonel Albert C. Wedemeyer, a promising army officer who had supervised much of the ground action planning without bothering to conceal his sympathies for America First. Ironically, given his distaste for the whole enterprise, Walter Trohan also came under surveillance. His home phones were tapped by the FBI, army and naval intelligence, and — in a bizarre subplot — the Anti-Defamation League, one of whose agents threatened to expose "that Nazi Manly."[63]

Despite intense grilling by FBI and military intelligence agents who questioned his patriotism, Manly refused to divulge his sources. One agent hinted that espionage charges might be forthcoming and warned of dire consequences if the pubic heard even a rumor linking the *Tribune*'s possession of the Victory Program to the Japanese attack on Pearl Harbor ("they would tear down that building in Chicago, and you know it"). Manly retorted that he had first glimpsed the report on December 2, long after the Japanese strike force had set sail with Hawaii as its target. He denied paying anyone for the information contained in his story.[64]

Attention shifted to Capitol Hill. A Missouri congressman was cleared of charges that he had bought the war plans from a government clerk. Attempts to connect Charles Lindbergh with the leak collapsed for want of credible evidence. Investigators settled on Burton Wheeler as their chief suspect. In his 1962 memoir, *Yankee From the West*, Wheeler employed arguments similar to those used in 1941 by the *Tribune*. He insisted that the Victory Program was not in fact "an operational war plan" but a mere prospectus of the manpower and other requirements on which American victory would depend.[65]

Perhaps the most curious response to the *Tribune* story came from the White House. At a December 5 press conference, Roosevelt made no direct comment on the security breach. Instead, he directed press inquiries to the War Department, where Secretary Stimson read a prepared statement castigating McCormick without mentioning him by name. Back at the White House, Steve Early blandly acknowledged the right of a free press to print whatever came into its possession. And the Office of War Information employed its shortwave radio to rush the offending story to enslaved Europe and Nazi Berlin (to which the "Roosevelt War Plan" had already been cabled by the German embassy in Washington).

At a cabinet meeting on December 6, Attorney General Francis Biddle observed that McCormick might be liable to prosecution under the World War I–era Espionage Act. Harold Ickes wanted to know if the Colonel was still a reserve officer and therefore subject to court-martial. Both men expected hearty agreement from the president. Yet Roosevelt seemed oddly detached. Could he know more than he was letting on? Was the story, so hastily disseminated abroad, a deliberate plant, designed to goad Hitler into a suicidal declaration of war on the United States? So asserted the author of *A Man Called Intrepid*. As William Stephenson had it, the Victory Program was a brilliant hoax concocted by British agents, then slipped to a credulous Senator Wheeler by a cooperative U.S. army officer and double agent.[66]

A still more cunning explanation was put forward by the historian Thomas Fleming in the December 1987 issue of *American Heritage*. Rejecting Stephenson's claims as fraudulent, Fleming did not deny that there had been a clandestine partnership involving Roosevelt and Churchill's master spy. He noted that the FBI investigation ordered by the White House had ended in a cloud of bureaucratic obfuscation. No fewer than 109 people in the War Department had had legitimate access to the Victory Program, wrote J. Edgar Hoover, and there were a comparable number of potential suspects in the Navy Department. Unwilling to take the case before a federal grand jury, on May 4, 1942, the Justice Department threw up its hands.[67]

Long after the war, assistant FBI director Louis Nichols admitted that the Bureau had been anything but exhaustive in its investigation. "When we got to Arnold, we quit," he confided to Frank Waldrop of the *Washington Times Herald.*[68]

In his *American Heritage* article, Fleming went well beyond this startling revelation. For example, he asked, if Hap Arnold was indeed culpable, then why did he retain the friendship and confidence of George Marshall, a figure of legendary probity (as did Albert Wedemeyer, to name just one officer whose career hung in the balance on the morning of December 4)?

And why did Roosevelt exhibit such uncharacteristic reluctance to punish the *Tribune,* and his administration such unwonted haste to trumpet the supposedly offensive story to any European, or European dictator, lacking access to the World's Greatest Newspaper? Did FDR enjoy a history-making joke at the expense of his bitterest adversary, a ruse made doubly satisfying because it discredited isolationist critics as it boosted slumping Allied morale? The theory is tantalizing — and unprovable.

What is beyond question is the unintended (by McCormick) consequence of the *Tribune*'s exposé. On December 11, the fox in the White House provoked the Berlin crow into a fatal miscalculation. On that date, Hitler appeared before the Reichstag to declare war on the United States. He justified the step — to the historian Martin Gilbert, "perhaps the greatest error, and certainly the most decisive act, of the Second World War" — as a preemptive measure to forestall the huge invasion described by the *Tribune* and its sister publications in New York and Washington.

By then McCormick was beating a hasty retreat. His congratulatory telegram disappeared from the walls of the Washington bureau. On a visit to the bureau a few days after Pearl Harbor, he affected ignorance of the scoop whose repercussions were still being felt halfway around the world. Claiming that he had yet to read the article he had earlier praised so lavishly, McCormick asked Ches Manly to show him a copy of the war plans story.[69]

This elaborate pantomime fooled no one, least of all Joe Patterson. His cousin had left explicit instructions with his Washington bureau, Patterson told the FBI agents who were quizzing him about the origins of the story. McCormick wanted "the hottest stories he could find" to shatter the journalistic lance of Marshall Field.[70]

14

At War

"We have plenty of information that the administration is out to get the *Tribune*. The *Sun* was founded for that sole purpose. It is conducted with its losses deducted from Marshall Field's income tax. It was promised the AP service and the AP is about to be sued in an effort to get the service that the members would not vote under pressure. There has not been such a fight for Freedom of the Press since Peter Zenger was tried in New York."

— Colonel McCormick, August 13, 1942

DECEMBER 7 was the last Sunday of the 1941 professional football season. For fans of the champion Chicago Bears, the afternoon promised a final chance to root for the home team before a long winter's hibernation. A huge radio audience was tuned in when, shortly after the first kickoff, an agitated announcer interrupted with news that Pearl Harbor was under heavy bombardment, presumably by Japanese planes.

McCormick, in Lake Bluff visiting Marion Claire, placed a call to Ward Quaal, a WGN announcer. He asked if Quaal's staff was up on Pacific geography and the pronunciation of strange names that would soon enough take on tragic familiarity. In Washington, Walter Trohan had spent an anxious Saturday night at the State Department, where the traffic in rumors was bumper to bumper. Elsewhere that Sunday afternoon, Cissy Patterson hastily convened her editors at the *Times-Herald* office on H Street. "Do you think *he* arranged this?" she sputtered.[1]

On December 11, the day Hitler formally declared war on the United States, Joe Patterson stood like a nervous schoolboy in the Oval Office of the White House. He had sought an appointment with FDR hoping to bury the past and offer his wartime services. He never got the chance. Instead, he was forced to absorb a presidential tongue-lashing that went on for fifteen blistering minutes. Afterward, he made for the nearest pay phone. Roosevelt, he informed McCormick, had told him to return to New York and reread anti-administration editorials from the *Daily News*, keeping in mind how many American lives would now be lost because war preparations had been slowed by malignant isolationism.[2]

The *Tribune* blamed "an insane clique of Japanese militants" for the war it had tried so hard to avert. Bygones were bygones — for two weeks. Then Patterson went to Hawaii. Speaking off the record, the disgraced commanders at Pearl Harbor held Washington responsible for their inability to resist the Japanese onslaught. This was enough for the *Tribune* to demand Knox's resignation. It should be unnecessary to point out, the paper said three days before Christmas, that the secretary's failure as a cabinet officer had been foreshadowed by his previous lack of success as a political candidate and newspaper publisher. Pleas for national unity were forgotten as McCormick expressed fears that the situation was tailor-made for economic dictatorship.[3]

Roosevelt, charged the *Tribune*, was running the war as "a bigger and gaudier WPA project." Military strategy had been entrusted to "nuts and dreamers" such as Harry Hopkins, whose woolly theories and reckless spending had contributed to the nation's vulnerability. McCormick continued to hope that Hitler and Stalin would destroy each other. "We cannot attack Germany in any effective way," he maintained, "but we can attack Japan." It naturally followed that American forces should be concentrated in the Pacific and not frittered away in pinprick assaults in Europe or North Africa.[4]

On February 19, 1942, a former *Tribune* employee named Jake Sawyer addressed an appeal to his old boss. Sawyer, a loyal Republican and regular *Tribune* reader, also happened to be an ardent Christian Scientist. In this capacity he beseeched McCormick, "while closeted in the sanctity of your prayers," to acknowledge a power greater than his own will. Only by putting aside personal hatred and bitterness, he wrote, could victory in the current war be hastened.

McCormick replied promptly with thanks for Sawyer's "very temperate letter." "What the most powerful propaganda organization in the world has misled you into believing was a campaign of hatred," he said, "has really been a constructive campaign without which this country would be lost. You do not know it, but the fact is that I introduced the R.O.T.C. into the schools; that I introduced machine guns into the army; that I introduced mechanization; I introduced automatic rifles; I was the first ground officer to go up in the air and observe artillery fire," an action he had since made regular army practice.

This impressive litany by no means exhausted McCormick's tribute to himself. "I was the first to advocate an alliance with Canada," he told Sawyer. "I forced the acquiring of the bases in the Atlantic Ocean." To be sure, he had experienced setbacks, having failed to obtain the fortification of Guam or prevent a divided, two-ocean navy. In addition, he said ruefully, "I was unable to persuade the navy and the administration that airplanes could destroy battleships . . . I did get the marines out of Shanghai, but was unsuccessful in trying to get the army out of the Philippines." Needless to say, he didn't expect that such efforts could be pursued free of criticism, "but in view of the accomplishment," he concluded, on a lofty note of self-approbation, "I can bear up under it."[5]

Seeking to determine the accuracy of McCormick's boasts, Sawyer naively submitted copies of this amazing document to other Chicago newspapers. The *Daily News*, rejecting Carl Sandburg's proposed heading, "And On the Seventh Day He Rested," as blasphemous, printed the letter under the caption "Whatta Man!" One reader playfully upbraided the *News* editors for overlooking other significant achievements for which McCormick might take credit:

1. He put the salt in the oceans.
2. He taught birds to fly.
3. He taught babies to say "goo-goo."
4. He sponsored "Curley" Brooks.[6]

No one laughed harder at the Colonel's discomfort than the president of the United States. With heavy sarcasm, Roosevelt paid mock tribute to "the most magnificent record of any Officer of the United States Army from Washington down to date. I think we should give Colonel Robert R. McCormick the next title higher than Field Marshal," he said to General Hap Arnold. Just to be on the safe side, Roosevelt asked Arnold to examine McCormick's claims regarding ROTC, army mechanization, and aerial surveillance of artillery fire. "I personally can take care of the other allegations," he concluded.[7]

It may be revealing that Roosevelt entrusted the assignment to Arnold, the air force chief of staff, who was even then under investigation for leaking the Victory Program to the *Tribune*. Demolishing McCormick's case was a piece of cake. Arnold reserved to himself the honor of being the first American soldier to observe artillery fire from the air. "Perhaps Colonel McCormick had a dream," he cracked to Roosevelt.[8]

Well aware that he had no one but himself to blame for the public ridicule, McCormick instructed his lawyers to find grounds for legal action against the *Daily News*. None existed. One brave attorney urged Weymouth Kirkland to confront McCormick with a detailed refutation of the Sawyer letter, "so that he won't get out on any more limbs." This was wishful thinking. As he aged, the uncompromising defender of the First

Amendment took a more selective view of press freedoms, forgetting them entirely when it was to his advantage.[9]

A few days before Halloween 1942, Kirkland's law firm received another angry blast from Tribune Tower. Enclosed was a recent *Daily News* cartoon from the caustic pen of Cecil Jensen. It showed a couple of street urchins conducting their own scrap-metal drive to aid the war effort and eying a set of iron gates in a posh Chicago neighborhood. "This is supposed to be my gate," the unamused McCormick notified his lawyers. "Cannot this be prosecuted as an incitement to do illegal acts?"[10]

❖ 2

The Sawyer letter gave birth to another Cecil Jensen creation, which satirized with deadly precision the Colonel's pose as the most profound military thinker since Hannibal. "The Adventures of Colonel McCosmic" were partly inspired by a long-forgotten Hearst strip ("King Gazooks and Loberino") that had made sport of the dictatorial Theodore Roosevelt and his compliant White House secretary. Commencing in March 1942, Colonel McCosmic appeared in the *Chicago Daily News* whenever his real-life counterpart issued some particularly outlandish claim or battlefield pronouncement.

As drawn by Jensen, McCosmic was a tall, chinless figure, potbellied and walrus-mustached. A silly tin hat crowned his head; binoculars perpetually dangled from his neck. His companion, a timid, fretful stooge addressed as Captain, was based on Maxwell Corpening, the polo-playing flunky who alternatively served McCormick's purposes and suffered his abuse. Pompous, opinionated, and eternally self-satisfied, Colonel McCosmic used pictures of FDR, Knox, and Stimson to perfect his dart-throwing skills. He conducted naval maneuvers in the bathtub and councils of war with marble busts of Washington, Grant, and Napoleon. In one typically wicked parody, the Colonel is at his desk, clutching a megaphone in one hand and a telephone in the other. He is barking advice to Admiral King while simultaneously taking credit for its success with the White House. "General Marshall," orders the Colonel, "stop worrying about Hitler" — a none too subtle dig at McCormick's Asia-first strategy. In the next breath he directs General MacArthur to get busy on winning the war in the Pacific.*

---

*After his escape from Bataan in March 1942, MacArthur received a congratulatory message from McCormick. With rather more courtesy than the situation required, the general expressed a wish that McCormick could join him in Australia. McCormick offered to drop what he was doing if MacArthur really wanted him. "I cannot pretend that I retain the physical capacity to command a regiment as it should be commanded," said the sixty-two-year-old publisher. When nothing came of the exchange, McCormick, characteristically, chose to blame FDR for excluding him from the Pacific theater.

In March 1942, shortly before MacArthur was forced to abandon the Philippines, the *Tribune* lamented the death of a former employee killed there by lambasting all those stateside who had gone "roaring up and down the country shouting for blood . . . it is time that those who willed the war were driven from their hiding places and sent to the front where they can share some of the agony they have created." McCormick pilloried Henry Luce, of combat age yet unwilling to fight the war drummed up by his publications, as White Feather. He had Luce tailed on a Chicago visit by his reporters, who returned with word that White Feather was carrying on with a woman in a Lake Shore Drive apartment. "My respect for the son of a bitch just went up," said McCormick.[11]

Actually, the Colonel's adversaries caused him fewer problems than some unwanted friends. Three weeks after lashing out at the administration for its conduct of the war, he heard his words played back for him by an approving Radio Tokyo. Roosevelt pounced on the event as a heaven-sent opportunity to isolate his domestic critics. In a nationwide broadcast on April 28, the president cautioned listeners to be wary of self-styled military experts. Colonel McCosmic came to mind. All smiles faded, however, as Roosevelt assailed "a few bogus patriots who use the sacred freedom of the press to echo the sentiments of the propagandists in Tokyo and Berlin."

That spring the Justice Department bore down on the Associated Press for withholding membership from Marshall Field and the *Chicago Sun*. In a meeting with the AP president, Robert McLean, publisher of the *Philadelphia Bulletin*, Attorney General Francis Biddle threatened legal action against the organization unless it voted to admit Field and changed its bylaws to elect future members by majority vote instead of the four fifths then required.[12]

McLean appealed to McCormick. "You eastern people do not understand the Middle West," he was told. "The idea that Chicago would welcome a man who shook its dust from his feet thirty years ago and has taken $100 million out of the community is fantastic." Equally absurd was the notion that Chicagoans would clasp to their bosom "a carpetbag publisher from Tennessee whose reputation, to say the least, is not above suspicion," or that they would stand in admiring awe of a magazine editor from New York, a managing editor "who already has two failures to his credit," or "a crooked city editor." Frankly, said McCormick, the people of Chicago resented a newspaper financed "by taking arms out of the hands of American soldiers and sailors" — this a reference to the mounting financial losses of the *Sun*, which were deducted from Field's wartime tax bill. Furthermore, the Colonel doubted whether history would look kindly upon an attorney general who used the power of his office to obtain "improper privileges" for a private business venture.[13]

A few weeks after Pearl Harbor, Roosevelt had told House majority leader John McCormack that the thirty-two page *Washington Post* ought to be reduced as a wartime conservation measure. Yet the pro-administration *Chicago Sun* went on printing 390,000 copies a day — three times the press run of the *Post* — and taking back 200,000 returns on each issue. Chicagoans were slow to embrace the new publication. However admirable objectivity was in principle, it proved colorless in print. Even readers sympathetic to the *Sun*'s politics found its editorials uninspired and its local news coverage barely adequate. Heavily touted columnists fell short of expectations. And whatever her other travails, Little Orphan Annie had nothing to fear from "Dinky Dinkerton" or other hastily improvised *Sun* comic strips.[14]

Any newspaper needs time to establish its identity; Field, needless to say, could afford to wait. But when it came to securing AP membership, he was a man in a hurry (the *Sun* already enjoyed access to the rival United Press). Calling on his friends in Washington, Field got Frank Knox to waive his right of protest as an AP member — hardly a sacrificial act, given the secretary's politics and personal stake in the success of the new paper. The plot thickened when the Justice Department dropped hints that it might prosecute *any* AP protest as a restraint of trade.

Attorney General Biddle had unwittingly given McCormick a club with which to beat Knox over the head, and the Morning Colonel didn't hesitate to use it. Prior to the AP meeting in New York scheduled for April 20–21, 1942, McCormick let it be known that he was thinking of starting an afternoon paper in competition with Knox's *Chicago Daily News*. In this way he could call Biddle's bluff while exposing Knox's hypocrisy.

Rather than indict his fellow cabinet officer, Biddle took a new tack. He intervened in the AP contest directly. Acting on orders from the attorney general, dozens of FBI agents fanned out across the country in March 1942. On St. Patrick's Day, a pair of G-men appeared on the twenty-fourth floor of Tribune Tower. McCormick refused to see them without a stenographer present to make a complete record of what was said.

The agents asked the Colonel why he wanted to deny the *Sun* an AP franchise.

"We don't need it here," McCormick told them.

The uninvited visitors pressed him on reports that *Tribune* representatives were seeking proxies from other AP members. One agent demanded the name of anyone soliciting votes against Field.

"All that is on record in Washington," said McCormick gruffly.[15]

The meeting ended abruptly. McCormick began hearing from other editors, many at small or struggling weeklies, who complained that FBI agents had sought to intimidate them. Some of Hoover's men seemed apologetic about carrying out so distasteful a political assignment. Others took a perverse joy in twisting arms. One woman, whose husband was away in the army, became so frightened by threats of antitrust action that she wrote her spouse to inquire whether, by giving the *Tribune* her proxy in the AP fight, she risked going to jail.[16]

At the end of March, McCormick had a cordial meeting with Thurman Arnold, the assistant attorney general in charge of his department's antitrust division. If no insults were hurled, no minds were changed. Tensions escalated. One week before the AP showdown in New York, the American Society of Newspaper Editors convened in the same city to hear from the poet Archibald MacLeish, who doubled as director of the federal Office of Facts and Figures. With McCormick in the audience, MacLeish expressed amazement that "a powerful publisher can publish without criticism from his colleagues a secret document of vital importance to the security of his country."

MacLeish repeated his comments before the full AP membership.* When he was through, Joe Knowland, the publisher of the *Oakland Tribune*, read a letter from Thurman Arnold reiterating the official view that the organization stood in violation of federal antitrust laws. Under threat of indictment, members eliminated the right of protest, adopted a simple majority for election, and imposed term limits on board members, including McCormick.

The intense battles over composition of the AP board and whether or not to admit Field attracted national interest. Rival camps buttonholed undecided members in the crowded halls of the Waldorf-Astoria. Anti-*Tribune* pamphlets were slipped beneath hotel room doors. The publisher of the *Chicago Herald-American* stoked the crowd's resentment by recounting his own sharp questioning by FBI agents when he refused to sell Field an AP membership valued at $1.4 million for $250,000. Cissy Patterson, true to form, tossed a lighted match on the powder keg by revealing a 1939 overture from none other than Thurman Arnold. "If you want AP membership I can get it for you," Arnold had promised her. All Cissy had to do was send a *Times-Herald* reporter around the country, stirring complaints from others papers shut out of the AP fraternity. She had declined to serve as a government Trojan horse. "I come from four generations of newspaper people," she told her fellow editors, "and I didn't like the smell of it."[17]

Tired of operating with a pistol cocked at their heads, members over-

---

*Attacked by McCormick because of his inflammatory speech, MacLeish received a letter from FDR welcoming him to the Society of the Immortals, inaugurated back in 1919, said the president, when the *Tribune* had published the Versailles Treaty without permission and gone on to break Woodrow Wilson's heart by targeting the League of Nations for destruction. Neither McCormick nor his Patterson cousins deserved hate or praise, concluded Roosevelt, "only pity for their unbalanced mentalities."

whelmingly reelected McCormick to the board of directors. They rejected Field's application. Joe Patterson said the result showed there was a limit to how far editors could be pushed around. McCormick hoped it meant that "the Gestapo is out of American newspapers forever."

Actually, the fight had only just begun. Roosevelt "didn't give a damn" about the AP bylaws, Robert McLean told McCormick. All the president wanted was membership for the *Chicago Sun*. In June, Thurman Arnold returned to the AP board, this time with more sticks than carrots. By granting Field the desired service immediately, said Arnold, the organization would face nothing worse than a civil suit filed under antitrust laws. Otherwise the directors risked prosecution under criminal statute.[18]

McCormick refused to back down. "If the attorney general can compel a news association to take in all applicants," he wrote as the case was being readied for trial — not before a jury, as he requested, but in front of a three-judge "expediting court," whose members were approved by the Justice Department — "he must have the corresponding right to compel a news association to furnish the kind of news that those applicants want." Either way, he reasoned, Biddle was shredding the First Amendment guarantee against legal restrictions on the press.[19]

✧ 3

Even paranoids have enemies. The old joke applied to no one more than McCormick. As the AP case dragged on, his feelings of persecution deepened. Treasury agents swooped down on Tribune Tower after the paper printed copies of government checks confirming a payroll scandal at the University of Illinois. No other journal that ran the story was bothered. In the fall of 1942, Harold Ickes reminded the president of an earlier proposal to requisition for military use the fleet of *Tribune* ships used to carry Canadian newsprint "to its place of defilement on the Chicago River." Now, said Ickes, he wished to offer Roosevelt some additional "bright little thoughts" at no cost. He understood that certain papers north of the border were taking vigorous exception to the *Tribune*'s war attitude. "Why could not the Canadian government be encouraged to shut off this newsprint at the source," Ickes inquired, "on the ground that when it gets to this country, it is put to a use that is of aid and comfort to the enemy?" (In fact, five of the company's eight ships were taken for government use. Three of Thorold's five paper machines were shut down by government-ordered power reductions. At the first board meeting after Pearl Harbor, the *Tribune*'s directors voluntarily decided to sell the company plane to Washington.)[20]

Ickes was too late. Previous attacks on the *Tribune* in the Canadian press, led by the *Montreal Star*, had produced a powerful rejoinder from Roy Howard, the president of the Scripps-Howard chain. Howard acknowledged his disagreement with many views espoused by Colonel McCormick. But he insisted on the right of any publisher to pursue an editorial line of his choice. And he warned of the consequences should Canadian politicians, bankers, or advertisers try to exert economic pressure on American newspapers.

Spared foreign retribution, the *Tribune* could not escape domestic controls on newsprint. Order L-240, promulgated by the War Production Board in 1942, established quotas that were loosely defined and unequally applied. The *Chicago Sun* was permitted to exceed its allotment without complaint from Washington. The federal appeals board granted additional supplies to the *Chicago Times* in recognition of increased news content — on the same day it rejected a *Tribune* request made on identical grounds.

For sheer hypocrisy, however, it was hard to beat the Navy Department, where Secretary Knox exploited rules of censorship to aid the *Chicago Daily News* and frustrate competitors. It was said that Knox sat on a big story "like a clucking hen until the publishing time of his own newspaper rolls around." For evidence of this, one need look no further than a full-page advertisement in the February 12, 1942, *Daily News*, promising readers exclusive coverage of a naval raid on the Marshall and Gilbert islands. The *New York Times*, having paid cable tolls on 7,000 words from its correspondent with the Pacific fleet, did not take kindly to being shut out of the story by an afternoon paper, especially one owned by the secretary of the navy. So loud was the protest that red-faced naval officials finally handed out a skeletal accounting of the battle, in which U.S. ships had sunk at least sixteen enemy vessels, for use in the morning papers on February 13.

For weeks the *Tribune* sought unsuccessfully to place a reporter in Alaska. The *Daily News* had greater luck. And when Knox ordered his Honolulu correspondent to come home, he directed Admiral Chester Nimitz to route all future news of Pacific submarine operations through the Navy Department in Washington.

Early in May 1942, a U.S. fleet tipped off to Japanese intentions by cryptographers who had broken the most sensitive of enemy codes fought a furious standoff in the Coral Sea, gateway to New Guinea and Australia. Technically, the encounter ended in a draw; the Americans were forced to scuttle the carrier *Lexington* after Japanese bombs had reduced the ship to a charred hulk. Strategically, however, the Battle of the Coral Sea marked a turning point, checking Japanese expansion to the south and setting the scene for a more decisive naval confrontation near Midway Island in the first week of June.

Journalists who suspected a big fight brewing in the Pacific found facts hard to come by. Ches Manly, now notorious for revealing the Victory

Program five months earlier, tapped into his most trusted Capitol Hill sources and came up empty-handed. Senator David Walsh, a Massachusetts Democrat who was a power on the Naval Affairs Committee, had been effectively silenced by press allegations linking him to a homosexual brothel in Brooklyn. Walsh swore the story was a New Deal smear, but his usefulness to the *Tribune* was at an end.[21]

Then, unexpectedly, Manly's editors struck pay dirt. On the afternoon of Wednesday, June 3, Pat Maloney returned an overnight call from Stanley Johnston, a McCormick favorite with an encyclopedic knowledge of fighting ships and an uncanny knack for turning up wherever the action was most intense. "I am back," said Johnston, barely able to contain his excitement. "I have got one of the greatest stories of the war so far."[22]

Mindful of naval restrictions, the reporter was tightlipped about his adventures. Not until a second call took place did he reluctantly admit that he had been present at the Battle of the Coral Sea. He couldn't say more, he told Maloney, until he had submitted his story to the Navy Department.

"Why don't you cable it to me," Maloney replied, "and we will submit it to Washington?"

Johnston didn't want to take the risk.

"Who won the battle?" pressed Maloney.

"We did."

"What did the enemy lose?"

"That I cannot tell you, Mr. Maloney, until I see you."

"What ships did we lose?"

"I cannot discuss it."[23]

Johnston, true to his word, left the outline of his Coral Sea stories with navy officials in San Diego, to be forwarded to Washington. He bought some clothes, called his wife in San Francisco, and prepared to leave for Chicago. The *Tribune* editors could hardly believe their luck. They had an exclusive eyewitness account of the war's greatest naval encounter from someone who had been on board the *Lexington* during her final hours.

Soon they would have even more. Before departing the West Coast, Johnston heard a radio report of a Japanese attack on Dutch Harbor, in the Aleutian Islands. He took the action to be a feint concealing enemy designs on Hawaii. In another phone conversation with Maloney, he told the managing editor that he had "some dope" pertinent to the latest action. He promised to write out this mysterious intelligence and mail it to the *Tribune*. Maloney, far more interested in the recently concluded battle, seemed inattentive. Johnston let the matter drop.

He arrived in Chicago at eight o'clock on Friday morning, June 5, the "dope" still in his pocket. He was rushed to a private office on the fourth floor of Tribune Tower. Outside, a guard paced, with strict orders to let no one intrude as Johnston pounded out a sensational series of stories recounting the life and death of the *Lexington* and his own heroic efforts to rescue badly burned sailors in the ship's hold. He was still working on the evening of the sixth, aided by the rewriting skills of the aviation editor, Wayne Thomis. Facing an eleven-thirty deadline, Johnston left the room to get some fortifying coffee. Instinct guided him to a clacking news ticker. His eyes widened as he read a communiqué from Admiral Nimitz describing a smashing American victory near Midway, a tiny outpost 1,000 miles west of Hawaii and 3,500 miles due east of Tokyo.[24]

As quoted by the Associated Press, Nimitz estimated Japanese losses to number five carriers destroyed or heavily damaged, as well as several battleships, cruisers, and transports. Johnston instantly grasped the significance of what he read. He couldn't understand why Maloney and his coworkers, still caught up in the frenzy of their Coral Sea exclusive, seemed blind to its implications. The Nimitz announcement also jogged his memory, reminding him of the dope he had promised to send Maloney three days earlier.

Johnston went off in search of a brief memo he had typed in San Diego. Deadline was an hour off when he found the piece of paper stashed in his coat pocket, still in its original envelope. And there it might have stayed, overshadowed by his Coral Sea dramatics, had it not been for fragmentary reports of a second, even larger battle in which the Japanese fleet had sustained crippling, if unknown, losses.

❖ 4

Elsewhere in Tribune Tower, McCormick was preparing for his regular broadcast stint with *The Chicago Theater of the Air*. Shortly before eight o'clock, he dropped by the fourth-floor newsroom to check up on the latest war news. His arrival coincided with fresh information pointing to a major American triumph in the central Pacific. Coming on the heels of earlier, pessimistic reports that Alaska might be the next object of Japanese aggression, the news buoyed McCormick's spirits. Discarding his planned text, he shared with his radio audience details hot off the wire concerning the Coral Sea and the still unfolding action around Midway. Afterward he retired to his office for a postbroadcast buffet supper with Marion Claire and other performers.

While the Colonel unwound with the cast, twenty floors below Johnston was handing over to Maloney the information he had first jotted down in San Diego. Typed on a small sheet of paper was Johnston's best estimate of the Japanese fleet, much of which, if Nimitz was to be believed, now lay on the bottom of the Pacific.

"Where did you get this?" said Maloney.

"I got it from the same place I got all of my information," replied Johnston, "from what I can figure out in my own head and from the conversations with the men I have been with on the boat."[25]

This was deliberately vague. Johnston said nothing about the close friendship he had struck up with Commander Morton Seligman, the *Lexington's* highest-ranking surviving officer. Working against the clock, he banged out a sidebar piece to the main Midway story detailing the composition of the shattered enemy fleet. He assured Maloney that he had checked the names of the warships involved against *Jane's Fighting Ships*, the bible of naval planners. Maloney was dissatisfied with the "muddy" style of Johnston's account, so he rewrote the first two paragraphs himself. When he was through, the article had a very different emphasis, reinforced by a headline that was anything but ambiguous:

NAVY HAD WORD OF JAP PLAN TO STRIKE AT SEA,
KNEW DUTCH HARBOR WAS A FEINT[26]

Thus far, Johnston had told less and Maloney more than either man knew for a fact. Maloney now committed two additional blunders, whether by accident or design, which landed McCormick and the *Tribune* in the dock on espionage charges. First, he incorrectly attributed the story to "reliable sources in the naval intelligence." Then he slapped a phony dateline of Washington, D.C., on the piece.

It was almost eleven-thirty in Chicago. Maloney had yet to submit Johnston's sidebar to naval censorship. In his office, he retrieved a copy of the censorship code and satisfied himself that there was nothing in naval regulations pertaining to the movement of hostile ships. This was only logical. Of what possible aid could it be to the enemy to read in print the whereabouts of his own vessels? To confirm his hunch, Maloney called Arthur Sears Henning in Washington. The bureau chief told him what he wanted to hear. The sidebar would run as revised by Maloney, falsely datelined and credited, unseen by naval censors.[27]

It was five o'clock Sunday morning when Stanley Johnston, exhausted, finally walked out of Tribune Tower. Picking up a copy of the first edition on the streets, he proudly read the main headline, which served as revenge for Pearl Harbor:

JAP FLEET SMASHED BY U.S.
2 CARRIERS SUNK AT MIDWAY

Casting his glance elsewhere on the front page, he was surprised to find his assessment of Japanese losses, headed by the stunning revelation that Nimitz and other American commanders had known of enemy plans. He was especially impressed, Johnston said afterward, by the speed with which naval censors had cleared his dope for publication.[28]

✧ 5

The *Tribune* exclusive delighted McCormick so much that he waived his copyright on the riveting series of articles, later turned into a best-selling book, *Queen of the Flattops.* Navy officials rubbing sleep from their eyes on Sunday morning, June 7, did not share the Colonel's feelings of triumph. Johnston had indeed produced the biggest story of the war, but it wasn't the story he thought he had written. His account of the Battle of the Coral Sea was dwarfed in their eyes by the sidebar, which they took to mean that Japanese codes had been breached. Sitting on the desk of naval commander-in-chief Admiral Ernest J. King was a draft citation recognizing Johnston for his heroic conduct on board the sinking *Lexington.* The award was never made.

Instead, the excitable King called an afternoon press conference, from which *Tribune* reporters were excluded. Before nightfall the navy had amended the code of censorship to keep advance knowledge of enemy movements from finding its way into print. By scurrying to close the barn door after the horse had escaped, the admirals grudgingly conceded that the *Tribune* had broken no law. Maloney said as much when he telephoned McCormick at seven o'clock Sunday evening. McCormick sounded less sanguine in a phone conversation with Arthur Sears Henning, to whom he entrusted delicate negotiations with naval officials.[29]

It was wrong, said McCormick, for Maloney to have credited the story to "an anonymous staff officer." Nevertheless, the article was flattering to the navy and good for public morale. McCormick couldn't see what all the fuss was about. It was only natural that the *Lexington*'s survivors would share their observations with the correspondent who had risked his life to pluck drowning sailors from the water. McCormick assured Henning that everyone at the *Tribune* would cooperate. He hoped the "misunderstanding" could be resolved quickly. Still, he wasn't about to take chances. Considering the many prior occasions on which Secretary Knox had used his official position to advance his interests and cause injury to the *Tribune,* McCormick was apprehensive. "If he intends to be tough," he said of Knox, "I can be just as tough." Any attempt to scapegoat him or the *Tribune* would produce demands for a congressional investigation of Knox's performance in office. As always with McCormick, the best defense was a good offense.[30]

His fears were well founded. Earlier that Sunday, Vice Admiral Charles M. "Savvy" Cooke, Admiral King's chief of staff, angrily informed staff officer Arthur McCollum that McCormick faced prosecution as "a god damn traitor . . . The president is buying into this thing and we're going to hang this guy higher than Haman."[31]

This was no exaggeration. Shortly before his death, King made a hospital room confession to Walter Trohan. According to the admiral, Roosevelt's initial reaction to the Midway story had been to send Marines to occupy Tribune Tower. When this failed to pass legal muster, the president, goaded by Knox, pressed for a charge of treason against McCormick. As Roosevelt well knew, this was a wartime offense punishable by death. Within the navy, there was sharp disagreement over the best course of action. Basking in the glow of Midway, most were prepared to let the controversy die with amendment of the censorship code. At the office of wartime censorship, Byron Price, a former AP bureau chief, opposed any sanctions on the *Tribune*. His view prevailed on June 9, when Arthur Sears Henning learned from naval censors that the *Tribune* was off the hook.[32]

But Byron Price did not occupy the Oval Office. It was also on June 9 that Roosevelt was notified by Knox that treason charges were unlikely to hold water. Knox, no less than the president, wanted to discredit McCormick. At the same time, neither man wished to leave his fingerprints on a punitive action. Recusing himself as a professional rival of McCormick's, Knox gladly entrusted the case to the Justice Department. Acting on orders from Roosevelt, he asked Attorney General Biddle to proceed with an indictment under the Espionage Act, carrying a possible $10,000 fine and up to ten years behind bars for anyone convicted.[33]

To justify dropping this hot potato in Biddle's lap, Knox dwelled at length on a May 31, 1942, communication from Nimitz to his fleet commanders. Based on decoded Japanese messages, the supersecret document had given advance notice of an enemy flotilla sailing straight into an American ambush at Midway. How, asked Roosevelt, Knox, and King, had this information reached Stanley Johnston?[34]

McCormick, unaware of the schemes being laid for his downfall, was nevertheless upset over "pettyfogging desk admirals" who were picking on an authentic war hero. His own offer of cooperation was curtly acknowledged on June 12 by Admiral King. The matter had been referred to Secretary Knox, King informed him, but the crusty old sailor could not let pass unchallenged McCormick's assertion that no harm had befallen national security. On the contrary, said King, in quoting verbatim from a highly sensitive enemy communication, Johnston had compromised future intelligence-gathering in the Pacific theater. McCormick was momentarily thrown for a loss. This was the first inkling he had, he wrote King, of any paper secrets. Until then, it simply hadn't occurred to him that Johnston's estimate of Japanese strength had been rooted in anything more "than ward-room conversation."[35]

As gently as possible, McCormick took Maloney to the woodshed. "Pat," he told him, "I don't want you as managing editor while this Johnston thing is on." Johnston spared himself an even worse fate by giving a long affidavit to the *Tribune*'s lawyers. Thus reassured, McCormick again wrote to King, this time taking a much harder line. It should be evident, he said, that no secret documents had been compromised. The story was the result of Johnston's "thoroughgoing knowledge of naval matters," gained from a lifetime of close study and wide experience.[36]

In effect, McCormick volunteered as a character witness for Stanley Johnston. It would be his word against that of J. Edgar Hoover, who on June 18 sent the White House an unflattering summary of gossip, hearsay, and innuendo regarding the reporter (and "his so-called wife," Barbara), which accused him of providing information to the Nazis while working in Holland for the *Tribune*'s Press Wireless Service. In his desire to curry favor with Roosevelt (the Johnston file was directed to the president's personal secretary, General Edwin "Pa" Watson), Hoover conveniently failed to mention that these and other allegations had been disproved a year earlier by military and naval intelligence, a must before McCormick would give Johnston full-time employment as a *Tribune* war correspondent.[37]

According to the FBI, even Colonel McCormick looked upon Johnston as "a phony." Nothing could be further from the truth. McCormick had taken an instant fancy to the native Australian, who had run away from home at fifteen, joined a field artillery unit that fought at Gallipoli and later in France, and been recommended for the Victoria Cross. Johnston's youthful exploits had inaugurated a passionate interest in naval and military matters rivaling that of his boss. At six feet, five inches tall, he could look the Colonel in the eye. A black mustache enhanced their resemblance.[38]

So did a picaresque background, testimony to Johnston's restless versatility. Champion sculler of Australia, he had gone on to master Morse code and to earn a fortune selling hair curlers to German hausfraus. Unable to export his earnings, he bought himself a castle on the Rhine. The property was confiscated by the Nazis at the outbreak of World War II. After a stint with the Press Wireless office in Amsterdam, Johnston had been hired by Larry Rue to spot incoming planes and ships from the English port of Dover, whose inhabitants in the autumn of 1940 expected a German invasion hourly. The brash Aussie impressed grizzled veterans by his ability to identify a Heinkel bomber or Messerschmitt 109 long before anyone else detected its presence. No one doubted his courage or pluck, either. When his seaside hotel was bombed to pieces, Johnston rode a bureau down six floors of the collapsing structure. Narrowly escaping death, he spent hours burrowing through wreckage in search of survivors and still managed to file a story before deadline.

His performance earned him an invitation to come to Chicago. Early in 1942, he talked himself into an assignment with the Pacific fleet, many of whose officers he had entertained as an Australian real estate broker. After the *Lexington* went down, Johnston and other survivors were herded onto the transport *Barnett* for passage back to the United States. In the over-crowded quarters of the ship the reporter heard, and overheard, nearly constant talk of battles concluded and contemplated. He spent much of the trip in the suite occupied by the *Lexington*'s commander, Mort Seligman. The two men established strong bonds of trust. As Seligman later explained to Pat Maloney, he never stopped to worry about John-ston's credentials, much less the politics of his newspaper. "If he comes from the Admiral," said Seligman in justifying his relaxed attitude toward the press, "he comes to get correct information and to give the public the benefit of his knowledge and experience." Seligman was too busy to watch reporters closely, and too honest to punish a man for doing his job. "If he happens to get information, that is his business," he told Maloney. "You or I or anybody else wouldn't employ a man who could not get information."[39]

Johnston knew his business, and there is every reason to believe that he was aided in it by Commander Seligman. As Johnston recounted his last hours on board the *Barnett,* he was in Seligman's cabin on the evening of June 2, polishing his Coral Sea stories. Pushing some books out of his way, he noticed a piece of blue lined paper on which someone had written the names of Japanese warships, transports, and other vessels, broken down under three headings: "Striking force," "Occupation force," and "Support force."[40]

Like any good reporter, Johnston found his curiosity getting the better of his scruples. He hastily copied the information, noticing as he did that several of the names had been scratched out and revised, as if to correct errors in the original transmission. Most of the ships he recognized as a devoted student of *Jane's Fighting Ships*, whose editor, Francis McMurtrie, had once occupied a London office adjoining his own. Johnston was still writing when a Marine orderly appeared in the doorway: Commander Seligman wanted him to pack and report to shore immediately. Johnston returned the list of Japanese ships to the place where he had found it. He typed out a brief memo to be sent to Pat Maloney, just in case such a force should be sighted by American sailors. The next day he left for Chi-cago.

The Midway story ran on Sunday, June 7. At nine o'clock that evening, Johnston was ordered by his superiors to catch the first available plane to Washington. The next morning he and Arthur Sears Henning walked into Admiral King's office, where they were confronted by King's chief of staff, Vice Admiral Russell Wilson, and several naval investigators. Back in Chicago, meanwhile, the story Johnston told to the *Tribune*'s lawyers was amended in ways that raised new questions about his relationship with Seligman. It turned out that a "high officer of the *Lexington*" had assigned Johnston to write a five- or six-hundred-word history of the ship, both to provide survivors of the battle with a souvenir and to serve them as a guidebook to help frame answers when grilled by stateside interrogators.⁴¹

Johnston was careful to downplay the significance of his shipboard discovery. He told Wilson that the sheet of scratch paper had contained nothing he did not already know. He also claimed to have destroyed the paper as soon as he copied its contents — in flat contradiction of his earlier account, in which he had replaced the document before leaving to join Seligman on the pier. Notwithstanding these discrepancies, there was every reason for the navy to close the books on an embarrassing chapter. King was especially anxious to hush up the fact (which only belatedly came to light) that his own public relations office had neglected to have Johnston sign the customary security pledge before he boarded the *Lexington*.⁴²

Knox, too, had second thoughts, caused by Biddle's argument that in order to convict the *Tribune*, the navy would have to present evidence of damage to the national security. The secretary was reluctant to affirm the cracking of the Japanese codes. But his caution was overcome by his eagerness to please Roosevelt. He pledged to cooperate with any grand jury proceeding. To lend the case a bipartisan aura, the administration recruited William D. Mitchell, a well-regarded New York lawyer and former attorney general under Herbert Hoover, to act as special prosecutor. Whatever happened from then on, Biddle informed the U.S. attorney in Chicago, was all Mitchell's show.⁴³

Early in July, Maloney and Johnston returned to Washington to be separately questioned by the special prosecutor. Both men appeared before Mitchell without benefit of defense counsel. They contradicted each other on the issue of naval censorship and on whether the offending story ought to have been submitted for official review. Maloney showed himself to be an artful dodger, not above eating a generous portion of humble pie when it served his cause. Mitchell, though far from satisfied with the answers he had elicited, concluded that the government could never meet the test of "willful intent" as spelled out by the Supreme Court. He advised Biddle against prosecution.

In due course, these findings reached the White House. Roosevelt returned the case file to the attorney general. He was certain, he said, that a closer examination of the evidence would lead to a different conclusion. Biddle reasserted his belief that no law had been broken. Again Roosevelt urged him to reconsider. Additional pressure came from the press. Alerted by administration sources, both *PM* and Walter Winchell accused the *Tribune* of betraying national secrets; Winchell went so far as to claim, wrongly, that the paper had knowingly based its Midway coverage on decoded Japanese messages.⁴⁴

Under the circumstances, Biddle had little choice but to reverse himself. Even then, however, he was careful to place the onus on Frank Knox, who meekly obeyed a presidential edict to recast the inquiry as an internal navy affair. On August 7, much to the surprise of the censors who had cleared the *Tribune* two months before, Mitchell announced plans to convene a Chicago grand jury. Breaking with tradition, the special prosecutor made no secret that his targets including Johnston, Maloney, and the *Tribune* itself.

✧ 6

Publicly, McCormick welcomed the challenge. For years the Roosevelt administration had sought "by one sly means or another" to weaken his influence and alienate his readers. Now at last the conspiracy was out in the open. "We have said and proved that we cannot be intimidated," the *Tribune* crowed on August 9, "and now, once again, we are going to prove it."

Others took up the cry of aggrieved victimhood. In the Senate, Robert Taft predicted that if the *Tribune* could be indicted, "no editor in the United States is safe." Burton Wheeler volunteered his legal services to the Colonel at no charge. On the other side, Congressman Elmer Holland of Pennsylvania accused the *Tribune*, the *New York Daily News*, and the *Washington Times-Herald* of working "consciously or unconsciously" under Hitler's orders to secure American defeat and enslavement. As the charges flew back and forth, Chicagoans were treated to a display of journalistic venom unmatched since Joe Medill and Wilbur Story had blasted away at each other in the nineteenth century.

Away from the public, however, McCormick could not conceal his fears. He invited Don Maxwell, temporarily editing the paper in the absence of Maloney, to visit Astor Street. "Don," he asked, "what are we going to do?" The question answered itself, said Maxwell. They would fight. More precisely, they would take the fight to their enemies.[45]

And so Bill Fulton was given the task of writing a hard-hitting series of articles portraying a decade-long pattern of White House vindictiveness toward the *Tribune*. Making good on his earlier threat to Arthur Scars Henning, McCormick now launched a broadside at Knox, whose bungling, favoritism, and greed received a full airing. By taking $60,000 a year to act in an "advisory capacity" with his newspaper, Knox made a mockery of wartime sacrifice. According to the *Tribune*, it was difficult to tell where the *Daily News* ended and the navy began. How much time the secretary put in on each of his jobs was apparently "a military secret."

The controversy cost McCormick a forty-year friendship with Ed Kelly. Recalling how he had stood publicly with Kelly when the mayor had faced ruin on tax evasion charges, McCormick asked him to return the favor by appearing as his guest at the *Tribune's* annual music festival. Kelly, fearful of incurring White House displeasure, sent his regrets. Although the two men avoided an open rupture, their relationship never recovered its old intimacy.[46]

In reconstructing the sequence of events leading up to the June 7 revelations, the *Tribune* made much of Maloney's World War I record and of Johnston's naval expertise. It contrasted both with the single month of stateside service, half of it coming after the November 11, 1918, armistice, credited to Biddle. Unmentioned by the paper was the critical memo describing the composition of Japanese forces, how Johnston came by it, and what use he made of it in preparing his story.

The grand jury began its work on August 16. At the eleventh hour, Frank Knox threw a monkey wrench into the government case by refusing to permit his officers to reveal how the *Tribune* had compromised national security. (In fact, U.S. cryptographers were continuing to read decoded Japanese messages, which suggested that the enemy hadn't caught on to the implications of the *Tribune* story.) It had not been a pleasant week for Mitchell, even before he learned that Washington was pulling the rug out from under him. One evening, answering a knock on the door of his room at the Blackstone Hotel, he had been confronted by Pat Maloney's eighty-year-old father, who had come to protest his son's innocence and beg Mitchell to put him on the stand.[47]

Behind the scenes, Mitchell resisted the idea of letting either defendant tell his story. "I've only a slim chance to get an indictment right now," he told U.S. attorney J. Albert Woll. If he permitted Maloney and Johnston the highly unusual privilege of addressing the grand jurors, even this would likely evaporate. Woll reminded Mitchell that if he couldn't obtain twelve votes for indictment from the eighteen-member grand jury panel, he could hardly expect to win a unanimous conviction from twelve trial jurors.[48]

What Mitchell didn't know was that the *Tribune's* lawyers were just as nervous about the prospect of Maloney and Johnston testifying. "God damn it all, there is no other way," argued Maloney. "We've got to go in there."[49]

First, however, the grand jurors heard from Frank Waldrop of the *Times-Herald*. Outside the jury room, Waldrop was asked if he would waive immunity, "a low and cheap shot even for FDR's goons," he concluded. Consultation with his lawyer persuaded him that he had nothing to fear. Clutching a copy of the offending *Times-Herald* story in one hand, Waldrop described for the jury how his paper had come by its account. He offered up the original wire copy, and before Mitchell could stop him, he exhibited a list of all the other papers that had published the same piece under identical circumstances.

Staying on the offensive, Waldrop inquired why he had been called before the grand jury and asked to waive immunity before supplying routine data that only confirmed his innocence. Mitchell took the bait. If he had known that the Johnston story would alert the Japanese to advance U.S. knowledge of their plans, pressed Mitchell, would he have run it? Waldrop squirmed convincingly, hesitated to answer hypothetical questions — and let Mitchell have it right between the eyes.

As it happened, he said, he hadn't been tipped off to the Battle of Midway by the *Tribune*. He had been told of the coming battle over an open telephone line by James Warner, an assistant to Byron Price in the office of war censorship. One day, lacking any news of significance, Waldrop had written what is known in the journalistic trade as a thumb-sucker — a speculative dissertation on the military significance of Alaska and the strategic potential of the Alcan Highway, which links the giant U.S. territory with Canada to the south. The following day his phone rang. It was Jim Warner, wondering for the record whether he had submitted the piece for clearance. Waldrop replied in salty language that he had not, and that he would like to know what justification Warner had for making such a request. Warner hastened to assure Waldrop that it wasn't his idea to register a complaint against the *Times-Herald*. "It's the navy," he confided. "They're all upset because they have a big battle coming up out in the Pacific Ocean and all of them are scared something will tip off the Japs. When they see a piece like yours in this morning's paper it gives them goosebumps."[50]

The jury foreman, a black upholsterer from Joliet named John Holmes, closely questioned Waldrop about the workings of the censorship system. Before they finished their exchange, Mitchell knew his case was in ruins.*

Not until August 18 did the grand jurors finally hear from Johnston and Maloney. The former explained that he had picked up the list of ships on board the *Barnett*. He minimized its importance, sticking to his earlier claim that his account was a composite of general knowledge and information gleaned from shipboard conversations and *Jane's Fighting Ships*. Maloney made an equally favorable impression. Jurors examined other news accounts of Midway, including stories printed in Knox's *Chicago Daily News*. Late on the afternoon of August 19, they dismissed all charges brought against the *Tribune* and its employees.

Johnston and Maloney were cheered as they entered the city room. An even greater roar greeted McCormick when he strode into the room a few

---

*In the course of the grand jury hearing, Holmes's sister died. The *Tribune*'s circulation manager, Louis Rose, learning that the dead woman had an insurance policy that had been offered as a *Tribune* promotion, cashed the policy and sent one of his staff members to deliver the $2,000 personally to the family of the deceased. Rose was not hesitant to claim credit for the ensuing grand jury action.

minutes after five o'clock. Typewriters fell silent; copyreaders set aside headlines in the making. Blinking nervously, the Colonel paid tribute to his assembled staff. "There never has been a bunch like the *Tribune* bunch," he said awkwardly. "Every member of the *Tribune* is a member of my family."[51]

The Colonel returned to the twenty-fourth floor, where Howard Wood found him surrounded by congratulatory telegrams and phone messages. "You know, Howard," he said, fighting back tears, "I had an amazing experience. I went down to the local room and they all stood up and cheered."[52]

Obscured for over fifty years, the truth behind the Midway story almost certainly implicates Commander Seligman as the source of Johnston's intelligence scoop. Most likely the commander had left the list of names in his quarters, where Johnston was sure to find and copy it. If, as now appears likely, the *Tribune* was trying to protect its confidential source, many things that are otherwise mysterious become clear. For example, Maloney's decision to attribute the original story to naval intelligence in Washington was a clumsy effort to throw naval investigators off the trail of the real perpetrator.

Such a theory would also explain the failure of the *Tribune* to mention the list of ships copied by Johnston and later described in various ways by him, depending on who was doing the questioning. Certainly the navy regarded Seligman as the culprit. Admiral King personally guaranteed that the commander, a twenty-eight-year veteran of the service, was never promoted. As for Johnston, his behavior under pressure earned him McCormick's lifelong trust. On his deathbed in the spring of 1955, the Colonel was attended by Stanley and Barbara Johnston, and it was Stanley who dressed the shrunken corpse in McCormick's World War I uniform, which had to be folded over his back.

✧ 7

According to Biddle, Roosevelt could hardly believe the news from Chicago. Presidential shock turned to anger, which turned to recriminations. In seeking a scapegoat, FDR didn't have far to look. "Knox pushed Biddle out on a limb," observed *Newsweek*, "followed him there, then sawed them both off."

In truth, Knox had walked the plank. Less Machiavellian than he imagined, by doing the president's bidding he had angered many in the navy, who wanted nothing more than to forget their humiliation. He had made a permanent enemy out of Biddle, who, by his own admission, felt like a fool. Knox remained in his post until his death in April 1944. But his stature was permanently diminished, and much of Washington echoed

Texas senator Tom Connally's assessment of him as "a two-cylinder engine in a four-cylinder job."

Knox's ego wasn't the only thing to suffer as a result of the botched investigation. The *Chicago Sun* had timed a tremendous circulation drive to coincide with the anticipated indictment of the *Tribune*. Costly billboards went up throughout Chicago promoting Field's paper as "the truth, the whole truth, and nothing but the truth." Then came the dismissal of charges. The advertising agent responsible for the campaign was furious, chortled McCormick, "because he spent all that money and nobody knows what he is talking about."[53]

By the autumn of 1942, the *Tribune* was selling a million copies a day, with Sunday circulation exceeding 1.3 million — triple that of its morning rival. Chaos reigned at the *Sun*. The editorial page editor, John L. White, was fired by the imperious Silliman Evans. White told friends that Evans had compromising photographs of Field with which he was prepared to blackmail the publisher if he got out of line (a story that reached the presidential secretary Jonathan Daniels). In the end, however, it was Evans, not Field, who was sent packing. Evans returned to Nashville in mid-1943, and Field stepped into his shoes.[54]

Weymouth Kirkland urged McCormick to lay off the competition. Let the full impact of Field's financial losses bring him to his senses, he argued. Cissy Patterson agreed. McCormick wouldn't listen to either of them. "Well," said Cissy, "it's Bertie against the world."[55]

True to this assessment, McCormick launched a series of personal attacks that demonized Field as a slacker, part of a cowardly "herd of hysterical effeminates." ("You are getting rattled, Colonel McCormick," the *Sun* responded.) A Field speech before a group of Canadian circulation managers angered McCormick, whose journalistic credentials far outstripped those of his morning competitor. "Marshall Field is an authority on horse racing, yacht racing, and grouse shooting," he said, "but he knows little about newspapers and nothing about the great constitutional subject of freedom of the press." The more he reflected, the madder he became, imagining that "some weasel-minded lawyer" had written Field "a disingenuous speech for him to declaim in a spot where freedom of the press does not exist."

The angry premier of Ontario declared McCormick mentally unbalanced. The *Montreal Herald* attacked him as "a Hitler-crazed Chicago publisher." McCormick was unfazed. New Dealers surprised by the *Tribune*'s continuing success were stupid people, he told his editors in September 1942. They should realize that Chicagoans wanted a newspaper reflecting their interests, "not those of eastern politicians and sports." Looking ahead to election day, he struck hard at wartime controls. Meat rationing was unnecessary, he argued, "unless the New Deal goes through with its plan to decimate agriculture." He was incensed over a war poster depicting a GI held captive in a Nazi prison camp. "Americans do not surrender," he intoned.[56]

McCormick was otherwise occupied touting the reelection of Senator C. Wayland "Curley" Brooks, a former Chicago prosecutor who had earned his undying loyalty by convicting Leo Brothers of the murder of Jake Lingle. With what *The Nation* called his "round, heavy, puckered face capped with tight curls which look as though they are held down with a patent hair concoction," Brooks inspired little enthusiasm among Illinois voters. Four times they had rejected him for statewide office. Then, in 1940, he had ridden the gubernatorial coattails of his fellow prosecutor, Dwight Green, to a seat in the Senate. A World War I hero with a clutch of medals and a spread-eagle platform style, Brooks rarely expressed a thought that hadn't first occurred to McCormick. In the Senate he toed the *Tribune* line in opposing lend-lease and the draft. He also gave outspoken support to America First.[57]

On December 6, 1941, Brooks's normally acute sense of timing deserted him. He chose that date to flood Illinois voters with franked copies of his recent Senate orations entitled "This Is Not Our War." Arriving in mailboxes days after Pearl Harbor, the speech did little to advance his reelection chances against an uninspiring New Deal congressman from Chicago, christened Small Potatoes McKeough by the *Tribune* after he accused McCormick of treason. Brooks evinced his gratitude by attacking the "Gestapo tactics" the administration had employed in its efforts to destroy the newspaper.

Making an issue of wartime controls, not the war, paid rich dividends on election day. Republicans everywhere scored major gains. Brooks defeated McKeough in Illinois. His isolationist soulmate, New York congressman Hamilton Fish, retained his House seat notwithstanding opposition from what McCormick called "the International Set . . . composed of women and effeminate men." Savoring its victory, the *Tribune* sought a post-election interview with White Feather Luce. The publisher of *Time* and *Life* said he would gladly prepare a statement of his views on the postwar world if McCormick honestly wished to acquaint his readers with them. "But I should like to be excused from answering such questions as: When did I stop thinking that Chicago ought to be handed over to the British Empire?"[58]

Luce, displeased with the result, retaliated by sending a *Life* reporter to Chicago in the summer of 1943 to ask the Colonel about his continuing opposition to a second front in Europe. The United States faced no danger from the Axis powers, who lacked a navy capable of menacing the New World, responded McCormick. The resulting article was as unflattering to the Colonel as the *Tribune* profile of Luce had been to him. McCormick got the last word, telling a friend, "I don't kick lap dogs when they yap at me, so why should I kick this perpendicular Pekingese?"[59]

❖ 8

On August 5, 1943, McCormick accepted an invitation from British consul general William Gallienne to attend the Chicago showing of the film *Desert Victory*. The Colonel was on his best behavior that night. He took five dozen red roses for the wife of his host. He also went out of his way to be introduced to several labor leaders at a pretheater cocktail party. Afterward, he asked Gallienne back to Astor Street for three hours of affable, well-lubricated conversation. He showed off his collection of paintings, spoke warmly of Amy's talent, and professed great admiration for Churchill. At one point he expressed the fear that hungry people in wartime might make off with Cantigny's chickens and cattle. A British guest observed that no such outrages had taken place in rural England. He was hardly surprised, said McCormick; the English were less enterprising than Americans.[60]

Later that month, in a tongue-in-cheek interview with *PM*, the Colonel proposed that as an alternative to the one-world internationalism espoused by Wendell Willkie, nations belonging to the British Commonwealth might wish to apply for American statehood. He returned to the subject in an April 25 editorial, "Hands Across the Sea." Any country hoping to benefit from U.S. foreign policy, trade, or defense commitments would be well advised to do what Texas had done a century earlier, he suggested — adopt a written constitution and petition Congress to join the American union. The advantages of such a course should be obvious, particularly to the British, who would at last be able to unburden themselves of a parasitical nobility. To be sure, the king would also have to go, but as his powers were limited and rarely exercised, the transition to a republican form of government shouldn't be too wrenching. In his own country, McCormick continued, the "hand-kissers and Tories" should welcome their increased representation in Congress, not to mention more intimate social and political ties to their English friends. Best of all, those admitted to the strongest, freest, and most stable nation on earth would have their liberties guaranteed via a written constitution containing a bill of rights.

Rarely had the Colonel employed his talent for mayhem to better effect. *Time* said it was hard to tell whether he was being sincere or just peculiar. George Bernard Shaw, who had humorously promoted just such a scheme in his 1929 play *The Apple Cart*, protested that McCormick had omitted Ireland from his plan of acquisition. Emmanuel Shinwell, a Labour MP, conveyed thanks to the Colonel for teaching Britons the meaning of the word *applesauce.* Delighted with the ruckus he had caused, McCormick said he would like to write an editorial "saying it is strange that the British Dominions will not accept the status of wife when they have been living as kept woman for several years — but that is not newspaper language." His real quarrel was with Americans who were willing to sign away their national sovereignty in pursuit of a world government that would junk the Constitution, jeopardize individual choice in matters of faith and expression, and reduce Washington's sphere to overseeing Yellowstone Park "and the agricultural experimental staions."[61]

On May 15, the black-owned *Chicago World* floated McCormick's name as a candidate for the White House. Six weeks later, 2,000 delegates styling themselves the Republican Nationalist Revival Committee met in Chicago to add their voices to the draft-McCormick movement. So did Wendell Willkie. By running in the Illinois primary, said Willkie, McCormick could make the contest a national referendum on America's role in the world and the need for liberal policies at home. In the *Chicago Daily News*, Colonel McCosmic reappeared long enough to burn stacked copies of Willkie's best-selling book *One World* and proclaim, "There isn't room in one world for the two of us."

McCormick refused to take the bait. "People who cannot see through Willkie, his self-interest, and his falsehoods," he told Alf Landon, "are not entitled to a free government." Besides, he said, anybody could beat Willkie, including Governor Green and Senator Brooks. His less than Shermanesque declination left journalists salivating at the thought of Willkie and McCormick jousting in Illinois cornfields. Richard Strout, writing in the *New Republic*, imagined the spectacle of McCormick's inaugural parade: "After the first motorcycle cops there would be a big black car . . . filled with all the members of the Dies Committee [named after its Communist-hunting chairman, Texas congressman Martin Dies]. Marching sturdily along on foot would come Ham Fish, promised the Secretaryship of State. Cissy and Colonel Patterson would ride in respective open barouches, with calliope attachments . . . And then finally would come the Colonel himself, astride his charger, with a placard fastened to the trappings on its flank telling how many more days were left in which to save the country."[62]

McCormick stepped up the pressure on Dwight Green to run as a favorite son. The governor was a reluctant warrior. Unwilling to put his own chances for reelection at risk, Green sang the virtues of Tom Dewey, who had scored a 1942 landslide to become New York's first Republican governor in a generation. Beneath his coy surface, Dewey calculated his 1944 prospects like a riverboat gambler. He worked through Joe Patterson to avert a Willkie-McCormick clash in Illinois that might revive the fading chances of "our fat friend." Douglas MacArthur was McCormick's first choice, but the charismatic general had yet to redeem his solemn pledge to return to the occupied Philippines. Another McCormick favorite was

Senator Robert Taft of Ohio. "He speaks for America," said the Colonel, "while Willkie and Roosevelt speak for American inferiority."[63]

Suitable candidates for 1944 might be in short supply, but there seemed to be no shortage of winning issues, beginning with shortages. The *Tribune* looked askance at the rationing of sugar, meat, and fuel. ("They won't get me," McCormick told Cissy Patterson. "I killed a beef.") The paper sympathized with merchants harassed by government price-fixers and with American housewives deprived of strawberry jam so that the British could enjoy the taste of jam for breakfast. On the subject of England, McCormick was half mad. "The English give the orders. We do the fighting. England gets the benefit of our victories," he fumed.[64]

Everywhere McCormick looked in the first days of September 1943, he saw dark conspiracies afoot. Churchill was at Harvard receiving a honorary degree from the university's "alien" president, James Conant. McCormick interpreted the prime minister's remarks before his academic audience as a brazen attempt to stampede Republicans assembled at Mackinac Island for a discussion of postwar objectives. In the many rooms of the Republican mansion, he allotted no space to internationalists. Tom Dewey formally endorsed a permanent Anglo-American alliance to keep the world's peace, leading the *Tribune* to read him and other "imitation Republicans" out of the party. The paper flailed Dewey as "a tragic example of a man who was not quite big enough to rise above his immediate environment."[65]

Speaking before the Detroit Athletic Club on December 15, 1943, McCormick unveiled a "confession of faith" that had all the earmarks of a campaign platform: "I believe in the American political doctrine as conceived by the great Virginia philosophers, as expressed by Thomas Jefferson in the Declaration of Independence, codified in the Constitution, perfected in the Bill of Rights, interpreted by John Marshall, and expounded by Abraham Lincoln." In his enthusiasm for the great-man school of history, McCormick betrayed a shaky grasp of some elemental facts. His admiration of the great Federalist chief justice as a worthy interpreter of Jeffersonian dogma would no doubt have astonished those bitter antagonists.

However, it was McCormick's reading of more recent history that landed him in hot water on both sides of the U.S.-Canadian border. Reminiscing about his post–World War I contributions to the U.S. Army General Staff, he bragged of helping draw up plans to resist a hypothetical invasion of the United States by 300,000 British regulars.

Agents of the British Information Service stationed in Chicago concluded that McCormick was suffering from dementia praecox. They downplayed his influence, maintaining that only one in ten *Tribune* subscribers bothered to read his editorials and that of these, only a small fraction believed what they read. In truth, the failed prosecution of the Midway leak had left the Colonel feeling more truculent than ever. "So nothing will ever be done to the paper or its owner during his lifetime," Anthony Eden was informed in January 1944, "except by the natural taking away of that life."[66]

⬧ 9

        Insulting wartime allies and questioning the loyalty of his president might not win McCormick popularity contests, but it got him and his paper talked about. Critics called the Colonel a twentieth-century Copperhead, as repellent as the disloyal northerners whom Joseph Medill had roasted in the pages of the *Tribune* eighty years before. Yet journalists making a pilgrimage to Tribune Tower found a shy, almost impish man, wholly at odds with his public image.

"It is silly to build him into a super-fuehrer," concluded the columnist Marquis Childs. McCormick simply reflected the desires of his readers for a simpler past. To the writer John Bartlow Martin, he was unique in successfully combining two divergent strains of American journalism, the flamboyant personal style employed by Joseph Medill and the shrewd businessman with a weather eye for profitability. Increasingly of late, wrote Martin in *Harper's*, big-city newspapers had fallen into the hands of industrial operatives, men who might as easily have mass-produced girdles as editorials and whose overriding concern could be summed up in the eternal grubby inquiry, will it pay? McCormick was different. With a firm grasp of what would sell and of how to manage his business, "he also knows what he believes and is willing to go to hell for it." Because he never stopped asking questions, McCormick often stumbled onto realities hidden from the more credulous.[67]

In the first days of January 1944, McCormick raised some hard choices for those advocating a postwar alliance between the United States, Russia, Great Britain, and China. To begin with, he wondered about the final disposition of boundary disputes involving Russia and China, an issue unresolved more than four decades later. Free of countervailing pressures from Germany and Japan, how would these two neighboring giants settle the future of Mongolia? "There is a strong Communist movement in China," he noted. "What are we to do if it opposes Chiang Kai-shek, with Russian Communist assistance?" And what of imperial Britain? "Churchill has as much as said that England will take back Hong Kong and reestablish Shanghai as a foreign-controlled settlement independent of China. Did anyone realistically believe, demanded McCormick, that such vexing conflicts could be resolved through lofty, meaningless phrases contrasting peace-loving and aggressive nations?[68]

A month later, on February 5, the Colonel told a national radio audience that Stalin would not be content to expel the Nazis from Mother Russia. In the past, Russian armies had occupied Vienna, Zurich, Genoa, Copenhagen, Paris, and Berlin. "Judging by the whole history of Russia and its imperial Roman doctrine inherited from the eastern empire, we may expect that Stalin will overrun the whole of Europe if he can."

Away from the microphone and the editorial page, McCormick lent what assistance he could to the war effort. Much of it was necessarily secret. Prior to Pearl Harbor, he had been dissuaded from evicting Japanese agents operating out of Tribune Tower by U.S. intelligence officers who had bugged the Japanese consulate there. Early in the war, he lent European correspondent Sam Brewer to the Office of Strategic Services. Badly singed by the Midway affair, he readily assented to a plea from Walter Trohan to kill a story enlightening *Tribune* readers about the military significance of radar. In Canada, the Ontario Paper Company did its bit by devising a synthetic rubber using grain alcohol distilled from sulfite and wood fibers.

Closer to home, nearly two million people attended *Tribune*-sponsored shows highlighting the various services and their firepower. In the first twelve months of the war, news from the front filled the equivalent of thirty-three daily issues. *Tribune* correspondents were among the earliest to recount in graphic detail the horrors of the Bataan death march, the daring of Jimmy Doolittle's Tokyo raid, the capture of Guadalcanal, and the sinking of the U.S. cruiser *Houston*. A *Tribune* man went along with the first wave of B-29s to drop their bombs on Japan. The Vichy correspondent David Darrah was imprisoned for over a year by the retreating Germans. Guy Murchie, seriously injured by a German bomb that demolished the English hotel in which he was staying, wrote up his story in a hospital bed while awaiting surgical attention.

In November 1942, John H. Thompson became the first American journalist to make a combat jump with paratroopers. The next time he leaped from a plane, as part of the Allied invasion of Sicily, he came away with a Purple Heart. McCormick raged at Bob Cromie, the Floyd Gibson of his era, for riding atop an American tank exposed to enemy fire at Guadalcanal. "We didn't send him over, for Christ sake, to get killed," the Colonel shouted at Pat Maloney. "We sent him over there to get news. Crazy fool — did you assign him?" Maloney ducked that one.[69]

As a rule, McCormick was far less involved in this war than he had been in its predecessor. The Great War had been his youthful adventure, his defining test of manhood. This time around, he confined himself to morale-boosting broadcasts while the *Tribune* collected cigarettes for battle-weary GIs in a Smokes for Yanks campaign. He guaranteed every *Tribune* worker in uniform as good a job or better on his return. For employees with families, the Colonel supplied the difference between military pay and the absent breadwinner's civilian income. Unmarried service members received cash bonuses.

An overseas edition was inaugurated in November 1943, a year after the *Tribune* first applied for a license to print a daily paper for GIs in Britain. As recounted by the historian David Reynolds, Roosevelt cabled Churchill asking that the request be denied because McCormick published "lies and deliberate misrepresentations in lieu of news." Douglas MacArthur was more accommodating. Yet even in the Pacific theater, the new paper failed to duplicate the success of the old *Army Tribune.*[70]

✧ 10

In March 1944, Drew Pearson got hold of a McCormick cable denouncing *Stars and Stripes,* the official armed forces journal, as "an out and out Communist New Deal paper." Pearson shared his find with listeners to his weekly radio broadcast. McCormick raged like Lear on the heath. He demanded a full investigation of the leak by the same government official who had earlier pursued the *Tribune* over the Victory Program and the Midway story. In the end, nothing was proved beyond the double standard enforced by an aging publisher where freedom of the press was at issue.[71]

For sheer squirming-in-the-seat embarrassment, nothing uttered by Pearson compared with propaganda broadcasts made over Radio Berlin by the renegade *Tribune* correspondent Donald Day. The *Chicago Times* was moved to sum up Day's career in six words: "From *Tribune* Fakir to Nazi Stooge." When a reporter for the *London Daily Express* cast aspersions on Chicago's patriotism and sobriety, McCormick upbraided its owner, Lord Beaverbrook. Beaverbrook had no right, said the Colonel, to condescend to the American heartland as he did to Lancashire or the Punjab.[72]

In April 1944, knowing full well that his request would be turned down, McCormick appealed to the War Production Board for newsprint with which to start a morning paper in Milwaukee. It was a ruse, he told Joe Patterson, "but it will put us in a better position to fight the *Sun*'s demand for paper." Besides needling Field, McCormick hoped to throw a scare into the *Milwaukee Journal,* which had been "pretty nasty" in taking the side of Wendell Willkie against the *Tribune* in the April 4 Wisconsin Republican primary. Willkie's crushing defeat left him a man without a party and McCormick a manager without a candidate. Puzzled by Dewey's growing internationalism, the Colonel briefly reconsidered his decision to remain on the political sidelines. He had no wish to lead a Stop Dewey movement, he told General Wood in May. "Perhaps we can convert him," he said of the New Yorker.[73]

His optimism was short-lived. "Dewey had the people with him four years ago and Wall Street knocked him out in four ballots," McCormick complained. "This time I think he is determined to have Wall Street and take his chances with the people." For McCormick, New York had become an urban anthill crawling with *Daily News* readers, alien masses with tabloid emotions and dubious loyalties. A 1944 *Tribune* appraisal of the nation's largest city was unabashedly racist. "The very sight of the New York crowd antagonizes the visitor who has come into New York from his farm or small town on the western plains," the paper claimed. "These frizzy heads, these broad, brutish cheekbones, these furtive, piggy eyes, these slacken mouths — the whole 'muffin-faced race' which he sees in the New York subway — how different from the well-marked features of his neighbors back in Iowa or Kansas."[74]

In June 1944, McCormick overcame his aversion to the place long enough to attend the wedding of his nephew Jimmy Patterson, a recent West Point graduate. Writing to Cissy in Washington, the father of the groom speculated on the comic possibilities the ceremony presented. The New Deal senator Robert Wagner was coming, as was Cousin Bertie. "These two ought to get on famously together." Perhaps, said Patterson, it was just as well that Triny Barnes, the black sheep of the family, had declined an invitation to attend. "Although if we could put these three at one table together," he concluded mischievously, "it ought to be good clean fun for the observers."[75]

The Allied invasion of Europe on June 6 did not take McCormick by surprise. He had been told of the operation in advance by General Levin Campbell, an old army friend, now head of ordnance. Three weeks after GIs stormed ashore at Normandy, Republicans meeting in Chicago nominated Dewey to run on a ticket that included the conservative governor of Ohio, John Bricker. Ruth Simms, part of the committee designated to escort Dewey to the podium to make his acceptance speech, was introduced as Mrs. Albert D. Simms. The point was not lost on her brother-in-law; the Dewey high command hoped to steer clear of McCormick-style isolationism.[76]

On July 8, the Colonel urged Dewey to debate FDR. Dewey thanked McCormick for his "very interesting suggestion." He also conveyed his frustration in running against the elusive commander-in-chief. "How can you challenge a will-of-the-wisp?" asked Dewey. "Roosevelt won't debate anything with anyone and will laugh at the proposals from his position at Pearl Harbor, Guadalcanal, or the White Cliffs of Dover." In choosing photos for the *Tribune* roto section, McCormick emphasized Dewey's youthful energy, in contrast with the haggard appearance of the president, whose health was to be the subject of intense speculation throughout the campaign. The Colonel turned down a Hollywood invitation from Hedda

Hopper, pleading the press of political business. "If we lose," he wrote whimsically, "I do not think there will be any travel for anybody until after the Revolution."[77]

The GOP effort left him predictably dissatisfied. His hopes rose briefly in late September, when Dewey belatedly took the gloves off in an Oklahoma City speech. The White House was jittery, McCormick learned from Walter Trohan, and Roosevelt was urging Jimmy Doolittle to repeat his electrifying Tokyo raid just before election day. Doolittle refused, telling those around the president, "You've made me a God damned hero and now you'll have to listen to me."[78]

On October 9, McCormick renewed his plea to have Dewey prosecute Roosevelt like a criminal in the dock. The candidate replied that he too leaned toward "the slugging type of campaign." Yet the two men remained poles apart on foreign policy and an international peacekeeping organization. In the third week of October, an exasperated McCormick sent word to Dewey through his reporter Hal Foust that he shouldn't cut his own throat by courting internationalist voters. Dewey replied that "I'm keeping my neck in." McCormick threw up his hands. "If Dewey is elected," he grumbled on October 28, "it will be in spite of his campaign."[79]

When the votes were counted on November 6, Dewey had held Roosevelt to his smallest margin in four races. Green narrowly won a second term as governor of Illinois. But voters rejected the isolationist congressman-at-large Stephen Day, along with the *Tribune*'s candidate for the Senate, a mossback named Richard J. Lyons. McCormick was too accustomed to losing to take the rejection personally. "I think it was a combination of a lot of minorities turned into a majority," he told Ruth Simms. This was a code for the city he loved to hate. Two weeks after the election, McCormick lashed out more explicitly at New York influence in the GOP. "If we cannot do better four years from now than we did in the last two elections," he wrote to Robert Taft on November 24, "we might as well give up the Republican Party as lost."[80]

✧ 11

        In the five years since Amy's death, McCormick had not lacked for female companionship. In October 1942, the British consul general in Chicago had notified his superiors that the Colonel was spending his Thursday nights with a sprightly, attractive mistress. Her name was Maryland Hooper. Seventeen years his junior, Maryland had much to recommend her. She was a dashing horsewoman, a stylish hostess, and a witty dinner partner. She had been Amy's best friend. And she was married, restively, to an alcoholic *mari complaisant* named Henry Hooper, who, like

Ed Adams before him, had appealed to McCormick to bail him out of his debts, with his wife as collateral.[81]

Henry Hooper laid claim to some distinguished New England ancestors, an uncertain future, and an unquenchable thirst. He befriended McCormick, a Wheaton neighbor, then became financially dependent on him. The *Tribune* bought coal from his Lake Shore Fuel Company, and McCormick personally endorsed $30,000 in bank loans to his improvident friend.[82]

Maryland, the only child of doting parents, was born in Baltimore in 1897. Her father, a prosperous businessman, had moved his little family to Chicago when his daughter reached adolescence. A childless aunt and uncle contributed to her indulgent upbringing. Maryland got from her eccentric Uncle Arthur, who kept a wildcat in his office and pheasants in his garden, a love of animals that endeared her to Amy McCormick when the two women met for the first time in 1922. Amy, still smarting from the petty snobberies of Lake Forest, saw Maryland as a kindred spirit, a younger version of herself, plagued by marital difficulties reminiscent of her own troubled life with Ed Adams.[83]

By the early thirties, Amy and Maryland were inseparable. The younger woman sat for her portrait; the older provided her with a ticket of admission to a lifestyle "poor Henry" could never hope to attain. Others in the Cantigny set were less accepting. They scorned Maryland as a social-climbing arriviste. They laughed knowingly when she rose before dawn to stake out a place at the head of the line waiting to take advantage of a rare sale at Bes Ben, Chicago's leading seller of women's hats.[84]

One time, a group of dowagers persuaded the Colonel to let them show off his flower beds. On the day of the tour, the heavens opened, forcing the organizers to seek refuge on the big screened veranda named for James Madison. Hearing Maryland's voice inside the house, one grande dame shuddered. "Well," she remarked on the unwanted guest, "maybe we could open the servants' porch."[85]

Such affronts only sharpened Maryland's desire to turn the tables. Her daughters, Alice and Ann, seemed genuinely fond of the man they called Uncle Bert. McCormick reciprocated. Maryland had interests that ran parallel to his own, even if some of her opinions were at a right angle to his. She enjoyed politics, taking a more pragmatic approach than her lover. She thought Robert Taft was hopelessly dull, for example, a view McCormick reluctantly embraced with time. She could make the Colonel laugh at himself, no easy task. She told him that Cecil Jensen, the satirist responsible for Colonel McCosmic, was "a damned good cartoonist. You ought to try and get him for the *Tribune*." She entertained his English friends and tried to reconcile his American enemies. Among the latter was Marshall Field. "Now listen," she told McCormick. "Let's try to be friends instead of this eternal throwing of mud at each other like you did at Knox."[86]

"He respected her judgment and he kept her amused," said one friend. Ward Quaal, an important figure at WGN radio and television, saw another aspect of the relationship, which eluded Maryland's detractors. "She had more than a little of the maternal instinct," recalls Quaal, who watched as the diminutive Maryland fussed over McCormick, making certain he didn't forget to wear his overcoat against the autumn chill. Well into his sixties, McCormick was still searching for a mother figure.[87]

The possibility that Maryland Hooper might become the second Mrs. Robert R. McCormick did not go over well at the *Tribune* law firm. Weymouth Kirkland viewed her as a gold digger, transparently eager to inherit McCormick's position and the wealth and status that accompanied it. He talked the Colonel out of settling a block of *Tribune* stock on her, but he couldn't save the Hooper marriage. A few weeks after Henry Hooper again thanked McCormick for coming to his financial aid, Hooper moved out of the Chicago apartment he shared with Maryland and their daughters. McCormick had his lawyers draw up a prenuptial agreement assuring Maryland of $1 million in the event of his death. The document was silent as to what, if any, role the future Mrs. McCormick might play at the *Tribune*.[88]

In November 1944, Maryland obtained a quick Mexican divorce. Not wishing to repeat the scandal surrounding his first marriage, McCormick insisted that the divorce be approved by a friendly Illinois judge. In a display of personal power intended to quell Maryland's lingering doubts — while in Mexico City, she had come close to backing out — he scheduled a private hearing at eight o'clock in the morning, too early for photographers to swarm the courthouse. Rather than go to the office of the county clerk, Richard J. Daley, McCormick had Daley bring the marriage license to him. Since the Colonel carried no money on his person, Weymouth Kirkland paid the $2 license fee.

The wedding ceremony, held at twilight on December 21, 1944, was a subdued affair. A dozen relatives and friends gathered at the Lake Shore Drive apartment of Chauncey McCormick; Joe Patterson was his cousin's best man. Observing from a distance, British consul general William Gallienne said he was mystified as to how the former Mrs. Hooper had managed to hook the Colonel — "not that he is much of a catch, except financially." According to friends of the groom, he was feeling his age, and a loneliness aggravated by the disappointing results of the recent election. "He has been sick mentally for years," concluded Gallienne, "and his fear of death is a neurosis. Mrs. Hooper is not likely to cure him: perhaps she will do the next best thing."[89]

Maryland wasted no time in redecorating Cantigny and the house on Astor Street. She gave away most of Amy's art collection, antique furniture, and carpets, replacing them with Chinese art and hideous Meissen Buddhas. She undertook to learn the full extent of McCormick's wealth.

Flying into town one day on his Lockheed Lodestar, which he preferred to fighting vehicular traffic, the Colonel buried his nose in the *Wall Street Journal.*

Maryland saw her chance. "Are you looking at the stock page?" she asked.

"Hrumph."

"Are you checking out IBM?"

"Hrumph."

"They say IBM is a great stock, Bertie. Do you have any IBM?"

McCormick's eyes never left his newspaper. "None of your goddamned business."[90]

❖ 12

Two weeks after his wedding, McCormick received a belated congratulatory note from Alf Landon. "I doubt if you will be able to enjoy the New Deal any better," Landon remarked. "I know you will enjoy life better."[91]

In these final months of the war, McCormick was increasingly preoccupied with the abuses of foreign colonial rule. On Thursday, April 12, 1945, he railed against European powers' domination of weaker nations such as India, which could offer no more than moral resistance to their white oppressors. In a sharply worded memo to the editorial writer Leon Stolz, he argued for a single, anti-imperialist standard. The United States must give the people of Puerto Rico the opportunity to have a government of their choosing. Both Alaska and Hawaii should be groomed for early statehood.[92]

After lunch, McCormick summoned Pat Maloney to his office, along with another editorial writer, Frank Hughes. The Colonel stood to greet them. A few minutes after two o'clock, the agitated figure of Genevieve Burke, his long-time personal secretary, appeared in the office doorway.

"Colonel, Roosevelt is dead."

"Turn the rules," said McCormick.[93]

It was a response that only a newspaperman could make or understand. The rules were metal dividers, thick at the bottom, hairline thin at the top, used to place a nearly imperceptible line of ink between vertical columns. When the rules were turned, the normal pattern was reversed, resulting in heavy black borders, symbolic of mourning.

Pat Maloney was less inclined to observe the proprieties. "Colonel," he barked, "the only honorable thing the son of a bitch ever did was to die on morning newspaper time."[94]

McCormick telephoned Maryland at Cantigny. In response to her query about a previously scheduled dinner party, he said that the only change would be to replace the usual champagne with a Montrachet; he didn't want Chicago gossiping that they were drinking champagne on the night of Roosevelt's death. Before leaving the building late that afternoon, he spontaneously handed out $10 bills to elevator operators and workmen in the press room.[95]

When he arrived at home, Maryland wanted to know what she should do about the flag outside the Colonel's library. Other flags were flying at half-staff. "There's no one I'd rather fly a flag at half-staff for," remarked McCormick.[96]

The Roosevelt-McCormick feud did not end with the death of the president. Haunted by the past, alarmed about the future, the Colonel found in controversy a unifying sense of self. His hatreds made him whole. They helped ward off depression, excuse his isolation, and keep him in the spotlight. Determined to uncover whatever secrets Roosevelt might have taken to his grave, the *Tribune* conducted an exhaustive probe of Pearl Harbor, and its findings were drastically at odds with those of the official inquiry. McCormick did not blame the military disaster on inept, overconfident Hawaiian commanders asleep at the switch. The fault lay with Roosevelt and Knox, he contended, each of whom had known of the Japanese attack in advance. Indeed, it was anxiety over the possible exposure of their treachery that had caused the premature deaths of both men.[97]

By the spring of 1946, according to the Colonel, half of Europe had been condemned to slavery, the other half to economic chaos. "I have no doubt that Roosevelt divided the world between Russia and England," he told Walter Trohan. A desire to win votes in New York accounted for the late president's Red sympathies; his English leanings reflected the bias of Groton and Harvard. Roosevelt had been shown up as "the boob of the century," said the *Tribune* on March 20. His diehard supporters might remain publicly faithful, "but in private their faces are very, very red."[98]

PART V

Some Private Sort *of* Greatness

1945–1955

"You want to know what I think of Charley Kane.
I suppose he had some private sort of greatness. If so he
kept it to himself . . . I don't suppose anybody ever
had so many opinions. But he never believed in anything
except Charley Kane. He never had a conviction
except Charley Kane in his life. I suppose he died without one. Must have been pretty unpleasant."

JED LELAND in *Citizen Kane*

15

The Last Leaf on the Tree

"I tell you there is such a thing as creative hate."

— Willa Cather

HE TRAGEDY of Franklin Roosevelt was that he died too soon; the tragedy of Robert McCormick was that he lived too long. As with Lincoln in another April, eighty years before, fate denied Roosevelt the chance to savor a victory or shape a peace largely realized through his efforts. Death may have been kind to his reputation, for just as Lincoln was spared the ordeal of Reconstruction, so time ran out before Roosevelt could be tested by Soviet imperialism and a precarious balance of nuclear terror. Both presidents died like heroes, their work incomplete, their memories wreathed in hopeful speculation.

Colonel McCormick was to be less fortunate. Outlasting the era of personal journalism, he lingered on to see television begin to homogenize America and destroy the regional loyalties on which the *Tribune* had built its power. Marooned in the second half of the twentieth century, he spent his final years in a harrowing reenactment of *Citizen Kane*, an erstwhile urban reformer, thwarted in politics and frustrated in love, irreconcilably alienated from the political party that had been synonymous with three generations of his family. With his newspaper in decline and his personal life in a shambles, the aging mogul stumbled from one disaster to the next.

Upon reading of the first atomic bomb dropped on Japan in August 1945, McCormick ripped out the page-one banner and sent it to an assistant with a scrawled note: "Find a remedy for this." But there was no remedy for changing popular tastes. From a peak daily circulation of

1,076,000 in 1946, the *Tribune* slipped below 900,000 in the final years of McCormick's life. A bombastic centennial observance in 1947 brought 300,000 celebrants to the lakefront for the greatest pyrotechnic display since the Chicago fire, complete with pinwheel portraits of Abraham Lincoln, Dick Tracy, and Little Orphan Annie, and a fiery climax recreating the destruction of Hiroshima in natural color. Soon after, the *Tribune* was embroiled in a typographers' strike. Before it ended twenty-two months later, the walkout had shattered the paternalistic myth that every *Tribune* worker was part of the Colonel's family.[1]

As the ranks of his contemporaries dwindled, McCormick looked in vain for a blood relation who would do his bidding, retain his confidence, and love him in the bargain. The impossible quest darkened his final years. Still, while history might be nearly through with him, he was far from being through with history. In 1945 he published *The American Revolution and Its Influence on World History*. In this slender volume the Colonel acknowledged the existence of political philosophers prior to the founding fathers, while claiming that "they did not get beyond essay writing." Giving full rein to his anglophobia, he explained that English titles of nobility were royally bestowed for services to the state. Thus the economist John Maynard Keynes had been created a baron "for his dominance of American affairs." McCormick credited Cecil Rhodes with the scholarship program that educated young Americans at Oxford, free of charge, before sending them home to act as "English cells boring from within."

That he had more than a little to learn about the nation he reviled became embarrassingly clear following the unexpected defeat of Winston Churchill in the general election of July 1945. McCormick stunned the British consul general in Chicago by observing that whatever the fate of the prime minister, he took consolation in knowing that no other member of the Conservative government would get the sack ("This from the man who nearly every day lectures us on the faults of our political system," marveled William Gallienne). More amazing still was McCormick's theory that the British government, bent on making Lord Louis Mountbatten a new German kaiser after the war, had sent him to Burma to kill Japanese and not Germans.[2]

McCormick was even less enamored of the United Nations than of the crumbling British empire. Each delegation attending the San Francisco organizing conference of the world body received a daily copy of the *Chicago Tribune*, courtesy of the Colonel. Apparently the exposure to pure Americanism fell short of its intended effect. McCormick, fearing the loss of American sovereignty, decried the United Nations Charter and the International Declaration of Human Rights as mortal threats to constitutional government. He viewed the first American delegation to the UN as a sorry lot. "[Edward] Stettinius represents predatory wealth," he wrote, "Eleanor Roosevelt petty graft in high office — Vandenberg and the other Republicans, men who sacrificed principle for enjoyable jobs."[3]

A mainstay of midwestern isolationism for most of his career, Arthur Vandenberg had been reborn by 1945 as a symbol of bipartisan foreign policy. This earned him the *Tribune*'s hatred. Denounced by the paper as a modern Benedict Arnold, Vandenberg waspishly claimed to be making progress. The last time he had come under editorial assault, he said, "I was Judas Iscariot."[4]

It will come as no surprise that McCormick repudiated international jurisprudence as carried out in the trials of alleged Nazi war criminals at Nuremberg. He accused Justice Robert Jackson and Attorney General Francis Biddle, "the two worst men in the United States," of practicing lynch war at Nuremberg, where Nazi leaders were tried for the newly invented crime of waging aggressive war. The Colonel's dissatisfaction with Biddle reached new heights on June 18,1945, when the Supreme Court by a single vote vindicated the government's long-held position in the Associated Press case arising out of Marshall Field's 1941 application for membership. He took what encouragement he could find from the narrowness of the result and the vigor with which dissenting justices, led by Chief Justice Harlan Stone, upheld his view that the First Amendment took precedence over antitrust laws.[5]

Refusing to accept defeat, McCormick elicited support from other AP directors for an appeal to Congress. In the meantime, a few weeks after the court ruling, he put on a show of gentlemanly sportsmanship by seconding Field's four-year-old application for AP membership. Election of a Republican Congress in 1946 raised his hopes that legislation to exempt the press from antitrust provisions might yet be enacted. But time had passed him by. Unable to rally solid support for the idea even within the AP, he saw his hoped-for remedy stall on Capitol Hill. There remained only the ritual of parting from an organization to which he had devoted twenty-one years as a director.

At his last board meeting, in 1948, McCormick was so overcome with emotion he couldn't speak. Only later did he reveal the valuable lesson he had gained from his membership in the group. "Never before," he said, "had I realized that friendship and integrity could go together." To one onlooker, the remark strangely illuminated this proud, distant man "who felt such need to hold himself apart in order that he might be true to his concept of newspapermaking."[6]

The AP's surrender to Field was one of several factors redrawing the lines of journalistic competition in Chicago. Nineteen forty-four saw the passing of both Frank Knox and Emory Thomason. Many questioned whether their newspapers could survive. The Knox estate lost no time in putting the *Daily News* on the auction block. Adlai Stevenson, Knox's Washington deputy and a rising figure in his own right, was the sentimental choice to carry off the prize. But the cautious Stevenson let himself be outbid and outmaneuvered by John S. Knight, an austere-looking man who already owned successful papers in Miami, Detroit, and his native Akron, Ohio. Knight enjoyed a deserved reputation for straight talk. He thought it a mistake to mix politics and publishing. "Tell both sides of the story" was his journalistic credo.

Before entering the field, Knight dropped by Tribune Tower to inquire whether McCormick had any objections to his bidding for the *Daily News*. The Colonel raised none. "But frankly," he told Knight, "I don't think it's much of a newspaper." "That's beside the point," said Knight.[7]

The new owner of the *Daily News* was equally plainspoken with department heads and editorial personnel. On his first day, he let it be known that he had bought a newspaper, not a war. "I fight my own fights, but I have no desire to inherit the quarrels of others," he remarked. He paused for effect. Colonel McCosmic was retired, "as of today."

McCormick respected Knight for his courtesy, his candor, and his personal stoicism. News that his son, John Junior, a paratroop lieutenant, had been killed in the closing weeks of World War II reached Knight on a Miami golf course. His partners wanted to call off the game, but the publisher refused. "I felt that I just had to keep going," he explained afterward. "It's just the way I do things."[8]

Knight's steely resolution made him a formidable competitor. The newcomer opened his purse strings, adding popular features to the stodgy *News,* conducting stunts (like a cross-Illinois race between a man and a pigeon), and winning a Pulitzer Prize for uncovering Springfield corruption during the gamy administration of Governor Green. *Daily News* readership leapt upward. At the *Sun,* meanwhile, Marshall Field appeared undeterred by the $10 million in losses he had sustained between 1942 and 1947. In July of the latter year, he spent another $7.8 million to buy the *Chicago Times.* He merged the two papers in 1948. Raiding the Tribune-New York Daily News Syndicate, Field made off with cartoonist Milton Caniff, the artist behind "Terry and the Pirates."

To counter the expansion of Field's foreign service, McCormick signed up with the British news agency Reuter's, whose dispatches he had once characterized as "poison copy." His wartime promises of job security for every returning veteran left the *Tribune* heavily overstaffed. Whereas one reporter had covered Springfield in the past, three were now assigned to the state government beat. A surplus of pressmen, printers, stereotypers, and editorial staff lent credence to reports that McCormick might soon inaugurate an afternoon paper or invade Milwaukee, Detroit, or Minneapolis.

✧ 2

The rumors were just that. Approaching his sixty-fifth birthday in July 1945, McCormick gave less thought to starting new papers than to perpetuating his hold over the *Tribune*. Seeking an heir, he settled on an heiress: his favorite niece, twenty-five-year-old Ruth "Bazy" McCormick Miller, the daughter of his late brother and Ruth Hanna McCormick Simms. From her mother, Bazy had inherited a love of politics and horses, not necessarily in that order. She was as ideologically conservative as her sister, Triny, was radical. At the time she was learning the journalistic ropes by running, together with her husband, Peter, a small daily in downstate LaSalle. Peter Miller's epilepsy marred their happiness, but only Uncle Bert could destroy it.

"I am now sixty-five years old," rumbled the Colonel shortly after reaching this milestone, "and occasionally I like to have my own way about something." To maintain the appearance of control, he converted Tribune Tower into a modern-day Potemkin village. One favorite in-house joke was the "seven o'clock edition," a few hundred copies of which were replated to incorporate stories breaking as late as an hour before McCormick arrived at work. "We wanted the Colonel to feel that he had the best staff in the world," remembers Donald Agrella, a rewrite man, "always on top of the news!" A network of informants throughout the building alerted elevator operators to McCormick's every move. Not for him the inconvenience suffered by other mortals, who had to wait for the doors to open.[9]

Always demanding, McCormick became even more arbitrary with age. His attention span narrowed. "You can't hold his interest if you change the subject on him," a *Tribune* executive acknowledged in 1947. "Got too much on his mind — logs in the rivers, paper at the mills, the new presses . . ." His growing deafness made conversation difficult. At editorial meetings, he digressed about problems at Cantigny ("Maybe we ought to tell people how to plant beans") or reminisced about "my wife," which those in attendance came to realize meant Amy, not Maryland McCormick. When a stray dog killed one of his sheep, the Colonel unleashed a full-bore campaign to rewrite Illinois rabies laws. He directed the medical editor, Theodore Van Dellen, to promote buttermilk, alert *Tribune* readers to the dangers posed by houseflies, and explore his thesis that American Indians committed murder by feeding their victims ground-up hair.[10]

Like the Colonel himself, the resulting mélange was entertaining, cheeky, and of questionable relevance. The *Louisville Courier*'s publisher, Mark Ethridge, asked to explain why the *Tribune* continued to lead the world in advertising, credited the paper's "animal vigor" rather than the comic strips popularly supposed to account for its phenomenal success. *Tribune* editors were quick to agree. "Comes the dawn, it ain't Orphan Annie," they declared, "it's the hair on our chest." McCormick advanced an odder theory. "It's the dull papers that make the money," he observed blandly, lumping together in this profitable category the *New York Times* and the *Tribune*.[11]

Did he believe it? Over the years, Robert Rutherford McCormick had all but disappeared into the semi-mythical figure of the Colonel, first created in the flippant 1920s to hold the world at bay. Among the handful still living who had known McCormick before he became a Public Character was Helen Dunn, the widow of his Ludgrove schoolmaster. In 1946, McCormick asked *Tribune* reporters in England to locate the old woman and present her with a canned ham and other delicacies that might ease the rigors of life in postwar, Labour-led Britain. "I will never forget how sweet you were to lonesome little boys," he plaintively told this substitute mother.[12]

McCormick's kindness to individual Britons was exceeded only by his continuing public abuse of their fading empire. In much the same way, he had formed a deep attachment to members of the Yale class of 1903 without ever being moved to make a gift to the university (he did give Northwestern property and cash worth over $1 million). In his more constructive moods, he imagined Chicago regaining its economic supremacy through air transport, especially between the American Midwest and Asia. He established an unlikely friendship with the Nobel laureate Ernest Lawrence and other scientists at the University of Chicago who had been pivotal in harnessing the atom. According to the *Tribune*, the super-weapon used to vaporize Hiroshima and Nagasaki had succeeded in transforming war "from irrationality to idiocy." A well-advertised campaign to convert the basement of Tribune Tower into a gigantic fallout shelter reaped notoriety and more than passing ridicule — at least until the *New York Times* proposed to create a bomb shelter of its own.

"I don't know whether it was age or just ignorance," said Carl Wiegman, who joined the *Tribune*'s editorial board in 1946, "but the Colonel did have some foolish ideas." McCormick scorned the League of Women Voters as a coterie of "fussy would-be political bosses." Governor Green, hankering after national office, had fallen in with bad (i.e., eastern, internationalist) company. Mayor Kelly was a putative dictator whose wings must be clipped in the 1947 municipal elections. If the CIO labor bosses came to power, God forbid, Americans could expect to be herded into concentration camps.[13]

And yet ... The canny McCormick realized, said Wiegman, "that because he was a national figure of sorts, when he did nutty things they were newsworthy." Well into his seventies, McCormick was not above playing the court jester — or *enfant terrible* — if it sold newspapers. His flair for self-promotion once led him to arrive at a Connecticut garden party hosted by Arthur Sulzberger in a helicopter whose sides had been painted over to advertise the *Chicago Tribune* — World's Greatest Newspaper. ("Well, if it's not," the Colonel replied to doubters, "nobody ever said which one *is*").[14]

Prodded by his new wife, McCormick stepped up his postwar entertaining. On Friday nights, Cantigny was the setting for buffets and film showings (at which the Colonel rarely sat through the first reel). Howard Hughes sent along a print of his sensational *The Outlaw* for private screening. McCormick insisted on reimbursing the eccentric tycoon, in line with the *Tribune*'s long-established ban on accepting services without paying for them. "You see it would be quite impossible for me to enforce this rule if I did not live up to it myself," he told Hughes. At lavish Christmas parties, the squire unbent long enough to lead guests in carols around the piano. Maryland's Christmas night champagne suppers ranked high on the list of Chicago's premier social events.[15]

Time exacted a harsh toll on McCormick's relations. Ruth Simms died on the last day of 1944, two months after fracturing her shoulder in a fall from a horse. The indomitable Cissy Patterson suffered a serious heart attack in July 1943, which was followed by recurrent spells that left her gasping and terrified of dying alone. These fears were insufficiently grave to curtail her three-pack-a-day cigarette habit, her use of cocaine, or her serious drinking, a problem that she passed along to her estranged daughter Felicia. Reversing the normal order of things, Felicia disowned her mother. Cissy then invited the forty-year-old to live with her in the Patterson mansion at 15 Dupont Circle. She promised Felicia a floor to herself and a generous allowance. "I'd rather starve to death than go down there," said Felicia. "I couldn't call my soul my own." During one reconciliation she did persuade her mother to go with her to a meeting of Alcoholics Anonymous. But Cissy never went back. "Joe says I'm too old to join," she rationalized.[16]

Exhausted and bored, Cissy toyed with the idea of entrusting the *Times-Herald* to Joe's daughter Alicia, the dynamic founder of the Long Island tabloid *Newsday* whom the Colonel looked upon as the best journalist in the family. "Stay away from Alicia," Joe ordered Cissy. "You'll only hurt her the way you've hurt everyone else."[17]

The truth was that Joe and Alicia had inflicted lasting scars on each other. As a child, Alicia had been sent by her warring parents to live with a German family on the pretext of learning their language. A Christian Scientist governess taught the girl to ignore pain. She adored her father, from whom she learned the joys of hunting and horses, and she and Joe earned their pilot licenses on the same day. Ever the nonconformist, Joe beamed when his daughter got herself expelled from two elegant finishing schools. But then, having raised a rebel in his own mold, he tried disastrously to dominate her life. Twice he married her off to men he liked and she didn't love. In 1939, Alicia incurred her father's wrath by wedding Harry Guggenheim, a millionaire mining heir and former U.S. ambassador to Cuba. Joe refused to meet his new son-in-law for a year. He made nasty remarks about Jews. He fired Alicia from her *Daily News* book column.[18]

With $70,000 of her husband's money, Alicia purchased an old press and six Linotype machines. The first 15,000 copies of *Newsday* were run off in a Hempstead garage. "I'm afraid it looks like Hell," moaned Alicia. Seven years and $750,000 later, Harry Guggenheim saw the first profit on his investment. By exploding the sedate conventions of suburban journalism, Alicia's tabloid did for Long Island what the original *Daily News* had done for Manhattan in the twenties. Her father predicted failure for *Newsday*. He ignored its success. Bitterly, Alicia accused Joe of favoring her stepbrother, Jimmy. "I couldn't help being a girl," she wrote in July 1943. "And I tried to overcome that handicap." She recited a catalogue of grievances, starting in childhood "when I jumped five feet six and you never gave me the horse you promised."[19]

Joe wouldn't be drawn into a fight. But he was quick to defend Jimmy, a West Point cadet who had washed out in basic training.

"We used to have such a helluva time," said a remorseful Alicia. "Are them days really gone forever?"[20]

Joe evaded the question. "I am too old to quarrel with you," he finally replied.[21]

His liver, ravaged by decades of heavy drinking, began to fail. In the autumn of 1945, obviously ill, Joe visited occupied Japan at the invitation of his World War I compatriot Douglas MacArthur. The journey taxed his dwindling strength. Early the next year he took to his bed. In April he dragged himself to an AP luncheon, where his appearance shocked McCormick. By then, rumors of his impending death and of family dissension had sent morale at the *Daily News* into a tailspin. "Rats desert a sinking ship," announced Harold Gray, the creator of "Little Orphan Annie," "and if I am a clever rat I am going first."[22]

In his last weeks, Joe converted to the Catholicism of his wife, Mary. Early in May 1946 he entered Doctors' Hospital. His room was the scene of terrible rows pitting Alicia's sister Josephine and a drunken Cissy Patterson against Mary. McCormick went to see his cousin, hoping to discuss ways to keep the restive Gray from carrying out his threat. He found Joe near death, unable to recognize him. Patterson died on May 26. Opinions about his legacy were as divided as his own family. "None could ever say," eulogized the *Washington Post*, "that he was ever the tool of any interest; he served nothing but the light as he saw it." A dry-eyed *New*

Yorker compared the post-Patterson *Daily News* to a steamroller whose operator had left in search of a beer without bothering to switch off the engine.[23]

The death of his cousin added immeasurably to McCormick's burdens. Even before leaving New York for Joe's funeral in Washington, he assured *News* executives that he had no intention of trying to run the paper himself. Neither would he entertain thoughts of selling it to outsiders. His decision was governed by more than sentiment. Any other course would risk having Joe's shares in the McCormick-Patterson Trust fall into unfriendly hands. The trust, organized to protect the cousins from the crushing burden of taxes, had become a straitjacket requiring their survivors to borrow huge sums with which to pay estate taxes and keep individual shares from going on the auction block.

Such concerns were put aside as the clan assembled at the Patterson mansion on Dupont Circle, where Joe's body lay in state pending burial at Arlington National Cemetery. Protocol was strictly observed as the procession of mourners pulled up at Cissy's front door. Mary King Patterson and her son, Jimmy, rode in the first car. Behind them came the Colonel and Maryland, designated the Royal Family by Cissy. Riding with the McCormicks was Felicia, the countess Gyzicka, who so dreaded the thought of spending time under her mother's roof that she had to be practically dragged from the car by Maryland McCormick.

Inside the house, Cissy was on the second-floor landing, rehearsing her big reconciliation scene. The Colonel liked to say that the world had lost its greatest ham actor when Cissy abandoned the stage for the monochromatic world of newspaper publishing. She wasn't about to disappoint her audience now. At the first sight of her trembling daughter on the grand staircase, she flung out her arms. "Felicia!" she cried. "My darling!"[24]

McCormick went from Washington directly to Canada, deliberately bypassing New York to give those left behind at the *Daily News* a chance to establish their credibility. Quickly he settled on Roy Holliss, a fifty-nine-year-old *News* vice president, to replace Joe. He told Cissy that he regarded the *News* succession as settled for the balance of his lifetime. Within three months, however, Holliss was killed in an automobile accident. Two other top executives at the paper died from natural causes. Adding to the sense of chaos, McCormick was dismayed to learn that advertising department employees had gone for years without a Christmas bonus. He corrected the oversight immediately.

Family squabbling broke out anew as Alicia and her sisters, angered by the way in which their father's estate had been apportioned, protested the naming of Mary and Jimmy Patterson as trustees. Cissy took Alicia's side, much to McCormick's annoyance. Control over the McCormick-Patterson Trust had never previously been in doubt, the Colonel reminded Cissy, because "everyone has been reasonable . . . the principle was simple enough while Joe and Ruth were alive, and Ruth's children were minors." But in 1936, Triny Barnes had liquidated her *Tribune* holdings to satisfy her political conscience. More recently, her stepfather, Albert Simms, had been forced to sell twenty-eight shares of the trust to meet the tax bill assessed against Ruth McCormick Simms's estate.[25]

A much greater test of ingenuity awaited Joe's executors. Warily, McCormick agreed that one of the Patterson children might be added to the board, but only if the newcomer was prepared "to work in entire harmony with the rest of us." This excluded Alicia, at least in his view. Having spent a lifetime battling Cissy, McCormick dreaded the thought of contending with yet another domineering Patterson female — and a liberal internationalist at that. Prolonged negotiations led to an uneasy truce. Under its terms, Cissy briefly chaired the *News* board before passing the gavel to F. M. "Jack" Flynn, the paper's business manager, who was to share oversight with the executive editor, Richard W. Clarke.[26]

McCormick took advantage of the rare lull in family acrimony to borrow enough funds to retire most of Joe's outstanding stock. This left him strapped and feeling vulnerable enough to ask Joe's first wife to keep her holdings off the market for at least five years. "At the end of that time I should have disposed of a considerable amount of my purchase among the employees," he told Cissy; after that, "very likely I will not care what happens anyway."[27]

✧ 3

For McCormick, the 1946 congressional campaign supplied a welcome respite from family politics. Addressing 11,000 GOP partisans at the Illinois state fair in August, he charged that Communist-led labor bosses held the Democratic party in a grip of iron. Democrats responded by casting the fall elections as a referendum on the malign influence of Boss McCormick. This was fine by the Colonel, who always thought it better to be despised than ignored. For the first time in sixteen years, *Tribune* predictions of a Republican sweep were borne out by the voters. In a stinging rebuke to the Truman administration, the GOP captured both houses of Congress.

Ballots were still being counted on November 6 when McCormick wired Cissy, "I wish Joe were here to share our triumph." Muting his joy was the continuing muscle of eastern "money-mad millionaires" within the Republican party. Throughout their long years in the political wilderness, McCormick and the *Tribune* had jealously guarded Republican purity like the vestal fires. Come January 1947, the Colonel anticipated that a Congress of the old faith would repeal the New Deal and reverse the flow of American sovereignty to international bodies such as the United Nations. His greatest fear was that the same forces responsible for Willkie and Dewey would fob off yet another "renegade westerner" to challenge the unpopular Truman in 1948.[28]

With his faith in democracy restored, McCormick formally joined the Presbyterian Church in December 1946. At a ceremony in nearby Wheaton, his knees shook as he responded "I do" to a series of doctrinal questions put to him by the Reverend Robert Stewart. Another local eccentric, Stewart favored Bermuda shorts over the usual ecclesiastical garb. He was rarely seen in public unaccompanied by his German wolfhound, Bruce, with whom he rode in an open car each year as part of Wheaton's Fourth of July pageantry. Steward coerced from McCormick more than a statement of faith. The Colonel donated funds for a chapel memorializing his father. He rarely visited the place himself, being too accustomed to preaching to enjoy being preached at.[29]

En route to Latin America in January 1947, he spent three days in Texas, virtually a foreign country itself. Here he found a raw energy and entrepreneurial zeal sadly missing from his hometown. He predicted that Houston would occupy a position in the twenty-first century analogous to that of Chicago in the nineteenth. As consolation, he also forecast that Los Angeles would surpass New York in wealth and influence, especially cultural influence.

McCormick tested his hypothesis in March, when he made his first visit to the City of Angels since 1932. Hedda Hopper adroitly steered him through a round of well-attended cocktail parties, movie premieres, and studio excursions. "He's a great man," gushed Frank Sinatra, as Lucille Ball, Cary Grant, and Lana Turner looked on from the deck of Hopper's swimming pool. Conspicuously left off the invitation list were Charlie Chaplin and Orson Welles, both men thought to be politically offensive to the guest of honor. Other Hollywood liberals who chanced to cross McCormick's path were neutralized through a charm few had anticipated. "I don't know why I was afraid of you," confessed the wife of producer Samuel Goldwyn. "Why, you're as comfortable as an old shoe."[30]

McCormick had more on his mind than Hollywood stargazing. Television was in its infancy, and he was determined to repeat in the new medium his earlier success with radio. By the summer of 1947, he had ordered broadcast equipment and secured a wavelength. He enlisted Hedda Hopper to obtain the programming he would need to satisfy television's voracious appetite. Under rules set out by the Federal Communications Commission, no company would be permitted to own more than

five broadcasting stations. This assured that television would exist independent of the major Hollywood studios. Yet the time was approaching,
McCormick told Hopper, when the moviemakers were bound to enter the
business of production. As for the *Tribune*, whose television station WGN
signed on the air in April 1948, "we would like to be the outlet for the best
of them."[31]

In the meantime, studios had to be constructed. An eight-story annex to
the existing WGN building was entrusted to a *Tribune* labor relations
expert named Harold Grumhaus. "I can't build that building," Grumhaus
protested. "I don't know a blueprint from a sheet of music."

"Well," replied the business manager, Elbert Antrim, "the Colonel"
thinks you can coordinate it."

Reluctantly, Grumhaus gave his assent. But he had no intention of
working late into the night six days a week, depriving himself of time with
his family and endangering his health. Wasn't it enough that he carried a
heavy load of negotiations aimed at preventing a printers' strike? What
more could any employer ask?

"And the word came," recalled Grumhaus long afterward, " 'If I were
Grumhaus, I'd want to work six days a week.' "[32]

Thereafter McCormick and Grumhaus met every Saturday morning at
eleven o'clock to examine the latest blueprints sans interfering architect or
engineer. Together they improvised a building housing not only television
and radio facilities but a modernized press layout. Grumhaus would report
the latest construction progress and problems. "Invariably we'd leave his
office and walk across the bridge and take a look at it from the south, and
go back and look at it from the north . . . We'd make our decisions right
there, as to the type of elevation we wanted, what type of roof, and whether
we wanted a cornice."

McCormick had long since come to enjoy his own mythology. In June
1947, he invited the public to a week-long extravaganza marking the *Tribune*'s centennial. *Time* thought the occasion worthy of a cover story, illustrated with a more than slightly ridiculous portrait of the Colonel wearing
the traditional pressman's cap as though an admiral of the fleet. The festivities matched the grandiosity of their impresario. Thousands of *Tribune*
employees and their families were fêted at the Medinah Temple. Large
crowds toured the unfinished WGN television studios. McCormick's normally cloaked emotions were put to the test at a dinner attended by 2,000
of the civic elite and presided over by Governor Green and Mayor Martin
Kennelly, Ed Kelly's gray successor at city hall.

Douglas MacArthur sent greetings from Tokyo. Additional messages
were received from Eddie Rickenbacker, Cecil B. De Mille, and dozens of
members of Congress. "I will have to wait to answer most . . . because there
are so many," McCormick wrote to Charles Summerall on June 9, "but

yours I answer immediately. All that I am, all that I have done, I owe to your example. I learned from you that duty comes first, and learned also from you how to build an unconquerable organization."

In the spirit of the occasion, professional rivalries were temporarily suspended. The *Chicago Daily News* under Jack Knight lauded the "fabulous saga" of McCormick and his *Tribune*. "Few American newspapers have fought so vigorously to preserve our traditional freedom of expression," said the *News*. Nor had any American publisher been subjected to greater abuse or more vicious character assassination. Yet no amount of slurs on the Colonel's patriotism or what Knight delicately labeled the "journalistic eccentricities" of his competitor could obscure the tenacious loyalty McCormick displayed to his city, his country, and his convictions. Hardly less fulsome was the tribute from Lord Rothermere, whose *London Daily Mail* joined with fifty-five other foreign newspapers in reproducing the front page of the June 10 centennial *Tribune* issue.

McCormick took pride in the technological ingenuity that enabled his views to be disseminated globally via radio facsimile, forerunner of the modern fax machine. But it was tradition, he maintained, particularly the egalitarian outlook of the old northwest, that was most responsible for a century of *Tribune* prosperity. As explained by McCormick, the "aristocratic press" of Joe Medill's day had failed to survive the onslaught of vulgar journalism as symbolized by Hearst. "The *Tribune* did, without sinking into vulgarity." McCormick found his formula for success in the words of his grandfather. "We go our own way, at our own time, in our own manner," Joseph Medill had written, "in company of our own choosing, knowing as we do that vindication will be sure to follow."[33]

❖ 4

For years McCormick had cultivated the aura of omniscience. His power appeared unlimited, like his appetite for work and his command of detail. But it was a confused and diminished figure who sought escape in the fall of 1947, when the *Tribune*'s printers threatened to rupture a labor peace that was almost as old as the *Tribune* itself. As part of the centennial observance, McCormick had accepted a laudatory scroll from Local 16 of the Chicago Typographical Union. Beneath a deferential surface, however, worker dissatisfaction was mounting, aimed less at McCormick than at the 80th Congress, responsible for the Taft-Hartley Act.

Adopted over a presidential veto in June, the bill had empowered states to outlaw closed shops monopolized by union labor. It also made unions financially liable for losses inflicted through wildcat strikes and secondary boycotts. To McCormick, the legislation merely redressed an imbalance of power between labor and management fostered by the New Deal. The unions, not surprisingly, saw Taft-Hartley as punitive and vengeful. The burden of compliance fell on no one more heavily than the International Typographical Union (ITU) and its gruff, table-pounding president, Woodruff Randolph. Skillfully, the ITU had exploited closed shops to gain a virtual hammerlock over newspaper production in major U.S. cities.

In the autumn of 1947, the ITU decided to make Chicago a test of strength. The union opposed technological changes that might eliminate jobs. It demanded the right to establish work rules in the composing room. ("Taking over management is what they were doing," claimed Harold Grumhaus.) Management, improbably led by Marshall Field, presented a solid front of opposition. At a meeting of his fellow publishers at the Chicago Club, Field took a while to grasp the full implications of what his employees were demanding. When they finally hit him full force, the publisher of the *Sun-Times* rose to his feet and exclaimed, "They can't tell *me* what to do."[34]

The rise of labor militancy left the Colonel more despairing than at any time since the death of young Medill McCormick. Unwilling to concede that the *Tribune* family might be dysfunctional, his courage gave out. "You run the strike," he told Jack Knight. "I'm going to Japan." Early in November, he fled the country.[35]

McCormick spent the next six weeks in Asia, traveling like a potentate. While in Manila, he was given a ride in a B-17 Flying Fortress, one of a fleet of military aircraft decommissioned since the war and converted for passenger use. On returning to Chicago, he made arrangements to buy an identical plane at the bargain price of $7,500, with four spare engines thrown in. He then poured thousands more into refitting the old bomber for maximum comfort, with a well-stocked library, portable bar, and wall-to-wall rugs.

It was just as well that the plane was unavailable to fly him to his next destination, Tokyo. There he enjoyed a pleasant stroll with Emperor Hirohito through the imperial gardens. He sampled more lavish hospitality from the country's occupying power, Douglas MacArthur. McCormick was still in the Japanese capital when he learned that the ITU printers had walked off the job. Sounding as if he knew something the union leaders didn't and should have, he said he hoped the strike wouldn't end anytime soon. His remark was in stark contrast to the mood of the departing workers, some of whom hadn't bothered to collect their clothes from their lockers.

McCormick hadn't the stomach for personal confrontation, at least not at this stage of his life, but that didn't mean he was unprepared for a strike or reluctant to engage in a test of wills with militant union leaders. Hidden from the ITU was the *Tribune*'s secret weapon: the VariTyper, an ungainly machine that produced columns of identical width in a typeface corresponding to the familiar Linotype process. First employed two years earlier to frustrate a work stoppage in San Antonio, the advanced typewriter represented the cutting edge of newspaper technology, which threatened the union and its members with obsolescence.

The *Tribune*'s news editor, Stewart Owen, was a good man to have by one's side in a journalistic knife fight. Fresh from a reconnaissance mission to San Antonio, Owen had joined forces with Pauline Ferber, head of the paper's stenographic department, to launch the whimsically titled Manhattan Project, a crash course secretly administered to twenty crack typists. Tripled in size and renamed Operation Musk Ox, the program came to be supplemented with copyreaders, who were taught the intricacies of an alternative method of setting headlines called Fototype, and with students from Northwestern, hired to set classified ads.[36]

On the night of November 24, 1947, as clattering typesetting machines in the composing room fell silent, Operation Musk Ox went into overdrive. Long wooden tables, hastily crafted in the *Tribune*'s carpentry shop, were set up in the fourth-floor newsroom. A ragtag force of stenographers, secretaries, and typists drafted from throughout Tribune Tower worked ten- or twelve-hour shifts at their VariTypers. The sound was deafening. To McCormick's relief, twenty-three unions stayed on the job, their loyalty exceeded only by their versatility. In the crunch, executives demonstrated hidden proletarian talents. Production bosses pushed carts of metal. Artists dropped brushes and pencils for scissors and paste pots.

The improvised *Tribune* relied on photoengraved copy in place of traditional printing plates. The obstacles to converting overnight to a new form of production were daunting. Yet the first strike issue ran twenty-four pages, double prestrike expectations. And as the VariTyper operators became comfortable with their machines, the paper gradually lost its haphazard appearance. The rest of the nation took notice. During the first month of the strike, representatives from forty-seven other newspapers visited Tribune Tower to verify rumors that McCormick and his staff had found a way to publish a professional-looking product without recourse to the printers, Linotypes, and composing machines that for nearly sixty years had been indispensable tools of the newspaper trade.

Feigning supreme indifference to the labor dispute, the Colonel remained in the Orient. He did not allow the grim tidings from Chicago to interfere with his pleasures. On a visit to Shanghai, the horse-loving Maryland McCormick took delight in some equestrian-theme wallpaper which she thought ideal for the formal dining room at Cantigny. Her husband was dubious. Cocking his head at the south end of a horse heading north, he said he didn't relish the thought of looking at Harry Truman every time he sat down to dinner.[37]

McCormick had a horse of his own entered in the 1948 Republican presidential sweepstakes. In Hong Kong he reiterated his belief that Robert Taft was the man best qualified to restore conservative rule to the White House. He took the uncharismatic Taft under his wing, hoping to teach the senator a thing or two about the medium of radio. "Broadcasting requires a technique quite different from addressing the Senate, or platform speaking," McCormick wrote to Taft. "Franklin Roosevelt was its greatest master, and Tom Dewey is a close second." Perhaps Taft would come by the WGN studios and make some test recordings before submitting to coaching by vocal experts?[38]

The logic was impeccable, but McCormick failed to reckon with Taft's stubborn resistance to politics as performance art. The Colonel decided to hedge his bets. He opened a back channel to MacArthur in Tokyo, advising the general to remain at his post while signaling to voters in the key primary state of Wisconsin his receptivity to a presidential draft. MacArthur followed this course to the letter. His reward was a humiliating defeat at the hands of former Minnesota governor Harold Stassen. By way of consolation, McCormick assured the general that if Taft fell by the wayside at the June 1948 convention in Philadelphia, Republican delegates would have only two alternatives to choose from: the hero MacArthur or a candidate endorsed by "the international bankers."[39]

In mid-December 1947, with his role as decoy at an end, the Colonel flew back to Chicago. "Twenty-five thousand miles over ocean does not seem so terrible," he wired Cissy Patterson, "when you are confident you were born to be hanged." That he had escaped yet another grisly fate became clear as McCormick reviewed the consequences of the typographers' strike. Amazingly, the *Tribune* had been able to retain its preeminent position in national circulation and advertising. "If this is not a strike to end all strikes," he told Cissy hopefully, "I think it will greatly reduce publishers' fear of them."[40]

Of more immediate concern was a fresh outbreak of family wrangling orchestrated by Cissy. Determined to show herself a force to be reckoned with, Mrs. P. took up the cause of her niece Alicia. The publisher of *Newsday* was "a smart little cookie," she argued to her Chicago cousin. "She has a lot to offer." McCormick resisted putting Alicia on the *Tribune* board, and Cissy taunted him mercilessly, saying that he wouldn't dare to oppose the idea if Joe was alive. "Joe's dead!" roared McCormick, seizing the arms of Cissy's chair and putting his contorted face close to hers. The message was lost on Cissy, a terminally weary woman whose mind was further clouded by alcohol and drugs.[41]

Delighted as ever to stir the pot, Cissy promised to leave her niece the

Washington Times-Herald on the condition that Alicia obtain a divorce from Harry Guggenheim. Her motives were even less creditable than they appeared on the surface. "I know all about Jews," she blurted, "I married one."[42]

Alicia spurned the bribe, in a show of independence that may well have inspired McCormick to make a conditional offer of his own. At a May 1948 meeting, he revealed his willingness to accept Alicia as a member of the Tribune Company board — in place of her erratic aunt. The deal was consummated on the spot. "I'll hand it to Cissy," McCormick allowed afterward. "She never turned a hair."[43]

But the Colonel was wrong. Cissy burned for revenge. The secret of her success as a publisher was also the source of her personal turmoil: the constant need to be noticed, at whatever cost in dignity or peace of mind. Overlooking their strained relationship, the McCormicks stayed with Cissy whenever they were in Washington. Early in July 1948, they arrived at 15 Dupont Circle for a short visit. The Colonel was provoked beyond measure by Cissy's bohemian lifestyle. Shortly after breakfast one morning, he walked into a third-floor room to find his wife sipping champagne with the mistress of the house. He demanded an explanation. "It's none of your goddamned business," snorted Cissy.[44]

The Royal Family returned to Chicago. On entering the Pump Room a few days later, Maryland had her own surprise: alone in Booth #2 sat a morose Cissy, nursing a scotch and soda and obviously spoiling for a fight. "You can tell that son of a bitch of a husband of yours that I'm gonna raise hell," she growled.[45]

McCormick laughed off the threat. At the time he was preparing to leave the country on a lengthy excursion to Europe and the British Isles. It was at this juncture that Frank Waldrop hand-carried to Cantigny a rambling eight-page diatribe in Cissy's hand. "I made up my mind that if you got tough with me," she wrote, in apparent reference to McCormick's unwillingness to supply desired financial statements from the McCormick-Patterson Trust, "I'd get tough with you — but good!" The letter went on to exhume ancient allegations of how *Tribune* influence had been improperly used to obtain a school department lease on valuable Chicago real estate. It cautioned McCormick against bullying tactics: "You should realize that you have never, and can never, *stampede* me off my chosen ground." And it raised the specter of a hostile combination in which Cissy and the Guggenheims joined forces to cut McCormick down to size. Near the end of her tirade, all fury spent, Cissy lapsed into cousinly affection, admonishing the Colonel, "Don't ever stop me loving you."[46]

The letter sat unopened after Waldrop delivered it to a butler. Maryland, beside herself with curiosity, urged her husband to break the seal. McCormick refused. "I'll let Kirkland read it," he said, confident that his trusted lawyer was more than a match for Cissy.[47]

A few days later, the Colonel and Maryland climbed into their newly refurbished Flying Fortress for a six-week European odyssey. Although it was nearly midnight when they touched down in Edinburgh, enough reporters were waiting at the airport to convene an impromptu press conference. Someone asked McCormick what he thought of the idea of Scotland applying for membership in the American union. "I think it would be a great thing for the United States," he replied, "but I don't know how good it would be for Scotland." From Edinburgh he went on to Dublin, where the president of the Irish republic, Eamon De Valera, feted the Colonel and his lady at an elaborate state dinner. In Londonderry, McCormick sought out Old Meg, the gigantic cannon fired by his eighteenth-century ancestor, Captain James McCormick, in the Protestant defense of the city.[48]

The more recent past enveloped McCormick in London. Within minutes of checking into Claridge's, he was off on a nostalgic ramble. Thanks to the intervention of U.S. ambassador Lew Douglas, a long-time friend, he was asked to a July 22 garden party at Buckingham Palace. Inside the royal enclosure, a tense moment ensued when Winston Churchill, feeling wronged by the *Tribune*'s mockery of the British empire before, during, and since the war, went out of his way to avoid McCormick. Churchill's natural warmth gradually thawed his resentment, until the two men were seen engaged in polite conversation. Afterward, McCormick commented favorably on the girlish charms of the princesses Elizabeth and Margaret Rose. The royal frolic capped a successful two-week visit to the British Isles. Preparing to fly to Paris on July 23, McCormick said he felt like a soldier emerging unscathed from battle.

In the French capital, he and Maryland stayed at the Ritz, another nostalgic landmark. On the twenty-fourth they spent several hours at Versailles, returning late in the day to find telephones ringing in every room of their suite. Maryland picked up a receiver and heard the insistent voice of an Associated Press reporter asking to speak to the Colonel. McCormick took the call in the bedroom. Maryland, observing closely, noticed that her husband had "the most benign look on his face." The conversation was brief on both ends. McCormick hung up the phone. "Cissy's dead," he said matter-of-factly.

He disappeared into the bathroom, from where his singing startled Maryland. She strained to catch the jaunty baritone rendition of an old Victorian tune: "I'm the Last Leaf on the Tree."[49]

❖ 5

The accidental presidency of Harry Truman had initially evoked feelings of sympathy and relief around Tribune Tower. As far as McCormick was concerned, Truman's salty candor and lack of pretense contrasted favorably with the guile and polish of his predecessor. The new president had served creditably as a captain of artillery in World War I, always a shining credential to one of the Colonel's outlook. As chairman of a Senate committee looking into military waste and mismanagement, Truman had earned high marks from the *Tribune*. To be sure, as Roosevelt's 1944 running mate, the man from Missouri had taken his lumps, particularly over his long-standing friendship with the Kansas City political boss Tom Pendergast. Democrats who entertained doubts about FDR's capacity to serve out his fourth term were faced, in the *Tribune*'s words, with "the grinning skeleton of Truman the bankrupt ... Truman the yes man and apologist in the Senate for political gangsters."[50]

The paper sang a different tune in April 1945. As a border-state Democrat culturally unattuned to the style and outlook of the New Dealers surrounding Roosevelt, Truman was expected to provide more conservative leadership. In any event, McCormick was much too busy prosecuting the ghost of Truman's predecessor to worry about the new man in the White House. "The incredible is true," he stormed less than a month after V-E Day. "We fought a great war; incurred a million casualties; frightfully bankrupted the country ... without any agreement as to what we were fighting for, or what would take place after victory." This harsh assessment overlooked what it did not distort: the entire thrust of Rooseveltian diplomacy, with its emphasis on collective security and international peacekeeping, which ran straight from the Atlantic Charter of 1941 to the United Nations Charter of 1945.[51]

Any inclination McCormick might feel to cut the new president some slack vanished abruptly with the Potsdam Conference in July 1945 and Truman's friendly allusion to "Old Joe" Stalin, his partner in negotiating the future of occupied Germany. Truman, raged the *Tribune*, was "as devoid of diplomatic skill as he is without understanding of the problems he has been dealing with." The president widened the breach by going before Congress early in September to unveil a domestic agenda virtually indistinguishable from the New Deal. Thereafter the administration was under constant fire. The Colonel accused Truman of bungling price controls and prolonging wartime taxes. He blamed the White House for accelerating inflation, crippling shortages, and labor unrest. A front-page cartoon in the *Tribune* showed the beleaguered chief executive as Little Truman Fauntleroy:

> Look at Little Truman now
> Muddy, battered bruised — and how!
> Victim of his misplaced trust,
> He has learned what good boys must
> In the alley after school,
> There just ain't no golden rule.[52]

McCormick trained his heaviest guns on Truman's foreign policy. He attacked the president for tacitly conceding Soviet domination of eastern Europe. With more passion than logic, he hurled allegations of appeasement at the Truman White House — an audacious gesture coming from one who had shown himself more than willing to feed the fascist crocodiles in the 1930s. It was hard to tell which McCormick hated most, Stalin or Europe. Clinging to his prewar isolationism, he offered only verbal resistance to the Red tide lapping at the shattered continent. Not that he was blind to the menace of Soviet communism. Convinced of his moral superiority, he was willing to dispense with military force. The *Tribune* continued to regard the Atlantic and the Pacific as divinely placed to shield the United States from the corrupting influence of an ideologically festering Old World.

McCormick emphatically disapproved of Truman's request for $3.8 billion in American aid to the tottering democracies of western Europe. "To hell with the Marshall Plan," said McCormick. "It's really a snob plan." His resentment grew with time. By the spring of 1948, he had convinced himself that what appeared on the surface to be a humane attempt to forestall a Communist Europe was in truth part of a much larger intrigue to communize the United States.* For McCormick, the catalogue of treachery had commenced with the Roosevelt-Stalin agreements reached at Tehran and Yalta. "The United Nations was formed as a fake to fool people as to Roosevelt's real reason for going to war," he argued in May 1948. "It was successful for this, but valueless as a war preventive. Hence, up came the Marshall Plan to bankrupt America in the name of war prevention." When this too failed in its objective, "up comes the seventy-group air force, conscription, and universal military training."[53]

Such gestures alarmed McCormick, for whom the greatest threat to individual liberty was an executive drunk with power. Adding to his dread of presidential aggrandizement were the postwar seizures of coal mines, railroads, meat-packing plants, and oil refineries — further evidence of Washington's intention to take over private industry — coupled with Truman's astonishingly ill-advised attempt in 1946 to draft workers deemed to be "on strike against their government."

Cold war liberals laughed bitterly at McCormick's premonitions of domestic tyranny. They accused him, not without provocation, of rolling the stone of right-wing paranoia up a familiar mountain. To McCormick the libertarian, however, the national security state fostered in the late

---

*He was equally disapproving of the North Atlantic Treaty Organization, overwhelmingly approved by the Senate in July 1949. It was a misreading of history, said McCormick, to classify the nations of Europe as either unified or democratic. Most had little in common besides Roman occupation and the Crusades. Moreover, half a dozen were monarchies, and at least one had the Communist party as its largest single political force.

1940s held no more appeal than the welfare state put in place by the New Deal. In both cases, he feared that government assurances would act like a narcotic upon the people, leaving them content to forgo their liberty in exchange for protection from the heartless logic of economic competition in the one case, the lurking terrors of Red domination or atomic destruction in the other. Rounding out a life full of paradox, McCormick the exemplar of the Old Right became simultaneously a forerunner of the New Left. To adherents of both movements, the promise of security carried an implicit risk to civil and economic liberties; whatever the illness for which such actions were being prescribed, it was less debilitating than the official cure.

✦ 6

McCormick's distaste for Truman, however pungent, did not cause him to underestimate the president's chances in 1948, especially if, as he predicted before a Los Angeles audience in the spring of 1947, "New York bankers" again controlled the GOP convention. "Dewey didn't want the Republican nomination for President the last time," the Colonel told the *New York Times* in September 1947. "He just wanted to go on being a New Yorker," which suited the same international financiers who had designated Wendell Willkie as their 1940 sacrificial lamb. As theorized by McCormick, "the bankers just wanted to save England and British imperialism and they knew that they could do it with that fellow Roosevelt in there, so they just put up Willkie and Dewey to get beaten . . . And that's what happened."[54]

Taft remained the Colonel's favorite for 1948, notwithstanding his somewhat arid personality. McCormick thought MacArthur was too old and California governor Earl Warren insufficiently well known except on the West Coast. Harold Stassen and Arthur Vandenberg bore the scarlet letter of internationalism as "Truman's candidates." Convinced that Dewey couldn't beat Truman, McCormick relayed an improbable offer to the White House through Attorney General Tom Clark. If Truman were to play his political cards "as close to his vest as he played his poker hands," in the well-chosen words of Walter Trohan, McCormick's emissary to Clark, the *Tribune* might stay neutral in a Dewey-Truman contest. The peace feeler was conveyed to the Oval Office, where it met instant, profane rejection.[55]

Spurned by the opposition, McCormick turned his attention to the Illinois GOP. He made certain that the fifty-eight-member delegation to the June convention in Philadelphia was pledged en bloc to Taft. If there was any fly in the ointment, it was the state's two-term Republican governor, Dwight Green, whose lukewarm attitude about a third term was mirrored by the electorate. Green went into the campaign seriously weakened by scandals in Springfield and the continuing fallout from a disastrous 1947 mine explosion which cost the lives of 111 coal miners in the downstate community of Centralia. Running against him was the eloquent Chicago lawyer-diplomat Adlai Stevenson. The *Tribune* maligned Stevenson as Striped Pants Adlai, a UN supporter who believed the world body had the right, as McCormick told Green in March 1948, "to enslave the American people or try American citizens in its courts."[56]

Never miserly with advice, the Colonel urged Green to attack Stevenson, bearer of one of the state's more distinguished political names, as a carpetbagger who preferred the company of eastern snobs to that of "simple middle westerners." This was a none-too-veiled allusion to Stevenson's ongoing love affair with his "indomitable little tiger," Alicia Patterson. Both Stevenson and Patterson were married to other partners in 1948; their relationship remained guarded and, ultimately, frustrating, even after Ellen Stevenson filed for divorce early in her husband's gubernatorial career.

Of more pressing concern to McCormick than Stevenson's love life was the surprisingly effective race the Democratic candidate was making against "Bertie's Boy," as he condescendingly labeled Green. Equally vulnerable was Senator Curley Brooks, who also had to face the voters in November 1948 and who looked on Green as a potential rival. Aiding Brooks in his mischief-making were Green's unconcealed national ambitions. The governor was a favorite of Herbert Brownell, Dewey's Nebraska-born campaign manager and former chairman of the Republican National Committee. From his earlier dealings with Green, Brownell came away convinced that the governor was a closet internationalist, concealing his true leanings out of deference to his patron at the *Tribune.*

Before his death in 1996, Brownell confided his scheme to unite the urban east and the conservative farm belt by pairing the politically attractive governors of New York and Illinois on the 1948 Republican ticket. Before approaching either Dewey or Green, he was careful to run the idea past the Illinois national committeeman Werner Schroeder and the committee's treasurer, Chicago insurance man James Kemper. Both men were close to McCormick and the *Tribune;* neither said anything to dampen Brownell's hopes. For his part, Brownell thought Dewey amenable to Green as his running mate. When convention organizers picked Green to be keynote speaker, affording the Illinois governor the perfect stage on which to make his national audition, Brownell had every reason to congratulate himself on a shrewd plan, skillfully executed.[57]

Except one. The deal-broker hadn't reckoned with McCormick, for whom the suggestion of a Dewey-Green ticket was anathema. Such a combination would never get a *Tribune* endorsement, McCormick told friends. Not that he anticipated confronting the issue anytime soon: Dewey's lieutenants had made so many promises, he said, that to honor them all would produce an exponential growth in the number of vice presidents and require attendance at cabinet meetings to be spread out over at least three shifts.

In the third week of June 1948, a thousand Republican delegates assembled in Philadelphia amid an atmosphere of decided optimism about the prospects for victory in November. McCormick's suite at the Warwick Hotel was a nest of intrigue. (Clare and Henry Luce were next door; McCormick thought the publisher of *Time* was "on the verge of a breakdown" over the failure of his candidate, Vandenberg, to catch fire.) At the center of the plotting was Curley Brooks. Together with his equally ambitious wife, Brooks sent word to the Colonel that he had been betrayed by the *Tribune*'s city editor, Don Maxwell, whom he accused of being in league with his fellow Hoosier, Dwight Green, to obtain for Green the vice presidency on a Dewey ticket. Brooks prevailed upon Alf Landon, another Taft supporter who should have known better, to convey the same grim message to the Colonel and Maryland McCormick.[58]

In fact, Green had already performed the political equivalent of self-immolation by submitting the draft of his keynote speech to the Colonel for his approval. Instead of vetting the mildly internationalist text, Mc-Cormick gutted it, thereby closing the door to Green's vice presidential ambitions. True to his word, McCormick held Illinois in line for Taft. At the end of the second ballot, with Dewey closing in on the prize and neither Taft nor Stassen willing to withdraw for the other, the Colonel resolved to suffer defeat rather than compromise. Dewey took the prize on the third ballot. Refusing to join in the customary motion to declare the nomination unanimous, McCormick strode out of the convention hall, barking "Dewey can't win."[59]

In his anger he came close to firing Maxwell for insubordination. Walter Trohan went to the Warwick to vouch for Maxwell's loyalty and convince the Colonel that Brooks was lying. He found Maryland in the bedroom of the suite, wearing a negligee and combing her hair. For half an hour they discussed the matter. Trohan was still arguing Maxwell's cause when the Colonel appeared in the doorway: "What in the hell are you and my wife up to?" Trohan didn't stay around long enough to answer.[60]

With Green eliminated from vice presidential consideration, the Midwest for the first time in history went unrepresented on a Republican national ticket. Second place went to Earl Warren, a lackadaisical campaigner whom Dewey privately derided as "that big dumb Swede." In the fall, Warren was unable to deliver California for the party, while the farm belt turned decisively against the bicoastal ticket. By vetoing Green's vice presidential hopes, McCormick may well have sealed his party's fate and, ironically, vindicated his own forecast of a Dewey loss.[61]

The Colonel made no attempt to conceal his disappointment over Taft's defeat and the internationalist leanings of congressional Republicans. "The final collapse on Marshall money and conscription was either a surrender to the New Deal," McCormick wrote to Taft on June 30, "or the New Dealers taking over the Republican party." Either way, he entertained diminishing hopes for the party his grandfather had helped to found and promote in defiance of eastern Tories. He told Taft that he was "looking forward to a dubious but interesting fortune."

✧ 7

Whatever else divided them, McCormick and Truman were as one in their aversion to understatement. Before the 1948 campaign ended, the *Tribune* castigated the president of the United States as "a nincompoop" — also a warmonger, coddler of Communists, and political hack unable to rise above his unsavory origins in the Kansas City machine run by Tom Pendergast. Truman hurled a few verbal Molotov cocktails of his own, calling McCormick's the worst newspaper in the country, skilled in character assassination, and its proprietor a right-wing crackpot fronting for native fascists.

That summer the nation was riveted to hearings held before the House Un-American Activities Committee, which explored — and exploited — fears of domestic subversion. On August 21, McCormick directed his editorial writers to go after "Roosevelt-Truman Communists" who took the Fifth Amendment, arguing that it was tantamount to confession. He pounced on Alger Hiss, a prominent New Deal State Department official who had accompanied FDR to Yalta and played a highly visible role in the formation of the UN, when Hiss was publicly denounced as a Soviet agent. McCormick was just as hard on Hiss's accuser, Whittaker Chambers, *Time*'s "ex-Communist editor-in-chief," who set out to expose his one-time friend in the murky Communist underground of the 1930s. Chambers's professional associations did not go unremarked on. "See what you can find about the Luces and fashionable radicalism," McCormick ordered his men. He also offered $10,000, unsuccessfully, for the notorious "pumpkin papers" Chambers had stashed on his farm as confirming evidence of his charge against Hiss.[62]

For the Colonel, the Hiss case proved to be a scandalous trifecta, tarnishing not only Truman and the Luce press but his own party's presidential candidate as well. Dewey might logically have framed the fall contest around Chambers's explosive allegations. Instead, he served up weightless rhetorical meringues about national unity. McCormick thought he knew why: John Foster Dulles, Dewey's top foreign policy adviser and, if the polls were to be believed, the next secretary of state, had strongly recommended Hiss, his fellow establishmentarian, for the presidency of the prestigious Carnegie Endowment for International Peace. With Dewey "entirely too close to the Communist conspiracy," McCormick feared that both Dwight Green and Curley Brooks might be dragged down to defeat. The truth was just the opposite — Green and Brooks were a dead weight on the top of their party's ticket. But by the fall of 1948 there was no one around Tribune Tower to call McCormick back to reality.[63]

In any event, few other Republicans shared his worries. Encouraged by polls showing Dewey way out in front, most were counting their money while still at the table. The political establishment shook its head in collective astonishment when the *Tribune* on October 8 broke the news of a desperate White House improvisation. Acting on the advice of a couple of speechwriters, Truman had persuaded Chief Justice Fred Vinson to fly to Moscow and plead America's peaceful intentions before Stalin. It was hoped that such a dramatic gesture, coming in the final weeks of the campaign, might blunt the peace-at-any-price appeal of former vice president Henry Wallace, who was running to the left of Truman as the candidate of the Progressive party.

But what, the embattled Truman might well ask himself, does it profit a president if he gain the Upper East Side of New York and lose his faithful secretary of state? The danger was real, for Truman hadn't bothered to clear the Vinson mission with Secretary George Marshall, who was in Paris trying to negotiate a united western front against Soviet aggression aimed at the divided city of Berlin. Once he learned of the scheme, Marshall blasted it out of the water. Truman told Vinson to unpack his bags. A half-hour of nationwide radio time requested by the White House was quietly shelved — but not before the story leaked to Walter Trohan and the *Tribune.* Truman's political and diplomatic initiative turned to ashes in his mouth.

For once McCormick resisted the urge to gloat over a fallen adversary. Pat Maloney, made timid by his brush with disaster over the Midway revelations, buried Trohan's latest scoop deep inside the paper. Only a congratulatory message from an alert AP editor caused Maloney to give the story the front page in later editions.

On October 12, Truman brought his high-voltage campaign to Springfield. The *Tribune* chose the occasion to open fire on Adlai Stevenson ("a socialite and former New Deal diplomat") as the unwitting pawn of the Chicago Democratic machine. "This lousy, contemptible editorial really makes one mad," Stevenson grumbled to Alicia Patterson. Truth be told, he displayed impressive name-calling prowess of his own, denouncing "Parlor Car Pete" and pledging to fumigate the state capitol after ridding it of "Greed, Grime, and Green." Echoing Truman's aggressive courtship of black voters, Stevenson promised a state Fair Employment Practices Act and an end to discrimination in Illinois schools and hospitals.

McCormick went considerably further, in theory, telling Ralph McGill of the *Atlanta Constitution* that he would repeal the poll tax and other discriminatory devices used to suppress black voting in the South. Otherwise he held decided, if not advanced, views on American race relations. In August 1948, he complained to the *Tribune* writer Joe Ator that "the Association of Broadcasters — I have not got the exact name — have changed the words in a number of old songs to avoid the word 'darky.' " It was absurd, said the Colonel, "for the classics of our language to be distorted by stupid radio managers" in deference to "professional leaders of minorities" who were merely stirring up racial discord for profit. (As late as 1952, McCormick asked his personal physician whether white people receiving blood transfusions from blacks would develop racial characteristics to match.)[64]

In the closing days of the campaign, Truman carried his fight onto McCormick's home turf. Twenty-five thousand screaming partisans filled Chicago Stadium on the night of October 24 to hear the president hint darkly that a Republican victory would usher in a totalitarian state. The crowd lustily booed McCormick as the unnamed but obvious target of Truman's scorn. Dewey made no effort to defend his reluctant ally. On a campaign visit to Chicago that same month, McCormick confided to Alf Landon, Dewey acted "as though he was not in his right mind. The Governor and Senator met him at the station and he put them in the fourth and fifth cars in the procession behind some New York state policemen. At the meeting, he came on the stage just as he was introduced and left immediately afterwards without speaking to anybody." Judging from the tone of the campaign to date, McCormick told another correspondent, "there may have to be an amalgamation of the American Republicans and the American Democrats against New Deweyism."[65]

Notwithstanding these reservations, on Sunday, October 31, the *Tribune* told its readers to "Mark It Straight Republican." That evening a crew drawn from the production, mechanical, and editorial staffs gathered in a special news assembly room in the unfurnished Tribune Tower annex to rehearse election night procedures. Under ideal circumstances, election coverage is an editor's nightmare. Hundreds of races must be monitored, trends spotted, and analysis supplied even as the votes cascade in. Speed and flexibility are essential. For the *Tribune* in 1948, as for its Chicago competitors, the challenge was magnified by the continuing effect of the typographers' strike. The cumbersome process whereby so-called monster type was set on the *Tribune*'s VariTyper machines, then rushed to the engravers so they could make a page plate, meant going to press long before the polls closed. In practical terms, recalled

Harold Grumhaus, "it took a good two hours to get a story into the paper."[66]

This was not expected to be more than an annoyance on the night of November 2–3, 1948. So confident of the outcome was Arthur Sears Henning, the seventy-one-year-old dean of the Washington press corps, that he wrote the *Tribune* lead confirming Dewey's victory before 9 A.M. on election day. The first actual returns came from the Republican bastion of Kansas. They showed Dewey clinging to a small lead. Editorial writer Leavering Cartwright heard the news on a radio he had brought along to the press room. "Your guy's in," he told the printers, Democrats to a man.[67]

A different logic prevailed in the composing room, where Stew Owen appeared with a pasteup of the eight-column headline DEWEY DEFEATS TRUMAN, just as Harold Grumhaus concluded a dispiriting phone conversation with his wife, who was attending a Republican victory party that more nearly resembled a wake. Grumhaus could barely credit what she was telling him. To rebut her gloom, he described the first-edition headline calling the race for Dewey.

"You must be talking to the wrong people," replied Helen Grumhaus.

"Oh, no," Owen piped up. "Arthur is right on this one."[68]

Pat Maloney had his doubts. As the evening wore on, Maloney gave less thought to scheduled poll closings than to the scheduled departure of trains to points throughout Chicagoland. On such nights, the *Tribune* was held hostage to its distant readers; successive editions had to be ready to go when trains pulled out for Dubuque and Grand Rapids.* Accepting Henning's unqualified prediction had led Maloney to kill stories reporting sweeping Democratic gains in Congress. Now, with Truman opening a firm lead in the presidential contest, Maloney modified the front page to suggest an upset in the making. Henning was "aghast," said Maloney, but too much of a gentleman to raise a fuss. In any event, Owen's headline awarding victory to Dewey remained unchanged.[69]

At 9 P.M., Robert Taft called Walter Trohan seeking a *Tribune* forecast of the final vote in Illinois. What he heard only confirmed him in his suspicion of a Republican debacle. Still Maloney held back, desperately wanting to believe Henning's thesis that the late-breaking farm vote would save Dewey — and the *Tribune*. McCormick entertained fewer illusions. At home that evening, he took grim satisfaction in an outcome he had predicted for months. Convinced that Truman had won, he went to bed at eleven o'clock. Afterward he told Alf Landon that he had never seen the early *Tribune* headline.[70]

---

*Eleven separate fifty-four-page editions were printed that night, with their lead stories rewritten four or five times to reflect the historic upset in the making. In addition, over three hundred election bulletins were set in the process known as Graphotype.

It was nearly midnight when Maloney left the *Tribune*, about the same time that Henning went before WGN-TV cameras to reiterate his belief in Dewey's election. Don Maxwell, slipping into the editor's chair vacated by Maloney, took advantage of Henning's absence to junk the embarrassing headline hailing President Dewey. For the rest of the night the *Tribune* emphasized state and local results. These were unlikely to enhance McCormick's mood on Wednesday morning, for while Dewey lost Illinois by a scant 33,000 votes, both Green and Brooks were routed. Adlai Stevenson smashed all records, outpolling Green by 572,000 votes and accomplishing the near-miracle of carrying the heavily Republican downstate region. Nor was Curley Brooks spared. He lost his Senate seat to Paul Douglas by almost 400,000 votes.

For McCormick, the election was an unmitigated disaster. His protégés in Springfield and Washington had been tossed from power. The next Congress would be heavily Democratic, internationalist, and sympathetic to organized labor. Most galling of all was the sight of Truman winning photographic immortality by holding aloft a copy of an early *Tribune* edition with its famously inaccurate headline declaring Dewey's election. What a jubilant Truman flashed from the rear platform of his train during a brief stop in St. Louis — "That's one for the books" — was already well on its way to becoming a collector's item.

All told, over 1.1 million copies of the *Tribune* were printed on election night. Some 150,000 — not 30,000, as McCormick tried to claim later — contained the "Dewey Defeats Truman" banner. There was precedent for the faux pas: the *Chicago Daily News* had mistakenly called Charles Evans Hughes the winner over Woodrow Wilson in 1916. But that was for the historians. A popular legend had been hatched, arrogant pollsters humbled, the unreliable press given its comeuppance. A Milwaukee woman made her feelings known to McCormick succinctly, in a ten-word telegram that spoke for millions: "HA HA HA HA HA HA HA HA HA HA." "Truly, 1948 has been a bad year for the Colonel," rejoiced the *Montreal Star*. "No one has asked him to run for President. No one has asked him to invent a machine gun or a tank. No one has given him secrets to betray to his country's enemies ... no one, indeed, has paid any attention to him at all — and that is hardest of all." The Colonel had been predicting imminent ruin for America since 1933. In defeat he might find consolation of sorts, for with the Democratic lease on the White House renewed for another four years, reflected the *Star,* he could revert to his favorite role as the gloomy Cassandra of Michigan Avenue: "The older the fiddle, the better the tune."[71]

Truman was nearly as jaunty in thanking a friend at the *Chicago Sun-Times* who had sent him a copy of the famous photo taken at the *Tribune's* expense. "I imagine they would give all the tea in China if they had that back," chortled the president. "It has created a laugh all over the country, but I imagine that Bertie will be just as mean as ever." Others reached a similar conclusion. As the sun rose on the morning of November 3 and McCormick got his first look at the front page that so delighted Truman, the embarrassed *Tribune* executives asked themselves whether heads would roll. Answers were not long in coming. That day McCormick telephoned Arthur Sears Henning to inform him that his long career with the newspaper was over. As of Inauguration Day 1949, Walter Trohan would be in charge of the Washington bureau, with Henning pensioned off at full salary.[72]

Maloney survived the election night fiasco, but not for long. In 1950, using Maloney's deteriorating health as a cover, McCormick told his managing editor to take a year off before returning to the twenty-fourth floor as a troubleshooter on his personal assignments. The door was thus opened to Don Maxwell to become the last and, in the view of many around the *Tribune*, the least of McCormick's managing editors. As recalled by the *Tribune* correspondent Robert P. Howard, Maloney was "one of the great newspapermen of his time," a fatherly, approachable workaholic who had managed to gratify the Colonel's whims without surrendering either his self-respect or his personal integrity. Howard had less regard for Maxwell, "a Chamber of Commerce type" who lacked the broad education of his predecessor and who was reputed to have a heart that beat slower than normal, thereby enabling him to drink more than anyone else in a thirsty profession.[73]

Once ensconced in the managing editorship, Maxwell all but divorced himself from his reporters. His habit of schmoozing with potential sources did not sit well with the working press, any more than did his callous disregard for old friends who were no longer in a position to advance his interests. On election night 1948, Maxwell rubbed salt into Dwight Green's wounds by letting the defeated candidate know he was expecting a visit from Adlai Stevenson. "You don't lose much time, do you?" muttered Green.[74]

To be fair to Maxwell, he thought there was little time to lose. Playing to his constituency of one, he realized that his unconcealed ambition would bring him into conflict with Maryland McCormick, a rival whose hopes for the *Tribune* succession fluttered every time her astringent husband verbally wrote off one of his executives as "a boob." With the Colonel perceptibly aging, a shadowy competition pitted Maryland against a triumvirate composed of Maxwell; the advertising director, Chesser Campbell, a brilliant salesman who had more than doubled the paper's advertising revenue; and Howard Wood, the company controller, who had impressed McCormick with his wartime oversight of the Canadian operations and who assumed many of Campbell's responsibilities following the latter's mild heart attack in 1949. In time the three men joined forces to secure their inheritance, powerfully backed by Weymouth Kirkland and the *Tribune* law firm.

That the old monarch remained secure on his throne was made clear one morning when the *Tribune*'s pilot, Dick Prendergast, parked his twin-engine Aero Commander, dubbed *Tribby* by its owner, at the end of a dirt runway a couple hundred yards from the main house at Cantigny. (Before buying the plane in 1946, McCormick had briefly contemplated making the daily commute to work via helicopter, with a landing pad atop Tribune Tower.) On this particular day, Prendergast and his mechanic, Hal Irwin, shut down their engines before 8 A.M. Outside the Colonel's bedroom ran a stairway with an iron railing. If McCormick was up and out of the shower, his towel was customarily draped over the railing by Shin, his valet. After making certain that no towel was visible from their landing site, Prendergast and Irwin headed for a nearby raspberry patch. Here Irwin, a farm boy from Ohio, helped himself to several handfuls of fruit.

Within a few minutes Shin appeared. The Colonel would like the men to join him on the Madison Porch. When they arrived, the pilots found their employer in an expansive mood.

"Sit down, boys, and have some breakfast with me," said McCormick. Out of the kitchen emerged two huge bowls brimming with raspberries. The Colonel had seen everything, Prendergast realized, and intended to teach them a lesson.

"Aren't those good raspberries, Hal?" boomed McCormick, savoring his little joke — and his unlimited authority over the men pretending to enjoy their second meal of the morning.

"Yes, sir, Colonel, they are delicious!"[75]

From then on McCormick's raspberry patch was secure from early morning raids.

16

April Fool

"Remember that when you do foolish things, worse than foolish things will be ascribed to you."

— Theodore Roosevelt

A NYONE EXPECTING Cissy Patterson to go gently into that good night was in for a rude shock. In death as in life, the flamboyant Mrs. P. remained a hot topic of gossip for Washingtonians inured to the sensations of the Hiss case and Harry Truman's rackety comeback. Within weeks of her death, her daughter Felicia, resentful that the *Washington Times-Herald* had been left to the paper's seven top executives while she had to make do on an annual income of $25,000, announced her intention to contest the will. At issue was an estate conservatively valued at $16.5 million (the *Times-Herald* alone was estimated to be worth $8 million) and the final disposition of a personal legend beyond price.

Many a conversation that winter revolved around the identity of prospective witnesses — cabinet members, Supreme Court justices, diplomats, financiers, senators, and disaffected relatives — who might be summoned to give testimony concerning the dead woman's state of mind in the unhappy twilight of her existence. At the last minute, the show was called off when Felicia agreed to an out-of-court settlement of $400,000. A new snag developed, however, as it became clear that there wasn't enough cash in the estate to honor Cissy's individual and charitable bequests, establish new trusts, pay off heavy estate taxes, and dispose of the *Times-Herald* in keeping with her testamentary wishes.

The only way to raise the necessary funds was to sell at least part of her 13 percent stake in the McCormick-Patterson Trust. Yet Colonel McCormick seemed oblivious to the threat when, in February 1946, he met with administrators of the Patterson estate in Washington. To Frank Waldrop, one of the lucky *Times-Herald* executives christened the Seven Dwarves, the Colonel evinced little interest in the fate of Cissy's newspaper. Actually, his thoughts lay elsewhere. In Washington, he boarded his converted Flying Fortress, outfitted with seven-foot beds in the bomb bay and a swivel chair before the picture-window nose, for a survey of South America.[1]

Like all his postwar travels, this 14,000-mile journey was intended to generate publicity for McCormick and discomfort for his enemies. It was a roaring success on both counts. Broadcasting from Santiago, Chile, he praised the republican character of Chileans, who, unlike "North American snobs," didn't go into raptures at the sight of European nobility. He also got in a nasty crack at the expense of an American naval attaché in Valparaiso, whom McCormick blamed for failing to hoist his country's flag over the graves of some Yankee seamen killed in a nineteenth-century skirmish with the British.[2]

Tribune readers familiar with the Colonel's distaste for American citizens who debased themselves by pocketing foreign decorations might have been surprised to learn that he rarely, if ever, rejected such honors if they came his way. In Buenos Aires, he gratefully accepted from dictator Juan Perón a medal struck in recognition of his journalistic achievements. (He justified a special trip to Seoul to pick up the ancient Order of Teigook from the South Korean president, Syngman Rhee, by telling Walter Trohan that South Korea was only a small nation.) Although he liked to portray his semiroyal progresses as fact-finding expeditions, the Colonel showed little intellectual curiosity about and even less understanding of the foreign cultures he glimpsed at breakneck pace, through jaundiced eyes. He once sent home a postcard from Libya reading: "No water in river and country full of wops."

In his final years, McCormick's flair for the outrageous bordered on self-parody. On February 19, 1950, he embarked on a 24,000-mile odyssey spanning thirteen nations in Europe, North Africa, and Asia. Four days later, he told reporters in Madrid that the dangers of atomic warfare had been grossly exaggerated. "It would be hard for little, concentrated countries like England," he readily conceded, but "in the United States we have lots of space." One McCormick dispatch home, beginning "I have just come from an interview with General Franco," didn't bother to reveal what, if anything, the Spanish leader had said to him. The Colonel's radio listeners were only marginally better informed. McCormick said that Franco's hunting lodge reminded him of the Chicago eyesore inhabited by the late Potter Palmer. He credited the generalissimo with the invention of dive-bombing and, aided by his no less original German and Italian allies, the blitzkrieg.[3]

McCormick denounced Spanish bullfighting as an insult to civilization. Going on to Cairo, he insulted the French Fourth Republic as "atheist and anarchic" and openly lamented the fate of France's "greatest hero," the senile collaborationist Marshal Pétain, exiled after the war to a remote island off the French coast. He did have the manners to wait until he reached the Pakistani capital, Karachi, to criticize the recently adopted Egyptian constitution as "a complete phony."[4]

The Indians, who had spurned their British colonial masters and joined the republican fraternity in 1947, received McCormick as a kindred spirit. Prime Minister Nehru went out of his way to compliment the *Tribune*'s anti-imperialist line. Yet even here, McCormick insisted on playing the Ugly American. In Bombay, for example, he modestly presented himself as a simple "reporter looking for news." So far, so good. He proceeded to spoil the favorable impression by confessing his total ignorance of the hotly disputed province of Kashmir. A United Press of India representative tried to set him straight as to the larger significance of the contested border between India and Pakistan. McCormick, tired and bored, said none of it mattered, or mattered enough to rouse Americans, who took little interest in events far from home. That his own thoughts were stateside became brutally clear when he was asked about Truman's civil rights program. Before this racially sensitive audience, McCormick condemned the presidential initiative as "a new form of slavery." Someone inquired whether India's neutralist ambassador to the United States was welcome at the White House. "I wouldn't know," replied the Colonel. "I am not welcome there myself."[5]

A world tour with the Colonel was unintentionally educational, if hardly relaxing. "I'll never forget one time — oh, we'd had a rough time with Percy Wood [a *Tribune* correspondent]," Maryland McCormick remembered. Hopscotching around India, Ceylon, and the Orient had left everyone on board the winged *Chicago Tribune* feeling tense and irritable. "The Colonel had gotten mad about something the pilot did . . . so we made a ten-hour trip" — in the process eliminating a planned stop in Iran — "which is quite a trip on that old B-17." On parting from their guide in Istanbul, Maryland said, "I'll bet you're going to get tight tonight." "I would," replied the frazzled Wood, "except I'm afraid you'll be back again. I'm going to wait until tomorrow night."[6]

Maryland complained that everyone else in their traveling party was deaf; she was losing her voice from screaming all the time. The Colonel was unapologetic. "I can't hear bells and I'm glad of it," he informed E. R. Noderer, a *Tribune* correspondent in charge of advance preparations for McCormick's lightning trip to Greece. The visitor played havoc with

Noderer's carefully devised itinerary. He was cordial enough to King George and Queen Fredericka, with whom he took tea at the royal palace, which he likened to a New England summer hotel. Less fortunate was Lieutenant General James Van Fleet, entrusted with coordinating U.S. military assistance to the regular Greek army in its ongoing battle with Communist rebels. The general was in the middle of a briefing when McCormick got up and walked out, leaving Van Fleet "with his mouth wide open, pointing at the situation map."[7]

Conduct once excused as charmingly eccentric was now bizarrely self-centered. On his first morning in Athens, McCormick wandered aimlessly around the royal suite of the Grand Bretagne Hotel clad in pajama bottoms, shirt, and tie. He ordered no breakfast but indulged himself, like a child, by plucking sausages off his wife's plate. He canceled his radio broadcast, telling Noderer he couldn't possibly stay up until midnight, the only time available on the wireless and cable services. He objected to the housing arrangements: it was wildly extravagant, said McCormick, for every member of his party to have a room of his own. To begin with, his secretary, Dorothy Murray, could sleep on a cot in front of the fireplace. "What?" shrieked Maryland. "And walk through our rooms to go to the bathroom?" Miss Murray retained her private quarters.[8]

McCormick announced his intention of taking a postbreakfast nap. Noderer, his services temporarily dispensed with, repaired to the hotel bar. The reporter was raising a whiskey glass to his lips when suddenly he spied "a great enormous fellow," wearing dark glasses, standing outside on the street corner. Noderer put down his glass and hastened to join his employer. "Who was the king of Greece in 1915?" inquired the Colonel.

A much greater test of Noderer's local knowledge was posed that evening, as McCormick made an early exit from a cocktail party in his honor at the American embassy. He had been invited by the prime minister to submit an article containing his impressions of the country, he told Noderer. But he was scheduled to leave Athens in the morning. "I don't have time to write that story," said the Colonel. "You pretend you're me, and you write it." There was a catch: "I want to see the story before I leave."

Noderer deposited his boss in the hotel restaurant before retreating to his room, where, fortified by five brandy-and-sodas, he banged out a wholly fictitious travelogue by 4 A.M. More than an excellent mimic, Noderer faithfully reproduced every McCormick bias and jingoistic kink. He pointed out the superiority of Greek highways built with American foreign aid to roads back in Illinois and blamed this on "the English wing of the State Department." Waxing poetic under the influence of brandy and the clock, he had the Colonel, "as I take off across the ancient battlefields," mouth the revolutionary verse of Byron:

> The mountains look on Marathon
> And Marathon looks at the sea;
> And musing there an hour alone,
> I dreamed that Greece might still be free.

At six in the morning, Noderer was back in McCormick's suite to receive a nod of approval for his literary marathon. Before leaving for the airport, Maryland dispatched the reporter to a nearby market to buy her a sponge as a souvenir of their Greek stopover. "You paid too much for it," she squawked to the reporter on his return.

Her husband used rougher language in rebuking anyone who fell short of his expectations. Returning from another European jaunt in March 1952, he landed at Gander, Newfoundland, in the middle of the night. No customs or immigration officials were on hand, nor were there ground crews available to refuel the Flying Fortress as it sat motionless in the frigid Canadian night. To speed the Colonel on his way, Terrence Flahiff, the *Tribune*'s man in Ottawa, interrupted the sleep of the minister of transport. The needed fuel magically appeared, but not before a wrathful McCormick appeared at the front of the plane spewing aspersions on the ancestry of Newfoundlanders ("in-bred bastards"). As the angry publisher departed from Canadian airspace, he left the offended inhabitants of Newfoundland to derive such consolation as they could from the knowledge that he had traduced civilizations more ancient and culturally advanced than theirs.[9]

✧ 2

As the Colonel approached his biblical allotment of three-score years plus ten, his frequent absences from Chicago contributed to a sense of drift at the *Tribune*. By the summer of 1949, the last thing McCormick needed or desired was additional responsibility. Leave it to Cissy Patterson to exact revenge from her grave by shackling her elderly cousin to a failing newspaper he didn't want in a city he couldn't abide. Under the terms of her will, the Seven Dwarves were free to run the paper as they saw fit. And if, as Mrs. P. no doubt had suspected, seven bosses proved to be six too many, the group was at liberty to place the *Times-Herald* on the market.

As it happened, there was no shortage of prospective buyers for what Howard Wood called "a fairly profitable little scandal sheet," beginning with young William Randolph Hearst, Junior, who was eager to rectify his father's mistake in selling out to Cissy in 1939. At the start of July 1949, the name of another, more ominous contender surfaced. During his long, trying career as Cissy's foil, Eugene Meyer had found that running the

Washington Post was more prestigious than profitable. Cissy's death and her tangled estate gave him the opening he had dreamed of. Executors of the estate had to come up with millions to pay taxes and honor bequests. The Seven Dwarves, lacking the resources to operate the *Times-Herald* on their own, were anxious to convert their paper legacies into cash. Meyer signified his willingness to purchase both the *Times-Herald* and Cissy's shares in the McCormick-Patterson Trust. Once the deal was consummated, the Seven Dwarves could expect a lucrative early retirement. The *Post* would rid itself of a pesky competitor and achieve overnight a position of dominance in Washington. And for the first time in his long career, McCormick would find himself saddled with a minority partner.[10]

It was a nightmare scenario he could no longer shrug off. On July 15, McCormick packed *Tribune* directors, executives, and their wives into three small planes and flew off to Manitoulin Island in Lake Huron, the site of a major timber limit recently added to the holdings of the Ontario Paper Company. What transpired next was eerily reminiscent of May 1914, when Jim Keeley had executed his midnight betrayal while McCormick was off looking for timber in Quebec. This time it was Maryland McCormick who was felled by illness; she had stayed behind in Chicago to undergo an emergency appendectomy. Also in Chicago was Weymouth Kirkland, who phoned the island with alarming news: Meyer was close to a deal, with potentially disastrous implications for the Tribune Company.[11]

The island retreat broke up. McCormick and his directors returned to Chicago. At a hastily convened meeting on July 18, they authorized spending $4.5 million for the *Times-Herald*. Out of his own pocket, McCormick paid $1.05 million for 30 units of the McCormick-Patterson Trust. Another 70 shares were parceled out among the Seven Dwarves, with most of the remaining 172 units marked for resale to employees of the Tribune Company.

Just how great a sacrifice this entailed emerged from a gloomy prospectus of the *Times-Herald* drawn up at McCormick's request by Walter Trohan. At 278,000 copies each weekday, the paper enjoyed the biggest circulation in Washington. But the raw numbers masked serious weakness. At one time or another, Cissy had managed to offend virtually every leading advertiser in Washington, with the result that her paper ranked third in ad revenue behind the *Star* and Meyer's *Post*. Trohan claimed that the *Times-Herald* under the Seven Dwarves had no soul or life blood. Its staff was mediocre, its columnists dismal, and its plant badly in need of modernizing. Yet he also acknowledged that the paper filled an important niche as the only sheet in town that could be counted on to oppose the Truman administration.[12]

In the end, the sale of the *Times-Herald* to McCormick was dictated by simple self-interest. Under McCormick, the paper would escape the death sentence sure to be imposed if it fell into Meyer's hands. A thousand jobs would be saved. And conservative Washingtonians could sleep soundly, knowing that in the morning a fresh blast of anti-Truman indignation would be on the doorstep.

Time, always glad to stick rhetorical pins in the Colonel, detected a certain irony in his belated invasion of the Washington market, observing that "He has always regarded anything east of Gary, Indiana, as a foreign country." News of the sale leaked out on the evening of July 20. Walter Trohan gleefully conveyed to McCormick the reactions voiced by guests at a dinner party hosted by Arthur Krock of the *New York Times*:

> Clark Clifford — Consternation
> John Foster Dulles — Horror
> Sen. [J.W.] Fulbright — Dejection
> Sen. Taft — Unconcealed delight.[13]

Trohan also reported glad tidings from Republicans in Congress and "almost universal rejoicing" in the defense establishment. A July 23 *Tribune* editorial linking the *Times-Herald* purchase to the "fatal ratification" of NATO by the Senate spelled out McCormick's unreconstructed nationalism. His new venture was intended as "an outpost of American principles" comparable to young George Washington's Fort Necessity (he overlooked the sad fate visited upon the pathetic stockade erected by the callow Washington during the French and Indian War). Having compared himself to the father of his country, McCormick was quick to take credit for the Civil War as well, reminding readers that "the *Tribune* was the most influential factor in making Lincoln president and in preserving the Union. It will now become the most important single factor in rescuing it."[14]

That McCormick had no intention of being a caretaker publisher became obvious during his first visit to Washington after the paper changed hands. A reporter reminded him that the nation's capital was widely thought to resemble a madhouse. "Yes," agreed McCormick, "and the inmates are running it. I find that the budget is not the only thing that's unbalanced in Washington." He intended to make people forget Cissy. To Howard Wood he expressed an intention to rename the paper the *Washington Tribune*. Wood broached the suggestion to the *Times-Herald*'s general manager, William Shelton, who counterproposed the *Washington Times-Herald-Tribune*. "Craziest idea I ever heard of," said Wood. "How are you going to sell the *Washington Times-Herald-Tribune* on the street?" Faced with such practical impediments, McCormick reluctantly dropped the idea. The *Times-Herald* retained its familiar name, even as it struggled to find a new identity.[15]

✧ 3

To command his latter-day Fort Necessity, McCormick turned to his niece Bazy Miller and her husband, Peter. Bazy was just twenty-eight at the time, her husband thirty. The Millers were the parents of two small children, to whom they were devoted. McCormick guessed that the jaded capital would be intrigued by these fresh young faces. Moreover, he thought that the Millers had shown "real capacity" in their two and a half years as publishers of the LaSalle, Illinois, *News-Tribune*, circulation 13,055.[16]

Both Millers were politically sound. In 1948, Bazy had taken the lead in organizing Twenties for Taft clubs throughout the Midwest. Much later, McCormick would say that he had installed his niece at the *Times-Herald* in order to show the dynastic flag. Real power, he contended in a 1951 court deposition taken as part of an unsuccessful libel suit by Drew Pearson, was to be reserved to such holdover *Times-Herald* executives as Frank Waldrop. But this was a retroactive claim, which scarcely concealed a much larger truth, namely, McCormick's refusal to empower anyone to exercise over the *Times-Herald* the more or less benevolent dictatorship that defined the *Tribune*. At the outset, the patronizing Colonel told Bazy that she would doubtlessly refrain from making changes "until you are thoroughly familiar with the paper. At the same time," he added, contradicting his stated wish to avoid management decisions, "I do not see any $150.00 a week value in 'Little Abner.' "[17]

Out of the other corner of his mouth, McCormick issued instructions to Waldrop. Boasting that he had in Carey Orr, Joseph Parrish, and Daniel Holland "the three best cartoonists in America," the Colonel decided to reproduce for readers in the nation's capital the biting front-page cartoons for which the *Tribune* was famous. He cautioned Waldrop against relying too greatly on editorials from the *New York Daily News*. These, he said without a hint of self-consciousness, were written "to be snappy and not accurate."[18]

Bazy took up her new post in the first week of October 1949. "I know you are taking a big chance sending me down here," she wrote to her uncle, "and I certainly hope you will be pleased and proud of your decision." Within a month, McCormick was egging her on to the kind of bitterly personal feud that was his stock in trade. At lunch with Virginia's reactionary senator Harry Byrd, the Colonel told Bazy, the discussion had touched on the violent internationalism of New York papers like the *Star*, successor to the ill-fated *PM*, and the venerable *Times*. McCormick thought he had an explanation. It all stemmed from "a Jew complex," he wrote, "perhaps social ambition. Iphigene Sulzberger is full of it. While she is an ardent professional Jew in the newspaper, she tries desperately to associate with Christians of social position and gets herself invited to Hobe Sound, which she cannot join." Because "you don't know your way around," McCormick counseled his niece, the present was no time to go looking for fights — "but perhaps if Meyer gives you one on international politics, you can comment on the weakness of a newspaper run for social ambition."[19]

Instead of this, Bazy came to have a special appreciation for Meyer's son-in-law, Phil Graham, after Graham tipped her off to the presence of a numbers game in the *Times-Herald* press room. The green Mrs. Miller feared sabotage when her pressmen produced an embarrassing and possibly costly typographical error. The paper went after Drew Pearson as a prominent New Deal columnist, a word that accidentally came out in print as *communist*. Amid talk of lawsuits, the liberal muckracker showed himself every bit as misogynistic as his ideological opposite in Tribune Tower. Summing up his most condescending manner, Pearson absolved the *Times-Herald* publisher of any deliberate smear attempt. "I used to dandle Bazy on my knee," he said.[20]

In January 1950, Frank Waldrop tendered his resignation over a minor dispute. McCormick nearly came unglued. He hated, he said, to "deplete" his own newspaper by sending an executive editor to Washington. Bazy promised to work out the organizational tangles, but McCormick went ahead on his own and successfully appealed to Waldrop to rescind his decision. Then, having denied that he could spare a senior man from Chicago, the Colonel assigned Pat Maloney, his recently retired managing editor, to be his eyes and ears around the *Times-Herald*. Maloney's hovering presence, ostensibly justified as a friendly source of assistance, was interpreted by many as a vote of no confidence in Bazy.[21]

Determined to remake Cissy's paper into a southern *Tribune*, the Colonel became ever more peremptory in his commands. Meyer's *Post* remained the object of his fixation, as McCormick made clear in a January 23, 1950, directive to his niece: "Run an editorial saying *Washington Post* is entirely too close to Hiss element, to express any opinions on public affairs until it has cleaned house itself. Put up the flag the next day." Front-page cartoons, Old Glory in the upper lefthand corner, an editorial policy that made the *Times-Herald* a singular bundle of well-focused rage: by the beginning of 1950, few Washingtonians would have been surprised to find a new masthead proclaiming Cissy's hand-me-down the World's Second Greatest Newspaper.

✧ 4

That same month, the media critic A. J. Liebling took three issues of *The New Yorker* to convey in full his caustic impressions of the *Tribune*, formed during a month the writer had spent immersed in Chicago's newspaper culture. Conceding that a daily encounter with the World's Greatest Newspaper was without doubt "the most invigorating feature of life" in America's second city, the outside observer implicitly questioned the wisdom of exporting McCormick-style journalism to the banks of the Potomac. In a world awash with change, where foreign dangers lurked in every news cycle, the Colonel offered the balm of certitude and the reassuring conviction that there was indeed no place like home.

Often this came at the expense of accurate reporting, since, according to Liebling, the *Tribune* rarely permitted news developments to interfere with its editorial intuitions. At the least, Chicagoans comparing the *Tribune* with the *Daily News* or *Sun-Times* were bound to experience some confusion; the only points on which the Colonel and his rivals were in agreement were those scored at basketball and hockey games. Faithful *Tribune* readers, meanwhile, were unsure which posed the greatest menace to the American Way of Life, Wall Street or Downing Street. In December 1949, McCormick gave page-one treatment to a water shortage afflicting residents of the Big Apple. He seized on the city's emergency conservation plan to reinforce Gotham's already seedy image: 8 MILLION SET FOR B.O. PLENTY DAY IN NEW YORK. Next to New York, "Truman Taxes," and shiftless Europeans milking Uncle Sam for Marshall Plan dollars, McCormick aimed his deadliest barbs at Britain, consistently portrayed in the *Tribune* as a nation of pink-coated, horn-blowing, supercilious bankrupts. Rare indeed was an issue of the *Tribune* without a derogatory story or two from Liebling's "chalk-cliffed hell." BISHOP ADVISES BRITAIN TO CURB ITS POPULATION introduced a clerical denunciation of the welfare state and the growing ranks of idle, slovenly Britons for whom every day, presumably, was B.O. Plenty Day. TAXES SO HEAVY KING'S NEPHEW MUST SELL LAND reported the Earl of Harewood's intention to put one fourth of his 25,000 acres on the market.[22]

Liebling thought the *Tribune* without peer in its use of cartoons to manipulate reader opinion. He was particularly taken with a front-page drawing, in eye-grabbing colors, that portrayed an impoverished Uncle Sam selling pencils against a backdrop teeming with crude ethnic stereotypes: the fat Dutchman in wooden shoes, an arrogant Frenchman, and the inevitable John Bull crying "Sucker" at the expense of his Yankee benefactor. Foreign aid, the *Tribune* insinuated, was part of a Communist scheme to pauperize Americans; "then Stalin can take over without firing a shot, or spending a 19 cent ruble."

Politics aside, Liebling detected in the *Tribune* a surprising tabloid sensibility, as if the ghost of Joe Patterson had returned to the twenty-fourth floor to put into practice the grimy commercial lessons he had learned on the streets of New York. Practicing the same blatant lack of objectivity for which he faulted the *Tribune*, Liebling attributed much of McCormick's success to his habit of "reaching out all over the world for entertaining crimes and then playing them as if they had happened in the lobby of the Tribune Tower." One result was to encourage a false belief among Chicagoans that more humans than pigs were slaughtered in their city. A special target of the Colonel's ire was the Illinois State Training School for Boys, a home for delinquent adolescents distressingly located a few miles from Cantigny. McCormick looked on the school as a criminal breeding ground only slightly less fearsome than Alcatraz. Having successfully campaigned for a high fence to be built around the school grounds, both to keep the boys inside and to drive their social-worker superintendent to quit, the *Tribune* kept a highly publicized tally of subsequent escapes to prove its claim that a fence was worthless without guard towers.[23]

To illustrate further what he called the paper's blend of "blood and fudge sundae," Liebling zeroed in on a single pre-Christmas front page, dominated by an eight-column streamer about the murder of a University of Iowa coed, who had been strangled by her sweetheart, a student of abnormal psychology, in his rooming house, "the ironically named Empty Arms." A less salacious, and correspondingly less prominent, headline attested to the robbery of the Palace Theater, and a full-color reproduction, three columns wide, of the painting *Madonna and Child* accompanied the first installment of Charles Dickens's *Life of Our Lord*. The page also included the heart-warming story of a small white dog, "from New York, of all places," that had received treatment at that city's Bellevue Hospital; an article about the tragic demise of some unsuspecting Californians (BIG ROCK SLAB FALLS ON PICNIC PARTY; 4 KILLED); and the latest dose of seasonal uplift from the "politeness" reporter, whose assignment was to roam Chicago streets in search of people who embodied the Christmas spirit.

Liebling's polemic was as selective as it was amusing. Yet he was too shrewd a satirist to settle for easy laughs. On the surface, the *Tribune* retained its cranky originality, the byproduct of McCormick's distrust of the world beyond Chicagoland. On closer look, however, the paper was losing its distinctiveness, as lines between tabloid journalism and the more traditional school of reporting blurred. By the early 1950s, it was becoming obvious that declining readership would lead to more sensationalism than the paper's conservative audience was accustomed to. McCormick summed up the new era in a seemingly casual remark to his Sunday editor, Mike Kennedy. At Kennedy's urging, the Colonel had carefully reviewed a women's fashion supplement that some thought was unnecessarily racy.

McCormick disagreed. "You can cut the blouse as low as you want," said the publisher who had once banned the depiction of human feet as aesthetically offensive, "only don't show the pink."[24]

✧ 5

Another kind of coarsening was overtaking American politics in the wake of Dewey's unexpected 1948 defeat and escalating fears of Communist subversion in bureaucratic and academic circles. Republicans made irresponsible by their continuing exclusion from the White House clashed bitterly with Democrats who had grown arrogant during their twenty-year monopoly of the executive branch. Foreign events added to domestic anxieties, spawning the impression of monolithic communism laying seige to vast parts of what would soon be known as the free world. Stalin exploded his first atomic bomb in September 1949. Before the year ended, Mao Tse-tung and his Communist followers had chased Chiang Kai-shek's Nationalist government from the Chinese mainland and forced Chiang to reestablish himself and his shadow regime on the island of Formosa. In the third week of January 1950, a New York jury convicted Alger Hiss, not on espionage charges but for having lied in denying knowledge of his original accuser, Whittaker Chambers.

Sensation followed sensation. Ten days after the Hiss verdict seemingly confirmed the existence of a Communist spy ring in New Deal Washington, Truman revealed plans for the United States to build a hydrogen bomb — and the British physicist Klaus Fuchs, part of the western team responsible for harnessing the atom's destructive power, was arrested on charges of spying for the Soviet Union. REDS GET OUR BOMB PLANS! howled the *Tribune* on February 4. J. Edgar Hoover exploited popular fears by telling members of Congress that the United States sheltered over half a million Communists and Communist sympathizers. So unstable was the political atmosphere by February that a single match, struck without regard for the consequences, could detonate civil liberties and civilized discourse with nuclear force.

Enter Senator Joseph R. McCarthy of Wisconsin, the bombastic, gamy grand inquisitor, whose name would become synonomous with fifties Red-baiting. Long before McCarthy became an ism, he was being observed closely by Willard Edwards, the *Tribune*'s Capitol Hill correspondent, who became, by his own admission, virtually an extension of the McCarthy staff. His reckless friend, said Edwards, was "irresponsible in the way that an overgrown boy is careless when his size belies his years." Far from having a plan to dominate the republic, McCarthy "never at 9 P.M. at night knew what he would be doing at 10 A.M. the next day." The junior senator from Wisconsin evinced something of the blowsy charm of that earlier demogogue Big Bill Thompson. This alone guaranteed that he and the Colonel would never become personally close. The aristocratic McCormick could only cringe at the crude practical joker who liked to subject visitors to his modest southeast Washington apartment to a humiliating game of his own devising. Victims were told to balance a marble on their forehead before trying to slot the marble into a funnel tucked inside their trouser belt. "At a strategic moment," said Edwards, "Joe would pour water into the funnel, to the accompaniment of raucous laughter."[25]

Up to this time, McCarthy and McCormick had met just once. As recounted by his biographer, Thomas Reeves, McCarthy had paid a brief visit to Tribune Tower in September 1946 at the urging of Jim Murphy, the Colonel's Milwaukee correspondent. Afterward, McCarthy replied, "Hell, no!" when asked by reporters whether he had been won over to McCormick's isolationist views as a result of their encounter. He told the truth. Before Republican audiences, McCarthy endorsed the United Nations and explicitly disavowed "the old America First crowd." He got *Tribune* support anyway, since the paper hated the domestic liberalism of his primary opponent, Phillip LaFollette, even more than it despised McCarthy's global outlook.[26]

McCarthy narrowly defeated LaFollette in the primary. He went on to win a landslide victory in the fall. For the next few years, "Tailgunner Joe" conducted himself in ways that stamped him as anything but the Colonel's soulmate. In the Senate, McCarthy quickly became identified with his party's internationalist wing. He solidified his liberal reputation by supporting Harold Stassen in the 1948 presidential race. He had powerful enemies within Wisconsin, however, especially in the press, and his 1952 reelection was anything but assured. This explained why, by the start of 1950, he was trolling for hot-button issues with which to ease the road to a second term. McCarthy briefly considered championing the unbuilt St. Lawrence Seaway, only to conclude that the gigantic public works project lacked political sex appeal. He dismissed as financially untenable a scheme to provide elderly Americans with $100 a month in federal pensions.

More encouraging was the public response to a series of anti-Communist speeches McCarthy delivered late in 1949. Yet even in the wake of the Hiss and Fuchs cases, Tailgunner Joe was inclined to hedge his bets. Accepting a string of second-tier Lincoln Day appearances before the Republican faithful, commencing on February 9, 1950, in Wheeling, West Virginia, McCarthy commissioned from his Senate staff a sober text addressing the nation's housing needs. As a crowd-pleasing alternative, he sought outside help in crafting a second speech, capitalizing on recent allegations of Communist influence in the State Department. His electrifying charge of diplomatic treason, first leveled in Wheeling, rested on flimsy evidence, much of it supplied by Ed Nellor, a *Washington Times-Herald* reporter who had covered the Hiss case, and George Waters, another *Times-Herald* man, whom McCarthy later hired as his press secretary.

About February 1, Waters approached Willard Edwards, an old friend and true believer who unhesitatingly turned over a thick file of his own work, including a contemporary series in the *Tribune* that featured the names of fifty-seven individual suspects, described by Edwards as "a libel-proof list of persons found guilty in court or official hearings of Communist party membership." One of Edwards's clippings detailed a 1946 attempt to screen some 3,000 State Department employees, of whom 285 were considered problem cases. Of the latter group, 79 were actually denied employment. Allowing for a slight mathematical error, this is how McCarthy came up with his sensational bill of complaint against 205 "known Communists" currently on the State Department payroll.[27]

McCarthy later modified his claims, telling reporters in Denver that he had in his possession the names of 207 "bad risks"; by the time he reached Reno, he had retreated to Edwards's original list of 57 "card-carrying Communists." For the meticulous Edwards, even this claim sacrificed accuracy for notoriety; American Communists had long since been told to dispense with formal membership cards.

❖ 6

Like his grandfather before him, McCormick suffered from encroaching deafness. His refusal to wear a hearing aid was imputed to an old man's vanity. It might just as well be said of the Colonel that he heard only what he wanted to, filtering out unpleasant facts that might divert him from his foregone conclusions. He had been casually listening to McCarthy for four years, not caring much for the senator's internationalist song. He grew noticeably more appreciative once McCarthy began lobbing charges of disloyalty against the Truman administration. Indeed, by 1950, McCormick might reasonably argue that it was McCarthy who had been converted to the *Tribune*'s outlook, not the other way around.

In truth, the Colonel cared little whether McCarthy caught any Communists in his net. Shrewder than the senator, he perceived a yawning gulf between McCarthy's professed belief in the projection of U.S. power overseas and his verbal pummeling of those under Roosevelt and Truman who had been the architects of American assertiveness. By knocking the props out from under the bipartisan foreign policy that was anathema to the *Tribune*, the senator from Wisconsin served McCormick's purposes. That he also helped to discredit the foreign policy establishment symbolized by Secretary of State Dean Acheson, the tweedy, elegant Grotonian who had refused to turn his back on his old friend Alger Hiss, made him a useful partner in a defamatory tag team.

On May 28, 1950, the *Tribune* borrowed a page out of McCarthy's book, alleging the existence of "a secret government" answerable to Justice Felix Frankfurter, New York senator Herbert Lehman, and former secretary of the treasury Henry Morgenthau. The plot thickened as the *Tribune* noted the defense of Hiss, another Frankfurter protégé, mounted by the *Washington Post*, whose president and publisher, Phillip Graham, was himself a former law clerk of Frankfurter's. Complaints that the article smacked of anti-semitism left the Colonel unmoved. His editors must not sound too conciliatory in their response to such criticism, he wrote, "because it will look as if we had been browbeaten. We do not intend to stand for censorship in the name of nondiscrimination."[28]

The Korean War, which began in the last week of June 1950 with the unprovoked invasion of South Korea by 90,000 troops from the Communist north, left McCormick sputtering with indignation — not at the North Koreans but at Harry Truman. The president, charged the *Tribune*, longed to be a dictator. Lawmakers should not indulge him in his fantasies. "The invasion of Korea should warn Congress against giving Mr. Truman the authority he was asking for to call conscripts to camp whenever he feels like doing so," McCormick editorialized on June 26. Declaring the Korean peninsula not worth the loss of a single American soldier, McCormick would extend sympathy and nothing more to the beleaguered South Koreans.

Truman maintained that the United States was not at war but was engaged in "a police action," a euphemism soon disproved by the enormous scale of U.S. response to Communist aggression. To McCormick, the real battleground was constitutional. Only Congress, he argued, could sanction American military involvement abroad, yet Truman seemed determined to fight an undeclared war on the Korean peninsula. Their differences did not end there. To the president, more than South Korean freedom was at stake. As a warm admirer of Woodrow Wilson, Truman was determined to uphold the principle of collective peacekeeping embodied in the United Nations.

McCormick, who had learned a very different lesson from the Wilsonian crusade, feared the loss of South Korean sovereignty to northern invaders far less than the loss of American sovereignty to the UN. He found himself badly outnumbered, and in the unlikeliest of places. Gloomily, he revealed that Ann Hooper, his wife's youngest daughter, was "war-minded" enough to volunteer as a nurse on the front. Ann's mother wanted him to conduct her personally to the battlefront, but McCormick refused. "I have had enough war," he wrote dejectedly.[29]

The only heartening news out of Washington was of Bazy Miller, whose progress at the *Times-Herald* vindicated McCormick's judgment even as it appeared to secure the *Tribune* succession. Writing to her uncle on July 17, Bazy depicted a capital city awash in confusion. From Defense Secretary Louis Johnson she had learned that the war's ultimate objectives seemed to fluctuate with the shifting fortunes of opposing armies.

July 30, 1950, marked McCormick's seventieth birthday. "I will hope to battle it along for a few years more," he assured Robert Taft. At the formal celebration, held at Cantigny, Weymouth Kirkland provoked knowing laughter when he explained how he had gotten along with the Colonel for so many years: when a question was put to him, said Kirkland, he asked his old friend what answer he wanted to hear — and then repeated it verbatim.[30]

McCormick used the occasion to show unmistakable signs of favor toward Bazy. While a guest at Cantigny, she stayed in the room her father had occupied as a boy. Knowing of her interest in horses, the Colonel presented her with an Arabian stallion, originally a gift to him from Saudi Arabia's King Ibn-Saud. She reciprocated, flattering McCormick on his weekly radio broadcasts and thanking him profusely for hours of instruction from *Tribune* executives.

The surest way to win McCormick's confidence was to share his political obsessions. In the summer of 1950, this meant aiding Joe McCarthy at every opportunity. By now, even some McCarthy well-wishers were starting to have second thoughts about the senator's tactics, if not his objectives. Walter Trohan declined to serve as a go-between when the FBI asked him to pass sensitive information from its files to the notoriously indiscreet McCarthy. Willard Edwards, in contrast, buried his doubts lest he forfeit his privileged status with McCarthy's office and the exclusive stories that flowed his way as a result. "All this time, the *Tribune* was editorializing vociferously in behalf of McCarthy," Edwards rationalized in a 1976 interview. "I would have appreciated some consultation on the subject, but not once in four years did an editorial writer call me to ask a question."[31]

In the resulting vacuum, the *Tribune*'s representatives in Washington were left to divine the wishes of their increasingly distracted boss. This was harder than one might imagine, for even the Colonel's ideological compass could waver under the magnetic force of personality. For example, his lifelong admiration of General Douglas MacArthur slightly mitigated his hostility to the Korean misadventure. MacArthur's daring amphibious assault on Inchon in September 1950 was a master stroke that effectively reversed the course of the war. The *Tribune* heaped laurels on the victor of Inchon. Just as predictably, it belittled Truman for restraining MacArthur from carrying the war to North Korea's Chinese allies.

For McCormick, politics remained war by other means. He resolved to crush Senate majority leader Scott Lucas, an Illinois Democrat, at the polls that fall, a task made immeasurably simpler by an old-fashioned police corruption scandal that tarred the Cook County Democratic leader, Jacob Avery, and tainted the entire Democratic ticket. To oust Lucas, McCormick was willing to make peace with Republican congressman Everett Dirksen, whose earlier flirtation with internationalist heresy was now forgiven in light of his strident attacks on Lucas and the alleged Communist conspiracy gripping Washington.

The long arm of the *Tribune* reached into Maryland politics as well. There Bazy Miller spearheaded a bare-knuckles campaign to retire McCarthy's nemesis, Millard Tydings. At first it looked like an impossible challenge; Tydings, a Democratic conservative, had survived an attempted purge by FDR in 1938, and his GOP opponent, a Baltimore lawyer named John Marshall Butler, was a political unknown whose most distinguishing claim was that he *looked* like a senator. Yet Butler could boast of some powerful friends, led by McCarthy himself, who raised money for the Republican candidate, campaigned in the state, and lent his entire Senate staff to the cause. His significant involvement in the race merely complimented the efforts of Mrs. Miller and the *Times-Herald*. It was Bazy who secured the appointment of Jon M. Jonkel, a Chicago public relations man well known to McCormick, as Butler's campaign manager.

Also imported from Chicago was the Colonel's faithful emissary to that city's black community, a one-man rotten borough with the marvelously baroque name of Roscoe Conklin Simmons. As the nephew of Booker T. Washington, Simmons had proved his value in propagandizing for Robert Taft and other McCormick favorites. Now he moved smartly to exploit Tydings's weakness among black Marylanders, making over fifty speeches on behalf of the Butler Campaign. If McCormick disapproved of any of this, it was a well-kept secret. In mid-October he expressed to Bazy the pleasure he felt "to see you making good and to know that you will carry the flag into the next generation."[32]

Simmons, for one, was quick to award the lion's share of credit for Butler's unexpected victory to "the great Bazy," whose appearances at Republican headquarters in Baltimore had given heart to the party faithful. "The Butler campaign was organized by Mrs. Miller," Simmons wrote to the Colonel one week after the November election, "directed by her; financed by her; led by her and none other." (Bazy merely allowed that Butler had been floundering before he was rescued by the *Times-Herald*. Her most tangible assistance took the form of a four-page tabloid publication entitled *From the Record*. This had been McCarthy's idea, Bazy explained to her uncle, "to take material out of the *Congressional Record* about the hearings and rewrite them into readable newspaper style. We produced it, making a slight profit, and 500,000 of them were distributed, which pretty well blankets Maryland."[33]

Prominently displayed in the tabloid, which was written by Frank M. Smith, the chief editorial writer for the *Times-Herald*, was a composite photograph, clearly labeled as such, showing Tydings intently listening to the Communist leader Earl Browder. Tydings and his supporters cried foul. Not one voter in ten, they argued, was likely to understand the meaning of the word *composite*.* Minimizing other factors that contributed to his loss, including dismal reports from Korea and widespread dissension among Maryland Democrats, Tydings singled out for criticism the *Times-Herald*, Bazy Miller, and, by extension, her uncle in Chicago. Mrs. Miller responded with a stinging post-election editorial entitled "Tydings, the Cry Baby."

Behind her wisecracking facade, Bazy entertained second thoughts. "Perhaps I was more active in this campaign than I should have been in my position," she wrote to McCormick on November 14. She enclosed a copy of the disputed tabloid. McCormick, fresh from a successful campaign to destroy Lucas, who lost to Everett Dirksen by over 200,000 votes, was in no position to lecture his niece on electioneering etiquette. Still, he began to have doubts about her judgment, mingled with unspoken resentment of her overnight success. Bazy's effusive admirer, Roscoe Conklin Simmons, didn't do her cause any good by rhapsodizing over her performance in the Butler campaign. Within the space of a single year, Simmons told McCormick, Mrs. Miller had transformed the political culture of Maryland. More impressive still, "she has successfully brought you and the *Tribune* to the puffed and hostile East and become a force and voice second to none."[34]

 ✦ 7

Like her mother before her, Ruth McCormick Miller had a mind of her own, and an inclination to use it in ways not always pleasing to the Colonel's male ego. As Washington marveled over Bazy's creation of a senator from Maryland, her uncle, an unlikely Pygmalion, began to wonder exactly what *he* had created. As Bazy recalls it, the Colonel was "ambivalent" about her performance with the *Times-Herald*. "Every once in a while he'd get tremendously proud of something I'd done. At other times I'd hear secondhand that he was saying, 'She's getting too big for her breeches.' He was jealous in a way. He didn't like to see a woman achieve too much."[35]

---

*Offensive as the faked photograph was — it eliminated the space between Tydings and Browder to create the impression that the two men were engaged in private conversation — it can be argued that Bazy Miller's worst crime was naiveté. One can scarcely imagine Hearst or his kind feeling honor-bound to reveal the trickery behind their manipulation of the news.

Responding to post-election rumórs that Bazy was about to call for the replacement of Guy Gabrielson, the Republican national chairman, McCormick tried to rein in his niece. "Our great problem is to prevent the nomination of Dewey or a Dewey stooge" in 1952, he reminded her. Gabrielson, for all his imperfections, was no friend to Dewey. As it happened, Bazy had already killed the offending editorial at the request of Taft and Maine senator Owen Brewster. But while she promised her uncle that she would give the chairmanship additional thought, she didn't retreat from her view that Gabrielson had to go.[36]

By this time, the issue of who ran the RNC was the least of her problems. Millard Tydings was out for blood, and the Senate Subcommittee on Privileges and Elections offered the ideal forum in which to discredit the tactics used to evict him from office after twenty-eight years on Capitol Hill. Three weeks after the election, McCormick told Bazy that while he had no wish to "butt in," he strongly advised her to do nothing in the Tydings matter without first obtaining approval from the Washington office of the *Tribune*'s law firm, Kirkland, Ellis. Perry Patterson, a young lawyer whose father had once been the Colonel's law partner, had been delegated by his Chicago elders to move to Washington, where he could keep a careful watch on developments at the *Times-Herald*.

Patterson was a busy man in the winter of 1950–51. It wasn't only that Bazy's newfound professional confidence was to be tested in the congressional hearing room. Her emotional life was in turmoil. "I had lunch with William Blair Sr. today," McCormick wrote to her on November 30, 1951. "He told me that one of his children said that you were to be divorced." The note was signed "Affectionately," but its tone was ominous. The Millers had in fact separated that autumn, their marriage a casualty of divergent interests, unforeseen passion, and the pressures — and attractions —of big-city journalism.

Ruminative and wryly intelligent, Peter Miller stood in marked contrast to Garvin Tankersley, the *Times-Herald*'s gruffly decisive city editor. Tank, as he was universally known, was a burly, self-assured figure ten years older than Bazy. His take-no-prisoners approach to the Maryland election had caused a storm of acrimony, but it had done nothing to diminish his appeal in Bazy's eyes. Flouting the journalistic ban on management-editorial romance (crudely restated by one grizzled veteran as "you don't get your meat where you get your bread"), Bazy and Tank courted danger as well as each other.[37]

Alarmed by the prospective scandal, McCormick became a more frequent visitor to the nation's capital. He was present at the elegant Sulgrave Club on the evening of December 12, when McCarthy, elated by his recent victories at the polls, baited Drew Pearson. The verbal confrontation escalated, and McCarthy kneed Pearson in the groin; senator-elect Richard

Nixon intervened to break up the fight. McCormick returned to the city to give testimony in Pearson's subsequent lawsuit, which blamed McCarthy, the *Times-Herald*, and a raft of right-wing operatives for his loss of a radio contract worth $5,000 a week. (Although the case never moved beyond preliminaries, it did afford Pearson and his lawyers the satisfaction of deposing McCormick and shedding embarrassing light not only on the bias of his newspapers but on the old man's seeming confusion over the *Times-Herald* and its operations.) Hoping to avoid an equally painful confrontation with his niece, McCormick entrusted a campaign of persuasion to his surrogates, Pat Maloney and Perry Patterson. Maloney, whose genial manner failed to conceal his role as the Colonel's agent and spy, encouraged Bazy to follow her uncle's wishes. "After all," he told her, "his experience of many years is worth having and he deserves your confidence."[38]

Patterson was more direct. Bluntly, he warned the unhappy young woman that unless she ended her affair with Tankersley, McCormick would remove her from the *Times-Herald*. "Uncle Bert would not do that to me," Bazy insisted. Uncle Bert, reflected Patterson, could be pretty firm when he made up his mind. "Journeyman journalists are interchangeable," McCormick wrote to Bazy at the end of January 1951. "It is the top that makes or destroys a property. Hearst was the greatest newspaperman of all time until he took up with Marion Davies. It has been an extraordinary romance and a marvel of constancy, but it ruined him . . . His papers have been on the decline ever since."[39]

In a weird turn of events, McCormick had stepped into the part played by his censorious mother almost forty years earlier, when Kate had sent her lovesick son to Russia in hopes of making him forget Amy Adams. Hypocritical though he might appear, he did not hesitate to reassign Tankersley from the *Times-Herald* to the *Tribune*. Bazy floundered. She missed Tank a great deal, she told her uncle, "both personally and on the paper"; nevertheless, she would try to bury her frustrations in work.[40]

On February 20, the special Senate committee named for its chairman, Guy Gillette, commenced six weeks of open hearings, during which members rehashed every questionable practice associated with the Maryland campaign. The committee had harsh words for those outside the state who had attempted to influence the Tydings-Butler race. Special censure was pronounced on the *Times-Herald* tabloid, with its composite image of Tydings and Browder. To the committee, the doctored photo represented "a shocking abuse of the spirit and intent of the First Amendment."

Not content to separate Bazy and her lover, McCormick now sent Weymouth Kirkland to see his wayward niece, "to take me to the top of the mountain," as she dryly put it. The lawyer painted a flattering picture. "If I agreed not to marry Tank, Uncle Bert would leave me Cantigny Farm,"

Bazy explained. "He would set me up to be chairman of the trust. I was to inherit the whole empire."[41]

In fact, Bazy didn't want the house, which she thought was a mausoleum, and she didn't want the empire. She didn't particularly want to spend her life in the news business. What she did want, most emphatically, was the freedom to marry the man of her choice. A showdown was at hand. "It may appear to you to be worth all that it costs," McCormick wrote bitterly of the impending marriage, "but to the *Times-Herald* it is nothing but a damaging scandal, the more damaging as it makes material for gossip and gossip columnists."[42]

A Chicago meeting was arranged for April 3. With both Weymouth Kirkland and Pat Maloney looking on in McCormick's office, the conversation was predictably strained. Both principals covered familiar territory. The Colonel reiterated that Bazy was at liberty to marry whomever she chose — just as he was free to exercise his authority over the *Times-Herald*. If she insisted on going ahead with this ill-advised marriage, she must surrender her current position, and with it the prospect of someday inheriting the *Tribune*.

"Why?" demanded Bazy. She had done nothing wrong. She wasn't living with Tankersley. To tell the truth, she hadn't finally decided to marry him. "But I must have the right to do so," she plaintively told her uncle.

This was out of the question, said McCormick, for "you would then become a divorced woman."

Bazy reminded the Colonel that two married women had obtained divorces in order to marry him.

"But *I* never got a divorce," replied McCormick.

So blatant a double standard caused Bazy to burst into tears of sheer frustration. "He couldn't handle that," she remembered. Taking advantage of his momentary discomfort, she asked him if he would sell her the *Times-Herald*. McCormick impulsively gave his assent. He instructed Kirkland on the spot to work out details with his distraught niece. As Bazy was escorted from the office, Kirkland stayed behind. When he emerged fifteen minutes later, it was to announce that the Colonel had changed his mind: the *Times-Herald* was not for sale.[43]

"I guess I'm through," Bazy told Kirkland.[44]

A notice was posted on the *Times-Herald* bulletin board: "To all staff members: I resign from the *Times-Herald* today. I tried to buy the paper but was unsuccessful. Ruth McCormick Miller." There remained only the business of putting the best face possible on the rupture. Publicly, Bazy attributed her departure to McCormick's failure to give her the measure of independent control he had promised when she took over the paper. They had parted company over "general policy," she explained, as well as the Pearson lawsuit and the Maryland campaign.

The Colonel differed in his recollections. As he reconstructed events for Pearson's lawyers, his hand had been forced by Pat Maloney's sudden illness in March 1951. With Maloney sidelined, he wanted the managing editor, Frank Waldrop, to supervise the *Times-Herald*, leaving Bazy as little more than a figurehead. Waldrop was to "substantially run the newspaper while Mrs. Miller would represent the family name." Unmentioned was the romance that had triggered Bazy's abrupt fall from grace. And in truth, his niece's impending divorce and remarriage may have simply provided McCormick with the excuse he was looking for to reassert his personal control over the *Times-Herald*. It wasn't his propriety that Bazy had offended, but his sense of proprietorship.

When the dust settled, McCormick wrote chillingly to the *Times-Herald*'s general manager, Bill Shelton, like Frank Waldrop a hardy survivor of earlier Patterson-McCormick family purges. The Colonel took issue with Shelton's latest revenue figures. "It seems to me that the showing ought to be better," he said. "Because of the departure of the Millers, we save five thousand a month, don't we?" He reduced operating expenses further by firing three employees who took part in Bazy's May wedding to Tankersley. He poured nearly $4 million into shiny new Goss presses and an expansion of the *Times-Herald* printing plant to house them. The equipment might be state-of-the-art, but what came off it bore striking resemblence to the tried-and-true formulas recognizable to every *Tribune* reader. Simplified spelling came to Washington, along with hardy Chicago perennials such as "Dr. Fax," "Vox Pop," and "Test Your Horse Sense."[45]

Most important of all, McCormick told Waldrop that he wanted the *Times-Herald*'s editorial page to be a faithful reflection of *Tribune* sentiments. These had most definitely not changed, as McCormick spelled them out to a reporter for the *St. Louis Post-Dispatch* in June 1951. Franklin Roosevelt had been a Communist, "although I don't know if he carried a card. Why else would he have given the Kurile Islands to the Russians if it wasn't to attack us?" Truman was a Socialist, "tremendously under Russian influence." England had gone to hell. McCarthy, although not of presidential caliber, was doing an "indispensable" job in exposing official traitors. Looking ahead to 1952, the Colonel disowned Dwight Eisenhower as "a Truman Republican, like Dewey and Willkie." His own preference ran to either Taft or MacArthur.[46]

McCormick took comfort from the failure of organized labor to stir worker resentment against employers. "They tried to work up class feeling in this country, but they didn't succeed," he declared smugly. "It is easy to work up class feeling in England because of ingrained social and economic distinctions, but that is not the case in the United States ... Why, I'll bet there's hardly a man on the *Tribune* who doesn't own a dinner coat."[47]

✧ 8

One week after McCormick fired his niece for alleged insubordination, Harry Truman pronounced the same sentence on his overreaching military commander in the Far East. So swiftly and completely had Bazy Miller been rejected by the culture of the *Times-Herald* that she might have been foreign tissue. Douglas MacArthur could hardly be removed so easily. Truman's advisers shared his exasperation with the general's free-lance diplomacy and open consorting with the president's enemies on Capitol Hill. The issue for them was not whether to sack MacArthur but how to do so in a way that would contain the public firestorm sure to follow. As humiliating as the news of his dismissal might be, it was essential that the proud old soldier learn of it from the White House directly and not from the press.

This eminently sensible view did not take into account an enterprising *Tribune* reporter named Lloyd Norman. On the evening of April 10, 1951, Norman solicited comment from top Pentagon brass on rumors out of Tokyo, where MacArthur had his headquarters, about an imminent "major resignation." Panic ensued among the generals. It soon engulfed the White House. At 10:30 P.M., Truman cut a hasty order notifying MacArthur of his removal from command. But its transmission was bungled, enhancing the general's martyrdom and bringing down on Truman's head a crushing wave of denunciation.

With foam-flecked lips, the *Tribune* tore into the president as "a fool who is surrounded by knaves." There was only one thing that McCormick desired more fervently than Truman's early impeachment, and that was MacArthur's early return to the United States. He wired Tokyo to this effect. Determined to stage-manage the general's homecoming, the Colonel told Walter Trohan to pull strings and arrange a joint session of Congress (a far better platform, thought McCormick, than the American Society of Newspaper Editors, who were just as eager to have MacArthur address their annual convention in Washington). Pat Maloney was dragged off a Pebble Beach golf course and dispatched to San Francisco to convey the Colonel's personal greetings to the returning hero. Unfortunately for Maloney, 250,000 delirious San Franciscans blocked his access to the general. The resourceful emissary somehow passed his message to a MacArthur aide; in return, McCormick got the desired assurances that Chicago would be included in the triumphal progress MacArthur planned on making after his address to Congress on April 19.[48]

McCormick was in the House gallery that day as the old soldier blasted Truman's Korea policy and tugged at the nation's heartstrings. Just as MacArthur swung into his emotionally charged peroration, McCormick got up and executed his own farewell. At the end of the speech, Trohan remembers, "there wasn't a dry eye in the house, nor an empty seat" — except that vacated by the Colonel.[49]

With an intimacy granted to few courtiers, Trohan observed McCormick in the final years of his life, when he spent considerable time in Washington trying to breathe life into the fading *Times-Herald*. As chief of the *Tribune*'s bureau in the capital, Trohan dreaded nothing more than his employer's periodic self-invitations to lunch with "you and the gang." Since the invariable sequel to these convivial gatherings was a demand for staff reductions, Trohan dug deep into his bag of tricks to orchestrate the table conversation and thereby dazzle McCormick with the gossip and expertise accumulated by his charges.[50]

The bureau remained intact, but the price of continued employment was eternal vigilance. For Trohan, this took many forms of servitude. He attended so many military funerals as McCormick's representative that in later years he could never drive by Arlington National Cemetery without a mournful rendition of "Taps" playing in his brain. He accepted invitations to join the Colonel on expeditions to Gettysburg and Bull Run, only to have McCormick order their driver to turn around before they reached their destination. Trohan personally arranged suites for McCormick's use in three of Washington's finest hotels. All were found wanting. So was a large rented apartment and two homes purchased with *Tribune* funds.

Believing that the Colonel was staying in his Rock Creek residence rather than his house in Kalorama, Trohan was astonished to receive an early morning phone call summoning him to McCormick's bedside at the Alban Towers Hotel on Wisconsin Avenue, to which the Colonel had repaired in hopes of escaping the city's blast-furnace heat. On his arrival, Trohan couldn't help but notice the steamy conditions in McCormick's supposed refuge. Checking a hunch, he informed his boss that hot air was pouring out of the room's air conditioner. "Get out, and don't come back until you acquire some sense," snapped McCormick.[51]

Those not on the *Tribune* payroll were less likely to indulge the old man's egocentricity. In the fall of 1951, the maverick Oregon senator Wayne Morse objected vociferously when McCormick tried to read him out of the Republican party. Rather than fight the 1952 campaign on a platform written in Tribune Tower, said Morse, he would bolt the GOP of his own volition (a threat he made good on, notwithstanding the nomination of Dwight Eisenhower, after Tom Dewey the Colonel's least favorite Republican). As for the publisher of the *Tribune*, Morse believed him so advanced in journalistic senility "that if a liberal thought could get through his cortex . . . he would die of a brain hemorrhage."[52]

This struck uncomfortably close to home for some around the *Tribune*, who shook their heads as they murmured of the Colonel's latest eccentricity. The story was told of how company directors had been summoned to a shipboard conference in the middle of the St. Lawrence River and then forced to conduct their business without specially prepared meeting documents; McCormick, in keeping with his lifelong habit, had casually tossed the papers overboard after reading them. [53]

Then there was the time that the Colonel, scheduled to leave Palm Beach late one evening, prudently arrived at the airport an hour and a half before his plane was to depart. Retiring to his cabin, he donned pajamas and climbed into bed. Sometime later he left the plane, without informing anyone, and wandered into the terminal in search of newspapers and a bathroom. He was still there when the plane took off without him. His unexplained disappearance touched off a frantic search by the crew. The pilot, hoping that McCormick hadn't contrived to fall into the Caribbean, executed a 180-degree turn. By then, McCormick was already asleep in his own bed. Oblivious to the airborne melodrama he had caused, he had calmly gone to the nearest pay phone and summoned his chauffeur to take him home.[54]

Occasionally the *Tribune* resembled a mighty battleship, with steam up and screws going and no rudder. Well into his seventies, McCormick continued to put in six days a week at Tribune Tower. But he rarely arrived on the twenty-fourth floor now before eleven-thirty in the morning, or stayed past four-thirty, when he joined Maryland for cocktails at the nearby Tavern Club before making the short flight home to Cantigny.

When he was there, the atmosphere of formality pervading the *Tribune* executive suite could be misleading. "You never knew what he was going to say or do," recalled Bess Vydra, whose unenviable task it was to replace Genevieve Burke, McCormick's devoted secretary for more than forty years. Seeing the Colonel's office door fly open one morning, Bess hurried in. She tripped over a German shepherd and went sprawling on the floor. "Bite her," McCormick instructed the dog, presumably in jest. (Later he made amends of a sort, telling Miss Vydra, "She wouldn't bite you anyway.")[55]

Aside from his daily editorial conferences and lunches at the Overset Club, McCormick's contact with the *Tribune* family was sporadic. He almost never attended a wedding or missed a funeral. He didn't entertain executives in his homes, contending that to do so would merely foster jealousies. Canada still exercised its perennial fascination. He was kept young, McCormick said, by the challenge of running three paper mills and as many steamship lines north of the border. Young or not, he was certainly kept prosperous by the booming success of his Canadian operations. Since the end of the war, *Tribune* circulation losses had been more than offset by a doubling of advertising. To avert a crippling newsprint shortage, McCormick expanded the production capabilities at his Thorold mill. He added 65,000 acres of harvestable timber on a pair of islands in Lake Huron.

With $35 million in holdings scattered from western Ontario to the Gulf of St. Lawrence, by the early 1950s McCormick was thought to be the single largest foreign investor in Canada. And he was far from through. In Quebec, his friend and sparring partner, Premier Maurice Duplessis, personally sponsored legislation to enable him to construct a $15 million hydroelectric dam and power plant near Baie Comeau. In return the Colonel agreed to help the premier realize his dream of economic development on the remote Gaspé Peninsula by sharing power generated at the new McCormick Dam.

Nearing the end of his career, McCormick was back where he had started with the Chicago Sanitary District, gouging the earth, defying the elements — an engineer at heart. Refuting critics of the modern corporation who held it to be a heartless juggernaut, devoid of risk or romance, McCormick cited the staggering tests of human imagination and persistence posed by his Canadian ventures. "There was nothing impersonal or accidental about our success," he reminded employees of the Ontario Paper Company when they assembled in February 1952 to mark the concern's fortieth anniversary.

In dedicating the new dam the following year, Maurice Duplessis chose to emphasize the parallels between himself and his equally contentious American counterpart. "We're both criticized," said Duplessis as McCormick looked on smilingly, "but we both do some good work."[56]

✧ 9

At the end of March 1952, Harry Truman announced that he would not be a candidate for reelection. In a venomous editorial largely written with his own pen, McCormick looked forward to the return of White House honor and patriotism after twenty years of Democratic betrayal. His public expressions of confidence were belied by private doubts. He had again enlisted in the Taft army, though without much enthusiasm. "I cannot see what Eisenhower has," he wrote to Hedda Hopper in mid-May, "but I certainly know what Taft lacks."[57]

To overcome his candidate's deficiencies in mass appeal and organizational muscle, McCormick dug for dirt with which to soil Eisenhower's heroic reputation. *Tribune* reporters checked out stories that the Eisenhower campaign was being funded by liquor interests. They found no evidence to support the claim. Nor was McCormick any more successful in gaining access to the wartime diary of General George Patton, said to contain evidence of Eisenhower's decision to divorce his wife, Mamie, and wed his wartime driver, Kay Summersby. The Eisenhower-Summersby relationship had long been a subject of prurient speculation. Acting on a tip from the New Hampshire publisher William Loeb, whose *Manchester Union-Leader* made the *Tribune* look moderate by comparison, McCormick dispatched his London correspondent, Bill Fulton, to call on Miss Summersby in person. Unfortunately for Taft partisans and conspiracy theorists, Fulton heard nothing in the course of his visit to sustain Loeb's allegation that Summersby was a spy as well as an adulteress.[58]

Another kind of bedroom politics divided the McCormick household. The elimination of Bazy Tankersley from the *Tribune* line of succession had brought Maryland McCormick one step nearer the throne. "She wanted to be made a trustee in the worst way," recalled Charles B. Wyngarden, a local physician who had been making house calls at Cantigny since the early 1940s. "There wasn't any love in that house," he said. But there was no lack of ambition. Thanks to the *Times-Herald*, Maryland had cut her teeth as a Washington hostess and putative kingmaker. Accompanying the Colonel to a meeting with Eisenhower at NATO headquarters outside Paris, she hadn't hesitated to upstage her husband by flashing an *I Like Ike* button pinned on the inside of her fur coat, for the benefit of onlookers.[59]

By the time GOP delegates met in Chicago in July 1952, Maryland's allegiance had shifted to MacArthur. On her own initiative, she appealed to Taft to withdraw his hopeless candidacy and throw his support to the more conservative general in the race. Taft was puzzled. Maryland had represented herself as her husband's emissary. Yet on the phone, the Colonel was telling him to stand fast, make no deals, and be prepared to go down with all flags flying. Maryland had a better contract than most *Tribune* executives, for whom such free agency would have been grounds for instant dismissal. But her meddling did not sit well with her husband, who began to doubt her discretion and even her loyalty.[60]

Eisenhower's nomination, and the tactics employed to bring it about, caused McCormick to rage against "Buster Dewey the cheap trickster and Lodge the New Dealer, who pretends to be a Republican." His anger led him to propose the unthinkable. As Truman's party met in Chicago to select its own presidential nominee, the Colonel told young Bill Hearst that he was prepared to endorse whomever the Democrats chose, so long as it wasn't Adlai Stevenson. Foiled a second time, McCormick sulked for much of the campaign, called for the formation of a third party, from which he would exclude all "Truman Republicans and Truman Democrats," and finally, tepidly, backed Eisenhower, to whom almost anybody else was preferable. "Unfortunately," the *Tribune* concluded in the last week of October, "almost anybody is not the opposing candidate, and Adlai Stevenson is."[61]

Three weeks after the election, McCormick renewed his call for a new American Party under whose brightly colored banners all true patriots

might assemble. He declared before the Yale Political Union that the president-elect owed his nomination to "a queer assortment of millionaire
Socialists in the East" and his election to Taft and vice presidential candidate Richard Nixon, whose spirited, nationally televised rejoinder to
attacks on his integrity had established him overnight as a force to be reckoned with. McCormick displayed a touch of whimsy, and a perspective few
credited him with, in writing to a Yale friend in advance of his fiftieth class
reunion: "I see in an old class history that when I was an undergraduate I
was considered very radical. Apparently I have gotten over it."[62]

In March 1953, he flew to Europe for a month. In London, he surprised
reporters by complimenting English manners and observing, "I think you
[British] are coming on a bit." He paid a sentimental visit to Ludgrove,
saying that "it was here that I learned how to be patriotic to one's
country." So mellow did the Colonel appear that Lord Beaverbrook's
Evening Standard pronounced him a closet anglophile. Even the Labourite
Daily Mirror managed a kind word of sorts. "Now he is with us once
more," said the working-class sheet, "and has been summing us up again.
Bless him. Bless his stupid old rancorous heart."[63]

✦ 10

Returning at the end of April, McCormick caught a heavy cold
in New York. It soon developed into pneumonia. It was his first real health
scare, and it left him deeply depressed. "I did not come so far from stepping out last week," he confided to Bazy on May 26. Even before his latest
overseas journey, the old man had moved to reconcile with his niece. He
waived the customary age requirement and made her a trustee of the
McCormick-Patterson Trust, authorized to act upon his death, resignation, or incapacity. "Everything and everyone is taken care of except you,"
McCormick informed his secretary, Dorothy Murray, at the end of May.
When the time came, Chesser Campbell would assume McCormick's title
of company president, with Don Maxwell oveseeing the editorial department and Howard Wood serving as treasurer and business manager.
Arthur Schmon was to have direction over all Canadian operations. Bazy
would see to it that the family retained a significant voice in company
affairs.[64]

One person with whom this did not sit well was Maryland McCormick.
Dr. Wyngarden now found himself sucked into the vortex of corporate —
and family — politics. He received a call from Weymouth Kirkland, who
invited him to come by the *Tribune* law firm for a frank discussion. "We're
in a quandary," said Kirkland. In her anxiety to be made a Tribune Company trustee, Maryland was "pestering the life out of the Colonel." For

months the old man had stalled her, but she refused to be put off. Her persistence instilled fears in Kirkland and others that she might take advantage of McCormick's failing health to get what she wanted. Bluntly, the lawyer asked Wyngarden whether the Colonel still possessed the mental acuity and judgment called for under the circumstances. "As far as I'm concerned, he does not," Wyngarden replied.[65]

His patient seemed to agree. "Years ago when they came to me to tell me a plan I had no trouble at all figuring it out," he confided to the *Tribune*'s medical director, Dr. Theodore Van Dellen. "Now I can't do it." Stanley Johnston's wife, Barbara, had an unsettling encounter with the Colonel in the Lake Shore Bank. McCormick failed to acknowledge her greeting, she told her husband. And he seemed to be moving very slowly, as if present in body only. "He's not very well," Stanley acknowledged.[66]

This was an understatement. A painful bladder condition required periodic treatments in which a catheter was used to stretch the ulcerated organ. The discomfort of the procedure was compounded by the indignity of frequent urination. The Colonel's chauffeur began to map out routes based on ready access to roadside rest stops. McCormick's occasional mental confusion was traceable to poor circulation. His increasingly sluggish movements bespoke a diseased liver. His friend and Florida neighbor Kent Cooper was sufficiently concerned to make the Colonel an unusual offer: he, Cooper, would forgo alcohol for a year if McCormick would do the same. But *he* had reasons for drinking, said the Colonel, which Cooper did not.[67]

McCormick wasn't worried about the future of the *Tribune* or most of the rest of his empire. He had already sold off the *Tribune*'s experimental farms and given his Astor Street property to Northwestern University (after unsuccessfully trying to interest the British consulate in the place). But the *Times-Herald* was literally killing him. He wished he had never heard of the paper, McCormick told Cooper. He hated living in Washington, and he feared that he would have to denude the *Tribune* of executive talent to rescue the ailing paper, into which he had already poured millions. For the first time in his business life, he confessed, he felt like a failure. He drank to numb the resulting pain and anguish.[68]

For some time it had been apparent that ammunition was running low at Fort Necessity. After turning marginal profits in 1949 and 1950, the *Times-Herald* had racked up increasing deficits — $592,000 for 1953 alone, with even greater losses projected in succeeding years. Frank Waldrop was fired in May 1953, three months before the paper's general manager, Bill Shelton, got the ax. With large capital expenditures staring him in the face and cash reserves running uncomfortably low, McCormick was in a receptive frame of mind when Kent Cooper began pressing him during the winter of 1953–54 to unload the property once and for all. Cooper asked

McCormick if he would let *him* sell the paper, making certain that the transaction was kept secret and that the Colonel recouped everything he had put into it. "Yes," said McCormick, "but who do you think would pay that much money?"

It was a question to which there could only be one answer. On January 23, 1954, Cooper wrote cryptically to Eugene Meyer. Three days later, Meyer and his son-in-law, Phil Graham, met with Cooper at the Brazilian Court Hotel in Palm Beach. Brushing aside an opening offer from McCormick to purchase the *Post* for consolidation with the *Times-Herald*, Meyer wanted to know what it would cost him to buy out the Colonel. Cooper answered $8.3 million, the figure authorized by McCormick. This did not include severance pay for *Times-Herald* workers or incidental expenses that could inflate the price to $10 million.

Under the circumstances, neither man was inclined to haggle. When Meyer tried to raise objections, Graham jumped in to remind him of what was at stake. "Let's not make it any harder for Kent to get us what we want by questioning the price," he remarked.

That evening, Cooper reported back to the Colonel, who agreed to call a meeting of the *Tribune* board in mid-March, at which time the deal could be consummated. In the meantime, the discussions must be kept an absolute secret. McCormick declined to explain his reasoning to Meyer personally, fearing the effect on morale at the *Times-Herald* if news of the impending sale leaked out and Meyer reneged on his word.

"In other words," said Cooper, "you want me to be the goat so you can deny it if my contact with Meyer becomes known."

McCormick smiled. "That's it."

Unknown to Cooper, McCormick had already tried and failed to interest Walter Annenberg in buying the *Times-Herald*. Annenberg had first met McCormick as a twelve-year-old accompanying his father, Moe, to the Colonel's Christmas luncheon for *Tribune* circulation men and newspaper agencies that marketed the paper. Later Annenberg became a regular at his annual Waldorf-Astoria luncheons, coinciding with the meeting of the American Newspaper Publishers Association. Before selling the *Times-Herald* to Meyer, whose politics he distrusted and whose son-in-law he regarded as emotionally unstable, McCormick offered the paper to Annenberg for the bargain price of $5 million. Though sympathetic to his friend's plight, Annenberg was too practical a businessman to overlook the red ink.[69]

McCormick's spirits lifted once he became reconciled to the deal with Meyer. He stopped thinking about, or even looking at, the newspaper that had caused him such distress. Incredibly, the secret held; not until March 13, two days before the scheduled board meeting in Washington, did the *Tribune*'s executives first learn of the pending sale. So apprehensive was

McCormick that Bazy might catch wind of what was going on and try to block the transaction that he withheld any information concerning his plan from Maryland and from Weymouth Kirkland.[70]

The night before the board meeting, an almost surreal scene played itself out at the F Street Club, where Bazy was throwing a retirement party for Elbert Antrim, the *Tribune*'s long-time business manager. The Colonel was present, but his mind seemed elsewhere. And Antrim's successor, Howard Wood, was nowhere to be seen.[71]

Periodically, Chess Campbell would leave the party and call Wood, who was in the midst of final negotiations with Phil Graham at the World Center Building on 16th Street. "The Colonel wants to see you," he told Wood.

Then McCormick would get on the phone. "Howard, close that deal," he said.

He couldn't close it just yet, Wood replied. He had more trading to do.

A half-hour later the phone would ring again. "Close that deal."[72]

The next day, Monday, March 15, McCormick stalled for time with the directors while Wood and Patterson nailed down final details on the sale. Lunch was delayed past the scheduled one o'clock start. The directors were getting restive when Wood walked in at one-thirty and nodded at the Colonel.

"I think Howard has an announcement to make."

The news stunned everyone around the table. Bazy's stomach "went hollow." She protested the sale as a betrayal of conservative principles. She asked her uncle for time in which to raise enough money to buy the paper herself. McCormick refused. Then Mary Patterson, known to admirers as "the conscience of the *Daily News*," rose dramatically from her seat to endorse Bazy's proposal. The Colonel executed a tactical retreat. He gave his niece forty-five hours to match Meyer's offer. That meant she had until 11 A.M. on Wednesday, March 17, to keep the *Times-Herald* from being history. He attached a further condition: she must not tell any of her prospective financial angels what she was raising money for.[73]

Meyer was playing hardball now, threatening to cancel the deal in the event news of it leaked prematurely. With the clock ticking, Bazy excused herself from the board meeting. Putting up $350,000 of her own funds as a deposit, she made a frantic round of calls to Texas oilmen H. L. Hunt, Sid Richardson, and Clint Murchison. By Wednesday morning, March 17, she had pledges of $4 million, but McCormick turned a deaf ear when she sought an extension. In her anger, reportedly, she declared that she hoped never to see her uncle again. And then, in a bold gesture of defiance that a younger McCormick would have envied, she took out black-bordered sympathy ads in the *Washington Star* and the *Washington News*.

Flying back to Chicago from Washington that afternoon, McCormick was a man transformed. He confided to the pilot, Fred Hotson, his intention to sink part of his *Times-Herald* windfall into the purchase of a new Convair.

On March 18, the first edition of the combined *Washington Post and Times-Herald* contained a front-page message from the Colonel justifying his decision as the result of doctors' orders following recent bouts with severe illness. "Mr. Meyer needs no endorsement from me," McCormick added, "but I bespeak for everybody the fullest possible cooperation" with the new owners. Meyer was no less gracious, declaring himself "pleased and proud" to print McCormick's words and wishing the Colonel better health now that he was relieved "from the burdens in Washington." Actually, McCormick was returning to Palm Beach "to get all cleared up," he informed Meyer, "and then I will be strong enough to fight Jack Dempsey."[74]

He would need all the strength he could muster. After netting a $2.2 million profit on the deal, he had to endure the cries of sellout from conservative activists — even General Robert Wood took his old friend to task for abandoning the Washington field to his enemies — and the no less offensive sounds of liberal gloating. "Hooray for the canary that swallowed the cat," declared Walter Lippmann. The columnist David Lawrence was more equivocal: "A feeling prevails that the anti-Communist crusade has lost its most articulate exponent in the nation's capital."[75]

On March 22, Alicia Patterson congratulated her uncle on his "magnificent" handling of the *Times-Herald* sale. The same day McCormick fired off an angry order to his lawyers. "I know that Bazy has certain rights under the agreement between me and her mother, but I had given her more than she was entitled to under the law," he wrote to Howard Ellis. "Now that she has made such a damn fool of herself, I want to reduce her to the minimum she is entitled to legally."[76]

❖   11

Standing outside Tribune Tower one day early in the 1950s, a friend looked up at the massive structure and remarked to the Colonel that he could take pride in building so lasting a memorial. McCormick answered that he expected the *Tribune* to last no more than ten years "the way I leave it." In fact, the paper was already changing in ways that would have astonished earlier generations of readers. Circulation was down almost 20 percent since 1946. "The odds seem to be against the extreme right wing," said Maryland McCormick in her column, "The Distaff Side." "It's very sad, but true, and why not face it?"[77]

Starting in July 1954, the *Tribune* initiated a new editorial department. "The Other Side" as its name implied, exposed readers to differing viewpoints. Front-page cartoons lost their political edge. The paper toyed with instituting a gossip column, something McCormick had previously disdained as the work of "keyhole-peepers." The Colonel maintained his staunch opposition to syndicated columnists, especially pundits such as Walter Lippmann and the Alsop brothers, who saw themselves as virtual government advisers. But he didn't hesitate to reproach Joe McCarthy for baiting the United States Army in his latest anti-Communist crusade. McCarthy, said the *Tribune*, would better serve his cause by distinguishing the role of investigator from that of avenging angel.[78]

In her column, the outspoken Maryland poked fun at "lords of the press" who exaggerated their power to shape public opinion while underestimating the talents of their women. She mocked chauvinistic *Tribune* editors who took umbrage over a column making light of the McCormick family dogs. She imagined their disapproving remarks made in solemn conclave: "Look at the trouble women have always made in the *Tribune* family. Cissy Patterson, then the colonel's niece, and now his wife." If only publishers' wives would "stay home and cook good, hot, nourishing meals, and perhaps do a little laundry, instead of infringing on their husbands' territory."[79]

McCormick resented the demands of Maryland's new career. "Your mother has developed a considerable literary capacity," he wrote to his stepdaughter Ann in July 1954, "and has to go to Washington and New York frequently because she does not think the Chicago and Wheaton people are worth a column." Exasperated and lonely, he complained to friends that Maryland was out "whoring around Chicago." Striding into his office one morning he was surprised to see her behind his desk, giving dictation to Bess Vydra. "That's *my* chair," he exclaimed. In the future, he said, his wife might confine her journalistic labors to their apartment at 209 Lake Shore Drive. Moreover, any requests for secretarial assistance should be directed to the *Tribune* pool.[80]

To Miss Vydra's colleague Dorothy Murray, the Colonel lamented that his wife seemed determined to run the *Tribune*. He was just as resolved that she would not. In December 1954, he poured out a story of violent squabbling over the family dinner table. As he recounted the incident, Maryland had lost her temper on hearing that Miss Murray would be joining them on an upcoming trip to Florida. The argument escalated until Maryland confronted her husband with a brutal list of demands: he must fire both Miss Murray and Miss Vydra, designate herself as an executor of his estate and chief trustee of the *Tribune*, establish substantial trust funds for her daughters, and grant her both $1 million and a divorce.

A shouting match ensued. He had done enough for her daughters, said McCormick. No one was going to dictate to him the identity of his trustees or secretaries. At one point he had fancied that his wife possessed executive ability, but he had rethought this conclusion as he discovered how thoroughly disliked she was by everyone at the *Tribune*. Hoping to avoid personal scandal, he told Maryland that she could remain in his household, but only if she stopped nagging him about the *Tribune* succession.[81]

A few days later he flew off to Palm Beach for Christmas. Two days before the holiday, he placed a call to Don Maxwell: "Don, I'm lonesome. I want you to come down and spend Christmas Day with me."

What about Mrs. McCormick? asked the wary Maxwell.

"She stayed up to be chairman of a ball or something." McCormick told Maxwell that he would send his Convair to pick him up. An hour later he called back. "I've been thinking this over," said the Colonel. "You can call my wife and tell her that she can come down with you." To Maxwell's protests, McCormick said, "You just do what I tell you. Just call her up."[82]

"What did the Colonel want?" Maryland asked the *Tribune*'s managing editor. Maxwell replied, truthfully enough, that he didn't have the slightest idea, other than to alleviate his loneliness.

Getting off the plane, Maryland went straight to Dr. Van Dellen, who had also been commandeered to spend the holiday at her husband's side. "What does the Colonel want of Maxwell?" she inquired anxiously.[83]

Over the holiday, McCormick signed papers disposing of his mile of Florida beachfront for $1 million. Maxwell flew back to Chicago. On January 3 he received instructions from the Colonel to run a story in the *Tribune* "saying I have left a large bequest to Northwestern Medical School to teach doctors to be on time."

"I am coming to the end," McCormick wrote to Bazy on January 16, "and hope that you and I can part as we used to be." The next day he returned to Chicago to be operated on for the removal of adhesions between his large intestine and bladder. Bazy conspired with Dr. Van Dellen to see her uncle without Maryland present. Driving all night, she made her way to Chicago and Passavant Hospital. There she found McCormick drowsy and sedated but grateful to see her. They held hands wordlessly. Then she went back to the Drake Hotel and bought a gold fishing knife, on which she had inscribed a fraternal sentiment from *The Three Musketeers*, "It's all for one, and one for all." McCormick cherished the gift. "Your visit was worth a tenth legion to me," he informed Bazy on Janaury 27.[84]

Ten days later McCormick had the Sunday *Tribune Magazine* reproduce the Christmas cards he had sent to Campbell, Maxwell, and Wood, his way of introducing readers to the three men "who stand at the right hand of the editor and publisher." He went back to Florida, where he slept much of the time. Even when awake, he appeared dazed and disoriented.

"Walter," he abruptly asked the visiting Trohan one morning, "what do you hear about my being senile?"

Unwilling to report that Maryland and his designated trustees had been the source of such allegations, Trohan reminded the Colonel of their previous night's discussion, in which he had spoken knowledgeably of Revolutionary and Civil War campaigns. Surely anyone in command of Phil Sheridan's movements in the Shenandoah Valley possessed self-command as well.[85]

McCormick retained his sense of humor to the end. "I came to the south for change and rest," McCormick informed a friend. "The waiters are taking the change and the hotels have taken the rest." On February 14, Howard Wood waited for two hours as the Colonel tried, with the help of a nurse, to dress himself. He gave up after managing to put on a shirt and tie. The dying man offered Wood assurances that his mind was at peace regarding the *Tribune* succession. McCormick was an unruly patient. During an earlier illness, he had called the *Tribune* in the middle of the night and demanded that he be released. Then he had leaped out of bed, intravenous tubes still in his arm, and marched out to where an improvised ambulance in the form of a station wagon modified to accommodate his long form waited to speed him home.[86]

Now McCormick gave instructions to build an apartment for his use on the twenty-seventh floor of Tribune Tower. He named the place "27 Bells," after an old drinking song he had first memorized as a Yale undergraduate. The plans never got off the drawing board. Another fixation involved his desire to fly to Tokyo and the resulting need to convert his dirt strip at Cantigny into a modern runway fully equipped to handle jet aircraft. "Have they started on my airstrip yet?" he asked repeatedly in the last weeks of his life. Back from the *Tribune* came the response, "Tell him that the ground is still frozen."[87]

Charles Wyngarden heard piteous cries for help coming from his patient's room whenever McCormick woke to find himself alone. To ease his terror, Stanley Johnston and other old *Tribune* hands formed a group they called the Watchmen of the Night, to remain by the Colonel's side as his life ebbed away.

Occasionally his mind flickered with something of its old inquisitiveness. On February 26, he wrote to Mike Kennedy, "It might be interesting to know when high heels came into use. We know that Cleopatra, who was very vain, had flat heels on her slippers. When the change to high heels came, I haven't the slightest idea." In the shadow of death, his thoughts were focused on life. "I wonder if this spring we can pick out some individual robin on the farm and follow it through to the full growth of the eggs?"

On March 17, convinced that McCormick's case was hopeless — he was suffering from heart disease and cirrhosis of the liver — his doctors sent him home to Cantigny, to the house he had known as a boy and had later

rebuilt to assert his claim to history's attention. One day Wood and Maxwell came calling with a special thirty-two-page *Tribune* insert scooping the *New York Times* with the complete text of the hitherto secret Yalta
agreements. McCormick greeted them lying on a sofa in the library. His
eyes remained shut, and his visitors were uncertain whether he had
absorbed what they had to tell him. Finally he stirred. "Gentlemen," he
said in a voice barely above a whisper, "I only wish I could adequately
express my appreciation."[88]

The death watch began in earnest. Not expecting her husband to leave
his room, Maryland gave a library sofa to the Reverend Robert Stewart, a
frequent visitor to the house in those weeks. She gratified Don Maxwell's
long-standing desire to possess a wooden Indian in full war regalia that
had been presented to the Colonel on one of his forays into Canada.
Whereupon the patient rose from his sickbed, discovered the missing
items, and demanded their immediate return.[89]

To the last, McCormick kept asking about his new airstrip and a specially designed automobile that he would not have to stoop low to enter.
Along with the doctors and nurses, the *Tribune* executives were on guard
lest Maryland take advantage of her husband's mental lapses to have him
revoke his earlier instructions and give her at the end the power she craved.

By the last days of March, McCormick was drifting in and out of consciousness. A hospital bed had been set up in a small ground-floor room.
Here he passed restless days, his agony only partially deadened by regular
injections of morphine. The situation, admittedly trying, did not bring out
the best in Maryland. "*He* can't sleep!" she told the doctors. "What about
me?" At the dinner table she spoke brusquely of the dying man, in the
third person: "What does *he* want now? How much has *he* had to eat?"
Worn down by the vigil, she turned to the prone, suffering figure on his
bed, his flesh turning yellow from liver failure, and moaned, "You know
you are going to die — why make it so hard on everyone else?"[90]

McCormick's pulse faded and he grew quiet on the night of March 31.
Midnight came. April Fool's Day. Forty-five years had elapsed since
Robert Patterson had taken his life in a Philadelphia hotel room, setting
up the unlikely sequence of events by which Kate McCormick's unloved
second son had risen to a position of absolute control over the *Tribune*.
Stanley Johnston alerted his wife, Barbara, that the end was at hand.
McCormick was moaning continuously now, watched over by his griev-
ing valet, Shin.

Maryland was in her own bed when, shortly before three A.M., Dr. Van
Dellen pronounced the Colonel dead. Stanley Johnston closed his friend's
eyes. Then he placed a phone call to a downtown Chicago funeral home
where McCormick several years earlier had purchased and stored an oversize casket — out of fear, he explained, that a regulation casket would not

accommodate his huge frame and an unscrupulous mortician would cut off his feet to make him fit.[91]

By the time Maryland woke, the Colonel had been embalmed and dresssed in his World War I uniform, which Johnston had contrived to drape over the wasted figure. The widow was asked if she would like to see the shrunken corpse lying in its mahogony box in the library, beneath the likeness of McCormick the soldier painted by Amy. Maryland declined. Better to remember the Colonel as he had been, she thought, than to see him as he was.[92]

Acknowledgments

"To live over people's lives is nothing," wrote Henry James, "unless we live over their perceptions, live over the growth, the change, the varying intensity of the same — since it was by these things they themselves lived." In the course of living over Robert R. McCormick's life, I have been the recipient of many kindnesses, both individual and institutional.

More than six years have elapsed since August 1990, when I first visited Tribune Tower at the urging of John McCutcheon, himself the bearer of a distinguished newspaper name, to make an initial survey of Colonel McCormick's papers. That Jack was in a position to guarantee me absolute independence in undertaking an intellectually rigorous accounting of McCormick's life reflected the personal and professional integrity I came to associate with Stanton Cook, then the Tribune Company chairman, and his successors, Charles Brumback and John Madigan. They promised me a totally free hand, and they honored their promise to the letter.

Although Jack McCutcheon left his position soon after, about the time the archives themselves left Tribune Tower for a magnificent new facility on the grounds of McCormick's Cantigny estate, his interest in the project has never flagged. He read early drafts of the manuscript with a generous eye, and his incisive comments have rescued me from numerous errors of fact and interpretation. Funding for the First Division Museum of Cantigny, which also houses the Colonel Robert R. McCormick Research Center, came from the Robert R. McCormick Tribune Foundation, whose visionary leader, General Neal Creighton, has become a valued friend. The same holds true for Neal's wife, Joan, who oversees the McCormick mansion with a hospitality that makes visiting there an unforgettable experience.

Colonel John Votaw, director of the First Division Museum, is a first-rate military historian. He is also a thoughtful host, supportive colleague, and seemingly inexhaustible sounding board. The archival riches housed at Cantigny are astonishing in their quality and bulk. Besides the personal and business papers of Colonel McCormick, I was able to draw on McCormick and Patterson family correspondence and diaries; a file cabinet brimming with previously unknown letters exchanged by McCormick and his globetrotting parents during their diplomatic rounds; unpublished histories of the McCormick-era *Tribune* and private memoirs of his associates; extensive files of information developed for projected biographies of the Colonel, including transcripts of taped interviews conducted by *Tribune* reporter Frank Hughes, who also extracted the Colonel's highly detailed instructions to his editors; letters, unseen until now, that detail the Civil War activities of Joseph Medill and Cyrus McCormick; and a complete set of the Colonel's writings and speeches, augmented by film and audio recordings.

If I did not drown in this sea of paper, it was due entirely to the guidance and sympathy of the Cantigny archivists, led by Eric Gillespie and Andrew Woods. Eric was a particular source of help, never hesitating to interrupt his own labors to retrieve a load of archival boxes, copy relevant documents, locate a rare volume, or track down the obituary of some long-dead Tribunite. He played a vital role in assembling the photographs. On top of all this, he laughed at my jokes and indulged me in unending biographical theorizing. What more could a researcher ask for?

Also to be found at Cantigny are nearly fifty interviews with McCormick associates conducted in the 1970s as part of the Tribune Oral History Project. I have drawn extensively on these conversations and wish to acknowledge my debt of gratitude to the late *Tribune* archivist Harold Hutchings, with whom I had the pleasure of discussing McCormick and his newspaper shortly before Hutchings died in 1994, and his colleague Lloyd Wendt, happily still here to be told of my admiration for his definitive 1979 history of the *Tribune*. The oral history treasure trove compiled by Hutchings and Wendt has been supplemented in recent years by a fresh round of interviews carried out by another *Tribune* veteran, Bob Wiedrich. Bob's tough-guy exterior cannot obscure his impish wit, or a slangy irreverence straight out of *The Front Page*. As a result, his interviews are as entertaining as they are informative.

The deeper I burrowed into McCormick's archival legacy, the greater was my admiration for earlier biographers, who produced sharply etched portraits notwithstanding their lack of access to the Colonel's papers. These include Frank Waldrop, Joseph Gies, and Gwen Morgan and Arthur Veysey. Thanks, too, to Jerome Edwards and James Schneider, who have added immeasurably to our knowledge of McCormick's isolationist politics and the degree to which his *Tribune* both reflected and shaped opinion throughout the American Midwest during the tense years preceding U.S. involvement in World War II.

Frank Waldrop graciously shared his insights into McCormick and his no less colorful Patterson relations in the course of two extensive interviews at his home in Washington, D.C. He supplied additional information by letter and throughout the life of the project has offered the sort of encouragement that any author craves. I am deeply grateful for his help.

The same holds true for Walter Trohan. "I do not want to intrude on the Colonel's life," he wrote to me in July 1992. "I cite my doings and opinions merely so you can estimate their value." At the age of eighty-nine, Trohan's mind was as keen as his eyesight was precarious. Laboriously he wrote out dozens of pages of notes in response to my questions. He also sat down for a lengthy interview with Dwight Miller, senior archivist of the Herbert Hoover Presidential Library, who had several years earlier persuaded Trohan to donate his papers to the Hoover facility.

Greater still is the debt I owe Kristie Miller. Through her superb biography of her grandmother, Ruth Hanna McCormick Simms, Kristie has disproved the assumption that McCormicks and objectivity go together like the devil and holy water. Over the years we have had countless discussions about the Colonel and the place he holds in her family and in *Tribune* history. Kristie has been of immense help in concentrating my thoughts and refining the raw ore mined in archival caverns.

Gwen Morgan and Arthur Veysey, former *Tribune* correspondents and for many years the devoted caretakers of McCormick's Cantigny estate, kindly welcomed me to their London home even as they were in the midst of preparing to leave their beloved England and take up permanent residence in New Zealand. Their book *Poor Little Rich Boy* is especially useful for the light it sheds on McCormick family intrigues and the semifeudal lifestyle the Colonel enjoyed at Cantigny.

At Lake Forest College, Art Miller proved an expert guide to the Joseph Patterson papers housed there. Douglas Brown, unofficial historian at the Groton School, turned up a rich harvest of previously unknown correspondence concerning the student career of young Robert McCormick. In London, Martin Lubowski uncovered valuable information in diplomatic files at the Public Records Office in Kew. Carol Mason, of the Naval Institute in Annapolis, helped track down material shedding light on the 1942 Midway controversy and the Roosevelt administration's efforts to punish McCormick and the *Tribune.* Lynda Schuler did an excellent job of combing relevant collections at the Library of Congress and the National Archives.

Barbara Johnston Wood followed up a memorable lunch in Lake Forest by providing extensive written comments on McCormick's final days and — Eureka! — page after page of contemporary notes made by Stanley Johnston (her husband at the time) as he lovingly watched over the dying Colonel in 1955. Thomas Swanson generously supplied copies of films shot by his father, capturing the Colonel's air and naval fleet. Professor Edward Coffman, a World War I scholar of the first rank, was kind enough to read my chapters on McCormick's wartime experiences and prevent me from betraying my too obvious limitations as a military historian. Thanks are due as well to the expert and helpful staffs of Yale's Sterling Memorial Library, Sangamon State University, the Illinois Regional Archives at Northeastern Illinois University, the Chicago Historical Society, and the Franklin D. Roosevelt and Harry S. Truman Presidential Libraries.

To fill remaining gaps, I conducted interviews and/or corresponded with the following people: Walter Annenberg, Herbert Brownell, Hal Bruno, Gerald R. Ford, Jack Fuller, Katharine Graham, Toni Gillman, Robert Hardesty, Harold Hutchings, Louise Hutchinson, John Karwoski, Bruce MacFarlane, Murrey Marder, Brooks McCormick, Kristie Miller, Peter Miller, Gwen Morgan, Richard Nixon, Perry Patterson, Ward Quaal, George Reedy, Don Reuben, Jeanette Reuben, Chalmers Roberts, Zifforah Snydecker, R. Douglas Stuart, Thomas Swanson, George Tagge, Bazy Tankersley, Theodore Van Dellen, Arthur Veysey, Bess Vydra, Frank Waldrop, Bob Wiedrich, Shirley Wickman, Carl Wiegman, Barbara Johnston Wood, and Charles Wyngarden.

My final acknowledgment is to my first and oldest friend, a Chicago journalist with a national audience and a stubborn, occasionally cranky integrity that no editorial page should be without. Steve Chapman has little in common with Robert McCormick except the First Amendment. No doubt much of what Steve writes in the current *Chicago Tribune* would give offense to the Colonel. But first it would make him think. And that, as McCormick would readily concede, is the surest sign that a newspaper is fulfilling its public obligation.

Notes

An early draft of this book in which virtually every statement of fact was annotated promised to extend an already lengthy manuscript to unmanageable proportions. In an effort to satisfy both the demands of scholarship and the preferences of the general reader, for whom the book is intended, I have followed a system that emphasizes primary sources, most of them previously untapped. Where possible, I have indicated the source of information within the text itself. Elsewhere, I refer readers interested in secondary sources to the bibliography. Unless otherwise identified, all materials cited below are to be found at the Colonel Robert R. McCormick Research Center of the First Division Museum at Cantigny.

Prologue. The Voice of America

1. *New York Times*, September 26, 1947.
2. "Mussolini, Moscow, or America," RRM speech, December 1, 1932. "To us," McCormick wrote to the financier Thomas Lamont in December 1943, "New York appears a halfway place between England and America. Having been to school at Groton and college at Yale and much in the east, I have observed that easterners tend to look up to England and down on the west."
3. *Time*, April 11, 1955; RRM–Tiffany Blake, February 16, 1931; interview with Frank Waldrop.
4. *Chicago Tribune*, September 1, 1950.
5. Waldrop interview.
6. "How many times can a man or woman be married without being a polyganist?" RRM–Tiffany Blake, February 16, 1931.
7. Harry S. Truman–Bess Truman, September 26, 1947, Truman Library.

8. RRM–Frank Hughes, April 3, 1944; Walter Trohan, "My Life with the Colonel," *Journal of the Illinois State Historical Society* (Winter 1959), pp. 477–502 (Trohan's original draft, slightly longer and even more revealing, is to be found at the MRC); interview with John R. Thompson for Chicago Tribune Oral History Project, henceforth cited as TOHP.
9. Interview with Dr. Theodore Van Dellen; Waldrop interview; RRM–Gail Compton, September 8, 1945.
10. *The New Yorker*, January 7, 1950.
11. Interview with Harold Hutchings.

1. The House of Medill

1. Joseph Medill–Mr. Baldwin, July 23, 1888.
2. Ibid.
3. Elmer Gertz, "The Beginnings," from unpublished McCormick biography, Gertz Papers, Library of Congress; Paul Gilbert and Charles Lee Bryson, *Chicago and Its Makers*, Chicago, 1929, p. 857.
4. *Cashocton Republican*, January 1850.
5. Sketch of Patrick ancestors, July 1931, sent to Colonel McCormick by Alicia Patterson, March 15, 1955.
6. *Chicago Tribune*, March 17, 1899.
7. Ibid.
8. Trohan, "My Life with the Colonel"; "The McCormick Tartan"; RRM–Edward McCormick, December 30, 1952.
9. Interview with Brooks McCormick; John Tebbel, *An American Dynasty*, New York, 1947, pp. 12–13.
10. R.R. McCormick radio memoirs, WGN, hereafter identified as Memoirs, p. 24.
11. *Chicago Times-Herald*, March 17, 1899.
12. Charles Collins, "Joseph Medill of the *Chicago Tribune*," *Sunday Tribune Magazine*, June 12, 1955, p. 50.
13. Abraham Lincoln–Charles H. Ray, June 27, 1858.
14. Elmer Gertz, "Joe Medill's War," unpublished ms., Gertz Papers, Library of Congress; Harold Holzer, *The Lincoln-Douglas Debates*, New York, 1993, p. 2.
15. Joseph Medill–Abraham Lincoln, *Confidential*, August 1858.
16. *Chicago Tribune*, October 11, 1858; Holzer, pp. 6–16.
17. *Chicago Times-Herald*, March 19, 1899.
18. Carl Sandburg, *Abraham Lincoln, The Prairie Years*, Vol. II, Norwalk, Conn., 1995, pp. 215–16.
19. "Booming the First Republican President," *Saturday Evening Post*, August 5, 1899.
20. *Chicago Tribune*, March 16, 1949.
21. "The Man of the People," *Chicago Tribune*, May 19, 1860.
22. Joseph Medill–Abraham Lincoln, June 19, August 9, 1860.
23. Cyrus W. McCormick–E. W. McComas, "Baltimore, 1860."
24. Tebbel, *An American Dynasty*, pp. 22.

25. Joseph Medill–Abraham Lincoln, December 18, 1860.

26. Joseph Logsdon, *Horace White, Nineteenth Century Liberal*, Westport, Conn., 1971, p. 69; Joseph Medill–Alfred Cowles, January 14, 1861.

27. Joseph Medill–Alfred Cowles, January 14, 1861.

28. Joseph Medill–Abraham Lincoln, December 26, 31, 1860; Joseph Medill–Alfred Cowles, February 24, 1861.

29. Joseph Medill–Abraham Lincoln, April 15, 1861.

30. Joseph Medill–Horace White, March 5, 1863; Joseph Medill–Abraham Lincoln, February 9, 1862.

31. Joseph Medill–Edwin M. Stanton, January 21, 1862.

32. *Chicago Sun-Times*, September 28, 1950, p. 23.

33. Ibid.

34. Joseph Medill–William Medill, May 24, 1863.

35. Ibid.

36. Joseph Medill–Abraham Lincoln, May 15, 1863.

37. November 1863 witnessed Lincoln's address on the Gettysburg battlefield. Wilbur Storey's *Chicago Times* accused the president of profaning a solemn occasion with his "silly, flat, and dish-watery utterances." The *Tribune*, by contrast, said that Lincoln's brief remarks "will live among the annals of man."

38. Joseph Medill–Abraham Lincoln, January 15, 1865.

39. Joseph Medill–Abraham Lincoln, April 14, 1865.

40. Lee was also characterized by the *Tribune* as "an average Virginia slaveholder in moral character, nothing more." Philip Kinsley, *The Chicago Tribune, Its First Hundred Years*, Vol. I, New York, 1943, p. 379.

41. Mike Kennedy–John Menaugh, November 27, 1951; Mary Ann McCormick–Nettie F. McCormick, January 31, 1865.

42. William S. McCormick–G. Walker, November 4, 1859.

43. Frank Waldrop, *McCormick of Chicago*, Englewood Cliffs, N.J., 1966, p. 18.

44. Henry Justin Smith, *Chicago's Great Century, 1833–1933*, Chicago, 1933, p. 67.

45. Kinsley, *Tribune, Its First Hundred Years*, Vol. II, p. 132.

46. *Reminiscences of Chicago During the Great Fire*, Chicago, 1915, pp. 87–88.

47. That Medill was available at all should have alerted voters to his high-handed ways, so offensive to his nominal partners at the *Tribune* that they were delighted to kick him upstairs.

48. "Feuds and Vendettas," unpublished ms., Gertz Papers, Library of Congress. Medill blamed the impoverishment of the working class on "their own proudness and lack of thrift." "Too many people are trying to get along without work," he told a Senate committee in 1873. "Those who do toil squander the greater part of their wages in drink and tobacco."

49. Ralph G. Martin, *Cissy*, New York, 1979, p. 15.

50. Katharine Medill–Joseph Medill, January 1, 1860.

51. Joan Chalmers–Edward S. Beck, July 18, 1932; Katharine Medill–"Kitty" Medill, undated.

52. Kate Medill–Katharine Medill, December 12, 1867.

53. Joseph Medill–Katharine Medill, September 20, 1873.

54. *The Chicago Times*, June 9, 1876.

55. *Cincinnati Daily Times*, undated, 1874; *Louisville Courier Journal*, November 2, 1874.
56. "About two thousand millionaires run the policies of the Rep[ublican] party and make its tariffs," Medill complained to Illinois senator Shelby M. Cullom, quoted in "Twenty Years of Stormy Weather," unpublished ms., Gertz papers, Library of Congress; undated editorial instructions from Joseph Medill to George Upton.
57. "Hugh Fullerton," undated ms., Joseph Medill, papers.
58. Gertz, "Feuds and Vendettas"; Medill to George P. Upton, undated editorial instructions.
59. Calvin Cobb–Kathleen Maddock, April 1, 1899.
60. *Time*, April 11, 1955; *Cincinnati Commercial Gazette*, April 1, 1893.
61. *The Indianapolis Journal*, July 26, 1879.
62. Ibid.

2. A Second Son

1. Nellie Patterson–Mrs. Robert W. Patterson, December 13, 1893.
2. Nellie Patterson–Mrs. Robert W. Patterson, undated.
3. Martin, *Cissy*, p. 17. Nellie easily justified her domination of the Patterson household, explaining, "After all, the *money* was all mine."
4. Robert S. McCormick-Cyrus H. McCormick, November 11, 1882.
5. Kate McCormick, "My dear Mamma," January 9, 1879.
6. Maryland McCormick interview, TOHP; R. R. McCormick, "Autobiography," March 18, 1947, hereafter referred to as Autobiography; Ginger Le Fevour–Harold Hutchings, October 24, 1976.
7. Frank Hughes, "The Man in the Tower," unpublished McCormick biography, p. 4; RRM–Judith C. Churchill, October 6, 1947.
8. Kate McCormick–Mrs. Joseph Medill, August 11, 1881.
9. Kate McCormick–Mrs. Joseph Medill, undated. The McCormicks and the Pattersons were much more faithful in writing to each other than in dating their correspondence. This complicates matters for their biographers, but in most instances it is possible to arrive at a fairly precise date.
10. Autobiography, p. 1.
11. Autobiography, pp. 1, 4. "The girls of our neighborhood were much more adventurous than the boys," McCormick remembered in February 1940. "I think I am the only one who went further than Clark Street."
12. Robert S. McCormick–Mrs. Joseph Medill, July 31, 1885; RRM–"Dear Grandma," undated.
13. Autobiography, p. 6.
14. Memoirs, pp. 7–8.
15. Robert S. McCormick–Mrs. Joseph Medill, September 18, 1889.
16. Robert S. McCormick–Robert Patterson, July 5, 1889; Robert S. McCormick–Mrs. Joseph Medill, November 12, 1889.
17. Kate McCormick–Mrs. Joseph Medill, August 12, 1889; Bertie McCor-

mick–Mrs. Joseph Medill, July 2, 1889. Writing to his Chicago grandmother in June 1892, thirteen-year-old Medill described New York City as "still the Purgatory it always is at this time of the year. You get all the heat and none of romantic surroundings of the original."

18. Robert S. McCormick–Mrs. Joseph Medill, February 2, 1891; Ralph Crawshaw–RRM, July 19, 1946; RRM–Joseph Patterson, March 7, 1891.

19. Robert S. McCormick–Mrs. Joseph Medill, March 9, 1891.

20. Robert S. McCormick–John G. Shortall, November 24, 1891; Robert S. McCormick–Mrs. Joseph Medill, August 31, 1891.

21. RRM–Joseph Patterson, August 6, 1891.

22. Robert S. McCormick–Mrs. Joseph Medill, October 26, 1892; Robert S. McCormick–Endicott Peabody, February 19, 1893, Groton Archives.

23. Robert R. McCormick interview, TOHR; Shane Leslie, *The Film of Memory*, London, 1938, p. 135.

24. Shane Leslie, *Men Were Different*, London, 1937, pp. 177, 151; *Barnet Times and Finchley Telegraph*, February 28, 1902.

25. Arthur Dunn–Robert S. McCormick, May 28, 1892; Medill McCormick–Mrs. Robert W. Patterson, July 27, 1892

26. "Literary Ambition," notes prepared for author by Walter Trohan; Autobiography, p. 6; RRM–Mrs. John Liddell, June 9, 1953.

27. Kate McCormick–Mrs. Joseph Medill, February 13, 1893, June 11, 1893.

28. Robert S. McCormick–Joseph Medill, May 9, 1893.

29. Memoirs, p. 10; RRM–Cliff Raymond, October 7, 1949.

30. Kate McCormick–Mrs. Joseph Medill, December 20, 1893; Kate McCormick–Endicott Peabody, February 1, 1894; Robert S. McCormick–Endicott Peabody, February 27, 1894, Groton Archives.

31. Autobiography, p. 7.

32. Frank Ashburn, *Peabody of Groton*, New York, 1944, p. 86.

33. Autobiography, p. 8.

34. John Walter Cross–Elmer Gertz, June 16, 1939, Gertz Papers, Library of Congress.

35. "My school English Teacher ... so belittled my capacity to write English," McCormick confided to a friend in 1948, "as to cause me not to [cover] the news." He was forever grateful to a later instructor at Yale who observed that while he was no Shakespeare, "I wrote as well as any average person."

36. Endicott Peabody–RRM, May 28, 1898, Groton Archives.

37. Joseph Patterson–"Dear Medill," March 22 (year unspecified).

38. RRM Groton essay books.

39. Ibid.

40. Ibid.

41. Joseph Medill to George Upton, undated editorial instructions.

42. Memoirs, p. 25.

43. Edward Bowditch–Elmer Gertz, July 3, 1939; Richard Derby–Gertz, July 19, 1939; Endicott Peabody–Gertz, July 21, 1939, Gertz Papers, Library of Congress.

44. RRM–Charles Dawes, October 12, 1950.
45. RRM–Endicott Peabody, April 8, 1932; McCormick interview, TOHP.
46. RRM–Archibald M. Brown, September 16, 1936.
47. RRM–Endicott Peabody, April 15, 1930; RRM–Archibald M. Brown, August 23, 1952.

3. Fitting In

1. Hutchings interview.
2. "The Colonel's Century," *Time*, June 9, 1947.
3. McCormick interview, TOHP; RRM speech before *Tribune* advertising department, January 4, 1928.
4. "The Fortunate Sons-in-Law," unpublished ms., Gertz Papers, Library of Congress, pp. 14–18.
5. Joseph Medill–Ione Maxwell, May 13, 1894.
6. "The Prospect for America," RRM speech, December 17, 1933; Autobiography, p. 9.
7. Joseph Medill–Robert W. Patterson, February 2, 1899.
8. RRM–Herma Clark, March 6, 1947; Memoirs, p. 37; Frederic Hartzell, "Reminiscent and Prophetic Words by Joseph Medill in the Closing Days of His Life." To the end, Medill remained resolutely anglophobic, predicting that within ten years Great Britain would acquiesce in American sovereignty over Mexico, Canada, and virtually all of Central America.
9. Interview with John McCutcheon; Memoirs, p. 36.
10. R. R. McCormick, "An Everyday Story of San Antonio."
11. RRM–"Dear Par," undated note.
12. *Chicago Tribune*, March 19, 1899.
13. John J. McPhaul, *Deadlines and Monkeyshines*, Englewood Cliffs, N.J., 1962, p. 238.
14. Memoirs, p. 41; Robert S. McCormick–Endicott Peabody, July 3, 1895, Groton Archives.
15. George W. Pierson, *Yale College, An Educational History, 1871–1921*, New Haven, 1952, pp. 111–20. Importuned to abolish campus football, Hadley refused, saying, "Mars takes more boys from Venus and Bacchus than he does from Minerva."
16. Memoirs, pp. 38–39; RRM–A. K. Oliver, June 6, 1953; RRM–Randolph Lyons, November 6, 1953.
17. McCormick interview, TOHP; Memoirs, p. 42.
18. Memoirs, p. 41; Pierson, *Yale*, pp. 274–75; A. G. Keller–RRM, May 21, 1952.
19. McCormick biographical material; unpublished ms. by Clifford Raymond.
20. W. A. Swanberg, *Citizen Hearst*, New York, 1961, p. 232.
21. "Newspaper Work," an address by James Keeley, November 26, 1912. "The man who thinks he can . . . let private interests dictate his policy, and at the same time secretly imagines he can pose as a leader of public opinion, an exponent of right and honesty, is fooling himself, not the public," Keeley told

his audience. In the journalistic as in the political world, he maintained, the day of "invisible government" was over.

22. Nellie Patterson–RRM, November 15, 1906.

23. Kate McCormick–Cissy Patterson, undated, autumn 1901.

24. Lorna Hogg, "Austro-Hungarian Empire," *Majesty*, October 1992; Memoirs, p. 9; Robert S. McCormick–Kate McCormick, May 3, 1901.

25. Kate McCormick–Nellie Patterson, October 28, December 26, 1901.

26. Robert S. McCormick–Nellie Patterson, November 27, 1901.

27. Memoirs, p. 35.

28. RRM Diary of Arctic Trip, July 18, 20, 1901.

29. To finance his Arctic adventure, McCormick originally approached his friend Jim Deering and asked to borrow $500. Deering refused, but the next day he went to Kate McCormick with a request of his own. "Why don't you give Bertie the $500 to go to the Arctic? Do you realize he's a very young boy, very susceptible, and this [Chicago] is one of the wickedest country clubs in America?" The next day Kate gave her son the money. Maryland McCormick interview, TOHP.

30. Medill McCormick–Kate McCormick, March 2, 1901, McCormick Papers, Library of Congress.

31. Ibid.

32. Memoirs, p. 55; "Save the Republic," RRM speech, August 1, 1935.

33. RRM–"Dear parents," undated letter from Yale University Club, New Haven; RRM–"Dear Excellencies!," undated.

34. RRM–"Dear Parents," undated.

35. RRM–"Your Excellencies!," undated; RRM–Cissy Patterson, undated letter from Yale University Club, New Haven.

36. Ibid.

37. *Chicago Tribune*, November 19, 1902; Memoirs, p. 53.

38. RRM–"Dear Parents," undated. McCormick told his parents that following his commencement in June 1903 he would be coming to visit them, accompanied by a classmate named Joseph Thomas. Thirty years later, McCormick's affair with Thomas's wife, Clara, would nearly wreck his marriage, itself the product of a scandalous liaison.

39. Ibid.

40. RRM–Ruth Hanna McCormick Simms, August 6, 1936.

4. Silk Stockings

1. RRM–"Dear Aunt Nellie," undated; RRM–Cliff Raymond, November 5, 1949.

2. Interview with Gottfried Hintersdorf, TOHP; RRM–"Dear Aunt Nellie," undated.

3. RRM–"Dear People," undated letter to parents.

4. Ibid.

5. Notwithstanding the ridicule excited by his activities in St. Petersburg, Rob McCormick felt very much at home there. "Nothing would induce Kate to

return to Vienna, except for a brief visit," he told his sister-in-law in February 1903. "The Russians are so much more sympathetic and we are treated with the most marked consideration." *Chicago Inter Ocean*, February 15, 1903; *Chicago American*, February 4, 1903.

6. Joseph Patterson–Nellie Patterson, undated.
7. Robert S. McCormick to Secretary of State John Hay, January 2, March 9, March 25, 1904, State Department records, National Archives.
8. R. D. Cahn–RRM, October 8, 1943. In excerpting the Spring-Rice–Roosevelt correspondence for the Colonel, Cahn fed his employer's anglophobia by quoting the British diplomat's October 7, 1904, lament to his friend in the White House: "I wish you had a really good Ambassador here." TR's response, "largely because of what you set forth," was to replace the well-intentioned amateur Robert S. McCormick with his trusted friend George Meyer.
9. To his secretary of state, John Hay, Roosevelt confided the view that "the Czar is a preposterous little creature as the absolute autocrat of 150,000,000 people." For another revealing episode in U.S.-Russo relations during McCormick's ambassadorship, see Stuart E. Knee, "The Diplomacy of Neutrality: Theodore Roosevelt and the Russian Pogroms of 1903–06," *Presidential Studies Quarterly*, Winter 1989, pp. 71–78.
10. McCormick interview, TOHP; Memoirs, p. 73; RRM–James Doherty, May 9, 1952.
11. *Chicago Inter-Ocean*, March 3, 1904.
12. *Chicago Record-Herald*, April 13, 1904.
13. *Chicago Tribune*, undated, March 1904.
14. *Chicago Tribune*, April 2, 1955.
15. *Chicago Examiner*, May 18, 1904.
16. *Chicago Inter-Ocean*, July 11, 1904.
17. R. R. McCormick Diary, April 1904.
18. Ibid.; Joanna H. Dorrat–RRM, October 3, 1905.
19. RRM–"Dear People," undated, Onwentsia Club, Lake Forest, Ill.
20. RRM–"Dear Aunt Nellie," undated. "I must stop now," concluded McCormick, anything but his phlegmatic self, "as I have made up my mind to buy a shirt and am too excited to sit still."
21. *Chicago Post*, August 24, 1904; *Chicago Examiner*, October 31, 1905.
22. Wayne Andrews, *The Battle for Chicago*, New York, 1946, p. 226.
23. Clifford Raymond, unpublished McCormick biography, Chap. 2, p. 7; Andrews, *The Battle for Chicago*, p. 224.
24. John Walter Cross–Elmer Gertz, June 16, 1939; James S. Cochrane–Elmer Gertz, June 24, 1939, Gertz Papers, Library of Congress.
25. Arthur Sears Henning–Cliff Raymond, October 27, 1949.
26. Robert S. McCormick–William G. Beale, March 21, 1905; Kate McCormick–Robert W. Patterson, March 26, 1905.
27. *Chicago Examiner*, December 8, 1905.
28. *Chicago American*, February 25, 1906.
29. Ibid.

30. RRM–Cliff Raymond, November 5, 1949; William Hard–Clifford Raymond, November 1, 1949; Maryland McCormick interview, TOHP.
31. *Chicago Examiner*, March 6, 1906.
32. Ibid.
33. Yale History of the Class of 1903, Triennial Edition, 1906, p. 183; "The Young Man's Opportunity in Politics," RRM speech, March 3, 1908.
34. Jack Alexander, "The World's Greatest Newspaper," *Saturday Evening Post*, July 26, 1941.
35. R. R. McCormick, "1906 President's Message," Chicago Sanitary District.
36. Kate McCormick–Medill McCormick, March 12, 1906.
37. RRM–"Dear Parents," March 1, 1906.
38. Kate McCormick–RRM, November 9, 1906. "I gave up all my journalistic ambition some years ago," McCormick wrote to his parents about thist ime. "Since then I have been traveling on my own feet and have journeyed far enough to know that the editor of a paper is not the only big man in the world." He had come to the realization that in "this day and generation the possession of a good-sized fortune is necessary not only to obtain the creature comforts of life but to maintain an honorable independent position ... and perhaps even avoid oppression from the powerful and unscrupulous."
39. Kate McCormick–RRM, October 30, 1906; Robert S. McCormick–RRM, March 6, 1907.
40. *Chicago American*, January 14, 1907; Robert S. McCormick–Kate McCormick, April 28, 1907.
41. *Chicago Record-Herald*, April 23, 1907.
42. *Chicago Examiner*, July 25, 1907. "There are two classes of officeholders," McCormick told a University of Chicago audience on March 3, 1908. "Those who lead in politics by reason of patriotism and those who lead in politics for the graft."
43. RRM–"Dear Folks," undated. In the same communication, McCormick informed his parents that he intended to "strike from the shoulder" in an upcoming speech about Insull. His reasons were twofold: "First, I will not compromise with my conscience at any cost, and Second, I do not believe it can ever be profitable to allow any man to force one to stultify oneself for his profit, be his power of coercion ever so strong."
44. Robert Conot, *A Streak of Luck*, New York, 1979, p. 229.
45. Harold L. Platt, "Samuel Insull and the Electric City," *Chicago History*, Spring 1986, p. 22; John Clayton, "An American Story," unpublished ms., p. 295.
46. Platt, "Samuel Insull," p. 22.
47. Clayton, "An American Story," p. 296.
48. *Chicago American*, November 25, 1908.
49. *Chicago Examiner*, August 14, 1907; *Chicago Inter-Ocean*, July 20, 1908; "1909 President's Message," Chicago Sanitary District.
50. *Chicago American*, November 25, 1907.
51. William G. Beale–James Keeley, October 14, 1910.
52. *Chicago Tribune*, October 21, 1910; interview with Toni Gilliman. "Years

later," McCormick asserted in his radio memoirs, "Insull was indicted under charges of defrauding his stockholders. He thought I was responsible. I was not. He was a political corruptionist, but I never thought he was dishonest to his associates."

5. *Into His Own*

1. Memoirs, p. 233. In a diary he kept for several weeks in the spring of 1909, McCormick described a much larger role for himself at the *Tribune* than he ever publicly acknowledged. On top of his legal practice, he immersed himself in the paper's finances and especially its editorial policies. The impression is unmistakable; for all his protestations of disinterest, he was readying himself for a career with the *Tribune*.
2. Confidential memo: "Robert R. McCormick's Assumption of Control of Tribune Company"; RRM–Kate McCormick, February 15, 1909.
3. Hughes–McCormick Project, Cliff Raymond ms.
4. RRM Diary, April 7, 9, 1909.
5. RRM–Kate McCormick, June 18, 1909. For all his limitations, Lawson was generously praised by McCormick as "perhaps, the greatest all-around publisher who ever lived."
6. William Hard–RRM, March 18, 1910. "Tell Medill to *shut up* on the subject of his *daemon*, his *polygamous nature*, and his incestuous moral relations!!" Kate instructed Bert in an undated letter from Paris. Such wild-eyed talk only confirmed the view that Medill was "bughouse." On one occasion Medill caused a sensation by running an editorial entitled "John Maynard Harlan Is a Liar." Harlan was a respected figure in Chicago, and a sworn foe of Charles T. Yerkes and other boodlers. Medill refused to back down, although he did concede that the privilege of calling a man a liar in print was a limited one, not to be exercised more than once a year.
7. William G. Beale–Kate McCormick, February 11, 1910; RRM–William G. Beale, February 4, 1910.
8. Kate McCormick–RRM, undated.
9. Kate McCormick-RRM, undated, but clearly on or about April 1, 1910.
10. McCormick interview, TOHP; RRM memo to Cliff Raymond, November 24, 1949.
11. RRM–Medill McCormick, April 7, 1910. "This position will always be open to you," McCormick assured his brother.
12. Nellie Patterson–RRM, undated.
13. Joseph Patterson–Nellie Patterson, April 12, 1910.
14. RRM–Kate McCormick, April 16, 1910.
15. Ibid.
16. RRM–Victor Lawson, July 11, 1910; McCormick interview, TOHP; Memoirs, p. 191.
17. Kate McCormick–RRM, August 3, 1910.
18. Arthur M. Evans, "Details of the Lorimer Fight," unpublished *Tribune* history.

19. James M. Cleary, "The Colonel and the Captain Take Command: The Chicago Tribune — 1900–1920," Chap. 10, p. 4.
20. *Chicago Tribune*, October 22, October 25, 1910.
21. RRM–R. A. Grannes, November 25, 1910, RRM–Medill McCormick, November 14, 1910.
22. Nettie F. McCormick–RRM, November 9, 1910; *Chicago Tribune*, September 28, 1911.
23. Carl Wiegman, *Trees to News*, Toronto, 1953, p. 21. McCormick was even blunter in his instructions to Elbert Antrim, then the *Tribune*'s traffic manager. He dispatched Antrim to Ontario with the parting words, "If you don't get the wood, you needn't come back."
24. Cliff Raymond, "The Annenbergs," unpublished ms., p. 3; Elmer Gertz, "The Wars for Dominance," unpublished ms., Gertz Papers, Library of Congress.
25. RRM–Kate McCormick, September 3, 1913.
26. Joseph Patterson–RRM, December, 1911; RRM–James Keeley, September 26, 1913.
27. Kate McCormick–RRM, undated, "The Plaza, New York."
28. RRM–Nellie Patterson, February 1, 1912.
29. RRM, "A Concise History of the National Republican Convention of 1912"; *Chicago Tribune*, October 28, 1912.
30. J. C. Howard–*Chicago Tribune*, July 31, 1913. Senator Lorimer's *Chicago Inter Ocean* was hardly more decorous in its comments about Medill, whom it described in July 1912 as "an alcoholic little cad who haunts sanitariums between debauches and whose pus-fed face for months turned men in disgust from his lunch table and caused them to avoid even the tableware which touched his lips."
31. Kate McCormick–RRM, undated, "Wednesday, Natural Bridge Hotel."
32. RRM Diary, May 1913.
33. Ruth Roberts interview, TOHP.
34. Kate McCormick–Medill McCormick, July 26, 1909.
35. Kate McCormick–RRM, January 22, 1910; Kate McCormick–Medill McCormick, undated, McCormick Family Papers.
36. Ruth Roberts interview, TOHP.
37. Ibid. Additional details of the McCormick-Adams liaison are to be found in *The Daybook*, a short-lived, adless Chicago newspaper, September 28, 1914.
38. Nellie Patterson–Medill McCormick, April 12, 1916.
39. Kate McCormick–Medill McCormick, undated, "The Greenbriar," McCormick Family Papers.
40. RRM–Kate McCormick August 2, 1910.
41. Nellie Patterson Diary, August 25, 1915.
42. RRM–Cliff Raymond, October 7, 1949; William H. Field–RRM, May 8, 1914. McCormick was hardly alone in his reaction. The gossipy publication *Town Topics* predicted disaster for the "three-ring circus" run by the green cousins.
43. RRM–Kate McCormick, June 25, 1914.
44. RRM Diary, June 4, 1913.
45. RRM–Kate McCormick, July 31, 1914.

46. Joseph Patterson–William G. Beale, August 3, 1914; RRM–Kate McCormick, August 5, 1914.

47. Kate McCormick–Medill McCormick, undated, McCormick Family Papers.

48. Nellie Patterson Diary, January 25, 1915; RRM–Sir Edward Grey, October 10, 1914, Public Records Office, Kew, hereafter referred to as PRO.

49. Cecil Spring-Rice–Sir Edward Grey, October 13, 20, 1914, PRO.

50. RRM–Kate McCormick, December 9, 12, 1914.

51. Interview with Don Reuben.

52. Kate McCormick–Medill McCormick, undated, "Blackstone Hotel." With every day her son continued his affair, said Kate, she was more convinced of the "impossibility" of his remaining at the *Tribune*.

6. *The Wine of Death*

1. *Chicago Tribune*, March 2, 1915.

2. Ibid.

3. Ibid.

4. *Chicago Tribune*, April 22, 1915.

5. Robert R. McCormick, *With the Russian Army*, New York, 1915, pp. 29–30.

6. RRM–Tiffany Blake, October 6, 1917.

7. RRM–Kate McCormick, March 11, 1915, McCormick Family Papers. "I love you as much as ever and will always," McCormick concluded his sharply worded appeal.

8. Kate McCormick–Medill McCormick, undated, McCormick Family Papers. According to Nellie Patterson, as recorded in her diary, Bert had hoped to keep his marriage to Amy a secret, at least until he wrote in explanation to Kate. Unfortunately, the news reached the press first. Her sister, Nellie observed, was "heartbroken" and violent in her epistolary efforts.

9. Nellie Patterson–Kate McCormick, December 9, 1915; *Time*, June 9, 1947.

10. Memoirs, p. 96; RRM Diary, March 17, 1915.

11. Amy McCormick, "From Tilbury Dock to Warsaw," March 13, 1913, hereafter referred to as AM Diary.

12. *Chicago Tribune*, April 28, 1915; RM Diary, March 28, 1915.

13. McCormick interview, TOHP; RM Diary, March 29, 1915; AM Diary.

14. AM Diary.

15. Ibid.; RM Diary, April 1–2, 1915.

16. AM Diary; RM Diary, April 5, 1915.

17. Memoirs, p. 99; RM Diary, April 9, 1915; Nellie Patterson Diary, June 14, 1916. "Poor Bertie!" Kate wrote to Medill about this time. "Does he yet realize what his wicked headstrong passion has cost him? His fortune, inheritences — social position, family loyalty, and affection all gone — Oh, what a tragedy!"

18. Memoirs, pp. 100–105.

19. RM Diary, April 11, 1915; Kate McCormick-Medill McCormick, undated.

20. *Chicago Tribune*, June 29, 1915; AM Diary.

21. AM Diary; RM Diary, April 17, 1915.

22. *Chicago Tribune*, June 1, 1915; RM Diary, April 20, 24, 1915; Memoirs, p. 107; McCormick, *With the Russian Army*, pp. 85–87.
23. Joseph Gies, *The Colonel of Chicago*, New York, 1979, p. 55. McCormick sang the praises of Russian artillery, transport, infantry attack tactics — even the Russian physique, which he called the first in Europe (RM Diary, April 26, 1915).
24. McCormick interview, TOHP.
25. RM Diary, May 1, 1915; Kate McCormick–RRM, undated.
26. RRM–Kate McCormick, May 1, 1915.
27. RRM–Kate McCormick, May 6, 1915.
28. Kate McCormick–Medill McCormick, Newport, Summer 1915. "Still worrying and raging" over her son's conduct, Kate wondered how Joe Patterson and the rest of the *Tribune* crowd felt about paying Bert's $20,000 in travel expenses, "apparently for a wedding journey."
29. Nellie Patterson–Kate McCormick, April 22, 1915, McCormick Family Papers.
30. Theodore Roosevelt–RRM, September 3, 1915.
31. RRM–Joseph Patterson, September 1, 1915.
32. Ibid.; RRM–Kate McCormick, September 18, 1915.
33. Theodore Roosevelt–RRM, September 3, 1915; Memoirs, p. 126.
34. Memoirs, p. 125.
35. RRM–George Bakhmetoff, October 16, 1915.
36. Wayne Andrews, *Battle for Chicago*, New York, 1946, p. 243; RRM, "Ripe for Conquest," *The Century*, April, 1916.
37. RRM–Lawrence Sherman, July 17, 1916.
38. RRM, "The Next President," *The Century*, June 1916.
39. Ibid.
40. RRM speech to *Tribune* advertising department, December, 1939; Memoirs, p. 207; Carl Wiegman, *Trees to News*, Toronto, 1953, p. 35.
41. RRM–Albert L. Mills, July 8, 1916.
42. Cliff Raymond, "Mexican Border," notes for McCormick biography.
43. Walter Trohan, *Political Animals*, Garden City, N.Y., 1975, p. 11.
44. Kate McCormick–Medill McCormick, July 30, 1916, McCormick Family Papers.
45. *Chicago Tribune*, October 26, 1916; "Universal Military Training," RRM Testimony before U.S. Senate Committee on Military Affairs, January 25, 1917.
46. *Chicago Herald*, August 30, 1916; Jack Alexander, "The Duke of Chicago," *Saturday Evening Post*, July 19, 1941; Memoirs, pp. 130–31.
47. *Chicago Tribune*, November 10, 1916.
48. RRM, "Universal Military Training."
49. *Chicago Tribune*, December 9, 1916.

7. Kaiser Bill, Kaiser Will

1. McCormick memo, May 18, 1922; Memoirs, pp. 81–82.

2. Joel Arthur Tarr, *A Study in Boss Politics, William Lorimer of Chicago*, Urbana, Illinois, 1971, p. 290.

3. Cleary, *The Colonel and the Captain Take Command*, Chap. 20, "Big Bill Thompson and the *Tribune*"; "Rise and Fall of Thompsonism," *Outlook*, April 22, 1931.

4. *Chicago Tribune*, January 17, 1923.

5. RRM–Franklin D. Roosevelt, March 6, 1917.

6. Franklin D. Roosevelt–RRM, March 9, 1917; RRM–Franklin D. Roosevelt, April 11, 1917. "We are at war and utterly unprepared," McCormick wrote. "You doubtless know much better than I what a failure the recruiting campaign is — and I do not envy your declining to put the navy to sea without men."

7. Arthur Sears Henning–RRM, April 6, 1917; Newton Baker–RRM, April 13, 1917; RRM–E. S. Beck, April 23, 1917.

8. McCormick interview, TOHP.

9. Kate McCormick–RRM, undated, "3000 Massachusetts Avenue, Washington, D.C."; RRM–R. D. Cahn, August 31, 1954.

10. Theodore Roosevelt–RRM, June 28, 1917.

11. McCormick interview, TOHP; McCormick Diary, July 9, 1917; Memoirs, pp. 137–38.

12. RRM Diary, July 11, 1917; Nellie Patterson Diary, notes "1917"; Joseph Gies, *The Colonel of Chicago*, New York, 1979, p. 67.

13. RRM–E. S. Beck, September 12, 1917.

14. RRM–William H. Field, September 2, 1917.

15. Memoirs, pp. 138–39.

16. RRM–Warren Curtis, August 9, 1917; RRM–Emory Thomason, August 26, 1917.

17. RRM–Joseph Patterson, July 31, 1917.

18. Memoirs, early draft, pp. 172–73.

19. McCormick interview, TOHP.

20. RRM–William H. Field, September 2, 1917; RRM Diary, September 13, 1917.

21. Writing to his law partner, Stuart Shepard, McCormick acknowledged that he was very much a stranger to the regular army organization. "Their ways are not my ways," he wrote (RRM–"Again dear partners," September 22, 1917).

22. RRM–Medill McCormick, October 31, 1917, McCormick Family Papers; RRM–Stuart Shepard, October 27, 1917.

23. RRM–Stuart Shepard, October 27, 1917; RRM Diary, October 17, 1917; Memoirs, p. 171.

24. RRM Diary, October 8, 1917; RRM–Medill McCormick, October 31, 1917.

25. RRM–Medill McCormick, October 31, 1917.

26. RRM–William H. Field, September 21, 1917.

27. RRM–"Dear Stuart and Emory," September 21, 1917; RRM–Medill McCormick, undated.

28. RRM–E. S. Beck, September 12, November 11, 1917.

29. RRM–E. S. Beck, December 1, 1917. "We must beat the American Bolsheviks," added McCormick "or they will destroy us. They are traitors and anarchists. Sometimes I think Wilson is Karensky."

30. John J. Pershing–RRM, March 20, 1918. In his diary, McCormick pronounced Pierson's conduct "unexplicable. He is clever business man. No books. No success. Probably all mixed up with women."

31. Elmer Gertz, "Colonel Bertie's First World War," unpublished ms., Gertz Papers, Library of Congress.

32. RRM Diary, December 8, 10, 1917.

33. Fox Connor–RRM, October 27, 1918.

34. In response to Murphy's complaints, Joe Patterson promised to find him work on another beat, with no reduction in salary. Murphy went on to postwar assignments in Paris and Vienna. He eventually landed a press job on the White House staff during FDR's second term.

35. RRM Diary, October 20, 1917; Clayton, "An American Story," pp. 66–67.

36. Gertz, "Colonel Bertie's First World War."

37. Consistent with his disdain for those at the rear, McCormick urged his *Tribune* colleagues to keep promoting universal military training. "This talk of destroying German militarism is just lovely talk ... but it ain't going to happen," he wrote to Tiffany Blake in December 1917. "Let us for the love of Pete *try* to see straight."

38. RRM Diary, November 26, 1917; RRM–Milton J. Foreman, December 28, 1917.

39. RRM Diary, February 11, 13, 1918.

40. RRM–Milton J. Foreman, December 28, 1917; RRM Diary, February 25, 1918.

41. Dwight Aultman, "Report on Operations of March 1, 1918, 5:40 AM to 7AM"; RRM Diary, March 1, 1918; McCormick interview, TOHP.

42. Memoirs, p. 164.

43. RRM–Tiffany Blake, March 16, 1918.

44. RRM Diary, March 25, 27, 1918; RRM–Maxwell Murphy, May 28, 1937.

45. RRM Diary, April 16, 1918.

46. Memoirs, p. 161.

47. RRM–Tiffany Blake, May 1918.

48. Memoirs, p. 165.

49. McCormick, *The Army of 1918*, New York, 1920, pp. 83–84.

50. RRM–Tiffany Blake, May 18, 1918.

51. Ibid.

52. Memorandum of Major Robert R. McCormick's service, 5th Field Artillery, June 23, 1921.

53. RRM Diary, May 4–7, 1918.

54. RRM–Colonel Robert Davis, May 21, 1918.

55. Dwight Aultman–RRM, August 10, 1918; RRM Diary, May 20, 1918; Henry Wales, "The First Time I Met Robert R. McCormick ... ," *New York Times*, April 5, 1955.

56. McCormick interview, TOHP; Memoirs, p. 166; Society of the First Division, *History of the First Division During the World War, 1917–1919*, Philadelphia, 1922, pp. 79–85.

57. Charles D. Bourcier–Maryland McCormick, April 6, 1955.

58. Arthur Schmon, "Report of Events During the Barrage on May 28, 1918," Schmon Diary; Arthur Schmon–John H. Thompson, February 25, 1959.

59. RRM–Major General George Bell, June 5, 1918.
60. Milton Foreman–Amy McCormick, July 24, 1918.
61. McCormick interview, TOHP.
62. *Chicago Herald-Examiner*, August 25, 1918.
63. RRM–Joseph Patterson, November 1, 1918; Joseph Patterson–RRM, November 8, 1918.
64. RRM–Floyd Gibbons, November 18, 1918.
65. RRM–Medill McCormick, November 6, 1918.
66. Franklin D. Roosevelt–Medill McCormick, October 31, 1919; Joseph Patterson–Medill McCormick, November 12, 1919; RRM–Medill McCormick, June 5, 1922, McCormick Family Papers; RRM–Charles P. Summerall, June 18, 1921.
67. Rascoe did not exaggerate his employer's martial posturing, or his battle-hardened attitude toward flawed humanity. "Man is an inefficient machine at best," McCormick wrote to Tiffany Blake on May 15, 1918. "Except for a number of spurts when he can work three-quarters of the time, he can only work half of the time. Every year beyond about 25 decreases his efficiency." In the same letter he expressed hope that the war would purge the United States of "lots of bad symptoms," including government control of farmland and railroads. "I sincerely trust that the drafting of a large number of men into the Army will develop orderliness and a rational demand for individual freedom after the restraints of military life have been lifted, rather than a mob control such as resulted in Russia."
68. Interview with Carl Wiegman.
69. Interview with Walter Trohan, Herbert Hoover Presidential Library.
70. RRM–Kate McCormick, October 9, 1919.
71. RRM–Helen Dunn, September 23, 1947.

8. *"We Seem to Be Fighting All the Time"*

1. Clayton, "An American Story," pp. 60–61.
2. *Chicago Tribune*, April 17, 1919; *Hinsdale Record*, April 19, 1919; Kate McCormick–RRM, "Tuesday, The Blackstone, Chicago."
3. Kate McCormick–Medill McCormick, July 25, 1919, McCormick Family Papers.
4. Clayton, "An American Story," pp. 63–64; J. M. Patterson–Medill McCormick, June 9, 1919.
5. *Tribune*–Spearman Lewis, June 9, 1919; *Chicago Tribune*, June 30, 1919.
6. Kate McCormick–"Dearest Bertie," "Saturday, The Greenbriar."
7. William H. Field–"Dear Bert and Joe," December 17, 1918, Joseph Patterson Papers, Lake Forest College, hereafter referred to as JPP. In a 1950 interview, McCormick ascribed the success of the *Daily News* to New York subway riders: "You see, at the time we started it, we didn't of course . . . have the Royal Family which is the pictures in all English papers. The army had been disbanded, the navy wasn't romantic in our estimation, the bathing beauties

hadn't come in, racing was outlawed." The tabloid took off when the Hearst paper went to three cents and the *Daily News* remained at two.

8. Cleary, *The Colonel and the Captain Take Command*, Chap. 34, "The Tribune Invades New York"; Jack Alexander, *"Vox Populi,"* I-II, *The New Yorker*, August 6, 13, 1938.

9. *Boston Evening Transcript*, August 9, 1919.

10. RRM–John W. Weeks, October 12, 1923.

11. RRM memo on Ford case, February 12, 1919.

12. Cliff Raymond, unpublished McCormick biography. Writing to Weymouth Kirkland on May 24, 1919, McCormick pressed his lawyers to emphasize Edsel Ford's draft deferment "as direct proof of anarchy. He used the entire influence of his enormous organization to keep his son from doing the duty that every poor man's son was compelled to perform. I think we should fight like the devil to get this in evidence."

13. *Chicago Tribune*, February 4, 1965, April 2, 1955.

14. Philip Kinsley, "Henry Ford and the *Chicago Tribune*," unpublished ms. Kinsley followed his instructions closely enough to prompt Weymouth Kirkland to ask him at one point during the trial, "Are you reporting this for the *Tribune* or for Ford?"

15. *Chicago Tribune*, April 2, 1955.

16. *Chicago Herald-Examiner*, July 10, 1919; RRM notes, "My grandfather, Joseph Medill," undated, Kirkland and Ellis files, Henry Ford lawsuit.

17. *Chicago Tribune*, July 10, 1919.

18. Kinsley, "Henry Ford and the *Chicago Tribune*," Chap. 22, "Henry Ford's Ordeal."

19. In an unusually candid article in the February 1923 *American Bar Association Journal*, Weymouth Kirkland conceded that the Ford trial was something of a legal charade, tried on practically everything but the ostensible issues of the case.

20. C. D. Hagerty–RRM, October 26, 1919. At McCormick's insistence, Hagerty interviewed every member of the jury and reconstructed each step in their deliberations.

21. Ibid.

22. RRM–John W. Weeks, October 12, 1923.

23. Interview with Harry N. King, TOHP.

24. *Chicago Tribune*, November 25, 1919.

25. RRM–Kate McCormick, November 28, 1919; RRM–David Lloyd George, November 26, 1919.

26. David Lloyd George–RRM, December 4, 1919.

27. Interview with Joseph Cerutti, TOHP.

28. Clayton, "An American Story," p. 115.

29. Ibid., p. 117.

30. Wales, "The First Time I Met Robert R. McCormick . . ."

31. Waverly Root, *The Paris Edition*, San Francisco, 1989, pp. 64–65.

32. Ibid., p. 62.

33. Ibid. pp. 63–64.

34. RRM–Joseph Patterson, November 4, 1921; RRM–Max Annenberg, February 26, 1916; King interview, TOHP.
35. RRM–Medill McCormick, October 6, 1921, McCormick Family Papers; *Chicago Tribune*, September 29, 1922.
36. King interview, TOHP.
37. Medill McCormick–Kate McCormick, August 1, 1920, McCormick Family Papers; RRM–Weymouth Kirkland, April 18, 1919.
38. RRM–Weymouth Kirkland, April 8, 1920; RRM–Floyd Gibbons, May 10, 1920.
39. RRM–"Dear Mother," undated, "McCormick, Kirkland, Patterson and Fleming."
40. RRM–Kate McCormick, June 11, 1921. Medill should inform his friends, McCormick told his brother in April 1921, that Lundin "is not only a political crook but a would-be revolutionary."
41. Martin B. Madden–Edward H. Wright, June 22, 1921. In a confidential letter dated June 17, Madden notified a lawyer for Frank Masce that he had raised the *Tribune* lawsuit with President Harding that morning and secured Harding's promise to "send for the secretary of the treasury within 30 minutes and convey his views" to the Chicago collector of revenue. Harding also pledged to restrain his appointees from making trouble for the Thompson organization. His action amounted to obstruction of justice, an impeachable offense.
42. RRM–Kate McCormick, September 27, 1921, McCormick Family Papers.
43. Ibid.
44. RRM–C. W. Raymond, September 21, 1921.
45. RRM–Kate McCormick, May 29, 1921, McCormick Family Papers.
46. Kate McCormick–Medill McCormick, June 12, 1921, McCormick Family Papers; Oswald Garrison Villard, "The World's Greatest Newspaper," *The Nation*, February 1, 1922. As if to confirm Villard's harsh strictures, McCormick complained to Patterson in January 1923 about the continuing English influence over American academics, clergyman, and writers.
47. Arthur Sears Henning recollections, McCormick biographical project; *Chicago Tribune*, May 27, 1946.
48. Kate McCormick–Medill McCormick, undated, McCormick Family Papers. "Joe, being a true Patterson," Kate assured Medill, "is seeking some way to knife you"; Henning recollections, McCormick biographical project.
49. Interview with Chester Gould, TOHP.
50. Ibid.

9. The Man in the Tower

1. *Chicago Tribune*, February 26, 1925; Kristie Miller, *Ruth Hanna McCormick, A Life in Politics*, Albuquerque, N.M., 1992, p. 151; Harold Hutchings–Stanton Cook, June 30, 1976.
2. Elmer Gertz, "Eccentric Titan, McCormick of the *Tribune*," *The Nation*, April 30, 1955, p. 362.

3. Katherine Solomonson, "Chicago Cathedral of Commerce," *Chicago History*, Spring 1989.

4. Francis C. Coughlin, "The Colonel," *The Chicagoan*, February 9, 1929.

5. Interview with Eleanor Nagle, TOHP; S. E. Thomason–Walter Sammis, July 25, 1926; Alexander, "The Duke of Chicago."

6. Robert L. Shebs, "What's Happening at the Tribune," *Chicago*, December 1954; Alexander, "The Duke of Chicago."

7. Interview with Carl Wiegman; interview with Robert P. Howard, Sangamon State University.

8. *Editor and Publisher*, January 25, 1969.

9. *Chicago Tribune*, April 2, 1955.

10. Interview with Don Maxwell, TOHP; Trohan, "My Life with the Colonel"; Greer Williams, "I Worked for McCormick," *The Nation*, October 10, 1942. Aviation writer Wayne Thomis, asked by the *Tribune* executive Howard Wood to make his stories more accessible to the general public, replied, "You don't understand. I'm doing it for Colonel McCormick — to interest him" (TOHP).

11. Williams, "I Worked for McCormick"; *Time*, April 11, 1955; interview with Howard Wood, TOHP.

12. Wood interview, TOHP.

13. Interview with William Fulton, TOHP; interview with Levering Cartwright, TOHP; Williams, "I Worked for McCormick"; *Time*, April 11, 1955.

14. RRM–Richard Orr, September 14, 17, 1951; Howard interview, Sangamon State University.

15. Maxwell interview, TOHP; interview with Willard Edwards, TOHP.

16. Alexander, "The Duke of Chicago."

17. Ibid.; interview with Fred Byington, TOHP.

18. Maxwell interview, TOHP.

19. Wood interview, TOHP.

20. RRM–Joseph Patterson, September 19, 1929.

21. Interview with Paul Fulton, TOHP; interview with A. M. Kennedy, TOHP.

22. Jack Fuller to author, January 2, 1995.

23. RRM–Ralph M. Shaw, December 29, 1942; Gwen Morgan and Arthur Veysey, *Poor Little Rich Boy*, Wheaton, Ill., 1985, p. 455.

24. Interview with Walter Trohan, Herbert Hoover Presidential Library.

25. Maxwell interview, TOHP.

26. Ibid.

27. Confidential source; interview with John Park, TOHP.

28. King interview, TOHP.

29. Hintersdorf interview, TOHP.

30. Interview with Eleanor Page, TOHP.

31. Interview with Dr. Theodore Van Dellen, TOHP.

32. Interview with Harry J. Hirsch, TOHP; King interview, TOHP; *Chicago Tribune*, April 2, 1955.

33. Morgan and Veysey, *Poor Little Rich Boy*, p. 455.

34. H. B. David, "The Troubled Travels of Colonel McCormick," *The Reporter*, August 4, 1953.

35. Joseph Patterson, memorandum, May 2, 1927; RRM–Joseph Patterson, March 27, 1927; Joseph Patterson–RRM, November 5, 1926.

36. Jack Alexander, "Vox Pop II," *The New Yorker*, August 13, 1938.

37. RRM–Joseph Patterson, December 17, 1933; RRM–Emory Thomason, January 18, 1928.

38. Interview with John Park, TOHP.

39. Charles McCabe, "Himself," *San Francisco Chronicle*, December 23, 1975; Lester Weinrott, "Chicago Radio: The Glory Days," *Chicago History*, Spring-Summer 1974.

40. RRM–Joseph Patterson, March 23, 1929.

41. Interview with J. Loy Maloney, TOHP.

42. Ibid.

43. *Chicago Tribune*, March 16, 1927.

44. John Kobler, *Capone*, New York, 1971, pp. 196–99.

45. *Chicago Herald and Examiner*, February 15, 1931; Kobler, *Capone*, p. 235.

46. E. M. Antrim–RRM, February 17, 1931; RRM–*Chicago Herald and Examiner*, February 19, 1931.

47. McCormick interview, TOHP.

48. RRM–William H. Thompson, May 22, 1927.

49. Lloyd Wendt, *Chicago Tribune*, Chicago, 1979, p. 518.

50. *Chicago Tribune*, April 14, 1928.

51. RRM–Herbert Hoover, August 13, 1928.

52. Herbert Hoover–RRM, August 16, 1928, RRM–Herbert Hoover, November 9, 1928; RRM–"Dearest mother," November 30, 1928.

53. Trohan, "My Life with the Colonel."

54. Herbert Hoover–RRM, "Confidential," March 30, 1929; RRM–Herbert Hoover, April 4, 1929. McCormick was genuinely outraged over Hoover's southern strategy, telling one editorial writer that if a child of his got into trouble, he would naturally hire the best lawyer in town to defend him: "AND HOOVER PROPOSED TO TAKE THIS AWAY FROM THEM" (Levering Cartwright–Clayton Kirkpatrick, May 13, 1974).

55. Hoover schedule, April 17, 1928, Hoover Library; Kobler, *Capone*, p. 276.

56. Arthur Sears Henning–RRM, April 17, 1929; RRM–Herbert Hoover, June 12, 1929.

57. "Scandal and Information!" American Civil Liberties Union, March 1931; *Chicago Tribune*, March 28, 1928.

58. RRM–Malcolm Bingay, February 25, 1935; Weymouth Kirkland–RRM, September 14, 1928.

59. Weymouth Kirkland–RRM, December 24, 1929.

60. J. M. Near–RRM, December 14, 1929.

61. RRM–Harry Chandler, December 23, 1929; Harry Chandler–RRM, January 1, 1930; RRM–E. H. Butler, January 18, 1930.

62. S. E. Thomason–RRM, February 14, 1930; RRM–M. V. Atwood, February 17, 1930; William E. MacFarlane–RRM, October 14, 1936.

63. RRM–Emory Thomason, February 18, 1930; RRM–Weymouth Kirkland, May 25, May 28, June 11, 1930.
64. J. M. Near–RRM, February 4, 1931.
65. RRM–Charles E. Hughes, June 2, 1931; RRM–C. B. Blethen, June 2, 1931.
66. RRM–Roger Baldwin, June 6, 1931; RRM–W. F. Hardy, June 26, 1931.
67. *Editor and Publisher*, October 24, 1931.
68. Ibid.; RRM–Leon Stolz, March 13, 1930.
69. Frank Parker Stockbridge, "The Great Artist Behind the W.G.N.," *American Press*, June 1931; *Editor and Publisher*, April 5, 1955. McCormick offered his own definition of freedom of the press in February 1935, when he told Detroit publisher Malcolm Bingay, "Freedom of the Press is the liberty guaranteed by the Constitution of the United States and by the constitutions of the several states to write for publication, to publish his writings, or to cause another to publish them upon any terms that may be agreeable to himself and a publisher, and to publish the writings of another upon terms agreeable to himself and the writer."

10. Hard Times

1. RRM–Joseph Patterson, November 27, 1929; Kate McCormick–RRM, January 11, 1931. Prior to the crash, the *Tribune* financial writer J. Howard Wood urged readers to buy bonds instead of stocks, in keeping with instructions from McCormick. Apparently he went too far. "I thought maybe you would just warn them a little," the Colonel remarked afterward, "that it might rain a little — not that the tide was out."
2. RRM–Kate McCormick, February 5, 1930; *Chicago Tribune*, March 7, 1930.
3. "An Address by Robert R. McCormick," September 14, 1931; RRM–Tiffany Blake, May 6, 1931.
4. *Chicago Tribune*, September 5, 15, 1930.
5. RRM–Edward Hurley, October 27, 1931; RRM–Tiffany Blake, December 28, 1931.
6. Draft *Tribune* advertisement, February 1931.
7. RRM–Westbrook Pegler, December 11, 1931; RRM–Tiffany Blake, January 15, November 29, 1930.
8. *Chicago Tribune*, March 8, April 11, 1930. McCormick deplored Hoover's "press agenting" on the unemployment situation. "The thing for him to do is to talk less and do more, especially on the Postoffice and the Illinois waterway" (RRM–Tiffany Blake, October 18, 1930). Not since TR, the Colonel complained in October 1930, had there been a true nationalist in the White House. As a result, the presidential office had been dominated by "internationalists and little Americans" (*Chicago Tribune*, October 17, 1930). Interestingly, McCormick opposed efforts in Congress to outlaw domestic Communists. "The empty stomach is the great revolutionary," declared the *Tribune* in January 1931, "and mere counter propaganda will not fill it . . . the answer is not argument or heedless repression, but a strong effort to improve

conditions, not only by well considered measures of public action, but by generous contribution of private means."

9. *Chicago Tribune*, April 2, 1955.

10. "Address by William Hale Thompson, Apollo Theater," October 31, 1930. George Reedy, whose father was a Thompson-era *Tribune* reporter, recalled for me one theory about the origins of the McCormick-Thompson feud. It was said that Big Bill, on learning that a *Tribune* loading dock encroached on city property by six inches, tried to shake down the Colonel, a tactic widely and profitably employed against countless Chicago businesses. McCormick refused to go along with the crude tradeoff; rather than pay a bribe to city hall, he tore down the fraction of the dock that intruded on municipal property. McCormick himself told Tiffany Blake in October 1930 that he was surprised by rumors suggesting an accord had been reached between the *Tribune* and "William the Obese . . . the worst Mayor Chicago his ever had . . . The *Tribune* did not fight the city hall corruption for all these years to lie down at the eleventh hour."

11. "The Tribune Shadow," Thompson campaign advertisement; Paul M. Green, "Anton J. Cermak," *The Mayors*, Carbondale, Ill., 1987.

12. Frank J. Wilson, "Undercover Man: He Trapped Capone," *Collier's*, April 26, 1947.

13. Cliff Raymond, "Jake Lingle," McCormick biographical files.

14. RRM memo, "Lingle." According to Walter Trohan, the Colonel was incensed over the tone adopted by the priest who conducted Lingle's June 12 funeral. "The priest, who obviously knew Jake, had his fingers crossed, saying it could be hoped he would be forgiven for the sins of his grown days" (Trohan notes prepared for author).

15. Memorandum, "Publisher's Meeting, Saturday, June 14, 1930."

16. Ibid.

17. *Chicago Tribune*, June 30, 1930.

18. Walter Fitzmaurice, "McCormick and His *Tribune*," *The Sign*, January 1947.

19. *Chicago Tribune*, July 23, 1930; D. M. Deininger, June 19, July 7, 1930; Maloney interview, TOHP. "Jake offered to take me to talk to Capone one time and I accepted it," recalled Maloney in 1975, "for which [Don] Maxwell said I was a damned fool." He went to Capone's headquarters in the Metropolitan Hotel but just missed his quarry. They later spoke on the telephone. "And it was funny," Maloney continued. "He had a woman with him that Jake later told me gave him the syphilis that killed him."

20. Maloney interview, TOHP; Joseph Patterson–RRM, August 18, 1930.

21. Interview with Wayne Thomis, TOHP. Corpening was described by *Fortune* in May 1934 as "one of those versatile young men who can handle details in business hours, play polo, converse charmingly, invariably make himself useful." Among the more offbeat assignments he received from McCormick was an investigation into the seeming infertility of two black swans at Cantigny of which the Colonel was especially proud. Corpening summoned experts, who informed him and his master that both of the creatures were males.

At the height of the Lingle controversy, McCormick summoned Moe Annenberg for a discussion of the floundering *Liberty* magazine. The Colonel, referring to the case of the murdered reporter, complained that no one in his organization ever told him things he should know until it was too late. Annenberg replied courageously that McCormick wouldn't believe bad news and would only punish its bearer.

22. An excellent contemporary account of the entire Lingle affair is to be found in Edward Dean Sullivan's *Chicago Surrenders*, New York, 1930.

23. "Statement of Leo V. Brothers, Monday, June 29, 1936," interrogated by William Hale Thompson. Lingle's mother, among others, wrote to Brothers in jail, absolving him of responsibility for the murder of her son.

24. *Time*, January 19, 1931; RRM–*Time* Inc., January 21, 1931; RRM–Charles Rathbun, March 16, 1931.

25. Interview with George Reedy. Pat Maloney probably came as close to the truth as anyone when he said, "I have no reason to believe that Brothers didn't do the job. I have every reason to believe that he didn't know Lingle from Adam's off ox."

26. George Seldes, "My Decade with Colonel McCormick," *Lost Generation Journal*, Fall 1974.

27. Ibid.

28. Root, *The Paris Edition*, p. 72.

29. Ibid., p. 67.

30. Ibid.

31. William L. Shirer, *The Start*, Boston, 1976, pp. 229–30.

32. Memoirs, pp. 310–12; Shirer, *The Start*, p. 298. James Thurber memorably described the *Paris Tribune* as "a country newspaper published in a great city."

33. Seldes, "My Decade with Colonel McCormick."

34. RRM–George Seldes, October 10, 1927; George Seldes–RRM, October 28, 1927. "In the days when Seldes was with THE TRIBUNE," McCormick wrote of the left-wing journalist in April 1949, "he was a reliable correspondent, but after he left us he found it more profitable to become a professional liar."

35. Clayton, "An American Story," p. 287.

36. Root, *The Paris Edition*, p. 75.

37. Shirer, *The Start*, pp. 377–78. Another version of the story, with a virtually identical punchline, appears in Alexander, "The World's Greatest Newspaper."

38. Shirer, *The Start*, pp. 511–14.

39. RRM–William L. Shirer, May 3, 1930.

40. RRM–Joseph Patterson, May 5, 1928.

41. RRM–Larry Rue, November 22, 1929.

42. William L. Shirer–RRM, November 19, 1930.

43. RRM–William L. Shirer, November 17, 1930.

44. RRM–William L. Shirer, July 2, 1931.

45. William L. Shirer–RRM, August 21, 1931; RRM–William L. Shirer, September 8, 1931.

46. RRM–William L. Shirer, April 27, 1932.

47. William L. Shirer–RRM, July 7, 1932.

48. William L. Shirer, *The Nightmare Years*, Boston, 1984, pp. 49–50.

49. William L. Shirer–RRM, October 20, 1932; William L. Shirer–E. S. Beck, October 19, 1932; RRM–Edmond Taylor, July 19, 1932.

50. RRM–William L. Shirer, December 30, 1932. Shirer complained to McCormick, in a letter dated December 23, 1932, that the thousand-dollar settlement the *Tribune* had been forced to make with Anna May Wong hardly justified his firing. "Your keeping me in India on a meager salary for a year cost me more than that out of my own pocket just to support my family. And to boot it ruined my health for years. And now you repay me like this."

51. Shirer, *The Nightmare Years*, p. 57; William L. Shirer–RRM, January 20, 1933.

52. Clayton, "An American Story," p. 215.

53. "Re Katharine Medill McCormick's Will," April 12, 1932; Shirer, *The Start*, pp. 366–67.

54. RRM–Kate McCormick, November 19, 1932; Marie Dougherty–RRM, October 31, 1927; RRM–Marie Dougherty, November 2, 1927; Kate McCormick–RRM, October 6, 1929, December 11, 1927, July 27, 1929. "Dearest Bertie," Kate wrote to her son in April 1931, "I am so glad you could get me the same rooms on the *France* which I had the last time. P.S. I was afraid I would not get them when I didn't hear from you so long."

55. Kate even relented — slightly — toward Amy McCormick, telling lawyers that she was changing her will to give her surviving son more *Tribune* stock in part because Amy had tried hard to comfort her husband, and because Bert had gone out of his way to visit his mother faithfully.

56. Ann McCarty–RRM, June 27, 1932.

57. RRM–John Minor, July 23, 1932; RRM–Edmund Gross, July 21, 1932; RRM–Joseph Patterson, July 6, 1932.

58. In the final years of her life, Kate remained capable of cutting remarks about her son. "Bertie's not quite right in the head," Waverly Root quoted her as saying in his memoir, *The Paris Edition*. "They'll have to put him away someday."

59. "On the Edge of Destruction," RRM speech, March 16, 1932.

60. "Help Save Your Country," RRM speech, July 19, 1932.

61. RRM–Professor William E. Dodd, August 20, 1932; RRM–E. S. Beck, December 2, 1929; *Chicago Tribune*, December 11, 1932.

62. *Chicago Tribune*, April 22, 1932.

63. RRM–Joseph Patterson, June 21, 1932; Franklin D. Roosevelt–RRM, June 24, 1932.

64. RRM–Franklin D. Roosevelt, June 29, 1932.

65. RRM–Franklin D. Roosevelt, August 6, 1932.

66. Ibid. "I am continually impressed that Hoover is a Jacobite," McCormick had complained. "The Jacobites were furious with the resistance to the royal will, but the royal will never had a will of its own. It was always directed by favorites around the throne, in foreign policies of Louix XIV just as Hoover in his foreign policy is directed by England." As the 1932 campaign lurched toward the finish line, the *Tribune* dismissed Hoover and Roosevelt as virtu-

ally indistinguishable. Hoover, McCormick told his editorial writers, "although at the head of a Marxian bureaucracy, still represents . . . the only candidacy for which a conservative . . . can vote. Mr. Roosevelt is drawn to the left by his support. If he is elected he will be under great pressure to bring a change in American government in the direction of Karl Marx."

67. RRM–E. S. Beck, November 14, 1932; RRM–A. F. Jacques, December 30, 1932.
68. RRM–Perley Boone, January 5, 1933; RRM–John Boettiger, January 10, 1933; *Chicago Tribune*, January 12, 1933.
69. John Boettiger–RRM, undated.
70. RRM–Franklin D. Roosevelt, February 23, 1933; RRM–Jim Farley, March 8, 1948.
71. John Boettiger–RRM, February 7, 1933.
72. Howard Wood interview, TOHP.
73. RRM–John Boettiger, March 20, 1933.
74. RRM–Joseph Patterson, March 8, 1933; RRM–Tiffany Blake, undated; "Aikin, So. Carolina," March 9, 1933.

11. The Duel

1. RRM–Tiffany Blake, March 28, 1933.
2. Ibid.; RRM–Tiffany Blake, November 27, July 17, 1933.
3. RRM–TIffany Blake, April 3, 1933. On April 4, McCormick, still in Aikin, told Blake, "We have got to give Roosevelt credit for cutting the veterans' costs."
4. *Chicago Tribune*, May 17, 1933; RRM–Tiffany Blake, April 3, 1933.
5. RRM–John Boettiger, May 4, 1933.
6. RRM–Franklin D. Roosevelt, May 6, 1933; Franklin D. Roosevelt–RRM, May 16, 1933.
7. RRM–Tiffany Blake, May 6, 1935; John Boettiger–RRM, May 8, 1933.
8. RRM–Tiffany Blake, May 31, 1933.
9. "Our Republic Is at Stake," RRM speech, February 15, 1940.
10. *Chicago Tribune*, July 12, 1933; Harold L. Ickes–RRM, July 14, 1933; RRM–Harold Ickes, July 17, 1933. Hugh Johnson, head of the industrial codes section of the NRA, was less fortunate than Ickes. McCormick instructed Boettiger to check out reports that Johnson was dictatorial by nature, "more of a Mussolini than an American."
11. RRM–John Boettiger, June 24, 1933. Thereafter, at McCormick's orders, the *Tribune* characterized all expenditures made under the NRA as "easy money" within its news columns.
12. L. B. Palmer–RRM, June 27, 1933.
13. Weymouth Kirkland–RRM, July 25, 1933.
14. RRM–Tiffany Blake, April 2, 1933.
15. RRM–Sigrid Schultz, May 5, 1933.
16. Sigrid Schultz–RRM, February 20, 1933; *Chicago Tribune*, August 10, 1933.
17. Interview with Sigrid Schultz, TOHP.
18. Ibid.

19. *Chicago Tribune*, August 12, 1933. McCormick saw little to distinguish German dictatorship from the Soviet model. Their principle difference, declared the *Tribune* on September 26, 1933, "is that Stalin speaks Russian and Hitler speaks German." Otherwise, "Stalin says a man with two coins is an enemy of Society and sends him off to forced labor in the arctic. Hitler says a Jew is an enemy of society and enforces a boycott against him." Both regimes deified central authority, made war on the political opposition, and exercised rigid control over the printed and spoken word.

20. Schultz interview, TOHP. "The treaty of Versailles lies like a trident in every German heart," McCormick declared in the *Tribune* on August 11, 1933. "Admission of the war guilt, loss of national self-respect and economic slavery have rankled day and night for 15 years . . . Reaction against world-wide abuse accounts for the wild applause that greets Hitler's platitudes about the greatness of the German soul. Reaction against the Versailles treaty explains their sobs when he refers to Germany's sufferings. Reaction against the poverty it imposed accounts for the plundering of the Jews."

21. Arthur Sears Henning–RRM, October 27, 1933.

22. RRM speech, November 4, 1933, released in newsreel form by Pathe Film Company; *Time*, November 13, 1933. With characteristic pith, Frank Waldrop described Carey Orr as "brutal and slugging an attacker as Thomas Nast" and his fellow cartoonist Joseph Parrish as "a born gifted master of sly observation that britches do slip. FDR merely hated Orr," Waldrop wrote in August 1993, "but Parrish shattered him."

23. *Chicago Tribune*, January 12, 1943.

24. Arthur Sears Henning–RRM, December 18, 12, 1933; RRM–Arthur Sears Henning, December 20, 1933.

25. John Boettiger–RRM, December 25, 1933; RRM–John Boettiger, January 2, 1934.

26. RRM–Tiffany Blake, February 14, 16, 1934; RRM–Tiffany Blake, October 31, 1933. A few weeks later, McCormick likened the NRA to the politically privileged "established churches" of Russian communism, German Nazism, and Italian fascism. "Query: Can we invoke against it the Constitutional provisions against an established church and disabilities of nonmembers?" This novel theory of constitutional interpretation did not find its way into print, but it does suggest both the intensity of McCormick's opposition to the New Deal and his willingness to construct the nation's organic law in ways scarcely imaginable to constitutional scholars or Supreme Court justices.

27. Wood interview, TOHP.

28. RRM–John Boettiger, March 1, 1934.

29. RRM–Tiffany Blake, March 31, 1934. McCormick felt vindicated in 1936, when he assured a black minister who had written to protest the unjust treatment of the Scottsboro boys (nine black farm workers sentenced to death on rape charges) that he intended to oppose "with every fiber of my body" the AAA and the "serfdom and bondage" imposed on southern tenant workers by the Democratic party.

30. Ibid.; *Chicago Tribune*, April 24, 1934.

31. Harold L. Ickes, *Autobiography of a Curmudgeon*, New York, 1948, p. 60. "I recognize my symptoms," McCormick wrote to Henry Pringle, the journalist-historian who had completed an extensive profile of the *Tribune* and its publisher in April 1934. "It had never occurred to me before that I was a kind of honest Noloch or irritable Galahad."

32. Williams, "I Worked for McCormick"; RRM–John Boettiger, September 21, 1934; RRM–Arthur Sears Henning, March 27, 1934.

33. RRM–John Boettiger, August 9, 1934.

34. *Chicago Tribune*, June 29, 1935; MES–Howard Schendorf, March 20, 1935.

35. James H. Berner–Louis M. Howe, June 6, 1934; Louis M. Howe–James H. Berner, June 13, 1934; A. W. Stevenson–Louis M. Howe, August 7, 1934; referred by Howe to Justice Department, September 11, 1934, Franklin D. Roosevelt Library.

36. RRM–Edward J. Kelly, December 24, 1934, June 5, 1935.

37. *Time*, May 2, 1934; RRM–T. Bentley Mott, May 15, 1934.

38. Waldrop interview.

39. RRM–Tiffany Blake, February 9, 15, 1935.

40. RRM–Raymond Hood, September 16, 1929.

41. RRM–Willis Irwin, March 24, November 30, 1930.

42. RRM–Willis Irwin, May 8, 1931.

43. RRM–Willis Irwin, June 7, 1934; RRM–Cora Clagstone, July 10, 1953.

44. Morgan and Veysey, *Poor Little Rich Boy*, p. 341.

45. Interview with Zeffy Snydecker; interview with Brooks McCormick.

46. Waldrop interview.

47. M. M. Cullom–RRM, February 10, 1948; RRM–M. M. Cullom, February 11, 1948.

48. Interview with A. M. Kennedy, TOHP.

49. Willard Edwards–RRM, March 25, 1935; Edwards interview, TOHP.

50. RRM memo, October 10, 1935. Before the year was out, McCormick instructed his editorial writers to warn that confiscatory taxes would not apply only to great personal fortunes. Inevitably the movement would lead to the breakup of foundations, colleges, hospitals — even churches. "While we will not even intimate it," he went on, getting in a dig at Chicago's liberal prelate, "I think this will give Cardinal Mundelein something to think about."

51. RRM–William Allen White, March 26, 1935. To a Pennsylvania newspaper publisher who urged him to seek the presidency, McCormick replied on February 1, 1936, that he was "emphatically" not interested. "Every resource at my command is devoted to defeating Roosevelt because I feel that his re-election will involve the destruction of the Republic. If I were to be even a receptive candidate, I am sure I would lose part of whatever effectiveness I have in this battle because I would then be thinking of myself and modifying my attack to suit my private ends."

52. RRM–Joseph Patterson, September 8, 1936; RRM–Fanny Butcher, March 18, 1936.

53. Walter Trohan, *Political Animals*, Garden City, N.Y., 1975, p. 147.

54. "Our Debatable Middle West," *Review of Reviews*, February 1936.

55. RRM–E. S. Beck, June 17, 1936 (a copy of McCormick's letter found its way to Roosevelt within three weeks); McCormick interview, TOHP; Julius Miner, "The National Convention of 1936," unpublished McCormick biography.
56. *Chicago Tribune*, June 20, 1936; RRM–Alfred M. Landon, July 8, 1936.
57. Edwards interview, TOHP.
58. RRM–E. S. Beck, July 18, August 29, 1936.
59. *Aero Digest*, October 4, 1936; *Chicago Tribune*, October 24, 1936; James Woolley, "Roosevelt Name Linked with Plan to Grab Airline Contracts," McClure Newspaper Syndicate, October 25, 1936.
60. J. Loy Maloney–RRM, undated.
61. RRM–Alfred M. Landon, September 21, 1936; Alfred M. Landon–RRM, September 21, 1936.
62. RRM–Alfred M. Landon, September 14, 1936; RRM–John B. Kennedy, October 8, 1936.
63. RRM–Thomas W. Lamont, October 16, 1936; RRM–Phillip Kinsley, October 13, 1936.
64. Sigrid Schultz, October 3, 1936; RRM–Alfred M. Landon, October 14, 1936.
65. RRM–Ruth Hanna McCormick Simms, October 8, 1936; *Time*, November 2, 1936; RRM–Joseph Patterson, October 16, 1936.
66. Undated petition to RRM; A. L. Messing–RRM, November 3, 1936; E. S. Beck–RRM, October 21, 1936; RRM–Alfred M. Landon, October 28, 1936.
67. RRM–Frank O. Lowden, October 26, 1936; RRM–Phillip Kinsley, November 2, 1936.
68. *Chicago Tribune*, April 2, 1955.
69. Constant Reader–RRM, November 4, 1936.
70. RRM–Alfred M. Landon, December 3, 1936.
71. Ibid.

12. Undominated

1. RRM–David Darrah, December 22, 1936. To McCormick, the abdication and subsequent remarriage of Edward VII was "the most sensational event that has happened since King David took Bathsheba."
2. Edmond Taylor–RRM, December 24, 1936; Alex Small–RRM, January 10, 1936.
3. Sigrid Schultz–RRM, April 12, 1937.
4. *Chicago Tribune*, August 22, 1937.
5. Chesser Campbell–RRM, February 26, 1943; *Time*, June 9, 1947.
6. *TIme*, February 20, 1939; RRM, "Why Advertisers Should Not Attempt to Influence Editorial Content," *Printer's Ink*, August 25, 1938.
7. RRM–Joseph Patterson, June 2, 1936; Trohan interview, Hoover Library.
8. RRM–Nathan Goldblatt, August 26, 1937.
9. John Bartlow Martin, "Colonel McCormick of the Tribune," *Harper's Magazine*, October 1944.
10. Trohan interview, Hoover Library.
11. Martin, "Colonel McCormick of the Tribune"; interview with Toni Gillman.

12. Martin, "Colonel McCormick of the Tribune."

13. India Edwards, *Pulling No Punches*, New York, 1977, pp. 67–68.

14. Arthur Sears Henning–RRM, February 10, 1937; RRM–C. K. Gregg, February 17, 1937; Kenneth S. Davis, *FDR: Into the Storm*, New York, 1993, p. 85.

15. RRM–Arthur Sears Henning, May 19, 1937.

16. Maloney interview, TOHP; *The Tribunit*, September 1938.

17. John J. McPhaul, *Deadlines and Monkeyshines: The Fabled World of Chicago Journalism*, New York, 1962, pp. 120–21.

18. RRM–E. S. Beck, December 8, 1937.

19. Trohan, *Political Animals*, pp. 68–69.

20. RRM–Dean Shailer Mathews, February 19, 1937.

21. RRM–Winston Churchill, November 18, 1937.

22. Maloney interview, TOHP.

23. Mrs. C. D. Barnes–RRM, October 26, 1943; RRM–Mrs. C. D. Barnes, February 5, 1937.

24. RRM–Joseph Patterson, May 8, 1937; RRM–Mrs. C. D. Barnes, December 3, 1936.

25. RRM–Mrs. C. D. Barnes, November 19, 1943.

26. RRM–Joseph Patterson, September 9, 1936.

27. *Newsweek*, November 12, 1945. Walter Winchell, for one, did not take Cissy's ridicule lying down. While Drew Pearson responded to her attacks by proposing a society for protection against ex-mothers-in-law, Winchell went for the jugular. "Very special bulletin!" he declared on his radio broadcast. "The craziest woman in Washington, D.C., is not yet confined at St. Elizabeth's Hospital for the Insane. She is, however, expected any edition."

28. RRM–Mrs. Elmer Schlesinger, July 16, 1928.

29. *Editor and Publisher*, May 13, 1944.

30. Ibid.; Stanley Walker, "Eleanor Patterson," *Saturday Evening Post*, May 6, 1939.

31. Joseph Patterson–Cissy Patterson, June 3, 1935. FDR gave as good as he got, attacking unnamed millionaire "parasites" in their twenty-room mansions on Massachusetts Avenue — a none too thinly veiled reference to Mrs. P.

32. Eleanor Patterson–RRM, September 1, 1939; RRM–Eleanor Patterson, October 10, 1939.

33. Maryland McCormick interview, TOHP.

34. RRM–Arthur Schmon, August 21, 1936; interview with Terrence Flahiff, TOHP.

35. Flahiff interview, TOHP.

36. Interview with H. Arthur Sewell, TOHP.

37. Ibid.

38. Franklin D. Roosevelt–Joseph Patterson, November 9, 1945.

39. J. E. Vallillee–William Fulton, June 30, 1945; Flahiff interview, TOHP; Sewell interview, TOHP; interview with Lawrence Richard Boys, TOHP.

40. Sewell interview, TOHP.

41. Ibid.; Ontario Paper Company publication, "The Facts about Baie Commeau."

42. Interview with Mrs. G. J. Lane, TOHP.

43. Sewell interview, TOHP.

44. RRM–Arthur Schmon, June 3, 1939; interview with Mrs. T. B. Fraser, TOHP; Byington interview, TOHP; interview with Bazy Tankersley.

45. Lane interview, TOHP.

46. Ibid. Alice Lane saw another side of the Colonel one night when her two-year-old grandson climbed into McCormick's lap and gave him a goodnight kiss. "The Colonel didn't say anything," she recalled. "But when Christmas came, he sent him the most elaborate electric train set you ever saw in your life. I'm sure there wasn't a thing that could be added to that electric train set . . . it had to be put away for years before he was able to play with it."

47. Lane interview, TOHP; RRM–James Lane, August 27, 1938.

48. Cissy Patterson–RRM, September 6, 1938. In anticipation of the visit, McCormick ordered up a lumberman's lunch of pea soup and trout, "rather than an effort at the Ritz."

49. Sigrid Schultz–RRM, March 29, 1938.

50. RRM–Sigrid Schultz, April 27, 1938.

51. Sir Ronald Lindsay–Right Honorable Anthony Eden, January 6, 1938, PRO.

52. Ibid.; interview with Paul C. Fulton, TOHP.

53. Interview with E. R. Noderer, TOHP; RRM–David Darrah, November 19, 1938.

54. Joseph Medill–George Upton, undated; Joseph Medill memo, July 30, 1896.

55. RRM–Joseph Ator, May 6, 1938.

56. RRM–E. S. Beck, September 26, 1938.

57. RRM–E. S. Beck, September 26, 1938. "The rest of the world is intent upon suicide," wrote McCormick. "It is our right and our duty to preserve sanity and civilization here."

58. RRM–Winston Churchill, September 14, 1938. In canceling his American visit, Churchill sent McCormick the latest volume of his Marlborough biography. "Welcome as it is, it is only less welcome than you would have been yourself," wrote McCormick in response. "May your international difficulties and our internal ones clear up with the New Year."

59. RRM–L. W. Cook, Jr., November 4, 1938.

60. RRM–Bainbridge Colby, November 14, 1938.

61. RRM–E. S. Beck, November 15, 25, 1938.

62. RRM–Joseph P. Kennedy, August 13, 1938.

63. Arthur Sears Henning–RRM, February 4, 1939. Henning's information came from Louis Glavis, former director of the investigating force of the Interior Department and Public Works Administration and no stranger to controversy. Glavis's accusations of wrongdoing against Secretary of the Interior Richard Ballinger had rocked the Taft administration twenty-five years earlier.

64. Ibid.; Trohan, *Political Animals*, pp. 144–46; James C. Schneider, *Should America Go to War?*, Chapel Hill, N. C., 1989, pp. 164–65.

65. Thomas E. Dewey–RRM, May 6, 1939; RRM–Thomas E. Dewey, July 27, 1939; Thomas E. Dewey–RRM, July 19, 1939.

66. Sigrid Schultz–RRM, May 16, 1939.

67. Ibid. "Schultz is our best correspondent," McCormick said after reading her

latest Berlin dispatches. "If she gets less than [David] Darrah, bring her up to him. If she gets the same, send her $100."

68. Sigrid Schultz–RRM, June 26, 1939.

69. Sigrid Schultz–RRM, July 9, 1939; RRM–E. S. Beck, July 8, 1939. "Then let us advocate making the CCC sissies into soldiers," McCormick added.

70. Sigrid Schultz–RRM, July 30, 1939.

71. Morgan and Veysey, *Poor Little Rich Boy*, pp. 356–57; Wood interview, TOHP.

72. Herbert Asbury, "High Wind in Chicago," *Collier's*, October 15, 1944.

73. Interview with Brooks McCormick.

74. "The Fabulous Colonel McCormick," *The Standard*, February 8, 1947; Brooks McCormick interview, TOHP.

75. Maxwell interview, TOHP; Wood interview, TOHP; Maryland McCormick interview, TOHP.

76. Morgan and Veysey, *Poor Little Rich Boy*, p. 348.

77. RRM–Joseph Patterson, February 15, 1938. Standing at the entrance to the ballroom of an elegant Palm Beach resort hotel one evening, McCormick was approached by an officious young man who warned him against venturing any further. "We do not allow people in white flannel trousers on the floor," he told the Colonel. "Tell the hicks on your committee I have forgotten more about dressing than they have ever known," replied McCormick. RRM–Mrs. Orville Taylor, January 19, 1954; Morgan and Veysey, *Poor Little Rich Boy*, p. 355.

78. RRM–May Birkhead, August 13, 1939; RRM–M. M. Corpening, August 13, 1939; RRM–Ruth Hanna McCormick Simms, August 13, 1939. "I am writing to keep busy," McCormick told his secretary, Genevieve Burke.

79. RRM–Joseph Patterson, August 14, 1939; Amy McCormick death certificate, August 14, 1939. McCormick's experiences at the bedside of his dying wife inspired a dread of hospitals and a strong interest in euthanasia.

80. RRM–Howard Ellis, December 12, 1939.

13. *America First*

1. Henry L. Stimson–RRM, September 7, 1939.

2. RRM–George C. Marshall, August 30, 1939, September 7, 1939.

3. RRM–R.C.H. DuClos, October 10, 1939. "Europe is back again at its old game of power politics and murderous wars," McCormick wrote on October 14, 1939. "We want no part of it." To those among his countrymen who felt a passionate attachment to one side or another in the current hostilities, he had some blunt advice: "If you have got the courage of your convictions, go over and fight. If you have not, shut up."

4. *Time*, April 11, 1955; Larry Rue–W. D. Maxwell, April 12, 1955. Taylor's behavior prompted McCormick to observe to Walter Trohan that foreign correspondents tended to become attached to the countries to which they were assigned. As partisans rather than reporters, he went on, "their effectiveness was greatly diminished."

5. RRM–E. S. Beck, September 29, 1939. Writing to Arthur Vandenberg in September 1939, McCormick dismissed cash-and-carry as a sophistry advanced by "war boilers . . . I think it very necessary to point out over and over again that the only issue is whether or not we are to allow arms and ammunition to be shipped abroad and challenge anybody to produce a reason why they could be helpful."

6. RRM–E. S. Beck, November 2, 1939.

7. RRM–Gifford Pinchot, November 20, 1939.

8. Sigrid Schultz–RRM, February 10, 1940.

9. RRM–William Allen White, March 6, 1940.

10. Interview with William J. Fulton, TOHP.

11. RRM–Charles G. Dawes, May 10, 1940; RRM–Cliff Raymond, May 10, 14, 1940.

12. Harold Hutchings, "Alfred M. Landon. Recollections of Colonel McCormick," April 22, 1977.

13. RRM–Leon Stolz, June 25, 1940.

14. RRM–Leon Stolz, June 29, 1940; Thomas E. Dewey–RRM, July 26, 1940; RRM–Thomas E. Dewey, August 1, 1940.

15. Interview with Frederick A. Nichols, TOHP; undated McCormick editorial instructions.

16. RRM–Cliff Raymond, July 3, 1940; Fanny Butcher, *Many Lives, One Love*, New York, 1972, p. 117.

17. Waldrop interview. McCormick told his New York cousin the story of a sixty-year-old man who let it be known that he intended to wed a twenty-year-old girl. His children were scandalized. They objected that in another twenty years he would be eighty and his bride forty. What then? "Hell," replied the lusty suitor, "I'd just get me another twenty-year-old."

18. Reuben interview; interview with Jack McCutcheon; Don Maxwell–Elbert Antrim, February 22, 1952. For the month of January 1952, described as "a light month" by the *Tribune*'s managing editor, Mrs. Pickering's expenses totaled $3,531. Long after McCormick's death, his onetime mistress was said to receive $400 a month.

19. Kennedy interview, TOHP; Dick Philbrick, "Memo re: Mrs. Pickering," February 27, 1975; interview with Eugene P. Struksacker, TOHP. Mrs. Pickering's temperamental nature was revealed by the call McCormick placed to Mike Kennedy, to whom the early *Tribune* fashion shows were entrusted. "Mrs. Pickering is here," said the Colonel, moments before the show was to begin, "and she says she won't show any of her gowns with a blue curtain. See what you can do about it." Kennedy eventually discovered that a skillful blend of lighting could transform a blue backdrop into virtually any color desired.

20. Claudia Cassidy, "Farewell, and Hail!" *Chicago Tribune*, August 10, 1947; Gillman interview; Howard Wood interview, TOHP.

21. Marion Claire–RRM, October 25, 1939; "The *Chicago Tribune*," RRM speech, December 13, 1939; RRM–Henry Weber, January 13, 1940.

22. A. J. Liebling, "Second City: At Her Feet the Slain Deer," *The New Yorker*, January 19, 1952; Trohan, "My Life with the Colonel"; Memo for the record, "Recollections of Jack Brickhouse," January 20, 1988.

23. RRM–Joseph Patterson, February 28, 1941; S. B. Field–RRM, undated; J. H. Brown–Jake Manasse, July 7, 1941; Marion Claire–J. L. Maloney, June 27, 1941; Marion Claire–Weymouth Kirkland, August 9, 1941.

24. *Chicago Tribune*, April 2, 1955.

25. RRM–Leon Stolz, September 17, 1940.

26. William J. Fulton interview, TOHP; RRM–Robert McCormick Adams, September 27, 1940.

27. RRM radio broadcast, September 29, 1940; Sigrid Schultz–RRM, October 8, 1940.

28. RRM–Joseph Patterson, November 1, 1940. On the eve of the voting, McCormick told his cousin that in the event of Roosevelt's triumph at the polls, "only the *News* can prevent our being prorated in Canada"; RRM–Sigrid Schultz, November 13, 1940.

29. RRM, undated editorial instructions.

30. Robert M. Hutchins–RRM, February 7, 1941; RRM–Arthur Vandenberg, February 12, 1941.

31. RRM–Arthur Vandenberg, February 12, 1941. "When has our country ever sought world leadership?" McCormick asked Landon on March 10, 1941. "For forty years, to my knowledge, it has been led around by the nose. Flunkies could not be more servile than our diplomats and secretaries of state have been, and are now."

32. *Time*, April 7, 1941; RRM–E. S. Beck, June 22, 1938.

33. RRM–Charles Lindbergh, March 7, 1941.

34. Ibid.

35. Charles Lindbergh–RRM, April 15, 1941.

36. Trohan, *Political Animals*, p. 137.

37. Ibid., p. 159.

38. William J. Fulton interview, TOHP.

39. Lillian Gish–RRM, undated; RRM–Lillian Gish, March 31, 1941.

40. RRM–Roy A. Roberts, May 6, 1941; interview with Hughston McBain, TOHP.

41. Interview with R. Douglas Stuart.

42. Ibid.

43. Ibid.

44. Interview with Katharine Graham.

45. RRM–Joseph Patterson, October 14, 1941.

46. "What Has Roosevelt Promised Churchill?" *Chicago Tribune*, August 15, 1941.

47. Alfred M. Landon–RRM, July 17, 1941.

48. John W. Park–RRM, June 6, 1941; J. L. Maloney–Mr. McMahon, June 6, 1941; J. L. Maloney–RRM, June 6, 1941.

49. Thomas Furlong–J. L. Maloney, August 1, 1941; RRM, "The *Sun*," February 19, 1942. "The *Chicago Daily News* and the *Sun* are like ham and eggs," wrote McCormick.

50. RRM–Chesly Manly, May 15, 1946.

51. Andrews, *Battle for Chicago*, pp. 296–305; *Time*, August 10, 1941; RRM–Cissy Patterson, June 26, 1942; RRM–J. D. Ferguson, October 11, 1943.

52. William Fulton–RRM, October 10, 1941. Almost a year earlier, McCormick

had asked his New York correspondent to check out reports of some "great faker . . . who runs Marshall Field, Jr. [sic]." He was referring to Zilboorg.

53. Arthur Sears Henning–RRM, October 21, 1941; J. L. Maloney–RRM, October 9, 1941; "Thumbnail Sketch of Jesse Jones, Silliman Evans," prepared by Luke Lea; Ted Morgan, *FDR*, New York, 1985, pp. 460–61.

54. *Fortune*, February 1942; Waldrop interview.

55. Harold Ickes, *The Lowering Clouds, 1939–1941*, New York, 1954, pp. 651–52; Stephen Early–L. B. Sherman, September 20, 1941, Roosevelt Library.

56. Trohan, *Political Animals*, pp. 139–40.

57. Nagle interview, TOHP.

58. *Atlanta Constitution*, August 25, 1944.

59. "War Plans Story," Trohan notes prepared for author.

60. Ibid.

61. RRM–Joseph Patterson, December 4, 1941.

62. *Chicago Tribune*, December 4, 1941; Trohan notes.

63. Thomas Fleming, "The Big Leak," *American Heritage*, December 1987; Trohan, *Political Animals*, p. 171. The investigative findings provided here are taken from FBI files, in particular from the reports of Joseph G. Genau, who supervised the bureau's probe of the war plans leak. Genau's reports are part of a thick dossier containing verbatim transcripts of interviews with Chesly Manly and Arthur Sears Henning, along with details of the investigation on Capitol Hill and within the military. Also within the FBI files are reports from various confidential informants, including one unnamed source who quoted Drew Pearson as saying that *he* had been offered a copy of the Victory Program a month before it appeared in the *Tribune*, by a War Department clerk who tried, unsuccessfully, to sell it to him for $400.

64. FBI interview with Chesly Manly, January 23, 1942. Asked if he put protecting sources above his patriotic obligations, Manly told his interrogators, "I don't consider this has anything to do with patriotism" (J. Edgar Hoover–William D. Mitchell, June 17, 1942). Hoover's "detailed summary" of the investigation, which entailed several hundred interviews, was made available to Frank Waldrop nearly a quarter-century later for use in preparing his biography of McCormick. It is cited here through the generous permission of Mr. Waldrop.

65. FBI summary, "Extent of FBI Investigations and Observations in Connection Therewith," June 23, 1942; Burton J. Wheeler, *Yankee From the West*, New York, 1962, p. 36.

66. Ickes, *The Lowering Clouds*, pp. 659–60; Lloyd Wendt–Clayton Kirkpatrick and Stanton Cook, July 17, 1976; William Stephenson, *A Man Called Intrepid*, New York, 1976, p. 298.

67. Fleming, "The Big Leak"; J. Edgar Hoover–Special Agent in Charge, Washington, D. C., May 11, 1942. On June 17, 1942, assistant attorney general Wendell Berge asked Hoover to supply the Bureau's findings on the war plans leak to the Criminal Division of the Justice Department — this barely a week after Stanley Johnston caused an uproar with his *Tribune* sidebar detailing the composition of a Japanese fleet shattered by a U.S. armada off Midway Island.

68. In a February 1993 interview, Waldrop repeated what he had earlier told

Fleming, and added a hunch that the FBI had been purposefully diverted from an investigative trail leading to the White House.

69. "The War Plans Story," Trohan notes.

70. FBI Memorandum, re: Unknown Subjects, June 15, 1942, pp. 4–5.

14. At War

1. Interview with Ward Quaal; Chalmers Roberts, ". . . And When We Heard," *Washington Post*, December 7, 1991. After somehow managing to slip some interventionist sentiments into the paper for which he toiled as Sunday editor, Roberts received a telegram from Cissy. "I think you are a nice young man but pretty fresh," it read.

2. Stephen T. Early, Memorandum for General Watson, December 10, 1941; E. M. W., Memorandum for the President, December 10, 1941, Roosevelt Library; Leo McGivena, *The News*, New York, 1969, pp. 311–12.

3. RRM–C. P. Summerall, March 11, 1942.

4. Robert Lasch, "Chicago Patriot," *Atlantic Monthly*, June 1942; RRM–Joseph Ator, March 6, 1942.

5. *Newsweek*, March 30, 1942. McCormick, it was said, looked upon the publication of his private correspondence as "a dirty trick."

6. *Chicago Daily News*, March 25, 1942.

7. Franklin D. Roosevelt, personal memorandum for General Arnold, March 26, 1942, Roosevelt Library.

8. H. H. Arnold, Memorandum for the President, April 4, 1942, Roosevelt Library.

9. Howard Ellis–Weymouth Kirkland, April 1, 1942; Howard Ellis–RRM, March 25, 1942.

10. RRM–Howard Ellis, October 23, 1942.

11. Confidential source.

12. RRM–Joseph Patterson, December 19, 1941.

13. Ibid.

14. R. D. Cahn, confidential memorandum to Colonel McCormick, "Summary of What I Learned on My Trip to Washington," January 26, 1942.

15. Transcript of FBI interview with RRM, March 17, 1942, made by Dorothy Murray, AP/*Chicago Sun* file, MRC. Writing to Joe Patterson on April 3, McCormick blamed Silliman Evans for calling out the FBI agents and urged his cousin to maintain an uncharacteristic silence in print over the affair. "We have been very successful in preventing Field from being sensational," he told Patterson. "Maybe making a big story over the FBI at this time would give him what he wanted."

16. Arthur Sears Henning–RRM, March 24, 1942; Joseph Patterson–RRM, March 31, 1942. Patterson passed on to his cousin in Chicago a list of nineteen papers in Illinois and Indiana that had been visited by FBI agents in connection with the AP case (W. E. MacFarlene–RRM, March 27, 1942). In an April 29, 1942, memorandum for J. Edgar Hoover, written in response to a recent

column by Frank Waldrop in the *Washington Times-Herald*, FBI official D. M. Ladd confirmed that "about two weeks prior to April 23, the Bureau received a specific request from the Attorney General, stating that the Bureau was to discontinue all inquiries in connection with this matter" — described earlier in the same document as an "investigation made by the FBI in an effort to force the Associated Press to grant membership in that organization to Marshall Field." Ladd wrote that "some thirty or forty" AP members had been contacted in seven states, among them the *New York Times, Baltimore Sun, Philadelphia Inquirer,* "and papers in Illinois."

17. *Chicago Tribune,* January 11, 1943; *New York Times,* April 21, 1942; RRM–Cissy Patterson, April 27, 1942. "I have heard so much about you all my life," Arnold wrote to McCormick on March 13, "I would esteem it a pleasure to meet you." In his memoirs, Arnold recounted his extraordinary encounter with McCormick before the AP gathering. The assistant attorney general flatly told the Colonel that his indictment was the object of the FBI investigation then under way. McCormick scoffed at the possibility, contending that Attorney General Biddle would never approve the prosecution of a newspaper. Arnold vowed to try anyway. McCormick expressed appreciation for his visitor's frankness. The entire visit lasted less than half an hour.

18. RRM–Joseph Patterson, April 3, June 17, 1942. For another view of McCormick's role in the AP controversy, see Waldrop, *McCormick of Chicago,* pp. 257–59.

19. RRM, "AP Litigation," December 23, 1943.

20. Wiegman, *Trees to News,* pp. 221–27; Harold Ickes–Franklin D. Roosevelt, October 17, 1942; RRM–Weymouth Kirkland, October 28, 1942.

21. J. L. Maloney–RRM, May 14, 1942.

22. Statement of J. Loy Maloney, managing editor, *Chicago Tribune,* Washington, D.C., July 9, 1942, p. 4, hereafter referred to as Maloney affadavit.

23. Ibid., p. 5.

24. Statement of Stanley Johnston, *Chicago Tribune* reporter, Washington, D.C., July 13, 1942, pp. 31–34, hereafter referred to as Johnston affadavit.

25. Maloney affadavit, p. 9.

26. Ibid., p. 12.

27. Ibid., pp. 13–15.

28. Johnston affadavit, pp. 4–8.

29. Don Maxwell–J. L. Maloney, June 8, 1942; Maloney affadavit, p. 15; "Maloney-Johnston Case Facts," November 5, 1954, p. 14.

30. RRM–Arthur Sears Henning, June 7, 1942.

31. Arthur H. McCollum Oral History, Naval Institute, p. 474.

32. Walter Trohan to J. L. Maloney, "This for your eyes and special perusal alone," January 27, 1948. Also on June 9, the day McCormick decreed that he would waive his copyright on Johnston's first three stories, he sent the following telegram, immediately transcribed by the FBI, to Cissy Patterson: "For your information when news of the AP election was telegraphed to Canada, the *Toronto Financial Post* sent a man to ask [Archibald] MacLeish the significance, and MacLeish replied, 'We are determined to control public opinion just the way we control steel or rubber.' It would be a very pleasant birthday

present to release the Coral Sea for tomorrow." In other words, McCormick hoped to needle MacLeish on his birthday by defying government efforts to suppress wartime reporting.

33. Frank Knox–Franklin D. Roosevelt, June 9, 1942, Roosevelt Library; "Confidential," Walter Trohan–Joseph Patterson, undated. Trohan spoke with naval officials, who confided Knox's role in the prosecution as well as FDR's intense personal interest in the case.

34. Frank Knox–Francis Biddle, June 9, 1942, Roosevelt Library.

35. RRM–Ernest J. King, June 15, 1942.

36. Maxwell interview, TOHP; RRM–Ernest J. King, June 16, 17, 1942.

37. J. Edgar Hoover–Edwin M. Watson, June 18, 1942; RRM–Marvin K. Hart, August 27, 1942.

38. Walter Trohan, "War Plans and Jap Code," notes prepared for author; *Chicago Tribune*, August 19, 1942.

39. In a July 16, 1942, phone conversation with Stanley Johnston, the contents of which Pat Maloney reported to Howard Ellis, a badly shaken Seligman took comfort from Johnston's assurance that none of the information used in his June 7 story had been obtained while at sea, but that the controversial sidebar "was all guesswork, surmise, opinion, and judgment, etc., as to what the makeup of the Jap fleet was." The two men even professed ignorance as to the origin of the now famous scrap of paper — an act presumably staged for the benefit of government agents listening into their conversation.

40. Stanley Johnston affadavit, Washington, D.C., June 9, 1942, given before naval investigators led by Vice Admiral Russell Willson; Clyde J. Van Arsdall, Jr., "Freedom of the Press or Treason," *U.S. Naval Institute Proceedings*, December 1977.

41. J. L. Maloney–Arthur Sears Henning, June 12, 1942.

42. Stanley Johnston affadavit, June 11, 1942. Yet another explanation of the mysterious scrap of paper was offered by John Clayton in his unpublished memoir, "An American Story." According to Clayton, on the morning of May 8, 1942, when the damaged *Lexington* was abandoned by its crew, Johnston and an unnamed signal officer were picked up by the destroyer *Phelps*. The officer had just completed decoding a long message giving the deployment of Japanese warships and enemy plans to attack Midway, intended for Admiral Frank Jack Fletcher and Admiral Aubrey Fitch, the fleet's highest-ranking commanders. As Clayton told it, the message, retrieved from the sinking *Lexington*, was carelessly left on a wardroom table of the *Phelps*, where it was seen and copied by Johnston. The story has one big hole in it: Johnston returned to the States on the troop carrier *Barnett*, not, as Clayton had it, by air.

43. E. Ken–J. L. Maloney, September 24, 1942. This memorandum recounting operations within Mitchell's shop was based on information gleaned at the time from U.S. Attorney Albert Woll as well as unnamed lawyers close to the federal probe.

44. Ibid.; *Newsweek*, August 24, 1942; Walter Trohan, "Confidential to Joseph Patterson." Trohan's chief source was Biddle himself. The attorney general confirmed that a "furious" Roosevelt directed Mitchell, through him, to convene

a grand jury and attribute the decision to Knox; Walter Trohan–R. J. Maloney, September 1, 1942; *PM*, June 23, 1942.

45. Maxwell interview, TOHP.

46. Howard Wood interview, TOHP.

47. Maxwell interview, TOHP.

48. Memo to Mr. Maloney, re: Wall, September 11, 1942, signed "Holt"; E. Ken–J. L. Maloney, September 24, 1942.

49. Thomis interview, TOHP.

50. Frank Waldrop, "Memorandum re: Midway," prepared for author, May 8, 1993.

51. *Time*, August 31, 1942; Page interview, TOHP.

52. Howard Wood interview, TOHP.

53. RRM–Cissy Patterson, August 21, 1942.

54. Jonathan Daniels, *White House Witness, 1942–1945*, Garden City, N.Y., pp. 199–200.

55. Waldrop, *McCormick of Chicago*, p. 246.

56. *Chicago Sun*, October 8, 1942; RRM–Joseph Ator, September 23, October 13, 1942.

57. Willard Shelton, "Boss McCormick's Men," *The Nation*, February 21, 1943; Walter Trohan, "Brooks," notes prepared for author.

58. RRM–Hamilton Fish, November 8, 1942; Henry Luce–RRM, December 13, 1942.

59. Don Maxwell–RRM, undated; RRM, "Answer Henry Luce the Squaw Man?" August 1943.

60. W. H. Gallienne, Memorandum, Colonel Robert McCormick, April 6, 1943, to Viscount Halifax, PRO.

61. *Time*, May 3, 1943; *PM*, April 22, 1943; RRM–William Benton, May 4, 1943; "Our Constitution in a World State," *Chicago Tribune*, May 8, 1943.

62. RRM–Alfred M. Landon, July 28, 1943; *Heard and Seen*, July 24, 1943; "Bertie on a White Horse," *New Republic*, July 26, 1943.

63. Dwight H. Green–RRM, July 16, 1943; RRM–Dwight H. Green, July 19, 1943; RRM–Joseph Ator, August 26, 1943. Writing to Dewey in March 1943, McCormick hedged his bets, telling the New York governor "that I consider anyone born in the Northwest Territory" — Dewey was a native of Owosso, Michigan — "to be one of us."

64. Waldrop, *McCormick of Chicago*, p. 260; RRM–Joseph Ator, September 7, 1943.

65. "Gov. Dewey Goes Anti-American," *Chicago Tribune*, September 7, 1943; RRM–Joseph Ator, September 8, 1943; *Time*, September 27, 1943.

66. D. Graham Hutton, British Information Services, on McCormick speech in Detroit, December 14, 1943, transmitted by Viscount Halifax to R. H. Anthony Eden, December 31, 1943, PRO.

67. Martin, "Colonel McCormick of the *Tribune*," *Harper's Magazine*, October 1944.

68. RRM instructions to editorial writers, January 8, 1944. Earlier, McCormick had asked Cliff Raymond to address the folly, as he saw it, of advocating a per-

manent U.S. alliance with China, "which has never had a government; Russia, which has never had a Constitution, and England, which has destroyed its Constitution."

69. Maloney interview, TOHP.
70. David Reynolds, *Rich Relations: The American Occupation of Britain, 1942-1945,* New York, 1955, p. 165.
71. RRM–Francis Biddle, March 20, 1944.
72. *Chicago Tribune,* April 12, 1944.
73. RRM–Joseph Patterson, April 11, 13, 1944; RRM–Joseph Patterson, April 10, 1944; Ruth Hanna McCormick Simms–Joseph Patterson, May 6, 1944; RRM–Robert E. Wood, May 15, 1944. "Field is an unfortunate man," McCormick wrote to Westbrook Pegler in March, 1944. "He inherits suicidal mania. His brother and father committed suicide and his grandmother died in confinement. I try to make allowances for him, but my associates, less versed in family history, sometimes go off the deep end."
74. RRM–A. J. Williams, May 18, 1944; Tebbel, *An American Dynasty,* p. 189.
75. Joseph Patterson–Cissy Patterson, May 31, 1944.
76. RRM–Joseph Patterson, July 8, 1944.
77. RRM–Thomas E. Dewey, July 8, 1944; Thomas E. Dewey–RRM, July 17, 1944; RRM–Thomas E. Dewey, July 24, 1944; RRM–Hedda Hopper, July 25, 1944.
78. RRM–Thomas E. Dewey, September 26, 1944; Walter Trohan to J. L. Maloney, undated. "This comes right out of the White House," Trohan wrote.
79. RRM–Thomas E. Dewey, October 9, 1944; Thomas E. Dewey–RRM, October 12, 1944; Hal Forest–J. L. Maloney, October 24, 1944; RRM–C. C. Muhs, October 28, 1944.
80. RRM–Ruth Hanna McCormick Simms, November 15, 1944; *Chicago Tribune,* April 1, 1955.
81. W. H. Gallienne to Earl of Halifax, "Marriage of Colonel McCormick," December 20, 1944, PRO.
82. Henry Hooper–RRM, November 26, 1940, April 23, 1943; RRM–Henry Hooper, April 27, 1943.
83. Maryland McCormick interview, TOHP.
84. Interview with Jeannette Hurley Reuben.
85. Snydecker interview.
86. Maryland McCormick interview, TOHP.
87. Interview with Warn Quaal.
88. Gwen Morgan and Arthur Veysey, "The Colonel," *Sunday Chicago Tribune Magazine,* April 7, 1985; Maryland McCormick prenuptial agreement, December 1944.
89. Gallienne–Hallifax, December 20, 1944, PRO.
90. Wiedrich interview.
91. Alfred M. Landon–RRM, January 9, 1945.
92. RRM–Leon Stolz, April 12, 1945.
93. Frank Hughes, "The Man in the Tower," unpublished ms., Chap. 1, p. 3.
94. Ibid., p. 5.
95. Maryland McCormick interview, TOHP. The story of McCormick's unseemly

celebration was told to me by Joyce Wenger, in 1945 a Northwestern University student working nights at Acme Newspictures, the newsphoto division of United Press International, which had its offices on the fourteenth floor of Tribune Tower. Arriving in the building's lobby at 5 P.M. on April 12, she was met by a friendly elevator operator who asked if she had received a $10 bill from the Colonel and who explained that McCormick had walked all over the building handing out cash and greeting employees with "It's a great day for America," or words to that effect. Asked if the elevator operator might be pulling her leg, Wenger recalled hearing the same story from workmen in the press room (Mrs. J. George Wenger to author, June 22, 1992, February 18, 1993).

96. Maryland McCormick interview, TOHP.
97. RRM–Arthur Sears Henning, September 10, 1945; RRM–Leon Stolz, November 7, 1945.
98. RRM–Walter Trohan, March 9, 1946; "Their Faces Are Red," *Chicago Tribune*, March 20, 1946.

15. The Last Leaf on the Tree

1. *Time*, April 11, 1955.
2. William H. Gallienne, Confidential memorandum, "Colonel McCormick," July 30, 1945, PRO.
3. RRM–Leon Stolz, April 7, December 21, 1945.
4. One story the *Tribune* did not run concerned Vandenberg's active and potentially risky extramarital life. In a suite adjoining his own at the Wardman Park Hotel in Washington, the senator installed first a Canadian and then a British sweetheart. The latter's reports to Churchill's U.S. agents, intercepted by the Office of Naval Intelligence, were reportedly shared with the White House.
5. *Montreal Star*, October 26, 1942; RRM–Leon Stolz, June 19, 1945.
6. *New York Times*, April 2, 1955.
7. Charles Whited, *Knight*, New York, 1988, p. 112.
8. *Newsweek*, April 25, 1955.
9. Waldrop interview; interview with Donald Agrella, TOHP; interview with Thomas Swanson.
10. *Time*, June 9, 1947; interview with Carl Wiegman, TOHP; RRM–Theodore Van Dellen, September 11, 1945; Theodore Van Dellen–RRM, October 11, 1945; RRM–Richard Orr, April 11, 1951. "Do bulls moo?" McCormick asked Orr in March 1952. *Bellow* would be a more appropriate description, replied Orr, unless the Colonel was thinking of stock-market bulls, in which case the most suitable word to characterize their communications was *growl*.
11. *Time*, June 9, 1947; Waldrop interview.
12. William Fulton interview, TOHP; RRM–Helen Dunn, August 23, 1947. "Small boys remember small things," McCormick told his Ludgrove classmate Shane Lesley.
13. Wiegman interview, TOHP; undated McCormick editorial instructions.
14. Waldrop interview; Graham interview.

15. RRM–Frank Young, August 23, 1947.

16. Maryland McCormick interview, TOHP.

17. Martin, *Cissy*, p. 458.

18. "Alicia in Wonderland," *Time*, September 13, 1954; Alicia Patterson–Joseph Patterson, undated, JPP.

19. Alicia Patterson–Joseph Patterson, undated, JPP.

20. Alicia Patterson–Joseph Patterson, undated, JPP.

21. Joseph Patterson–Alicia Patterson, August 9, 1943, JPP.

22. RRM–Cissy Patterson, August 5, 1946.

23. Maryland McCormick interview, TOHP.

24. Ibid.

25. RRM–Cissy Patterson, August 5, 1946.

26. RRM–Cissy Patterson, September 9, 1946.

27. RRM–Cissy Patterson, June 5, 1947.

28. RRM–Cissy Patterson, November 6, 1946; *Time*, August 26, 1946.

29. Allison Crittenden–Claude A. Smith, January 13, 1988; Gertz, "Eccentric Titan," *The Nation*, April 30, 1955, p. 363.

30. *Life*, April 7, 1947.

31. RRM–Hedda Hopper, July 5, 1947.

32. Interview with Harold F. Grumhaus, TOHP.

33. "From These Beginnings," *Chicago Tribune*, June 10, 1947.

34. Grumhaus interview, TOHP; Wood interview, TOHP.

35. Whited, *Knight*, p. 152.

36. Clayton Kirkpatrick, "History of the Production of the *Chicago Tribune* During the 1947–48 Strike of Printers," unpublished ms.; Grumhaus interview, TOHP; "Full Speed Ahead after a Quick Change Over!" *The Trib*, Christmas issue, 1947.

37. Morgan and Veysey, *Poor Little Rich Boy*, p. 405.

38. *Time*, November 17, 1947; RRM–Robert A. Taft, October 7, 1947.

39. RRM–Douglas MacArthur, December 12, 1947, May 8, 1947.

40. RRM–Cissy Patterson, December 15, 1947, January 28, 1948.

41. Martin, *Cissy*, p. 456.

42. Maryland McCormick interview, TOHP.

43. Paul Healey, *Cissy*, Garden City, N.Y., p. 377; Maryland McCormick interview, TOHP.

44. Maryland McCormick interview, TOHP.

45. Ibid.

46. Waldrop interview; RRM–Cissy Patterson, June 25, 1948; Martin, *Cissy*, pp. 358–59. "If a Trustee should connive at the election of a director who was not working for the best interest of the company," McCormick told Cissy, "or if a Trustee should profit from his trusteeship, it would be a breach of trust. I hope I have now made this crystal-clear to you."

47. Maryland McCormick interview.

48. *Newsweek*, August 2, 1948; William Fulton interview, TOHP.

49. Maryland McCormick interview, TOHP.

50. David McCullough, *Truman*, New York, 1992, pp. 330–31.

51. RRM–Leon Stolz, May 29, 1945.

52. McCullough, *Truman*, p. 482.

53. *Time*, April 11, 1955; RRM–Joseph Ator, May 7, 1948.

54. *New York Times*, September 26, 1947.

55. Trohan, *Political Animals*, pp. 229–30.

56. RRM–Dwight Green, March 18, 1948.

57. Herbert Brownell to author, February 4, 1993.

58. Trohan, *Political Animals*, pp. 232–33.

59. Robert P. Howard interview, Sangamon State University. McCormick told Taft that he was "very much pleased" by the way in which Green had withstood temptation.

60. Trohan, *Political Animals*, p. 233.

61. Richard Norton Smith, *Thomas E. Dewey and His Times*, New York, 1982, p. 608.

62. RRM–Joseph Ator, August 26, 1948; Sam Tanenhaus, *Whittaker Chambers*, New York, 1977, pp. 304-5.

63. RRM–J. L. Bentley, August 30, 1948.

64. RRM–Joseph Ator, August 21, 1948; RRM–Theodore Van Dellen, November 25, 1952.

65. RRM–Alfred M. Landon, November 5, 1948; RRM–James Thompson, October 29, 1948.

66. Kirkpatrick, "History of the Production"; Grumhaus interview, TOHP.

67. Interview with Levering Cartwright, TOHP.

68. Grumhaus interview, TOHP.

69. Maloney interview, TOHP; Maxwell interview, TOHP.

70. Trohan, *Political Animals*, pp. 243–44; RRM–Alfred M. Landon, November 5, 1948.

71. Catherine Anthony–RRM, November 3, 1948; J. W. McConnell–Harry S. Truman, December 1, 1948, Truman Library.

72. Harry S. Truman–William Max, November 15, 1948, Truman Library; Trohan interview, Hoover Library. "You are the best reporter of us all," Trohan wrote to the Colonel on November 6. "You were the only one to say Dewey could not win."

73. Wendt, *Chicago Tribune*, p. 689; Howard interview, Sangamon State University.

74. Trohan notes prepared for author.

75. Interview with Richard Prendergast, TOHP.

16. April Fool

1. Waldrop interview; Fred W. Hotson, "The Colonel and His Aircraft," *AAHS Journal*, Summer 1996, p. 86.

2. I. M. Leche, British Embassy, Santiago, Chile, March 4, 1949, PRO.

3. "The Colonel Looks on Marathon," *The New Yorker*, March 25, 1950.

4. Ibid.

5. Ibid.; *Time*, March 20, 1950.
6. Maryland McCormick interview, TOHP.
7. Noderer inteview, TOHP.
8. Ibid.
9. Flahiff interview, TOHP; Morgan and Veysey, *Poor Little Rich Boy*, p. 417.
10. Howard Wood interview, TOHP; *Newsweek*, August 1, 1949.
11. Howard Wood interview, TOHP; Wiegman, *Trees to News*, p. 327.
12. Walter Trohan–Pat Maloney, July 17, 1949.
13. Walter Trohan–Pat Maloney, July 21, 1949.
14. *Time*, August 1, 1949.
15. Julius Miner, unpublished McCormick biography; Howard Wood interview, TOHP.
16. RRM–F. M. Flynn, July 23, 1949.
17. *Chicago Tribune*, August 3, 1950; RRM–Bazy Miller, September 12, 1949.
18. RRM–Frank Waldrop, August 29, September 27, 1949.
19. Bazy Miller–RRM, October 4, 1949; RRM–Bazy Miller, November 3, 1949.
20. Interview with Kristie Miller.
21. RRM–J. L. Maloney, January 20, 1950.
22. "Cassandra on Lake Michigan," *The New Yorker*, January 14, 1950.
23. "The Colonel's Formula," *The New Yorker*, January 21, 1950.
24. Interview with Arthur Veysey.
25. Edwards interview, TOHP.
26. Thomas Reeves, *The Life and Times of Joe McCarthy*, New York, 1982, pp. 98–99.
27. Edwards interview, TOHP; Reeves, *The Life and Times of Joe McCarthy*, pp. 224–30. "Listen, you bastards," McCarthy told skeptical reporters in Madison, Wisconsin, who tried unsuccessfully to flush out his evidence. "I'm not going to tell you anything. I just want you to know I've got a pailful of shit, and I'm going to use it where it does me the most good."
28. RRM–"Dear Pat," June 10, 1950.
29. RRM–Bazy Miller, July 10, 1950.
30. RRM–Robert Taft, August 3, 1950; interview with Perry Patterson.
31. Trohan, *Political Animals*, p. 249; Edwards interview, TOHP.
32. Reeves, *The Life and Times of Joe McCarthy*, p. 337; RRM–Bazy Miller, October 13, 1950.
33. Roscoe Conklin Simmons–RRM, November 14, 1950; Bazy Miller–RRM, November 14, 1950.
34. Roscoe Conklin Simmons–RRM, November 14, 1950.
35. Tankersley interview.
36. RRM–Bazy Miller, November 11, 1950; Bazy Miller–RRM, November 14, 1950.
37. Confidential source.
38. Pat Maloney–Bazy Miller, December 28, 1950.
39. Patterson interview; RRM–Bazy Miller, January 31, 1951.
40. Bazy–"Dear Uncle Bert," undated, but clearly written in response to McCormick's January 31 letter comparing her romance to the Hearst-Davies affair.

41. Tankersley interview.
42. Ibid.; RRM–Bazy Miller, March 4, 1951.
43. Tankersley interview.
44. Pat Maloney–RRM Memo No. 10, in conjunction with McCormick's deposition in the fall of 1950, relating to Drew Pearson's unsuccessful libel action against the *Times-Herald*, among others.
45. RRM–William Shelton, May 1, 1951; *Newsweek*, September 17, 1951.
46. RRM–Frank Waldrop, July 16, 1951; *St. Louis Post-Dispatch*, June 24, 1951.
47. *St. Louis Post-Dispatch*, June 24, 1951.
48. RRM–Douglas MacArthur, April 12, 1951; Maloney interview, TOHP.
49. Trohan, *Political Animals*, p. 254.
50. Trohan, "My Life with the Colonel."
51. Trohan, *Political Animals*, p. 258.
52. *The Nation*, October 6, 1951.
53. Byington interview, TOHP.
54. Interview with Richard Prendergast, TOHP.
55. Interview with Bess Vydra.
56. *Time*, July 27, 1953.
57. RRM–Hedda Hopper, May 16, 1952.
58. RRM–W. D. Maxwell, June 4, 1952; Joe Cerutti–RRM, June 6, 1952.
59. Interview with Charles B. Wyngarden.
60. Trohan, "My Life with the Colonel."
61. *Time*, August 11, 1952; Clayton Kirkpatrick–Stanton Cook, May 9, 1974; *Newsweek*, September 1, November 2, 1952. Asked by a reporter following the GOP convention whether he would endorse Eisenhower, McCormick was noncommittal. "Hell," he said, "I supported Dewey."
62. RRM–Carlos Stoddard, December 4, 1952.
63. *Time*, April 6, 1953.
64. RRM–Bazy Tankersley, March 6, 1953; Bazy Tankersley–RRM, undated; Maryland McCormick, May 23, 1953; Dorothy Murray memo to Howard Wood, November 24, 1955.
65. Wyngarden interview.
66. Van Dellen interview, TOHP; interview with Barbara Johnston Wood.
67. Kent Cooper–J. Howard Wood, February 3, 1956.
68. RRM–Berkeley Gage, May 4, 1951; Kent Cooper–J. Howard Wood, February 3, 1956.
69. Walter H. Annenberg to author, July 19, 1993.
70. Patterson interview.
71. Howard Wood interview, TOHP.
72. Ibid.
73. Tankersley interview; *New York Times*, March 18, 1954.
74. *Editor and Publisher*, March 20, 1954; RRM–Eugene Meyer, March 17, 1954; Eugene Meyer–RRM, March 17, 1954.
75. Robert E. Wood, March 19, 1954.
76. RRM–Howard Ellis, March 22, 1954.
77. Trohan, "My Life with the Colonel"; *Time*, March 8, 1954.

78. *Time*, July 26, 1954; *Newsweek*, March 8, 1954.

79. *Newsweek*, May 3, 1954.

80. RRM–Ann H. Warner, July 14, 1954; Trohan notes prepared for author; Vydra interview; Dorothy Murray memo, November 24, 1955.

81. Dorothy Murray memo, November 24, 1955.

82. Maxwell interview, TOHP.

83. Ibid.

84. Tankersley interview; Miller interview.

85. "I was taken back," Trohan recalled nearly forty years later. "He had often surprised me but never so greatly ... My observations satisfied him. He then went on to tell me again he was not happy with his will, saying Campbell was dying, Maxwell was a boob, and Wood would not leave a woman safe on the North Shore."

86. J. Howard Wood–Weymouth Kirkland, May 24, 1955; Van Dellen interview, TOHP.

87. Barbara Johnston Wood interview; Stanley Johnston notes, February 1954. According to Walter Trohan, McCormick exacerbated his bladder condition by mixing whiskey and sleeping pills, gulping the latter as if they were peanuts.

88. Howard Wood interview.

89. Barbara Johnston Wood to author, August 29, 1993; Wyngarden interview.

90. Doctor's notes, March, 1955.

91. Barbara Johnston Wood to author, August 29, 1993; Doctor's notes; Park interview, TOHP; King interview, TOHP.

92. Barbara Johnston Wood to author, August 29, 1993.

Bibliography

Adler, Selig. *The Isolationist Impulse.* London and New York, 1957.

Allsop, Kenneth. *The Bootleggers: The Story of Prohibition.* Garden City, N.Y., 1961.

Alsop, Joseph W. *I've Seen the Best of It.* New York, 1992.

Andrews, Wayne. *The Battle for Chicago.* New York, 1946.

Angle, Paul M. *The Great Chicago Fire.* Chicago, 1946.

Asbury, Herbert. *Gem of the Prairie.* New York, 1940.

Ashburn, Frank D. *Peabody of Groton.* New York, 1944.

Bailey, Thomas A. *Woodrow Wilson and the Great Betrayal.* New York, 1945.

Baker, Jean H. *The Stevensons: An American Family.* New York, 1996.

Beasley, Norman. *Frank Knox.* New York, 1936.

Becker, Stephen D. *Marshall Field III.* New York, 1964.

Beckson, Karl. *London in the 1890s: A Cultural History.* New York, 1992.

Bennett, James O'Donnell. *Chicago Gang Land: The True Story of Chicago Crime.* Chicago, 1929.

———. *Joseph Medill.* Chicago, 1947.

Biddle, Francis. *In Brief Authority.* Garden City, N.Y., 1962.

Boettiger, John. *Jake Lingle.* New York, 1931.

Boettiger, John R. *A Love in Shadow.* New York, 1978.

Bright, John. *Hizzoner Big Bill Thompson: An Idyll of Chicago.* New York, 1930.

Bross, William. *History of Chicago.* Chicago, 1876.

Brown, Douglas V. *Groton School, 1884–1985.* Groton, Mass., 1986.

Butcher, Fanny. *Many Lives, One Love.* New York, 1972.

Chapman, John. *Tell It to Sweeney.* Garden City, N.Y., 1961.

Chicago Tribune. *A Century of Tribune Editorials, 1847–1947.* Chicago, 1947.

———. *Picture Encyclopedia of the World's Greatest Newspaper.* Chicago, 1928.

———. *The Thunder of the Prairies.* Chicago, 1944.

———. *Tribune Tower.* Chicago, 1924.

————. *The W.G.N.* Chicago, 1922.

Churchill, Allen. *The Liberty Years, 1924–1950.* Englewood Cliffs, N.J., 1969.

Clark, Herma. *The Elegant Eighties.* Chicago, 1941.

Clayton, John. "An American Story." Robert R. McCormick Research Center (hereafter identified as MRC).

Cleary, James. "The Colonel and the Captain Take Command, 1900–1920." 3 vols., MRC.

Coffman, Edward M. *The War to End All Wars.* Madison, 1986.

Cohen, Bernard C. *The Press and Foreign Policy.* Princeton, 1963.

Colbert, Elias, and Chamberlain, Everett. *Chicago and the Great Conflagration.* Chicago, 1871.

Cole, Wayne. *America First: The Battle Against Intervention, 1940–1941.* Madison, 1953.

Collier, Peter, and Horowitz, David. *The Fords.* New York, 1987.

Conot, Robert. *A Streak of Luck.* New York, 1979.

Considine, Bob. *It's All News to Me.* New York, 1967.

Cook, Frederic Francis. *Bygone Days in Chicago.* Chicago, 1910.

Cooney, John. *The Annenbergs.* New York, 1982.

Cooper, Kent. *Kent Cooper and the Associated Press.* New York, 1959.

Cray, Ed. *General of the Army: George C. Marshall, Soldier and Statesman.* New York, 1990.

Cromie, Robert. *The Great Chicago Fire.* New York, 1958.

Cronon, William. *Nature's Metropolis: Chicago and the Great West.* New York, 1991.

Daniels, Jonathan. *The Time Between the Wars.* Garden City, N.Y., 1966.

————. *White House Witness, 1942–1945.* Garden City, N.Y., 1975.

Davis, Kenneth S. *FDR: The Beckoning of Destiny, 1882–1928.* New York, 1971.

————. *The New Deal Years, 1933–1937.* New York, 1986.

————. *Into the Storm, 1937–1940.* New York, 1993.

Dedmon, Emmet. *Fabulous Chicago.* New York, 1953.

Demeris, Ovid. *Captive City: Chicago in Chains.* New York, 1969.

Dennis, Charles H. *Victor Lawson: His Time and His Work.* Chicago, 1935.

Desmond, Robert W. *The Press and World Affairs.* New York, 1937.

Drewey, John E. *Post Biographies of Famous Journalists.* Athens, Ga., 1942.

Edwards, India. *Pulling No Punches.* New York, 1977.

Edwards, Jerome. *The Foreign Policy of Colonel McCormick's Tribune, 1929–1941.* Reno, Nev., 1971.

Evans, Arthur M. "Details of the Lorimer Fight." MRC.

Fair, Finis. *Chicago.* New Rochelle, 1973.

Faw, Volney. "The *Chicago Tribune* and Its Control." Master's thesis, University of Chicago, 1940.

Fink, John. *WGN — a Pictorial History.* Chicago, 1961.

Friedel, Frank. *Franklin D. Roosevelt: the Apprenticeship.* Boston, 1952.

Friendly, Fred W. *Minnesota Rag.* New York, 1981.

Gelderman, Carol. *Henry Ford, the Wayward Capitalist.* New York, 1981.

Gibbons, Edward. *Floyd Gibbons, Your Headline Hunter.* New York, 1953.

Gies, Joseph. *The Colonel of Chicago.* New York, 1979.

Gilbert, Martin. *The First World War.* New York, 1994.

Gilbert, Paul, and Bryson, Charles Lee. *Chicago and Its Makers.* Chicago, 1929.

Goodwin, Doris Kearns. *No Ordinary Time.* New York, 1994.

Goren, Dina. "Communication Intelligence and the Freedom of the Press: The *Chicago Tribune*'s Battle of Midway Dispatch and the Breaking of the Japanese Code." Thesis, Yale Law School, May 1978.

Gottfried, Alex. *Boss Cermak of Chicago.* Seattle, 1962.

Gramling, Oliver. *AP: The Story of News.* New York, 1940.

Green, Paul M., and Holli, Melvin G. *The Mayors: The Chicago Political Tradition.* Carbondale, Ill., 1987.

Gunther, John. *Inside USA.* New York, 1947.

Harbord, James G. *The American Army in France, 1917–1919.* Boston, 1936.

Harrison, Carter H. *Stormy Years.* Indianapolis, 1935.

Hartzel, Frederic. *Reminscent and Prophetic Words by Joseph Medill in the Closing Days of His Life.* Chicago, 1925.

Healy, Paul. *Cissy.* Garden City, N.Y., 1966.

Hoffman, George C. "Big Bill Thompson, His Mayoral Campaigns and Voting Strength." Master's thesis, University of Chicago, 1956.

Hoge, Alice Albright. *Cissy Patterson.* New York, 1966.

Howard, Robert P. *Illinois: A History of the Prairie State.* Grand Rapids, 1972.

———. *Mostly Good and Competent Men: Illinois Governors 1818–1988.* Springfield, Ill., 1988.

Howells, John M., and Hood, Raymond. "The Tribune Tower, Chicago." MRC.

Hutchinson, William T. *Cyrus Hall McCormick.* New York, 1930.

Ickes, Harold. *America's House of Lords.* New York, 1939.

———. *Autobiography of a Curmudgeon,* New York, 1948.

———. *Freedom of the Press Today.* New York, 1941.

———. *The Secret Diary of Harold Ickes.* 3 vols., New York, 1953, 1954.

Ingersoll, Ralph. *Top Secret.* New York, 1946.

Irey, Elmer, L., and Slocum, William J. *The Tax Dodgers.* New York, 1948.

Jenkins, Warren G. "The Foreign Policy of the *Chicago Tribune*, 1914–1917: A Program of National Self-Interest." Ph.D. dissertation, University of Wisconsin, 1943.

Johns, Elizabeth Dewey. "Chicago's Newspapers and the News: A Study of Public Communication in a Metropolis." Ph.D. dissertation, University of Chicago, 1942.

Johnson, Walter. *The Battle Against Isolation.* Chicago, 1944.

Johnston, Stanley. *Queen of the Flat-Tops: The U.S.S. Lexington and the Coral Sea Battle.* New York, 1942.

King, Ernest J., and Whitehill, Walter Muir. *Fleet Admiral King.* New York, 1952.

Kinsley, Philip. *The Chicago Tribune, Its First Hundred Years.* New York, 1943.

———. *Liberty and the Press: A History of the Chicago Tribune's Fight to Preserve a Free Press for the American People.* Chicago, 1944.

Kirkpatrick, Clayton. "History of the Production of the *Chicago Tribune* During the 1947–48 Strike of Printers." MRC.

Kobler, John. *Capone: The Life and World of Al Capone.* New York, 1971.

Kogan, Herman, and Kogan, Rick. *Yesterday's Chicago.* Miami, 1976.

———and Wendt, Lloyd. *Chicago.* New York, 1958.

Lacey, Robert. *Ford: The Men and the Machine.* Boston, 1986.

Leighton, Isabel. *The Aspirin Age, 1919–1941.* New York, 1946.

Leslie, Shane. *The Film of Memory.* London, 1938.

———. *Men Were Different.* London, 1937.

Leuchtenburg, William E. *Franklin D. Roosevelt and the New Deal.* New York, 1963.

Lewis, Lloyd, and Smith, Henry Justin. *Chicago: The History of Its Reputation.* New York, 1929.

Liebling, A. J. *Chicago: Second City.* New York, 1952.

Linn, James Webber. *James Keeley, Newspaperman.* Indianapolis, 1937.

Logsdon, Joseph. *Horace White, Nineteenth-Century Liberal.* Westport, Conn., 1971.

Longstreet, Stephen. *Chicago 1860–1919.* New York, 1973.

Lundberg, Ferdinand. *Imperial Hearst.* New York, 1936.

Luthin, Reinhard H. *American Demagogues.* Boston, 1954.

Lyle, John H. *The Dry and Lawless Years.* Englewood Cliffs, N.J., 1960.

Martin, John Bartlow. *Adlai Stevenson of Illinois.* Garden City, N.Y., 1976.

Martin, Ralph. *Cissy.* New York, 1979.

Mayer, Harold M., and Wade, Richard C. *Chicago: Growth of a Metropolis.* Chicago, 1969.

McCormick, Robert R. *The American Empire.* Chicago, 1952.

———. *The American Revolution and Its Influence on World Civilization.* Chicago, 1945.

———. *The Army of 1918.* New York, 1926.

———. *Freedom of the Press.* New York, 1936.

———. 1906 Message, Sanitary District of Chicago.

———. 1907 Message, Sanitary District of Chicago.

———. 1908 Message, Sanitary District of Chicago.

———. 1909 Message, Sanitary District of Chicago.

———. 1910 Message, Sanitary District of Chicago.

———. *Ulysses S. Grant: The Great Soldier of America.* New York, 1934.

———. *With the Russian Army.* New York, 1915.

McCoy, Donald R. *Landon of Kansas.* Lincoln, Neb., 1966.

McCullough, David. *Truman,* New York, 1992.

McCutcheon, John T. *Drawn From Memory.* Indianapolis, 1956.

McElvaine, Robert S. *The Great Depression.* New York, 1984.

McGivena, Leo E. *The News: The First Fifty Years of New York's Picture Newspaper.* New York, 1969.

McPhaul, John J. *Deadlines and Monkeyshines: The Fabled World of Chicago Journalism.* New York, 1962.

Mencken, H. L. *The Bathtub Hoax and Other Blasts and Bravos from the Chicago Tribune.* New York, 1958.

Miller, Kristie. *Ruth Hanna McCormick, A Life in Politics.* Albuquerque, N.M., 1992.

Morgan, Gwen, and Veysey, Arthur. *Poor Little Rich Boy.* Wheaton, Ill., 1985.

Morgan, Ted. *FDR*. New York, 1985.

Moriarity, Frank T. "The Life and Service of Joseph Medill." Master's dissertation, Northwestern University, 1933.

Mosley, Leonard. *Lindbergh*. New York, 1977.

Mott, Thomas B. *Twenty Years as Military Attaché*. New York, 1937.

Munson, Lester E. *The Chicago Tribune Fights World War II*. Princeton, 1962.

Murray, George. *The Madhouse on Madison Street*. Chicago, 1965.

O'Reilly, Alice M. "Colonel Robert Rutherford McCormick, His *Tribune* and Mayor William Hale Thompson." Master's thesis, University of Chicago, 1963.

Pasley, Fred D. *Al Capone: The Biography of a Self-Made Man*. New York, 1930.

Patterson, James T. *Mr. Republican: A Biography of Robert A. Taft*. New York, 1972.

Patterson, Joseph M. *A Little Brother of the Rich*. Chicago, 1908.

———. *The Notebook of a Neutral*. New York, 1916.

Peterson, Virgil W. *Barbarians in Our Midst: A History of Chicago Crime and Politics*. Boston, 1952.

Pierce, Bessie L. *A History of Chicago*. 3 vols., New York, 1937–1957.

Pierson, George W. *Yale College: An Educational History, 1871–1921*. New Haven, 1952.

Poole, Ernest. *Giants Gone: Men Who Made Chicago*. New York, 1943.

Pusey, Merlo J. *Eugene Meyer*. New York, 1974.

Ralphson, George H. *Over There with Pershing's Heroes at Cantigny*. Chicago, 1919.

Rascoe, Burton. *Before I Forget*. New York, 1937.

Reynolds, David. *Rich Relations: The American Occupation of Britain, 1942–1945*. New York, 1995.

Robinson, Jerry. *The Comics: An Illustrated History of Comic Strip Art*. New York, 1974.

Roderick, Stella. *Nettie Fowler McCormick*. Rindge, N.H., 1956.

Rue, Larry. *I Fly for News*. New York, 1932.

Saunders, Hilary St. George. *Pioneers! O Pioneers!* New York, 1944.

Schlesinger, Arthur, Jr. *The Crisis of the Old Order*. Boston, 1956.

———. *The Coming of the New Deal*. Boston, 1959.

———. *The Politics of Upheaval*. Boston, 1960.

Schneider, James C. *Should America Go to War?* Chapel Hill, N.C., 1989.

Schultz, Sigrid. *Germany Will Try It Again*. New York, 1944.

Seldes, George. *Lords of the Press*. New York, 1938.

———. *You Can't Say That!* New York, 1939.

Shirer, William L. *The Start, 1904–1930*. Boston, 1976.

———. *The Nightmare Years, 1930–1940*. Boston, 1984.

Shogan, Robert. *Hard Bargain*. New York, 1995.

Sirotek, Robert L. *The Wayne-DuPage Hunt*. Broadview, Ill., 1980.

Smith, Harvey H. *Shelter Bay: Tales of the Quebec North Shore*. Toronto, 1964.

Smith, Henry Justin. *Chicago's Great Century, 1833–1933*. Chicago, 1933.

Smith, Richard Norton. *Thomas E. Dewey and His Times*. New York, 1982.

———. *An Uncommon Man: The Triumph of Herbert Hoover*. New York, 1984.

Stewart, Kenneth, and Tebbel, John. *Makers of Modern Journalism.* New York, 1952.

Stone, Ralph. *The Irreconcilables: The Fight Against the League of Nations.* New York, 1973.

Strevey, Tracy E. "Joseph Medill and the *Chicago Tribune* During the Civil War Period." Ph.D. dissertation, University of Chicago, 1930.

Stuart, William H. *Twenty Incredible Years.* Chicago, 1935.

Swanberg, W. A. *Citizen Hearst.* New York, 1961.

———. *Luce and His Empire.* New York, 1972.

Tarr, Joel Arthur. *A Study in Boss Politics.* Urbana, Ill., 1971.

Tebbel, John. *An American Dynasty.* Garden City, N.Y., 1947.

———. *The Compact History of the American Newspaper.* New York, 1963.

———. *The Marshall Fields: A Study in Wealth.* New York, 1947.

Trohan, Walter. *Political Animals.* Garden City, N.Y., 1975.

Union for Democratic Action. *The People Versus the Chicago Tribune.* Chicago, 1942.

Villard, Oswald Garrison. *The Disappearing Daily.* New York, 1952.

Waldrop, Frank. *McCormick of Chicago.* Englewood Cliffs, N.J., 1966.

Ward, Geoffrey. *Before the Trumpet.* New York, 1985.

Welch, Lewis Sheldon, and Camp, Walter. *Yale: Her Campus, Classrooms, and Athletics.* Boston, 1899.

Wendt, Lloyd. *Chicago Tribune: The Rise of a Great American Newspaper.* Chicago, 1979.

———and Kogan, Herman. *Big Bill of Chicago.* Indianapolis, 1953.

Wheeler, Burton K. *Yankee From the West.* Garden City, N.Y., 1962.

Wiegman, Carl. *Trees to News.* Toronto, 1953.

———. Unpublished history of the *Chicago Tribune.* MRC.

Yale University, Class of 1903. *Class Book, 1903.* New Haven, 1903.

———. History of the Class of 1903, Vol. I Triennial, New Haven, 1906.

Index